Children's
Literature
Review

Guide to Gale Literary Criticism Series

When you need to review criticism of literary works, these are the Gale series to use:

If the author's death date is: **You should turn to:**

After Dec. 31, 1959
(or author is still living)

CONTEMPORARY LITERARY CRITICISM

for example: Jorge Luis Borges, Anthony Burgess,
William Faulkner, Mary Gordon,
Ernest Hemingway, Iris Murdoch

1900 through 1959

TWENTIETH-CENTURY LITERARY CRITICISM

for example: Willa Cather, F. Scott Fitzgerald,
Henry James, Mark Twain, Virginia Woolf

1800 through 1899

NINETEENTH-CENTURY LITERATURE CRITICISM

for example: Fyodor Dostoevsky, Nathaniel Hawthorne,
George Sand, William Wordsworth

1400 through 1799

***LITERATURE CRITICISM FROM 1400 TO 1800
(excluding Shakespeare)***

for example: Anne Bradstreet, Daniel Defoe,
Alexander Pope, François Rabelais,
Jonathan Swift, Phillis Wheatley

SHAKESPEAREAN CRITICISM

Shakespeare's plays and poetry

Antiquity through 1399

CLASSICAL AND MEDIEVAL LITERATURE CRITICISM

for example: Dante, Homer, Plato, Sophocles, Vergil,
the Beowulf Poet

Gale also publishes related criticism series:

CHILDREN'S LITERATURE REVIEW

This series covers authors of all eras who have written for the preschool through high school audience.

SHORT STORY CRITICISM

This series covers the major short fiction writers of all nationalities and periods of literary history.

POETRY CRITICISM

This series covers poets of all nationalities and periods of literary history.

ISSN 0362-4145

volume 24

Children's Literature Review

Excerpts from Reviews,
Criticism, and Commentary
on Books for Children
and Young People

Gerard J. Senick
Editor

Sharon R. Gunton
Associate Editor

Gale Research Inc. · DETROIT · LONDON

STAFF

Gerard J. Senick, *Editor*

Sharon R. Gunton, *Associate Editor*

Jeanne A. Gough, *Permissions & Production Manager*
Linda M. Pugliese, *Production Supervisor*
Maureen A. Puhl, Jennifer VanSickle, *Editorial Associates*
Donna Craft, Paul Lewon, Lorna Mabunda, Camille Robinson, Sheila
Walencewicz, *Editorial Assistants*

Maureen Richards, *Research Supervisor*
Paula Cutcher-Jackson, Judy L. Gale, Robin Lupa, *Editorial Associates*
Jennifer Brostrom, Amy Kaechele, Mary Beth McElmeel, Tamara Nott,
Editorial Assistants

Sandra C. Davis, *Permissions Supervisor* (*Text*)
Josephine M. Keene, Kimberly F. Smilay, *Permissions Associates*
Maria Franklin, Michele M. Lonoconus, Shalice Shah, Nancy Sheridan,
Denise M. Singleton, Rebecca A. Stanko, *Permissions Assistants*

Patricia A. Seefelt, *Permissions Supervisor* (*Pictures*)
Margaret A. Chamberlain, Pamela A. Hayes, *Permissions Associate*
Keith Reed, *Permissions Assistant*

Mary Beth Trimper, *Production Manager*
Evi Seoud, *Assistant Production Manager*

Arthur Chartow, *Art Director*
C. J. Jonik, *Keyliner*

Contents

Preface

Children's literature has evolved into both a respected branch of creative writing and a successful industry. Currently, books for young readers are considered the most popular segment of publishing, while criticism of juvenile literature is instrumental in recording the literary or artistic development of the creators of children's books as well as the trends and controversies that result from changing values or attitudes about young people and their literature. Designed to provide a permanent, accessible record of this ongoing scholarship, *Children's Literature Review* (*CLR*) presents parents, teachers, and librarians—those responsible for bringing children and books together—with the opportunity to make informed choices when selecting reading materials for the young. This audience will find balanced overviews of the careers of the authors and illustrators of the books that they and their children are reading; these entries, which contain excerpts from published criticism in books and periodicals, assist users by sparking ideas for papers and assignments and suggesting supplementary and classroom reading. Ann L. Kalkhoff, president and editor of *Children's Book Review Service Inc.,* writes that "*CLR* has filled a gap in the field of children's books, and it is one series that will never lose its validity or importance."

Scope of the Series

Each volume of *CLR* profiles the careers of authors and illustrators of books for children from preschool through high school. Author lists in each volume reflect these elements:

- author lists are international in scope.

- approximately fifteen authors of all eras are represented.

- author lists represent the variety of genres covered by children's literature: picture books, fiction, nonfiction, poetry, folklore, and drama.

Although earlier volumes of *CLR* emphasized critical material published after 1960, successive volumes have expanded their coverage to encompass important criticism written before 1960. Since many of the authors included in *CLR* are living and continue to write, it is necessary to update their entries periodically. Thus, future volumes will supplement the entries of selected authors covered in earlier volumes as well as include criticism on the works of authors new to the series.

Organization of This Book

An author section consists of the following elements: author heading, author portrait, author introduction, excerpts of criticism (each followed by a bibliographical citation), and illustrations, when available.

- The **author heading** consists of the author's name followed by birth and death dates. The portion of the name outside the parentheses denotes the form under which the author is most frequently published. If the majority of the author's works for children were written under a pseudonym, the pseudonym will be listed in the author heading and the real name given on the first line of the author introduction. Also located at the beginning of the introduction are any other pseudonyms used by the author in writing for children and any name variations, including transliterated forms for authors whose languages use nonroman alphabets. Uncertainty as to a birth or death date is indicated by question marks.

- An **author portrait** is included when available.

- The **author introduction** contains information designed to introduce an author to *CLR* users by presenting an overview of the author's themes and styles, occasional biographical facts that relate to the author's literary career or critical responses to the author's works, and information about major awards and prizes the author has received. Introductions also list a group of representative titles for which the author or illustrator being profiled is best known; this section, which begins with the words "major works include," follows the genre line of the introduction. Where applicable, introductions conclude with references to additional entries in biographical and critical reference series published by Gale Research Inc. These sources include past volumes of *CLR* as well as *Authors & Artists for Young Adults, Contemporary Authors, Contemporary Literary Criticism, Dictionary of Literary Biography, Nineteenth-Century Literature Criticism, Short Story Criti-*

cism, Something about the Author, Something about the Author Autobiography Series, Twentieth-Century Literary Criticism, and *Yesterday's Authors of Books for Children.*

• **Criticism** is located in three sections: **author's commentary** (when available), **general commentary** (when available), and **title commentary** (in which commentary on specific titles appears). Centered headings introduce each section, in which criticism is arranged chronologically. Titles by authors being profiled are highlighted in boldface type within the text for easier access by readers.

The **author's commentary** presents background material written by the author or by an interviewer. This commentary may cover a specific work or several works. Author's commentary on more than one work appears after the author introduction, while commentary on an individual book follows the title entry heading.

The **general commentary** consists of critical excerpts that consider more than one work by the author or illustrator being profiled. General commentary is preceded by the critic's name in boldface type or, in the case of unsigned criticism, by the title of the journal. Occasionally, *CLR* features entries that emphasize general criticism on the overall career of an author or illustrator. When appropriate, a selection of reviews is included to supplement the general commentary.

The **title commentary** begins with title entry headings, which precede the criticism on a title and cite publication information on the work being reviewed. Title headings list the title of the work as it appeared in its first English-language edition. The first English-language publication date of each work is listed in parentheses following the title. Differing U.S. and British titles follow the publication date within the parentheses.

Entries in each title commentary section consist of critical excerpts on the author's individual works, arranged chronologically by publication date. The entries generally contain two to six reviews per title, depending on the stature of the book and the amount of criticism it has generated. The editors select titles that reflect the entire scope of the author's literary contribution, covering each genre and subject. An effort is made to reprint criticism that represents the full range of each title's reception—from the year of its initial publication to current assessments. Thus, the reader is provided with a record of the author's critical history. Publication information (such as publisher names and book prices) and parenthetical numerical references (such as footnotes or page and line references to specific editions of works) have been deleted at the editor's discretion to provide smoother reading of the text.

• Selected excerpts are preceded by **explanatory notes,** which provide information on the critic or work of criticism to enhance the reader's understanding of the excerpt.

• A complete **bibliographical citation** designed to facilitate the location of the original book or article follows each piece of criticism.

• Numerous **illustrations** are featured in *CLR.* For entries on illustrators, an effort has been made to include illustrations that reflect the characteristics discussed in the criticism. Entries on major authors who do not illustrate their own works may also include photographs and other illustrative material pertinent to the authors' careers.

Special Features

Entries on authors who are also illustrators will occasionally feature commentary on selected works illustrated but not written by the author being profiled. These works are strongly associated with the illustrator and have received critical acclaim for their art. By including critical comment on works of this type, the editors wish to provide a more complete representation of the author's total career. Criticism on these works has been chosen to stress artistic, rather than literary, contributions. Title entry headings for works illustrated by the author being profiled are arranged chronologically within the entry by date of publication and include notes identifying the author of the illustrated work. In order to provide easier access for users, all titles illustrated by the subject of the entry will be boldfaced.

CLR also includes entries on prominent illustrators who have contributed to the field of children's literature. These entries are designed to represent the development of the illustrator as an artist rather than as a literary stylist. The illustrator's section is organized like that of an author, with two exceptions: the introduction presents an overview of the illustrator's styles and techniques rather than outlining his or her literary background, and the commentary written by the illustrator on his or her works is called illustrator's commentary rather than author's commentary. Title entry headings are followed by explanatory notes identifying the author of the illustrated work. All titles of books containing illustrations by the artist being profiled as well as individual illustrations from these books are highlighted in boldface type.

Other Features

• An **acknowledgments,** which immediately follows the preface, lists the sources from which material has been reprinted in the volume. It does not, however, list every book or periodical consulted for the volume.

• The **cumulative index to authors** lists authors who have appeared in *CLR* and includes cross-references to *Authors & Artists for Young Adults, Contemporary Authors, Contemporary Literary Criticism, Dictionary of Literary Biography, Nineteenth-Century Literature Criticism, Short Story Criticism, Something about the Author, Something about the Author Autobiography Series, Twentieth-Century Literary Criticism,* and *Yesterday's Authors of Books for Children.*

• The **cumulative nationality index** lists authors alphabetically under their respective nationalities. Author names are followed by the volume number(s) in which they appear. Authors who have changed citizenship or whose current citizenship is not reflected in biographical sources appear under both their original nationality and that of their current residence.

• The **cumulative title index** lists titles covered in *CLR* followed by the volume and page number where criticism begins.

A Note to the Reader

When writing papers, students who quote directly from any volume in the Literature Criticism Series may use the following general forms to footnote reprinted criticism. The first example pertains to material drawn from periodicals, the second to material reprinted from books.

[1] T. S. Eliot, "John Donne," *The Nation and the Athenaeum,* 33 (9 June 1923), 321-32; excerpted and reprinted in *Literature Criticism from 1400 to 1800,* Vol. 10, ed. James E. Person, Jr. (Detroit: Gale Research, 1989), pp. 28-9.

[1] Henry Brooke, *Leslie Brooke and Johnny Crow* (Frederick Warne, 1982); excerpted and reprinted in *Children's Literature Review,* Vol. 20, ed. Gerard J. Senick (Detroit: Gale Research, 1990), p. 47.

Suggestions Are Welcome

In response to various suggestions, several features have been added to *CLR* since the series began, including author entries on retellers of traditional literature as well as those who have been the first to record oral tales and other folklore; entries on prominent illustrators featuring commentary on their styles and techniques; entries on authors whose works are considered controversial or have been challenged; occasional entries devoted to criticism on a single work by a major author; sections in author introductions that list major works by the author or illustrator being profiled; explanatory notes that provide information on the critic or work of criticism to enhance the usefulness of the excerpt; more extensive illustrative material, such as holographs of manuscript pages and photographs of people and places pertinent to the authors' careers; a cumulative nationality index for easy access to authors by nationality; and occasional guest essays written specifically for *CLR* by prominent critics on subjects of their choice.

Readers who wish to suggest authors to appear in future volumes, or who have other suggestions, are cordially invited to write the editor.

Acknowledgments

The editors wish to thank the copyright holders of the excerpted criticism included in this volume, the permissions managers of many book and magazine publishing companies for assisting us in securing reprint rights, and Anthony Bogucki for assistance with copyright research. We are also grateful to the staffs of the Detroit Public Library, the Library of Congress, the University of Detroit Library, Wayne State University Purdy/Kresge Library Complex, and the University of Michigan Libraries for making their resources available to us. Following is a list of the copyright holders who have granted us permission to reprint material in this volume of *CLR*. Every effort has been made to trace copyright, but if omissions have been made, please let us know.

THE EXCERPTS IN *CLR*, VOLUME 24, WERE REPRINTED FROM THE FOLLOWING PERIODICALS:

The Alan Review, v. 10, Fall, 1982; v. 10, Spring, 1983; v. 11, Winter, 1984; v. 12, Spring, 1985. All reprinted by permission of the publisher.—*Appraisal: Children's Science Books,* v. 12, Spring, 1979; v. 13, Fall, 1980; v. 15, Winter, 1982. Copyright © 1979, 1980, 1982 by the Children's Science Book Review Committee. All reprinted by permission of the publisher.—*Appraisal: Science Books for Young People,* v. 15, Winter, 1982; v. 17, Spring-Summer, 1984; v. 18, Spring, 1985; v. 18, Autumn, 1985; v. 19, Spring, 1986; v. 19, Summer, 1986; v. 20, Winter, 1987; v. 22, Winter & Spring, 1989. Copyright © 1982, 1984, 1985, 1986, 1987, 1989 by the Children's Science Book Review Committee. All reprinted by permission of the publisher.—*The Art Bulletin,* v. LVII, September, 1975 for a review of "Humorous but Wholesome: A History of Palmer Cox and the Brownies" by David Kunzle. Reprinted by permission of the College Art Association, Inc. and the author.—*Best Sellers,* v. 37, June, 1977; v. 39, September, 1979; v. 40, June, 1980; v. 42, May, 1982; v. 44, December, 1984; v. 44, January, 1985. Copyright © 1977, 1979, 1980, 1982, 1984, 1985 Helen Dwight Reid Educational Foundation. All reprinted by permission of the publisher.—*Book World—The Washington Post,* May 10, 1981; May 9, 1982; November 6, 1983; July 9, 1989. © 1981, 1982, 1983, 1989, *The Washington Post.* All reprinted by permission of the publisher.—*Books for Keeps,* n. 47, November, 1987; n. 50, May, 1988; n. 63, July, 1990. © School Bookshop Association 1987, 1988, 1990. All reprinted by permission of the publisher.—*Bookbird,* n. 3, September 15, 1964; v. 6, March 15, 1968; v. VI, September 15, 1968; v. VIII, June 15, 1970; v. IX, June 15, 1971; v. XI, March 15, 1973; n. 3, September 15, 1980. All reprinted by permission of the publisher.—*Booklist,* v. 73, May 15, 1977; v. 74, March 15, 1978; v. 75, September 1, 1978; v. 75, December 1, 1978; v. 75, March 1, 1979; v. 75, July 15, 1979; v. 76, June 15, 1980; v. 76, July 1, 1980; v. 76, July 15, 1980; v. 77, November 15, 1980; v. 77, December 15, 1980; v. 77, July 1, 1981; v. 78, September 1, 1981; v. 78, October 15, 1981; v. 78, November 15, 1981; v. 78, June 1, 1982; v. 79, October 1, 1982; v. 79, December 15, 1982; v. 79, August, 1983; v. 80, September, 1983; v. 80, October 1, 1983; v. 80, November 15, 1983; v. 80, April 1, 1984; v. 80, June 1, 1984; v. 81, October 15, 1984; v. 81, November 15, 1984; v. 81, May 1, 1985; v. 81, May 15, 1985; v. 82, June 15, 1986; v. 83, September 15, 1986; v. 83, November 1, 1986; v. 83, November 15, 1986; v. 83, May 1, 1987; v. 83, August, 1987; v. 84, September 1, 1987; v. 85, September 15, 1988; v. 85, October 1, 1988; v. 85, October 15, 1988; v. 85, February 15, 1989; v. 85, March 1, 1989; v. 86, September 15, 1989; v. 86, October 1, 1989; v. 86, October 15, 1989; v. 86, November 1, 1989; v. 86, April 1, 1990; v. 86, April 15, 1990; v. 86, May 1, 1990; v. 86, May 15, 1990. Copyright © 1977, 1978, 1979, 1980, 1981, 1982, 1983, 1984, 1985, 1986, 1987, 1988, 1989, 1990 by the American Library Association. All reprinted by permission of the publisher.—*The Booklist,* v. 68, February 15, 1972; v. 69, December 15, 1972. Copyright © 1972 by the American Library Association. Both reprinted by permission of the publisher.—*Bulletin of the Center for Children's Books,* v. XVIII, February, 1965; v. 25, September, 1971; v. 26, March, 1973; v. 27, January, 1974; v. 28, February, 1975; v. 29, July-August, 1976; v. 31, July-August, 1978; v. 33, September, 1979; v. 33, December, 1979; v. 34, September, 1980; v. 34, October, 1980; v. 34, November, 1980; v. 35, October, 1981; v. 35, March, 1982; v. 36, September, 1982; v. 37, September, 1983; v. 37, February, 1984; v. 37, June, 1984; v. 38, October, 1984; v. 39, January, 1986; v. 39, February, 1986; v. 39, March, 1986; v. 39, July-August, 1986; v. 40, September, 1986; v. 40, October, 1986; v. 40, December, 1986; v. 40, January, 1987; v. 40, April, 1987; v. 41, September, 1987; v. 41, October, 1987; v. 41, December, 1987; v. 41, April, 1988; v. 41, May, 1988; v. 42, September, 1988; v. 42, March, 1989; v. 42, July-August, 1989; v. 43, October, 1989. Copyright © 1965, 1971, 1973, 1974, 1975, 1976, 1978, 1979, 1980, 1981, 1982, 1983, 1984, 1986, 1987, 1988, 1989 by The University of Chicago. All reprinted by permission of The University of Chicago Press.—*Catholic Library World,* v. 51, August/September, 1979; v. 56, March, 1985. Both reprinted by permission of the publisher.—*Chicago Tribune,* November 14, 1954. Copyrighted 1954, renewed 1982 Chicago Tribune Company. All rights reserved./ July 1, 1956. © copyrighted 1956, renewed 1984 Chicago Tribune Company. All rights reserved. Used with permission.—*Children's Book News,* London, v. 3, May-June, 1968. Copyright © 1968 by Baker Book Services Ltd. Reprinted by permission of the publisher.—*Children's Book Review,* v. I, April, 1971; v. I, October, 1971; v. I, December, 1971; v. II, February, 1972; v. II, December, 1972; v. III, June,

THE EXCERPTS IN *CLR,* VOLUME 24, WERE REPRINTED FROM THE FOLLOWING BOOKS:

Group, Inc./ Illustration by Maud and Miska Petersham from their ***The Christ Child, as Told by Matthew and Luke.*** Doubleday, Doran and Company, 1931. Pictures copyright 1931 by Maud and Miska Petersham. Used by permission of Doubleday, a division of Bantam Doubleday Dell Publishing Group, Inc./ Illustration by Maud and Miska Petersham from their ***The Story Book of Things We Use.*** The John C. Winston Company, 1933. Copyright, 1933, by the John C. Winston Co. Reprinted by permission of Marjorie Petersham./ Illustration by Maud and Miska Petersham from their ***The Rooster Crows: A Book of American Rhymes and Jingles.*** The Macmillan Company, 1955. Copyright 1945 by Macmillan Publishing Company, renewed © 1973 by Miska F. Petersham. Reprinted with permission of Macmillan Publishing Company./ Illustration by Maud and Miska Petersham from their ***An American ABC.*** The Macmillan Company, 1946. Copyright 1941 by Macmillan Publishing Company, renewed © 1969 by Maud Petersham. Reprinted with permission of Macmillan Publishing Company./ Illustration by Helen Roney Sattler from her ***Holiday Gifts, Favors, and Decorations That You Can Make.*** Lothrop, Lee & Shepard Company, 1971. Copyright © 1971 by Helen Roney Sattler. Reprinted by permission of Lothrop, Lee & Shepard Books, a division of William Morrow & Company, Inc./ Illustration by Helen Roney Sattler from her ***Sock Craft: Toys, Gifts, and Other Things to Make.*** Lothrop, Lee & Shepard Co., 1972. Copyright © 1972 by Helen Roney Sattler. Reprinted by permission of Lothrop, Lee & Shepard Books, a division of William Morrow & Company, Inc. Illustration by Helen Roney Sattler from ***Jar and Bottle Craft,*** by Helen Roney Sattler. Lothrop, Lee & Shepard Company, 1974. Copyright © 1074 by Helen Roney Sattler. Reprinted by permission of Lothrop, Lee & Shepard Books, a division of William Morrow & Company, Inc.

PHOTOGRAPHS APPEARING IN *CLR*, VOLUME 24, WERE RECEIVED FROM THE FOLLOWING SOURCES:

Photograph by David Gullette. Courtesy of Avi Wortis: **p. 1**; Photograph by Rosemary Ranck. Courtesy of Avi Wortis: **p. 7**; Photograph by Al Cetta: **p. 61**; © Jon Gilbert Fox. Courtesy of Tomie dePaola: **p. 84**; Photograph by Ken Salls: **p. 105**; Courtesy of Christobel Mattingley: **pp. 117, 123**; Courtesy of Advertiser Newspapers Limited: **p. 128**; Courtesy of Marjorie R. Petersham: **pp. 155; 168**; Courtesy of Bookbird: **p. 180**; © Jerry Bauer: **p. 186**; Courtesy of William Morrow & Company, Inc.: **p. 212**; Photograph by Polly Thompson. Courtesy of Julian F. Thompson: **p. 226**.

Children's
Literature
Review

Avi

1937-

(Full name Avi Wortis) American author of fiction and short stories.

Major works include *Emily Upham's Revenge; or, How Deadwood Dick Saved the Banker's Niece: A Massachusetts Adventure* (1978), *Encounter at Easton* (1980), *The Fighting Ground* (1984), *S.O.R. Losers* (1984), *The Man Who Was Poe* (1989), *The True Confessions of Charlotte Doyle* (1990).

Considered one of the most popular and versatile writers of literature for young people, Avi is acknowledged for successfully contributing to a variety of genres for the early, middle, and upper grades; although most of his works are historical fiction, both serious and comic, he is also the creator of contemporary realistic fiction, mysteries, fantasies, psychological thrillers, adventure stories, and short stories. He is often credited with investing his lively yet sensitive works with spirited plots, believable characters, vivid atmosphere, accurate historical detail, and considerable irony and wit. Writing in a literary style which ranges from terse to richly textured, Avi is praised for addressing complex issues with sensitivity and skill. He characteristically explores the thoughts and feelings of young people faced with moral dilemmas and asks both his readers and the protagonists of his novels to question conventional values. Although several of his books explore the darker sides of both the natural and supernatural worlds, Avi is also the author of a number of comic stories and parodies filled with nonsense and tongue-in-cheek humor.

A librarian and storyteller who is also a teacher and reviewer of children's literature, Avi is especially well known for his historical and realistic fiction. Among his most acclaimed works are parodies such as *Emily Upham's Revenge* and *The History of Helpless Harry* (1980), spoofs of nineteenth-century melodramas featuring convoluted plots and happy endings; young adult historical novels such as *The Fighting Ground*, which presents a personalized view of war and its conflicting emotions against the background of the American Revolution; *Night Journeys* (1979) and its sequel *Encounter at Easton*, adventures for middle graders which center on the escape of two youthful indentured servants and on the reactions of the characters, both young and old, with whom they come in contact; and *The Man Who Was Poe*, a thriller for middle graders set in nineteenth-century Baltimore which describes how eleven-year-old Edmund enlists the help of Edgar Allan Poe in locating his missing mother and sister. In addition to these works, Avi is well known as the author of the contemporary stories *S.O.R. Losers* and its sequel *Romeo and Juliet—Together (and Alive!)—at Last* (1987), humorous fiction for middle graders about the students at South Orange River Middle School which are especially popular with young readers. Recently, Avi has re-

ceived acclaim for his historical novel *The True Confessions of Charlotte Doyle,* an adventure story about how teenage Charlotte becomes involved with a brutal captain and his mutinous crew on a sea journey in 1832; *Charlotte Doyle* was named a Newbery Medal honor book in 1991. Three of Avi's works were runners–up for the Edgar Allan Poe Award: *No More Magic* in 1976, *Emily Upham's Revenge* in 1979, and *Shadrach's Crossing* in 1984. He also received the Christopher Award for *Encounter at Easton* in 1981 and the Scott O'Dell Award for *The Fighting Ground* in 1984.

(See also *Something about the Author,* Vol. 14; *Contemporary Authors New Revision Series,* Vol. 12; and *Contemporary Authors,* Vols. 69-72.)

AUTHOR'S COMMENTARY

It's always difficult for me to set down a coherent plan that will describe how I write my books for young people. (p. 18)

The question that's addressed to me more than any other (adults as well as kids, by the way) is: "Where do you get your ideas?" The answer is, everywhere. Ideas do not come whole cloth. They are amalgams of random thoughts, observations, moods, squeezed into shape by the way I look upon the world.

For example, my book, **Sometimes I Think I Hear My Name** is based on a) the particular living circumstances of a kid I knew; b) a remark about locale by a writer friend; c) a passing reference by my wife to the way some kids were living; d) the offchance remark of another friend about a parent, and e) a quote from Ross MacDonald, "Most fiction is shaped by geography and permeated by autobiography, even when it is trying not to be."

Clearly, all these elements did not come together in one explosion. They rattled about in my head until they were linked. How so? This, I suspect, is the crucial part. My primary perception of the world is that of story. Because I have always read a great deal (still do), I have taught myself to think about people, circumstances, events, not in terms of singular occurrences, but in the context of evolving narratives that contain beginnings, endings, tensions, and locales. This means I am never without ideas. I've got six books in my head right now.

I think that each person has a way of looking at the world. I'll bet your dentist, upon meeting someone, notices teeth. The clothing designer will measure your cut, taste, and budget. . . . In just the same fashion, you can learn to look at the world from a novelist's point of view. It does require you to read a great deal and to think novelistically. Even that can be further defined; it's the 19th century novel that holds me.

Out of a rather casual, *on-going* observation of things in a narrative fashion, I move on to constructing my novels. The key question for me has always been, not, how do I find ideas, but rather, how do I choose the ones I wish to work on? Not all ideas make good books for me.

I do it by building a brief outline that consists, in the main, of a series of *events,* usually no more than twenty. Since my perception of plot has to do with interlocking events that have a culmination, in time these events become chapter concepts. (pp. 18-19)

The outline is . . . crude, and much of it sits in my head, rather than on paper. In that sense, the outline helps me recall my thoughts.

Usually, for a while, I don't go beyond the construction of an outline. I sit back and think and think, and having done that, think a while more. Occasionally I've jumped in quickly upon the page with a new idea, but more often than not, I'll think it over for a period of months, maybe a couple of years. I will fuss with that event-outline a good bit, adding, subtracting, but always keeping it brief, to the point, and focused on *events.* I make no notes about persons, places, characters. I think about it. Above all, I try hard not to think what I *mean.* (p. 19)

As for getting around to writing, that start is focused on the first chapter, the first page. I do believe that with the children's book, that first page, that first paragraph, is crucial. The kids don't give you much time to set your hook, and if you provide too much information they simply can't absorb it all. I strive for a quick sense of conflicting forces, an unanswered question, a loss of balance. I labor a great deal over these opening words and pages, not just for their readability but because they set the tone, the mood, the pace, even—and this is *very* crucial to me—the rhythm.

Given the opening gambit (which I think is exactly the right word here), I set to work from page one, right on through, with one eye on that "event" outline. But the fact is I'm never really sure where I am going. For example, when I wrote **The History of Helpless Harry,** I was intent on composing a grim, relentless tragedy about a kid whose fearfulness made him positively evil. There was not the slightest notion of anything funny. After a crucial suggestion by my astute agent—many, many rewrites and three years later—one reviewer wrote: "This is an invitation to farce, and farcical indeed is the web of misconstructions that follow." Wrote another critic of my would-be demonic youth: "This tale offers . . . a hero who makes the reader stand up and cheer."

So much for my relentless tragedy.

This kind of thing happens to me often because I allow myself to react to the books as I write them. I write, I have a suspicion, to discover what will happen. It's a journey. I read my books as I write them, responding to that reading, making countless adjustments, major and minor, as my *developing* perception of what I am writing evolves. Not infrequently I'll work on a book for months before I describe a character's physical being. It takes that long to see.

Just the other day, typing a manuscript for perhaps the tenth time, I was pounding toward the climax when I suddenly realized that my main character would *not* be saying what *I* had him saying. What he wanted to say was . . . and so he did, in the eleventh rewrite. (pp. 19-20)

[I] describe myself as a very slow writer who works quickly. Fifteen rewrites for me is not uncommon, and the difference between first and last version is day and night. My first drafts are simply awful. I wouldn't show them to my cat. What *emerges* can be, and often is, O.K. But good Lord, there are times I feel as if I'm not writing, not for fun anyway, until I'm into the manuscript for six months.

It is here that my conceptual view of the novel's form becomes so critical. I reread what I rewrite endlessly. I respond to my work as *listener,* seeking that right voice, tone, flow. I read my books out loud so I can hear them. Amazing what you hear. Read to a class of young people, and that relentless, restless shifting of feet is every bit as eloquent, as critical as a major media review. Considering its place in the process, it's usually more helpful.

How long does this entire evolution take? It varies. Generally speaking, I find that my best books are written in two phases. First, a fast, intense period of writing in which an entire crude first draft is made complete. This is followed by a long, slow period, during which time I untangle or realize that draft's potential. On the one hand, there is the emotional uniformity of that mad dash toward the finish; on the other, the often difficult, sometimes tedious, technical process during which I labor to make the emotional base readable. And, believe me, it's an everyday effort.

The crux of all this is a kind of hard honesty. If the work doesn't feel right, I *must* respond accordingly. Sometimes, I suppose, I try to fool myself, but I know. If you are not going to be absolutely honest with yourself, forget it. It will never go. And I'm not just thinking of plot and character, but of words, rhythm, that slender, silken, but always *spoken* thread that beads your vision into an ornament of articulation.

Betty Miles, one of our best writers for young people, once described to me that time after the book is essentially done, when one is free (and relaxed) to make those countless changes, those tiny touches that transform adequacy into an adventure. How true she spoke. At last one feels that one is truly playing the writer's craft. (pp. 20, 28)

Young people have an essentially empirical understanding of the world. Their cognitive development is founded not on abstract ideas, but on their concrete experiences, experiences centered on self. It is that characteristic that makes kids naïve, blunt, crude, insulting, cruel, refreshing, candid . . . depending on your perspective. The point is that they bring this critical apparatus to the books we write for them. They are much more demanding than the average adult reader. A hard audience to please: Give them a world they can understand and they will read you. Give them a world that expands, or better, defines, their often unspoken, often hidden perceptions and extraordinary sensibilities, and they will embrace you. (p. 28)

> *Avi, "Writing Books for Young People," in* The Writer, *Vol. 95, No. 3, March, 1982, pp. 18-20, 28.*

GENERAL COMMENTARY

Susan Stan

This year, Avi . . . is teaching a course in children's literature at Simmons College in Boston. "I choose a number of important writers. We read everything by them in chronological sequence and then discuss the books—as a body of work—in class. Finally, we meet with each author for an intense three-hour discussion. It's tremendously difficult and tremendously exciting," he says. "This is an attempt to get people to read in a different way, to see work as a whole, to see development, the evolution of ideas and themes."

Ironically, to Avi's knowledge no one has ever looked at *his* work that way. People constantly remark on the variety of books he has written, which include ghost stories, contemporary and historical adventures, comedies, mysteries, and even fantasy, but no one has moved past the genres to explore reoccurring themes.

Although his work has been described as innovative— especially *The Man Who Was Poe* . . .—Avi has neither attempted to be innovative nor considered himself so. Instead, he begins with a premise or conflict and chooses his vehicle: "I look at the story and ask, How can I most effectively tell it?" He has, he notes, been very fortunate in having editors who encourage this approach. "It's made writing hard in the best way, and I love that."

S.O.R. Losers, one of Avi's most popular books with young readers, is the story of a motley assortment of smart, talented, but unathletic seventh-graders who are turned, despite their wishes, into a soccer team. The humor is found in the situation (they don't know how to play soccer and are coached by a history teacher whose soccer knowledge comes out of a manual) as well as in the language. One of the eleven players narrates (his last name is the same as Avi's spelled backwards); his clever observations and allusions, which can cause the reader to laugh out loud, are perfectly in character. The premise, though, is not particularly funny: too great an emphasis is placed on participating in and winning at sports, while accomplishments in other areas, whether academic or artistic, are undervalued.

In *The Man Who Was Poe,* set in Rhode Island in 1848, a young boy runs headlong into Poe in a dark street. Poe agrees to help the boy find his lost sister, and as the complicated story progresses, Poe's motives slowly come to light. Avi explains the origin of the story in this way: "Poe is an incredible and complex figure who's absolutely adored by many young people. What happens if you confront him—this crazy, alcoholic, weird, brilliant man— with a kid? That's a historical question, but after that, it's about the relationship, not about history or the moment in history. One could have written the story today about what it's like to depend on someone who's an alcoholic. You can tell that story in a hundred different ways."

Another of Avi's historical novels, *The Fighting Ground,* is set during the Revolutionary War. The entire action spans only one day, and while the battlefield is the setting, the conflict occurs in a young boy's heart and mind. . . .

Historical fiction, so popular for many years, lost favor among readers during the past couple of decades, quite possibly reflecting a declining interest in history itself. Today historical fiction is once again being written and read. . . .

As Avi astutely points out, modern works of historical fiction must necessarily be different from their predecessors. Every era looks at history differently, in the context of its own time. "If you read a book like *Johnny Tremain,* written in a different period, the forties, you see the tendency to glorify the ideals and values of the American Revolution. I don't think we would look at it in the same simple, unconflicted way today." In fact, *The Fighting Ground,* as noted previously, offers a decidedly conflicted view of war.

Avi writes full time now, but until a little more than four years ago, his writing schedule had to be flexible enough to fit around his career as librarian. Then, too, he has been a reviewer, and he is keenly aware of the needs and responsibilities of all three groups of people. As an author, he asks for longer, more extensive reviews that give consideration to a book's quality of writing as well as its plot and content. As he wrote in a controversial *School Library Journal* article [in March of 1986], "I hope reviewers will remember that children's literature *is* literature, not merely material for a teaching unit, a resource for homework."

Susan Stan, "Conversations: Avi," in The Five Owls, *Vol. III, No. 3, January-February, 1990, p. 45.*

TITLE COMMENTARY

Things That Sometimes Happen: Very Short Stories for Very Young Readers   (1970)

Short stories? Thirty long shots—missing every mark: child-style rambunctious set-ups with punchlines limper than a soggy shaggy dog. To wit, there's **"Dancing"**: Little Girl, then Papa, Cat, Fish, Horse, join Mama bowing, bouncing, stretching, jumping . . . "Then they took naps." And there's **"Talking to the Stars"** to find out if there's sunshine in store for a trip to the country: the Star says there is so the children stop worrying; "Next morning the weather was fine. They did go to the country. The Star had told them the weather." Etcetera . . . whether the nameless 'protagonist' be Little Boy or Girl or angry Fire Engine or (most popularly) Hippopotamus, the same thing happens: nothing.

A review of "Things That Sometimes Happen: Very Short Stories for Very Young Readers," in Kirkus Reviews, *Vol. XXXVIII, No. 23, December 1, 1970, p. 1288.*

Thirty of the briefest stories (about one page each) that are whimsical with the matter-of-fact, illogical conjunction of reality and fantasy characteristic of the very young. They sound like a first grader's first story efforts, but they are not as spontaneous and show the contol of an adult writer: "A Little Girl was walking down the street, not looking where she was going. Before she knew it she walked right into the huge mouth of an enormous Hippopotamus, who happened to be yawning himself to sleep." . . . [This] could be a useful book for teachers working with creative writing in the primary grades—the titles alone suggest great possibilities: **"Making the Mouse Feel Better"**; **"How the Goldfish Spent the Day"**; **"The Visiting Giant."** This would also be a suitable read-aloud for pre-schoolers with the shortest attention spans.

Marjorie Lewis, in a review of "Things That Sometimes Happen," in School Library Journal, *Vol. 17, No. 7, March, 1971, p. 116.*

Snail Tale: The Adventures of a Rather Small Snail (1972)

The workings of snail and ant minds will not hold the interest of youngsters in this overly wordy tale. Because books have convinced Avon Snail that happiness is only possible through adventure, he and his friend Edward Ant set out on a journey. A newt, a salamander and other small creatures encountered along the way fail to provide the friends with opportunities for real heroism. Ultimately, they come upon a "magic castle" which exactly resembles Avon's own home. The episodes are disjointed and, although there is some humor, the fantasy is never fully realized.

Marianne Hough, in a review of "Snail Tale:

The Adventures of a Rather Small Snail," in School Library Journal, *Vol. 19, No. 5, January, 1973, p. 65.*

[**Snail Tale** has] little concern with reality, consisting mainly of long conversations between an ant and a snail. No news may be good news, as Avon the snail says, but it makes a very quiet book. There are some easy jokes about creativity and relativity and beginnings and ends, and even one about Neasden Wanderers which seems to have strayed in from *Private Eye*.

"Rewards and Fairies," in The Times Literary Supplement, *No. 3734, September 28, 1973, p. 1122.*

You can if you wish read [**Snail Tale**] as a light-hearted satire on the way a writer manipulates reality. Avon's reverential belief in the infallibility of traditional literature is seen to be relevant to this approach. Hearing a sound of woe in the distance, he announces "I think we should stop . . . That's what they do in the books"; heedless of Edward's warning ("Never rush into anything which may want rushing out of "), he moves forward, to find a worm tightly curled and needing someone to distinguish between its front and its back. When the two friends are safely ensconced in the "Magic Castle" Avon is about to tell the Chameleon about his adventure with the Frog when "he remembered just in time that he never did have an adventure with a Frog". Edward, as always, has a solution; he can put it in an appendix—"It's what you put at the back of the book when the front is too thin". Adults who read this brief, sparkling tale to small children will certainly enjoy its intellectual humour. . . .

As for the young, some will appreciate the unobtrusive way the joke of the circular journey is built up through the narrative. Some will enjoy the way the two characters are revealed in their conversation and in the striking difference between their respective forms of locomotion; at one point Edward leaves Avon for three days and three nights, having dashed ahead to relieve knees aching with the effort to match his speed to that of the snail. Some will enjoy the snatches of natural history—the meeting with the caterpillar, for example, and her reappearance from her cocoon as a butterfly (incidentally, another neat way of indicating the passage of time). . . . Altogether this tiny exercise in nonsense, . . . is to be warmly welcomed. . . . (p. 2964)

Margery Fisher, in a review of "Snail Tale," in Growing Point, *Vol. 15, No. 4, October, 1976, pp. 2963-64.*

No More Magic   (1975)

Chris' stolen bike, Muffin's missing warlock costume winning the Halloween parade for a mystery marcher, even the disappearance of Muffin's parents . . . creates a tangled puzzle that Chris sets out to solve logically according to the system of his librarian dad. According to Chris, who delivers his findings in a hang-loose first person report, evidence of magic at work becomes undeniable and it looks like the local junk dealer, Mr. Bullens, must be a practicing warlock. But even a witch couldn't anticipate the final twists of this plot, and though the solution isn't quite cricket by detective novel rules, it works an amusing twist on those by now routine manifestations of the supernatural in suburbia.

> *A review of "No More Magic," in* Kirkus Reviews, *Vol. XLIII, No. 12, June 15, 1975, p. 659.*

No More Magic doesn't have any in the first place but tricks readers into expecting some. It's all about a stolen green bike (the color makes it "magical" to young Chris) and a missing Halloween warlock costume. The author tries to spice it up with a mysterious Druid design woven into a coat and Chris' friend Muffin's father alluding to the magic being gone from his marriage before he takes off in search of her missing mother. But in essence there's just a lot of racing around town on bikes looking for clues to the whereabouts of the missing items, which of course are found at the end. The main virtue of the story is the depiction of how children look and hope for magic in their daily lives, by pretending and/or believing; but this relevant theme is not explored far enough.

> *Cherie LaGess Zarookian, in a review of "No More Magic," in* School Library Journal, *Vol. 22, No. 2, October, 1975, p. 94.*

The story is amusing even though the narrative is spun out with stock characters, a good share of false leads, and obviously contrived incidents. Chris and Muffin are individualized and winning, and their strong belief in magic seems typical of imaginative children of mid-elementary-school age and adds a distinctive twist and some humor, much of it adult, to what would otherwise be a rather conventional mystery for middle readers. The use of short sentences and phrases produces an appropriately conversational tone. The slight subplot about Muffin's parents' marriage contributes human interest and a little suspense.

> *Alethea K. Helbig and Agnes Regan Perkins, in a review of "No More Magic," in their* Dictionary of American Children's Fiction, 1960-1984: Recent Books of Recognized Merit, *Greenwood Press, 1986, p. 476.*

Captain Grey (1977)

Young Kevin Cartwright, his sister, and his insane father are attacked by the mysterious Captain Grey and his band of pirates in the pine forests of New Jersey. His father killed and his sister seemingly having met the same fate, Kevin is taken by the Captain and given the choice of death or joining the band of pirates. It is not that much to the benefit of the reader that Kevin chooses to continue. Nonetheless, chapter by chapter, a passenger pigeon here, an answered message there, Kevin and his sister (how'd you guess) literally stand aside as the story winds itself down like some return of an old television serial.

I couldn't help but get the feeling as I read this effort by Avi . . . that it was in fact a script for a prime-time television series. Another Space Family Robinson in the mak-

ing. "Be with us next week when Kevin discovers who's been answering his messages."

That, of course, is my objection here. The plot offers a few interesting turns to keep a young person going with this book, but in the end he'll find it about as rewarding as the commercialized prefabrications he faces on the tube every night.

Come on Avi . . . if you're going to take the responsibility of offering a good alternative to the tube for our kids, at least give them something they can sink their teeth into.

> *Larry Stoiaken, in a review of "Captain Grey," in* Best Sellers, *Vol. 37, No. 3, June, 1977, p. 94.*

This is a robust pirate adventure with a neat twist. Instead of piling his raggle-taggle band aboard a standard pirate ship, Avi has his crew living as a "Free Nation" on the wild, uninhabited coast of New Jersey (this is 1783, remember). By means of a floating raft of cannons, the marauders plunder passing ships, then cram their makeshift huts with stolen loot. Except for the missing Jolly Roger, however, all other conventions of buccaneering are closely observed: there's the requisite iron-hearted captain of the title; a couple of bloody fights at sea; and, of course, a young kidnap victim—11-year-old Kevin who, accepted as one of the men, is given a crash course in piracy, only to bring about the fall of the "Free Nation." From start to finish, Avi keeps a taut line on the action. Anyone looking for a hearty old-fashioned swashbuckler should certainly sign on with **Captain Grey.**

> *Jane O'Connor, in a review of "Captain Grey," in* The New York Times Book Review, *September 11, 1977, p. 30.*

For younger YAs who like adventure, here is a tale which provides action on every page. The setting is the New Jersey coast in the 1780s with most of the excitement taking place in and around a pirate settlement. Two children, Kevin (11) and his sister Catherine (13), are seized by pirates. The latter are a mixed lot with sympathetic characteristics as well as the expected villainous traits. One point worth special mention is the fact that Catherine is exceedingly courageous, inventive and strong (not a weak sister who needs to be protected), so the book provides some good, healthy escape reading for both sexes.

> *A review of "Captain Grey," in* Kliatt Young Adult Paperback Book Guide, *Vol. XIII, No. 1, Winter, 1979, p. 5.*

Emily Upham's Revenge: Or, How Deadwood Dick Saved the Banker's Niece: A Massachusetts Adventure (1978)

A cheerful, amusing story set in 19th-Century Massachusetts. Young Emily Upham, a proper little lady, afraid of getting her clothes dirty, has been sent to North Brookfield to stay with her wealthy (but nasty) uncle. Instead of meeting him, however, she encounters mischievous (but innocent) Seth Marple, a happy-go-lucky Huckleberry Finn-type. Their interchange sets off a chain of events, with several hairpin twists and turns of plot. Emily's new experiences leave her less prissy but she never really gets a chance to show her stuff, and the ending is as syrupy and moralistic as were the children's books of the era in which this is set. Nevertheless, the story . . . will be good, light reading for those looking for laughs, adventure, and a happy ending.

> *Cyrisse Jaffee, in a review of "Emily Upham's Revenge or How Deadwood Dick Saved the Banker's Niece: A Massachusetts Adventure," in* School Library Journal, *Vol. 24, No. 7, March, 1978, p. 124.*

As a spoof of books of the Alger vintage, [**Emily Upham's Revenge**] it is just a bit overdrawn, and the appropriate audience for the book is probably too young to appreciate the fact that it is a spoof; taken at face value it has, despite some humor and more than enough action, good style but a tortuous plot.

> *Zena Sutherland, in a review of "Emily Upham's Revenge; or, How Deadwood Dick Saved the Banker's Niece," in* Bulletin of the Center for Children's Books, *Vol. 31, No. 11, July-August, 1978, p. 170.*

[When Emily and Seth conspire to rob Mr. Upham's bank for train fare to Boston, they] are astounded to observe a robbery already in progress. Seth recognizes the robber as Emily's own father, but out of consideration for the little girl's feelings he keeps his knowledge to himself. An exciting and amusing assortment of misadventures and entanglements follows, involving blackmail, fraud, and treachery, as resourceful Seth strives to keep from being blamed for the robbery and at the same time maintain naive Emily's innocence concerning her father's part in this nefarious affair. Events reach a grand climax when all best-laid plans to entrap and inveigle go hilariously awry and only the suddenly assertive Emily knows the whereabouts of the $4,000 in loot, and she stubbornly refuses to tell. Seth emerges as noble hero, banker Upham gets his comeuppance, Emily's father acknowledges the error of his ways, and Emily secretly and righteously donates the money to charity, it having been abundantly proved once again that "money is the root of all evil." The inventively convoluted plot is rich with ironies and surprises. It quicksteps along for what on one level is an engaging spoof on the old dime novels, on another is just deliciously good entertainment.

> *Alethea K. Helbig and Agnes Regan Perkins, in a review of "Emily Upham's Revenge," in their* Dictionary of American Children's Fiction, 1960-1984: Recent Books of Recognized Merit, *Greenwood Press, 1986, p. 191.*

Night Journeys (1979)

Looking back on his youth, the narrator, Peter York, tells of an episode during his adolescence in colonial Pennsylvania which proved to be a turning point in his life. Orphaned, he had been sent to live with a family of kindly but undemonstrative Quakers whose ways he did not understand and whom he consequently resented, thinking

that they did not care for him. When two children who had been indentured servants to a harsh master in a nearby county make a bid for freedom, both Peter and his foster father are called upon to help capture them. Though at first they cooperate, each for very different reasons, they both soon come to realize that no matter what the cost they must heed their consciences rather than uphold the law. As each becomes aware of the other's faltering but persistent struggle toward integrity, the distance between them closes and they begin a new warm and supportive relationship. Though the plot is a slim one, it manages to convey a commendable message without being obtrusively didactic, and contains enough tension to retain readers' interest. The author's strength here is his insightful portrayal of appealing, uncommon characters and the generally believable growth which they experience as the story progresses.

> *Chuck Schacht, in a review of "Night Journeys," in* School Library Journal, *Vol. 25, No. 8, April, 1979, p. 52.*

An efficiently worked-out object lesson, communicated in Colonial-ese. . . . [Farmer Shinn's tacturnity stands] between him and Peter when they become involved in trying to apprehend two escaped bondsmen. First, Peter can't understand Shinn's reluctance to go after the sizable reward, his insistence on doing no more than his duty as Justice of the Peace; then, after Peter himself warms to their plight—one is a young girl whom he hastily, horrifyingly shoots, the other a still younger boy—Shinn seems to him callous for being willing to turn the two in. . . . There is a central action sequence but even when Peter and the girl are in mortal danger the book has no grip: it moves along on a conceptual level with prototypical characters and not a single stray feeling or purposeless thought. Worthy, then, but vacuum-packed.

> *A review of "Night Journeys," in* Kirkus Reviews, *Vol. XLVII, No. 9, May 1, 1979, p. 517.*

There is much that is dramatic in the story, and the writing style is competent, but the book is weakened by a slow pace and by the fact that there is little depth of characterization; there is motivation, there is message, and there is action, but Peter and Shinn are superficial figures.

> *Zena Sutherland, in a review of "Night Journeys," in* Bulletin of the Center for Children's Books, *Vol. 33, No. 1, September, 1979, p. 2.*

Encounter at Easton (1980)

Nathaniel Hill, a local gambler and bully, is hired by a Trenton, N.J. gentleman to track and trap two young runaway indentured servants, Robert Linnly and Elizabeth Mawes, last seen fleeing toward freedom in the author's **Night Journeys.** An infected bullet wound renders the girl delirious, and fate brings the boy into his cruel pursuer's clutches as employee. What's a game to the mercenary hunter is life and death to his prey, and there is little hope for the child outlaws or for Mad Moll, who shelters them in her cave. All are marked victims, but Robert is saved by a kindly tapman at the inn, witness to his ordeal. Set

Avi at his typewriter.

in the spring of 1768, the tale is told through alternating testimonies of the major parties involved, comprising a court investigation of the events described. In his terse style, Avi manipulates these narratives with skill, sustaining suspense and reminding readers of more modern events with the disavowing refrains: "Rest perfectly assured that what happened had nothing to do with me. . ." and "I acted only in accordance with the laws . . . "

> *Laura Geringer, in a review of "Encounter at Easton," in* School Library Journal, *Vol. 26, No. 9, May, 1980, p. 64.*

Good adolescent literature can foster sophisticated adult reading habits and should, therefore, be more than just a story. *Encounter at Easton* fits the bill nicely. It has a lot going for it. It is an historical novel set in the pre-Revolutionary War colonies. Though in the past, the characters would not be all that out of place today. . . .

Encounter at Easton is not overly complex, nor is it so simple as to be demeaning to younger readers. The book gives the reader characters and situations which may or may not have parallels today; the young reader gets to think and render his own judgment. Avi must be given

credit for not underestimating the potential of his audience.

One only hopes that books of this quality continue and that the kids read them!

> *A. Siaulys, in a review of "Encounter at Easton," in* Best Sellers, *Vol. 40, No. 3, June, 1980, p. 115.*

Though the author threads his story line with a keen sense of timing and pace, his manner of telling will impede all but the special reader. The plot, which unfolds through a series of testimonies, is forced through changes in point of view as Robert, Hill, and Constable Clagget take up the story. Those caught up in the destinies of Elizabeth and Robert will find the adventure worth pursuing.

> *Barbara Elleman, in a review of "Encounter at Easton," in* Booklist, *Vol. 76, No. 20, June 15, 1980, p. 1528.*

Robert Linnly and Elizabeth Mawes, the boy and girl runaways aided by orphan Peter York in *Night Journeys,* continue their flight in this crisp chronicle, which is presented as testimony by a number of those involved in the story. (Avi whets curiosity by plunging straight into the testimony, without indicating what exactly is being investigated in the 1768 hearing.) . . . The story's pace is brisk and Avi's testimonial format gives a clean, unsentimental tone to the sentimental-melodrama content. It also tends to perpetuate the problem with **Night Journeys**—namely, the absence of any personal observation, feeling, or quality that would not show up in well-edited court records.

A review of "Encounter at Easton," in Kirkus Reviews, *Vol. XLVIII, No. 12, June 15, 1980, p. 778.*

Characters skillfully revealed by their own accounts of what they have said and done, a subtly realized setting with just enough detail of landscape, customs, and the ethic of the time to keep the reader informed and interested, a plot carefully calculated for suspense and irony, and an energetic, understated, slightly formal style that heightens the tension and underscores the tragic climax combine for a powerful exploration of both period and human nature. (p. 195)

Alethea K. Helbig and Agnes Regan Perkins, in a review of "Encounter at Easton," in their Dictionary of American Children's Fiction, 1960-1984: Recent Books of Recognized Merit, *Greenwood Press, 1986, pp. 194-95.*

Man from the Sky (1980)

In a gripping story that will engage reluctant readers, 11-year-old Jamie's inability to read (he has a learning disability) leads him to a favorite activity: making up tales about the figures he sees in clouds. One day, he notices a parachute drop from a plane. The parachutist, a thief who has planned a clever means of stealing—in midair—one million dollars in payroll money, has not planned on being seen. Avi keeps his story line simple, yet his characters are complex enough to be real. Jamie, in particular, finds his special gift has added value, not only for himself but also in the eyes of others.

Judith Goldberger, in a review of "Man from the Sky," in Booklist, *Vol. 76, No. 22, July 15, 1980, p. 1678.*

Eleven-year-old, learning disabled Jamie Peters, sees a man parachute from an airplane. Ed Goddard, who has stolen a million-dollar payroll from the cargo hold, drops the satchel during his descent and is then blown off course. The satchel is found by a young girl who is captured by Goddard and forced to lead him to the nearest town. Gillian manages to write the first four letters of their destination in the dirt. Jamie must read those letters if he is to guide the police to Gillian's rescue. Though the author treats Jamie's problems in a sensitive way, the real strength of the book is the alternating chapters telling Goddard's and then Jamie's story in uncluttered prose.

Drew Stevenson, in a review of "Man from the Sky," in School Library Journal, *Vol. 27, No. 4, December, 1980, p. 72.*

The History of Helpless Harry: To Which Is Added a Variety of Amusing and Entertaining Adventures (1980)

Harry is eleven, he does not like to be addressed as Horatio (his name), he does not like Miss Trowbridge, and he particularly does not like the fact that his parents are leaving Miss Trowbridge in charge of their son and home while they go on a trip. All of the trouble that ensues in this volatile situation is due to Harry's density; to the fact that Miss Trowbridge is secretly married; the fact that Constable Narbut doesn't know she is married, proposes, and is infuriated and vengeful at her rejection of his proposal; the fact that a sanctimonious and mercenary quack, Mr. Skatch, is about; and—most particularly—the fact that Harry's father had left information as to the whereabouts of his money box. This is an invitation to farce, and farcical indeed is the web of misconstructions that follows, with hapless Harry as the dupe of Skatch and the remorseless accuser of innocent Miss Trowbridge. This has a good deal of nonsense, a good deal of fun with the orotund language of the period (1845), and a good deal of action; it is weakened somewhat by the fact that nobody (particularly Harry) can see through anything.

Zena Sutherland, in a review of "The History of Helpless Harry: To Which Is Added a Variety of Amusing and Entertaining Adventures," in Bulletin of the Center for Children's Books, *Vol. 34, No. 3, November, 1980, p. 46.*

Though not quite as deft as Garfield in a twist-of-fate escapade, Avi nevertheless provides a well-paced blend of wit and suspense. . . . The author's comments to his audience are overdone in places but the overall tone effects a mischievous flair; executed in a style similar to his **Emily Upham's Revenge.**

Barbara Elleman, in a review of "The History of Helpless Harry: To Which Is Added a Variety of Amusing and Entertaining Adventures," in Booklist, *Vol. 77, No. 8, December 15, 1980, p. 569.*

A literary conceit, mocking the conventions and sentiments of old-time fiction, has precious little chance with youngsters of nine or so. But this one self-destructs in the first couple of pages—when we're asked to think of eleven-year-old Harry, child of overprotective parents, as a "small boy" whose "soft eyes and appealing mouth" have caused him to be taken as helpless. And throughout the ensuing events, he hasn't indeed a clue to what we, the readers, know. . . . Harry just resents Miss Trowbridge (because his parents went off); is taken in by Mr. Skatch (because he calls him "brave, bold," etc.); and never does get straightened out until the last pages . . . of a book that's mostly making fun of itself (and not a little of poor Harry). A dubious undertaking not very well executed.

A review of "The History of Helpless Harry," in Kirkus Reviews, *Vol. XLIX, No. 4, February 15, 1981, p. 212.*

A Place Called Ugly (1981)

Avi Wortis, who writes under his given name, may be

starting a whole new trend in novels for young people. His hero, 14-year-old Owen Coughlin, is not on drugs, doesn't drink, likes his college-bound brother and sister when they are around, and lives with parents who do not exhibit signs of getting divorced. His folks are in the same boat as are most adults who encounter Owen. They don't understand him.

As for young Owen, he doesn't understand himself, either. And why should he? He has just entered that impossible spot between a hard place and a rock called adolescence, where one's vision of the world is completely out of kilter with everyone else's.

Owen's dramatic break with childhood comes at the end of the 10th and last summer he will spend in a ramshackle rented beach cottage in a magnificent and isolated spot on Grenlow's Island called East Neck. For two seasons now, his brother and sister have been too busy to join their parents. Owen would like to believe that, for him, the idyllic summers will continue forever, no matter how many times his father's work takes them to new cities, no matter how many schools he has to attend.

The boy's dream is shattered when he learns that a new hotel complex is going up in East Neck, right on the spot where the house stands. Two days before Labor Day the bulldozer is in position behind a clump of marshgrass, waiting for the occupants to vacate.

Acting on an impulse he does not understand, Owen decides to stay on the island. He will save the house.

In the often humorous, sometimes tender, and even brutal events that follow, Owen proves to be an inventive and sympathetic David fighting the Goliaths of change. If he loses the original battle, he wins the much bigger one as he grows to understand the reasons for his intransigence. And he gives the islanders a memory of splendiferous youth they will not forget. I found myself cheering Owen on all the way.

> *Bryna J. Fireside, in a review of "A Place Called Ugly," in* The New York Times Book Review, *March 1, 1981, p. 24.*

In [this book's] dramatic ending, Owen, having resigned himself to the loss of the cottage, makes himself the instrument of its destruction. The wrenching sadness of lost dreams and times that will not come again is mitigated by Owen's humor, his first love and a fast-paced plot that will keep readers interested. Alternating chapters that intercut Owen's account of his battle with his fond memories emphasize the bittersweetness of this fine book.

> *Marjorie Lewis, in a review of "A Place Called Ugly," in* School Library Journal, *Vol. 27, No. 8, April, 1981, p. 136.*

[At the end of **A Place Called Ugly** Owen makes a] dramatic move, blowing the house up so that at least he and not the bulldozer will finish it off. Meanwhile he acquires some sensitivity to the year-rounders' position, but that is peripheral. Interspersed with the action are Owen's memories from summers past—and those, he realizes in the end, will outlive the house. But neither they nor the story have much force or dimension as fiction. Owen's cause is

less than compelling to readers, yet Avi asks us to take the struggle and the two-dimensional characters as seriously as Owen does.

> *A review of "A Place Called Ugly," in* Kirkus Reviews, *Vol. XLIX, No. 7, April 1, 1981, p. 436.*

Who Stole the Wizard of Oz? (1981)

Who stole *The Wizard of Oz?* As Becky was asking for it just before the used copy disappeared from the library with four other second-hand children's classics, she is questioned by a suspicious policeman. To clear her name, then, Becky and her brother Toby determine to find the real thief. The books, they discover, were owned by a supposedly rich old lady who willed them to her ungrateful niece. The niece in turn gave them to the library. As the books themselves aren't valuable, the children decide they must contain clues to something of value. After reading all five, Becky and Toby use their maps and other clues to track down a rare *Alice in Wonderland* hidden behind a mirror in the library . . . where they then wait in the dark of night to trap the thief. There are no thrills, no personalities to speak of, no secondary rewards of any sort— just a one-dimensional mystery. Within that limit, Avi does keep readers puzzling and piecing out the solution at Becky and Toby's pace.

> *A review of "Who Stole the Wizard of Oz?" in* Kirkus Reviews, *Vol. XLIX, No. 19, October 1, 1981, p. 1235.*

Sometimes I Think I Hear My Name (1982)

Isaac Singer occasionally abandons his adult audience and writes for children. He knows that they are too discerning to tolerate pretentious literary artifice, but that they are impressed with compression, involvement and discovery. Singer gladly accepted this challenge and so does Avi. Once again this Christopher Medalist has produced a fine novel.

Thirteen year old Conrad Murray is the third party in a divorce, the vulnerable only child. He is not sure why all of this has happened and he is not sure he wants to be. He lives in St. Louis with his aunt and uncle, happy, if not a bit smothered by love, but bewildered about why his parents are sending him to England for the summer instead of to New York. Nancy, the enigmatic girl from St. Louis, is also from New York. They meet there during spring vacation from their respective schools and thereby hangs the tale.

Nancy's problem is different from Conrad's. She and her flaky older sister have been divorced from their parents who live in the same building. They have set both of them up in their own apartment. Conrad and Nancy try to deal with their own world. They don't make sense out of it, but they do at least come to a point of some understanding and acceptance—they are both beginning to "pass over."

Sometimes I Think I Hear My Name is a gentle novel of

maturing. Conrad is easy to know, easy to relate to. Nancy, with her strange butterfly tattoo, is elusive enough to add subtle mystery. As with his other excellent books, **Man From the Sky** and **A Place Called Ugly,** Avi has not forgotten what Isaac Singer believes.

> *H. T. Anderson, in a review of "Sometimes I Think I Hear My Name," in* Best Sellers, *Vol. 42, No. 2, May, 1982, p. 76.*

Avi offers an almost surrealistic view of family life. His friend Nancy, whose butterfly tattoo is the only part of herself she considers "real," lives with her punk-culture sister in a Central Park apartment. Her snobbish parents, who wish to be neither distressed nor bothered by their children, live upstairs. Conrad's own parents, luckless childlike actors, have no place in their lives for a teenage boy. Each character here is an original, uniquely crafted. Nuggets of humor continually turn up in what is otherwise rough but memorable terrain.

> *Ilene Cooper, in a review of "Sometimes I Think I Hear My Name," in* Booklist, *Vol. 78, No. 19, June 1, 1982, p. 1308.*

This is a novel of controlled exaggerations. The openness of Conrad's thoughts in his first person narrative are sharply contrasted to the deadpan emotions of Nancy who befriends him. Nancy's relationship to her parents, her guilt about their unhappy marriage, and her retreat from anything that would make her feel alive offer Conrad and the reader a measuring stick for questions of love, honesty, and self-acceptance.

> *Maryellen Hains, in a review of "Sometimes I Think I Hear My Name," in* The ALAN Review, *Vol. 10, No. 1, Fall, 1982, p. 19.*

Shadrach's Crossing (1983)

A Prohibition/Depression mystery, with a message about standing up to terrorist smugglers, that's as remote and stark (and upright) as Avi's colonial adventures. It's 1932 on otherwise-unidentified "Lucker's Island," and the out-of-work inhabitants, including 15-year-old Shad Faherty's father, are at the mercy of smuggler-boss Kinlow and his cohorts. When Shad rashly goes out one night to watch the liquor being landed, Kinlow threatens his parents—who, to his dismay, just take it "like . . . slaves." Shad, vowing to "get Kinlow," fixes his further suspicions on "rich-yachtsman" newcomer Nevill (who apparently disabled his own boat), and fixes his hopes on "government-agent" Sheraton, ostensibly on the island to check a rain gauge. As the reader will guess on the instant, the two mysterious strangers are the opposite of what they seem to Shad—though he does have a hand in Kinlow's capture and, more important to him, gets Kinlow to *apologize* to his parents. The plotting won't get Avi a passing grade in mystery circles; the theme seems superimposed on the circumstances; and Shad (like other Avi heroes) is a high-minded stick. But some kids would probably respond to the spectacle of a boy facing down his parents to restore their lost honor.

> *A review of "Shadrach's Crossing," in* Kirkus

Reviews, *Vol. LI, No. 12, June 15, 1983, p. 662.*

A tiny sand-swept island is the setting for a story of the Prohibition era. . . . By giving the island and its people an anonymity, the author focuses on Shad and his isolation as he pursues his quest. And although the plot's twists and surprises maintain suspense to the very end, the book is less an adventure story than a novel about a boy's refusal to give in to the pervading hopelessness of his people. (pp. 439-40)

> *Kate M. Flanagan, in a review of "Shadrach's Crossing," in* The Horn Book Magazine, *Vol. LIX, No. 4, August, 1983, pp. 439-40.*

Once again, Avi makes use of an historical backdrop for a fast-moving plot involving a heroic young person. . . . Shadrach Faherty, disgusted by the passivity of his family and neighbors, decides to take on single-handedly a group of liquor smugglers who are terrorizing his poor island home. His attempts to discover the identities and foil the plans of the smugglers produce some gripping scenes and provide the narrative with most of its substance. A sense of oppressive poverty and impotent anger—paralyzing the community and forcing Shad's father to admit his helplessness to his son—is sustained throughout. Readers might be puzzled by the author's portrayal of the Coast Guard, who seem rather timid and unknowledgeable in the ways of catching smugglers red-handed: Shad, with his shrewdness and stubborn courage, outshines them by far. This exciting story will appeal to a wide range of ages and abilities, particularly to those who shy away from heavier historical fiction.

> *Linda Wicher, in a review of "Shadrach's Crossing," in* School Library Journal, *Vol. 29, No. 10, August, 1983, p. 61.*

[**Shadrach's Crossing** is a] realistic novel of suspense covering about a week's time in 1932 on a tiny, impoverished, sparsely populated, offshore Atlantic island, in which a determined and courageous youth brings criminals to justice and restores his community's self-respect. . . . Though the plot is typical of the genre and offers the usual full measure of red herrings and twists, much of the interest comes from the reader's perception of the irony of the situation. The smugglers' activities sustain the islanders' precarious economy and make it possible for them to continue living there in spite of the increasingly hard times.

Shad's idealism—he maintains it is a free country and the islanders ought to stand up for their rights and do what they wish—brings him into conflict with his parents and neighbors who maintain a more pragmatic view. Tension runs high from the very beginning, made so by short, pithy sentences, curt dialogue, superb pacing, and plenty of action. (pp. 590-91)

> *Alethea K. Helbig and Agnes Regan Perkins, in a review of "Shadrach's Crossing," in their* Dictionary of American Children's Fiction, 1960-1984: Recent Books of Recognized Merit, *Greenwood Press, 1986, pp. 590-91.*

The Fighting Ground (1984)

A small stunner. Thirteen-year-old Jonathan has longed to go to war against the hated British, and one morning, April 3, 1778 at 11:00 a.m., he gets his chance. Joining a small band of American soldiers he skirmishes with Hessians near Rocktown, New Jersey, and is captured: "Jonathan tried to rekindle his hatred, but all he could muster was the desire to stand close to them, to be taken care of." What is superb is the control. The story takes place in one day, detailed minute by minute. There is constant closeness—huddled soldiers, Jonathan hiding—tightly held and suffocated by darkness or fog. Readers hear the Hessians as Jonathan does, only speaking German, frightening and disorienting. All this makes the war personal and immediate: not history or event, but experience; near and within oneself, and horrible.

> *Zena Sutherland, in a review of "The Fighting Ground," in* Bulletin of the Center for Children's Books, *Vol. 37, No. 10, June, 1984, p. 180.*

Though fast-paced, the story is fairly predictable, and frequent notations of the time of day interrupt the narrative and dull rather than heighten the suspenseful mood Avi creates. Conversations between the Hessians appear in German, although English translations are supplied in an appendix. An interesting contrast to the more usual panoramic historical novel, this is a vivid telling of a brief and intensely personal moment of history in which a young boy grows up much too fast. The thematic similarity with the Colliers' classic *My Brother Sam Is Dead* could be an intriguing starting point for discussion with more mature readers. (pp. 1395-96)

> *Karen Stang Hanley, in a review of "The Fighting Ground," in* Booklist, *Vol. 80, No. 19, June 1, 1984, pp. 1395-96.*

The pace of the novel is slow, as it would be for a youngster living through the waiting, the fear and the horror that Jonathan encounters over the day; that slow pace may deter some readers. The literary beauty often found in Avi's books is not found here; the author points up the harshness of his subject with appropriate severity of language. The German dialogue of the Hessian soldiers is interspersed throughout the text; readers may be confused by it and surprised to find its translation, unexpectedly, at the end of the book. But Avi has accomplished his intent: to have readers experience, minute by minute, what it's like to be involved in war.

> *Susan F. Marcus, in a review of "The Fighting Ground," in* School Library Journal, *Vol. 31, No. 1, September, 1984, p. 125.*

Avi has again written a tale that, through the moral dilemmas faced by an ordinary, believable youngster, makes the past vividly real. The story grips imagination and emotion till the last words. Particularly poignant are those of the Germans. Untranslated in the text, the German speech evokes fear. Translated at the end, it reveals the confusion, bluster, and fear in these men, too. War, the author reminds us, is a human activity, and nothing human is clear-cut.

> *Elsa Marston, in a review of "The Fighting Ground," in* Voice of Youth Advocates, *Vol. 7, No. 6, February, 1985, p. 321.*

Jonathan's desire to experience battle is all-too-quickly satiated and in the space of a single day he learns—much like Adam Cooper of *April Morning*—that war really means pain, senseless brutality and death. Like Tim Meeker of *My Brother Sam Is Dead,* Jonathan learns that good and evil are to be found on both sides of the bitter conflict; that even the universally detested Hessians are capable of compassion.

Avi has written a taut, fast-paced novel that builds to a shattering climax. His protagonist's painful, inner struggle to understand the intense and conflicting emotions brought on by a war that spares no one is central to this finely crafted novel. Also deserving note is a translation of the German spoken by the Hessians which provides the novel with a stunning postscript. Read on its own, or in conjunction with books like *Johnny Tremain* or those mentioned above, **The Fighting Ground** will provide readers with important insight into the Revolution and the very different ways authors have interpreted it.

> *Joel Taxel, in a review of "The Fighting Ground," in* The ALAN Review, *Vol. 12, No. 3, Spring, 1985, p. 23.*

Devil's Race (1984)

A more sophisticated version of the theme used by Kin Platt in his hi/lo success *The Ape Inside Me* (Harper, 1979), this mystery suspense story with eerie, supernatural overtones is turned into a taut—albeit simplistic—psychological thriller. John Proud's great-great-great-great grandfather and namesake was hanged in 1854 for being a demon and a murderer. Motivated by a perverse, intense desire to find out the truth about his evil ancestor, 16-year-old John is led to his remote graveside by his uncle. His cousin Ann aids him as he becomes involved in a dangerous struggle with the demon spirit who is trying to replace John on Earth. As real as this spirit is, however, John ultimately comes to see the struggle as an interior war between the good and bad within himself, and once he accepts the confrontation as a metaphor of his divided self, he knows how to fight the demon successfully. Except for some wooden storytelling early in the novel and an unexplained and sudden happy ending, this is a good story, as well as being fast moving and *very* easy (around fourth-grade reading level).

> *Jack Forman, in a review of "Devil's Race," in* School Library Journal, *Vol. 31, No. 2, October, 1984, p. 164.*

This story of John and his namesake ancestor provides a suspenseful ghost story with supernatural overtones, and hints of the good and evil within us all. . . .

Devil's Race is a ghost story that moves along at a reasonable pace, but slows down as it draws to a close. And it wraps up almost too quickly, leaving a few incidents unexplained.

The philosophical ramblings in the last chapters are confusing and empty. They needlessly complicate what might have been a simple ghost story.

> *Patricia A. Morgans, in a review of "Devil's Race," in* Best Sellers, *Vol. 44, No. 9, December, 1984, p. 356.*

S.O.R. Losers (1984)

To every kid who's hated trotting out on an athletic field—this one's for you. Narrator Ed Sitrow is one of the 11 seventh graders chosen to play on a specially created soccer team. The requirement for being chosen is having avoided athletic teams all through South Orange River Middle School. These boys—nonjock artists, writers, and poets coached by an earnest history teacher—come together to make the worst team in the history of the school. They are losing by scores of 30 or 40 to 0. Oddly, the more inept they prove to be, the more principals, teachers, and parents insist that they go out and give it the old middle-school try. In a blow for independence, the boys prove that being happy with what you are is its own virtue, and that losers can be winners, too. Characterizations are slight, but action is the name of the game. Unfortunately, the adults are portrayed as uniformly rah-rah; surely there would be one among them who'd put the situation into perspective. Realism aside, this is fast paced and funny. Nonathletes will feel vindicated after reading it.

> *Ilene Cooper, in a review of "S.O.R. Losers," in* Booklist, *Vol. 81, No. 4, October 15, 1984, p. 303.*

Described by team captain Ed Sitrow, the chronicle of the S. O. R. losers is one of the funniest and most original sports sagas on record. Short, pithy chapters highlighting key events maintain the pace necessary for successful comedy. As in a Charlie Chaplin movie, emphasis is on individual episodes—each distinct, yet organically related to an overall idea. The style is vivid, believably articulate, for the narrator and his teammates may be deficient athletically but not intellectually. Certainly, the team manifesto " 'People have a right to be losers' " is as refreshing as it is iconoclastic.

> *Mary M. Burns, in a review of "S.O.R. Losers," in* The Horn Book Magazine, *Vol. LXI, No. 1, January-February, 1985, p. 49.*

Bright Shadow (1985)

A sensitively written tale which poses philosophical questions about selfishness, selflessness and the terrible burdens of what first appear to be wonderful gifts. Young Morwenna, upon the death of an ancient wizard, finds herself in possession of the world's last five wishes. She soon discovers that this gift is a lonely burden. By a curious trick of fate, a beloved but rather simple and selfish friend believes himself to be in possession of the wishes and constantly gets himself into situations from which Morwenna must extricate him. Freed from his foolishness through his death, Morwenna must live with the knowledge that she could have saved him had she been willing to use her final wish, thus giving up her own life in return. In a straightforward manner, Avi presents a fascinating balance between the simplistic and the complex. The inner conflict constantly taking place within the more mature (though chronologically younger) Morwenna is well contrasted with that of the unsophisticated Swen. A compact and well-told story that should inspire much debate about Morwenna's predicament and what readers would do in her circumstances.

> *Karen P. Smith, in a review of "Bright Shadow," in* School Library Journal, *Vol. 32, No. 4, December, 1985, p. 86.*

The writing is not as smooth as Avi's usual, with informal conversation slightly out of sync with the high fantasy tone, and a couple of contrived scenes. Yet the fast pace, easy-to-read style, and challenging conclusion will hook a fair share of readers.

> *A review of "Bright Shadow," in* Bulletin of the Center for Children's Books, *Vol. 39, No. 6, February 1986, p. 102.*

[Avi] offers readers aged 10-12 an unusual fantasy. . . .

This is a cautionary tale that emphasizes the young heroine's frustration at her inability to control her own fate despite the power she possesses; while doubtless a salutary lesson to heedless youth, its appeal may be limited. Libraries with sizeable holdings for younger readers should consider it.

> *Ray Thompson, "The Burden of Power," in* Fantasy Review, *Vol. 9, No. 3, March, 1986, p. 26.*

Wolf Rider: A Tale of Terror (1986)

A charged beginning electrifies a plot that sizzles with suspense every inch of the way. Avi fortifies this excitement with staccato dialogue and a fast pace, but at times neglects the understructure. Whys and wherefores, however, fall away in the face of immediate action as 15-year-old Andy Zadinski attempts to ferret out the identity of a telephone caller who says his name is Zeke and claims to have killed Nina Klemmer. Very much alive, Nina, a student at the college where Dr. Zadinski teaches, interprets Andy's warnings as harassment, and Andy's father simply wants him to lay off. Thinking he is the only one to save Nina from certain death, Andy continues his investigations until his search backfires and he finds himself in the hands of psychotic Zeke. In addition to being a simple tale of terror, as the subtitle indicates, this is also a more complex story of a father-son relationship. Their closeness, a result of Andy's mother's recent death, begins to crumble as Dr. Zadinski becomes involved with a new woman, as he fails to believe Andy's story, and as Andy refuses to follow his father's orders to forget the matter. Then, in an ironically structured conclusion, the two recognize the depth of their mutual feelings while unnecessarily attempting to protect each other. Motivations are not entirely clear here but for those readers who don't analyze plots, the emotion and release of so much tension will be more than enough. (pp. 505-06)

> *Barbara Elleman, in a review of "Wolf Rider: A Tale of Terror," in* Booklist, *Vol. 83, No. 6, November 15, 1986, pp. 505-06.*

The story is harrowing on two counts: one, the deepening trouble Andy gets into with authorities who believe he is disturbed as a result of his mother's recent death; and two, the approach of the inevitable encounter with the potential killer, who turns out to be a model professor in the mathematics department where Andy's father teaches. The ending is not a standard mystery wrap-up, but a disturbing, ambiguous parting of father and son. Perhaps just a touch too cold and calculating, this is nevertheless a gripping and above-average YA thriller.

> *Betsy Hearne, in a review of "Wolf Rider: A Tale of Terror," in* Bulletin of the Center for Children's Books, *Vol. 40, No. 4, December, 1986, p. 61.*

Andy's heightening confusion and fear, and his increasing alienation from the adults in his world, are conveyed convincingly in an understated style with lots of dialogue. Unfortunately the adult characters' behavior is not as believable. Andy's father and the counselor seem too ready to distrust his story, and the mysterious caller's motive and behavior are not explained. It seems as if Avi could not decide between plots, a conventional mystery with all the threads tied neatly at the end, or a psychological study raising as many questions as it answers. While the print is large and the vocabulary is not difficult, the tone and tension of the story make it more appropriate for older readers, as does the inconclusive ending. (pp. 111-12)

> *Ruth S. Vose, in a review of "Wolf Rider: A Tale of Terror," in* School Library Journal, *Vol. 33, No. 4, December, 1986, pp. 111-12.*

Romeo and Juliet—Together (and Alive!) at Last (1987)

The kids from South Orange River are back, now in eighth grade and putting on a much-abridged, student-run, unintentionally slapstick version of Shakespeare's play.

When their friends discover that Pete Saltz and Anabell Stackpoole are sweet on each other but too shy even to converse, they arrange a first kiss through the elaborate and thoroughly implausible device of putting on *Romeo and Juliet* and electing them to the title roles. Their school principal agrees to everything, including a performance date only two weeks away. Most of the book is taken up with the actual production, a junior version of Frayn's *Noises Off* in which everything that can go wrong deservedly does, and the original objective is achieved.

This lighthearted farce achieves what must have been Avi's objective—a fast-moving, genuinely funny, enjoyable read. Kids won't be able to resist the humor, even if they miss the full import of the malapropisms; they may even absorb the message that Shakespeare can be approachable.

> *A review of "Romeo and Juliet—Together*

> *(and Alive!) at Last," in* Kirkus Reviews, *Vol. LV, No. 12, July 1, 1987, p. 987.*

When Shakespeare penned the line "a poor player that struts and frets his hour upon the stage," he surely couldn't know to what lengths the strutting and fretting would be carried in this imaginative, cleverly written, laugh-out-loud story centered on one of the Bard's creations. . . . Everything that could possibly go wrong does; the resulting chaos, which could have resulted in overdone slapstick, is handled with finesse. Avi's on-target, snappy dialogue (Ed's advice to Saltz on kissing is priceless), sense of timing, and use of language (Romeo mistakenly asks about Juliet "Is she a catapult?") will make this comic romp a middle-school favorite for years to come.

> *Barbara Elleman, in a review of "Romeo and Juliet: Together (and Alive) at Last!" in* Booklist, *Vol. 83, No. 22, August, 1987, p. 1740.*

Avi's heart is in the right place; he devotes an entire book to the well-intentioned efforts of a group of good friends to bring a boy and girl together, but fans of his historical fiction may find this a light repast. The story strains credibility, but no matter; Avi proves that stories don't have to be believable to be fun.

> *A review of "Romeo and Juliet, Together (and Alive!) at Last," in* Publishers Weekly, *Vol. 232, No. 9, August 28, 1987, p. 81.*

Something Upstairs: A Tale of Ghosts (1988)

A suspenseful tale of multiple hauntings, time travel, and murder in old Rhode Island.

Young Kenny Huldorf's room in an 18th-century Providence house comes complete with bloodstained floor and the ghost of Caleb, a slave murdered nearly 200 years ago. Naturally prompted to do some research in the local historical-society library, Kenny meets the crabbed, sinister Pardon Willinghast, who seems to know more about Kenny's house than he'll tell. Caleb appears repeatedly, claiming that he will never rest until his killer is discovered; he cajoles a reluctant Kenny into promising help, then takes him back to that fateful night in 1800— whereupon, in effect, *Kenny* becomes the ghost. He also receives a dreadful shock: Willinghast is there, waiting for him—it seems that Caleb has brought back others before, but Willinghast is absolutely determined that Caleb should die. Kenny is given the same choice as his predecessors: kill Caleb or stay trapped in the past.

As always, Avi weaves accurate historical detail into his story and builds up tension expertly. Kenny escapes his dilemma by shooting Willinghast; he returns to the present confused, disturbed, and still haunted, this time by the memory of his own act of violence. The author presents this as a true story, told to him on a school visit by a young fan, and indeed it does have a realistically indeterminate end. A thoughtful, spooky, ingenious treat for ghost-story fans. (pp. 1145-46)

> *A review of "Something Upstairs: A Tale of*

Ghosts," in Kirkus Reviews, *Vol. LVI, No. 15,*
August 1, 1988, pp. 1145-46.

Cleverly introducing his story as one he heard from the protagonist while on a school visit, Avi here constructs a ghost/time-slip story that takes Kenny Huldorf back to eighteenth-century Providence to change the ghastly fate of Caleb, a young black slave murdered in the attic (now Kenny's bedroom) of the Huldorf's house. Caleb the ghost is too self-aware of the circumstances of his haunting ("If a person dies in an unnatural or unjust way, that person's memory stays fixed in time and space"), especially for a self-proclaimed "memory," but his anger at whites and suspicion of Kenny's motives and courage add human and historical tension. In fact, the core and interest of the story are found in the realistic scenes set in the past rather than in the supernatural element, which is fogged by inconsistencies and a shaky structure. This would have been better off as straight historical fiction; for that element, the book is certainly worth reading.

> *Roger Sutton, in a review of "Something Up-*
> *stairs: A Tale of Ghosts," in* Bulletin of the
> Center for Children's Books, *Vol. 42, No. 1,*
> *September, 1988, p. 2.*

A ghost story of redeeming social value: when 12-year-old Kenny Huldorf moves with his family to Providence, Rhode Island, he finds himself embroiled in the century-old murder of a teenage slave named Caleb. Not only is Kenny haunted by the injustice of the murder, but also by the ghost of Caleb himself, who summons Kenny back in time to the early 19th Century, where the boy must solve Caleb's murder to return to his own century. How Kenny does this is the stuff of a somber and ambiguous conclusion upon which Avi intrudes himself as a character as he has earlier done at the book's beginning. Why Avi has chosen to do this is debatable—perhaps to reinforce the reality of the social issue, slavery, which drives the narrative. In any event, as a literary device it compromises an otherwise carefully constructed tale, just as the too obvious employment of Caleb as both character and symbol tends to compromise his viability as a character. Nevertheless **Something Upstairs** is an intelligent and well-intentioned effort. It can provoke discussion of the issues articulated above as well as how, finally, violence visits the lives of both Caleb and Kenny and how Kenny, through choice and circumstance, may have become a slave himself. (pp. 138, 143)

> *Michael Cart, in a review of "Something Up-*
> *stairs: A Tale of Ghosts," in* School Library
> Journal, *Vol. 35, No. 2, October, 1988, pp. 138,*
> *143.*

The Man Who Was Poe (1989)

Eleven-year-old Edmund has lost his sister, and Edgar Allan Poe has lost his inspiration. Can they help each other? Informing an intricate detective story with the lurking menace of the real Poe's short stories, Avi has crafted a complex, atmospheric thriller. First mother, then aunt, then Sis having disappeared, a despairing Edmund turns for help to a stranger in the street. "Auguste Dupin" senses a story, as well as some disturbing parallels to his own life, and agrees to investigate. Callous, alcoholic, pursued by private demons, Dupin (Poe) is only intermittently helpful, and just as often hindering, forcing Edmund to do his own searching among shadows he only half comprehends. Avi recreates the gloom of 1840's Baltimore with a storyteller's ease, blending drama, history, and mystery without a hint of pastiche or calculation. And, as in the best mystery stories, readers will be left in the end with both the comfort of puzzles solved and the unease of mysteries remaining.

> *Roger Sutton, in a review of "The Man Who*
> *Was Poe," in* Bulletin of the Center for Chil-
> dren's Books, *Vol. 43, No. 2, October, 1989, p.*
> *27.*

Many will be familiar with Avi's work, and no one can say he has let himself be pigeonholed. His books have ranged from upbeat, contemporary stories such as **Romeo and Juliet—Together (and Alive!) at Last!** to historical adventures like the recent **Something Upstairs.** In **The Man Who Was Poe,** Avi attempts something very complex: a character study of a famous figure, wrapped in a mystery and knotted with questions about the nature of reality. . . .

Technically, as a mystery, the book falters. Complicated, at times confusing, the serpentine plot may be difficult to follow, even for better readers. The very premise of Edmund's relationship with Poe is questionable as well; he tells Poe he has no one else to help him, yet later in the book it is established that Edmund is friends with a local sea captain, surely a more logical source of aid.

What is intriguing is Avi's depiction of Poe, a genius who has difficulty differentiating between the people he is meeting and the characters he is writing about in his story. Surly, quixotic, stumbling in and out of reality, Avi's Poe is mesmerizing. Yet whether young people, who may or may not be familiar with Poe and his work (a brief concluding note about Poe appears), will appreciate the representation, is something that remains to be seen. The same is true of Avi's innovative subtext—Poe's fascination with death and its link to his writing. Throughout, his motives are suspect, until it becomes clear that Poe is merely tracking events so he will have something to write about. And Poe knows full well how he wants his story to end. As Edmund concludes, "You never did want to save my sister, did you? . . . You only wanted to make sure she'd die." But Poe counters, " . . . in what fashion will your sister live longer? In her life? Or in this, my story that would have been." . . .

Ambitious on every front, including its use of narrative as a manipulator of events, the novel's problems are almost balanced by its strengths. To use this book to best effect, it needs to be introduced in conjunction with the works of Poe in a classroom situation; there, its intricacies will have a chance to be fully explored.

> *Ilene Cooper, "Focus: 'The Man Who Was*
> *Poe', by Avi and 'Shabanu: Daughter of the*
> *Wind', by Suzanne Fisher Staples," in* Book-
> list, *Vol. 86, No. 3, October 1, 1989, p. 345.*

The author uses the period before Edgar Allan Poe's death, when he was courting a widow in Providence, as the springboard to this mystery. As the narrative shifts from Edmund to Poe (Auguste Dupin), the reader comprehends Poe's growing madness and his fascination with the boy whose life nearly parallels his own. Unfortunately, this story offers too little too late. Poe unravels an improbable mystery in the last few pages and 11 year old Edmund is allowed precocious insight into a man about whom he previously understood nothing. This story is rich in atmosphere, but, ultimately, disappointing; even the brief biographical epilogue sheds little light on "the man who was Poe."

> *Catherine Clancy, in a review of "The Man Who Was Poe," in* Voice of Youth Advocates, *Vol. 12, No. 6, February, 1990, p. 340.*

The True Confessions of Charlotte Doyle   (1990)

A breathtaking seafaring adventure, set in 1832. Charlotte Doyle, 13, returning from school in England to join her family in Rhode Island, is deposited on a seedy ship with a ruthless, mad captain and a mutinous crew. Refusing to heed warnings about Captain Jaggery's brutality, Charlotte seeks his guidance and approval only to become his victim, a pariah to the entire crew, and a convicted felon for the murder of the first mate. There is no doubt that she will survive, however, for the telling is all hers, masterfully related in a voice that perfectly suits the period and the heroine. At first, Charlotte exudes the haughty self-confidence and the need for propriety that only those of privilege and wealth can pull off, yet she also exhibits the naivete of an adolescent taught to respect and not question her elders—as long as they are of her class. As she sees the insane captain for what he is, she switches allegiances—thus endangering her life—and becomes part of the crew, passing their rugged tests and proving that she can become as adept as any of them. Her changing views and personality from a prim and proper pain to respected friend and mate are aptly reflected in her narrative, and the point of view gives Avi excellent opportunities for some fine foreshadowing. The irony at the end—that indeed her beloved papa is very much like the captain, tyrannical and unyielding—will leave readers agape, and they will sigh with relief when she deserts her very rigid family and returns home—to the ship. A sensuous novel, evoking the sights, sounds, and smells of the ship and the sea; the moods of captain and crew; the terror and bloodshed caused by the captain; and the nature of friendship and loyalty. (pp. 221, 224)

> *Trev Jones, in a review of "The True Confessions of Charlotte Doyle," in* School Library Journal, *Vol. 36, No. 9, September, 1990, pp. 221, 224.*

"Not every thirteen-year-old girl is accused of murder, brought to trial, and found guilty." This direct opening line powerfully launches a novel of extraordinary achievement and resonance. . . .

Avi tells this story in the first person, unfolding Charlotte's forceful characterization in honest journal entries. He subtly reveals Charlotte's metamorphosis on numerous levels. The journal catalogs her growing suspicions and questions. She exchanges her polished boots and high-buttoned collars for common sailor's garb. She assumes first the duties, then the attitudes of a crew member and holds onto the dagger given to her by the ship's cook. Charlotte faces grim realizations and mortal moral decisions, but her voice never wavers. Control and refinement mark her language and similarly distinguish Avi's stylistic expertise.

As she slowly reacts to the crew's volatile temperament and witnesses Jaggery's cruelties, Charlotte reaches a jolting epiphany: she most choose between her romantic ideals and humane mutiny. The tempestuous sea echoes the turbulence on the ship and within Charlotte's heart and mind. Her struggle will fully engage readers, who will find themselves cheering the improbable but deeply satisfying conclusion.

Avi blends an innovative mixture of history and fiction, as seen previously in **The Fighting Ground** and **The Man Who Was Poe,** with the chilling realism of **Wolf Rider** to create this accomplished novel. Expertly crafted and consistently involving, it is sure to excite, enthrall, and challenge readers. (pp. 56-7)

> *Cathryn M. Mercier, in a review of "The True Confessions of Charlotte Doyle," in* The Five Owls, *Vol. V, No. 3, January-February, 1991, pp. 56-7.*

A rousing adventure story set in times past, this tale featuring a female protagonist has all the suspense, derring-do, and pacing of Stevenson's *Kidnapped.* . . . [Charlotte's] transformation from prim schoolgirl to sailor is handled with élan. Since it was not unusual in the nineteenth century for very young boys to serve aboard sailing ships, Charlotte's ability to perform ably as an ordinary sailor at age thirteen is as believable as it is fascinating. The novel, narrated in the first person, retains the diction of a well-bred young lady, offering a brilliant contrast to the events which it records. And the conclusion—based on the decision Charlotte must make when she returns once again to the now stultifying role of dutiful daughter—seems as inevitable as it is satisfying. (pp. 65-6)

> *Mary M. Burns, in a review of "The True Confessions of Charlotte Doyle," in* The Horn Book Magazine, *Vol. LXVII, No. 1, January-February, 1991, pp. 65-6.*

Angela Banner

1923-

(Real name Angela Mary Maddison) English author and illustrator of picture books.

Major works include *Ant and Bee: An Alphabetical Story for Tiny Tots* (1950), *One, Two, Three with Ant and Bee: A Counting Story* (1958), *Happy Birthday with Ant and Bee* (1964), *Ant and Bee and the ABC* (1966).

Banner is well known as the creator of the "Ant and Bee" series, internationally popular informational books for preschoolers and young readers in the early grades. Featuring the insect friends Ant and Bee and their human and animal acquaintances in a variety of domestic situations, the series introduces children to such concepts as the alphabet, numbers, colors, and shapes as well as to such subjects as going shopping, going to school, and seeing the doctor. Considered both instructive and entertaining, the books are characterized by their lively action and humor and use of both familiar and unfamiliar elements. They are also acknowledged for suggesting to children that books are accessible and that reading is an enjoyable experience. Banner, who created her characters so that her children could avoid her fear of insects, builds her stories around key words from a limited vocabulary. Writing in a simple yet evocative style and often including sophisticated words such as "Asia" and "urn", she repeats these words throughout her stories and highlights them in red in order to aid preschoolers in recognition. Published in a small format, the books are intended to encourage a shared reading experience between small children and their older siblings or adults. Perhaps Banner's most popular book is *Happy Birthday with Ant and Bee;* designed to resemble a wrapped package and filled with presents, games, and party favors, the story teaches children to identify the days of the week while providing information on appropriate behavior for birthday parties. The series is also noted for its illustrations: initially, Bryan Ward provided pictures which defined Ant and Bee as expressive, anthropomorphic characters attired in hats and boots. In 1969, Banner began illustrating her texts with cartoonlike pictures in a similar style. She is also the creator of two books about Kind Dog, a character who appears in many of the Ant and Bee stories, as well as several picture books outside of the Ant and Bee series.

(See also *Something about the Author,* Vol. 10 and *Contemporary Authors,* Vols. 53-56.)

GENERAL COMMENTARY

The Times Literary Supplement

In this Beatrix Potter centenary year it requires a certain temerity to consider the work of another writer of small books for small children. It is only sixteen years since the first Ant and Bee book was published: the ninth is due out this month. There is no need to predict that they will still be read in the twenty-first century. It is enough to say that they have so far sold nearly half a million copies, and that, in a world of Noddy, Andy Pandy, Blackberry Farm and Janet and John, this is a wholly healthy thing.

There are plenty of exciting big books for small children, rich with pictures by Wildsmith and John Burningham, Ardizzone and Celestino Piatti. But these are special occasion books, birthday presents from godmothers, Christmas presents from uncles. Ant and Bee books are everyday books. Like the Potter books before them, they are cheap enough . . . for a mother to buy when she happens to be in a newsagents. And most of the books in this category are junk.

The author, Angela Banner, tells us that she chose an ant and a bee because she used to be terribly afraid of insects, and she hoped her children would be different. But in fact their "insectness" is merely incidental. Their smallness is nicely exploited and Bee does a good deal of flying about, often with Ant on his back. But they are not insects in the way that Mr. Jackson is a toad or Samuel Whiskers a rat. And they are not trying to be. They are a splendid alternative to those mice in frilly frocks and bunnies playing truant, the pale emasculated versions of Beatrix Potter's characters that crop up everywhere. What a relief it is to be out of that sub-Potter world of hedgerows and cottage doors (and out of that sub-Toytown world of Noddy and Big Ears) into a place where things are really surprising. Ant and Bee are zany, a little vulgar, fun. They come in small, fat, colourful packets, as tempting and as contemporary as a box of Smarties.

The publishers make much of the fact that this is an educational series. Indeed, in the early days Edmund Ward had some difficulty in promoting the series, perhaps "due to the fact that so many book outlets thought in terms of what is purely educational and what is bookshop material". But in the end, of course, it was this that proved their strength, for "from the time that ***Ant and Bee*** was first published there has been a strong feeling by parents to help their children along with basic learning outside school hours". Ant and Bee books appeal not only to the child but also to the same instinct in the parents that makes so many of them easy prey for door-to-door salesmen with their encyclopedias.

For reading-at-bedtime mothers, used to the cadences and subtleties of Beatrix Potter, the text is tedious stuff. But we should not make the comparison. The real comparison is with Janet and John, those ubiquitous children who dominate the learning-to-read scene. Read first:

> Come, little dog.
> You may look too.
> See, Janet.

Here is something red.
Can you see it?

Then read:

On the path in front of <u>dog</u> and <u>bee</u> and <u>ant</u> there
sat an <u>egg</u>. <u>Dog</u> and <u>bee</u> and <u>ant</u> could not see
the <u>egg</u> because there was a thick fog.

Simple, indeed, but there is a situation, fraught with interest. For the four or five-year-old shouting out the three-letter words that appear in red (underlined here) it is heady stuff. What will happen to that egg? Yes, it does. "Slip, slish and a big boomp!" Dog not only treads on the <u>egg</u> but bangs into a <u>gun</u> in the <u>fog</u>. Poor dog. It is his <u>hat</u> that gets squashed, of course. And so it goes on.

This is the original 1950 ***Ant and Bee,*** since reissued many times and revised to fit in with the concentration on lower-case letters which gives the beginning reader only 26 symbols to learn initially instead of 40. Now the new Ant and Bee . . . is to become the first book in the series. It is called ***Ant and Bee and the ABC*** (or perhaps one should say *abc*). It tells how Ant and Bee first meet and learn the alphabet in the process of investigating a sort of glorified Lost Property Office.

In this book the story is completely subordinate to the pictures, but it is still pure Angela Banner. Her method is to give the most detailed written directions to her illustrator. Sample instructions go like this:

Ant now pictured upright in little boots—he has
a cape but no hat and is more like the Ant of
later books. His eyes are wide with lack of
knowledge of Bee. . . .

Fortunately Angela Banner's bizarre imagination is well matched by Bryan Ward's dexterity and humour. The pictures, gay, hard, a little crude (he is particularly weak at women and children), are marvels of ingenuity. All children have their favourites which they turn to again and again. It may be a complex picture, such as that of the construction of Kind Dog's birthday cake, with dog-biscuits lifted into place by a crane and cemented together with sandwich filling, or a simple one, such as Ant and Bee in their little warm vests. It may be Ant playing patience to while away the long flight to Australia (on Bee's back, of course), or the list in ***One, Two, Three*** of the contents of the shopping-basket. Adults particularly enjoy the surrealism of the lily in the vase at the crossroads, and the strange oven on the desert island. The variety and the wit of the books are amazing.

Some of the titles are, of course, more successful than others. Probably the best-selling book of all, taking into consideration that it has been out for only two years, is ***Happy Birthday with Ant and Bee.*** This is the least overtly educational, as it happens, but it makes up for this by its subject. Designed ostensibly to teach the child the days of the week, it is in fact more of a juvenile guide to the proper conduct of a birthday party. And birthday parties play a large part in most children's lives. ***Happy Birthday,*** designed to look like a striped parcel tied up with blue ribbon, is full of talk of presents and games and prizes and balloons. And the child will probably get extra pleasure

from discovering one of the few errors in the series: Ant and Bee, after buying themselves new ties on Friday especially for the party, can be seen arriving on Saturday *not wearing their new ties.*

Kind Dog, whose birthday is thus celebrated, appears in most of the books, though he varies in appearance considerably. He is far fluffier and fatter in ***One, Two, Three,*** for instance. ***One, Two, Three*** is perhaps the least attractive visually, though one of the best so far as the series goes. The invention is unflagging and owners of the book will quickly learn not only how to count but also how to write and read their numbers. It is in this book that Ant is "sad in bed"—a simple statement that has the inevitability to make it a family catchphrase.

There are in the series at present four reading books. While lacking some of the panache of the Dr. Seuss books, they are much nicer. There is a very definite human mind behind them, not just a computer or a dictionary. Miss Banner's formula, with only the key (red) words from a limited vocabulary, allows her a certain flexibility. She chooses these key words first. "Like cooking ingredients", she says. She constructs the story from the words she has in the house. Some of her ingredients are very odd. There are the difficult letters, of course, where she rightly gives herself a little licence, and we have a pig's tail that looks just like a *Q,* and *X Word,* for instance. But *Asia* seems an unnecessarily obscure four-letter word beginning with *A.* Admittedly *adze* and *acre* and *atom* and *ally* would not be any better. But how about *arch* or *Alps?* If you meet a four-year-old who knows a *yew*-tree and a tea-*urn* when he sees them, you can be sure he is an Ant and Bee reader. *Pail* is all right for bucket (after all, everyone knows Jack and Jill), but *jail* is still surely rare compared with prison. *I* is also a tricky letter, but it is a difficult task to persuade a child that *isle* does not spell island, when that is what the picture shows.

Apart from the four reading books, the new alphabet book, the number book, and the birthday book with its days of the week, there are ***Ant and Bee and the Rainbow,*** a story about colours, and ***Around the World with Ant and Bee,*** a sort of infants' geography book. There is also, outside the Ant and Bee series but with the same author and artist, a time story, ***Mr. Fork and Curly Fork.*** But this is surprisingly confusing, unattractive, and unreadable. . . .

In the Rainbow story, Ant and Bee have a lot of fun painting an old half-buried rubber tyre, knocking over paint pots, to produce green from blue and yellow, and enjoying the changing colours of the sky. But it has a rather lame ending, and is altogether one of the weakest in the series.

Around the World with Ant and Bee, on the other hand, is one of the richest. The publishers claim that it will give a child "a vivid impression of the world around him" and that it will familiarize him with "important concepts of the earth's shape and size". This is nonsense. In fact it will familiarize him with some clichés. If he is taking it seriously he will imagine a world full of people in fancy dress carrying on in a most odd way. France he will see crowded with men in berets, gesticulating madly and waving

French bread aloft in the shadow of the Eiffel Tower. But of course no child will think he is learning important concepts. He will get to know the names of the countries and he will get the idea that geography is fun.

That is really the effect of the whole of this series. Books are fun. The Ant and Bee reader knows that books are small, friendly objects. They are not things that belong mainly to school or things to be kept on a high shelf and treated reverently. They are made to be handled and pored over. The detail in the pictures is there for the smallest child to enjoy on his own, but the books encourage the co-operative effort. Miss Banner believes strongly that what attracts children to early reading is the companionship and attention of the parent or teacher. And an excellent substitute for the busy adult is an older brother or sister. She wants young children to help one another to read, and certainly the Ant and Bee books are perfectly designed for this. The six or seven-year-old will read the black words while the five-year-old shouts out the red ones. The older child's enjoyment is increased as he becomes aware of Miss Banner's ingenuity—the alphabetical progression and the turning of the story to accomplish the constant repetition of the words already learnt.

Ant and Bee, once introduced to a child, become part of his life. Starting on the pictures at fifteen months, he may well still be surprised, amused, stimulated at seven. The books may be ephemera. Certainly no one would talk about literary and artistic masterpieces. They could be called vulgar, brash, unsubtle, limited, marred by over-emphatic punctuation. But they combine that mixture of the rational and irrational, the strange and the familiar, which children everywhere delight in. They are lively, inventive, funny and instructive. And that is a lot for which to be thankful.

> *"More and More Ant and Bee," in* The Times Literary Supplement, *No. 3378, November 24, 1966, p. 1076.*

Margery Fisher

Ant and Bee and the ABC, which describes [Ant and Bee's] first meeting, was not in fact the first book in which these two cheerful and useful insects were introduced to the preschool world. The first story, *Ant and Bee,* is cleverly planned so that children can learn to read a few simple three-letter words; these are displayed singly and also fitted into the narrative, always being marked out by red type. The formula is repeated in three more books; later there are lively, painless introductions to counting, geography, colour, the days of the week, time, money, school and medical care, all with Ant and Bee in the centre. These two, with their amiable friend Kind Dog, are turned into tiny people by virtue of hats and accessories and neatly contrived faces which hardly alter their insect appearance. It is the idiosyncratic illustrations which have established them among the hotchpotch of human, animal and inanimate 'characters' cherished by the very young. (p. 24)

[The] cheerful little book [*Mr Fork and Curly Fork*] has a simpler approach to that landmark of the nursery years, telling the time, than the Ant and Bee book on the same subject. The personification of inanimate objects has sel-

dom been more charming, direct and cheerfully comical than in this brief tale, in which both dialogue and pictures contribute to the credibility of the inhabitants of the kitchen drawer. (p. 77)

> *Margery Fisher, "Who's Who in Children's Books: Ant and Bee," in her* Who's Who in Children's Books: A Treasury of the Familiar Characters of Childhood, *Holt, Rinehart and Winston, 1975, pp. 24, 77.*

TITLE COMMENTARY

Ant and Bee: An Alphabetical Story for Tiny Tots (1950)

An ingenious story set in alphabetical form about an 'A-ant' and a 'B-bee' who live in a 'C-cup' and go for a ride on a 'D-dog'. It isn't quite as contrived as *My Aunt's Alphabet* as the author seems content to leave just one word for each object, which is printed in red to help the child to pick it out in the context of the story.

> *Pat Garrett, in a review of "Ant and Bee: An Alphabetical Story for Tiny Tots," in* Children's Book Review, *Vol. I, No. 2, April, 1971, p. v.*

One, Two, Three with Ant and Bee: A Counting Story (1958)

Another of those popular stories featuring that unlikely combination Ant and Bee, who, attired in boots and hats, set off on another of their incredible adventures. This one involves many experiences with numbers and invitations to count. Ant and Bee go shopping and with so many items, (enough to provide objects 1 to 10) the basket falls causing Ant to fall too. Fortunately kind friends send presents to help him recover which offer more opportunities for counting. Numerals and words to 10 are used but not necessarily in order.

> *Pat Garrett, in a review of "One, Two, Three with Ant and Bee," in* Children's Book Review, *Vol. I, No. 5, October, 1971, p. vi.*

More and More Ant and Bee: Another Alphabetical Story (1961)

The new volume is based on five-letter words introduced in red type as landmarks in a continuous story. Children delight in these books above all for the moment when the page is turned to show the new word by itself, and if they feel industrious they can track these new words (still in red) throughout the story. They are jolly, sensible little books that deserve their popularity.

> *Margery Fisher, in a review of "More and More Ant and Bee," in* Growing Point, *Vol. 1, No. 2, July, 1962, p. 25.*

Ant and Bee and Kind Dog: An Alphabetical Story (1963)

From letters to simple words, in the latest Ant and Bee story. These pleasing little books, with their engaging insect heroes, are always a little handicapped by their scheme. In each book the single words picked out in red are chosen to illustrate the letters of the alphabet in order. In the past this has meant agreeably inconsequent tales, but in the new volume rational children may well object to this, for the insects set out with a dog friend to track down a smell which they never find. These books are most useful, though, for children just starting to read, and their humour is always fresh.

> *Margery Fisher, in a review of "Ant and Bee and Kind Dog," in* Growing Point, *Vol. 2, No. 9, April, 1964, p. 298.*

Happy Birthday with Ant and Bee (1964)

There can be few people now who have not met the Ant and Bee series, which can be read aloud or used for children who can read just a little. It will be enough to say that this new book deals with the days of the week, with a neat little story and a trick with inset pictures [by Bryan Ward] which is both economical and amusing. After many years, these little books are as good as ever.

> *Margery Fisher, in a review of "Happy Birthday with Ant and Bee," in* Growing Point, *Vol. 3, No. 4, October, 1964, p. 385.*

Ant and Bee and the ABC (1966)

The alphabet has a new look here. Ant and Bee (now at last we know how they first met) lose their hats and go to the Lost Property Office where goods are stored in boxes. "Their lost hats were not in box A. What was in box A?" (Pictures with tags attached show ark, apple, animals: letters are in red). Finishing with Z, with no luck, they open an extra box of Funny Things, find their hats, swop for better fit. Useful, utterly irresistible.

> *Margery Fisher, in a review of "Ant and Bee and the A.B.C.," in* Growing Point, *Vol. 5, No. 8, March, 1967, p. 867.*

Ant and Bee Time (1969)

Two popular insects return to help children to tell the time. Using her customary device of alternate red and black type to stress the important words and phrases, the author works through a festive day at the Zoo; games and contests are arranged and every incident is ruled by the clock. Hour and minute hands are separated in the pictures so that children can understand the different ways the hands move.

> *Margery Fisher, in a review of "Ant and Bee Time," in* Growing Point, *Vol. 8, No. 5, November, 1969, p. 1421.*

Ant and Bee and the Secret (1970)

Nowadays books don't come with titles like Angela Banner's—***Ant and Bee: An Alphabetical Story for Tiny Tots***—except as a spoof. And they don't have illustrations like hers either. Take the matter-of-fact drawing that announces L is for Leg. Leg is a Briton's leg, pictured from the knee down, clad in purple tweed knickerbockers. The knickers are stuffed into heavy socks, the whole terminating in splendidly sturdy laced shoes.

Ant and Bee crossed the Atlantic about seven years ago, and, despite its English English (T for Tap, V for Van), it has become one of its publisher's best sellers. An even surer testimonial is the state of the battered, food-stained copy I have wrested from the third in a succession of loving young owners. Apparently, in the eyes of American children the qualities of clarity and unsophistication offset Ant and Bee's London nursery air.

Besides, neither author nor illustrator (Bryan Ward illustrated the first books) is trying to show off in the ant and bee books. The 1920-ish drawings are literal and bright, the larger-than-life-size ant and bee have friendly charm. So does Kind Dog. Besides Miss Banner always has the easy words printed in red. A small child sharing the book with an adult can chime in every time one of "his" red words appears.

The latest in the series is ***Ant and Bee and the Secret,*** a piece of unsubtle propaganda about the advantages of going to school. The title-pages, but not the drawings, reveal that Miss Banner is now doing her own illustrations.

Of course size has something to do with Ant and Bee's popularity too. All the books (there are now 11 of them) are fascinatingly tiny.

> *"Buzzing to Literacy," in* The Christian Science Monitor, *November 12, 1970, p. B5.*

The Ant and Bee Big Buy Bag (1971)

A sturdy pack of games and puzzle pictures to suit children around six to nine (and younger with help), with bright colour and ingenious variations on trad. games like Snakes and Ladders, and Lotto, Ant and Bee and Kind Dog playing their part. Some of the games need to be copied on to paper or card before they can actually be played; the pictures with stories on the back are frustrating, since you need two copies to be able to look at picture and story at the same time. But on the whole a welcome package for wet days and holidays, offering familiarity spiced with surprises.

> *Margery Fisher, in a review of "The Ant and Bee Big Buy Bag," in* Growing Point, *Vol. 10, No. 5, November, 1971, p. 1829.*

Ant and Bee and the Doctor (1971)

Considering the popularity of this series with both parents and children, it is hardly a surprise to find that this is the eleventh volume, and it comes as a useful present for the child who is kept in bed through illness. For besides being an entertaining instructional book in two of the three R's, it has a few suggestions for the bored child who is temporarily isolated from his friends; and it is always nice to know that old acquaintances like Ant and Bee can have similar afflictions to oneself. The repetition of word and phrase, the endearingly ugly pictures, are all here as before and as welcome as ever. But one can hardly agree with the note on the flap, "you'll want to read ALL the Ant and Bee books", for if they are as useful as they seem to be, the average child should, after the first half dozen, be demanding something a bit more meaty.

> *C. Martin, in a review of "Ant and Bee and the Doctor," in* The Junior Bookshelf, *Vol. 35, No. 6, December, 1971, p. 371.*

One feels that the intention behind Angela Banner's 'Ant and Bee' stories is wholly admirable, but somehow, between the idea and its execution, something is lost. The books' small measurements ensure a perfect fit into the small hands that use them, but one cannot but feel that they would have been easier to use if they had been rotated a quarter turn so that their width became their length. Many deal with important educational concepts such as telling the time, or the days of the week, and they also include an 'A B C' and 'Counting' book amongst their number. They are designed to be read with an older brother or sister, with sections for the younger child to join in; they also employ a limited vocabulary and have a certain amount of repetition, all of which would seem to be perfect for the young child starting to read. However, as with some other series with a limited story-line, the text often suffers and, although the books deal with two animals that children often worry about, yet, these animals can look grotesque and sometimes even unpleasant. The repetition, which can take the form of underlining, capital letters, printing words in red, or italic, often all at once on the same page, can also cause confusion where greater clarity was intended.

This example (***Ant and Bee and the Doctor***) is typical of the series and here children are to be reassured about their visits to the doctor. When Bee sneezes, he goes to the Doctor and then goes to bed to get well again, with faithful Ant working his feelers to the bone looking after him, so that inevitably, once Bee is well again, Ant falls prey to the dreaded red lumps and, unlike Bee, is a very bad patient. They are quite blatantly moral books and I think this is what worries me most. If *only* the point wasn't so insistently pushed home.

> *Pat Garrett, in a review of "Ant and Bee and the Doctor," in* Children's Book Review, *Vol. II, No. 1, February, 1972, p. 9.*

Ant and Bee Go Shopping   (1972)

Implied lessons on how to spend wisely, in a jaunty sequence of adventures in a large store; as always, Kind Dog is ready to make good inevitable mistakes and his gift of two secret parcels (reduced price clearly stated) rounds the book off cosily. The author/artist has been as generous as usual in providing surprises in her pictures.

> *Margery Fisher, in a review of "Ant and Bee Go Shopping," in* Growing Point, *Vol. 11, No. 4, October, 1972, p. 2021.*

A tiny book, illustrated in pedestrian style, is used for some thinly disguised lessons wrapped in a meandering story. Ant and Bee divide their shopping list, each takes money from the bank, they go shopping and all their goods are squashed in the new shopping bag. Their guest, Kind Dog, takes them shopping and each item is (unrealistically, even within the framework of the story) put in a large plastic box. Everything is intact when they get home and they have a good time playing with the bricks that Kind Dog has brought as a surprise. The story attempts to teach round, square, flat, and "fat" as concepts, as well as suggest care in transporting groceries; its appeal may be in the busy picturing of objects that small children can pore over and name.

> *Zena Sutherland, in a review of "Ant and Bee Go Shopping," in* Bulletin of the Center for Children's Books, *Vol. 26, No. 7, March, 1973, p. 101.*

Frances Hodgson Burnett

1849-1924

English-born American author of fiction and plays and journalist.

Major works include *Little Lord Fauntleroy* (1886), *A Little Princess, Being the Whole Story of Sara Crewe Now Told for the First Time* (1905), *The Secret Garden* (1911), *The Lost Prince* (1915).

The following entry presents criticism of *The Secret Garden.*

Acclaimed as one of the greatest writers of literature for children, Burnett is celebrated for her strength as a story-teller as well as for her understanding of young people and for the authenticity of her characterizations. The author of realistic fiction, fantasy, and plays adapted from her stories, she was also the creator of adult fiction that achieved best seller status during her lifetime. Burnett is now recognized almost exclusively for her contributions to juvenile literature, of which *Little Lord Fauntleroy,* the popular story of an American boy who discovers that he is heir to an English fortune, and *The Secret Garden* are the best known. Regarded as a classic of children's literature as well as Burnett's best book, *The Secret Garden* describes how ten-year-old Mary Lennox, a sallow, unhappy, and disagreeable orphan, arrives at the isolated Yorkshire mansion owned by her uncle and is restored to emotional health through her care for the walled rose garden, the key to which she finds by following a friendly robin, that has been locked for the ten years since her aunt's accidental death. A subplot in the book is the restoration to physical health of Mary's invalid cousin Colin Craven, also ten, who has been abandoned by his father and spoiled by the house staff. Aided by the maid Martha, her Pan-like brother Dickon, their mother Susan, and the crusty gardener Ben Weatherstaff, the protagonists recover their strength, learn self-reliance, and discover a renewed joy in living through a combination of fresh air, exercise, the companionship of other children, and kinship with the natural world. Often considered the first modern novel for children, *The Secret Garden* presents a departure from the idealized attitude toward childhood that was popular in much of the literature of the nineteenth and early twentieth centuries: Burnett characterizes Mary and Colin as initially unattractive children whose transformation into wholeness is accomplished mainly through their own efforts, not those of adults.

Burnett wrote *The Secret Garden,* in the words of her younger son and biographer Vivian Burnett, "as an expression of her love for growing things and her desire to tell the world to be happy." Influenced by the works of the Brontës, especially *Jane Eyre,* and her interest in the philosophies of the time that focused on the power of the mind, Burnett created the book out of her memories of Maytham Hall, her beloved home in Kent where a rose garden served as her workroom, and the experience of

planting a new garden at her new home on Long Island. Observers also note that the character of Colin is based on Burnett's elder son, Lionel, who died of consumption at fifteen, and offer the theory that Colin's recovery is perhaps Burnett's fulfillment of her own fantasy for her son. First published as a serial in the *American Magazine* in 1909, *The Secret Garden* was not an initial success. However, the book has been consistently popular among generations of children and is especially appreciated by adults; called by critic Marghanita Laski "the most satisfying children's book I know," *The Secret Garden* is often regarded by many children's literature professionals as the outstanding story of their early reading. The novel is also considered an important influence on subsequent literature for both children and adults; for example, several observers believe that *The Secret Garden* foreshadows T. S. Eliot's poem "Burnt Norton," which also features an enclosed rose garden. Although mixed in their reception of the second half of the book, when Burnett transfers her focus from Mary to Colin, reviewers consistently praise *The Secret Garden* for its charm, optimism, literary quality, and lack of sentimentality. Most observers also point to Burnett's original, insightful, and believable characterization of Mary Lennox as a refreshing heroine with whom readers can easily identify as the main reason for both the longevity and the current appeal of the novel. *The Secret Garden* received the Lewis Carroll Shelf Award in 1959.

(See also *Yesterday's Authors of Books for Children,* Vol. 2; *Contemporary Authors,* Vol. 108; and *Dictionary of Literary Biography,* Vol. 9.)

AUTHOR'S COMMENTARY

There came to me among the letters I received last spring one which touched me very closely. It was a letter full of delightful things but the delightful thing which so reached my soul was a question. The writer had been reading *The Secret Garden* and her question was this: "Did you own the original of the robin? He could not have been a mere creature of fantasy. I feel sure you owned him." I was thrilled to the centre of my being. Here was some one who plainly had been intimate with robins—English robins. I wrote and explained as far as one could in a letter what I am now going to relate in detail.

I did not own the robin—he owned me—or perhaps we owned each other.

He was an English robin and he was a *person*—not a mere bird. An English robin differs greatly from the American one. He is much smaller and quite differently shaped. His body is daintily round and plump, his legs are delicately slender. He is a graceful little patrician with an astonishing allurement of bearing. His eye is large and dark and dewy; he wears a tight little red satin waistcoat on his full round breast and every tilt of his head, every flirt of his wing is instinct with dramatic significance. He is fascinatingly conceited—he burns with curiosity—he is determined to engage in social relations at almost any cost and his raging jealousy of attention paid to less worthy objects than himself drives him at times to efforts to charm and distract which are irresistible. An intimacy with a robin—an English robin—is a liberal education.

This particular one I knew in my rose-garden in Kent. I feel sure he was born there and for a summer at least believed it to be the world. It was a lovesome, mystic place, shut in partly by old red brick walls against which fruit trees were trained and partly by a laurel hedge with a wood behind it. It was my habit to sit and write there under an aged writhen tree, gray with lichen and festooned with roses. The soft silence of it—the remote aloofness—were the most perfect ever dreamed of. But let me not be led astray by the garden. I must be firm and confine myself to the Robin. The garden shall be another story.

There were so many people in this garden—people with feathers, or fur—who, because I sat so quietly, did not mind me in the least, that it was not a surprising thing when I looked up one summer morning to see a small bird hopping about the grass a yard or so away from me. The surprise was not that he was there but that he *stayed* there—or rather he continued to hop—with short reflective-looking hops and that while hopping he looked at me—not in a furtive flighty way but rather as a person might tentatively regard a very new acquaintance. The ab-

solute truth of the matter I had reason to believe later was that he did not know I was a person. I may have been the first of my species he had seen in this rose-garden world of his and he thought I was only another kind of robin. I was too—though that was a secret of mine and nobody but myself knew it. Because of this fact I had the power of holding myself *still*—quite *still* and filling myself with softly alluring tenderness of the tenderest when any little wild thing came near me.

"What do you do to make him come to you like that?" some one asked me a month or so later. "What do you *do?*"

"I don't know what I do exactly," I said. "Except that I hold myself very still and feel like a robin."

You can only do that with a tiny wild thing by being so tender of him—of his little timidities and feelings—so adoringly anxious not to startle him or suggest by any movement the possibility of your being a creature who *could hurt*—that your very yearning to understand his tiny hopes and fears and desires makes you for the time cease to be quite a mere human thing and gives you another and more exquisite sense which speaks for you without speech.

As I sat and watched him I held myself softly still and felt just that. I did not know he was a robin. The truth was that he was too young at that time to look like one, but I did not know that either. He was plainly not a thrush, or a linnet or a sparrow or a starling or a blackbird. He was a little indeterminate-colored bird and he had no red on his breast. And as I sat and gazed at him he gazed at me as one quite without prejudice unless it might be with the slightest tinge of favor—and hopped—and hopped—and hopped.

That was the thrill and wonder of it. No bird, however evident his acknowledgement of my harmlessness, had ever hopped and *remained.* Many had perched for a moment in the grass or on a nearby bough, had trilled or chirped or secured a scurrying gold and green beetle and flown away. But none had stayed to inquire—to reflect—even to seem—if one dared be so bold as to hope such a thing—to make mysterious, almost occult advances towards intimacy. Also I had never before heard of such a thing happening to any one howsoever bird loving. Birds are creatures who must be wooed and it must be delicate and careful wooing which allures them into friendship.

I held my soft stillness. Would he stay? Could it be that the last hop was nearer? Yes, it was. The moment was a breathless one. Dare one believe that the next was nearer still—and the next—and the next—and that the two yards of distance had become scarcely one—and that within that radius he was soberly hopping round my very feet with his quite unafraid eye full upon me. This was what was happening. It may not seem exciting but it was. That a little wild thing should come to one unasked was of a thrillingness touched with awe.

Without stirring a muscle I began to make low, soft, little sounds to him—very low and very caressing indeed—softer than one makes to a baby. I wanted to weave a spell—to establish mental communication—to make

Magic. And as I uttered the tiny sounds he hopped nearer and nearer.

"Oh! to think that you will come as near as that!" I whispered to him. "You *know*. You know that nothing in the world would make me put out my hand or startle you in the least tiniest way. You know it because you are a real person as well as a lovely—lovely little bird thing. You know it because you are a soul."

Because of this first morning I knew—years later—that this was what Mistress Mary thought when she bent down in the Long Walk and "tried to make robin sounds."

I said it all in a whisper and I think the words must have sounded like robin sounds because he listened with interest and at last—miracle of miracles as it seemed to me—he actually fluttered up on to a small shrub not two yards away from my knee and sat there as one who was pleased with the topic of conversation.

I did not move of course, I sat still and waited his pleasure. Not for mines of rubies would I have lifted a finger.

I think he stayed near me altogether about half an hour. Then he disappeared. Where or even exactly when I did not know. One moment he was hopping among some of the rose bushes and then he was gone.

This, in fact, was his little mysterious way from first to last. Through all the months of our delicious intimacy he never let me know where he lived. I knew it was in the rose-garden—but that was all. His extraordinary freedom from timorousness was something to think over. After reflecting upon him a good deal I thought I had reached an explanation. He had been born in the rose-garden and being of a home-loving nature he had declined to follow the rest of his family when they had made their first flight over the wall into the rose-walk or over the laurel hedge into the pheasant cover behind. He had stayed in the rose world and then had felt lonely. Without father or mother or sisters or brothers desolateness of spirit fell upon him. He saw a creature—I insist on believing that he thought it another order of robin—and approached to see what it would say.

Its whole bearing was confidence inspiring. It made softly alluring—if unexplainable—sounds. He felt its friendliness and affection. It was curious to look at and far too large for any ordinary nest. It plainly could not fly. But there was not a shadow of inimical sentiment in it. Instinct told him that. It admired him, it wanted him to remain near, there was a certain comfort in its caressing atmosphere. He liked it and felt less desolate. He would return to it again.

The next day summer rains kept me in the house. The next I went to the rose-garden in the morning and sat down under my tree to work. I had not been there half an hour when I felt I must lift my eyes and look. A little indeterminate-colored bird was hopping quietly about in the grass—quite aware of me as his dew-bright eye manifested. He had come again—of intention—because we were mates.

It was the beginning of an intimacy not to be described unless one filled a small volume. From that moment we never doubted each other for one second. He knew and I knew. Each morning when I came into the rose-garden he came to call on me and discover things he wanted to know concerning robins of my size and unusual physical conformation. He did not understand but he was attracted by me. Each day I held myself still and tried to make robin sounds expressive of adoring tenderness and he came each day a little nearer. At last arrived a day when as I softly left my seat and moved about the garden he actually quietly hopped after me.

I wish I could remember exactly what length of time elapsed before I knew he was really a robin. An ornithologist would doubtless know but I do not. But one morning I was bending over a bed of Laurette Messimy roses and I became aware that he had arrived in his usual mysterious way without warning. He was standing in the grass and when I turned my eyes upon him I only just saved myself from starting—which would have meant disaster. I saw upon his breast the first dawning of a flush of color—more tawny than actual red at that stage—but it hinted at revelations.

"Further subterfuge is useless," I said to him. "You are betrayed. You are a robin."

And he did not attempt to deny it either then or at any future time. In less than two weeks he revealed a tight, glossy little bright red satin waistcoat and with it a certain youthful maturity such as one beholds in the wearer of a first dress suit. His movements were more brisk and certain. He began to make little flights and little sounds though for some time he made no attempt to sing. Instead of appearing suddenly in the grass at my feet, a heavenly little rush of wings would bring him to a bough over my head or a twig quite near me where he would tilt daintily, taking his silent but quite responsive part in the conversations which always took place between us. It was I who talked—telling him how I loved him—how satin red his waistcoat was—how large and bright his eyes—how delicate and elegant his slender legs. I flattered him a great deal. He adored flattery and I am sure he loved me most when I told him that it was impossible to say anything which *could* flatter him. It gave him confidence in my good taste.

One morning—a heavenly sunny one—I was conversing with him by the Laurette Messimys again and he was evidently much pleased with the things I said. Perhaps he liked my hat which was a large white one with a wreath of roses round its crown. I saw him look at it and I gently hinted that I had worn it in the hope that he would approve. I had broken off a handful of coral pink Laurettes and was arranging them idly when—he spread his wings in a sudden upward flight—a tiny swift flight which ended—among the roses on my hat—the very hat on my head.

Did I make myself still then? Did I stir by a single hairbreadth? Who does not know? I scarcely let myself breathe. I could not believe that such a thing of pure joy could be true.

But in a minute I realized that he at least was not afraid to move. He was perfectly at home. He hopped about the brim and examined the roses with delicate pecks. That I was under the hat apparently only gave him confidence. He knew me as well as that. He stayed until he had learned all he wished to know about garden hats and then he lightly flew away.

From that time each day drew us closer to each other. He began to perch on twigs only a few inches from my face and listen while I whispered to him—yes, he *listened* and made answer with chirps. Nothing else would describe it. As I wrote he would alight on my manuscript paper and try to read. Sometimes I thought he was a little offended because he found my handwriting so bad that he could not understand it. He would take crumbs out of my hand, he would alight on my chair or my shoulder. The instant I opened the little door in the leaf-covered garden wall I would be greeted by the darling little rush of wings and he was beside me. And he always came from nowhere and disappeared into space.

That, through the whole summer—was his rarest fascination. Perhaps he was not a real robin. Perhaps he was a fairy. Who knows? . . . (pp. 1-22)

I will not attempt to deceive. He was jealous beyond bounds. It was necessary for me to be most discreet in my demeanor towards the head gardener with whom I was obliged to consult frequently. When he came into the rose-garden for orders Tweetie at once appeared.

He followed us, hopping in the grass or from rose bush to rose bush. No word of ours escaped him. If our conversation on the enthralling subjects of fertilizers and aphides seemed in its earnest absorption to verge upon the emotional and tender he interfered at once. He commanded my attention. He perched on nearby boughs and endeavored to distract me. He fluttered about and called me with chirps. His last resource was always to fly to the topmost twig of an apple tree and begin to sing his most brilliant song in his most thrilling tone and with an affected manner. Naturally we were obliged to listen and talk about him. Even old Barton's weather-beaten apple face would wrinkle into smiles.

"He's doin' that to make us look at him," he would say. "That's what he's doin' it for. He can't abide not to be noticed."

But it was not only his vanity which drew him to me. He loved me. The low song trilled in his little pulsating scarlet throat was mine. He sang it only to me—and he would never sing it when any one else was there to hear. When we were quite alone with only roses and bees and sunshine and silence about us, when he swung on some spray quite close to me and I stood and talked to him in whispers—then he would answer me—each time I paused—with the little "far away" sounding trills—the sweetest, most wonderful little sounds in the world. A clever person who knew more of the habits of birds than I did told me a most curious thing.

"That is his little mating song," he said. "You have inspired a hopeless passion in a robin."

Perhaps so. He thought the rose-garden was the world and it seemed to me he never went out of it during the summer

months. At whatsoever hour I appeared and called him he came out of bushes but from a different point each time. In late autumn however, one afternoon I *saw* him fly to me from over a wall dividing the enclosed garden from the open ones. I thought he looked guilty and fluttered when he alighted near me. I think he did not want me to know.

"You have been making the acquaintance of a young lady robin," I said to him. "Perhaps you are already engaged to her for the next season."

He tried to persuade me that it was not true but I felt he was not entirely frank.

After that it was plain that he had discovered that the rose-garden was not *all* the world. He knew about the other side of the wall. But it did not absorb him altogether. He was seldom absent when I came and he never failed to answer my call. I talked to him often about the young lady robin but though he showed a gentlemanly reticence on the subject I knew quite well he loved me best. He loved my robin sounds, he loved my whispers, his dewy dark eyes looked into mine as if he knew we two understood strange tender things others did not.

I was only a mere tenant of the beautiful place I had had for nine years and that winter the owner sold the estate. In December I was to go to Montreux for a couple of months; in March I was to return to Maytham and close it before leaving it finally. Until I left for Switzerland I saw my robin every day. Before I went away I called him to me and told him where I was going.

He was such a little thing. Two or three months might seem a lifetime to him. He might not remember me so long. I was not a real robin. I was only a human being. I said a great many things to him—wondering if he would even be in the garden when I came back. I went away wondering.

When I returned from the world of winter sports, of mountain snows, of tobogganing and skis I felt as if I had been absent a long time. There had been snow even in Kent and the park and gardens were white. I arrived in the evening. The next morning I threw on my red frieze garden cloak and went down the flagged terrace and the Long Walk through the walled gardens to the beloved place where the rose bushes stood dark and slender and leafless among the whiteness. I went to my own tree and stood under it and called.

"Are you gone," I said in my heart; "are you gone, little Soul? Shall I never see you again?"

After the call I waited—and I had never waited before. The roses were gone and he was not in the rose-world. I called again. The call was sometimes a soft whistle as near a robin sound as I could make it—sometimes it was a chirp—sometimes it was a quick clear repetition of "Sweet! Sweet! Sweetie"—which I fancied he liked best. I made one after the other—and then—something scarlet flashed across the lawn, across the rose-walk—over the wall and he was there. He had not forgotten, it had not been too long, he alighted on the snowy brown grass at my feet.

Then I knew he was a little Soul and not only a bird and the real parting which must come in a few weeks' time loomed up before me a strange tragic thing.

I do not often allow myself to think of it. It was too final. And there was nothing to be done. I was going thousands of miles across the sea. A little warm thing of scarlet and brown feathers and pulsating trilling throat lives such a brief life. The little soul in its black dew-drop eye—one knows nothing about it. For myself I sometimes believe strange things. We two were something weirdly near to each other.

At the end I went down to the bare world of roses one soft damp day and stood under the tree and called him for the last time. He did not keep me waiting and he flew to a twig very near my face. I could not write all I said to him. I tried with all my heart to explain and he answered me—between his listenings—with the "far away" love note. I talked to him as if he knew all I knew. He put his head on one side and listened so intently that I felt that he understood. I told him that I must go away and that we should not see each other again and I told him why.

"But you must not think when I do not come back it is because I have forgotten you," I said. "Never since I was born have I loved anything as I have loved you—except my two babies. Never shall I love anything so much again so long as I am in the world. You are a little Soul and I am a little Soul and we shall love each other forever and ever. We won't say Goodbye. We have been too near to each other—nearer than human beings are. I love you and love you and love you—little Soul."

Then I went out of the rose-garden. I shall never go into it again. (pp. 32-42)

> *Frances Hodgson Burnett, in her* My Robin, *Frederick A. Stokes Company, 1912, 42 p.*

Literary Digest

The Secret Garden will charm every one from the children to the grown-ups.

It has the allurement of mystery, the fascination of child-life, and the same joyous and sane philosophy of life that made *Glad* lovable and *The Dawn of To-morrow* popular.

When ten-year-old Mary Lennox was brought, an orphan from India, to the estate of her guardian uncle at Misselthwaite Manor, no more disagreeable child could be imagined, but the author has cleverly made her regeneration, as well as her original heritage, the natural result of environment and inherent power. The mystery of the garden which had been closed for ten years, and the part it played in the life of the children—Mary, Dickon, and Colin—(the other mystery) are described with tender imagination, while the reader is kept in suspense to the end about the outcome of the "White Magic"—the power of will in compelling health.

There is more than an analogy between the garden that "comes alive" and the life and character of Colin and Mary. The reader learns to love sensible Susan Sowerby,

Dickon, the animal-charmer, Ben Weatherstaff, and the dear, pert little robin.

To describe adequately the delights of the story would deprive the reader of the joy and pleasure of first discovery—the sensation of surprize.

> *A review of "The Secret Garden," in* Literary Digest, *New York, Vol. 43, No. 10, September 2, 1911, p. 361.*

The New York Times

Many authors can write delightful books for children; a few can write entertaining books about children for adults; but it is only the exceptional author who can write a book about children with sufficient skill, charm, simplicity, and significance to make it acceptable to both young and old. Mrs. Burnett is one of the few thus gifted, and her new story will be read with equal pleasure by young people and by those of their elders who love young things, for whom literary craftsmanship is a source of enjoyment and a quiet, beautiful tale attractive. . . .

The material of the book is as simple as it could well be, and those who demand much plot and plenty of excitement in their fiction probably will not be able to "see anything in it."

But readers who appreciate other qualities in fiction will find in it such thorough understanding of the heart of childhood, such loving pleasure in the beauty of the out-of-doors and such conviction of its power to heal the human spirit, whether old or young, such skill in the management of simple materials and such charm of style that they will care for it a great deal. The book is in every way superior to *Little Lord Fauntleroy.* The sloppiness of sentiment, the goody-goodiness and the artificiality which characterized that highly popular story do not mar *The Secret Garden,* whose underlying philosophy of the beneficent power of good thoughts and wholesome action is expressed through their influence upon the two children simply and without any trace of mawkish sentiment.

> *"What Was Hid in a Garden," in* The New York Times, *September 3, 1911, p. 526.*

R. A. Whay

The *Secret Garden* is more than a mere story of children; underlying it there is a deep vein of symbolism. But regarded purely as romance, it is an exceedingly pretty tale, full of the pathos of sheer happiness, a tale which no one could possibly associate with any other name than that of Mrs. Burnett. (p. 184)

> *R. A. Whay, "Frances Hodgson Burnett's 'The Secret Garden'," in* The Bookman, *London, Vol. XXXIV, No. 2, October, 1911, pp. 183-84.*

Katharine Tynan

[*The Secret Garden*] is a *hortus inclusus* of a book—a very fragrant book, sweet with the sweets of the Hidden Garden, and with certain other flowers that grow in the soil of the human heart. It is a privilege when such a writer as Mrs. Burnett gives her fresh and living art to writing stories for children. Indeed this is a book which elders too may read with delight. . . . Altogether this is a very tender idyll, quite in the line of succession to *Little Lord Fauntleroy,* with just that touch of the grown-up heart and experience about it that makes it belong almost as much to general literature as to the literature of the schoolroom. From seven to seventy-seven one might read *The Secret Garden* with delight and profit. (pp. 102-03)

Katharine Tynan, "In Fairy-Book Land," in The Bookman, *London, Vol. XLI, December, 1911, pp. 102-03.*

Vivian Burnett

[*Vivian Burnett, the younger son of Frances Hodgson Burnett, served as the model for Little Lord Fauntleroy; he later became a journalist and editor.*]

In February [of 1909] Mrs. Burnett was back in Maytham, but making plans to return to America. Vivian was asked to find a place on Long Island, near enough to be a home, or at least a resting-spot for all the "day laborers" in the family. In June she was in the United States again, having waved a rather undecided good-by to Maytham, for her lease there was about to expire, and she was beginning to feel that, despite all its advantages in giving her, under favorable conditions, the life that best suited her working mood, it was an extravagance.

She found herself located in a strange little furnished cottage in the centre of the fashionable Sands Point district of Long Island. . . .

She began after the passage of months to find the Long Island district attractive to her—albeit in a way distinctly different from the hoary and romantic way of Maytham, and just before departing the next spring for a "cure" at Doctor Lampe's sanitarium, in Frankfort, Germany, she purchased land at Plandome, Long Island, and approved the plans for a house to be built while she was away. (p. 323)

With her moving into the Plandome house she became The Passionate Gardener indeed. The magic of making flowers grow, coaxing them to bloom their best, and bring their happiness into the landscape, became her chief distraction. From this time on she was never thoroughly well, and any real exertion tired her. She had not, in fact, the strength for social activities, and about the most she could do was to go occasionally to the theatre. But she could always plan her gardens, revel in the future possibilities of bloom, and, in the out-door weather days, spend an hour or more with her gardener, superintending the tucking in of plants and bulbs. (pp. 326-27)

By autumn, a real miracle had been accomplished. The brand-new house stood on its terraces amid green lawns, surrounded by shading trees and thickets of flowering bushes. The "perennial borders" were stuffed with every conceivable "hardy" plant ready to burst forth in the spring—and were even then ablaze with a riot of hardy chrysanthemums.

Mrs. Burnett's pen had been keeping step with her outside work. The people who had bought Maytham (England) had immediately (so she was told) torn down all the ancient brick garden walls, ploughed up the ground and

turned to market gardening. This was, as a matter of fact, not so. The new owners proved themselves quite as enthusiastic garden-makers as herself; with greater means at their command, in the course of time making the Maytham gardens among the most beautiful in Kent, itself known as the "garden county of England." Mrs. Burnett's cherished rose-garden was changed, it is true, but transformed into a delphinium-bed of unbelievable size and beauty. But Mrs. Burnett never revisited the district, and was to carry with her always the picture of her rose-garden reduced to rows of cabbages and turnips and lettuces under "cloches." Out of her regretful feeling about her rose-garden grew one of her best-beloved books, *The Secret Garden.* It came along naturally for older juveniles, as an expression of her love for growing things, and her desire to tell the world to "be happy." It struck a note of love for the outdoors and the health-giving power of happy thoughts that was enthusiastically welcomed. (pp. 327-28)

Vivian Burnett, in his The Romantick Lady (Frances Hodgson Burnett): The Life Story of an Imagination, *Charles Scribner's Sons, 1927, 423 p.*

Marghanita Laski

Just as *A Little Princess* is infinitely better than *Little Lord Fauntleroy,* so *The Secret Garden* . . . represents a considerable advance on either. (p. 87)

This is a book for introspective town children. I was just such a child myself, and it is therefore the most satisfying children's book I know.

Most children's books are written both about and for children who are uncomplicated extroverts. This is really most unfair. In character children are not really different from adults, and many of them are moody, imaginative, fearful, emotional, conscious of maladjustments with the external world. I suppose that most writers avoid such children for heroes and heroines in the belief that glimpses of the well-adjusted norm are likely to produce a correspondingly healthy frame of mind in the reader. They are wrong. This literary procession of good cheerful toughs only increases the sense of isolation in the mind of the child who is not such a one. I do not know of any children's book other than *The Secret Garden* that frankly poses this problem of the introspective unlikeable child in terms that children can understand and then offers an acceptable solution.

There are, I know, plenty of children's books in which the central character is an unpopular child who gains popularity through a spectacular act of moral or physical courage. These do not touch the problem. The children in such books long to be like the herd and are only accidentally different from it. They become accepted into the herd by their acceptance of a simple challenge that accidentally comes their way. These stories offer no help to the child who already dislikes the herd and yet longs to be happy.

Then there are the books about children who are unhappy because they have not yet learned that happiness comes from unselfishness and obedience. Mrs. Molesworth wrote many such, and both Jo March and Ethel May are prototypes of such heroines. But many children find obedience to external authority intolerable; it is only to something inside themselves that they can give obedience.

On the simplest plane, Mrs. Burnett's answer to these children is *cultiver votre jardin*. She is, of course, right. No one who has become interested in tending a garden has ever remained wholly unhappy. But there is more to it than that. She shows that the advice is to be taken in a metaphorical sense as well, that happiness will come with the constructive development of the individual personality.

I think Mrs. Burnett has put into **The Secret Garden** more than she herself intended. Her own religious beliefs were incoherent and muddled. At the time she wrote this book she was strongly influenced by Christian Science, and clearly intended to refer to this when she made the children believe in a pervading power they called "Magic" that could, so long as they had faith in it, make the roses grow and Colin become strong. But because she was too good a writer to twist a story awry for propaganda's sake, "Magic" comes to mean simply the need to have faith in yourself and show kindness to others. It is a moral book in a different sense from those of Mrs. Ewing and Mrs. Molesworth, where fundamentally morality sprang from a belief in the Christian faith, in, that is to say, authoritative power outside and superior to the child. Mrs. Burnett's book teaches a child to depend on a power that is inside himself; and are we not coming increasingly to believe that this is the teaching we should wish our children to have?

Quite apart from its moral teaching, **The Secret Garden** is a charming book, with many unforgettable pictures—the tapestry in Mary's bedroom with the hunting scene on it; the portrait in the deserted room of the little girl in the brocade dress with a green parrot on her finger; and the discovery of Colin, in the middle of the night, in the "carved four-poster bed hung with brocade". And then, in contrast to these strangely sombre scenes indoors, there is the lovely garden with the roses hanging over it like a green mist and the bulbs pushing up through the neglected earth and the sudden coming of spring. **The Secret Garden** is altogether a delightful book. (pp. 88-90)

[**Little Lord Fauntleroy, A Little Princess,** and **The Secret Garden**] represent all that is important in Mrs. Burnett's contribution to children's literature. She wrote much else for them. . . . But it is for **Fauntleroy, A Little Princess** and **The Secret Garden,** and for the delight and comfort these have given to children, that she deserves to be gratefully remembered. And for **The Secret Garden** in particular she is owed a very special debt of gratitude from those introspective children at war with themselves and the world whom no other children's writer has ever helped and comforted. (pp. 90-1)

> *Marghanita Laski, "Mrs. Hodgson Burnett,"*
> *in her* Mrs. Ewing, Mrs. Molesworth, and
> Mrs. Hodgson Burnett, *Arthur Barker Ltd.,*
> *1950, pp. 73-91.*

Roger Lancelyn Green

This story of two spoilt and introspective children living solitary lives in a big house in Yorkshire, finding each

other by chance and meeting secretly in the garden to which no one knows that they have entry, is the best loved of Mrs Burnett's stories. Although Mrs Molesworth had written in books like *Sheila's Mystery* (1895) of unpleasant children who did not fit into their surroundings and became introspective, she had always worked out their salvation with the aid of outside influences. Mrs Burnett seems to be the first writer for children to have produced a memorable story which turns on a salvation wrought by the child—or in this case the two children on themselves and each other, without any aid from adults.

With great skill she has made the story gripping and compelling without the aid of her usual melodramatic plot, and at the same time created in Mary and Colin real and believable people with whom the child reader can identify her- or himself—even if it is with a subconscious 'Here, but for the Grace of God, go I'. At the same time, she avoids morbidity and is careful not to indulge in any of the obvious soul-searching which even Mrs Molesworth would have felt it her duty to introduce in like circumstances. (pp. 120-21)

> *Roger Lancelyn Green, "Mrs. Hodgson and*
> *Frances E. Crompton," in his* Tellers of Tales,
> *revised edition, 1965. Reprint by Kaye &*
> *Ward, Ltd., 1969, pp. 116-26.*

Elizabeth Nesbitt

The age [of the years 1890-1920] is one frequently characterized by our own, usually in accents of scorn, as one inclined toward sentimentality and idealized romanticism, even in its realism. This is too superficial a view. . . . In any case, it is natural that the realism of the Victorian Age, undergoing the discipline of actuality, should still retain at times the idealization and sentiment characteristic of the period.

The combination of the old and the new is seen in Mrs. Frances Hodgson Burnett's **The Secret Garden.** The setting and background of the story are highly romanticized; the moors, with their strange beauty and fascination; the old house with its many rooms filled with curious and exotic things; the almost unearthly beauty of the secret garden and the tantalizing quality of the mystery concerning it; the Arcadian simplicity of the boy Dickon and his friendship with animals and birds. In the midst of all this there is a problem . . . rarely attacked by writers for children. It is the conversion into mental and physical health of two children, one introspective, withdrawn, inimical to people, and the other a confirmed hypochondriac, ungoverned and hysterical. The conversion is accomplished by a combination of self-development, the healing qualities of the outdoors and the self-forgetting love of growing things and, of all things, the principles of mental healing. And all of it is more plausible than it may sound, and it is plausible because basically Mrs. Burnett is right. Oversimplified and idealized as her presentation may be, her thesis is the same as that of Laura Richards, of Kate Douglas Wiggin, and of others before and since her time—a happy and normal child must care for something and must be cared for. (pp. 352-53)

> *Elizabeth Nesbitt, "Romance and Actuality,"*

Maytham Hall, Rolvenden, Kent, where Burnett lived from 1898 to 1907.

in A Critical History of Children's Literature *by Cornelia Meigs and others, edited by Cornelia Meigs, revised edition, Macmillan Publishing Company, 1969, pp. 349-62.*

Alison White

The taproot maintained by writers and readers into their "first world" goes also into a submerged literature, for some of the world's most influential books are below visibility. Unremembered for themselves they continue doing their work upon minds that may cast them aside but cannot cast them out. Even though the books themselves are left behind in the nursery, the marks they make on a reader's sensibility are lasting. Their stratum is basic, and one who reads of Death's twilight kingdom or the Chapel Perilous may carry into his perception unrecognized images from North Wind and Golden River allegory, or from the hazards and heavens of the children's Kingsley, Ingelow, or Andersen. (p. 74)

In the "first world" of *Burnt Norton* in Eliot's *Four Quartets,* an enclosed rose-garden figures prominently. It is autumn, but the roses are blooming, the pool is filled with water come out of sunlight, and behind a "door we never opened" . . . "the leaves were full of children, / Hidden excitedly, containing laughter." The insistence of *first:—*

"Through the first gate," "Into our first world," and again, "into our first world" thrusts the mind back to the *time past* which according to *Burnt Norton*'s opening oxymoron contains its precipitated self. In its backward search for a rose garden of the "first world," the reader's mind may encounter a symbolic enclosed garden of the "submerged" literature of childhood—***The Secret Garden***. . . . This novel has as its last scene the reunion of a father and son, brought about by the telepathic summons of a bird and the child's dead mother. As in *Burnt Norton* it is autumn in the rose-garden. The leaves are "full of children / Hidden excitedly, containing laughter." . . . Once the memory has spanned the garden of *Burnt Norton* and that of Mrs. Burnett's Yorkshire rose-garden, other parallels suggest themselves. Eliot's "door we never opened into the rose-garden" recalls the insistent, repeated image of a child looking for the garden door:

> . . . if she could find out where the door was, she could perhaps open it and see what was inside the walls, and what had happened to the old rose-trees . . . nobody would ever know where she was, but would think the door was still locked and the key buried in the earth.

and, at the end of the tale, of the father summoned from Lake Como:

He thought that as he sat and breathed in the scent of the late roses and listened to the lapping of the water at his feet he heard a voice calling. It was sweet and clear and happy and far away . . . "In the garden," it came back like a sound from a golden flute. "In the garden!"

In *Burnt Norton* a bird is the summoning voice: "Other echoes inhabit the garden . . . Quick, said the bird, find them, find them." In *The Secret Garden* a bird lives in the rose-garden, leads the children to it, shows them the hidden key and the overgrown door in the wall. To the most perceiving of them, however, and to the brooding master of the house, it is the ghost of the garden's dead mistress who used the bird's voice in calling the children, her own voice only to her husband. "Happen she's been in the garden," says the boy Dickon, "an' happen it was her set us to work, an' told us to bring him here."

The "deception of the thrush" (*Burnt Norton*) recalls two passages in the story where secretiveness and pretense in respect to the garden are rationalized:

"If tha' was a missel thrush an' showed me where thy nest was, does tha' think I'd tell any one? Not me," he said. "Tha' art as safe as a missel thrush."

and

" . . . If we called it our garden and pretended that—that we were missel thrushes and it was our next . . . "

The children's first entrances into the secret garden suggest:

Into our first world
There they were, dignified, invisible,
Moving without pressure, over the dead leaves.
(*Burnt Norton*)

(Dickon) began to walk about softly, even more lightly than Mary had walked the first time she had found herself inside the four walls . . . There were neither leaves nor roses on them now and Mary did not know whether they were dead or alive, but their thin gray or brown branches and sprays looked like a sort of hazy mantle . . . She moved away from the door . . . She was glad that there was grass under her feet and that her steps made no sound.

In the garden of *Burnt Norton* "water out of sunlight" fills the drained pool. Twice in *The Secret Garden* water and sunlight are doubly yoked, as here: "It is the sun shining on the rain and the rain falling on the sunshine." There is a pool also, and the formality of the garden suggests *Burnt Norton's* "empty alley" and "box circle" where the surface of the pool "glittered out of heart of light." Mary and Dickon passed "through the shrubbery gate . . . down winding walks with clipped borders . . . evergreens clipped into strange shapes, and a large pool with an old gray fountain in its midst . . . and the fountain was not playing."

All of these images in *Burnt Norton* are natural, accessible to any reader who can see or imagine rose-gardens in autumn and hear children laughing among the leaves. But to many a reader the evocativeness of these images is intensified by their connoting also the symbolic, subjective use to which they were put in one of the first novels he encountered in his life. *The Secret Garden* and other children's books of its lyric intensity do their work early in preparing the reader's mind for the experience of poetry. To enforce its implications of spiritual waning and gradual regeneration through the "Great Magic," *The Secret Garden* introduced rose-garden, prophet bird, water out of sunlight, and children as symbolic properties. Such a complex of images can carry over from childhood's "first world" of reading, to the adult's encounter with such poetry as *Burnt Norton.* For him the images are then not merely natural, generalized, drawn out of random experience. And Eliot's poem gains in implication through such use of a set of images the more highly subjective by virtue of this allusiveness. (pp. 74-6)

Alison White, "Tap-Roots into a Rose Garden," in Children's Literature: Annual of the Modern Language Association Seminar on Children's Literature and The Children's Literature Association, *Vol. 1, 1972, pp. 74-6.*

Alison Lurie

The conviction that every life should be full of natural splendid happiness is [a driving force behind] *The Secret Garden.* Like *Little Lord Fauntleroy,* it is about a psychological miracle: the complete regeneration of in this case two thoroughly disagreeable and self-centered people. Mary and Colin, like the old Earl of Dorincourt, are converted to goodness and joy. But also, like Cedric, they are restored to their natural birthright, which in this case is not temporal but spiritual; not money and position, but the natural heritage of mankind.

One of the interesting things about *The Secret Garden,* as Ann Thwaite remarks [in her *Waiting for the Party: The Life of Frances Hodgson Burnett*] is that the children are not reformed through the intervention of some wise and kind other person, but mainly through their own efforts, something very uncommon in earlier children's books. They do get some help from a local boy, Dickon, but only after they are well on their way.

And Mary and Colin are not just ordinary sulky or naughty children; they are severely neurotic. Today Mary, with her odd private games and cold indifference to her parents' death, might be diagnosed as pre-schizoid; bedridden Colin, with his imaginary hunchback, as a classic hysteric with conversion symptoms. Mrs. Burnett's presentation of their cases is astonishingly complete by contemporary standards, and plausibly grounded in the treatment both have received since birth.

The plot of the book centers around the children's discovery and cultivation of a long-neglected garden which becomes a metaphor for the hidden potentialities within themselves. The image is also latently sexual, though Mrs. Burnett may not have been aware of this: a walled rose-garden in which a girl and a boy, working together, make things grow.

In many ways *The Secret Garden* is very much of its time. Colin's self-hypnotic chanting recalls the rituals of Christian Science or New Thought, in both of which Mrs. Burnett was interested. Dickon, the farm boy who spends whole days on the moors talking to plants and animals, is a sort of cross between Kipling's Mowgli and the many incarnations of the nature spirit or rural Pan which appear in Edwardian fiction, rescuing Forster's heroines, and later Lawrence's, from death-in-life.

Yet when it appeared in 1911, *The Secret Garden* was only moderately successful—perhaps because it was ahead of its time, for since then its fame has grown steadily. Lately in fact it seems to have become something of a cult book among high-school and college students in America. (More of my students had read it than had read *Alice* or *The Wind in the Willows.*) And it isn't hard to see why, considering that *The Secret Garden* is the story of two unhappy, sickly, overcivilized children who achieve health and happiness through a combination of communal gardening, mystical faith, daily exercises, encounter-group-type confrontation, and a health-food diet. (pp. 40-1)

> *Alison Lurie, "Happy Endings," in* The New York Review of Books, *Vol. XXI, No. 19, November 12, 1974, pp. 39-41.*

Ann Thwaite

It was [the] spring of 1909 that Frances began her most loved book, *The Secret Garden.* This title leaps to the lips of great numbers of people between the ages of seventy and seven when asked to name the favourite book of their childhood. (pp. 219-20)

Vivian believed that the book "grew out of a regretful feeling" when Frances heard (mistakenly as it happened) that the new owners of [her former home in Kent, Maytham Hall,] had turned the Rose Garden into a market garden, with rows and rows of cabbages and turnips, and lettuces under glass cloches. But, as Philippa Pearce has pointed out, "the last thing *The Secret Garden* can have grown out of is a regretful feeling". She first drew my attention to that earlier garden near Islington Square, Salford, [Manchester,] which Frances knew in her childhood, with "the little green door in the high wall which surrounded the garden". This was the cindery desert where the weeds were transformed, by the child's imagination, into a carpet of flowers.

Seeds of *The Secret Garden* had undoubtedly been growing in Frances' mind for nearly fifty years. It may have been at about the same time Frances saw the Manchester garden that she read *Jane Eyre* for the first time. Mary's arrival at Misselthwaite is too reminiscent of Jane's arrival at Thronfield to be coincidental. Both girls were plain young orphans who were starting a new life in a mysterious manor house on the Yorkshire moors, a house where the master was abroad most of the time and the place run by servants. There is also the parallel between Mrs Rochester's tragic laugh and Colin's curious cry, both puzzling the listener beyond the closed door.

Maytham had provided the lamb, the rose garden and the robin. The Brontës (Mary "hated the wind and its wuthering") and Frances' visit to Lord Crewe's house in 1895 had provided the Yorkshire setting. Frances' interest in

the New Thought, as they called the new realization of the power of the mind, had provided the plot. But the most original thing about the book was that its heroine and one of its heroes were both thoroughly unattractive children. The first sentence makes it compulsive reading: "When Mary Lennox was sent to Misselthwaite Manor to live with her uncle, everybody said she was the most disagreeable-looking child ever seen." And Colin, of course, is a hysterical hypochondriac. It is the entirely convincing transformation of these two unhappy children that gives the story its tremendous appeal, even to children who do not find the natural world particularly attractive.

It was a long time since the heroines and heroes of a children's book had had to be as flat and perfect as creatures in a medieval morality play. Fifty years before, Charlotte M. Yonge had broken that pattern but it was still very unusual for them to be actively disagreeable. They might have their small faults, they might be careless and untidy, but they always had merry eyes. Mary and Colin did not have merry eyes.

The treatment of Mary is quite astonishingly accurate to our own much greater understanding of child behaviour. Other Victorian writers had made deprived children behave quite inappropriately, but Frances' instinct has since been confirmed by child psychologists. A child denied love does behave as Mary behaved. But *The Secret Garden* is far more than a parable or a demonstration of child behaviour. With Frances, as always, the story comes first and she was far too good a writer to spoil it with propaganda. Only at the beginning of chapter twenty-seven does she lapse into sententiousness, with explicit explanations of her symbolism and a bald definition of what the rest of the book conveys so subtly and brilliantly: "To let a sad thought or a bad one get into your mind is as dangerous as letting a scarlet fever germ get into your body." "Whatsoever things are honest, just, pure, lovely and of good report—think on these things" has been part of our collective wisdom for a very long time but it has seldom been put into more delightful form.

The Secret Garden is a book of the new century. Far from encouraging the attitudes instilled in Frances as a child ("Speak when you're spoken to, come when you're called . . . "), it suggested children should be self-reliant and have faith in themselves, that they should listen not to their elders and betters, but to their own hearts and consciences. Someone once said that you could learn the elements of pruning roses from *The Secret Garden,* and another large part of the attraction of the book is its exactly accurate descriptions of real gardening. Frances was always good at detail. She knew children liked it. It is not enough to mention they have tea, she once said, you must specify the muffins. It is the detail of things that makes them interesting. To Colin, the moor is bare and dreary. To Dickon, who knows its every detail, the moor is alive with activity and interest. Frances never lost her appetite for quiddities. (pp. 220-22)

> *Ann Thwaite, in her* Waiting for the Party: The Life of Frances Hodgson Burnett, 1849-1924, *Charles Scribner's Sons, 1974, 274 p.*

Margery Fisher

Colin's unhappy situation, if it is read in period context, can be seen to parallel Mary's, and in a sense the characters of the two children are complementary. The book divides naturally into two parts, the first concerned with the way Mary changes from a cross little girl to an eager, responsive one, the second concerned with Colin's discovery that he is not an invalid and his struggle towards health. The dual pattern is not repetitive, for the characters of the children are carefully distinguished. Mary comes to life through a deep love of plants and natural things. Colin's strong will transfers easily from tantrums to commands. (p. 72)

Childlike and yet precocious, Colin rationalizes to his satisfaction the simple discovery that his cure depends on himself. Pride is always a virtue in Mrs Hodgson Burnett's eyes, a virtue connected with birth and breeding but one which Mary and Colin and Sara Crewe and Cedric Errol cultivate by themselves and justify by their efforts. (pp. 72-3)

There are many reasons why *The Secret Garden* is one of the best-loved of all stories for children. The garden itself, locked away for ten years, with bulbs and roses waiting to be released into life; the fresh simplicity and feeling of excitement running through the book; the two ruthless egotists in confrontation; the actual and subliminal change from dark to light, from stuffiness to fresh air, from misery to joy. Above all, here are three characters who are completely real and recognizable. Mary's tough, obstinate, wayward temperament has something basically good about it that only needs the right circumstances for it to bloom into energy and usefulness, as quickly as her sallow face freshens to a healthy pink. Frances Hodgson Burnett is surely remembering her own childhood when she describes the little gardens Mary contrived in India with a patch of mud and a handful of withered flowers and when she makes her heroine free of a garden as secret and dormant as the one she had found herself behind 'the little green door which was never unclosed' in Manchester. There are clues in the early chapters that make it perfectly natural that Mary should climb out of the depths of gloom into the sunshine through her delight in weeding and sowing and freeing the old rose trees from tangled undergrowth. We can readily accept that a child like this should storm at Colin for his selfishness instead of being afraid of his hysterical fits, as the rest of the household are. We can appreciate that a child who has been both spoiled and neglected in childhood should actually have to *learn* to be interested in other people—and so forget herself. Nor will any young reader fail to see the absolute logic of Mary's remark to Dickon that he makes the fifth person that she likes. The others are his mother and Martha 'and the robin and Ben Weatherstaff'. This grouping seems no more odd to her than the fact that she has only liked five people in her life; it is one of many points through which the author shows that the change in her is subtly different from that in Colin, whose story runs parallel with hers. (pp. 211-15)

Margery Fisher, "Who's Who in Children's Books: 'The Secret Garden'," in her Who's Who in Children's Books: A Treasury of the

Familiar Characters of Childhood, *Holt, Rinehart and Winston, 1975, pp. 72-3, 211-15.*

Laura Hoffeld

The enchanted forest, *locus amoenus,* the sacred wood, the jolly greenwood, Wonderland. There was a year of my childhood when I cared for nothing else, when I read all the magical literature for children I could find. That year I found *The Secret Garden* and fell forever under the spell of that abandoned spot of cultivated wildness which had the power to change sallow, joyless children into beautiful, ecstatic creatures. Years later, in my hidebound adolescence, I saw a movie called *The Enchanted Cottage* and had a dim but moving memory of the Garden. In the movie two cruelly plain and embittered people, forsaking and forsaken by the world, are magically transformed in the cottage—by love—into beautiful people. Half this wonderful old black and white film is in soft focus: the characters fairly glow with inner light. I suppose it was made in the 1940's, when people could still be "resplendent."

Looking back I realize that what stirred me was the presence of both romance and magical transformation, that the two presences became allied forever in my girlish mind, and in fact, that an important lesson of our culture was encoded therein. Moreover, that what was exciting about the presentation was the way it moved adroitly between "fantasy" and "reality," playing with the categories until the benighted viewer was pleasantly unsure of which was which. Were the man and woman beautiful only to each other? Would an outsider, pathetically out of love, see their real faces? Which *were* their real faces?

It is this toying at the edge, this sense of the boundary, which made the fantasies I loved in childhood both appealing and valuable, because it is precisely at the place where the two worlds meet that they have significance for each other. The best books were the ones that lingered there, and returned there, that made the boundary their point of reference, and these were best because, unfailingly, they illuminated the real world. The world I was stuck in. (pp. 4-5)

The special bit of land in the tales I love is a place of human magic and human freedom, a place that enlarges and illuminates the unconscious mind, and is therefore a place of deep satisfactions and unrestraint. There is the element of courtly love in *Robin Hood* and there are coy hints at courtship among the birds and between the children in *The Secret Garden.* But these are present not just as a trap for the unwary female child, but because the magical transformation depends for its magic not on wizardry or deviltry but on the light: the life force. White magic, Nature, fecundity. The human response to the uncontrollable quality of procreation and growth. (pp. 5-6)

Generally, the more fabulous the fantasy, the more pagan and sexual the magic is, even in the ones expressly for children, like the book Frances Hodgson Burnett first published in 1911. In *The Secret Garden*—though the book is horribly littered with moralisms about unselfishness and covert references to God, though Mary gets prettier as she learns to care for others—Burnett's passion for Nature is the emphatic element, and her God is God the Joy Maker. Dickon, who charms without force, a boy who foregoes political power in favor of the power of love and tenderness, can sing "Praise God from whom all blessings flow" all he likes, so long as he is also a little poet-Pan:

> "Eh," he said. "I was up long before the sun. How could I have stayed abed! Th' world's all fair begun again this mornin', it has. An' it's workin' an' scratchin' and pipin' an' nest-buildin' an' breathin' out scents, till you've got to be out on it 'stead of lyin' on your back. When the sun did jump up, th' moor went mad for joy, an' I run mad myself, shoutin' and singin'.''

There is a quality of rebellion against convention in all this, even if it is small, confined to the context of Christianity, just as the prince and princess' rebellion in *The Sleeping Beauty* is defined quite narrowly as that of one generation unsurping the power and position of the one preceding, and assuming their roles. In Burnett's world Mary, the ugly little newcomer, must defy her supervisors, she must sneak and lie and follow her own instincts, in order to ensure her own growth and ordain health and beauty for herself and for the invalid Colin. Adults must be divided and classified: the foolish snobs who cannot see *real* good (that is to say, the potential for magic) must be disobeyed, and only the earthy, jolly ones—a classless category—sensual and unspoiled enough to see what the children can, may be allowed into the secret.

It is a tame and charming rebellion. (pp. 8-9)

> *Laura Hoffeld, "Where Magic Begins," in* The Lion and the Unicorn, *Vol. 3, No. 1, Spring, 1979, pp. 4-13.*

Stephen D. Roxburgh

[In "Tap-Roots into a Rose Garden," the article to which Roxburgh says "I owe the inspiration for this discussion," Alison White] shows remarkable restraint in not insisting on the influence of Burnett's book on [T. S. Eliot's poem "Burnt Norton"]—I am far more willing to commit myself on that point—but the present discussion is not a source study. It is, rather, an examination of the archetypal mode that "Burnt Norton" and *The Secret Garden* represent, and, more specifically, an evaluation of Burnett's book—Eliot's poem has many champions—in the terms of Northrop Frye's theory of myths.

Like "Burnt Norton," *The Secret Garden* is an extraordinarily complete summary of the symbols of the analogy of innocence. The "secret garden" of the title is Edenic. Set between Misselthwaite Manor—the Craven's ancestral home—and the cottage inhabited by the Sowerby clan, the rose-garden provides a meeting ground for the inhabitants of both. . . . The world of the Yorkshire moors and the "secret garden" is an animistic, magical, spirit-inhabited world, in which the Pan-like Dickon roams. Chastity, in the romantic sense of unviolated identity and the traditional sense of purity, informs the story, and "Magic"—the children's name for the complex of healing forces they experience—effects the rejuvenation and recovery of the earth and characters. These elements combine to form one of what Frye calls "significant con-

stellations of images"—specifically, the analogy of innocence.

"The meaning of a poem, its structure of imagery," according to Frye, "is a static pattern." The analogy of innocence and of other, similar structures of meaning "are, to use a musical analogy, the *keys* in which [works] are written and finally resolve; but narrative involves movement from one structure to another." Thus, the analogy of innocence portrays not "*the* garden at the final goal of human vision, but the process of . . . planting," the fundamental form of which is cyclical movement. *The Secret Garden* is, perhaps, as undisplaced a version of the "process of planting" as one is likely to find in literature; it approaches the mythic, the archetypal. An examination of the "secret garden" itself, the enclosed rose-garden, as an image, a metaphor, and a symbol, enables us to appreciate the levels of meaning and the narrative movement of Burnett's book.

Human activity is an attempt to impose order on the world around it, and Frye suggests that one "form imposed by human work and desire on the vegetable world" is the garden. Of the "secret garden," we learn that it was built by an adoring husband for his young wife, who tended it and made it their retreat. Because of an accident in the garden, which killed his wife, Archibald Craven locked the door, buried the key, and ordered that no one ever enter the garden again. By the time Mary Lennox arrives at Misselthwaite Manor, ten years have passed, the door to the garden is hidden behind a wall of ivy, and the garden has become a "secret," known of but not known in itself. Long before Mary enters this garden, however, before she ever sees it, she is associated with gardens. (pp. 121-22)

Mary soon becomes obsessed with the hidden garden, making it the object of a search which she pursues with an extraordinary tenacity and single-mindedness until, with the help of the robin, she succeeds in entering it. (p. 122)

The lonely, friendless child has a terrible need for something she can call her own. . . . [When] Mary confronts the dilemma of revealing her secret to Dickon, the significance of the "secret garden" is made clearer in her defense of her right to keep it.

> "Could you keep a secret, if I told you one? It's a great secret. I don't know what I should do if any one found it out. I believe I should die! . . . I've stolen a garden. . . . It isn't mine. It isn't anybody's. Nobody wants it, nobody cares for it, nobody ever goes into it. Perhaps everything is dead in it already; I don't know. . . . I don't care, I don't care! Nobody has any right to take it from me when I care about it and they don't. They're letting it die, all shut in by itself. I've nothing to do. . . . Nothing belongs to me. I found it myself and I got into it myself. I was only just like the robin, and they wouldn't take it from the robin. . . . It's this, . . . It's a secret garden, and I'm the only one in the world who wants it to be alive."

This long, impassioned plea indicates the extent to which

Mary has committed herself to the garden; should her "secret" be found out, she feels that she would die. To fully appreciate the seriousness of Mary's attachment to the garden and the real meaning of what appears to be a childish hyperbole, the association of Mary's condition with the rose-garden's must be examined.

The similarities between the "secret garden" and Mary suggest—in fact, they force—the metaphorical identification of the two. Like the garden, Mary was hidden away, denied to everyone's sight, by her parents, a harrassed colonial administrator and his flighty, irresponsible wife. When Mary is discovered in the deserted bungalow, she is identified as "the child no one ever saw," who had "actually been forgotten". Mary's question, "Why was I forgotten?" has implications beyond those suggested by the immediate circumstances. The little girl was uncared for, left in the hands of mindlessly subservient natives who deserted her. Ignored by her parents while they were alive, she was orphaned in a hostile world at their death. Her "guardian," the distracted widower Archibald Craven, hardly fills the role he legally holds. His first words to her, after she has been in his care for six months, were "I forgot you. How could I remember you? I intended to send you a governess or a nurse, or someone of that sort, but I forgot." Like the "secret garden," Mary existed but was uncared for; she was known of, but not known in herself.

The implied comparison of Mary's condition and the garden's is so strongly insisted on in the book that the most naive reader—using Frye's definition of "naive" as having limited previous verbal experience—can appreciate it. What is not as readily apparent, however, is the special significance the garden has assumed for Mary because of its secrecy. Physically, a "secret" garden is not essentially different from any other garden; that is, the image is the same. The symbolic implications of Mary's "secret" transcend the metaphorical level of meaning and suggest, I think, the romantic concerns at the core of Burnett's book.

Frye tells us that the romantic heroine's insistence on her virginity presents "a vision of human integrity imprisoned in a world it is in but not of, often forced by weakness into all kinds of ruses and stratagems, yet always managing to avoid the one fate which really is worse than death, the annihilation of one's identity." I see the "secret garden" as analogous to the virginity motif that pervades romance. The portrayal of imperilled virginity in explicitly sexual terms is inappropriate to the key of *The Secret Garden*—to use Frye's metaphor for the analogy of innocence. However, Mary's insistence that the garden remain secret, her dread that Colin will have the servants open it up, and that it will be trampled, violated, implies an analogous identification of the "secret garden" with Mary's emerging self-awareness, her embryonic selfhood. Viewed in this way, Mary's story is a quest for identity, actually it is the growth of an identity, and, thus, it partakes of the central concerns of the romance tradition.

Mary's action conforms to the structure of romance when she discovers Colin, the invalid son of Mr. Craven, who in Frye's terms is the demonic double Mary encounters as she descends into the labyrinthine night world of the twisting corridors and the "hundred locked rooms" within Misselthwaite Manor. Mary eventually comes to recognize her own faults, her selfishness and callousness, in Colin, thus emphasizing the *doppelganger* or "twin" motif so often seen in romance, in which the doubles are manifestations of two sides of the same individual. Just as Colin is Mary's nightworld counterpart, the dark, tapestried room in which she finds him is a demonic parody of the garden; it is a womb, like the garden, but in it the child is not nurtured, he is suffocated. While the garden is open to the sky and to the fresh air and breezes that sweep the moors, Colin's room is a black, stifling hole, heated by the fire that continuously burns in the grate, located in the depths of Misselthwaite Manor. When Mary descends into this pit, her story takes on a symbolic level of meaning that informs the rest of the book and places it firmly in the romance tradition.

Colin, however, is more than one of the cyphers of the myth. He is anything but a quietly suffering victim bound to a sacrificial rock. He is, in fact, a fully developed character whose action, while it partakes of the romantic structure of the quest for identity in much the same way that Mary's does, also involves elements that are more accurately described as comedic. Unlike Mary, Colin's identity crisis is not caused by his being forgotten, nor does it stem from a lack of identity. Rather, it is the result of an arbitrarily imposed identity, a negative self-image, or—to be more precise—a self-negating image. Colin's self-estimation is clearly linked with his father's opinion of him, which Colin summarizes when he tells Mary, "My mother died when I was born and it makes him wretched to look at me. He thinks I don't know, but I've heard people talking. He almost hates me". From conversations he has overheard, Colin knows that his father fears that he will develop into a cripple and that he will never live to grow up. These thoughts obsess the boy; they are the "hysterical night fears" that cause his tantrums; they are slowly killing him. Thus, when Mary inadvertently refers to the garden, he seizes on it. First, he threatens to have it opened, but then he succumbs to Mary's imaginative vision of it as a "secret" place, all their own. Colin's response to Mary's appeal again suggests the symbolic implications of the "secret garden:"

> He dropped back on his pillow and lay there with an odd expression on his face.
>
> "I never had a secret," he said, "except that one about not living to grow up. They don't know I know that, so it is a sort of secret. But I like this kind better."

Mary gives Colin a secret about the possibility of life which replaces his secret about the probability of death, and he immediately begins to recover. He, too, forges a new identity out of the image of the "secret garden" as Mary describes it to him. Like Mary, by the time he actually enters his mother's rose-garden—two thirds of the way through the book—he is well on his way to recovery. It is particularly significant that only images of the "secret garden" sustain him—the vividly colored pictures of gardens in his books do not—just as later in the story we see that the natural beauties of Europe are inadequate to soothe the wandering Mr. Craven. Only the "secret garden" and the association each character brings to it, the meaning each character invests it with, bring about their recovery.

As the garden "quickens"—a Yorkshire term for coming alive—we see a similar "quickening" of the children. Dickon points out the change in the garden to Mary: "Why!" she cried, "the grey wall is changing. It is as if a green mist were creeping over it. It's almost like a green gauze veil". This image is repeated and applied to Colin as well as the garden when he finally enters it; as he was pushed into the garden,

> . . . he had covered his eyes with his hands and held them there shutting out everything until they were inside and the chair stopped as if by magic and the door was closed. Not till then did he take them away and look round and round as Dickon and Mary had done. And over walls and trees and swinging sprays and tendrils the fair green veil of tender little leaves had crept, . . . And the sun fell warm upon his face like a hand with a lovely touch. And in wonder Mary and Dickon stood and stared at him. He looked strange and different because a pink glow of color had actually crept all over him—ivory face and neck and hands and all.
>
> "I shall get well! I shall get well!" he cried out. "Mary! Dickon! I shall get well! And I shall live forever and ever and ever!"

From this moment in Chapter 20 of *The Secret Garden* until the middle of the next-to-last chapter, when Colin realizes that he has recovered his health and cries out to Mary and Dickon and Ben Weatherstaff, "I'm well—I'm well!", we watch the process of growing in the garden and its inhabitants.

In terms of the structure of romance, these chapters clearly describe the children's ascent out of a night world. This movement is reflected in the transformation of the labyrinth that contains Colin's room. After Mary's initial descent into the heart of Misselthwaite Manor, she begins to gain control over it; it is still a maze, but she learns the way through it as her visits to Colin became more and more frequent. After her second trip to the corridor which leads to his room, she never loses her way again. Eventually, the corridors and locked rooms of the Manor become a haven for the children, which allows them to continue their recovery in the house and also allows their deception of the household staff and the physician attending Colin. The final stage of this metamorphosis is the transformation of Colin's self-imposed tomb into a kind of surrogate garden when Dickon brings his animals into the house. The curtains are drawn and the windows are opened, allowing sunshine and fresh air in, and Colin permanently unveils the portrait of his mother, whose laughing face overlooks the children at play. Burnett has shown the children returning from a lower world without leaving the confines of the room. By the end of the next-to-last chapter of *The Secret Garden,* the children have recovered both physically and mentally, they have established identities, and all that remains to be done is for their stories to be resolved in a way that confirms their achievement.

Frye tells us that the concerns and structures of comedy and romance are substantially the same until their actions are resolved. In *The Secret Garden,* Burnett suggests the alternatives offered by the romantic and comic visions in Mary and Colin's final positions in relation to the "secret garden." Without insisting on an absolute distinction between the romantic and comic aspects of the book, it is worthwhile, I think, to differentiate the final emphasis of each child's position in the world of the book and to consider the symbolic implications of the "secret garden" in terms of that emphasis.

When Colin exclaims, "I'm well—I'm well!", Mary Lennox's story has achieved a climax; and, when moments later she is assured by Mrs. Sowerby, Dickon's mother, "Tha'lt be like a blush rose when tha' grows up, my little lass, bless thee", her story can appropriately end. Her commitment to Colin manifests the complete change in character which Mary has undergone. Although our attention in the final chapters of the book is almost entirely on Colin, his recovery constitutes Mary's real achievement.

In the next-to-last chapter, Mary, Dickon, Colin, Ben Weatherstaff, the robin, and Dickon's animals are gathered in the "secret garden," where the human inhabitants sing the "Doxology." Meanwhile,

> the door in the ivied wall had been pushed gently open and a woman had entered. She had come in with the last line of their song and had stood listening and looking at them. With the ivy behind her, the sunlight drifting through the trees and dappling her long blue cloak, and her nice fresh face smiling across the greenery she was rather like a softly colored illustration in one of Colin's books. She had wonderful affectionate eyes which seemed to take everything in—all of them, even Ben Weatherstaff and the "creatures" and every flower that was in bloom. Unexpectedly as she had appeared, not one of them felt that she was an intruder at all.

In the specifically Christian imagery describing Mrs. Sowerby's appearance in the "secret garden," we see—using the terms of Frye's formulation of the analogy of innocence—a close approximation of "the symbol of the body of the Virgin as a *hortus conclusus*" [i.e., enclosed garden]. In a mythic context, Mary has moved from the isolation and alienation of the Indian wasteland to communion and fulfillment in a fertile paradise. In the context of romance, this scene exemplifies Frye's statement that "the closer romance comes to a world of original identity, the more clearly something of the symbolism of the garden of Eden reappears, with the social setting reduced to the love of individual men and women within an order of nature which has been reconciled to humanity." Thus, Mary's final place in the world of *The Secret Garden* represents the fulfillment of the promise of romance.

The contrast between the wasteland and the garden of Eden apparent in Mary's story is also symbolically present in the contrast between Mr. Craven and Mrs. Sowerby, who, although associated specifically with the Virgin, evokes a considerably older mythic type, the Corn-mother of primitive ritual who represents fertility incarnate and who guarantees the harvest.

The mythic qualities of this displaced matriarch of the Yorkshire moors add symbolic dimension to *The Secret Garden.* However, the immediate context of the book is not myth or fertility rite. It is distinctly social, and Mrs. Sowerby's relations with Mr. Craven are set in a clearly defined social structure; he is a local squire, a landowner, and she is a tenant, a peasant. This context is crucial in the book because it accounts for the resolution of Colin's story.

The reconciliation that takes place between Colin and his father in the last chapter of *The Secret Garden* is a common comedic convention, as is the classic *anagnorisis* or *cognitio,* the discovery or recognition, which gives the final sentence of the book its effectiveness. In fact, Colin's entire story, viewed in terms of Frye's discussion of the structure, conforms to the "fourth phase of comedy," that is, "the drama of the green world" in which the plot is "assimilated to the ritual theme of the triumph of life and love over the waste land." Using Shakespeare's early comedies as his focus, Frye notes that the symbol of the "green world charges the comedies with the symbolism of the victory of summer over winter," and that it frequently incorporates "the folklore motif of the healing of the impotent king." Moreover, the green world has "analogies, not only to the fertile world of ritual, but to the dream world that we create out of own desires." Romance and comedy share many symbols, and Burnett's use of them in *The Secret Garden* is significant because she accommodates the divergent traditions of the *hortus conclusus* of romance and the "green world" of comedy, thus allowing for the alternative resolutions of the children's actions. The significance of the former is that it is an end in itself, an end that Mary achieves. The latter is the means to an end, an end that Colin achieves when he is reconciled with his father.

It has already been suggested that Colin's original condition was the result of his father's demented fears, which were transferred to the boy and reinforced by the people around him. Thus, the household of Misselthwaite Manor is a microcosmic society based on an arbitrary principle or law. With Mary's help, Colin is able to escape from this society into the "secret garden," where he is able to heal and grow strong enough to return to the society from which he came and reform it. This is the promise of the comic vision. Frye tells us that there are "two ways of developing the form of comedy: one is to throw the main emphasis on the blocking characters; the other is to throw it forward on the scenes of discovery and reconciliation." Obviously, *The Secret Garden* exemplifies the latter.

In the final chapter of the book, the focus of our attention is on Mr. Craven and Colin. We learn that the moment Colin cries out "I am going to live forever and ever and ever!" (upon entering the garden), Mr. Craven, then traveling hundreds of miles away on the Continent, experiences a "singular calmness" and "slept a new reposeful sleep". At first these quiet moments are intermittent, but "Slowly—slowly—for no reason that he knew of—he was 'coming alive' with the garden". One night Mr. Craven had a mystical experience: "He did not know when he fell asleep and when he began to dream; his dream was so real that he did not feel as if he were dreaming". Here we see the "dream world"/"green world" analogy that Frye points out. Mr. Craven's dead wife calls to him in a "real voice," and when he asks, "Lilias, where are you?" the voice in the dream answers, "In the garden . . . In the garden!". The day Mr. Craven receives the letter recalling him to England, "he was remembering the dream—the real—real dream". When he finally returns to Misselthwaite Manor it is Autumn. He approaches the garden:

> The ivy hung thick over the door, the key was buried deep under the shrubs, no human being had passed that portal for ten lonely years—and yet inside the garden there were sounds. They were the sounds of running, scuffing feet seeming to chase round and round under the trees, they were strange sounds of lowered suppressed voices—exclamations and smothered joyous cries. It seemed actually like the laughter of young things, the uncontrollable laughter of children who were trying not to be heard but who in a moment or so—as their excitement mounted—would burst forth. What in heaven's name was he dreaming of—what in heaven's name did he hear? Was he losing his reason and thinking he heard things which were not for human ears? Was it that the far clear voice had meant?

Suddenly a transformed Colin bursts out of the garden into his father's arms. As the boy leads his father back into the garden, the past is recreated; Mr. Craven remembers when the roses in the garden were planted. Colin's story ends with a significant statement about the garden: "Now, it need not be a secret any more. . . . I shall walk back with you, Father—to the house".

In respect to the distinction between the comedic and romantic elements in Burnett's novel, it is noteworthy that Colin and his father are reunited outside of the garden and that Colin no longer needs—or wants—to keep the garden a secret. As a secret, it provided a place where he could recover unwatched and unencumbered by the restrictive society around him, a "green world." However, once he assumes his rightful place, the garden can be abandoned. Frye tells us that at the end of comedy, a new society is formed around the hero, and "the moment when this crystallization occurs is the point of the resolution in the action, the comic discovery." This is the implication, if not the fact, of the last few paragraphs of *The Secret Garden,* which are, significantly, narrated from the point of view of the household servants who are awaiting the outcome of Mr. Craven's search for Colin.

The final paragraph of the book is couched entirely in the language of social identity:

> Across the lawn came the Master of Misselthwaite and he looked as many of them had never seen him. And by his side with his head up in the air and his eyes full of laughter walked as strongly and steadily as any boy in Yorkshire—Master Colin.

Finally, however, the vision of the book is romantic in its

portrayal of a present where "past and future are gathered," to cite Eliot's poem. I suggest that a quarter of a century before Eliot wrote the *Four Quartets,* Frances Hodgson Burnett not only showed us something very much like the world of "Burnt Norton," but also anticipated the realization Eliot was to come to much later in the concluding lines of "Little Gidding":

> We shall not cease from exploration
> And the end of all our exploring
> Will be to arrive where we started
> And know the place for the first time.
> Through the unknown, remembered gate
> When the last of earth left to discover
> Is that which was the beginning;

This is, perhaps, what was meant by the "far clear voice" that beckoned the wanderer to the garden. (pp. 123-30)

> *Stephen D. Roxburgh, "'Our First World': Form and Meaning in 'The Secret Garden',"* in Children's literature in education, *Vol. 10, No. 3, Autumn, 1979, pp. 120-30.*

Madelon Sprengnether

[*The following excerpt is from an essay originally attributed to Madelon S. Gohlke.*]

To me, the most immediately striking feature of *The Secret Garden* is that it begins with death. Mary, the lonely heroine of the book, is orphaned by an epidemic in India. Even more curious perhaps is the fact that she hardly seems to react. She is remarkably cool in the face of what would seem a devastating event in the life of any child. To all appearances, she is an imperious, self-willed, and otherwise unresponsive child. The only signs of inner activity are her tantrums, angry outbursts against a world which refuses to be controlled by her, and her vain attempts to construct a garden, first in the sand outside her house in India, and later in the yard of the unsympathetic family of a clergyman who offers her shelter until she can be escorted to the home of her uncle in England. From this point, the narrative documents the process of her awakening, first to the world, then to other people, and simultaneously to her own feelings.

The garden at the house of Mary's uncle, Archibald Craven, is clearly the symbolic center of the book. It is both the scene of a tragedy, resulting in the near destruction of a family, and the place of regeneration and restoration of a family. Mrs. Craven had been sitting in the garden when she was struck by a falling branch which brought on the premature labor and delivery of her son Colin and ultimately caused her death. It is as though the natural processes of life and growth, through this incident, are seen to be destructive. Mr. Craven, in his grief, has the garden closed, and leaves the child whom he blames for his wife's death to be cared for by servants. Not wishing to be reminded of his wife, through the garden and the child, he is in fact obsessed by her and remains in a paralyzed state of unacknowledged mourning. Mary's interest in his story is generated by her intuitive and sympathetic response to someone who is hurting like herself.

Her concern about the state of the garden thus directly reflects her concerns about herself. Her first questions are crucial: " 'I wonder if they are all quite dead,' she said. 'Is it all a quite dead garden? I wish it wasn't.' " Here Mary's pain and sense of abandonment are balanced by her fierce desire to live. . . . Mary's association with Dickon gives her an appreciation of how it feels to mother and to be mothered, something she had missed in her relation to her biological mother, who was too preoccupied with her social life to attend to the needs of her child. Taking care of the neglected garden, moreover, is a step towards the development of Mary's capacity to take care of other people. Colin, the other sick and lonely child in the book, enters the narrative at the point at which Mary is sufficiently healthy to care for and about someone else. She is also able at this point to confront a reflection of her former self.

Mary becomes aware of the presence of Colin through his crying in the night, through the part of herself, I would say, that is grieving. The narrator, entering Mary's consciousness, observes that he is "too much like herself". For both of them the world of dreams and stories represents the innermost processes of their minds. Each thinks initially that the other may be a ghost. Colin, in particular, sometimes has difficulty distinguishing dream from reality. . . . Colin's uncertainty about reality is accompanied by an emotional precocity which allows him to give expression to conflicts which in Mary are less immediately conscious. His statement about his mother, for instance, is extraordinarily direct. "I don't see why she died. Sometimes I hate her for doing it". In Colin, the struggle between the desire to live and the desire to die is explicit and urgent. (pp. 895-96)

The conversations between Mary and the uncanny Colin in which she systematically opposes his conviction that he is going to die parallel the coming of spring and the awakening of life in the garden, and together they form the crux of the narrative. The turning point for Colin occurs at the height of a tantrum generated by an overwhelming fear of becoming hunchbacked, the signal of his inevitable decline, in which Mary angrily denies the existence of any such deformity.

> "You didn't feel a lump!" contradicted Mary fiercely. "If you did it was only a hysterical lump. Hysterics makes lumps. There's nothing the matter with your horrid back—nothing but hysterics! Turn over and let me look at it!"

In the face of Mary's bedrock certainty, Colin's habit of translating fear into reality evaporates, bringing a "curious great relief," followed by tears and the tentative question "Do you think—I could—live to grow up?"

A book so obviously preoccupied with death and with a heroine who says things like "I hate you! Everybody hates you! I wish everybody would run out of the house and let you scream yourself to death!" may seem an odd candidate for children's literature. The narrator herself at one point observes that Colin and Mary were perhaps "both of them thinking strange things children do not usually think of ". Yet *The Secret Garden* is an acknowledged children's classic. It is one of the few books from my own childhood that I carried in memory with me into adulthood, not to be displaced by the books of greater density and magnitude which I read as I grew older. My curiosity about this fact led me on a journey into my own past in an attempt to reconstruct the child reader in me who so loved this book.

Like many children, though not all, I became a reader during a period of forced inactivity. I had, as a child, three bouts with rheumatic fever, at the ages of seven, nine, and eleven. (pp. 896-97)

My third round of rheumatic fever was far more serious than the first two. Every part of my body seemed to hurt. This time I knew that I was ill. I could hear the concern in my mother's voice when she called in a second doctor to advise her about the kind of treatment I was receiving. I had somehow formed the private opinion that if I got sick again at thirteen, in the sequence of alternate years, that I would die. I was equally convinced that if I survived my thirteenth year, I would never have rheumatic fever again. I was in the grip of the kind of magical thinking that appeals to people who have no active control over their lives and that flourished for me in the atmosphere of a heavily ritualized Catholicism.

I was a serious believer. . . . I went with my class to confession every month and tried to make communion on nine successive first Fridays. I was stunned by the notion of a plenary indulgence, when the slate of one's past sins would be wiped clean, and I was tempted by the thought that if I died at such a moment I would go straight to heaven. If I stepped in front of a car while crossing the street after such a confession, I thought, I would be assured of salvation. This idea conflicted, of course, with the darker realization that for a Catholic, suicide is the one unforgivable sin. It is the duty of a Catholic to live, regardless of the circumstances of one's life. Suicide, for a Catholic, is a terrible luxury. I think I took this hard lesson to heart despite the fact that my faith in other religious matters was badly shaken by the death of my father. (pp. 897-98)

I have often wondered why I became so ill with the third episode of rheumatic fever, but it was not until recently that my mother revealed to me the timing of my illness in relation to my father's death. I had already been sick twice by age nine when my father died. By the third time, I had been made vulnerable in a new way. Probably, it was during this period that I read **The Secret Garden.**

The power of my reaction, I believe, was based on recognition. I saw aspects of myself in the wilful, disagreeable, and frightened Mary, in the same way that she sees her own reflection in the sickly Colin. The debate in which she engages with Colin, though not typical of childhood, was one which moved me because of my own uncertainties. Just as Colin articulates the battle over life and death with which Mary herself has struggled, the book as a whole made explicit for me, and, in a fictional sense at least, resolved what was a question in my own mind about whether I wanted to live or die.

The Secret Garden is about the completion of a process of mourning. It is the completion of this process, for Mary, for Colin, and for Colin's father, moreover, which makes possible the image of the family restored with which the book concludes. At the center of this image, of course, is the garden, the place where the secrets of life, growth, and

The Secret Garden at Maytham Hall, Kent.

all the richness of feeling are located and then revealed. Colin, whose physical health is restored through the garden, sees it as a magical place, when of course what he is describing is the magic of his renewed hope in his capacity to live and to grow up.

> "Then I will chant," he said. And he began, looking like a strange boy spirit. "The sun is shining—the sun is shining. That is the Magic. The flowers are growing—the roots are stirring. That is the Magic. Being alive is the Magic—being strong is the Magic. The Magic is in me—the Magic is in me. It is in me—it is in me. It's in every one of us. It's in Ben Weatherstaff's back. Magic! Magic! Come and help!"

I believe that, as a child who had been seriously ill, partly in response to the death of a much loved parent, I knew what this was about. I would like to argue further that this awareness, resting as it does on inference and the supposition of a nonverbal and even unconscious reaction, represented, for me as a child, a genuine engagement with the text. What I want to suggest, finally, is that the process of recovery of meaning in which I have been involved in this essay is not wholly foreign to what literary critics more conventionally, though less explicitly, practice. (pp. 898-99)

By choosing a book to which I know that I responded powerfully as a child, I have perhaps artificially dissociated affect from articulation. The usefulness of this division, however, may outweigh its disadvantages in that it may serve to clarify the relation between the two. A powerful response to a reading experience, even on the part of a child, acts as a sign of engagement, or what [Wolfgang] Iser would call the reader's "entanglement" with a text. My own "entanglement" with *The Secret Garden,* I now believe, was based on my emotional needs at the time of reading and certain parallels between the plot of the book and the narrative of my own life. I experienced these aspects of the book with a peculiar intensity, an intensity which persisted through twenty-five years into the conscious attempt at articulation represented by the writing of this essay. Iser describes the process of articulation as represented by literary criticism in the following manner:

> This is why, when we have been particularly impressed by a book, we feel the need to talk about it; we do not want to get away from it by talking about it—we simply want to understand more clearly what it is in which we have been entangled. We have undergone an experience, and now we want to know consciously what we have experienced. Perhaps this is the prime usefulness of literary criticism—it helps to make conscious those aspects of the text which would otherwise remain concealed in the subconscious; it satisfies (or helps to satisfy) our desire to talk about what we have read.

While Iser stresses the role of the text, which realizes itself in the mind of the reader, one can also regard this description as a model of interaction in which the reader, through the process of articulation, simultaneously organizes a self. The "entanglement" with the text occurs at a preconscious or unconscious level. It is the process of articulation, talking or writing, by which one is moved, organized, altered. Again, the implicit view of interpretation offered by Iser is that of the completion of a gestalt.

The analogy between the process of making what is unconscious conscious and that of psychotherapy is both obvious and relevant, except for the fact that initially it is the patient who provides and the therapist who interprets the text. The process of therapy can be seen as one in which one learns through a specialized form of relationship to read oneself. To be in relation, moreover, is the obverse of solipsism, the danger generally ascribed to affective modes of criticism. The true solipsist is not the reader who finds himself or herself revealed by a text, but the psychotic who lives in a world of more or less closed metaphoric constructions. It is Colin, in *The Secret Garden,* who solipsistically reads the text of the world, isolated as he is from nature and from other people. It is his capacity, on the other hand, to form a relation, to have a clear and intense response to Mary, which releases him from this half-life. His ability to experience his feelings towards another person, even if they are initially ones of rage, establishes his relation to reality.

A response, however incomplete, may be viewed as an implicit interpretation. My daughter, once, when I was extremely distracted and unresponsive to her attempts to engage my attention, threw a small rock at me. By reacting in this way, she was, I believe, interpreting her situation, as well as attempting to influence it. Our fictions of interpretation often prevent us from seeing what is fairly evident in dramatic terms, namely, that actions and feelings are as much interpretive gestures as are statements of cause and effect. What distinguishes the process of literary criticism from the actions of my daughter is that the former involves the bringing of a background awareness into the foreground of consciousness by means of articulation.

The process of articulation in literary criticism completes the cycle of perception which begins with the reader's entanglement with a text. My own entanglement with *The Secret Garden* occurred so long ago that my reconstruction of it has necessarily been hypothetical. What I can state with some assurance, however, is the power of the book in my imagination, a power which I have attempted to understand in part by recalling myself as a child. This process of recovery is of course inextricably bound to the present, to the person I am now, moved and altered by my recognition of myself in Mary, or to the parts of myself, persisting into adulthood, which are childlike and perhaps hurting. The issues raised by this book for me have also become more urgent since I have become a parent, given the significance of the garden as an image of parental- as well as self-nurturing. In bringing some of these preoccupations into the foreground of my awareness through the process of writing, I have come to understand not only my attachment to this book, but also the extent to which it still informs my life.

I would like to extend this meditation a little to describe literary experience, in one of its aspects, at least, as a form of inner movement. I want to suggest as readers that we may be activated by literary events, much as we are activated by events in our lives, that we may inscribe our relations with fictional characters into our memories, as we inscribe our relations with people. Not to participate fully in one's own life, is, of course, to deaden one's experience, and the same holds true for literature. To discover the ways in which we have been moved, at the same time, is to discover and perhaps to recover a self, to move through literary experience rather than to remain trapped in patterns of sterile repetition. Literary interpretation, as such, is a complex sign of relation, and like the other relations in our lives, one in which we may deepen and enrich our experience. Literature, as Cathy in *Wuthering Heights* says of dreams, passes through and through us, "like wine through water." Each convergence of reader and text is personal, autobiographical. To write about the intersection between personal and literary narrative, as I have done in this essay, is simultaneously to acknowledge a relation and to integrate it into a new narrative, one which has allowed me here to weave the history of a troubled child into the life of an adult. (pp. 900-02)

> *Madelon Sprengnether, "Re-reading 'The Secret Garden'," in* College English, *Vol. 41, No. 8, April, 1980, pp. 894-902.*

John Seelye

If Frances Hodgson Burnett's best book for children, *The Secret Garden,* was written in the Rousseauistic tradition, being intended as a treatise on how a child might be reformed by means of the Burpee seed catalogue, it also contains a thoroughly subversive dimension. For all of its pious horticulture, *The Secret Garden* also satisfies a child's deep psychic needs, because the important thing about the garden is not its flowers but its *secrecy*. Little girls need blooms of their own. The subversive element is the thing children seek in whatever literature they read, whether meant for adults or for themselves. (pp. 179-80)

> *John Seelye, "Notes on the Waist-High Culture," in* Children's Literature: Annual of the Modern Language Association Seminar on Children's Literature and The Children's Literature Association, *Vol. 9, 1981, pp. 178-82.*

Fred Inglis

[*The Secret Garden*] catches and intensifies in its central image all the energy which the Victorians directed at the home. The garden cherishes those strong, glad, positive qualities which were driven from the man's business world and left to the tender but passive care of the mother. But Frances Hodgson Burnett has a greater ambition for her book. She seeks not only to cherish the values of the garden, but to imagine them restored to the new public life of an ideal social order. 'An ideal social order' is just a slogan, of course, and yet my earlier assertion stands: implicit in every good story we tell to our children (setting aside the storytellers who are rancid with cynicism) is the moral: 'Look, this is how the world ought to be. Try to make it like that when you're grown up. We haven't managed it, we older ones; perhaps you will.' Whatever has happened to the idea of beauty and happiness in adult art, our children must keep faith with their radical innocence. That is our own, and the novelist's, act of faith for the future. It expresses our faith that our children will *have* a future.

But *The Secret Garden* . . . seeks to imagine the finest life possible and to use it to criticize and improve the life being lived around it at the time. Frances Hodgson Burnett wrote straight from the well-springs of Romanticism; the influence of the Brontës is felt on every page of the novel. She takes the great convictions of the Romantics that the 'nature', not, so to speak, of Edmund but of Edgar and Cordelia, needs only to be given a breathing-space to express itself in pure and excellent lives. But she turns certain expectations back to front in order to celebrate this commonplace. First, sensing (in 1911) the oppression and etiolation of family life, she removes her hero and heroine from their parents' care by making one an orphan, and the other, Colin, abandoned by his widower father in despair. She gives the children an ideal mother in Mrs Sowerby, instinctively sagacious, upright, compassionate; and in a brilliant insight makes Colin into a hypochondriac hysteric, thus providing a real consequence and a metaphor for the distortions wrought by Victorian family life. Frances Hodgson Burnett reinvents a pagan Garden of Eden for the children where culture is detached from labour and returned to creativeness, and which Dickon, the Pan-boy, tends and understands in the name of the mystery which Romanticism sought to keep intact from science. In this Eden, nature dissolves class—gardener and Pan-boy share the broadly human vocation of nursing the invalid boy to straight health, and helping the queer, difficult, yellow-faced little girl back into her natural fresh-cheeked shape.

I have spoken as though the book were a dull diagram

from an old myth-kitty. In fact, it is alive and quick, full of warm, sympathetic strength of feeling. The Sowerby family are at times too close to picture-postcard peasants for comfort, but the great joy which anybody must feel as spring swings round again is marvellously recreated for the little girl who has never seen it and has known only the arid limitlessness of the Indian plains. . . . The great strength of this book is the life it gives to these moving commonplaces. Mrs Burnett starts from the positives of Romanticism and goes on to turn these positives into solid details—the garden itself combines the ideal remembered holiday in a golden age, potent to children and adults alike, with a classless, reasonable, and joyous Utopia of the future. Only forty years later, Philippa Pearce wrote her great threnody, *Tom's Midnight Garden,* over that same vision. But Mrs Pearce . . . is not only a writer of genius, but she has the benefit of knowing what happened to some of the Edwardian visions, and how they died. Mrs Burnett's fine book speaks with an optimism which it is notoriously difficult to recover. (pp. 111-13)

> *Fred Inglis, "The Lesser Great Tradition," in his* The Promise of Happiness: Value and Meaning in Children's Fiction, *Cambridge University Press, 1981, pp. 101-23.*

Elizabeth Lennox Keyser

> When Mary Lennox was sent to Misselthwaite Manor to live with her uncle everybody said she was the most disagreeable-looking child ever seen.
>
>   (p. 1)

Unattractive, unlikeable, disagreeable—these are the ways in which the critics and the author herself characterize Mary Lennox and the way in which the critics at least characterize Colin Craven. But I want to examine closely what the term "disagreeable" really means in connection with the heroine, Mary, and to distinguish between the ways in which the two children are unattractive or unlikeable.

Mary initially "disagrees" with the adult characters in the story not only because her looks and manners fail to please them but also because she refuses to accept their authority. From the outset, however, she is by no means "thoroughly unattractive" to the narrator, who, in the passage quoted above, conveys sympathy as well as antipathy for Mary by mingling the child's point of view with the omniscient. . . . As the book proceeds, Mary becomes at least moderately agreeable, both to others in the novel and to the narrator, who grants her a grudging approval. But as Mary ostensibly "improves," her role in the book diminishes, and she loses for the reader her main appeal. Instead the other "thoroughly unattractive" child, Master Colin, increasingly gains the center of the stage.

Colin, I would argue, is never as unattractive to the narrator as Mary, nor is he ever as attractive to the reader. Unlike Mary, who is never described as more than "almost pretty" even when she gains flesh and color, Colin, though far more fretful and selfish, is described from the beginning as having a "sharp, delicate face the color of ivory" and great black-fringed eyes like those of his dead mother.

The narrator tells us that Colin, having had the advantage of "wonderful books and pictures," is more imaginative than Mary, and as he recovers his health he acquires both extraordinary physical beauty and a charismatic power. At the end of *The Secret Garden* we see Colin besting Mary in a footrace, and, indeed, he has already run away with, or been allowed to dominate, the final third of the book.

The race is not always to the swift, however. Ask an adult what he or she remembers from a childhood reading of *The Secret Garden.* Memories will differ, of course. But what I remembered before I re-read it recently was Mary's first finding and awakening the garden and then, in a reversal of the "Sleeping Beauty" story, her finding and awakening Colin. I remembered Mary exploring the winding paths and gardens within gardens, and indoors the winding corridors with their many locked rooms. And I remembered Mary as stubborn and defiant in her attitude toward adult authority and even toward Colin, but also tender and nurturing. I remembered Colin, too, but always as lying in his room being comforted by Mary or being wheeled by her into the garden. And I remembered his first faltering steps, supported by Mary, but I did not remember his digging, his running, and his calisthenics. And I certainly did not remember his expounding on magic and science. In fact, if my memory serves me, the more conventionally attractive that Colin grew and the more he came to dominate the book, the less memorable both he, and it, became.

Burnett seems to have intended to evoke sympathy for both Mary and Colin while at the same time portraying them as genuinely disagreeable children—children who treat others hatefully and are hated in turn because, having never known love, they feel hatred for themselves. She then apparently meant to show their transformation from self-hating and hateful to loving and lovable through the acquisition of self-esteem. For reasons which I will suggest later, however, Burnett makes Mary too attractive in her disagreeableness and Colin too unattractive in his agreeableness. As Mary becomes less disagreeable, she becomes, after a certain point, less interesting. And Colin, as he becomes more agreeable in some ways, becomes something of a prig and a bore. But before speculating as to why Burnett allows both characters to get out of control, let us consider how Mary, despite—or rather because of—authorial severity, becomes such a compelling figure.

An early example of Mary's unpleasantness earns her the nickname "Mistress Mary Quite Contrary." As a little boy named Basil watches Mary "making heaps of earth and paths for a garden," he suggests that they make a rockery. She spurns his offer, but what strikes us is not so much Mary's ill temper at what she takes to be his interference as her attempt, literally and metaphorically, to make something grow from barren ground. Although the narrator later tells us that Mary is less imaginative than Colin, we, having witnessed her persistent efforts to bring forth life, tend to disbelieve the narrator or at least to question her use of the word *imagination.* True, Mary must overcome the distrustfulness that makes her contrary with well-meaning people like Basil. And she succeeds by ad-

mitting first Dickon and then Colin to her secret garden. After admitting Dickon, she tells him about the incident with Basil. He replies, in characteristic fashion, "There doesn't seem to be no need for no one to be contrary when there's flowers an' such like". But Dickon is, in some respects, more naive than Mary, who knows there is more to the world than flowers and friendly wild things. Sometimes, as it was for Mary in India, contrariness is necessary for self-preservation; and sometimes, as for Mary in England, it is even necessary for self-renewal.

We can sympathize with Mary even though she is not a "nice sympathetic child" in part because of the deprivation she has endured. Her mistreatment of the Indian servants, though shocking, seems excusable, since she has been left almost entirely to their care by an apathetic, invalid father and a vain, frivolous mother. When, after her parents' death, she is passed from one reluctant guardian to another, her suspiciousness seems justified. And when, on arriving at Misselthwaite Manor, she overhears the housekeeper, Mrs. Medlock, being warned to keep her out of her uncle's sight and confined to her own two rooms, we can understand why Mary "perhaps never felt quite so contrary in all her life". Yet while we can see that Mary's unhappiness gives rise to her naughtiness, the narrator, by saying that Mary never belonged to anyone because she was a disagreeable child, implies that the reverse is true. In fact, the narrator's refusal to intervene on behalf of Mary, as she does on behalf of Colin, forces us into the position of defending her ourselves.

If Mary's contrariness consisted of mere sullenness, we might agree with the narrator and the adult characters' assessment of her. But there is, as I have suggested, a positive side to her contrariness, which is supported by other characters in the book as well. On her first morning at Misselthwaite, Mary awakens to find the servant Martha in her room. There had been no reciprocity in Mary's relationship with her Indian servants. She could verbally, and even physically, abuse her ayah with impunity. On meeting Martha, however, Mary wonders how she would react to being slapped. Something tells her that Martha would slap her right back. Sure enough, when Mary calls her a "daughter of a pig," as she was wont to insult her ayah, Martha reproves her. The way Martha reacts to and affects Mary resembles the way in which Mary later reacts to and affects Colin. When Martha forces Mary to make at least some effort to dress herself, the narrator comments: "If Martha had been a well-trained fine young lady's maid she would have been more subservient and respectful and would have known that it was her business to brush hair, and button boots, and pick things up and lay them away. She was, however, only an untrained Yorkshire rustic". When Mary later tells Colin that she hates him and contradicts him when, in a bid for her pity, he says he feels a lump on his back, the narrator similarly comments: "A nice sympathetic child could neither have thought nor said such things". But in fact both the untrained Yorkshire rustic and "savage little Mary" have a salutary effect on those who are used to being coddled, and the ironic treatment of Mary's antitypes—the well-trained maid, the fine young lady, and the nice sympathetic child—suggests both the author's need to condemn plain-spokenness and her even stronger desire to condone it.

Martha insists that the reluctant Mary play out-of-doors, where she meets another character whose contrariness matches her own. Ben Weatherstaff, the crusty gardener, "had a surly old face, and did not seem at all pleased to see her—but then she was displeased with his garden and wore her 'quite contrary' expression, and certainly did not seem at all pleased to see him". But when Mary mentions a robin and Ben describes how it was abandoned by its parents, she is able for the first time to recognize and admit her own loneliness. Like Martha, Ben Weatherstaff is given to plainspokenness. He says to Mary: "We was wove out of th' same cloth. We're neither of us good lookin' an' we're both of us as sour as we look. We've got the same nasty tempers, both of us, I'll warrant". Mary is taken aback and contrasts him, like Martha, with the native servants who always "salaamed and submitted to you, whatever you did." But Ben's bluntness, too, helps Mary both to know herself and to see herself as others see her.

Dickon, with his intuitive understanding of nature, and his mother, with her equally wonderful understanding of human nature, not only aid Mary but also counter the asperity of the narrator toward her. But in doing justice to Dickon and his mother, one tends to forget that it is Ben who befriends the robin, whose plight was analogous to Mary's and Colin's, and that it is Ben who kept the garden alive during the ten years it was locked up. It is also Ben who, along with Martha, piques Mary's curiosity about the garden but refuses to satisfy it, thus arousing by *his* contrariness all her stubborn determination to seek it out. And during the time that Mary searches for an entrance to the garden, Ben and Martha provide her with the insights necessary to appreciate her eventual discovery. In the chapter in which Mary finds the key, Martha forces Mary to consider the possibility that perhaps she does not really like herself. In the chapter in which Mary finds the gate, Martha, with her gift of a skipping-rope, persuades Mary that she is likeable and that she, in turn, is capable of liking others. Thus encouraged, Mary actively seeks and gains Ben's approval, so that by the time "the robin shows the way," Ben and Martha have already helped her find the key to her own heart.

Contrariness then, of the kind that Mary gradually loses, originates in sourness, irritability, an unwillingness to be interested or pleased. But the kind of contrariness that Mary retains, at least until Colin comes to dominate the book, arises from emotional honesty and reliance on one's own judgment. Mary finds both the garden and Colin largely because "she was not a child who had been trained to ask permission or consult her elders about things." Despite repeated denials by Martha that Mary hears crying in the night, and despite repeated warnings from Mrs. Medlock against exploring the house, Mary continues to believe the evidence of her own senses and to search for the source of the cries she hears. What she finds is a boy very similar to herself. Like Mary, Colin has been rejected by his father and has become used to overhearing terrible things about himself, many of which he now believes.

Even more than Mary, he has become a tyrant to those who are paid to wait on him. Given everything he ever requested, never forced to do what he didn't wish, he is the object of pity but also of dislike and disgust. But because Mary has also played the tyrant out of misery, acting the little ranee to her ayah, and because she is not afraid to impose her will on others, she is able to do for Colin what no doctor or even Dickon can.

Mary not only encourages Colin to believe that he can live; she persuades him that he need not live as a chronic invalid. In order to do so Mary must oppose her contrariness to Colin's own and act in a way not "nice" by conventional standards. When Colin unjustly accuses Mary of neglecting him, she becomes angry but, after reflection, relents. When she awakens to hear Colin in hysterics, however, she becomes enraged at the way her emotions, and those of everyone else in the house, are being manipulated. In expressing to Colin what no nice child would say or, according to the narrator, even feel—namely, that Colin is an emotional rather than a physical cripple whose self-centeredness has made him an object of contempt and loathing—Mary is actually expressing what everyone, including the reader, is feeling or would feel in similar circumstances. Her "savagery," as the narrator calls it, her ability to set aside the civilized veneer which has thinly disguised everyone else's hostility towards Colin, has a purgative effect on the entire household. And by disclosing what the nurse and doctor have long known but feared to say, that Colin is only weak from lying in bed and indulging in self-pity, Mary relieves him of his morbid fear and sets him on the road to recovery.

Gradually, with Mary's and Dickon's help, Colin gains enough strength to enter the garden. But although Dickon plants the suggestion that Colin will one day be able to walk, it is plain-spoken Ben Weatherstaff who brings him to his feet. Like Mary, Weatherstaff will express the unmentionable thoughts in everyone's minds: on finding the children in the secret garden, he blurts out, "But tha'rt th' poor cripple". And he is condemned as "ignorant" and "tactless" just as Mary is castigated for being "savage" and not "nice." But his bluntness also has a salutary effect on Colin. "The strength which Colin usually threw into his tantrums rushed through him now in a new way. . . . His anger and insulted pride made him forget everything but this one moment and filled him with a power he had never known before, an almost unnatural strength". Though "magic" later enables him to run and perform calisthenics, it is his passionate desire to refute Ben that enables him to take his first steps.

After watching Colin stand and walk, and after examining his legs, Ben decides that Colin, far from being "th' poor cripple," " 'It make a mon yet". From that point on Colin's athletic prowess, his leadership ability, his interest in science, and his magical powers all seem meant to prove Ben right. In the early chapters the narrator often reminded us of Mary's unattractiveness and unpleasantness; now she stresses Colin's beauty and charisma. At one point the narrator intervenes to tell us that Colin "was somehow a very convincing sort of boy," and it is doubtless this convincing quality that is meant to convince *us* of Colin's ascendancy over Ben, Dickon, and even Mary. Whereas earlier Colin had been a peevish little tyrant, he now becomes a benevolent despot, a combination rajah and priest. Colin, "fired by recollections of fakirs and devotees in illustrations," arranges the group cross-legged in a circle under a tree which makes "a sort of temple". Later Colin heads the rajah's procession "with Dickon on one side and Mary on the other. Ben Weatherstaff walked behind, and the 'creatures' trailed after them" It has been argued [by Fred Inglis] that "in this Eden, nature dissolves class—gardner and Pan-boy share the broadly human vocation of nursing the invalid boy to straight health." These doings in the garden, however, suggest a definite hierarchy, one that includes sex as well as class.

During Colin's lectures, "Mistress Mary" is described as feeling "solemnly enraptured" and listening "entranced". Although we are doubtless meant to be as charmed by Colin as the other characters are and to see in his domination of the little group the promise of his future manhood, we are in fact disenchanted to find Mary little more than a worshipful Huck to the antics of Colin's Tom Sawyer. Yet Mary and Huck are the truly imaginative and convincing children who do not, like Colin and Tom, need the stimulus of books in order to have real adventures and solve real problems. Huck's escape from Pap and his flight down the river with Jim, Mary's discoveries of Colin and the garden, and, above all, her self-discoveries, make Tom's "evasion" and Colin's "magic" anticlimactic. And just as Jim loses stature because of the indignities inflicted on him by Tom, so the roles of Martha and Ben Weatherstaff, so important to Mary's development, diminish. Martha, as remarkable in her way as Dickon and their mother, simply disappears from the final chapters; but since she is the first person for whom Mary feels anything like trust and affection, it is hard to believe that Mary would forget her. Ben, like Mrs. Sowerby a party to the secret in the garden, is treated condescendingly by Colin—and by the author. When Ben makes a joke at the expense of Colin's "scientific discoveries," Colin snubs him, a snub which Ben—acting out of character—takes humbly. But at least at the end of Twain's book we are left with its true hero. In ***The Secret Garden*** Burnett shifts from Mary's to Colin's point of view shortly after the scene in which Mary confronts him with his cowardice and hypochondria. From there on Mary slips into the background until she disappears entirely from the final chapter. The novel ends with the master of Misselthwaite and his son, Master Colin, crossing the lawn before their servants' admiring eyes.

Perhaps the analogy between Mary and Huck can do more than suggest why the final third of ***The Secret Garden*** is so unsatisfying. Huck is a memorable, even magical, creation not only because he is a very convincing boy (so is Tom, for that matter), but because he is, at the same time, unconventional. He resists being civilized in a way that Tom, for all his infatuation with outlaws, does not. Mary, too, is a more memorable creation than Colin because she is both recognizably human and refreshingly different. [Critics Anne Thwaite and Marghanita Laski] have tried to link this difference with her unpleasantness, but I be-

lieve it lies more in her freedom from sex-role stereotypes. (pp. 1-9)

From the first Mary is an independent, self-contained, yet self-assertive child. Unlike Colin, she discovers and enters the secret garden all by herself, and she defies adult authority in order to find, befriend, and liberate Colin. Unlike her mother, she is never vain of her appearance; she is proud when she finds herself getting plump, rosy, and glossy-haired, but only because these are signs of her growing strength. When she receives a present from Mr. Craven, she is delighted to find books rather than dolls, and she works and exercises in the garden along with Colin and Dickon. She does not wish to have a nurse or governess but seems to thrive on an active life out-of-doors. Early in the relationship with Colin she is the leader, and even when he is able to run about, it is she who, on a rainy day, suggests that they explore his house. Colin, when we first meet him, is a hysterical invalid, and his father, as the name "Craven" signifies, is a weak and cowardly man, still mourning after ten years his dead wife and, in doing so, neglecting their living son. It is as though Burnett so generously endowed Mary at the expense of Colin and his father that she had to compensate for it by stressing Mary's disagreeable traits and exaggerating Colin's charm. And in the final chapter Colin's ascendancy suggests that if he becomes a "mon," as Ben predicts, then Mary will have to become a woman—quiet, passive, subordinate, and self-effacing. Huck at the end of *Huckleberry Finn* cannot escape civilization; Mary cannot escape the role that civilization has assigned her.

Burnett's ambivalence toward Mary and her indulgence of Colin probably reflect lifelong conflicts. As a child Burnett was encouraged by her widowed mother to cultivate genteel and ladylike manners. And as a young married woman she is described by Thwaite as "obviously trying her best . . . to appear as the nineteenth century's ideal of womanhood". Often, especially during these early years, Burnett regarded her writing as a necessary, even sacrificial task, performed for the sake of her husband, struggling to establish himself as an ophthalmologist, and their sons. Yet Burnett continued to write long after Dr. Swan Burnett was well able to support his family. By then, however, writing, and the fame and fortune which attended it, seems to have become a psychological necessity. Her favorite image of herself was that of a fairy godmother, and the power as well as the magnanimity of that role must have appealed to her. So like many successful women writers, including Louisa May Alcott and Burnett's prolific friend Mrs. Humphry Ward, she tried to rationalize her writing as unselfish service, and, when she could not ignore its self-assertive and self-serving role, punished herself with ill health. And finally, again like other women writers (great ones such as the Brontës and George Eliot as well as minor ones such as Alcott and Ward), she chastened her self-assertive female characters.

The Secret Garden, written in 1911 toward the end of a long, successful career, seems to suggest not only self-condemnation and self-punishment in its treatment of Mary but an attempted reparation for wrongs Burnett may have felt she inflicted on the males closest to her.

Most obviously, the idealized Colin seems to represent her elder son, Lionel, and his recovery a wish-fulfilling revision of what actually happened. After the extraordinary success of *Little Lord Fauntleroy* in 1886, Burnett began to spend much of each year abroad. Although she was a doting mother, able from her earnings to give her sons whatever their hearts desired, she may have felt that even these luxuries, like those Colin's father provides for him, could not compensate for her absence. And when, during one of these absences, Lionel became consumptive, her guilt must have been intensified. To assuage it she nursed Lionel devotedly and especially prided herself on protecting him from the knowledge that he was dying. But in a notebook entry, written a few months after Lionel's death, she asks: "Did I do right to hide from you that you were dying? It seemed to me that I *must* not give you the terror of knowing." The situation in *The Secret Garden* is significantly reversed: Colin is kept in ignorance not of his imminent death but of his capacity for life; Mary, by breaking the conspiracy of silence, enables him to live.

The figure of Colin is reminiscent not only of Lionel but also of Swan Burnett and of Mrs. Burnett's second husband, Stephen Townesend. Swan, himself crippled in his youth, became a successful eye specialist, but the marriage seems never to have been a happy one. Two years after their divorce, Burnett married Townesend, a doctor and aspiring actor ten years younger than herself. Burnett had long attempted to use her theatrical connections to further his acting career, especially after Townesend helped her to nurse Lionel through his fatal illness. As her son Vivian wrote: "This was one of the few solaces that Dearest had in her dark hours, making her feel that surely some good had come out of her wish to help her older—disappointed—Stephen boy." And as Burnett wrote to her friend Kitty Hall, "If I had done no other one thing in my life but help Lionel to die as he did, I should feel as if I ought to be grateful to God for letting me live to do it—but if I can help Stephen to *live,* that will be another beautiful thing to have done." As these quotations suggest, Burnett's interest in Stephen Townesend was largely maternal, a desire to play fairy godmother as she had in the lives of her sons. To use her fortune and influence to aid a struggling young man would somehow justify her possession of it. But although Stephen, unlike Lionel, survived, she never succeeded in helping either him or their marriage to "live."

Thus *The Secret Garden,* far from combining [in Fred Inglis's words] "the ideal remembered holiday in a golden age . . . with a classless, reasonable, and joyous Utopia for the future," reflects its author's ambivalence about sex roles. On the one hand, she vindicates Mary's self-assertiveness and her own career by allowing Mary to bring the garden, Colin, and, eventually, Mr. Craven back to life. On the other hand, she chastens herself and Mary by permitting the narrator to intervene only to reprove her and by making her subordinate to Colin in the final chapters of the book. By idealizing Colin at the expense of Mary she seems to be affirming male supremacy, and the final version of the master of Misselthwaite with his son, Master Colin, further suggests a defense of patriarchal authority. While Mr. Craven can be seen as the neglectful,

erring parent of either sex—and thus still another means by which Burnett atones for her material failings—he, like the peevish invalid Colin, can also be viewed as an expression of her impatience with male weakness. And her attempts to glorify Colin are unsuccessful enough to make us wonder if even here her ambivalence—even her resentment and hostility—does not show through. For all her efforts to make Mary disagreeable and to efface her, Mary remains a moving and memorable creation, whereas Colin's "magic" never amounts to more than a mere trick. Mary, like the author herself, seems to have both gained and lost from her contrariness, and *The Secret Garden* succeeds and fails accordingly. (pp. 9-12)

> *Elizabeth Lennox Keyser, " 'Quite Contrary': Frances Hodgson Burnett's 'The Secret Garden'," in* Children's Literature: Annual of the Modern Language Association Seminar on Children's Literature and The Children's Literature Association, *Vol. 11, 1983, pp. 1-13.*

U. C. Knoepflmacher

The expression of anger by female writers has become of increasing interest to literary critics. We are now far more aware of the rich implications—cultural, biographical, artistic—that this subject entails, especially for our understanding of nineteenth-century women writers who faced simultaneously new freedoms and new restraints on their creativity. Still, when, in *The Madwoman in the Attic,* Gilbert and Gubar insist on separating the "decorous and ladylike facade" of Jane Austen or Maria Edgeworth from the more overt (and hence somehow more valued) depiction of aggressive impulses by those who " 'fell' into the gothic/Satanic mode," even the most comprehensive discussion of the subject remains slightly distorted.

The decorous and lady-like women who dominated the field of Victorian children's literature—such as Mrs. Gatty, Mrs. Ewing, Mrs. Molesworth, Jean Ingelow, Frances Hodgson Burnett, and others—were hardly gothic Satanists. As gentlewomen writing for middle-class juveniles, they, even more than an Austen or an Edgeworth, needed to maintain restraint and decorum. Paradoxically, the mode of fantasy also freed the same aggressive impulses that their fictions ostensibly tried to domesticate. Especially after 1865, with the playful anarchy of Lewis Carroll's *Alice's Adventures in Wonderland* before them as a foil as well as a model, women writers began to portray little girls who were allowed to express hostility without the curbs on female rebelliousness that had been placed earlier, in children's literature as well as in adult fiction. The fairy-tale realms depicted in Juliana Horatia Ewing's "Amelia and the Dwarfs" (1870), in Burnett's *The Secret Garden,* and in Burnett's earlier, less well-known, but delightful fantasy, **"Behind the White Brick"** (1874), thus serve a double purpose. The surreal setting is enlisted, on the one hand, to mute the hostile behavior of girls on the road to socialization and maturity; on the other hand, however, it permits their creators to turn their own satiric energies against the deficiencies or complacencies of a society that frowned on expressions of female anger. (pp. 14-15)

Like Jean Ingelow, who countered Alice in *Mopsa the Fairy* (1869), and Madeleine L'Engle, who still evokes

Carroll in *A Wrinkle in Time* (1962), Ewing and Burnett follow—yet also subvert—their male predecessor by transporting their intemperate heroines into realms of open aggression. (p. 15)

While Ewing's invalid condition forced her to live apart, during her last years, from her dashing military husband, Burnett twice divorced the weak men she first attracted and then repelled. In March 1898, after she had instituted divorce proceedings against her first husband, Dr. Swan Burnett, the *New York Herald* rather cruelly contrasted her forceful person to the husband whose effeminate first name she had always hated: "Mrs. Burnett is a woman of pleasing appearance and much personal magnetism, while her husband is of less than ordinary stature and a cripple."

The Secret Garden, written some years after Burnett's separation from her second husband—the young secretary she had married apparently as surrogate for an older son who had died of consumption—ends on an all-masculine note. Archibald Craven, the hunchback master of Misselthwaite Manor, a neurotic weakling, is amazed to discover that his once-deformed son now walks "as strongly and steadily as any boy in Yorkshire—Master Colin!" Burnett, whom a contemporary described as "a masculine, matter-of-fact person," was clearly fascinated by the strong male identity attained by Colin in his dead mother's magical garden. Describing her own practices as a gardener, Burnett confessed, "I should always have preferred to have been at least two strong men in one. . . . I love to dig. I love to kneel down on the grass at the edge of the flower bed and pull out the weeds fiercely. . . . I love to fight with those who can spring up again almost in a night and taunt me. I tear them up by the roots again and again, and when at last . . . it seems as if I had beaten them for a time at least, I go away feeling like an army with banners."

Yet if *The Secret Garden* ends as the story of Colin's mastery, a weak boy's recovery from an imaginary curvature of the spine, the book begins—and usually is remembered—as the story of the tough and indestructible Mary Lennox, a garden-builder from the very start. Indeed, the book was originally to be called *Mistress Mary.* And, though its opening sentence describes Mary as "the most disagreeable-looking child ever seen," it soon becomes evident that this asocial creature, uninterested "in anyone but herself", engages our sympathies even more than [Ewing's] Amelia did. Like Amelia, who tyrannizes her governess, Mary berates her Indian ayah as "Pig! Daughter of pigs!". Although Burnett returns the compliment by calling Mary as "selfish a little pig as ever lived", she shows us that Mary's aggressiveness is her sole defense against the deprivations she has suffered by being "kept out of the way", by her indifferent parents. Unlike the excessively indulged Amelia, Mary is ignored by her flighty mother and her ill and absent father. She is not allowed to hate her parents openly. Yet her anger at the absent ayah, who, unbeknownst to her, has died of the plague, masks her real anger at parents who also soon will die in the same epidemic. To compensate for her desolation, she makes a pretend flowerbed by sticking "big scarlet hibis-cus blossoms into little heaps of earth, all the time growing more and more angry".

Mary's anger proves emotionally therapeutic. It is a sign of her hardiness. While the adults around her perish, she survives. The abandoned child fearlessly stares "at a little snake gliding along and watching her with eyes like jewels". Deprivation has made her as tough as it has made her cousin Colin soft, we soon discover. Transported from Kipling's India to Brontë's Yorkshire, Mary will prove to be as hardy as a Mowgli or a Jane Eyre. And when, like Jane, she hears mysterious night-cries in the gothic manor house, she bravely ventures into the hidden chamber, to find not a raving Bertha Mason, the madwoman in the attic, but a whimpering, effeminate little boy, her weaker cousin and alter ego. Colin, to be sure, is also a tyrant, "a young *Rajah.*" Like the aggressive Amelia who terrorizes adults, the screaming boy intimidates Mrs. Medlock the housekeeper, Martha the servant, Dr. Craven his physician, and his attendant nurse.

Knowing Mary's own aggressive powers, however, these adults enlist her to subdue the hysterical boy. Her hostility now serves a purpose. Unused to "any one's tempers but her own," Mary decides to frighten Colin as "he was frightening her". She stamps her foot and runs along the corridor, feeling "quite wicked" by the time she reaches Colin's door. She slaps it open and runs to the four-poster bed:

> "You stop!" she almost shouted. "You stop! I hate you! Everybody hates you! I wish everybody would run out of the house and let you scream yourself to death! You *will* scream yourself to death in a minute, and I wish you would!"
>
> A nice sympathetic child could neither have thought nor said such things, but it just happened that the shock of hearing them was the best possible thing for this hysterical boy whom no one had ever dared to restrain or contradict. . . .
>
> (pp. 21-3)

Colin protests that he has felt a lump on his back; he is sure he is to become a hunchback like his father and then, like his mother, die. But Mary fiercely contradicts him. She orders the startled nurse to bare the boy's back and then clinically inspects it. "There's not a lump as big as a pin," she triumphantly declares, "except backbone lumps, and you can only feel them because you're thin. I've got backbone lumps myself, and they used to stick out as much as yours do, until I began to get fatter". Colin is shocked into submission by the obstinacy of this "angry unsympathetic little girl". The adults that he had cowed are surprised—yet highly pleased—by her outburst.

Burnett, too, obviously relishes Mary's "savage" behavior. The relentless ferocity with which the little girl sets out to assure Colin that the growth on Colin's back is imaginary seems identical to the determined pulling of weeds that spring up at night to taunt and choke the healthy, daylight growth of unencumbered plants. Burnett implies that growth, whether of plants or of little girls, involves both healthy anger and healthy nurturance. Mary can threaten Colin with hatred, the removal of love, but she also can and does soothe him by singing a lullaby. She soon transports the boy to the secret garden. There, fattened by the maternal Mrs. Sowerby, . . . he gradually attains the vitality that Mary the garden-builder has all along possessed.

In the last third of the book Burnett cedes the garden to her little Adam. The creator of Little Lord Fauntleroy suddenly becomes more interested in Colin's silly push-ups and acts of physical prowess than in Mary's instinctual need to actualize the imaginary gardens she had built in India. Mistress Mary, the book's seeming protagonist, slips into an increasingly subsidiary role. The garden becomes the boy's preserve, the place where his fragile mother (Mary's paternal aunt) had sustained her fatal injury. It is his to reclaim. He is the future master of Misselthwaite; he is a male. Mary's sudden subordination, though sanctioned by the plot, nevertheless remains more disturbing than Amelia's conversion into "Amy," the beloved. Her displacement, to be sure, seems more offensive to the adult than to the juvenile reader. Children, especially girls, who have the story read to them are not so perturbed, for Burnett provides them with some means whereby they can disregard, even screen out, the importance she accords to Colin's vigorous eugenic exercises. (pp. 24-5)

U. C. Knoepflmacher, "Little Girls without Their Curls: Female Aggression in Victorian Children's Literature," in Children's Literature: Annual of the Modern Language Association Seminar on Children's Literature and The Children's Literature Association, *Vol. 11, 1983, pp. 14-31.*

Phyllis Bixler

Generally recognized as Burnett's best work for children, **The Secret Garden** combines plot formulas from her earlier well-known child romances. In **Little Lord Fauntleroy,** she had portrayed a child reunited with his estranged family, and in **Little Princess,** she had portrayed an orphan who finds a new family. **The Secret Garden** has both. After her parents die in India, Mary Lennox goes to live with her uncle in the Yorkshire moors; there, she befriends her hypochondriac cousin, Colin Craven, who is alienated from his embittered father; in the end, the two children and the adult form a reunited and expanded family. As in previous romances, Burnett uses motifs from the Cinderella tale. In some variants of that tale, Cinderella's dead mother aids her through a plant growing on her grave or an animal she had given to Cinderella before she died. Through her portrayal of the secret garden and a robin who lives there, Burnett uses both of these motifs. Before she died giving birth to Colin, Mrs. Craven—who is also Mary Lennox's aunt—had cultivated a rose garden, where she had had a serious fall just before Colin was born. Archibald Craven blames the garden and the child for his wife's death and tries to shut both out of his life. He has the garden locked and abandoned, and he avoids the child both because Colin looks like his mother and because Craven fears the boy will inherit his own crippled

back. The secret garden and the robin who inhabits it become primary agents which break the enchantment of illness and alienation which came upon the Craven family when the mother died. (pp. 94-5)

While the Cinderella tale provides an archetypal substructure for **The Secret Garden,** the first-time reader is more aware of Burnett's portrayal of her child characters and of the garden itself. In Mary Lennox, Burnett created her most complex fictional child. Complex characterization is especially difficult in children's fiction; much less than in adult fiction can the author use abstract analysis of a character's feelings and motives; internal complexities must be expressed primarily through external actions and concrete images; character change must be dramatized or symbolically suggested rather than directly described. Burnett's experience writing for the stage—learning to use dialogue and scene effectively—was put to good use in **The Secret Garden,** and nowhere in her fiction were her talents as a symbolist more fully engaged. Mary Lennox's psychological change is dramatized through a succession of encounters with physical and natural objects, animals, and persons within her expanding environment. Her environment often reflects her own internal state, and her occasional recognition of this correspondence dramatizes her growth in self-awareness as she changes. (pp. 95-6)

By learning to respect the housemaid Martha, by befriending the robin and Ben Weatherstaff, and by taking loving charge of the secret garden, Mary gradually gains touch with her own feelings and breaks out of her earlier isolation; this inner healing is reflected in increasing physical health and energy.

Having undergone these changes, Mary encounters the most complete picture of the child she once was in the isolated, sick, temperamental Colin. Because Colin believes he is becoming a cripple who will soon die, he stays in a remote room of the mansion where he will be seen by no one but the servants, whom he can tyrannize because they fear his tantrums may precipitate his death. In an effective example of Burnett's ability to find physical correlatives for psychological processes, she has Mary's gradual discovery of Colin symbolically suggest her own search for the unhappy self hidden inside her. Several times Mary searches the mansion for the source of a remote cry, "a curious sound—it seemed almost as if a child were crying somewhere". That the children are in some senses alter egos is suggested also by their perception of each other as ghosts when they first meet. They soon break out of such solipsistic fantasies, however, for their nasty tempers make each recognize the other as a person outside his or her control. (pp. 96-7)

[Mary is able to call Colin's bluff and thus release him from his irrational fears] not only because she was angry but also because she recognized that Colin was using manipulative strategies she herself had once used.

Having dramatized the stages by which Mary breaks free from her own isolation and then springs Colin from his similar trap, Burnett portrays the completion of their psychological and physical healing primarily symbolically, through their work in the secret garden. To explain the

Burnett and her eldest granddaughter Verity at Burnett's home "Fairseat," or Maytham, at Plandome Park, Long Island.

marvelous changes the children undergo there, Burnett uses a metaphor from her earlier works, magic. She employs magic to describe the power of nature to effect changes in human beings much as it brings new life in spring after the death of winter; in doing so, Burnett draws on a literary pastoral tradition at least as old as Vergil's *Georgics* and allows her usual use of the fairy tale to be transformed into myth. Like Vergil in his *Georgics* and Thoreau in *Walden,* Burnett uses the seasonal cycle to give form to her work as well as to symbolically underscore human rebirth. Mary arrives at Misselthwaite in late winter; the two children enter the garden together in early spring; during the summer they fully recover; and in the autumn Colin's father returns to share their harvest of health. This emphasis on the seasonal cycle presents the children with nature as ever changing, ever new; most often, the children marvel at the changes spring brings continually to the garden. But the realization that nature's cycles are themselves unchanging also brings the children occasional glimpses of what Spenser called the "eterne in mutabilitie." At times, their hearts stand "still at the strange unchanging majesty of the rising sun—which has been happening every morning for thousands and thousands of years." Colin thus perceives the mystery of nature when he learns he can walk and exclaims, "I shall live forever and ever and ever!"

Also like Vergil and Thoreau, Burnett stresses the importance of work, the human cooperation needed if nature is to achieve its best results. By describing nature's healing power as "Magic," the children acknowledge that it is par-

tially outside their control—the healing of themselves and their garden needs the fresh air and warmer temperatures of spring. But the children also know that this "Magic works best when you work yourself," as Colin puts it. And so they till the garden, do physical exercises, and engage in magic experiments to help Colin get well—they call on nature's power through incantations and by sitting and processing in a "Mystic circle". This georgic reciprocity between man and nature—described in Wordsworth's *Prelude* as being both "willing to work and to be wrought upon," of being "creator and receiver both"—is reflected by the lyrical and incantational style of Burnett's book; language is used to celebrate what the characters receive, and it also provides a tool with which they can work or create. After they begin witnessing spring work its "magic" in their garden and in themselves, Mary and Colin frequently burst into lyrics of joy. Similarly, paeans to nature rise from the lips of the Yorkshire folk the children meet, especially Ben Weatherstaff and Martha's brother, Dickon, both of whom join the children's secret garden community. Occasionally, these paeans become incantatory as well as lyrical, as when Mary soothes Colin to sleep after a tantrum with a description of spring entering the garden. Possibly incantatory as well is the children's use in the garden of the Yorkshire dialect, a language made potent by its use by the folk who have long lived intimately with nature. Language is a tool for doing also since it is a transmitter of the proverbial wisdom Hesiod and Vergil had established as part of the georgic pastoral tradition. In bringing healing to themselves and their garden, the children are aided by the lore of Ben Weatherstaff, Dickon, and especially Dickon's mother, whose proverbial wisdom is quoted often throughout the narrative.

Burnett's use of the Yorkshire folk, especially Dickon and his mother, gives mythic resonance to her work as does her use of the seasonal cycle to symbolize rebirth. Twelve-year-old Dickon is an unself-conscious nature child; first presented sitting under a tree and playing a pipe for some attending animals, he is obviously meant to suggest the nature deity Pan. Mother Sowerby, a "comfortable wonderful mother creature", on the other hand, has the aura of the archetypal Earth Mother. The twelve children she has fattened on "th' air of th' moor" and "th' grass same as th' wild ponies" suggests her fertility. In addition, Mother Sowerby works behind the scenes on behalf of her adopted children, Mary and Colin, until she finally appears to bless their revived garden and their healthy selves. In a sense, Mother Sowerby, like the garden and its robin, is an agent for the spirit of Colin's dead mother; she is like the fairy godmother who helps Cinderella in some versions of the tale. Mother Sowerby herself points to the links in this chain of female benevolence by telling the healthy Colin, "Thy own mother's in this 'ere very garden, I do believe. She couldna' keep out of it." Adding that "Thy father mun come back to thee," Mother Sowerby sends a letter calling Craven to return, at about the same time as Craven's dead wife calls to him in a dream.

Burnett's portrayal of a quasi-mystical relationship between Colin's dead mother, Mother Sowerby, and the secret garden connects this juvenile classic to other works in which Burnett gave a divine aura to female power, such as *The Pretty Sister of José* and *A Lady of Quality*. *The Secret Garden* also has a significant number of parallels to Charlotte Brontë's *Jane Eyre.* . . . (pp. 97-100)

As Sandra M. Gilbert and Susan Gubar have pointed out, *Jane Eyre* contains many of the symbolic motifs prevalent in nineteenth-century literature written by women; the relationship of *The Secret Garden* to this tradition can be seen by an analysis of Burnett's use and adaptation of these motifs. Gilbert and Gubar note the frequent depiction by female writers of "maddened doubles" or "asocial surrogates" for their protagonists, "obsessive depictions of diseases like anorexia," "metaphors" of "physical discomfort," and "images of enclosure and escape"—symbolic expressions of the disintegration of the psyche, negation of the body, and psychological and physical imprisonment caused by narrow socially approved roles for women. Both Mary and her "double" Colin are sickly when they first appear, and Burnett stresses their thinness and lack of appetite. The initially dying garden provides a "metaphor" for their "physical discomfort," and its "enclosure"—the high, locked walls around it—images the physical and psychological isolation of both children when they first appear in the book. Congruent with her mode of comic romance, however, Burnett transforms these motifs of despair into images of female celebration. Through crucial adaptations of her protagonist's "double" and her "image of enclosure," Burnett allies herself with the feminist writers of the late-nineteenth century who, as Elaine Showalter has pointed out, "made the maternal instinct the basis of their ideology" and saw in this "female influence," especially over males, "a genuine source of power."

Burnett exalts the maternal instinct first by making Mary's "double" a boy she can nurture; her role in Colin's recovery places Mary in the romance's chain of female power along with Colin's dead mother, Mother Sowerby, and the secret garden. Moreover, by making her "enclosure" a garden, Burnett is able to transform it from tomb to womb. It is approximately nine months from the time Mary first enters the garden, in late winter, until the children publicly exit it in the fall—happily, Burnett does not call this symbolic reinforcement to her reader's attention; it remains part of the romance's mythic substructure, of which Burnett herself was probably only partially aware. Similarly subtle but present are the suggestions of human birth in Burnett's description of the children's exit from the garden which concludes the romance. The exodus is less an "escape" than a bursting forth of an exuberant, secret life that can no longer be contained. As he approaches the garden, the returning Archibald Craven hears "the laughter of young things, the uncontrollable laughter of children who were trying not to be heard but who in a moment or so—as their excitement mounted—would burst forth." The door of the garden is suddenly "flung wide open"; and out from the walls Craven had sealed as his wife's tomb comes his healthy son Colin, "full speed" in an "unseeing dash." Following Colin is Craven's new "daughter," Mary. Dramatically, this final reunion is a sentimental cliché. Nevertheless, the reader who is sensitive to the symbolic resonance of its setting, the secret garden, is likely to be moved. For by now that central trope unites Burnett's chain of specifically female nurturant power with the larger mythic theme of seasonal death and rebirth in nature and in human lives, regardless of sex or age.

The Secret Garden has its flaws. Some readers might object to its sentimental idealization of poverty and the class system in its portrayal of the Sowerby family and the gardener, Ben Weatherstaff. In a brief, uncharacteristic foray into fantasy, Burnett shows events in the garden through the consciousness of the robin and his mate, and she approaches her frequent silliness when personifying animals. Near the end, Burnett mechanically and unnecessarily interprets the garden as a symbol for the human mind; this discussion of the mind's power—the danger of locking it up, the necessity of weeding out bad thoughts to plant good ones—is undoubtedly the reason some contemporary readers considered *The Secret Garden* a Christian Science book. Most readers have been willing to forgive these lapses, however, because of the romance's many layers of symbolic meaning. Clearly the best of Burnett's works for children, *The Secret Garden* is also one of the richest, most complex, and most resonant of recognized children's classics. (pp. 100-01)

> *Phyllis Bixler, in her* Frances Hodgson Burnett, *Twayne Publishers, 1984, 147 p.*

Humphrey Carpenter

One would hardly expect it to have been Frances Hodgson Burnett who, seven years after the first performance of

Peter Pan and three after the appearance of *The Wind in the Willows,* should create a work of fiction which, more clearly than any other single book, describes and celebrates the central symbol of the Arcadian movement in English writing for children. Mrs Burnett seems a figure belonging entirely to the heyday of the Beautiful Child, to the late Victorian saccharine portrayal of children at its worst. Was she not the creator of the most notorious work of that period and type [*Little Lord Fauntleroy*]? Yet in 1911 came from her pen *The Secret Garden.* (p. 189)

The story of Mary Lennox's experiences at Misselthwaite Manor in Yorkshire, where she discovers a hidden walled garden and brings it back to life, is remembered by many people as one of the most satisfying books of their childhood, and at first it is hard to believe that it came from the same author as *Fauntleroy.* Mrs Burnett herself seems to have realised that she was doing something very different here, for she begins the story by destroying all the stereotypes of her earlier work. Mary is Cedric Errol reversed, the precise opposite of the Beautiful Child: 'the most disagreeable-looking child ever seen'. Her guardian, to whom she is sent after the death of her parents in India, has much the same function as the old Earl in *Fauntleroy,* but he is presented as physically repulsive, a hunchback who shuns other people because of his deformity. Other details seem to have been picked up casually from handy sources. There is a good deal of allusion to the wind 'wuthering' round the manor; the country lad Dickon, who becomes Mary's friend and helper, is a kind of Heathcliff-gone-right; and Colin, the hunchback's bedridden son, is first discovered hidden away in a remote bedroom after Mary hears a cry like that of Mrs Rochester in *Jane Eyre.* George MacDonald's influence seems to be present too: Misselthwaite Manor with its immense numbers of unexplored and uninhabited rooms, and its endless corridors and statues, is surely the castle from *The Princess and the Goblin,* while Mary's discovery of the key and her search for the lock that will fit it recalls MacDonald's 'The Golden Key'. . . . Mary and Dickon's cure of Colin, whom they persuade to walk again, seems to have been suggested by the passage in Johanna Spyri's *Heidi* where Heidi and Peter teach Clara Sesemann to use her legs. And *The Secret Garden,* besides being made up largely of borrowings, is written in Mrs Burnett's usual careless manner. Characters are crudely drawn and predictable, and the prose style is sloppy. Yet the book is lifted above all this by its choice of central image, the walled rose garden.

Such an image has preoccupied poets and writers from *The Romance of the Rose* to *Four Quartets,* but only on this occasion does it specifically enter children's literature. Something powerful and apparently not fully understood by Mrs Burnett herself comes into the book when Mary finds the door and turns the key:

> She took a long breath and looked behind her up the long walk to see if anyone was coming . . . She held back the swinging curtain of ivy and pushed back the door which opened slowly— slowly.
>
> Then she slipped through it, and shut it behind her, and stood with her back against it, looking

about her and breathing quite fast with excitement, and wonder, and delight . . .

> 'How still it is!' she whispered. 'How still.'

Mrs Burnett of all people has brought us to the centre of Arcadia, to the 'place of making' that lies at the heart of the Wild Wood. And is not the garden, dead and overgrown when Mary first finds it, reminiscent of another ancient symbol, the Waste Land? Its dead state seems profoundly related to the sickness of Colin, who is a kind of wounded Fisher King. No wonder that the revival of the garden, as Mary tends and weeds and clears away the undergrowth, brings him back to health. Mrs Burnett seems scarcely to understand why this should be so, and tries to suggest that some sort of supernatural 'life-force' is at work:

> Colin's face was not even crossed by a shadow. He was thinking only of the Magic . . . 'The sun is shining—the sun is shining. That is the Magic. The flowers are growing—the roots are stirring. That is the Magic. Being alive is the Magic— being spring is the Magic. The Magic is in me— the Magic is in me. It is in me—it is in me. It's in every one of us.'

Mrs Burnett cannot comprehend that no Magic is needed to explain the potency of the Secret Garden. But then the Garden, the Enchanted Place itself, is a symbol which greater children's writers than her only dared treat with the utmost delicacy, hinting at it and reaching out towards it rather than grasping it. No wonder that she, having picked it up in her hand, is scarcely sure what she is holding. (pp. 189-90)

> *Humphrey Carpenter, "A. A. Milne and 'Winnie-the-Pooh': Farewell to the Enchanted Places," in his* Secret Gardens: A Study of the Golden Age of Children's Literature, *Houghton Mifflin Company, 1985, pp. 188-209.*

Heather Murray

The Secret Garden made its first appearance to modest reviews, but its persistent popularity in book and film versions, and its inclusion in the early critical treatments of children's literature, soon categorized it as a "classic." (p. 37)

Yet *The Secret Garden* is in many ways an unlikely candidate for the position of classic, for it is a book which is disturbed as well as disturbing. (A reason for its continuing status may be the ease with which it has withstood transitions in the evaluative criteria for juvenile literature: what once was Edwardian fantasy may now be read as American hyper-realism.) "Mary and Colin," writes Alison Lurie, "are not just ordinary sulky or naughty children, they are severely neurotic. Today Mary, with her odd private games and cold indifference to her parents' death, might be diagnosed as preschizoid; bedridden Colin, with his imaginary hunchback, as a classic hysteric with conversion symptoms". Continuing as devil's advocate, Lurie notes the cult status of the book among 1970s high school and college students; "And it isn't hard to see why, considering that *The Secret Garden* is the story of two unhappy, sickly, overcivilized children who achieve health and happiness through a combination of communal gardening, mystical faith, daily exercises, encounter-group-type confrontation, and a health food diet".

The curious admixture which Lurie notes—jarring, too, in its seeming modernity—is in fact consonant with the literature of its time. Raymond Williams has noted of Georgian literature the "clear and intense" observation to which there is an "inrush of alien imagery," Pans, peasants, churches, demigods, seasons and all: "If it had not been lived, in a discoverable development, it would be impossible to deduce this extraordinary collocation". To Williams' list we may add elements of spiritualism or Christian scientism, visible here and in much other period literature, linked to the pastoral and idyll with themes of healing, inspiration, and Nature's beneficence.

But Lurie's irony alerts us, as well, the fact that the adult reader has a necessarily double perspective on *The Secret Garden,* for what we read is not what we remember. "My unrefreshed adult memory of the book," writes Madelon S. Gohlke in her reader-response analysis, "included an impression of a sickly and unpleasant little girl, a boy who loves animals and knows how to make things grow, another boy who is very ill, the finding of the key to the locked and neglected garden, and a vivid image of the reanimated garden". What startles us, I suspect, are not simply the disconsonances which Lurie notes, but the fact that we do not recall them. And there are other, less easily-glossed, contradictions. No one ever tells Colin why the garden has been kept locked, even when he asks about the broken tree. A trip to the Sowerby cottage, twice planned and often mentioned, is not undertaken; and Mary never sets foot on the moors which lie all around, and which intrigue her. The reason for Colin's mother's death is not made clear, whether this was from the fall which brought on childbirth or from the birth itself. (Throughout the story, Mary comes increasingly to resemble the portrait of Colin's mother.) Colin, although raised almost solely by servants and nurses, has no Yorkshire or other regional accent; and he is a remarkably accomplished autodidact (although at one point he doesn't know what a flower bulb is). The opposition between Rajah-like and Dickon-like behaviour is set out explicitly by Mary and implicitly by the narration, but in direct denial of our expectations Colin continues as Rajah to the end, becoming more suited to and more deserving of that role, and gaining a gradual assent from children and servants to his natural superiority. (The maternal Susan Sowerby however, in a moment of emotion, calls him "dear lad" rather than "Mester Colin.") And we note that the narratorial voice becomes increasingly heard, as in the passage on Archibald Craven's conversion, where the narrator enters as "I" to shore up our belief in "Magic." Rhapsodies on life's beauties and mysteries, and a whimsical passage about robins and nests which gives a birds'-eye view of the children, are more than intrusions—they are the signals of the breakdown of the close narrator/character/reader bond into a one-way relationship of interpretation and instruction.

These shifts in tone should be viewed as more than lapses in aesthetic quality. It is no coincidence that "I" enters when we are in the adult world of Europe and Archibald Craven; nor is it a coincidence that from this point the action will be seen through the eyes of adults—father, servants, a narrator whose identity has touched the author's and now is identifiably grown-up.

Nor is it happenstance that after this interlude Mary fades from the story. The most obvious sign of her marginalization is her loss of the foot-race: more subtle is the grammatical displacement, her own movement and endeavour shunted into a relative clause in a sentence whose purpose is to convey information about Colin: "Mary, who had been running with him, and had dashed through the door too, believed that he managed to make himself look taller than he had ever looked before . . . " This is the only direct mention of her in the concluding pages of the novel, in a conversion of Mary as actor to Mary as viewer. Her name occurs only once more, in Colin's story, to which she is a silent spectator. And then she is named no longer—present but not present, ghostlike, a marking absence. When Colin and his father walk back to the house, we do not know: does Mary walk behind them? does she go back to the garden? or is she standing in some intermediate place, between the manor and the garden?

Mary shrinks; Colin grows; the natural order cedes to the social. The first myth of *The Secret Garden,* the one we remember, is the romance of the vital, renewing, "wick" place which makes whole the broken heart. The second myth of *The Secret Garden,* the one that we forget (that renders us forgetful?) is the real story of the patriarchal order—generationally coherent, socially hierarchic, reassuringly benevolent—whose restoration heals the hurts and calms the crises in the narrative. The two are closely related. (pp. 37-40)

[In] the end, *The Secret Garden* blurs its own traces in the sweep from natural to social in the movement of organ(ic)ization. Insofar as the social order grows from the garden, it is natural; and the closing pages, with vibrant authorial voice and the happy rush to the story's conclusion, provide an equally "natural" aesthetic and narrative closure. The garden is ordered; the order is naturalized; everything and everyone are in their places. *The Secret Garden* "succeeds" because of its power to harmonize discordancies, to quell its own rebellions.

What are we to make of a woman-authored text which so validates the *status quo,* which erases the presence of the lower-class boy of the moors, and so disposes of its heroine? A tendency has been to refer this question to biography, to the facts of Burnett's dead son and estranged husband; we may as easily have recourse to the evidence of her wide-ranging sympathies and her non-conformity. Is Burnett here descriptive rather than prescriptive, telling us the way of the world rather than how it ought to be? And if we believe so, what are we to make of the irrefutably enthusiastic tone of the conclusion, the final authorial *imprimatur?* Is Mary, in her middle place, a mediator between classes and sexes, between nature and culture; or is she simply, now, a young woman?

The child reader leaps through the horns of this dilemma in a return to the garden through selectivity of reading and remembrance. And criticism has for the most part made the same turn, focussing on the story's pastoral, playful and juvenile aspects. We have, it would seem, saved the garden and salvaged the novel's Utopian potential. Yet this escape to the natural, the apolitical, the imaginary, is in precisely the direction the text has ordered. When the world cannot be changed, we seek the walled garden: haven, or ghetto, we do not know.

Jack Zipes has initiated an examination into the liberating possibilities of folk and fairy tales and their literary successors; Jacqueline Rose has asked whether stories for children can ever be other than constricting and controlling, given the inherent inequality of the author/reader relationship. Within this most current enquiry *The Secret Garden* may provide us with a new ground on which to assess the children's canon and its classics. (pp. 40-1)

> Heather Murray, "Frances Hodgson Burnett's 'The Secret Garden': The Organ(ic)ized World," in Touchstones: Reflections on the Best in Children's Literature, Vol. I, edited by Perry Nodelman, Children's Literature Association, 1985, pp. 30-43.

Michele Landsberg

There are some books, most loved by girls . . . , that invite a swooning rapture over landscape. Years afterward, one remembers not so much the characters as the colors of things, the heightened emotionalism that seemed to rise like a dizzying perfume from the grass, the trees, the flowers drowsing in hot sunshine. *Anne of Green Gables, Heidi,* and *The Secret Garden* are three that seem curiously linked in this way. As the English psychologist Nicholas Tucker points out, all three share a basic plot with heavily Oedipal overtones: A clever, spunky little girl with more ardor than beauty to recommend her wins over a gruff, remote older man by the sheer power of personality. I wonder if the overwhelming seductiveness of the landscape in these novels is the result of an awakening sensuality, unconsciously displaced onto the birds and the bees. (p. 107)

[Anne and Heidi share] an entirely unnatural artlessness. Both are given to gleeful leaping, singing, and spritelike dancing. But no matter how extreme their response to the landscape, no matter how poetic or exalted, they are never tortured by self-conscious embarrassment. This, of course, is because they are written from outside, seen through the sentimentalizing eyes of an adult. Though Anne and Heidi (and Mary Lennox in her secret garden and Jo of *Little Women*) are loved by girl readers, there is a half-suppressed guilty twinge of envy and alienation that accompanies one's admiration of these idealized heroines.

Was Anne Shirley never ashamed of her outrageous showing off? Did the poison of self-consciousness never cloud Heidi's sunlit days as she lisped to the trees? Nevertheless, the author's sensuous evocation of house and landscape is unforgettable; so is the secret Eden discovered by Mary Lennox, the cross little orphan girl who was healed by nature on those romantic windswept moors so loved by the Brontes.

The Secret Garden . . . still works its magic, even more strongly than *Heidi* or *Anne,* because Mary is not auto-

matically adored. Before she can win over her stubborn old man, she must forge a new character for herself, and she is helped in this difficult task by a wonderful Pan-boy, Dickon. He is as soft-spoken, sweet, and nurturing as no true adolescent boy who has existed ever before or since, and not only speaks in an enchantingly rustic Yorkshire dialect, but also can charm the birds and the animals with his pan pipes.

Mary brings the long-neglected garden back to life, and in return, the garden bestows on her a serene and giving temperament, a healthy appetite, and a new delight in life. It is this possibility of transformation that takes hold of the reader's imagination—a wholesome growth, nurtured and applauded by a whole chorus of earthily wise, rosy-cheeked peasants who know the virtues of hard work and self-sufficiency.

To reread *The Secret Garden* as an adult is to discover with a nasty shock, however, that though the spell of the garden remains intact, the book goes seriously off the rails toward the end, when Mary sets out to heal her hypochondriac cousin, Colin.

This boy is crippled and bedridden by sheer hysterical dread of death. Helping him, Mary learns new reserves of patience and generosity. Once Colin begins to regain his health, though, Mary disappointingly disappears from the story. The moment of her eclipse is even marked by the author: As Mary's crotchety uncle Archibald returns to his Yorkshire mansion, he is amazed to see his hated, sickly son all healed, racing toward him. "I can beat Mary in a race," Colin yells, and, in a fever of omnipotence, "I'm going to live forever and ever!" Colin has developed into an arrogant, high-strung little minister of pantheism. He actually leads the forelock-tugging servants (the gardener, Ben Weatherstaff, blinks away tears of admiration) in singing the Doxology in the garden. If Burnett had a weakness for Christlike little boys, she was more realistic and surer of touch in depicting Mary, a flawed soul who courageously healed herself. It is for that transformation that the book is remembered and loved. (pp. 108-09)

> Michele Landsberg, "The Quest for Identity," in her Reading for the Love of It: Best Books for Young Readers, Prentice Hall Press, 1987, pp. 99-128.

Lois Lowry

I talked to my twenty-four-year-old daughter the other day, and I asked her whether, when she was younger, she had ever read *The Secret Garden.* I remembered her bedroom from those years, strewn with dirty jeans, the petrified remains of peanut-butter sandwiches, and books about untamable horses, girl detectives, and complicated civilizations on distant planets. But I didn't remember her reading *The Secret Garden.*

"Oh, Mom," she replied. "Of *course* I read it. It was one of my favorite books. I wanted to be Colin."

"Colin?" I was amazed. "Didn't you want to be Mary? *I* wanted to be Mary when I was young. To be all alone, and wandering around, and to find that wonderful gar—"

But she interrupted me. "No, no. Mary was okay. But what was really neat was Colin. I wanted to be lying crippled in a bed, demanding things. Having everybody running around, waiting on me hand and foot, so that I wouldn't have tantrums."

Well, of course. Her answer shouldn't have surprised me. Mary was an appealing character, certainly, and it wasn't surprising that she was my favorite when I was young, since I, like Mary, was a secretive loner of a child. But Colin, too: what an enticing role, that of the demanding invalid calling the shots, manipulating an entire household of servants and nurses hired to do his bidding.

And both of them—Mary and Colin—without a parent anywhere around. Thinking of that made me remember something else: myself as a young mother, standing in the kitchen one summer afternoon, and overhearing, through an open window, the voices of my then six-year-old son, Ben, and his best friend, Jeff, as they played with their trucks in the grass.

"Wouldn't it be great," Jeff suggested, "if we didn't have any parents? We could do whatever we wanted, and nobody would tell us not to."

I smiled, waiting smugly to hear my son's response, knowing in advance what my sweet, affectionate Ben would say: maybe something along the lines of, "Oh, my mom is so wonderful that I can't imagine not having her around."

But instead, Ben answered matter-of-factly, "Yeah, wouldn't that be great? No parents!"

Well, it wasn't the first time—nor would it be the last—that I was duly humbled by one of my own offspring.

When *The Secret Garden* was published in 1909, *Booklist,* the prestigious review journal of the American Library Association, described it as a book "dealing almost wholly with abnormal people."

Abnormal? Mary, a spoiled, unattractive, petulant ten-year-old girl? Colin, a whining, manipulative hypochondriac? Dickon, an ingratiatingly nice little boy obsessed by flowers and animals? You could find all three of them in any sixth grade classroom today.

Abnormal my foot.

The only thing abnormal, if you ask me, is that Frances Hodgson Burnett, a very ordinary, meagerly-educated woman from a less-than-literary background, created the three of them and placed them in a plot that, whatever its flaws, incorporates every single element guaranteed to captivate young readers not only at the turn of the century, but seventy-five years later as well.

Orphanhood—how kids love it. More than love it—*yearn* for it, at least in the abstract, as my own traitorous six-year-old had reminded me. What a dream: freedom from parents! To prowl about on one's own, to pry into forbidden things, as Mary did. To deceive, and prove adults wrong, and say "Nyah, nyah," as Colin did. (Okay, I'll concede that he was nicer than that—almost repulsively so—by the end of the book. But let's face it, when he stood up and walked, when he proved all the adult predictions

wrong, it was a "Nyah, nyah" of the first order; a bravura nose-thumbing.)

It's tough for a contemporary writer to get rid of parents. We *want* to, often (count the number of kids' books set in summer camps; that's no accident), but there aren't too many ways to do it without taking on the trappings of tragedy and psychological ramifications. Personally, I've always stood in awe of Roald Dahl's *James and the Giant Peach,* or at least of these two wonderful sentences: "Then, one day, James's mother and father went to London to do some shopping, and there a terrible thing happened. Both of them suddenly got eaten up (in full daylight, mind you, and on a crowded street) by an enormous angry rhinoceros which had escaped from the London Zoo."

Would that we authors could all just let loose an enormous angry rhinoceros on page one and go on from there.

Mrs. Burnett had no such dilemmas to face. In 1909, orphanhood was not an aberrant circumstance (she herself had lost her father when she was four). A cholera epidemic might very well have felled a British child's parents in India; influenza was to do the same in the United States within only nine years.

What *was* unusual, in children's literature of that or any era, was the character she created in Mary Lennox: a sullen, homely brat. We've all known them, of course, in real life; but very few of us writers have had the nerve to install one as the protagonist in a full-length novel. Sure, we're clever enough to draw "well-rounded" characters, so that our heroines pout now and then or tell lies (small ones) or are rude to their mothers. But let's face it, they all have hearts of gold; their mischief is well-intentioned, and they only need to be prodded gently from a sulk to a smile.

But not Mary. Mary Lennox, when we meet her at the beginning of *The Secret Garden,* is already suffering from an advanced case of terminal obnoxiousness.

And so, it turns out, is Colin when we encounter him for the first time not many pages later, whining and crying in his impostor's bed of pain.

Unappealing? No doubt, if we had to live with them. But they're immensely appealing to young readers, every one of whom would give a great deal to get away with that kind of behavior, the way Mary and Colin do. I confess, myself, to a shiver of glee when Mary, aged ten—TEN!—demands to be dressed by the maid in the morning. And the maid obeys! How on earth did the author, writing it, have both the nerve to make that maid *obey,* and the intuition to know that the reader would still adore Mary Lennox?

Frances Hodgson Burnett was not, on the whole, a terribly original writer. She stole plot devices like crazy from earlier authors: Mary and Dickon helping Colin to walk on his own comes straight from Spyri's *Heidi,* which had been published thirty years earlier; remember Heidi and Peter urging Clara up out of her wheeled chair? Mary's arrival as a woebegone orphan, to take up a new life in a vast, eerie mansion presided over by its mostly absent owner, is unadulterated *Jane Eyre*—as, in fact, are the remote cries of Colin from a distant bedroom. And the wuthering sound of the moors? Burnett must have had her Brontë close at hand while she wrote.

But we, as readers, can forgive her plot-plundering for several reasons. First of all, unoriginality is by no means an original sin with Frances Burnett; among her predecessors in the act we can count Shakespeare, no slouch as a writer. Stealing stories is perhaps one of the few crimes in which the end *does* justify the means. In short, she made it work.

More important, she created one of the most seductive pieces of imagery ever to appear in literature for children. The gate to it opens for the first time in chapter 9 with the words "It was the sweetest, most mysterious-looking place any one could imagine. The high walls which shut it in were covered with the leafless stems of climbing roses. . . . "

The image of a garden as an inviolate space, a place for withdrawals, renewals, and beginnings, is one that spans the history of literature. Sometimes a serpent intrudes, as in the Genesis account of Eden. But slithery interlopers notwithstanding, these sacrosanct enclosures flourish in Shakespeare, Mother Goose, Voltaire, Eliot, and in Gothic novels by authors with aristocratic-sounding pseudonyms. I created one myself in a novel called *Taking Care of Terrific*. . . . (pp. v-viii)

Personally, I've always felt that Lady Chatterley was as attracted to the freedom of the gamekeeper's earthy domain, a pleasant contrast to her well-ordered mansion, as she was to the gamekeeper himself, given his tendency to be a bit brusque and laconic. Lawrence's other work confirms that, as again and again characters escape from strictures imposed by either poverty or wealth for the respite offered by nature.

Kids, of course, couldn't care less about literary devices or the nature symbolism that abounds in fiction following the industrial revolution. But they care about enclosed spaces that belong solely to them: ask any five-year-old who has ever made himself a house out of the carton the new refrigerator came in. They care about gardening, at least to the extent that they'll water their Sunday School marigold in order to enjoy a sense of creative power when new blossoms appear. . . . Most of all, kids are passionate about secrecy.

The secrecy is the thing. Picture the same book with a truncated title: *The Garden.* Picture old Ben Weatherstaff handing Mary a key, maybe suggesting, "Here's a nice little garden you might like to weed and clean up." Picture Mary saying, "Let's take the wall down so that everybody can *see* the garden."

Ruins the whole thing, doesn't it? Turns it right into a dull how-to book about the niceties of horticulture and the fun of sharing, which everybody knows is no fun at all.

Children's lives are bordered by secrecy, but it is almost always unilaterally effective. Parents keep things secret from kids. So do teachers. But when kids themselves try to have secrets, the secrets are always phony and they know it, because they know that Mom cleans the room where the birthday gift is hidden and that the hideout in

the garage is right there where Dad parks the car every night.

No wonder that they're captivated by a book in which first one child, and then two child collaborators, have—and keep—a real secret from adults. "As each day passed, Colin had become more and more fixed in his feeling that the mystery surrounding the garden was one of its greatest charms. Nothing must spoil that. No one must ever suspect that they had a secret. . . . It was almost as serious and elaborately thought out as the plans of march made by great generals in time of war."

And it *was* a kind of war: a war against adults, the most appealing kind of war for children to wage. Such a war was justified, as well—and young readers need that, for the war to be justified; they have a strong sense of fair play—because the adults were unfair. Frances Burnett made sure of that.

Archibald Craven, Mary's uncle, has her brought to his home, because it is his duty, but on her arrival, the servants are instructed, " 'He doesn't want to see her' " and she is installed in an opulent but gloomy room without any concessions to a child. No toys. No playmates. Unfair? Of course.

Mrs. Medlock, the housekeeper, provides for the basic needs of a child in residence and leaves Mary otherwise alone. When Mary wanders curiously about the mansion, she is told by Mrs. Medlock, " 'You come along back to your own nursery or I'll box your ears' " and " 'Stay where you're told or you'll find yourself locked up.' "

Ben Weatherstaff, the elderly gardener, tells Mary, " 'Don't you be a meddlesome wench.' "

Darn right it's unfair. With such an accumulation of adversaries, of course war must be waged. What a wonderful battle has been set: three kids with legitimate axes to grind, against a powerful phalanx of insensitive adults.

I said three. But when my daughter and I argued the respective merits of Mary versus Colin as an alter ego, neither of us mentioned Dickon. And I realize that I've postponed much mention of him here.

Well, let's face it: Frances Hodgson Burnett was not a flawless writer, and Dickon represents one of her flaws.

He has attributes, certainly. His kinship with the land, with growing things, and with animals and birds is appealing, albeit somewhat unrealistic. But after a few chapters of it I began to hear the ghost of Nat King Cole crooning that remarkably asinine song, "Nature Boy," in my head.

Biographers recount that Mrs. Burnett considered her own two sons somewhere up there on the order of saints and dressed them in velvet suits to boot. As a mother, I can forgive her for that—all but the velvet suits—having felt that way about my own oldest son until a policeman brought him home by the scruff of the neck when he was twelve, and I was forced to reshape my maternal viewpoint into something more realistic.

But it's tough to forgive her relentlessly saccharine portrayal of Dickon. An editor should have insisted that Mrs.

Burnett reshape him—just a little would have done it. As published, he is simply too monotonously good. We can stand him. We even like him. But we don't want to *be* him; nobody wants to be that saintly. It can't be any *fun*.

Moreover, unwritten rules of fiction writing demand that major characters undergo some change, some growth if they are to hold our interest through three hundred pages.

But we are introduced to Dickon early on, through the housemaid Martha, his sister, as she describes him to Mary. " 'Dickon's a kind lad an' animals likes him,' " Martha says first.

Then: " 'Our Dickon goes off on th' moor by himself an' plays for hours.' "

And: " 'However little there is to eat, he always saves a bit o' his bread to coax his pets.' "

So we know a bit about Dickon before we meet him. We know that he is kind, that animals like him, that he plays contentedly alone, and that he is self-sacrificing. Frankly, I am already a little mistrustful.

When we encounter him later, for the first time, we find that he is clean, smiles a lot, and smells good, too.

And by the end of the book, we also know that he is extremely kind to his mother and has a fine singing voice. We find out about the voice when he spontaneously sings the doxology.

By then even kids, who are notoriously tolerant, are turned off. It's hard to stomach someone who not only obeys the Boy Scout laws to the letter, but who also smiles—who has barely ever *stopped* smiling—and bursts into "Praise God from whom—" because things are going well.

It certainly wasn't that Frances Burnett didn't know how to create a realistic, multifaceted character. Dickon's sister, Martha, is one of the most interesting people in the book. She falls neither into the camp of the children, guarding their secret, nor the adults, against whom it must be guarded. Martha is a human, likable, down-to-earth being who falls victim to impatience and bad temper from time to time. She has common sense and a pragmatic desire to hand on to her job. She doesn't change throughout the book, but she doesn't need to change; she is not one of the major characters, and she has been presented as a stable and normal young woman from the beginning.

Mary and Colin change, of course. They have to, because otherwise the secret garden has no raison d'être. By the conclusion of the book, Mary Lennox has changed, by virtue of the fresh air and exercise, into a more attractive child with a little weight on her previously skinny body and some color to her previously sallow complexion. We can believe that. Her personality has changed as well, and the changes are wrought by some practical altruism and a lot of necessary self-sufficiency; believable changes as well.

I have a little more trouble accepting the changes in Colin. Though I wish Mrs. Burnett had reached a little farther with the character of Dickon, I *yearn* for her to have re-

strained herself with Colin. He was doing just fine while he sneaked about with Mary, rehearsing himself out of invalidism into normal boyhood, but, oh, how I wish that she had quit when she was ahead, when Colin got out of his wheelchair and proved the dire predictions of his father wrong.

Suddenly, in those concluding chapters of the book, Colin turns into such a sanctimonious, sermonizing bore that I keep wishing that Mary would tell him to knock it off.

But I have to remind myself that Frances Burnett was writing in an era when religiosity and didacticism were routinely part of fiction. She couldn't predict a future, seventy-five years later, when even children would be sophisticated enough as readers to be able to discern the moral lessons of a story without being whacked over the head. She couldn't have known that today's teachers of writing implore their students not to *tell* it, but to *show* it.

The irony is that she had already shown it so very, very well.

She had shown it, passionately, throughout the book, as she wrote about the garden. She had shown that care, attention, nurture, love—the things of which the garden (and the children) had been brutally deprived—are the things that create growth and bloom.

The deft handling of the Yorkshire speech is a remarkable feat on the part of Mrs. Burnett, given the fact that she had left Britain for Tennessee at age fifteen, returning only much later and occasionally as a visitor. She had a sure ear and a skillful hand with the use of dialect, always a risky undertaking for a writer.

It is one of the Yorkshire passages that, for me, remains the most moving moment in the book, combining the flavor of the region as reflected in its speech with the ingenuous quality of Mary Lennox and weaving the two together into the central metaphor of the book itself:

> "That one?" she said. "Is that one alive—quite?"
> Dickon curved his wide smiling mouth.
> "It's as wick as you or me," he said; and Mary remembered that Martha had told her that "wick" meant "alive" or "lively."
> "I'm glad it's wick!" she cried out in her whisper. "I want them all to be wick. . . . "

Despite my desire to edit that passage—to eliminate the wide smiling curve of a mouth that creates a Kermit the Frog out of Dickon in my imagination, and to change "cried out in a whisper" into something less oxymoronic—I am moved by it. I am moved by snobbish little Mary's unconscious adoption of the Yorkshire idiom, and I am moved by her wish for "them all to be wick." The reader does, too: wants them to be wick—not only the neglected trees and flowers, waiting there in the secret garden such a long time to be cared for, but the lonely children burdened by their almost lost dreams of normal life, waiting as well. . . . (pp. viii-xiii)

Frances Hodgson Burnett handled the telling of the story the way an old-fashioned gardener might have created a bed of perennials: no half-grown plants from Burpee's catalog, paid for by credit card; instead, seeds carefully sown in prepared soil, patiently tended—eventually a mixture of textures and hues form a treasure that will last and delight audiences for years. The satisfaction of feeling all the inhabitants of the secret garden—rosebushes, fruit trees, and children—emerge with tantalizing slowness into new growth and finally into lush bloom, has lasted for generations of readers now. I expect it will flourish for generations to come. (pp. xiii-xiv)

Lois Lowry, in an introduction to The Secret Garden *by Frances Hodgson Burnett, Bantam Books, 1987, pp. v-xiv.*

John Rowe Townsend

Frances Hodgson Burnett was a more powerful, and I believe a more important, writer than Mrs Ewing or Mrs Molesworth. She has suffered in reputation—unfairly, I think—from the notoriety of *Little Lord Fauntleroy,* which hangs like an albatross round her neck. (p. 68)

Mrs Hodgson Burnett's last important book, *The Secret Garden,* was published in 1911—twenty-five years after *Fauntleroy.* Much had happened to her, both as woman and as artist, in the years between. There is an interesting growth of complexity from the one-dimensional *Fauntleroy,* through the more subtle *Little Princess,* to the rich texture of *The Secret Garden.* And there is a corresponding increase in depth of the central child characters. Fauntleroy simply and effortlessly *is* a hero; Sara Crewe is shown by circumstances to be a heroine; but Mary Lennox in *The Secret Garden* has to struggle all the way to achieve a true heroine's status. (p. 71)

There is something about *The Secret Garden* that has a powerful effect on children's imaginations: something to do with their instinctive feeling for things that grow, something to do with their longing for real, important, adult-level achievement. Self-reliance and cooperation in *making* something are the virtues that Mary and Colin painfully attain. These are not Victorian virtues. The Victorian ideal was that children should be good and do as they were told. . . . It was no part of this ideal that children should be self-reliant, constructive, inner-directed. Perhaps it required somebody like Mrs Hodgson Burnett, who was no simple Christian (she dabbled in various unorthodoxies, and *The Secret Garden* contains clear indications of belief in some kind of Life Force) to bring forward this new, significant and potentially subversive doctrine. (pp. 71-2)

John Rowe Townsend, "Domestic Dramas," in his Written for Children: An Outline of English-Language Children's Literature, *third revised edition, J. B. Lippincott, 1987, pp. 59-72.*

Rosemary Threadgold

Few people today associate Frances Hodgson Burnett with adult novels, yet between 1876 and 1922 she produced a succession of best-sellers. She was hailed as a second Mrs Gaskell when her first novel, *That Lass o'Lowrie's,* appeared in 1876, but her literary promise remained unfulfilled. She was lured by the prospect of finan-

cial security into the world of the popular novel and, while reflecting much of the society in which she lived, failed to develop away from the formula that had brought her so much success.

However, in her writing for children, the picture is rather different. Instead of being a follower of fashion, she is something of a leader. Her attention to detail, her gifts as a storyteller, and her interest in children all stand her in good stead. The result is three or four children's books that are read and remembered when all her other novels have been forgotten.

One of her most successful children's books is *The Secret Garden,* which was originally published in 1911 and is still in print. Closer examination of this book reveals that the same qualities which mar Mrs Burnett's adult novels and relegate her to the lower ranks of novelists can be strengths in books written for children.

The Secret Garden was not widely acclaimed when it was published in 1911, although it seems to have been taken immediately to heart by some of its readers. It certainly did not have the rapturous reception that *Little Lord Fauntleroy* had provoked in 1886. Today, *Little Lord Fauntleroy* is known chiefly by reputation—or from television—whereas *The Secret Garden* is still widely read. Its popularity has remained undiminished over three generations. . . . Its lasting popularity despite its lukewarm initial reception can be explained, in part, by the book's modern qualities. *The Secret Garden* is not a morality tale of the conventional nineteenth century kind, although it does have its own subtle message. Its main characters are a pair of disagreeable children whose rather pathetic personalities are plainly accounted for by their upbringing; both are deprived of the comforting security of a loving family. The moral of the book is that self-reliance is a good thing in children and that listening to one's conscience may be wiser than listening to one's elders, advice that was heresy to many adults then and now. The way in which Mrs Burnett expresses her ideas is to demonstrate how the awakening of self-awareness changes two unlikable and precocious children for the better.

The theme of *The Secret Garden* is yet another variation of the Cinderella story of which Mrs Burnett was so fond. Two miserable lives are transformed into happy ones. *A Little Princess* and *Little Lord Fauntleroy* had already followed the rags-to-riches pattern, although the change in those was a physical rather than a moral one. Both Sara Crewe and Cedric Erroll retain throughout their polite and even-tempered natures; only their circumstances alter.

In *The Secret Garden,* the change in fortune is more subtle. Mary Lennox and Colin Craven already have all the material comforts that they require, but that does not bring them happiness; it is an adult fallacy that it does. The improvement in the lives of the two children is solely in terms of self-fulfillment and affection and, as such, is more satisfying to the reader than all the legacies and "good" marriages that sprinkle the adult novels.

Since it lacks the extravagances of plot found in some of Mrs Burnett's other books—for *Little Lord Fauntleroy,*

A Little Princess, and *The Lost Prince* are no less fantastic than some of the adult novels—the success of *The Secret Garden* lies largely in the characterisation and the style, which are more apparent than in a more involved tale. The children themselves are of the utmost importance, and here the author's habits of observation and her eye for detail stand her in good stead. The simplicity of the plot brings detail into greater prominence than usual. The main characters and the setting are created from the experience of the author, which enables her to portray incidents with an accuracy that is pleasing to both child and adult readers.

The portrayal of Mary and Colin is central to the success of the story. Fortunately, Mrs Burnett did not subscribe to the old adage that children should be seen and not heard. Mrs Burnett seems to have had a genuine interest in children. She enjoyed their company and they seem to have enjoyed hers, suggesting a sympathetic understanding of the way in which children think.

In *The Secret Garden*, she puts this understanding to good use when she plays the part of the omniscient author and reveals Mary Lennox's thoughts to the reader in the kind of ordered and articulate way that the child herself could never express. This gives a privileged insight into the character, which is essential if the book is to be convincingly realistic. One example of the technique is the way in which Mary's emotions are expressed when she has quarrelled with Colin and returned to her room. Her thoughts are in a turmoil which a child would not stop to analyse, but which the author is able to describe to the reader. In language which is not inconsistent with the character, Mrs Burnett reveals a little more of the secret personality of Mary, which is as complex as any adult's:

> She was cross and disappointed, but not at all sorry for Colin. She had looked forward to telling him a great many things . . . but now she had changed her mind entirely . . . he could stay in his room and never get any fresh air and die if he liked! It would serve him right! She felt so sour and unrelenting that for a few minutes she almost forgot about Dickon and the green veil creeping over the world.

The shifting point of view in this extract demonstrates the way in which Mrs Burnett manages to create a character who engages the reader's sympathy, while remaining plainly disagreeable to those who know her. For much of the book, the reader follows Mary, seeing things through her eyes, overhearing her conversation, glimpsing her thoughts. Occasionally, there is an objective view of her—a plain, spoiled little girl whose unpleasantness arises not from any original sin, but from lack of understanding by the adults who have brought her up. The technique of shifting perspectives can be seen in the description of Mary when she first sees the robin in the wintry garden at Misselthwaite:

> She stopped and listened to him, and somehow his cheerful, friendly whistle gave her a pleased feeling—even a disagreeable little girl may be lonely, and the big closed house and big bare moor and big bare gardens had made this one feel as if there was no one left in the world but

herself. If she had been an affectionate child, who had been used to being loved, she would have broken her heart, but even though she was 'Mistress Mary Quite Contrary' she was desolate, and the bright-breasted little bird brought a look into her sour little face which was almost a smile.

Colin Craven is portrayed in the same sort of way. He is a hysterical hypochondriac who "never had a fight with anyone like himself in his life" until Mary came along and like met like.

The technique of shifting viewpoint used in the characterisation of the two children is not a new one for Mrs Burnett. Janey Briarley in *Haworth's* and Tummas Hibblethwaite in *T. Tembarom* are successful examples of other children realised in a similar way. However, the technique will only work when the author has conceived a fully rounded and convincing character, which—in Mrs Burnett's case—generally means that she was writing from fairly direct experience. Her affection for children has been recorded, but she also entertained a specific interest in handicapped and disadvantaged children.

Tummas Hibblethwaite is a good example of an accurately observed portrait of a spoiled but frustrated and unhappy boy whose physical limitations have given him a sharp tongue and a demanding, cynical personality. Colin Craven is also portrayed sympathetically, but without any hint of sentimentality. The ability to characterise such children without condescending pity seems to have arisen from a genuine and practical concern for the needs of deprived children. This had its origins in Mrs Burnett's attempts to assuage her grief over her son Lionel's death by devoting time and money to various children's organisations.

Reliance on her own experience is similarly evident in her storytelling technique. One of the satisfactory things in *The Secret Garden* is the amount of circumstantial detail which occurs unobtrusively to fill the imagination of the reader. Mrs Burnett has recorded that as a child she was storyteller-in-chief to her school friends, so it is likely that she soon learned that children clamour for details of inconsequential things like food, clothing, and furnishings. Such details may have no real importance in the story, but they feed the imagination of the listener and add credibility to the rest of the tale. In her adult novels, the attention to details of dress and furnishings are of minor importance to the plot and chiefly provide an interesting feature for the social historian, but in a book such as *The Secret Garden,* the technique is part of the skill of the storyteller. It helps to hold the attention of the child reader and satisfy her curiosity. The reality of the story and its characters is reinforced by knowing that:

> In one room, which looked like a lady's sitting-room, the hangings were all embroidered velvet, and in a cabinet were about a hundred little elephants made out of ivory. They were of different sizes, and some had their mahouts on palanquins on their backs. Some were much bigger than the others and some were so tiny that they seemed only babies. Mary had seen carved ivory in India and she knew all about the elephants. She

opened the door of the cabinet and stood on a footstool and played with these for quite a long time. When she got tired she set the elephants in order and shut the door of the cabinet.

The detail of "she set the elephants in order," so typical of a little girl's behaviour, is typical of the realism of the book. All of Mrs Burnett's child heroes and heroines act and think like children, rather than scaled-down adults. They do not always do as they are told and, although they eventually emerge unscathed, they are likely to get themselves into unpleasant or even dangerous situations. They are not always approved of by adults, are sometimes not liked by other children, and are by no means always attractive physically. Cedric Erroll is the exception in Mrs Burnett's gallery of children—he is handsome, polite, loving, obedient, and fortunate. Generally, the children have some failing with which a child reader might identify, as well as some good qualities that might inspire emulation. (pp. 113-17)

Despite the unevenness of their fortunes, all the children arrive at a happy ending as Mrs Burnett's readers would expect. Like her adult novels, her children's stories follow a familiar pattern of a linear tale with easily recognisable heroes and heroines, plenty of circumstantial detail, and

Mary, Colin, and Dickon in the Secret Garden. Illustration by Charles Robinson from the first edition (1911).

conversation rather than long descriptive passages. Unlike her adult novels, Mrs Burnett's children's books are not merely a refurbishing of other people's ideas; she takes her storyteller's framework and integrates into it a realistic and original approach to children's characters and behaviour. The fairy-tale formula becomes a strength rather than a weakness by providing a familiar and timeless structure upon which to build, preventing the stories from becoming merely a reflection of their own generation.

There are details which date even such a long-standing favourite as *The Secret Garden,* but they do not have the same effect as the mass of social convention that exists in the adult novels and that, to the modern reader, seems indicative of another age. The one idiosyncrasy of the author which might have spoiled *The Secret Garden,* as it marred some of her later novels, is the Spiritualist-Christian-Science element. Fortunately, its influence is limited, and the only unsatisfactory section is Mr Craven's psychic experience in Switzerland, which brings him peace of mind and the desire to return to Misselthwaite. Otherwise, the "Magic" so often referred to can be understood to mean Nature and commonsense, and not whatever spiritual forces the author herself had in mind.

The Secret Garden has been a lasting success because it unites the strengths of the author. Her shrewd power of observation is combined with her ability to tell a story well, and, perhaps because she was writing for her own pleasure and for a readership that she would not pander to or exploit, all the trite and snobbish conventions that narrow the scope of her adult novels are absent. One cannot but feel that Mrs Burnett herself might have been secretly pleased to have achieved fame through her books for children, for in her autobiography written for young people she declared:

> I have so often wished that I could see the minds of young things with a sight stronger than that of very interested eyes, which can only see from the outside. There must be so many thoughts for which child courage and child longing have not the exact words.

In *The Secret Garden* she comes close to achieving that insight. (pp. 118-19)

> *Rosemary Threadgold, " 'The Secret Garden': An Appreciation of Frances Hodgson Burnett as a Novelist for Children," in* Children's literature in education, *Vol. 19, No. 3, Fall, 1988, pp. 113-19.*

Nina Bawden

When I was young, Frances Hodgson Burnett's *The Secret Garden* was my favourite book. I read and reread it, as I read other much-loved stories, *Black Beauty* and *Little Lord Fauntleroy* among them. But *The Secret Garden* gave me the deepest pleasure because it seemed most "real" to me. I felt comfortably at home with the character of Mary, that disagreeable and thoroughly contrary girl who, at the age of six, was "as tyrannical and selfish a little pig as ever lived." I had a low opinion of myself, and was greatly cheered to read about a character who was even less lovable than I felt myself to be. She was certainly ruder—I had never called anyone "Pig! Pig! Daughter of Pigs!"—and probably uglier, with her yellow skin and sour, pinched mouth. And the things that happened to her were things I could imagine happening to me. When Mary's beautiful mother died of cholera, I thought it served her right because she had been so horrible to Mary. My mother was beautiful, too, and although she loved me, and never neglected me, I sometimes felt she loved my brothers more. I didn't want her to die of cholera, of course, but it was safe to contemplate the possibility, since we didn't live in India.

Reading *The Secret Garden* as an adult, responding to the craftsmanship, the magic of the tale, I find myself admiring most of all the way that Frances Hodgson Burnett has managed to create a heroine who is consistently unattractive in her manners and her thinking, and yet retains the reader's sympathy. It is, of course, partly Mary's situation: tragically orphaned and despatched from her home in India to live with strangers on the Yorkshire moors. But more important to my mind is the author's unsentimental honesty. She makes no excuses for Mary. There are no condescending, authorial explanations for her bad behaviour.

> "I wonder [says Martha, the Yorkshire housemaid] what Dickon would think of thee."
>
> "He wouldn't like me," said Mary in her stiff, cold little, way. "No one does."
>
> Martha looked reflective again.
>
> "How does tha' like thyself?" she inquired, really quite as if she were curious to know.
>
> Mary hesitated a moment and thought it over.
>
> "Not at all—really," she answered. "But I never thought of that before."
>
> Martha grinned a little as if at some homely recollection.
>
> "Mother said that to me once," she said. "She was at her washtub an' I was in a bad temper an' talking' ill of folk, an' she turns on me an' says 'Tha' young vixen, tha'! There tha' stands saying tha' doesn't like this one and tha' doesn't like that one. How does tha' like thysel?' It made me laugh an' it brought me to my senses in a minute."

This is most delicately and neatly done; a point made, but not laboured, presented simply as a piece of common sense from a good-natured country girl. Martha is the first person Mary makes a proper contact with in her new home, and although she doesn't always understand her broad Yorkshire accent, she has no hesitation in asking her to repeat what she has said. "In India the natives spoke different dialects which only a few people understood so she was not surprised when Martha used words she did not know." And, to begin with, Mary treats Martha as she would have treated her ayah, wondering a little at Martha's "freedom of manner," and expecting this servant to dress her, as if she were a stiff little doll. . . . (pp. 165-66)

It is Martha's ignorance and innocence that makes her treat this awkward and troubled child so naturally and straightforwardly. And there is psychological truth in the way that Mary learns to like and trust Martha and, later, Ben Weatherstaff, the grumpy old gardener. Neither is afraid of her. They are both simple people, and they provide simple and effective therapy. Martha buys her a skipping rope, and Ben Weatherstaff introduces her to his tame robin. And it is the robin that leads Mary to find the key to the garden, which is "the sweetest and most mysterious place anyone could imagine."

Mary reflects that she is "the first person to have spoken here for ten years," and the magic of that idea caught my imagination when I was young, and catches it still. And her fear that if the grown-ups find out she has been there, Mr. Craven, her guardian, will put a new lock on the door in the wall, has the same ring of truth. Whisper a secret and you will have lost it forever. I think this is the point where the reader's identification with and sympathy for Mary is confirmed. She has found what we all long to find: a safe, private place, perfect freedom.

Mary's discovery does not change her, or not immediately. She remains exactly the same tough, and essentially very brave, child she has always been. She explores the large, half-empty house on her own, investigates the strange sound of weeping she hears in the night. Her first meeting with Colin is as touching and magical as the finding of the garden; her behaviour when, later on, he flies into one of his terrifying tantrums, is entirely in character. A little alarmed to begin with, she soon becomes angry. Fetched by the nurse,

> She flew along the corridor and the nearer she got to the screams the higher her temper mounted. She felt quite wicked when she reached the door. . . . "You stop! I hate you! Everybody hates you! I wish everybody would run out of the house and let you scream yourself to death!"

As the author notes,

> A nice sympathetic child would neither have thought nor have said such things, but it just happened that the shock of hearing them was the best possible thing for this hysterical boy whom no one had ever dared to restrain or contradict.

Set a thief to catch a thief, in fact. Or one spoiled brat to cure another.

The scene that follows is both funny and poignant. Colin believes there is a lump on his spine, that he is growing into a hunchback. He has lived in an atmosphere "heavy with the fears of people who were most of them ignorant and tired of him," and even if it seems a little surprising that no one has ever tried to reassure him, it is entirely possible that this cross little girl could be the first person he would have believed. "There's not a lump except backbone lumps, and you can only feel them because you are thin. . . . There's not a lump as big as a pin! If you ever say there is again I shall laugh!"

From this point on the story develops into an excellent comedy. The way the two children plot and plan to defeat the adults around them, persuading the housekeeper and the doctor to allow Colin out with Mary and Dickon, satisfying their growing hunger as they grow healthier with the milk and bread and potatoes supplied by Dickon's good mother so that they can send the meals they are served in the house back to the kitchen, is a simple joke that can be enjoyed by any reader from eight to eighty. More subtle is the way that they manipulate the situation while remaining true to their characters. Mary is a child who has suffered what any modern writer would be inclined to treat as a terrible trauma: the loss of both parents, the loss of her home. But she remains, throughout, independent and spirited. She doesn't whine. She scowls. She is afraid of no one. She keeps her dignity always. When she "forgets herself " for a minute and speaks to the doctor in the Yorkshire dialect Dickon has taught her, she rebukes him for laughing most effectively: "I'm learning it as if it was French. . . . It's like a native dialect in India. Very clever people try to learn them. I like it and so does Colin."

Because of her Indian background, she interprets Colin's autocratic behaviour as that of a young Rajah. Eventually she comes to realise

> that he did not know in the least what a rude little brute he was with his way of ordering people about. He had lived on a sort of desert island all his life and as he had been the king of it he had made his own manners and had had no one to compare himself with. Mary had indeed been rather like that herself and since she had been at Misselthwaite had gradually discovered that her own manners had not been of the kind which is usual or popular.

And having made this discovery she feels bound to tell Colin what a rude boy he is—a revelation which he accepts with fair equanimity. But neither the doctor, the nurse, nor the housekeeper deserve much respect, and any reader, child or adult, who has ever felt weak or defenceless—as in a real sense, after all, Colin is—will relish the haughty way he speaks to these people who are supposed to look after him and have so signally failed him.

In contrast, the simpler folk who live outside the huge, closed, claustrophic house, Susan Sowerby, Dickon, and Ben Weatherstaff, treat him with a healthily amused tenderness. It is the Natural World that is going to restore Colin to life, and they are part of it. Dickon is a Good Creature out of an old fairy tale. His mother is the mother Colin never had. And although to Ben Weatherstaff the boy is still "Master Colin," and Ben will take orders from him, he is a tart and tactless old man who stands up for himself very nicely: "What's tha' been doin' with thysel—hidin' out of sight and letting folk think tha' was cripple an' half-witted?"

But these good people are not merely symbols. They are sturdy and well-rounded characters, and it is their sound common sense that saves **The Secret Garden** from sentimentality. . . . Rereading **The Secret Garden,** I felt I could have done without Mr. Craven's dead wife speaking to him in a Norwegian fiord; it seemed to me (as, indeed, it had seemed to me as a child) that if she were capable of intervening from beyond the grave, she might have made an effort to do so before. But it is really Susan Sower-

by's sensible letter that brings Colin's father home to find that his invalid son has grown into a healthy and happy boy, and the "magic" that has brought this about is really very matter-of-fact: the companionship of other children, an absorbing and healthy interest, fresh air and exercise. The true and abiding magic of this novel, I think, lies in its instinctive and unself-conscious expression of a basic human longing for life as it should be, and the concept of a "secret garden" where everything is happy and peaceful and growing and good expresses this longing simply but perfectly. (pp. 166-69)

> *Nina Bawden, "Returning to 'The Secret Garden',"* in *Children's literature in education, Vol. 19, No. 3, Fall, 1988, pp. 165-69.*

M. Sarah Smedman

Many children's books which inspire hope do so, at least partially, because they create a time-out-of-time, transcending the instant and making it possible for the child protagonist and reader to live, however briefly, in that "'span' of time" which integrates past and future in the present. Because the stories I focus on [in this essay] are not fantasies but "realistic" novels, their characters live in clock time, but those stories also put readers in touch with sacred time, that decisive, ontological time when, as Madeleine L'Engle says, we will be known not by "some cybernetic salad at the bottom left-hand corner of a check, or [a] social security number or [a] passport number. In *kairos* [we] will be known by [our] name[s]", that is, by our "isness," our essence.

Before we turn to specific novels for young people which evoke hope by tapping sacred time, it is appropriate to remember that response to any particular work is individual, personal; this response is not only inevitable but desirable. Norman Holland speaks directly to the necessity that any integral criticism take cognizance of the transaction between the reader and the text, frankly acknowledge, accept, and use the critic's role in her own experience as well as the literary text. In *Patterns of Grace: Human Experience as Word of God,* Tom Driver emphasizes that any story requires its hearer (reader) to locate that story with respect to herself at the time of the hearing. Because the story unfolds in an individual's imagination, that individual must recognize its gestalt—its structured, unified whole—its shape which arises from chaos. And she must judge now whether it is a true story for her or a lie, or whether it speciously attempts to dazzle her in order to distract her from making that judgment. Consequently, no one may assume that the books which inspire her with hope and with a reverent joy will affect every reader similarly; even myths do not speak alike to all. However, one can argue that, because certain books recover primordial time for some readers, intrinsically they have a mythic dimension.

Eliade says, "myths describe the various and sometimes dramatic breakthrough of the sacred (or the 'supernatural') into the world. It is this sudden breakthrough of the sacred that really *establishes* the World and makes it what it is today". When we consider the similar power of the creative imagination to establish worlds, we see that literary techniques allow for patterns of reality within those fictional worlds which "wrinkle" or transcend chronological time and space. Though it is structurally easier for fantasy than for realistic novels to embody the mythic, yet, like those rituals which are imitative rather than subversive, realistic novels can in some ways more credibly involve readers in their recreation of kairos and offer a tempered hope.

Within this context, I would like to look first at **The Secret Garden,** the first book which deeply affected me with joy, hope, and a sense of transcendence. As Madelon Gohlke pointed out when she wrote from the perspective of an adult critic of her profound experience as a child with **The Secret Garden,** "powerful response to a reading, even on the part of a child, acts as a sign of engagement, or what Iser would call the reader's 'entanglement' with a text". I too can affirm the power of the book on the imagination of my child self. The summer I was eight I discovered the book in my grandmother's basement and for several summers thereafter made a ritual of unpacking the book from storage, rereading it, and returning it to the basement at the end of my vacation. As an adult critic I too wished to know consciously why the book so impressed me. When many years later I reread **The Secret Garden,** recalling few of its details but vividly remembering the aura of the enclosed garden, a secret and a saving place for two abandoned children, I was able to recognize it as a story of regeneration. Rereading **The Secret Garden** now with the same satisfaction, I see that the book does indeed incorporate a ritual of status reversal, does recover Eliade's mythic time and Macquarrie's span of time. Perhaps, indeed, it is **The Secret Garden**'s retrieval of primordial time which renders it timeless: an acknowledged children's classic in continuous publication; a perennial favorite among child readers, with the power to evoke a spark, even a blaze, of emotion among adult readers when they recollect their earlier "entanglement" with the book.

Mary Lennox finds a garden, the archetypal symbol of life and growth, which has been shut up for ten years; all but dead, it is described as a world of its own: . . . "Everything was strange and silent and she seemed to be hundreds of miles away from any one, but somehow she did not feel lonely at all. All that troubled her was her wish that she knew whether all the roses were dead". Mary's concern for the roses is significant, for the rose traditionally symbolizes the essence of completion, consummate achievement, perfection. Discovering that "even if the roses are dead, there are other things alive," Mary, in an act of reverent recreation, kneels down and, with a sharp stick, digs and weeds, making "nice little clear places around" the "green points pushing their way through the earth. 'Now they look as if they could breathe,' she said".

As the garden, including the roses, blooms, so do Mary and her frail cousin, Colin, whom Mary has unlocked as she has the garden itself. One fresh morning when Mary had "unchained and unbolted and unlocked" the door and bounded into the greening, "uncurling" world, "she clasped her hands for pure joy and . . . felt as if she must flute and sing aloud herself and knew that thrushes and robins and skylarks could not possibly help it. She ran around the shrubs and paths toward the secret garden".

After Colin has been introduced to the garden, "he looked so strange and different because a pink flow of color had actually crept all over him—ivory face and neck and hands and all"; " 'I shall get well!' he cried out. . . . 'And I shall live forever and ever and ever' ".

Mary and Colin can know on an experiential level the sacredness of such moments of being, but, as children, they cannot articulate what they feel. Therefore, the author-narrator steps in to verbalize for them and us the continuity between chronos and kairos, between profane and sacred time, between time and eternity:

> One of the strange things about living in the world is that it is only now and then one is quite sure one is going to live forever and ever. One knows it sometimes when one gets up in the tender solemn dawn-time and goes out and stands alone and throws one's head far back and looks up and up and watches the pale sky slowly changing and flushing and marvelous unknown things happening until the East almost makes one cry out and one's heart stands still at the strange unchanging majesty of the rising of the sun. . . . Then sometimes the immense quiet of the dark blue at night with millions of stars waiting and watching makes one sure; and sometimes a sound of far-off music makes it true; and sometimes a look in someone's eyes.

Before the story is complete, the characters name the power at the center of their cosmos. In mythic cultures, to recognize, to know, the sacred power is primary. Knowledge of the power is symbolized by the ability to name it. What one can name, one has power over, for naming indicates knowledge of the essence. Mary and Colin do not call the power God; perhaps because they recognize it as "Mystery" but yet inherent in nature, they call it "Magic," and Colin plans to grow up to analyze it scientifically, to have power over it in another way. By whatever name, however, the reader recognizes the power as life transcendent and creative: "Magic is always pushing and drawing and making things out of nothing". Having named the creative power, the characters perform a ritual of praise. Joining in a circle, that symbol of wholeness and of eternity, they chant a virtual Te Deum: "The sun is shining. . . . The flowers are growing—the roots are stirring. That is the Magic. Being alive is the Magic—being strong is the Magic. The magic is in me. . . . It's in everyone of us. . . . Magic! Come and help!"

The book ends with the return of Mr. Craven and the recreation of at least a partial family in which the children are parents to the man. Mary's, then Colin's, discernment of the regenerative force in physical and human nature has fostered an independence which will empower them to use their awareness of "Magic," the sacred immanent in the world, to change the stunted futures which seemed to lie ahead for themselves and Mr. Craven at the beginning of the book. Through the characters, readers, too, are put in touch with kairos and recognize in themselves, no matter how weak or contrary, the potential for moving into a mode of living where they also can shape their futures toward their dreams. For the reader, as for Mary and Colin, kairos, with the changing seasons, subsumes chronos in hope. (pp. 94-8)

> *M. Sarah Smedman, "Springs of Hope: Recovery of Primordial Time in 'Mythic' Novels for Young Readers," in* Children's Literature: Annual of the Modern Language Association Seminar on Children's Literature and The Children's Literature Association, *Vol. 16, 1988, pp. 91-107.*

Jeannette Caines

19??-

Black American author of picture books.

Major works include *Abby* (1973), *Daddy* (1977), *Just Us Women* (1982), *Chilly Stomach* (1986).

Praised for writing positive stories about black life that reflect her understanding of the feelings and perceptions of children, Caines is the creator of realistic picture books that stress the warm and caring relationships shared by her child protagonists and their families. Written in a casual style that incorporates a minimum of text and a lightly humorous tone, the books are commended for their universality and for their honest portrayals of sometimes unconventional but consistently supportive black families. Caines addresses some harsh issues in her works, such as divorce and child molestation, and her stories do not always end neatly; however, she underscores her books with the sense that loving relationships can persist under the most difficult conditions. Caines characteristically portrays black characters who enjoy themselves, their children, and their lives, and several of her stories are noted for being among the few picture books to portray black males in a positive light. With her first book, *Abby,* Caines drew on the experience of her own family to create a story told in dialogue about an adopted preschooler and the older brother who realizes his importance in making his sister feel good about herself. Caines is also the author of several works that portray strong female relationships; in *Window Wishing* (1980), for example, she describes the strong bond between the young female narrator and her nonconformist grandmother, while in *Just Us Women* Caines evokes the relaxed and happy journey shared by Aunt Martha and her niece. With *Chilly Stomach,* Caines departs from her portrayal of the black experience to feature Sandy, a small white girl who is uncomfortable when her uncle hugs and kisses her. Caines received the Certificate of Merit and Appreciation from the National Black Child Development Institute for her works.

(See also *Something about the Author,* Vol. 43.)

GENERAL COMMENTARY

Allen Raymond

"Windy," the little girl who is the object of Daddy's affection in the Jeannette Caines book, **Daddy,** always gets wrinkles in her stomach before Daddy makes his every-Saturday visit. Windy is nervous, afraid Daddy won't show. She lives from week to week waiting for daddy's visits.

> Before Daddy comes to get me I get wrinkles in my stomach

> Sometimes I have wrinkles every night and at school worrying about him

> Then on Saturday morning he rings one short and one long and my wrinkles go away

The author of these words, Jeannette Caines is deeply religious. Inside her we'd guess there burns a heart quietly aching at the misfortunes of others. "I have so much," she says. "Not just money, but a job, children. I'm an author—a minority, black author. Imagine!"

While vacationing in Mexico recently she saw poverty the like of which she hadn't seen. "I grew up in Harlem," she said. "We didn't have poverty like that!" She decided to see if she could help. "We have lots of people at Harper's who would send money, clothes, other things people need," she said. She also went to the local church to see a priest. He was "taking a siesta" and wouldn't see her. She went back the next day at a different time. He wouldn't see her. "That made me angry," she said in her quiet, but determined voice.

No, she never saw the priest. No climax, no neat finish. Just a story with an ending that leaves a lot to our own imaginations. But it helps us get to know the Jeannette

Caines who is something more than an author, something a lot more.

Like the story she told us of her visit to Mexico, Jeannette's books for children don't finish neat, either. There are few words, big pictures. Each story is simply a tiny vignette, a minuscule peek into the lives of others. We can read her books in four or five minutes; if we pause to look at the pictures more carefully, maybe ten minutes. If we discuss the books in the classroom, who knows how long we can spend?

Whether it's a story about an adopted girl (*Abby*), a grandmother who wears sneakers and goes window shopping (*Window Wishing*), or an aunt who likes to take trips in her new car (*Just Us Women*), the Caines books are filled with gentle humor and tell us the author lived what she writes. "Yes, I lived it," she says. "Part of my life is in each one of the books." (p. 24)

She was in fourth grade when the book bug bit her. She had checked out *Call Me Charley* by Jesse Jackson. That book turned her into an avid reader and she's never stopped. She's almost never without a book, whether she's on the subway, at home, at the grocery store or bank, or eating lunch. . . .

Jeannette has written six books and is working on her seventh. Four have been published, the fifth is coming out in 1983, the sixth is awaiting acceptance by her publisher. Writing comes easily to her. It's the ideas that sometimes come hard. "I have my lulls when I can't think of anything," she laments. But when the ideas come, she's ready.

One of her ideas, for the book, *Abby,* came while she was in her doctor's office. She wrote it while riding home on the "D" train of the New York Subway.

"Once I have the idea, I can just sit down and write. It's a God-given talent." One knows, or suspects, that she's silently saying a prayer and thanking God—and meaning it.

Jeannette looks upon herself as a role model for black kids. When she visits schools children swarm around her. As she talked to us her pride showed, and it was nice to see. "I think it's important that I'm listed as a black writer, that the illustrations in my books are of black children. There aren't many books about black kids, there aren't many black authors going around talking to kids. I like it."

This woman who wanted to be a writer for so many years ("I have rejection slips of all kinds, including lots from *The New Yorker* magazine for stories I now think are terrible," she said with a smile), didn't always want to be a writer. "I wanted to be a foot doctor," she says quietly. It didn't happen, probably because it wasn't "the right time."

Unless there is something we weren't told, it appears the "right time" may never come. The world will have to get along with one less foot doctor, one more author (a black one, at that), and thousands of satisfied kids. (p. 25)

Allen Raymond, "Jeanette Caines: A Proud

Author, with Good Reason," in Early Years, *Vol. 13, No. 7, March, 1983, pp. 24-5.*

TITLE COMMENTARY

Abby (1973)

This story of a warm and loving black family living in a city apartment could be used to introduce the subject of adoption. Abby, a pre-schooler, likes looking at her baby book that tells of her adoption. Her older brother, Kevin, is too busy with football to read the book to her until he realizes the importance of helping her feel special and important. Abby is reassured when Kevin announces he wants to take her to show-and-tell at school and brag that ". . . . we get to keep [her] forever."

Phyllis Galt, in a review of "Abby," in School Library Journal, *Vol. 20, No. 3, November, 1973, p. 36.*

A story told in dialogue is simple, amusing, and disarmingly sweet and natural. Abby is a very small black girl who is looking at her baby book and asks, "Ma, where did I come from?" "Manhattan." "How old was I when you and Daddy got me?" "Eleven months and thirteen days." Abby's older brother comes in, she makes overtures, he is busy, she feels rejected; he weakens, and sits down with her. When he leaves, Abby suggests they adopt a boy for Kevin. The story is charming in itself, and as a story about adoption, it is far more effective than most. (pp. 74-5)

Zena Sutherland, in a review of "Abby," in Bulletin of the Center for Children's Books, *Vol. 27, No. 5, January, 1974, pp. 74-5.*

Daddy (1977)

In *Daddy,* life is a broken home with visitation rights for fathers on Saturdays, and this book is a warm-hearted effort to show that, even in such circumstances, a little girl can still stay close to her daddy.

I suppose that a *real* slice of life might point out that daddies often don't show up on Saturdays, that they're often less loving and thoughtful than Windy's dad and also that tensions, not tenderness, may frequently exist between a daddy's daughter and lady-friend. But the book, with its really quite wonderful illustrations [by Ronald Himler] (the faces are black but the feelings are everyone's) is a valid acknowledgment of divorced family life. And in saying that caring relationships can, under such conditions, persist and grow, it offers a certain comfort, a certain truth.

Judith Viorst, in a review of "Daddy," in The New York Times Book Review, *April 17, 1977, p. 50.*

The joy-infused faces generate an all-pervasive warmth that's totally in tune with this little girl's account of Saturday visits with her father. Her big daddy is gentle, teasing as they talk, getting down and coloring with her (certainly one of the most incongruously loving scenes in the story), cooking up chocolate pudding, or watching her dress up in a costume. . . . Very real and very nice; hats off to Himler for his astute eye in visually interpreting this two-some's bond.

> *Denise M. Wilms, in a review of "Daddy," in* Booklist, *Vol. 73, No. 18, May 15, 1977, p. 1418.*

Children of single parents recognize through their own daily experience that there are varying and viable family structures. No longer does the two-parent family structure constitute the only "legitimate" one.

Historically, Black families have been misrepresented in both media and literature, and some of these misconceptions prevail in contemporary children's books. [There are] a few suitable children's books about single-parent, separated and divorced Black families. These books are realistic, positive depictions of Black family life and are highly recommended for their theme of family love and unity. . . .

[*Daddy*] is a warm story of a young girl and the activities she shares with her separated father every Saturday. Even though her father now lives with his new mate, he never fails to visit her and to make her feel special.

Books mold and shape young minds. It's important to expose your child to family-oriented children's books that speak in language they understand and that can help them see that families come in all shapes and sizes.

> *Beryl Graham Kalisa, in a review of "Daddy," in* Essence, *Vol. 15, No. 6, October, 1984, p. 142.*

Window Wishing (1980)

In contrast to Rhondy's grandmama [in Eloise Greenfield's *Grandmama's Joy*], who must cope with the pressures of urban living, the carefree and enchanting Grandma Mag in Jeannette Caines' **Window Wishing** shares some of the adventures of rural life with her two grandchildren.

Grandma Mag isn't your ordinary grandmother. She wears sneakers all the time, makes the best lemonade, raises worms for fishing, makes kites and doesn't like to cook. When Bootsie and his sister visit her during summer vacation, she's like one of the gang because she plays just as intensely as they do. She'll take them downtown after dinner on their bikes to window wish, and Grandma Mag thinks the cemetery is the most peaceful place there is to have a picnic. Any child would enjoy visiting this energetic and humorous grandmother who wears slacks and casual shirts and claims to be the same age as Orphan Annie. This brief narrative coupled with stunning, life-like illustrations [by Kevin Brooks] that greatly enhance the text, makes for a joyous picture book.

As two very different stories about caring, attractive grandmothers, both *Grandmama's Joy* and **Window Wishing** are honest representations of black life and are recommended for their central themes: family unity and love. (p. 68)

> *Nieda Spigner, "Honest Pictures of Black Life," in* Freedomways, *Vol. 21, No. 1, first quarter, 1981, pp. 67-8.*

This is not a story but rather a sequence of events in an easy-to-read picture book about Grandma Mag and her relationship with her two grandchildren. . . . The realistic black-and-white pencil drawings are as cold and unappealing as the text. The merit of the book is the positive relationship between the children and the grandmother, but Greenfield's *Grandmama's Joy* (Philomel, 1980) is far superior in story, pictures and sensitivity.

> *Betty Valdes, in a review of "Window Wishing," in* School Library Journal, *Vol. 27, No. 7, March, 1981, p. 129.*

Window Wishing successfully captures the spirit of the halcyon days that many children spend in the company of a beloved grandparent. What's particularly attractive is the book's portrait of an unconventional grandmother who raises worms, goes fishing, flies kites and wears sneakers. (And she doesn't like to cook!) She's a person who not only enters into the activities of her grandchildren, but plans a lively agenda of her own.

Grandma Mag has an eccentric fondness for Saturday picnics at the cemetery, where Grandpa Ben is buried. This may make some parents uneasy and provoke thoughtful questions from young readers. This is a lovely book that encourages children to view older people in a non-ageist way. I also like the way that Grandma Mag teaches the children to enjoy simple pleasures and activities, using imagination as the key to interest and fun.

Finally, the book is a refreshing portrait of African American people, young and old, who enjoy themselves and each other.

> *Ismat Abdal-Haqq, in a review of "Window Wishing," in* Interracial Books for Children Bulletin, *Vol. 12, No. 3, 1981, p. 17.*

Just Us Women (1982)

Smiling confidently from the heavily drawn cover illustration [by Pat Cummings] are a young black woman at the wheel of a convertible and a little-girl passenger of nine or ten—suggesting, as does the title, that this will be a glowing evocation of sisterhood. And so it proves. The little girl and her Aunt Martha are about to depart for North Carolina (presumably from New York, judging by the states they go through), and this is the little girl's future-tense anticipation of their unhurried stops . . . to shop at roadside markets, walk in the rain, pick mushrooms ("but we have to be careful not to pick the poisonous ones"), and so on. The pictures are similarly idealized, to the point where there is no life in the proceedings. Cummings is good at translating vague expectations to concrete scenes, but these scenes are all coated over with her cloying affirmation that being black and female together is a warming and wonderful thing. For that message, the book is sure to be praised and listed. But the message is imposed at the expense of a shared experience. (pp. 793-94)

A review of "Just Us Women," in Kirkus Reviews, *Vol. L, No. 14, July 15, 1982, pp. 793-94.*

This has only incidental action, as the small black girl who tells the story of what they'll do on their trip to North Carolina anticipates the freedom and companionship they'll enjoy. Nobody to hurry them, time to stop at roadside stands and have picnics, or to go to fancy restaurants, or even just stop to walk in the rain. The text has a warm, happy tone; it's written in a free, casual style and concludes with the response to the North Carolina relatives who might ask, "What took you so long?" "We'll just tell them we had a lot of girl talk to do between the two of us. No boys and no men—just us women." (pp. 4-5)

> *Zena Sutherland, in a review of "Just Us Women," in* Bulletin of the Center for Children's Books, *Vol. 36, No. 1, September, 1982, pp. 4-5.*

Chilly Stomach (1986)

When Sandy's Uncle Jim tickles and kisses her, she gets what she calls a chilly stomach—she wants to avoid him, but doesn't know how.

In this simple picture-book treatment of a common trouble, Sandy easily differentiates between Uncle Jim's unwelcome attention and the more appropriate affection of her parents, which makes her feel "nice and happy and cuddly." Her friend Jill urges Sandy to tell her parents; Sandy is reluctant, lest they be angry or not believe her, and the book stops as she is trying to decide what to do. This leaves the way open for good discussion, which will be aided by the story's well-chosed details: Jill, too, has an Uncle, loving and trustworthy; the straightforwardly realistic illustrations [by Pat Cummings] accentuate the open friendliness in both families, Sandy's distress, and the fact that her oblivious parents are too busy to notice what's going on.

A healthy, non-threatening approach to the difficult problem of child molesting.

> *A review of "Chilly Stomach," in* Kirkus Reviews, *Vol. LIV, No. 12, June 15, 1986, p. 936.*

Sandy is not comfortable around her Uncle Jim: "Sometimes he hugs me and kisses me on the lips, and I get a chilly stomach." Jim never does anything overt, nothing Sandy's parents would see as being amiss; nevertheless, "When Uncle Jim tickles me, I don't like it." While this picture book gets high marks for its consistently child-like perspective, there are serious problems with its resolution. During a sleepover at best friend Jill's house (Sandy always tries to go there when Uncle Jim stays over), Sandy confides her secret fears. Jill says she is going to tell her mother, and that Sandy should tell her parents, too. Sandy is afraid to tell: "Maybe Mommy and Daddy won't like me anymore." Last page: "But I want them to know." The picture shows a fearful Sandy, Dad waving goodbye to Jim, and Mom picking up the phone. The implication, one supposes, is that Jill's mother is calling, but this is too subtle for young children. More of a problem is that Sandy's fears—that her parents won't believe her or love her—are not resolved. The author's message may be that it doesn't matter how scared you are, *tell someone,* but the abrupt finish will only lead readers to think that a page is missing.

> *A review of "Chilly Stomach," in* Bulletin of the Center for Children's Books, *Vol. 39, No. 11, July-August, 1986, p. 203.*

The book is bibliotherapy rather than story, and the open ending that raises Sandy's concerns but does not alleviate them makes the book one that demands discussion between adult and child. This book should not be dumped in the picture book section; it belongs in parents' or teachers' collections. Linda W. Girard's *My Body Is Private* (Albert Whitman, 1984) is also very good and informative but is more encompassing and for older children.

> *Karen K. Radtke, in a review of "Chilly Stomach," in* School Library Journal, *Vol. 32, No. 10, August, 1986, p. 79.*

I Need a Lunch Box (1988)

A little boy's big sister has just gotten a lunch box, and he wants one too. Mama says no, because unlike his sister, he isn't about to start school. Still, the boy covets one, thinking about what he could keep in it—his crayons, marbles, bug collection, or toy animals—and dreaming of a different model for each day of the week. All that wishing pays off, because on the morning his sister begins first grade, Daddy surprises the boy with the lunch box he so dearly wants. The family portrayed here is black, but their experience is universal. . . . [The] book's strength is its portrayal of the yearnings that siblings often feel when they're excluded from the realm of their elder brothers or sisters. . . .

> *Denise M. Wilms, in a review of "I Need a Lunch Box," in* Booklist, *Vol. 85, No. 2, September 15, 1988, p. 156.*

[The] rather slim plot is fleshed out through a sequence in which the narrator dreams of a brightly-colored, imaginatively-shaped lunch box for each weekday. At last, on his sister's first day of school, their father surprises the boy with a spaceship lunch box of his own. . . . The simple text makes the story suitable for preschoolers. The drama of family relationships is honestly portrayed, although the issue of whether the father has contradicted the mother, which may bother some parents, is buried in the happy ending.

> *Leda Schubert, in a review of "I Need a Lunch Box," in* School Library Journal, *Vol. 35, No. 4, December, 1988, p. 83.*

Palmer Cox

1840-1924

Canadian-born American author and illustrator of fiction and playwright.

Major works include *The Brownies, Their Book* (1887), *Queer People with Paws and Claws, and Their Kweer Capers* (1888), *The Brownies Around the World* (1894), *The Brownies in the Philippines* (1904).

The following entry emphasizes general criticism of Cox's career. It also includes a selection of reviews to supplement the general criticism.

Considered the Walt Disney of the nineteenth century, Cox is best known as the creator of the Brownies, a band of more than fifty sprites whose national and international adventures are documented in thirteen humorous books in verse for early and middle graders. Acknowledged as a pioneer in the writing of imaginative and nondidactic literature for children as well as in the marketing of his characters, Cox is regarded as an especially original illustrator and storyteller whose works, extremely popular in their time, successfully reflect his understanding of his audience and what appeals to them. Cox created a complete and self-contained world with the Brownies, an ethnically diverse and almost entirely male group characterized by oval heads, big ears, wide eyes, smiling mouths, pot bellies, and spindle legs as well as by their unity and democratic approach. Although the Brownies are supernatural in origin and are always pictured as a group, Cox presents them with particular nationalities, vocations, costumes, and personalities; the Brownie band includes such members as a policeman, a cowboy, a sailor, a bellhop, and a clown as well as ethnic types from North and South America, Europe, and the Middle East; the most popular of the Brownies is the Dude, a monocled, top-hatted dandy in a swallow-tailed coat who carries a walking stick and often loses his pride as well as his hat and stick. Inspired by the stories he heard about brownies as a child from the Scottish settlers in his birthplace of Granby, Quebec, Cox retained only two features for his characters from their traditional sources: their helpfulness to humans and the rule that they must return home from their adventures by dawn. Cox created a utopian society for the Brownies that is filled with joy and fellowship; fascinated by humanity and prompted by their sincere desire to benefit it, the characters build, aid, and repair while investigating the contemporary world in an exuberant and childlike fashion. Engaging in a variety of activities, including sports, games, international travel, and visiting national landmarks, the Brownies encounter perils and hardships as a result of their investigations but always save themselves through their inventiveness and camaraderie. In addition to investing his works with positive values and an appreciation for nature and the arts, Cox provides information on history and geography and introduces his young readers to the latest technological advancements of the time, such as the bi-

cycle and the airship, through the exploits of his characters.

Basically a self-trained artist, Cox began drawing elves as a schoolboy; after coming to the United States and working in a variety of jobs he became a journalist and cartoonist, contributing to Western newspapers and periodicals and publishing his first book of adult humor. Moving to New York City, Cox contributed cartoons and verse, much of it political, to national periodicals and wrote and illustrated three more books of comic verse for adults. In the early 1880s his work began appearing regularly in children's magazines such as *Harper's Young People* and *St. Nicholas,* in which the first Brownie story, "The Brownies' Ride," appeared in February, 1883. After the publication of his first work for children, *The Brownies, Their Book,* Cox devoted himself almost exclusively to describing the adventures of his characters in straightforward, fast-paced tetrameters and black-and-white illustrations noted for their charm, action, and intricate detail. In addition to his stories in verse about the Brownies, Cox wrote a cantata, *The Brownies in Fairyland* (1894), which was later published in book form, and a three-act play, *Palmer Cox's Brownies,* which opened in 1894 in New York, ran for one hundred consecutive performances, and toured for five years across the United States, Canada, and England. The play, which features a flying ballet as well as several mechanical and electrical devices, describes the marriage of the Queen of Fairies to the adopted son of the King of the Brownies and was later published in prose as *The Brownies and Prince Florimel; or, Brownieland, Fairyland, and Dreamland* (1918). Cox is also the creator of the "Queer People" series, three books in which he teaches children about both real and imaginary creatures; in addition, he provided the text and illustrations for *The Palmer Cox Brownie Primer* (1906), a popular reader by Mary C. Judd, and the illustrations for several other books with texts by other authors which capitalized on the popularity of the Brownies. As well as creating a Brownie comic strip for newspapers, a new venture for its time, Cox marketed his creations in songs and advertisements and on toys, clothing, educational items, jewelry, figurines, wallpaper, stationery, kitchen utensils, glassware, food products, and other items now prized by collectors. The Brownies achieved an unprecedented popularity: over a million copies of the books about them were sold, and the creatures prompted a fad among the public that lasted for several years; in addition, the Brownie books were always among the most requested titles in the children's sections of libraries. With the advent of World War II, the popularity of the Brownies began to diminish; however, several of the books were republished in Dover paperback editions beginning in the mid-1960s and *Bugaboo Bill, the Giant* (1971), a tale by Cox that was originally published in *St. Nicholas,* made its first appearance in book form with illustrations by William Curtis Holdsworth. Although not extensively analyzed by reviewers, Cox is usually thought to be deserving of the reputation outlined by the motto which graces his tombstone, "In creating the Brownies, he bestowed a priceless heritage on childhood."

(See also *Something about the Author,* Vol. 24; *Contemporary Authors,* Vol. 111; and *Dictionary of Literary Biography,* Vol. 42.)

AUTHOR'S COMMENTARY

[*The following excerpt is from an interview by Joyce Kilmer.*]

With his pictures and rhymes of the Brownies at work and play, Palmer Cox has given pleasure to more children than has perhaps any other living man. Therefore his opinion as to what constitutes the best sort of book for children, and his observations on the changes in the kind of literature published for children, are of importance.

"In stories, rhymes, and pictures intended to amuse children," he said, "there must be no death and no pain. The children will find sorrow and suffering enough as they go on through life; these things ought not to be obtruded on their notice by the people who are writing and drawing for them.

"I have noticed a growing tendency in the colored pictures designed primarily to amuse children to make the point of the joke a matter of assault and battery, or a mean trick of some sort. Two little boys empty a pail of water on an old man's head, or saw a plank half-way through so that some one will fall into a ditch. This can have only a bad effect on the minds of the children who see it week after week.

"I see no reason why the comic artist who is drawing pictures to amuse children should think it necessary always to show childhood at its worst. A picture can be just as funny and yet not be a celebration of juvenile depravity; indeed, a picture can be just as funny, can give pleasure to an even greater number of children, and yet actually point a moral.

"Of course, the moral must not be so strongly emphasized in any picture or story that it will frighten the children away. He who writes or draws for children must not preach—that would be a fatal mistake! But he can make the characters whom he draws do the preaching by their words, or preferably by their actions—and the children will get the moral lesson without knowing that they are getting it.

"As a matter of fact," said Palmer Cox, with a whimsical smile, "I think that my criticism of the colored pictures made to amuse children applies equally well to some of the books and plays made to amuse, or to edify, grown people. There are too much pain and death in our novels and our plays. There are too many corpses in our literature. Not every corpse is like the corpse of Caesar lying by Pompey's Pillar, a thing to inspire Marc Antony's eloquence!

"The Brownies, you know, never give pain, nor do they ever suffer real pain. They are often in danger, but they always escape. I think that every story or poem for children should leave a pleasant impression on its reader's mind, should even make him want to commit it to memory. The Brownies do good, and they do it just for the sake of doing good, not for the sake of any reward. There are now nine Brownie books, and every one of them is packed with morals. But the children who read them don't know that they are reading morals, any more than their fathers knew it when they read them. You see, I hid my own personality; I myself didn't seem to do any preaching. But the preaching is there.

"You know," said Palmer Cox, suddenly, "the Brownies might have averted this war, if they had been permitted! There has never been a German translation of the Brownie books. If there were, and if the Kaiser and the other leaders of Germany had been brought up on it, and had really absorbed its message, then they never could have sent their armies into Belgium. They would have had the tender hearts of the Brownies, and their love for justice and truth.

"I don't want to seem to make light of the war—I couldn't make light of it. I am a Canadian by birth, you know, although I am a naturalized American citizen. But I honestly believe that the allied armies are fighting for those ideals of honesty and faith which I have tried, in my humble way, to make my Brownies establish in the minds of little children."

Palmer Cox was not always a maker of rhymes and pictures for children. In his "young youth" (as his Celtic neighbors in Granby might say) he went to California and there followed various trades, working on the railroads for some years, and also following the picturesque occupation of ship's carpentering. . . . [When] Palmer Cox was in California he did not let his work on the trains and ships win him wholly away from the Muses. He said:

"I used to write humorous verses for some of the California papers—The Golden Era and The San Francisco Examiner. I remember a long poem I wrote about a Chinaman who stole a currant pie. The baker and the police and a lot of other people ran after him and he decided to make sure of the pie by eating it as he ran. But the cook had accidentally dropped a rag in the pie and the Chinaman choked to death on it."

"That," said Palmer Cox, laughing, "is the sort of thing I used to write when I lived in California. But you see I had the Chinaman die as the result of his theft, so I must have been a moralist even before I began to write about the Brownies. (p. 19)

"I came to New York in 1876 with nothing but a pencil to make my living with.

"I wanted to do nothing but make humorous pictures and write verses. I found that there were several humorous publications that would buy my stuff. There was Wild Oats, and there was a paper called Merry Man's Weekly. The jokes and drawings which they printed were very broad, and had, of course, no moral at all.

"The chief source of humor in those days was drunkenness. In nearly every issue of these funny papers there would be a picture of a man getting drunk and throwing furniture at his wife, or being carried home in a wheelbarrow.

"Of course, it was chiefly to the children that this sort of publication appealed, and yet these drawings and verses were not made with the children in mind. I saw that this sort of thing was bad for the children, and I saw that the people who were writing and drawing for the children seemed deliberately to avoid any suspicion of humor.

"I saw no reason why humor could not be fresh and clean. And I saw no reason why people who were making pictures and stories and poems for children should not put as much fun in their work as if they were trying to entertain grown people.

"Although I was working for the humorous weeklies, like Wild Oats, I felt that my humor was not exactly in line with their humor. My work was more literary than they usually printed; I thought that every joke should have an idea back of it, that all humor should have a reason for its existence. I thought that the humorist should show life, not at its worst but at its best. And I still think that of the humorists and of every other sort of writer or artist.

"Nevertheless, I saw that all the printed humor was so broad, and I had just come from California, where the humor was even broader, that I did not think I could make a success with humorous drawings and verses that would be really fit for children to see. But some friends of mine,

some engravers who had reproduced some of my work, told me that I was wasting my time in writing and drawing for Wild Oats and Merry Man's Weekly and the rest.

"'There is a need for some one to make pictures and verses that will amuse the children,' they said. 'Why don't you do it? You can make four times as much money at it as you can from what you are doing now. You can make your work funny and yet give it a sort of a moral purpose.'

"Well, I thought I'd see if I could follow out their suggestion. I was sitting out in Prospect Park, Brooklyn, one afternoon in 1878. It was a fine summer day, and the bees were buzzing about some flowers that had been planted along the borders of the walk near the bench on which I sat. I like bees, I have been brought up in the country, you know. And I thought I'd try to write something about the bees which would amuse the children. So that afternoon I wrote **'The Wasp and the Bee.'**

"I used the old fable style in that poem. I tried to make it funny, and I also tried to put a moral in it. But I myself did not preach, I made the wasp and the bee do the preaching.

"And that is the key to all my work. I never preach, but I make the Brownies preach. In fact, although no Brownie appears in **'The Wasp and the Bee,'** I think that I may call that the first of the Brownie poems, because it is the first poem that I wrote for children, and the first in which I used the method which I used in every one of the Brownie poems. (pp. 19-20)

"That was the beginning," said Palmer Cox, with a reminiscent smile, "and it brought me a new experience. I had been accustomed to climb up the stairs to the offices of the editors of these little weekly humorous papers—this was before the day of elevators, you know—and stand trembling, hat in hand, to find out whether or not my work had been accepted. But I sent **'The Wasp and the Bee'** to St. Nicholas, and the editor, Mrs. Mary Mapes Dodge, sent a man down to see me, to have me make some more drawings to go with the poem, and to ask me to write some more for St. Nicholas.

"And I got four times as much as I would have got from one of the humorous weeklies. So all my engraver friends said 'I told you so!' and from that time on I did all my work for the children."

There is a paragraph which has been familiar to more than one generation of children—it is printed in the fore part of every one of the Brownie books. Palmer Cox believes that it expresses the central idea of all his work, so he repeated it to me. It is:

> Brownies, like fairies and goblins, are imaginary
> little sprites who are supposed to delight in
> harmless pranks and helpful deeds. They work
> and sport when weary households sleep, and
> never allow themselves to be seen by mortal
> eyes.

"Harmless and helpful," he repeated. "Harmless and helpful. That's what the Brownies are. And that's what I've tried to make my books about the Brownies." (p. 20)

Joyce Kilmer, "Palmer Cox of Brownie Castle Comes to Town," in The New York Times Magazine, *January 16, 1916, pp. 19-20.*

The New York Times

Countless are the little ones who have followed the adventures of those sprites Mr. Palmer Cox has drawn. [In **The Brownies: Their Book,** those] Brownies do all kinds of things, just like other children. They go to school, they glide on skates, they tear past on bicycles, they play lawn tennis and baseball, they slide down hills on toboggans, they go to the circus, to the toy shop, and they canoe. All humanity finds a place in these bright sketches. There is the Chinaman, the dude, the Dutch, the Scotch, and the military Brownie. The pictures are cram full of pleasant fun, and the verses well describe the events. It is an original kind of humor peculiar to Mr. Cox. We have had the ceremonious fairy with her gossamer wings and scepter, and now we have the less conventional sprites, and this is an invention, for which Mr. Palmer Cox has the patent. The Kobold of the German may be first cousin to the Brownie, but through long usage we have become a little tired of him: so long live the American elfkinship, the Palmer Cox Brownie.

A review of "The Brownies: Their Book," in The New York Times, *October 24, 1887, p. 2.*

The judge selected for the case
Ran here and there about the place
With warning cries and gesture wide,
And seemed unable to decide.

And there they might be tugging still,
With equal strength and equal will —
But while they struggled, stars withdrew
And hints of morning broader grew,
Till arrows from the rising sun
Soon made them drop the rope and run.

From The Brownies: Their Book, *written and illustrated by Palmer Cox.*

The Dial, Chicago

The swiftest peep into Palmer Cox's **The Brownies, Their Book** reveals the wealth of amusement it contains. Hordes of grotesque and comical little elves swarm on every page, intent upon some form of mischief or merry-making. Every one of the little fellows is so well-drawn that one can tell at a glance the part he takes in the general merriment. It is a masterly piece of pictorial delineation, humorous, vivid, and clever to the last degree. Rhymed stories accompany the illustrations,—accompany in the right sense of the term, for the drawings are by far the most interesting portion of the work.

A review of "The Brownies, Their Book," in The Dial, *Chicago, Vol. 8, No. 92, December, 1887, p. 193.*

The Dial, Chicago

Mr. Palmer Cox issues the third of his popular Brownie books, this time **The Brownies at Home.** It seems to belie its name, however, or to prove the cosmopolitanism of these midgets, for the author describes their wanderings through the South, Washington, New York, and the World's Fair. The latter episode is badly treated, however, and the drawings illustrating it are not only inaccurate, but inartistic, which is much worse. The Brownies themselves, though, are amusing, and their comical expressions and costumes will serve to entertain many idle half hours.

A review of "The Brownies at Home," in The Dial, *Chicago, Vol. 15, No. 179, December 1, 1893, p. 348.*

The Dial, Chicago

Mr. Palmer Cox, inimitable as ever, has this year sent **The Brownies around the World.** Poor sprites! They look dreadfully ill on their democratic raft, but they learn the sage lesson that

You can't through foreign countries roam
And have the comforts of a home.

They scale the Alps, they ride the crocodile; they moralize soberly on the follies of idol-worship while toying with the gold ear-ring of Buddha; but in the end they reach home safely, after having made the world their own. Adventures like these are sure to please the children. Mr. Cox, as usual, furnishes his own capital illustrations.

A review of "The Brownies around the World," in The Dial, *Chicago, Vol. XVII, No. 203, December 1, 1894, p. 339.*

The Nation, New York

It might be more of a geography lesson than would go down even with the appetizing Brownie sauce if every State were visited [in **The Brownies through the Union**], so the Brownies wisely content themselves with fourteen, well scattered, and manage to find something interesting in each. The youngsters will enjoy picking out their old favorites in the pictures to see what new antics they are up to.

> *A review of "The Brownies through the Union," in* The Nation, *New York, Vol. LXI, No. 1587, November 28, 1895, p. 393.*

The New York Times Book Review

It must be that Christmas is approaching once more, for here come Palmer Cox and his Brownies again. It is the same jovial, helpful, spindle-legged band as ever, whose exploits their historian tells in **The Brownies' Latest Adventures.** As time passes and Mr. Cox and his readers get better acquainted with his little people, he individualizes them more and more, and this time, in addition to the dude and the policeman and the Chinaman and the other favorite personalities, he has introduced a lot more who stand out with individual characteristics. But all alike are bent on doing useful things for humans, and they harvest ice, build baby-carriages, make a quilt, aid a hospital, repair the streets, improve the milk supply, and find many other ways in which to keep themselves as busy as bees. As usual, the pictures on every page furnish a goodly portion of the book's entertainment.

> *"The Brownies Again," in* The New York Times Book Review, *December 3, 1910, p. 687.*

The Nation, New York

The characters [in **The Brownies' Latest Adventures**] are virtually the same as have graced the pages of *St. Nicholas* for many years. But these gnomes are never behind the times; they always undertake the latest social work, this year being very ambitious in their civic activity.

> *A review of "The Brownies Latest Adventures," in* The Nation, *New York, Vol. XCI, No. 237, December 8, 1910, p. 555.*

Rose O'Neill

[*An American author and illustrator, O'Neill is the creator of the Kewpies, winged, chubby, fairylike creatures that, like the Brownies, were successful outside of the books in which they first appeared. The following excerpt is from the essay "The Coming of the Kewpies" which was originally published in the January, 1914 issue of the* Woman's Home Companion.]

In my childhood I had greatly loved the Brownies of Mr. Palmer Cox, and one of the delightful things about them was that one always reposed on the feeling that, whatever they did they 'meant well' by it. So the Kewpies, who I have liked to think might be young, toddling cousins of that earlier illustrious family. A Kewpie meeting a Brownie, I'm sure, would be almost overcome with respect.

> *Rose O'Neill, in an extract in* Humorous but Wholesome: A History of Palmer Cox and the Brownies, *by Roger W. Cummins, Century House Americana Publishers, 1973, p. 108.*

The Nation, New York

Grotesqueness is in the mode [of **The Brownies and Prince Florimel**], and overwhelms the original ludicrousness of the Brownies. Though old friends may still be recognized among them, the new ones make little appeal, and the plain prose of the present is a poor substitute for merry jingles of the past.

> *A review of "The Brownies and Prince Florimel," in* The Nation, *New York, Vol. CVII, No. 2787, November 30, 1918, p. 657.*

The New York Times

It is doubtful whether any fashion in children's literature has ever swept the country so completely as Palmer Cox's Brownies took possession of American childhood in the early '80s. The imagination of the Canadian-born Scotchman opened up a new continent of faery into which the young entered by the millions. The tests of popularity which we think peculiar to the present age were in evidence more than a generation ago. The Brownies lived for their public not only in books and the monthly pages, but on the pencil boxes and school rulers, on the wall-papers of the nurseries, on handkerchiefs, scarfs, pins, toys and stationery. Some notion of the vogue of these spindle-legged and pot-bellied folk is suggested by the teddy-bear of more recent times or by the Brownies' more direct descendants in the form of Miss O'Neill's kewpies and their numerous blood-relations.

Another contemporary superstition which a study of Palmer Cox would dispose of is the notion that Victorian childhood in the United States stood remote from life. What had thirty years ago to show in comparison with our present zealous efforts to "correlate" child life with the world around it and the world it will have ultimately to live in? Well, in the gallery of Brownies the adult life of that time was presented to the eye and mind of childhood with a greater fidelity to the grown-up fact than is to be found today in the grotesques of the comic sheet. Supernatural in origin, the Brownies nevertheless managed to take on the form of policemen, dudes, cowboys, Irishmen, Italians, and what not. They presented, in their own terms, the American scene, as Henry James would have called it. And for all Palmer Cox's resolve that there should be no pain or crime in his pictures and metric chronicles, he managed to convey a deeper suggestion of reality than we supply today for a childhood that must not be "sheltered."

In the realm of the young imagination during the last half century it is not altogether a coincidence that the supposedly dour Scotch soul should have supplied the richest and tenderest creations. Palmer Cox, Robert Louis Stevenson and the author of "Peter Pan" make up a galaxy against which we can set only Brer Rabbit. They are of the same family. They hark back to Lewis Carroll's Alice. And by no excessive torturing of the facts we may put in the same class, though the audience was a different one, W. S. Gilbert who began writing his librettos about the time Palmer Cox gave the Brownies to the world. Gilbert's lord chancellors, admirals and pirates are of the same race as Cox's cops and dandies. They all dwell in worlds of a grotesque whimsy that suggest the real world we live in more faithfully and more graciously than do the comics of today.

"Palmer Cox," in The New York Times, *July 25, 1924, p. 12.*

The Nation, New York

Palmer Cox is dead; the Brownies have lost their father. A generation now sedate in middle age was surprised to learn that the creator of its childhood friends had lived so long. The Brownies had become almost as authentic and universal a part of American childhood as Cooper's red Indians. For nearly half a century Cox's whimsical genius had been equipping their thin-legged bodies with dress suits and policemen's garb, stocking caps and nautical dress, and sending them forth on high adventures. Generations of children and ex-children lose a friend.

Cox's must have been a rarely happy life. He was one of those fortunate persons whose talents rescue them from a life of dull business. He grew up in a Scotch settlement in Quebec, but early wandered to California, where he made two false starts toward the happiness he achieved in the days when his Brownies were making *St. Nicholas* famous. Eleven of his thirteen Brownie-books are still in print: and hardly a year passes without a reissue of one or another of them. Their royalties made it possible for him to build and live in a Brownie castle in his boyhood home.

Strictly speaking, of course, Palmer Cox did not "create" the Brownies. They crossed the ocean when his ancestors came from Scotland. Cornwall knows Brownies, and Scotch tradition swarms with them. Medieval German houses bear carved figures of Kobolds obviously related to the creatures of Cox's fancy. Rome and Arabia were peopled with similar beings. But he rescued them from the byways of folk-lore and made their antics a living part of contemporary life; his Brownies were as much his own creations as the Kewpies are Rose O'Neill's, and that their popularity survives his death at eighty-four is eloquent tribute to his genius. For the fancies of childhood are fleeting, and it is rare that one generation will read the favorites of its parents' youth.

"The Father of the Brownies," in The Nation, *New York, Vol. CXIX, No. 3083, August 6, 1924, p. 137.*

The Outlook

When *St. Nicholas* came, we looked first of all to see what the Brownies were doing. Just as some readers of the morning newspapers to-day turn instantly to hunt for the "Gumps" or for "Mutt and Jeff," we opened our favorite magazine in the '80's and '90's to find out what sort of scrape Palmer Cox had devised for his crew of elves, and how he got them safely out of it. Now that the creator of the Brownies has died in the town in the Province of Quebec where he was born more than eighty years ago, thousands of men and women are going back to their Brownie

books or to the old numbers of *St. Nicholas* to see those fascinating creatures again. Not Frank Stockton's nor J. T. Trowbridge's stories, not even A. B. Frost's nor J. G. Francis's pictures, were more alluring.

Mr. Cox had been brought up, of course, upon legends of those Scottish sprites, the brownies, whose midnight pranks are humorous but kindly. But he developed them into a recognized band of adventurers, a collection of individuals, each with his pleasing characteristics. They had certain fixed laws. They had to be back—wherever that was—by dawn. And they were seldom, if ever, seen by mortals. And there were no females among them. The place for the girl or woman Brownie was plainly in the home. They could not repeat any action—and this nearly put an end to them. For when shipwrecked upon an island, they were estopped from building a ship or a raft since they had already built both, it looked as if the Brownies might have to stay on that island forever. Luckily, it was the resort of swarms of sea-birds, strong-winged and powerful. To these carriers (as they roosted on crags, sleeping, with fatuous smiles) the Brownies repaired, and, climbing on the birds' backs, were soon conveyed to the mainland.

In the verses accompanying the pictures (verses which, perhaps, many admirers never read) there is seldom any reference to individuals. The Brownies were a communistic group. But the pictures sharply differentiated various personages, and we all had our favorites. We looked eagerly and were not happy until we had found the King, the Irishman (with his coat tails), the Policeman (with his billy), the Uncle Sam, the Turk, the Chinaman (usually in misfortune), or the Jockey. The King, for all his crown, did not seem to have any special authority, nor be able to enforce law and order half so well as the Policeman. One or another of these important Brownies was always in a position of great danger or embarrassment. He had fallen overboard and was in imminent peril from a shark, or he had tumbled out of the balloon only to be caught by his coat tails at the very last second. But none of them ever came to grief. Like the animals in Mr. Burgess's *Bedtime Stories,* they always escape unhappy endings.

But of all the favored Brownies, for his mirth-provoking qualities and his exciting escapes, the Dude was easily chief. . . . The Dude among the Brownies was always high in our estimation; he got in more difficulties than all the rest, and he gave us more amusement than any other. We loved him, although we would have been ashamed to admit it. (pp. 532-33)

"The Brownies," in The Outlook, *Vol. 137, No. 14, August 6, 1924, pp. 532-33.*

Current Opinion

Of the same tribe as Lewis Carroll and Joel Chandler Harris was Palmer Cox. . . . His Brownies belong with "Alice in Wonderland" and "Brer Rabbit." He opened up a new world to the imagination. From the time, forty-four years ago, when these elfs first appeared in the pages of *St.*

Nicholas magazine, his art has continued to make its own unique appeal. . . .

Strictly speaking, of course, Palmer Cox popularized, rather than created, the Brownies. . . . But in Cox's imagination they took on peculiar shapes and characters. . . .

The idea that haunted Cox was of serviceable Brownies. . . . Palmer Cox had the notion of democratizing the Brownie; this system of one Brownie to a family seemed to him to savor of special privilege. So he organized the Brownies—even socialized them—and sent them out to do good in the world. (p. 314)

> *"The Father of the Brownies," in* Current Opinion, *Vol. 77, September, 1924, pp. 314-15.*

Malcolm Douglas

[*Douglas provided the music for two stage plays written by Cox that were produced in 1894: the cantata* The Brownies in Fairyland *and* Palmer Cox's Brownies, *which was billed as a fairy spectacle; Cox's last book* The Brownies and Prince Florimel *(1918) was based on the plot of this play.*]

[The Brownies are] a very strange little band of night-sprites; tiny, neckless creatures with big ears, pop-eyes, wide, smiling mouths, fat, round paunches, spindling legs, and long, tapering feet. Fairies, goblins, gnomes, and other mythical characters had all been depicted before by many illustrators according to their fancies, but never Brownies. These queer little supernatural beings, with traits that irresistibly appealed to one's sense of the ridiculous, were absolutely the sole idea of their creator. . . . (p. 1288)

Palmer Cox loved all children. His life was consecrated to them. . . . (p. 1289)

Not long since the whole English-speaking world was grieved to hear of the passing away, in his Brownie Castle, of Palmer Cox. . . . But it is good to think that his life-work was fully completed, and there was nothing that he had left undone. In all the years to come his name will be associated with those of Hans Christian Andersen, the Brothers Grimm, and Lewis Carroll; for, like these others, he bestowed a priceless heritage on childhood. (p. 1290)

> *Malcolm Douglas, "Palmer Cox, the 'Brownie Man'," in* St. Nicholas, *Vol. LI, No. 12, October, 1924, pp. 1288-90.*

William Murrell

Palmer Cox had a lively comic talent before he invented the "Brownies" in 1883 and was thereafter condemned to ink them. . . . [In] his youth he went to San Francisco, tried his hand at many things, among them humorous drawing and verse-making, and came East in the early seventies after the *New York Daily Graphic* had accepted some of his work sent by mail. A few years later he was author and illustrator of **Hans von Pelter's Trip to Gotham**, **How Columbus Found America**, **That Stanley!**, and two collections of Western tales. His range included the wildest slapstick and the most delicate satire, and graphic humor lost "a fellow of constant jest and infinite variety"

when he limited himself to the Brownies and illustration for children's magazines. (p. 31)

For the readers of *St. Nicholas Magazine* in the early eighties, Palmer Cox invented his "Brownies," whose antics were followed with delight by at least two generations. The Brownies, impish-looking, wide-mouthed, oval-headed little fellows, came from Dunbrownie, North Britain, according to their author, and later they were joined by the O'Brownies from Ireland, the Brownskis from Russia, the Ah-Brown-Ees from China, and many others. And they greatly increased in numbers, although there was never a sign of a lady or an infant Brownie. But, as was hinted earlier, Palmer Cox was from now on a prisoner; neither the children nor the Brownies would allow him to escape, and while he may quite possibly have taken pride and pleasure in the joy he brought to hundreds of thousands of children, it is not improbable that he sighed for the good old days when he illustrated **Hans von Pelter, That Stanley!** and **How Columbus Found America.** (p. 103)

> *William Murrell, "Chapter II" and "Chapter V," in his* A History of American Graphic Humor (1865-1938), *1938. Reprint by Cooper Square Publishers, Inc., 1967, pp. 23-42, 85-106.*

M. McLeish

Does anyone now own a copy of **The Brownies** by Palmer Cox? No wonders of draughtsmanship nor of decoration here, but the marvellous undertakings of these little people are set out with a kind of painstaking pleasure. Every brownie may be known and the details of his adventures pored over with that gimlet-eyed attention to detail special to children. (p. 19)

> *M. McLeish, "Picture Books—Yesterday and To-day," in* The Junior Bookshelf, *Vol. 8, No. 1, March, 1944, pp. 16-22.*

Robert Lawson

Cox seems now quite forgotten; he is little mentioned in reference books, yet during his heyday the *Brownie Books* were tremendously popular with children. I cannot venture to say how good or bad they were artistically, but they had one quality which children love in their pictures and which no one else has quite approached. Each character of this large band was unmistakably drawn, was easily recognizable in every drawing, and was always consistent in behavior. Thus children could, and invariably did, identify each of the characters with someone they knew in real life and follow each one through all the various adventures. I can remember well with what joy we endowed the Dutchman, the Frenchman, the Dude and all the others with the identities of each other, our uncles, cousins, friends and playmates, and how eagerly we followed them throughout the book. (p. 113)

> *Robert Lawson, "Howard Pyle and His Times," in* Illustrators of Children's Books, 1774-1945, *edited by Bertha E. Mahony, Louise Payson Latimer, and Beulah Folmsbee, The Horn Book Inc., 1947, pp. 103-22.*

Rita S. Gottesman

Palmer Cox was the Walt Disney of his day. His drawings of animated animals led to many orders for advertising illustrations, but his first ideas were soon superseded by an even more ingenious one. In 1883 he created the Brownies, performers of good deeds merely for the joy of doing good. He drew his Brownies with pop-eyes to show keen vision. He gave them big ears to signify sharp hearing. He made their stomachs round so they appeared comfortable and well fed. Their spindly legs and long tapering feet indicated that they were fleet of foot. With these little figures Palmer Cox added rhymes that sold many products. (p. 42)

> *Rita S. Gottesman, "Early Commercial Art," in* Art in America, *Vol. 43, No. 4, December, 1955, pp. 34-42, 55.*

May Hill Arbuthnot

Small children are generally not assumed to see details in a picture, but they do. For the older generation, half the charm of the pictures in the Palmer Cox Brownie books lay in their details. The illustrations seemed to have hundreds of Brownies, each doing something different, but every child always looked for his favorites, the Dude or the Policeman or the Cowboy. (p. 24)

Although neither great literature nor art, these books have a charm that their descendants, the comics, have never achieved. (p. 59)

> *May Hill Arbuthnot, "The Adult and the Child's Books" and "The Artist and the Child's Books," in her* Children and Books, *third edition, Scott, Foresman and Company, 1964, pp. 16-29, 52-75.*

Museum News

The Brownies are back, and Dover's got 'em. And for a sales desk item or a library must, order your copy [of ***The Brownies: Their Book***] right away. . . .

The Brownies: Their Book was the first of the Brownie books, and some consider it the best. Twenty-four of the free spirits' adventures are catalogued—all refreshing and nostalgic. All, of course, are illustrated by the author and just the sight of the pictures are enough to bring back a flood of memories. . . .

[The innocent Brownie tales are] often corny, always with a not-so-hidden moral. Still, maybe that's not so bad after all.

> *N. C. B., in a review of "The Brownies: Their Book," in* Museum News, *Vol. 44, No. 9, May, 1966, p. 38.*

The Junior Bookshelf

First published in the late nineteenth century, when it was received with great pleasure, [***The Brownies at Home***] is the third book of the Brownie adventures to be reprinted in [the] attractive and interesting paperback series [published by Dover]. The Brownies had a great appeal for the children of those days, but it is doubtful whether the present generation will react to the tale—told in rhyming couplets—of their escapades in the same way. The verse, and the very detailed black-and-white drawings are so unlike children's books of to-day that it is unlikely that the majority of children will appreciate the art that went into their creation. To the student of children's literature, however, this book like many others in the Dover series, is of considerable interest.

> *A review of "The Brownies at Home," in* The Junior Bookshelf, *Vol. 33, No. 2, April, 1969, p. 96.*

Elizabeth Nesbitt

To many middle-aged people, the mention of Palmer Cox's ***The Brownies: Their Book*** calls up an astonishingly clear memory of the pages of the picture books which showed the adventures of the brownies at home and abroad. These books had tremendous popularity which must have been due to the pictures, since they are remembered vividly, while the text and its content are forgotten, except for the fact that the text is in verse. Cox took the habits of his brownies from folklore, in that they "delight in harmless pranks and helpful deeds [and] work and sport while many households sleep." He adds a novel touch in the individualization he imparts to them. . . . It is probable that each child has his favorite and experiences a thrill of satisfaction as he finds that particular brownie in every picture, proof that Palmer Cox was wise in the ways of children. The large pictures and the little merry sketches of single brownies, caught in all sorts of postures and actions, have a fascination difficult to capture in words. It is something akin to the spell exerted by *The Night Before Christmas,* a thrill that only a child can experience. Yet once experienced, the feel of it is never forgotten, and an adult, turning the pages of the Brownie books, comes close to recapturing, for a moment, that lovely excitement which he felt as a child. (p. 371)

> *Elizabeth Nesbitt, "The March of Picture Books," in* A Critical History of Children's Literature *by Cornelia Meigs and others, edited by Cornelia Meigs, revised edition, Macmillan Publishing Company, 1969, pp. 369-76.*

Kirkus Reviews

Still satisfyingly tall and well-versed after almost a hundred years, [***Bugaboo Bill***] is the tale from *St. Nicholas* magazine about how some put-upon farmers finally rally to rid themselves of "A daring marauder, as strong as a moose, / Who lived on the best that the land could produce." Come each season's harvest, he'd head from his hill (where the sign reads, without any fanfare, 'B. Bill'), till "At length one remarked, who had studied his case: / 'No giant so strong but he has a weak place— / . . . / Now try a new method—invite him to dine: / Bring forth tempting dishes and flagons of wine, / . . . / And when he grows drowsy, as surely he will, / We'll easily manage this Bugaboo Bill.' " So they do, inventively (also charitably), by flying him off in "a monster balloon": "They

Brownie Castle, Granby, Quebec. Cox designed this home and had his studio in the tower.

never discovered, and little they cared / In what place he alighted, or just how he fared." The last picture carries another sign, 'Castle for rent,' typifying [illustrator William Curtis] Holdsworth's reserve: since *The Gingerbread Boy* and *The Little Red Hen* his soft greys have taken on more modulation and the composition here is solid, figures more defined; but his drawings still bespeak uncommon deference to the text's inherent humor—even his giant is not so much large as the various farmers are small. The restraint by itself is a sight for young eyes bored to tears or sore to saturation with the more exploitative design techniques.

> *A review of "Bugaboo Bill," in* Kirkus Reviews, *Vol. XXXIX, No. 6, March 15, 1971, p. 285.*

Marilyn McCulloch

Unfortunately, the poem [in *Bugaboo Bill*] is not written in a style which would appeal to young readers of today. And, the pictures are not sufficient to redeem it: the giant himself is not large enough in comparison with the size of the villagers, and hence the ending and his banishment via balloon are simply not believable. On the whole, an unnecessary item for any library.

> *Marilyn McCulloch, in a review of "Bugaboo Bill," in* School Library Journal, *Vol. 17, No. 8, April, 1971, p. 123.*

Roger W. Cummins

From ancient lore and from the Grampian legends he had heard as a child, Palmer Cox took the Brownies, individualized them, and made them a part of the contemporary scene. (p. 55)

Cox emphasized the best qualities found in the legendary brownie, and although he never alludes directly to the origin of his own Brownies in the stories, there are a few indications of their heritage. Each Brownie book begins with a foreword describing their habits: "BROWNIES, like fairies and goblins, are imaginary little sprites, who are supposed to delight in harmless pranks and helpful deeds. They work and sport while weary households sleep, and never allow themselves to be seen by mortal eyes." In the third Brownie book, *The Brownies at Home,* this foreword is preceded by a drawing of a Brownie in Scottish costume, holding an open book entitled *Old Scotch Traditions,* and in a later Brownie book, *The Brownies' Many More Nights,* the foreword is surrounded by torn pages on which appear words such as "Middle Ages," "Old Folk Lore," "Brownies," "Goblins," "Elves," "Old Traditions," "Tenth Century." Although his Brownies followed contemporary trends, they never lost sight of their ancestral beginnings.

As Cox developed his own Brownies, he retained characteristics found in the brownies of folklore, but he made notable changes. Whereas the Scottish brownie is usually a solitary being who remains in one household performing his domestic chores or field work, Cox's Brownies are gregarious, always banding together and moving from place to place for their frolics and deeds of kindness. In these respects they resemble the Cornish piskies (pixies) who, although more mischievous, also live in groups, travel about, and occasionally do helpful deeds. (pp. 62-3)

Rather than confine themselves to domestic work, Palmer Cox's Brownies spend much of their time cavorting and frolicking, engaging in a variety of sports, games, new adventures, and other activities, as well as traveling extensively. This is not to say that they disdain lowly tasks or disregard the needs of others. Quite the contrary, "They're not above the humblest deeds / They think the situation needs." Hearing of someone in want or dire circumstances, they are quick to respond, in spite of discomfort or danger, and they desire no reward: "Do good for goodness' sake always, / Not for reward on earth, or praise."

Cox gave his Brownies distinctive personalities. Much of the success of his books can be attributed to his treatment of the characters, who portray human nature with its goodness and strength and also its follies, but never its baseness. (p. 63)

The Brownies in the first stories were slender creatures, some with bald heads, curly antennae, and in general all alike. Only two were different from the others, the twins—bearded old men with wrinkled faces who always participated in the activities of the band and displayed a solicitous attitude toward the other members. They continued to appear throughout all the Brownie books. After the twins, the Dude, Chinaman, and Irishman were the earliest distinctive Brownies to emerge. Gradually new characters with expressive faces and appropriate attire were added, until numerous nationalities and vocations were represented. Among these were a Scotsman in native regalia, a soldier with precise military bearing, a policeman with a big stick who was popular with the boys, a sailor, an American Indian, a clown, an Arab and a Turk in colorful garb, a Japanese, an Eskimo, a German, and a Dutchman. The Brownie Cowboy, one of the later characters to be added, was proposed by Theodore Roosevelt, who was a follower and admirer of Cox's Brownie band.

The Brownies were eager to investigate anything new. During the last two decades of the nineteenth century the velocipede or bicycle began to enjoy a remarkable popularity, especially after the Centennial Exposition of 1876 in Philadelphia. . . . With characteristic alertness to current interests, Palmer Cox had the Brownies riding bicycles as early as November, 1885. Likewise, when automobiles were entering the American scene, a full page illustration by Cox appeared in *Century Magazine* of August, 1902, showing Brownies driving, repairing, having collisions, or simply riding along as they tried out the new machines.

When travel by air was still a novelty, the Brownies built their own airship (1893) "made with wings and tail and all / To steer its way through roughest squall" to cross the English Channel. While some members of the band were fearful and preferred not to go to France "than there in such a fixture get / That has not been perfected yet," the more persistent prevailed and landing was made safely. Had Cox lived in the 1960's he very likely would have had the Brownies traveling to the moon. That he did not is wholly characteristic: he preferred throughout his work not to write pure fantasy but to make those features of the times which were new—and sometimes mysterious—familiar and believable for his young readers.

Fewer than ten years after the completion of the Brooklyn Bridge, Cox writes a story about it, **'The Brownies in June'**. . . . Both his drawing of the bridge, festooned with Brownies, and the detailed description of their investigation of its features would have taught a child much about this marvel of the age. . . . (pp. 64-6)

Contemporary as they might be and far removed from the brown and shaggy creatures of legend, the Cox Brownies possess supernatural gifts which they use with ease:

> A shovel little wonder brings
> When in the human hand it swings
> But in a Brownie's hands—ah me!
> A different touch we see. . . .

If they use a householder's supplies, more is replaced than taken:

> The miller never missed his flour,
> For Brownies hold a mystic power:
> Whate'er they take they can restore
> In greater plenty than before.

This mystic power is never misused and is limited. The Brownies could not wish themselves in a different place and immediately find themselves there; initiative, ingenuity, and industriousness are always necessary.

The Brownies are childlike in enthusiasm and love of fun and adventure, yet they display mature judgment and live by certain laws (one of which requires them to return to their own habitation by dawn). Thoroughly honest, they never condone malicious deception. This integrity dominates their activities. . . . They nourish a spirit of fortitude in the face of danger and bear misfortunes without complaint. . . . Other distinguishing characteristics are courage and loyalty which lead to democratic conclusions. . . . (pp. 66-8)

Conventional morality and standards of conduct prevail in the world of the Brownies. Children who carefully read about the Brownies learned that it was important to make proper use of their time, to realize that the world can be marked by misfortune ("Few joys through life one may obtain / That are not balanced well with pain"), to practice the customary virtues, and to do good. But Cox kept the Brownies from seeming priggish or stuffy by never permitting the moral lessons and serious reflections drawn from their experiences to detract from the spirit of merriment and good fellowship. Readers could admire them and identify themselves with them, for the Cox Brownies were neither impossibly good nor drearily decorous.

They could succumb to very human temptations, as when in an Irish bay, eyeing the fishermen's nets hanging to dry, they feel the urge

To shoot the net and make a haul,
In fact, so strong temptation pressed,
They yielded, as might well be guessed;
For Brownies are like mortals still,
In reason strong, but weak of will.

On a visit to the White House they try out the "bed of state" gleefully until it breaks down with their weight. True to character, they reconstruct it in spite of confusion and injuries, and afterwards they discuss the results of superficial aims. Yet the moral maxims which conclude the story grow naturally from it, and there is no feeling that it was written to teach a lesson. What emerges from all of the Brownie tales is nothing strident, prescriptive, or condemnatory, but something gentle and humane:

Whatever gives a lift or start
To any enterprise or art,
Seems to the Brownie's helpful mind
A chance to benefit mankind.

Palmer Cox took the small, brown creatures of Scottish folklore and transformed them into engaging, merry beings. They retained that chief Brownie trait of their predecessors, helpfulness, but they united a beneficent cast of mind with a delight in simple pleasures and adventures and had become part of the modern age. For his thousands of readers, the combination proved irresistible—after years of obscurity he became a person known to children and their elders throughout the world. (pp. 69-70)

Designed in a deluxe format that is aesthetically pleasing, [*The Brownies, Their Book*] and its successors have exceptionally attractive, classic title pages, many illustrations, and wide margins which, especially in later volumes, are embellished with Brownies in typical poses. The books are a delight to behold as well as to read. (p. 76)

A striking aspect of the entire series of Brownie stories is the degree to which they appeal not only to a child's love of adventure and fun, but to his natural curiosity, his sense of history, and his intellect. Cox inculcated an appreciation of nature, a respect for the literature, art, and handiwork of mankind in former ages, and an interest in contemporary life. An attentive child learned much geography and history. . . . But names of people, events, and places of historical significance arise naturally from the tales themselves. There are never simple narrations of facts or tedious passages of elaboration and clarification; neither is there a patronizing tone. Cox respected the minds of his readers and was likely to leave it to the child himself to seek further information about subjects of the stories. When the Brownies play at being actors and when they visit Scotland, Cox assumes his readers' familiarity with the literature:

'T was strange to see old Egypt's queen,
Macbeth, and Trilby in one scene.
But what cared they for day or date,
Or mixing early scenes with late?
'T was fine to stalk like Banquo's ghost;
Like bulky Falstaff drink and boast;
Like Hamlet leap into the grave. . . .
They traveled many miles to see
Where Macbeth met the witches three
While he returned from battle-plain
A hero free from sinful stain.

The factual and educational aspects of the books become more pronounced in some of the later stories. In these tales, too, there is less emphasis on the Brownies' having to disappear into the forest at daybreak, and by the seventh book, *The Brownies in the Philippines,* each adventure ends on its own terms with no mention of quasi-magical disappearance. Knowing that the illustrations held great interest for even the youngest children, Cox perhaps intentionally made the subject matter more stimulating for older children as he watched his first readers mature. The humor, also, becomes slightly more sophisticated in later stories.

Humor, sometimes gentle, sometimes satirical, is present throughout Cox's writings. Referring to *The Brownies, Their Book* as "one of the first humorous American children's books," May Hill Arbuthnot says in her study of children's literature that "cheerfulness" became more and more dominant in books written for children during the nineteenth century. Cox was in the vanguard of his times. At the conclusion of one story three Brownies hold up a plaque which reads, "We've had enough of this story." While the Brownies cling perilously to a raft, the reader learns:

"The artist paints and poet raves
About the ocean's tinted waves,
But, let me tell you, when you stand
'Twixt sky and water, far from land,
With gales behind and squalls before,
And angry ocean in full roar,
You're not so likely to 'enthuse'
About its 'cradles,' or its hues."

No matter what the occasion, Cox could find a phrase which would amuse, delight, and instruct. . . . To the Brownie stories he brought a kindly, refreshing humor and a freedom of imagination that helped mark a new era in writing for children. The Brownie books were to achieve a permanent place in the world of children's literature. (pp. 83-6)

[From] beginning to end the Brownie books consist of dialogue, interspersed with matter of fact comment that never bores, and extraordinary pictures. Children too young to read were as entranced by the pictures as were their older brothers and sisters, who could follow the text. (p. 111)

There are several reasons for the Brownies' capturing the United States and other countries to an extent that was unprecedented. Foremost, perhaps, is that Cox was incapable of condescension. What distinguishes his work from that of many of his contemporaries is the sustained, straightforward tone that eschews all forms of coyness and makes no false appeals to the emotions. Despite his wishing to write stories with morals, stories that would inculcate good actions, the morals or lessons never obtrude. Instead, his readers are presented with a direct, quick-paced narrative which is easy to understand, never extended to dreary lengths, focused on a specific topic, and couched in rhyming verses which, if predictable in their rhythms, are pleasing to the ear. Not the least among Cox's gifts was his ability to write story after story, year after year, in verses which, however similar in form, are carefully crafted and read well aloud. Cox does not strive for special effects: it was enough to state as clearly and simply as possible what he wanted to say. What he wanted to say was what his young readers wanted to hear.

The Brownie band is thoroughly democratic. Except in *Palmer Cox's Brownies* (the play), *The Brownies and Prince Florimel*, and *The Brownie Clown of Brownietown*, none of the group is singled out as a permanent commander, leader, or guide. The Brownie Policeman, moreover, is scarcely a figure of fearsome authority but simply another member of the band. Through the Brownies a child learned that it was possible for a group of disparate members—the range of nationalities and occupations is large—to live together in harmony. Indeed, the very differences among the Brownies constitute a major source for the gaiety and happiness of the band. Though the Brownies are apolitical and emerge nightly from a region which is never geographically defined, to anyone who reads even a few of the Brownie books it is obvious that the world of the Brownies not only is utopian but embodies characteristics commonly associated with the American dream. The Brownies are not brothers of Pollyanna, and Cox never becomes saccharine, but there is no death or sickness in the world he describes, and happiness prevails in a democratic setting. The happiness does not come easily at all times, but the Brownies believe in working for the common good while retaining their individuality, and their efforts result in felicity: the Brownies embody the American dream of combining individualism with the idea of the good society. By not insisting on their Americanism, however, by not making explicit what so often is implicit, Cox gave the Brownies wider appeal.

He also realized that children might tire of books which showed nothing but an harmonious group performing kind deeds. The Brownies do become afraid on occasion, and Cox was astute in not avoiding such episodes: children were far more likely to identify themselves with (and thereby learn from) creatures who face at least some perils and difficulties than with those who perpetually smile.

The books are full of accidents, mistakes, and uncertainties. In the *Brownie Year Book* alone there are several major mishaps: in January, a toboggan laden with Brownies goes awry and Brownies are thrown in all directions; in February, twelve Brownies fall through the ice while skating; in June, a boat filled with Brownies capsizes on a rock at the edge of a waterfall; and in July, a hammock packed with Brownies breaks open in the middle. The world of the Brownies, to be sure, is not entirely realistic, and none of them is seriously hurt. The Dude may need a bandage, but readers knew that no matter what the appearances, the Brownies would all be alive and well for their next adventure. The hardships and calamities they face, moreover, are generally natural ones, not the result of man's inhumanity to man. Cox himself said:

> One thing . . . I resolved on was that my work for children would always have happy endings. So if the cat was chasing the mouse, I would let them hustle around for a bit, maybe, but the mouse would always escape in the end. I would let the cat go hungry rather than have the mouse eaten. It is time enough for children when they get big to learn that a reckoning must be made with suffering and bloodshed.

The lives of the Brownies, nonetheless, are full of realistic misadventure.

If the world of the Brownies is not entirely like that of their readers—and that it is not is part of its obvious appeal—it is, nevertheless, not a false version of the world the children know. Cox felt that stories for children should be happy and not emphasize cruelty, but he does not imply that unpleasantness does not exist. It exists, the Brownies discover, but it can be rectified. Cox's stories, furthermore, do not suggest that one receives rewards by doing good. From some of the children's literature of the day, a reader might deduce that by living a wholesome life one would receive money, acclaim, or both. The ethic in the Brownie stories is very different and resembles a traditional religious distinction: one does good and refrains from doing evil not because of the consequences but from the love of the good itself. The Brownies would have been happier as friends of Robin Hood than of the good boys in the Horatio Alger books.

There is no sentimentality in Cox's world and what poignancy exists comes not from the Brownies' everyday experiences but from their contemplation of past times. Whimsy is tempered by common sense. The supernatural is unobtrusive, and nothing is cloying. Cox never goes to the point of saying that there are Brownies at the bottom of the garden. By not insisting on their supernatural powers—the adjective seems almost peculiar in reference to them—Cox made them particularly accessible to his young readers. Their enormous inquisitiveness and their readiness to try anything once, no matter how unsuited they might be for it, made their view of the world much like that of their admirers. The world of the Brownies is appealing, happy, joyful. It is also believable. (pp. 113-16)

In diverging from the traditional brownie of legend and folktale, Cox showed an understanding of the minds of children, an acute awareness of the needs of the age, and sound judgment. That extraordinary English illustrator, George Cruikshank, had helped bring fairies to the forefront, and in the British Isles and America, children's stories about supernatural beings received increasing favor. By the time Cox introduced his Brownies, fairies were not unusual on the pages of children's literature. His genius lay in recognizing that neither more beautiful, ethereal, almost transparent winged creatures, nor more gnarled and oddly grotesque gnomes were required. In the growing plethora of children's books there was a need for something which appealed to the imagination and yet which allowed children to identify themselves to some degree with the creatures in front of them. The Brownies supplied that need. (pp. 116-17)

The Cox Brownies are all good creatures and their stories inculcate sound virtues, but they do not insist on their goodness; they are not heroes who ostentatiously point to virtues—indeed, the heroism exists on a small scale—and much of the time they engage simply in adventures and merry games. The Brownies provided children with a world which was close to their own but more fascinating.

From Another Brownie Book, *written and illustrated by Palmer Cox.*

This was the point: Cox had created an entire world—compelling, distinct, and unique.

By following his instincts about what children liked rather than what they were supposed to like, by refusing to make the magic and the folklore itself paramount in his stories, and by giving free play to his imagination without making the stories confusingly subtle or over-elaborate, Cox established a special place for himself among children's writers. His achievement rests not only on the concept of the Brownies and the stories themselves, however, but upon that accomplishment for which he would be best remembered: his drawings.

Speaking of illustrations he had drawn many years before, Cox said in 1918, "I think my natural gift ran more in that direction, but writing was forced upon me, on account of the need of something to illustrate." He probably was right. More than one of his readers has wondered what direction his talents might have taken had the Brownie books not been so popular. Once the series started, he drew and wrote about almost nothing else but Brownies for the rest of his life. The last Brownies he portrayed show all of their characteristics as clearly and deftly as had the first.

Superb illustrators of children's literature abounded in the nineteenth century: Randolph Caldecott, Walter Crane, George Cruikshank, A. B. Frost, Kate Greenaway, E. W. Kemble, Howard Pyle, Arthur Rackham, Frederick Remington, Sir John Tenniel. To this distinguished list Cox belongs. But for the work of some of these persons, and certainly for Cox, the term 'illustrated book' is a misnomer:

the texts, like those of Beatrix Potter, cannot be separated from the drawings.

A primary reason for the enormous success of the Brownies is the skillful joining of picture and words. Without the illustrations the tetrameter couplets would have become tedious; without a text, the illustrations could not have been extended indefinitely. Together they formed a wholly complementary unit, and a happy one for children's books. Who can think of the Pooh stories, after all, without remembering E. H. Shepard's illustrations? But unlike A. A. Milne books, the Brownie episodes needed drawings to give them real substance, and Cox's illustrations showed an infinite variety. Readers would watch for their favorite Brownies in new situations, which appeared to be endless. (pp. 117-18)

[Cox's] attention to detail is unerring. A typical Cox drawing is filled with Brownies, yet each one seems individually drawn. All appear to be participating in the scene, and the foreground is always full. The world of the Brownie is convivial, gregarious, and festive. The Brownie physiognomy would not suggest much possibility for variation, yet Cox gave his Brownies distinctive personalities. From consternation to eagerness, their faces show a wide range of emotional response. The constant variations in mood through facial expression and bodily movement had much to do in sustaining a reader's interest.

Cox preferred to lead rather than to challenge the imagination. He is matter-of-fact, straightforward, clear. He does not portray dream-like settings, nor is he impressionistic, and he does little with backgrounds or landscapes. Probably he was incapable of drawing a cherubic child. His is not the English countryside and garden mellowness of a Beatrix Potter or the ethereal enchantment and mystery of an Arthur Rackham. There is nothing haunting, sad, or ominous in Cox's pictures. There is much that is merry, surprising, and joyful. And whatever the drawing, it perfectly fits the text.

Cox holds a special place among writers and illustrators. Successfully to write books and also to illustrate them is a rare accomplishment. Some exceptions come to mind—Thackeray and Howard Pyle, Beatrix Potter and Hugh Lofting, to name disparate examples—but seldom have the pen and the drawing pencil been so complementary. To his gifts as a caricaturist and illustrator Cox had added his abilities as a poet and his memories of stories told to him as a child. The combination was felicitous.

In writing and illustrating children's books which were designed to appeal to the imagination rather than explicitly to instruct, to be primarily enjoyed rather than studied, Cox takes his place with other nineteenth-century authors who were gradually and sometimes splendidly breaking the hold of pure didacticism on literature for children, and he stands as a precursor of later writers who have established 'children's literature' as a distinctive genre. A pertinent parallel may be drawn between Cox and Theodore Seuss Geisel: both affirm, in their works, the validity of verse as a wholly appropriate form of narration for children, and in the Cox Brownie books as in the Dr. Seuss books a sense of the unity of text and illustration obtains.

Indeed, although the contents of the Brownie books differ considerably from those of Dr. Seuss's, and though Geisel is more experimental in language, both of these author-illustrators have created a literature based on non-didactic fantasy, and the enormous popularity of Dr. Seuss's series of illustrated books is strongly reminiscent of the enthusiasm generated by Cox's books from the eighties on.

Though the world of Cox's Brownies lacks the subtlety and intellectual brilliance of Alice's and that mixture of splendor, vision, and the commonplace which permeates the world of Rat, Mole, and Toad, Cox, like the best of children's writers, knew that to let the fancy roam was a noble and necessary activity. Fantasy and everyday life, impossibilities and simple pleasures were so intertwined in the Brownie stories that the result was enchanting and believable. Like Lewis Carroll, Kenneth Grahame, A. A. Milne, Hugh Lofting, and Frank Baum, Cox achieved that unusual feat of filling a landscape with rare beings of his own creation, endowing them with distinguishing characteristics, and showing that a literature of the imagination can exist in its own right. (pp. 118-20)

> *Roger W. Cummins, in his* Humorous but Wholesome: A History of Palmer Cox and The Brownies, *Century House Americana Publishers, 1973, 254 p.*

David Kunzle

[*The following excerpt is from a review of the biography* Humorous but Wholesome: A History of Palmer Cox and the Brownies *by Roger W. Cummins.*]

The fame of Palmer Cox, very considerable in his lifetime, lasted in diminished form up to World War II. His critical reputation has since radically declined; he has received only cursory notices in recent major manuals of the history of children's literature. Undoubtedly much critical resurrection of the classic children's artists and writers remains to be done; biographies and critiques are lacking for many of Cox's contemporaries whose work has stood the test of time better than his, e.g., Walter Crane, Kate Greenaway, or Arthur Rackham. Unfortunately, scrutiny of children's literature has been inhibited by the fear that any kind of "scientific analysis" would break the magic spell, or by the belief that stringent criteria for literary and artistic merit are inapplicable to the "intuitive" and "childlike" genius that supposedly generates the best juvenile literature. (p. 454)

Even a superficial comparison of Cox's work with that of his contemporaries shows his production, verse and pictures alike, to be rather flat. The verse is not unskilled, but it is wholly uninventive and, for a humorist, singularly lacking in the slightest hint of wit. One supposes that Cox provided the standard fare of the children's magazines of the period. His style is monotonous, heavy, and didactic. . . . Indeed, in the light of the innovations of the 1860's pioneered by Lewis Carroll—simpler language, playfulness, and amorality—Cox's constant interjection of moral tags appears downright retrograde. Many Brownie Book pages recall the walls of some early Victorian orphanage, with moral exhortations posted about gratuitously and adventitiously. Some of the slogans promote

the fiercest kind of Victorian bourgeois-capitalist morality: "The World is cold / to those who fail / So keep your hold with tooth and nail"; or, "Be fair but foremost in the race / And having won it hold your place."

Cummins does not offer a relative evaluation of verse and drawings, preferring to fall back on the familiar notions of "inseparability" and "interdependence"; these are always convenient when neither text nor illustration is demonstrably superior. But it is easy to imagine that young children, ignoring the text, were held by the drawings, which do have a kind of hypnotic charm that, to the modern adult eye, quickly palls. Cox was certainly no good draftsman. His line is slack, his shading messy, his lighting non-existent. He neither models nor composes: he simply amasses, deliberately, I think, and consciously excluding all pictorial "magic" effects. His Brownies are neither in form nor character supernatural creatures. They continue a process of demythification that began pictorially in mid-century with Richard Doyle, whose pretty style broke with the spooky effects conjured up by George Cruikshank in his famous illustrations to Grimm. Traditionally fairies are creatures able to straddle two worlds, the supernatural and human, investing the human with signs of powers derived from the supernatural. Palmer Cox, concentrating exclusively upon a sub-species of fairy noted for its human-domestic virtues, subjects it to a strictly human process of socialization and thereby robs the fairy world of its magical powers and appearances. His Brownies are wholly mundane, and, stripped of their supernatural powers, they deny those very forms of imaginative escape that may be considered the quintessence of fairy literature. These are Brownies bent upon the accumulation of worldly Brownie Points.

Cox must be one of the very few successful children's illustrators who shows no interest in the depiction of non-human nature. His Brownies theoretically return after each episode to whence they theoretically came, to some non-human environment. That they are so rarely shown disporting themselves in forest, mountain, or meadow is an index of the completeness of their urbanization, and, presumably, of that of their audience. Cox was more interested in the depiction of architecture and machinery: typically the Brownies pit themselves against machinery. When he is unable to avoid a natural environment, Cox becomes extremely perfunctory, although early drawings indicate that he was quite good at animals, which, unfortunately, he seldom drew once he was cast as the Brownie-master. One is tempted to compare Cox with the slightly younger master of fairy illustration, Arthur Rackham, who gave common things a "magical" vibrancy and conceived nature as a fount of wonder. Not only Rackham, but Walter Crane, Kate Greenaway, and Howard Pyle all show much superior sensitivity to the particular character of environments. But perhaps the comparison is unfair; after all, the environments of these other artists are literally colored, while Cox's remain black and white. The mundanity of Cox's vision might have been relieved had he had the opportunity to work in color. Cummins ignores the anomalous fact that this major children's writer and illustrator worked almost exclusively in black and white in the 1880's and 1890's, the very time when the color picture-book was making unprecedented technical and artistic advances. One may speculate whether, once harnessed to the cheaper book market, he had no escape; the sociological implications would be worth pursuing.

The word "cute," popularized in the United States at this time, originally meant smart (via "acute"); more recently it has come to mean childish charm. Both senses of "cute" spring to mind in describing Brownie physiognomy: neither really ugly nor pretty, just cute, all of them, unchangeably, hypnotically, all the time, with the same kind of cuteness. Like the formula for Disney cuteness, that of the Brownies is easy for children to imitate graphically. The formula may be one key to their success, and the formula does not, cannot, change. It is noteworthy that from this period onwards children's literature, like modern popular literature of all sorts, is governed by the principle of inertia; characters are immobilized in their original form for a generation and more. So it was with Palmer Cox.

The monotony that we experience as we pass from book to book and illustration to illustration also extends to the illustrations taken singly. Essentially the Brownies are a numerous band, but Cox never masses or scales or relates them to the background in an interesting way. For all the variety of their activities, they always move in amorphous blobs. They have no leader, no hierarchy. The principle of egalitarianism that governs them prevents any single Brownie from ever stepping into the foreground, from aspiring to command attention or give direction. Compositionally they are anarchists; politically, primitive communists. Physically and physiognomically identical, the Brownies suffer from great pathognomic inflexibility; they have basically only four expressive rictusses, of fear, surprise, glumness, and pleasure, for which the tiny scale may in part be responsible. Worse is the limitation that Cox placed on the Brownies' freedom of action. He rarely thinks up witty exploits or funny predicaments for individual figures. Their relation to a situation always remains general, never sharpened in particular and personal ways. Notwithstanding Cummins's unexplained assertion that the Brownies "retain their individuality in their actions," they behave like sheep.

Within their identical basic physical data, the Brownies are distinguished from each other only by their clothing, which marks them as an international, ethnically diverse band. This is generally cited as Cox's most original trait and the one which facilitated identification on the part of children. The Brownies' internationalism is indeed perhaps the single most culturally revealing factor in Cox's work, but comment upon this is conspicuous by its absence from Cummins's book. Onto an old folk and broadsheet tradition of representing the various estates or professions, Cox grafted a new, global range of ethnic types, recognizable, like the professions, by symbolic costume: Arab, East Indian, Red Indian, Chinese, Russian, Irishman, Eskimo, etc. The whole ethnic world is here but for one major and significant omission, the Negro. Before Helen Bannerman had made a Little Black Sambo acceptable to infant whites, the black man was apparently too real and too problematic for inclusion in the merry and harmonious band of Brownies. Another but different

omission from this "model society" is the female. It would be ironic indeed—but perhaps fitting from a feminist viewpoint—if the choice of the name "Brownie" for the youngest Girl Scouts were connected with Cox's all-male band, by far the most famous group operating under that name at the time the Girl Scout movement was started.

The internationalism of the Brownie band is almost exclusively expressed in the illustrations, it is seldom picked up in the verses and it does not provide for individualization of activity. Thus one might argue that the ethnic costuming signified nothing more than relief of the monotony of form. Such a view, however, would ignore the ultimate purpose of Cox's work, which is the same as that of *St. Nicholas,* the magazine in which the Brownies began and always first appeared.

St. Nicholas was expressly designed to foster "patriotism, home, nature and truth, . . . to prepare boys and girls for life as it is, . . . to stimulate ambition." In the later 19th century this purpose and these terms implied, among other things, belief in the "manifest destiny" of the United States, towards international influence and expansion. It is no accident that the absorption of massive waves of foreign immigrants and the fervor for annexation of the Philippines, Cuba, and Panama run parallel to the popularity of the international band of Brownies. With no more conscious intent to politicize children than the parents who bought and read aloud the stories, in 1904 Cox devoted a whole book to the Brownies in the Philippines, recruiting for the purpose a new Brownie, a Rough Rider bespectacled like the hero of the new expanding empire, Theodore Roosevelt. In the pages of *St. Nicholas,* cheek by jowl with Cox, whom he admired, Roosevelt himself wrote in celebration of the extermination of the buffalo; in the *Winning of the West,* which was also read by children, he justified the extermination of the Indian. The ruthless thrust for Empire was defended then, as now, as the generous sharing of the American democratic experience with the foreigner, as the solving of problems in happy mutuality. Cox illustrated the concept of universal brotherhood with Uncle Sam and Chinaman falling into the same rapids and helping each other out.

Even disregarding its internationalism, we can view the pluralistic, unstratified, leaderless Brownie society as a miniature ideal democracy, the kind towards which the United States was supposedly striving and, in the belief of many, nearly if not actually achieving. Children's literature in America was not a casual party to the creation of the American political mythology, for it offered in the view of a prominent historian of the United States and editor of two *St. Nicholas* anthologies [Henry Steele Commager], humanitarianism, equalitarianism, and "adventure that makes for . . . democracy." This contrasts with the class-biased, ethnocentric, and chauvinistic children's literature in England at the same period.

The Brownies are utopian democracy in action. They are constantly engaged in socially improving works, and if the poor hover in the background somewhere, they are there because there must be people to improve. Brownies do not need to quarrel, for their interests are the same. They applaud their agreement and the superfluity of debate:

" 'You speak our minds so full and fair / One loudly cried, 'that speech we'll spare.' " The superfluousness of the remark is as typical of Cox as is its elegant and archaic phrasing. Without sparing speech himself, Cox occasionally criticizes what he evidently considers an endemic fault of American democracy: the tendency to talk instead of act. He conjures up a political utopia where unity of purpose renders constant debate unnecessary: "But happily the Brownie band / Was under some mild system planned / With hearts and hopes and aims the same. / One has small reason to declaim / Or speechify to bring about / Sweet harmony ere they set out. / Oh, many a year and trying age / May pass away ere on the stage / Another band like them will rise. . . . "

Among authors for children, Cox was not of course alone in his internationalism. Global travelogue tales flowered in the 1880's and 1890's. But only in Cox do the foreigners become the protagonists. When they travel, the Brownies are good tourists in their own lands, for all lands are their lands. The Brownies assiduously gather scraps of local history and custom. (pp. 454-55)

Brownies show early symptoms of the tourist-collector-consumer syndrome, of the world as a supermarket-cum-junk-store where one shops for novelties.

Children's literature also served the expansion of consumer industries. Cox himself wrote and designed a number of advertisements, for soap, medicines, and other products, that featured the Brownies. They appeared on all manner of foodstuffs and household, nursery, and school-room articles. . . . The idea of the infant consumer lured by the bait of a favorite story-book character, which has since been exploited to such a horrendous degree, is regarded by Cummins with complaisance: "The Brownies smiled with *particular* warmth on the burgeoning world of American advertising" (my stress).

The chapter on Brownie merchandising closes on a description of Cox as "the Walt Disney of his day." This exalting allusion to that man of our times who has done more than any other to turn children into consumers and children's culture into merchandise opens up a whole Pandora's box of analogies and comparisons; these touch upon the tactics of cultural industries at different periods in the development of capitalism, and the ideology of different generations. Naturally we turn to Disney in search of characters whose innocence or apparent innocence may be compared with Cox's benign Brownies. In both, of course, infantile innocence is a mask for essentially adult preoccupations, for all children's literature is a projection of adult values and we can summarily dismiss the obvious nonsense of Cummins's statement that "what he [Cox] wanted to say was what his young readers wanted to hear." In both Cox and Disney, then, the moral characteristics are adult and so are the activities, usually some kind of contest, for mastery of a natural or mechanical obstacle in the case of Cox and for social dominance or wealth in the case of Disney. Adult characteristics are especially evident in those Disney comic-book characters capable of appealing to the relatively broad age-group reached by Cox, say four to twelve years, who are also the most baby-like in appearance: Donald Duck's little nephews, Huey,

Dewey, and Louie. Like the Brownies, they represent a kind of ideal cub-scout; like the Brownies they are democratic, for they have no leader and take all decisions by collective osmosis. Brownies and Ducks alike show industry and resourcefulness. These virtues constantly lead them into physical danger, which they courageously overcome. Wise beyond their apparent years, they are clearly designed to assure child-readers that they, too, will grow into masterful, independent adults. But there are major structural differences between Brownie and Duck society: where Huey, Dewey, and Louie, egalitarian among themselves, are in fact locked into a hierarchical and authoritarian family structure headed by the tyrant Uncle Scrooge, the Brownies are responsible to no one but themselves. They represent the concept of autonomous society and, at the same time of course, autonomous childhood, one that replicates but does not interact with the existing adult world. In this respect, they prefigure the happily adultless realms first created by Kenneth Grahame and Arthur Ransome. This difference reflects, I believe, a basic shift in social and political experience.

Absolute faith in the harmonious, universal enactment of democratic theory could still be professed in the late 19th century. By mid-20th century the culture of capitalist democracy had to defend a system rent by evident failures in practice, demonstrated by world wars, by revolutions, and in countless individual defeats. The comics of today,

Cox with a group of children in his studio at Brownie Castle.

Disney's included, have reflected the physical and social violence accompanying these failures. The physical violence in Cox is more farcical than painful or frightening, and it is never *social.* A profound cynicism also marks the Disney comic in the unremitting quest for status and gold, particularly acute in the most popular of all the series, *Uncle Scrooge,* where all activity and all the other personalities are subjected to the lusts of a tyrannical, capitalist multi-millionaire. Cox's Brownies live in a happily money-free, hatred-free, and envy-free society. Charitable, altruistic, and fun-oriented rather than goal-oriented, the Brownies decline material rewards; in this respect, they resemble Mickey Mouse rather than the Ducks. But Mickey is negatively defined as the opponent of omnipresent evil and crime. In their velvet three-fingered gloves, the heroes of Disney comics conceal the iron fist of a cynical and pessimistic bourgeois philosophy that assumes that greed rules the world. The Brownies posit a pre-bourgeois purity that in the Disney comics is projected onto the natives of the exotic lands visited by Mickey and Donald, usually in search of plunder. Cummins rightly stresses the altruism and moral purity of the Brownies, but he does so rather as if these same virtues had survived intact in children's literature today.

Understanding this, we can appreciate why it was possible in the 19th, but not in the mid-20th century, to incorporate the native and the foreigner into a collective leadership. The Brownie American and the Brownie Chinaman were posited as equal and compatible partners in improving and exploring the world. The myth has since been so shattered that not even the mass media can sustain it. Instead they establish a mythology of mortal conflict. Donald, Mickey, Superman, and Tintin are called to invade hostile territories fraught with criminality; they are locked in battle for control of wealth and world. They become part of a gigantic power struggle in which the true nature of the contestants is, as a rule, carefully masked. The Brownies did not seek power, either over each other or an outside world. They engaged in problem-solving, like learning to ride a bicycle, in an ambiance of relatively primitive technology and of relatively mild, human accident and natural mishap. They have neither the will nor the means for mass destruction. In an authentically positivist and optimistic spirit, with a genuine innocence, they believed that problems could be solved by the application of intelligence and altruism. And there seemed little, before 1914 and 1917, to prove them wrong. We need a greater virtue now than that of Brownie Points and greater intelligence than that which applies itself to technological problems. Nor does the solution lie in the super-virtues and super-science of the modern comic. (pp. 455-56)

> *David Kunzle, in a review of "Humorous But Wholesome: A History of Palmer Cox and the Brownies," in* The Art Bulletin, *Vol. LVII, No. 3, September, 1975, pp. 454-56.*

Margery Fisher

[The Brownies] are not at first sight obvious descendants of the traditional brownies of Scottish folk tale to whom the author had been introduced in his Canadian childhood. Certainly their mischievous, inquisitive natures belong to folk lore; they ride the farmer's mare by night, and in their role as helpers they harvest crops for a sick farmer and collect a winter's supply of wood for the parson. But their chief delight is to try out human sports and machines and to investigate the habits and imitate the customs of men. . . . Their grotesque appearance, with bulbous heads and skinny limbs, is as much a part of the humour as their lively facial expressions as they rush from one scene to another in a jostling, chattering horde. (p. 56)

> *Margery Fisher, "Who's Who in Children's Books: 'The Brownies'," in her* Who's Who in Children's Books: A Treasury of the Familiar Characters of Childhood, *Holt, Rinehart and Winston, 1975, pp. 54-6.*

Roy Nuhn

Nearly a century ago, the youthful readers of Mary Mapes Dodges' superb *St. Nicholas* magazine were treated for the first time to the wondrous adventures of a jolly, happy-go-lucky tribe of forest dwellers. . . . Appearing for the first time in the February, 1883 issue of America's leading juvenile publication, the Brownies caught the public's fancy like nothing had ever done before. The nation went Brownie-mad, unable to get enough to satisfy their appetite, devouring well over 1,000,000 copies of various Brownie books while eagerly awaiting each new episode of the elf-like creatures' adventures for the next 25 years in *St. Nicholas.* They spawned not only vast numbers of novelties, but lent their names to a host of products and things. Their heritage is still with us today whenever we speak of Kodak's Brownie box camera and the Girl Scouts' junior partners, the Brownies.

Palmer Cox's Brownies inspired many future illustrators and cartoonists, such as Rose O'Neill and her "Kewpieville," the Nimble Knicks from the Massachusetts-based publishing firm of Whitney, and a direct descendent, "The Teenies Weenies," a Sunday colored comic panel appearing during the 1940s. They are considered one of the significant forerunners of the comic strip itself.

Palmer Cox was a very talented illustrator, poet, and all-around good yarn spinner. He had a gift to be able to entertain, a gift that also brought him handsome rewards for his talent. His merchandising of the Brownie name would do proud any modern-day Madison Avenue advertising agency. (p. 90)

"The Brownies Ride" was Cox's first use of his elves and their arrival upon the American scene in that February, 1883, issue of *St. Nicholas* is a momentous event in the development of both comic art history and children's literature. These earliest Brownies were vastly different from even those who came a few months later. In that premier poem-story, they were without personality, most were naked, and they all lacked the characteristics and mannerisms later associated with them.

It took Palmer Cox only a few months to finalize his conception of his little people, and for the next quarter-century there were no dramatic changes.

Much discussion has been held in the past about the actual origins of the Brownies and the reasons for their name.

The best answer to both of these questions can be found in the October, 1910 issue of *St. Nicholas* . . . :

> Mr. Cox's interest in Brownies dates back to his boyhood days, when his Scotch-Canadian neighbors entertained him with folk-lore tales.

(pp. 91-2)

It took nearly three decades for these childhood experiences to surface in Cox's mind and be translated onto paper and into the hearts of this country's children, but when they were, a very important event occurred. The Brownies blossomed into delightful elfin beings, full of affection and warm humor. Their world was one without serious crime or trouble, only laughter and joy mixed with good fellowship. Cox truly loved and cherished each and every one of his Brownies, a fondness which is easily seen in all his work.

The Brownies lived in an imaginary, fantasy society that was at the same time separate, yet a part of our own. If they were not helping mankind in one way or the other, such as repairing an important dam or manufacturing babies' carriages in a factory closed-down, they visited the sea shore or toured American historical landmarks. In this way they were similar to Eaton's Roosevelt Bears (1906) and Cracker Jack's mischievous bears (1905).

All the Brownies looked alike—with their little paunches, matchstick legs and pointed toes—yet each had his own personality and characteristics, ones which were carried on for many years. The cast of characters exceeds fifty, and over the decades Cox continued to introduce them, one by one. There was the policeman, mayor, Indian, Uncle Sam, cowboy, Orientals, and many others who were actually a caricature microcosm of the real world. The Dude is generally recognized as being Teddy Roosevelt. At first, they were all males, as told by the ancient legends, but gradually a few females, such as a nurse, joined the band.

They were inimitable, pleasure loving, and helpful little elves who lived life to the fullest. They had no peers and were without equal anywhere. (pp. 92-3)

[From] the deep and mysterious forest strode the brave little tykes on daily missions to aid the human beings who lived near and around them, but were totally unaware of their existence. . . .

In his drawing of the Brownies, Cox paid much attention to each component part. Each and every elf was drawn as a separate work of art, and no detail was left incomplete or only partially sketched. It is possible to spend an hour studying each cartoon and finding familiar Brownie characters we recognize from past stories. In such detailing Norman Rockwell would also excel in the following century. Perhaps Cox's most important successor in this style was Harrison Cady, whose covers for *The American Boy* are in the same vein.

Folks all around the world sent to Cox their own Brownie handmade creations. His studio, now called "Brownie Land," was littered with them. The fad for Brownies was growing—in 1895 a 3-act play opened in the United States and Canada—*Palmer Cox Brownies* had a five-year run.

A song, "Frisky Frolics," based on the imps, enjoyed successful sales. The first Brownie book appeared in 1887; *The Brownies, Their Book* . . . , was followed three years later by *Another Brownie Book* in 1890, *The Brownies at Home* in 1893, *The Brownies around the World* in 1894, and close to a dozen more over the next two decades. Cox also authored many other non-Brownie illustrated works from 1875 to 1888, particularly the "Queer People" series.

The majority of the Brownie books, if not all, were merely reprints of the monthly escapades appearing in *St. Nicholas.* Most Brownie books were published by the Century Company, publishers of *St. Nicholas.* It is conceivable that they, and not Cox, owned the rights to the little people. This would also help to explain the emergence of other Brownie literature between 1890 and 1910 that was not written by Cox, but E. Veale and others. Cox was the illustrator of such stories, however, even though the text of some of them did tend to digress a bit from his basic conceptual image of the Brownies and their universe.

It may be said with a fair degree of historical accuracy that the Palmer Cox Brownies were the very first massive commercial exploitation, nationwide, of an imaginary person or creature from the comic art world of American literature. They paved the way followed by Outcault's "Yellow Kid" and "Buster Brown," Corbett's "Sunbonnet Babies," and many others all the way through the years, until the current favorite, the "Peanuts" gang, shares the same significant financial rewards and popularity.

Muslin sheets, playing cards, games, pins, handkerchiefs, children's building blocks, tea sets, juvenile silverware and dishware, stationery, and all sorts of printed writing materials are but a very few of the many products either bearing the name of the Brownies or advertised and decorated by them. Dolls of all types were marketed throughout the country in attempts to satisfy the demands of children for Brownie playthings. The Arnold Print Works, located in North Adams, Massachusetts, sold yard lengths of cloth printed with Brownie designs, meant to be cut out and stuffed so as to create rag dolls. Each yard came complete with 12 small figures, each 7" high, and representing one of the distinctive Brownie characters—i.e., Uncle Sam, John Bull, sailor, policeman. . . .

There were many, many advertising booklets distributed either as premiums or handouts by various manufacturing firms doing general merchandising or food business. Newspapers also found these excellent as supplements, one of the earliest forerunners of the Sunday Supplement idea which came to a full blossom during the 1890s. . . .

Palmer Cox also did artwork for advertising almanacs, notably one for the C. G. Green (patent medicine) Company in 1890. For this firm he created a pack of "Greenies" who were seen taking a world-wide tour on behalf of the product, "German Syrup." Cox apparently did not want to taint the moral character of his Brownies, so he gave birth to a similar group. This was in 1890, when the advertising application of his imaginary tribe to the advertising world was a new idea. As time progressed and the offers started piling up, Cox's reservations disappeared.

Cox also did a considerable amount of advertising artwork

using bears, foxes, and other animals for a long list of companies, such as Ivory and Tarrant's. He even found time to bring his Brownies to the Montgomery Ward catalogs of the mid-1890s where many Brownie items were being sold. . . .

Palmer Cox and his Brownies stand tall in the golden age of American illustration and comic art. Their contributions were mighty, both to their own era and to the legacy they left later generations. Cox emerges as one of the greats of American illustration. (p. 93)

> *Roy Nuhn, "Palmer Cox and His Band of Merry Elves," in* Hobbies, *Vol. 86, No. 6, August, 1981, pp. 90-3.*

Tomie dePaola

1934-

(Born Thomas Anthony dePaola) American author and illustrator of picture books and nonfiction, reteller, and editor.

Major works include *Nana Upstairs and Nana Downstairs* (1973), *"Charlie Needs a Cloak"* (1973), *Strega Nona: An Old Tale* (1975), *The Clown of God* (1978), *Giorgio's Village* (1982), *Tomie dePaola's Mother Goose* (1985).

Perhaps the most prolific and popular creator of books for children in the early and middle grades, dePaola is recognized as an original, versatile, and inventive writer and artist whose works reflect his personal background and affection for his audience. The author and illustrator of approximately seventy-five books and the illustrator of another seventy-five by other writers, all of which have been published at the rate of three or four times per year, dePaola is the creator of retellings in which he often draws on his Italian and Irish heritage; original stories based on traditional and continental literature; fantasies featuring both real and imaginary animals; realistic stories, several of which contain autobiographical elements; informational books that combine humor and concise facts in a fictional storyline; retellings of Biblical stories and religious legends that reflect his Roman Catholic background; and wordless, pop-up, and board books. DePaola's works characteristically address such themes as friendship, family relationships, ecology, courage and personal sacrifice, and the importance of individuality and equality; although many of his titles are humorous or whimsical, dePaola is often acknowledged for treating subjects such as old age and death in a sensitive and affectionate fashion. As an illustrator, dePaola characteristically provides paintings for his works in soft pastel watercolors or brightly colored inks; he also includes pencil and charcoal drawings, etchings, and other forms that highlight his varied use of line. Influenced by pre-Renaissance Italian artists such as Fra Angelico and Giotto, Romanesque art, folk motifs, and techniques from film and the theater, dePaola is recognized for developing a distinctive, easily identifiable style featuring solid figures, strong outlines, authentic architectural elements, and a stylized design that suggests a stage or film performance.

A painter, muralist, designer, and art teacher who has also worked with children's theater, dePaola began contributing to juvenile literature as the illustrator of the works of other authors; he has provided pictures for books by such writers as Norma Farber, Jean Fritz, Daniel Pinkwater, Patricia MacLachlan, Clement Clarke Moore, Jane Yolen, Valentine Davies, Nancy Willard, and Robert Bly. DePaola first received special acclaim in the early 1970s for such works as *Nana Upstairs and Nana Downstairs,* a book about the relationship between a small boy and his two grandmothers that was the first of his books to relate directly to dePaola's own life; *"Charlie Needs a Cloak",*

which introduces his blend of fiction and nonfiction by describing the process by which yarn is made through the experiences of shepherd Charlie and his playful sheep companion; and *Strega Nona,* a witty variation on the folktale theme of the magic cooking pot which features an Italian setting and the popular characters Strega Nona (Grandmother Witch) and her hapless helper Big Anthony. Since that time, dePaola has written and illustrated many other titles in a similar vein, including three additional Strega Nona books, several other stories that incorporate details of his own life, two picture books about the crocodile Bill and his friend-cum-toothbrush Pete, and nonfiction on such subjects as holidays, food, clouds, and cats. He is also the creator of a variety of retellings and original works from Biblical, religious, and native American sources as well as books in a nontraditional format of which the pop-up book *Giorgio's Village* is especially well-received; dePaola is also respected as an anthologist for his collections of poetry, Mother Goose rhymes, Bible stories, and Christmas carols. DePaola has received many awards for his books: among them are the Nakamore Prize (Japan) in 1978 for *Strega Nona,* a work which was also named a Caldecott honor book in 1976, the Golden Kite Award for *Giorgio's Village* in 1982 and for *Marianna*

May and Nursey (1983) in 1983, and The Critic in Erba commendation from the Bologna Biennale in 1983 for *The Friendly Beasts* (1981), a work which was also named a *Boston Globe-Horn Book* honor book for its illustrations in 1982; a number of dePaola's other titles have been named best and notable books by professional organizations. He received the Kerlan Award in 1981 and the Regina Medal in 1983, both for his body of work, and has also received many child-selected awards. In addition, dePaola is the recipient of several prizes for his art and has held many national and international exhibitions.

(See also *CLR,* Vol. 4; *Something about the Author,* Vols. 11, 59; *Contemporary Authors New Revision Series,* Vol. 2; *Contemporary Authors,* Vols. 49-52; and *Dictionary of Literary Biography,* Vol. 61.)

AUTHOR'S COMMENTARY

[The following excerpt is from an interview by Phyllis Boyson.]

[Phyllis Boyson]: Tomie, you once said: 'We can feed the intellect, but if we don't feed the soul as well, the intellect is going to starve to death.' In what ways do you feel that your books are 'feeding the soul'?

[Tomie dePaola]: Art, music, literature poetry, painting and sculpture are necessary to the soul. The visual imagery in my books helps feed the soul. Even my concept books which are filled with information and fun are also visually interesting. If I didn't have the words, the windows to look through, I'd be starving my soul. In my books, I pay a great deal of attention to the sound of words because I write my books to be read aloud. I'm interested in the audio-visual sense. That auditory thing is like music—I work with editors who have that same feeling, a feeling for poetic language.

The content, I believe, is what will interest children, and as Ben Shahn says in *The Shape of Content,* form follows content. Good drawings, fine compositions and human qualities that evoke human emotions are important.

There is a dangerous proliferation of children's books that aren't really children's books. University students buy 'arty' children's books. These sophisticated illustrated books belong to another category; I would hate to see them taking over the children's field. The decisions for buying the books are not in children's hands, and I recognise the importance of appealing to adults. I try to find elements that will appeal to adults and that will have real meaning for the children who read the books.

P.B.: It has often been stated that a writer of children's books is 'in touch with the child inside himself (herself).' Are you in touch with that child and if so, in what ways does this affect your writing?

T.d.: Yes. I am. But I wasn't always. I had locked the little child up and didn't give it a chance. I didn't pay attention to my childhood memories and experiences until 1971. I was feeling very ineffective: I had been teaching for 10 years, getting a Masters Degree and had already published 15-20 books. But I felt that I had a block in my work, and

I went into group therapy with Margaret Fringe Keyes who uses a lot of art as a means of therapy. I realized that I had locked up the child so effectively that it wasn't getting any say. I was a 'terrible' child in school—a problem! But not at home; I had very supportive parents. Through therapy, I realized that I had shoved the child in me into a closet. I had a feeling of loss—but no, I hadn't lost it. I finally opened the door and let it out of the closet. I remet my child and let it live again, and then I wrote **Nana Upstairs, Nana Downstairs.** (pp. 76-7)

With **Nana,** instead of making up a story, I took the risk of telling the truth. Looking back, . . . my works before that were much less honest, more influenced by others than myself, the REAL GUTS. As you know, **Nana** is part one of my autobiography; **Oliver Button is a Sissy** part two; and part three is **Now one foot, now the Other.** (p. 77)

P.B.: You deal with serious issues in a whimsical way in your books. Do people just see the whimsy and not the seriousness? . . . the depth or the exposure of tender feelings?

T.d.: Yes . . . some people do just that . . . Some people just say 'that's cute' and miss why it made them cry. It's their way of not dealing with real feelings! But the children don't dismiss the issues.

P.B.: From past discussions, I know that you appreciate and are interested in many of the artists and writers from times past. Who are some of your favorites?

T.d.: I look at painters more than specifically children's works. All of my 'household gods' were in a sense storytellers with their pictures: Fra Angelico, Giotto, Romanesque works. As for writers, the stories that I like best are the folk fairy tales.

P.B.: Talking about fairy tales, how do you feel about Bruno Bettelheim's statement in *The Uses of Enchantment* that 'each fairy tale is a magic mirror which reflects some aspects of our inner world and of the steps required by our evolution from immaturity to maturity?', and do you believe, like Bettelheim, children should be exposed to fairy tales?

T.d.: I still like fairy tales and I agree with Bruno Bettelheim that children should be exposed to them. But I'm less Freudian and more Jungian than Bettelheim. I believe that they have specific uses for children. I think it's a form that touches children of any era. Children have always had the same basic concerns, and folktales, although set in different cultures during different times, address those basic concerns. A fairy tale is like a mirror—it's timeless and deals with human situations. I think, by the way, the reason that *Star Wars* is so popular with children is because it's really a good old fashioned Fairy Tale with good and evil clearly defined values. It's a Folk Fairy Tale—that's why the movie captured the imagination of so many children including my own nephew.

P.B.: On the subject of values, Rex Andrews, an educationist at Goldsmiths' College, England, has suggested that: ' . . . in the twentieth century, literature is by far a safer and more beneficial means of value-acquisition than dogma and ideology.' Would you like to comment on that statement?

T.d.: I think it has always been true—not just in the twentieth century. Dogma and ideology change all the time. The true artist is digging deep to find constant and universal values.

P.B.: Which brings us back to fairy tales?

T.d.: Yes. When I was thinking of being an artist, I thought of the fairy tales. I was thrilled when I was given the opportunity to do them. Fairy Tales are very basic. I found this to be true when I was doing my research for writing a *Porridge Pot* story. One version has the main character as a servant girl: being a feminist, I changed that. I also changed 'porridge' because I didn't think many of today's children would relate to that! I wondered if the tale appeared in other countries and tried to find the 'root' tale. I found *The Rice Pot in India*. I'm half Italian and I found that there was a great lack in Italian tales. There was no Italian variant. In the tradition of the storyteller, I would have to tell it for my own village: porridge became pasta: the place became Italy; and the character became Strega Nona, who was my own creation. That was when I became aware of folk tale variants.

P.B.: As an artist yourself, how do you feel about Bettelheim's view that 'pictures limit the child's imagining' and that children should be read fairy tales without pictures?

T.d.: I can see what he's saying—if the tale is illustrated the child's imagination might be stifled. But I see pictures as stimulating rather than stifling. In the pictures, there are all kinds of elements which can send the child into a further embroidering of ideas. I think the artist makes the invisible-visible, the image has great power. In Europe and in Asia, I think that the image is considered much more important than in America. Bettelheim isn't leaving room for the child who is stimulated by images. Reading the pictures—visual literacy—is important.

P.B.: Only part of your body of work is based directly on folk/fairy tales. However, many of your other works have a similar universal appeal—they deal with basic personal concerns and human relationships. A common theme in your books seems to be 'acceptance'—it's O.K. to be who you are—is this on an awareness level?

T.d.: I avoid being self-conscious because once I become self-conscious I become a critic rather than a creator. But there IS acceptance in my books: even Big Anthony is loveable, though he messes things up. An idea for me must be 'heartfelt'—something that rings true for me—something worthy to share with children. As you know, I write a lot for children between three and seven years old; and young children can tell right away when you're not being honest. If a message rings true, they will sit and listen. My guess is that children respond to my work because it's simple and honest. (pp. 77-8)

P.B.: What would you like to see happen in the field of children's literature on the International level?

T.d.: I would like to see everyone 'hanging in' while facing the rising costs of everything. I'd hate to see production coming to an end. We don't seem to put money with the young child. One solution would be co-production. The field is healthy creatively; it is in danger of being overridden by unhealthy economics.

I would like to see editors take more of a chance with books of a particular culture: because something doesn't exist in one culture: doesn't mean that children of another culture won't understand it or benefit from it. Take my book *Oliver Button is a Sissy*—it's about a boy who tap dances. Some cultures may not have tap dancing; however, the book is about a child who is doing what he really wants to do, despite peer pressure. The book deals with absolutely human concerns, cross-cultural concerns; Oliver Button is universal. Fairy Tales deal with these same kind of concerns—that's why they work all over the world. As for selection, I would like to see regions form selection committees and to see more book examination centers; the more they are exposed, the more knowledge is gained.

It's a shame that a greater number of books about the specifics in a culture aren't translated more; it is a wonderful way for people around the world to find out about different cultures. (pp. 79-80)

Tomie dePaola and Phyllis Boyson in The New Era, *Vol. 62, No. 3, May-June, 1981, pp. 76-80.*

GENERAL COMMENTARY

Susan Ingrid Hepler

Charlie Needs a Cloak [was] de Paola's first informational book which he both authored and illustrated.

In soft greens, reds, golds and his familiar brown lines, de Paola explained how Charlie made his new red cloak. The text provided information but the illustrations enlarged upon his words by showing Charlie wrestling with, then shearing a sheep, washing, carding, spinning and dyeing the wool, and finally weaving, cutting out, and sewing the cloth. Humor, an ample part of all de Paola's books, was supplied both by a small packrat who carried off Charlie's yarn, dishes, a shoe and tools, and by the disgruntled sheep who nibbled at everything Charlie made. The sheep finished where he began—nibbling on Charlie's cloak.

De Paola was making education fun—a recurring theme for him. "I didn't know I was doing something that for awhile had been *verboten*—which was to try to present information as a story. In fact, a lot of children don't realize it's an instructional book until it's too late! I think humor can sometimes get more points across than seriousness." . . .

Because of its format, perhaps *The Popcorn Book* seems the most obviously educational of de Paola's several informational books. Twins become interested in popcorn and one reads from the encyclopedia while the other goes out into the kitchen and makes popcorn. Two different kinds of lettering help the reader separate information from dialogue. And the humor? A little too much popcorn in the pan produces a near "snowstorm" in the kitchen. "Two Terrific Ways to Pop Corn (*Be sure to ask a grown-up first)" conclude the text. De Paola and his editor do careful research to make sure that the information in these books is accurate and up-to-date. (p. 297)

[One] resource de Paola draws upon is his Italian/Irish family background. Born in Connecticut in 1934, he knew both his grandmothers and his Irish great-grandmother. Out of his memories of time spent with them, he has created two very personal books.

"Nana Upstairs & Nana Downstairs is a very important book to me because it's totally autobiographical. And, it was the first time I'd ever had a picture block. I found I was having a hard time drawing the pictures because I kept on worrying about my family saying '*That* isn't the way it was. *That* doesn't look like Nana.' So I finally went ahead and drew the pictures and said I wasn't going to make *anybody* look like *anybody.* And when I finished the book, everyone looked the way they did! That's one of my very favorite books." The small gentle story concerns his relationships with his own grandmother and great-grandmother and his reactions to their aging and eventual deaths. (p. 299)

Watch Out For the Chicken Feet in Your Soup, Joey warns Eugene when they go visit Joey's (Tomie's) Italian grandmother. Grandma uses their warm coats to help raise the bread dough, serves chicken soup and spaghetti and praises "Eugeney" for eating all of his dinner. While Joey fights to choke down the remaining spaghetti, Grandma and Eugene make braided bread dolls. Joey, having completed his dinner and back in Grandma's good graces, earns a hug and a special bread doll from his loving grandmother. De Paola's illustrations drew on fondly remembered details of his grandmother's bric-a-brac-filled house. He also included directions for making her braided bread dolls.

Tomie de Paola's Italian background emerges in much of his other artwork. *Strega Nona* is set in Calabria, the source of de Paola's name, as well. The influence of Fra Angelico and Giotto, artists whose work has greatly affected de Paola's own, may be seen in *The Clown of God.* What de Paola takes from these two pre-Renaissance Italian artists, he says, is "the absolute simplicity. And, I really care about the two dimensional design. I do what the Sienese painters do but not in the same way. I almost reduce features to a symbol. And yet I think of my faces as good and warm. I try to show expression in very few lines. If you look at Fra Angelico and Giotto, they're able to do that with very stylized—I don't want to say 'formula'—convention. I really like the design, simplicity, and tranquility of their characters. And, of course, they all use line very simply."

Line is a most important component of de Paola's work, so much so that he uses several different techniques and media in applying line to drawing. In *The Clown of God* for instance, he drew in pencil lines on special watercolor paper. He then went over the pencil sketch with a raw sienna waterproof ink followed by a second brown pencil line. Finally he went over the whole drawing with a brown ink he mixed himself. This, he says, gives his lines a certain quality which he can't get any other way. Watercolors and inks complete the full-color artwork.

Most of his artwork for book illustration is preseparated, however, and this means that each picture is composed of plastic overlays. (pp. 299-300)

For the past three years, de Paola has taught theater design and developed a children's theater program at Colby-Sawyer College in New Hampshire. Although the job consumed quantities of time, he enjoyed the experience. "I think theater training is very good for an illustrator. There are so many ways picture books are like theater—scenes, settings, characterization. A double page spread can be like a stage." Action is often presented in de Paola's illustration as if it were staged. The audience, at eye level, does not see, then, an aerial view or a close-up and each illustration always shows the action against a setting or backdrop.

In two of his books, *Charlie* and *Chicken Feet,* de Paola has placed the first page of the text before the title page, thus incorporating the title itself as part of the text. This "action during the titles" comes from films, suggests dePaola. Other books such as the easy-to-read *Andy (That's My Name)* are also framed in such a way as to suggest film. Andy's friends construct words from parts of his name but the action never escapes or intrudes upon the green borders of each page. In *Strega Nona,* however, the borders of the pictures are assaulted by the rampaging pasta, as if to suggest action which goes beyond the page.

Tomie de Paola often visits schools where he talks to children or reads to them. Although he never tries his books out on children before they are published, he does try them out on his tape recorder. "I read them aloud to myself in the final stages because I think that's very important—how they sound aloud. I *do* write my books to be read aloud."

He believes children should be given more options in visual imagery. There is certainly "lots of room for lots of different imagery, and that's the way it must be. Why expose young people to only one way of looking at things? Who knows, we may be helping to form some sort of visual taste—why limit it?" He also thinks that children deserve more options in behavior. While there are now plenty of books which portray little girls as tomboys, there are no books which portray little boys as sissies. He's working on a book tentatively titled *Oliver Button Is a Sissy.* (pp. 300-01)

Tomie de Paola cares about children and the books which are produced for them. He believes that, although artists should never talk down to children, "there is no room for self-indulgence, cleverness-for-the-sake-of-cleverness, ego-pyrotechnics, and over-sophisticated images."

One summer, he spent time as a student of Ben Shahn at Skowhegan, Maine. He took from Shahn a credo which has guided his artwork ever since: "No matter what you do—a Christmas card, a mural in a church, a painting, illustrations for a book—you bring the same kind of energy to it. It seems there's always been this great fight between the fine artist and the commercial artist—because something is going to be sold, it isn't *real art.* This is a bunch of hogwash! I really try to bring the *same* energy, the *same* intensity, to whatever I do."

Enthusiasm, intensity, a twinkling sense of humor—Tomie de Paola brings all of these to whatever he does. In illustrations and in words, he invites us into his books—to laugh, to learn, to see the world, if only for a few moments, through the eyes of a shaggy-haired, sweat-shirted child. (p. 301)

> *Susan Ingrid Hepler, "Profile: Tomie de Paola, A Gift to Children," in* Language Arts, *Vol. 56, No. 3, March, 1979, pp. 296-301.*

M. Crouch

Tomie de Paola is well on the way to becoming my favourite picture-book artist in the world today. He continues to explore new themes and forms, and brings to every book a keen eye and a fine technique. In **Sing, Pierrot, Sing** he gives us a wordless book, not because it is rather fashionable to do such things but because the subject demands it. Words have no place in the ageless story of Pierrot, Harlequin and Columbine, only the expressive communication of mime. Mr. de Paola's lovely moonlit drawings, with their predominating blues, bring home both the surface humour and the underlying melancholy of the story.

There is no room for humour in the story of the Magi, or indeed for human passion. [In Mr. dePaola's **The Story of the Three Wise Kings** even] Herod's anger is of a stylized kind. The whole book is presented in a series of grave formal designs. Mr. de Paola has drawn heavily on illuminated versions of the early Gospels as well as on such work as the Bayeux Tapestry, influences which are best seen in the fiery comet that leads the kings to their goal and in the lovely, serene picture of the Virgin and Child which greets them. The accompanying text is of the briefest and has no discordant note in it.

> *M. Crouch, in a review of "Sing, Pierrot, Sing" and "The Story of the Three Wise Kings," in* The Junior Bookshelf, *Vol. 48, No. 2, April, 1984, p. 59.*

TITLE COMMENTARY

The Comic Adventures of Old Mother Hubbard and Her Dog (1981)

[**The Comic Adventures of Old Mother Hubbard and Her Dog,** an] imaginative and thoroughly engaging version of the popular, early-nineteenth-century nursery rhyme, places two familiar and beloved characters in a theatrical setting lavish with magnificent costumes and props. Spectators in box seats attending to the trials of the solicitous, beribboned dame and her mischievous poodle include Humpty Dumpty, the King and Queen of Hearts, and Little Bo Peep, while the stage curtains are decorated with scenes from the stories of still other well-known Mother Goose characters. The fun and action of the story are captured perfectly in a series of large, framed illustrations. Typical de Paola humor, muted colors, and a folk-art style that brings to life an old English town combine for an ele-

From Francis: The Poor Man of Assisi, *written and illustrated by Tomie dePaola.*

gant and ingenious recreation of a childhood classic that should provide pleasure for many readings and viewings.

> *Alethea K. Helbig, in a review of "The Comic Adventures of Old Mother Hubbard and Her Dog," in* Children's Book Review Service, *Vol. 9, No. 11, June, 1981, p. 91.*

Old Mother Hubbard is set out as a stage play, watched by characters from nursery rhymes. The first picture shows the curtain, bearing the credits, the last Mother Hubbard and her dog taking a curtain call, one bedecked with flowers, the other clutching a bone tied with a pink bow. Tomie de Paola's pictures are as comic as ever—the hyperactive poodle, balancing on his lap an insulted cat wearing a ruffed baby gown, brought howls of glee from everyone.

> *Kicki Moxon Browne, "Artists and Writers," in* The Times Literary Supplement, *No. 4086, July, 24, 1981, p. 840.*

By coincidence we have together two examples of the work of one of the major illustrators of the world [**The Comic Adventures of Old Mother Hubbard and Her Dog** and **Fin M'Coul, the Giant of Knockmany Hill**]. . . .

For **Old Mother Hubbard** the American/Irish/Italian artist uses the traditional verses in all their grave, elegant absurdity. He finds designs which match precisely their Regency mood. The story is pursued as if on the stage, the characters framed by a procenium arch, on the pillars of which appear scenes from nursery rhymes. The preliminaries reveal that the distinguished audience for the drama include the King and Queen of Hearts, Bo Peep, Humpty Dumpty and Mother Goose herself. Rarely have fun and wit been conveyed with such admirable taste as well as spirit.

M. Crouch, in a review of "The Comic Adventures of Old Mother Hubbard and Her Dog," in The Junior Bookshelf, *Vol. 45, No. 4 August, 1981, p. 144.*

The Hunter and the Animals: A Wordless Picture Book (1981)

Though subtitled "A Wordless Picture Book," de Paola illustrates a fable with this clear moral: animals are friends and should not be hunted. The easily accessible story involves a lad who goes into the forest to hunt. His actions are watched and announced to the animals by a blue jay. The animals elude the hunter; he falls asleep; they steal his pouch and gun. When he awakens, the hunter is frightened, dashes wildly about and loses his hat. The animals pity the hunter and return his gun and pouch; they bring a gift of fruit in his hat. They have a bad moment when the hunter points his gun at them, but then he breaks his gun in two, and the story ends with a friendship tableau. The book should have a much broader appeal than such recent, pictures-only books as Molly Bang's *The Grey Lady and the Strawberry Snatcher* (Four Winds: Scholastic, 1980) or Graham Oakley's totally different *Magical Changes* (Atheneum, 1980).

George Gleason, in a review of "The Hunter and the Animals," in School Library Journal, *Vol. 28, No. 1, September, 1981, p. 105.*

[A] book that is frank in message but decorative and inviting in appearance. . . . Stories told entirely in pictures have proliferated, with varying success, in the past few decades; the most acceptable ones are those in which both the narrative line and the emotional tone are clearly defined. The artist has achieved a kind of colorful sobriety by telling the tale in a series of stylized tableaux of various sizes and shapes—from small blocks, discreetly numbered for clarity, to double-page spreads.

Ethel L. Heins, in a review of "The Hunter and the Animals: A Wordless Picture Book," in The Horn Book Magazine, *Vol. LVIII, No. 1, February, 1982, p. 33.*

A cut-out painted wood panel was the inspiration for a picture-book whose chunky figures and brilliant use of grouping make the story the artist has devised extremely clear in its topical application. . . . The technique of over-painted paper on which subtly related, soft colours are deployed is especially well used to add the emotional and intellectual values normally provided by a text to the aesthetic values (and these are considerable) of the fine pictures.

Margery Fisher, in a review of "The Hunter and the Animals," in Growing Point, *Vol. 21, No. 1, May, 1982, p. 3908.*

The Friendly Beasts: An Old English Christmas Carol (1981)

The simple strains of this old Christmas melody are superbly reflected in the graceful, delicate, yet strong images that de Paola brings to the page. The nativity setting is evoked with slender conical trees, a small pile of stones, the distant domes of Bethlehem, and sturdy, crude rafters, judiciously placed to frame the eloquent manger scenes. As the verses proclaim the contributions of donkey, cow, sheep, and dove to the baby Jesus' comfort (" 'I,' said the dove, from the rafters high. / 'I cooed him to sleep so he would not cry' "), the animal is prominently highlighted against plain white space, with only a few well-chosen symbols for balance. On each page following, the beast appears in appropriate perspective (e.g., the doves cooing from the rafters over the manger), which carries on the action. Three candle-bearing choirboys open and close the story, bringing a final cohesion to the work. A Christmas remembrance to be long treasured. Music with verses appended.

Barbara Elleman, in a review of "The Friendly Beasts: An Old English Christmas Carol," in Booklist, *Vol. 78, No. 1, September 1, 1981, p. 44.*

As in his other religious picture books, de Paola's treatment of this old English carol reduces people and animals to sugar-candy dimension, yet sacrifices human and creaturely charm for a distancing holy-card piety. First, choir boys (?) bearing candles parody stylized poses as the opening words tell how "Jesus our brother, strong and good / Was humbly born in a stable rude." Then each beast—donkey, cow, sheep, and dove—takes the stage to tell of its gift to the child, while alternating wordless double pages show human visitors paying their respects. In all of these posed, pastel tableaux, the animals and worshipping visitors have at best a nursery-decoration cuteness, while the Holy Family seems merely lugubrious.

A review of "The Friendly Beasts: An Old English Christmas Carol," in Kirkus Reviews, *Vol. XLIX, No. 18, September 15, 1981, p. 1156.*

It takes great skill to take a minor carol that can be found in many songbooks and turn it into a full-fledged book. Tomie de Paola shows that he deserves his reputation as an important illustrator with **The Friendly Beasts: an Old English Christmas Carol.** The text is printed by hand and is large enough to read aloud easily. The illustrations are reminiscent of a Renaissance masque, with three choirboys introducing a cast of animal and human characters that finally appears together in a double-page Nativity scene. The people, who are dressed in costumes of the early Renaissance, appear in formal stylized poses suggestive of a tableau vivant. Their faces are almost expressionless, while their clothing falls in decorative folds. The animals are carefully drawn and somewhat idealized. Meticulous attention has been paid to every detail of design, color and layout.

Jean Hammond Zimmerman, in a review of

"The Friendly Beasts: An Old English Christmas Carol," in School Library Journal, *Vol. 28, No. 2, October, 1981, p. 155.*

A beautiful Christmas book with the verses of a familiar carol for the text. . . . The striking paintings—done in outlined washes of colored ink—show the manger scenes filled with warmth and serenity; and as awed visitors come to welcome the Christ Child, the joyous but hushed spirit of the miraculous event is obvious. Because a carol is meant to be sung, the verses seem somewhat stilted when used as a text. . . .

Nancy Sheridan, in a review of "The Friendly Beasts: An Old English Christmas Carol," in The Horn Book Magazine, *Vol. LVII, No. 6, December, 1981, p. 653.*

Francis: The Poor Man of Assisi (1982)

Tomie de Paola's style is nearly always the same, but it suits his newest book, **Francis, the Poor Man of Assisi,** wonderfully well. This work was a sheer labor of love, for the author's note tells us that de Paola has had a life-long interest in St. Francis and has for years been planning to write about him. The book has appeared on the 800th anniversary of the saint's birth and has, throughout, a glow that can only come from the deepest concern for the subject.

The author's note also tells us that the book is a distillation arrived at after reading everything available on the lives of Francis and his companion saint, Clare. If so, the decisions as to what to include and what to leave out have been good ones, for the book moves well from event to event, each one a mini-chapter contained on a single left-hand page with illuminated opening capital and a simple scene at the bottom, while on the right a full-page illustration occupies the same kind of nicely balanced space.

The impression here given of Francis is that of a flesh-and-blood human, in spite of all the legendary miracles that surround him, and that is something of a miracle in itself. In simple, direct prose, de Paola tells of an unruly boy, son of a rich man, whose life is slowed by two long illnesses and then forever altered by a vision of the voice of the Lord from a crucifix in an old church near Assisi. The first steps that lead Francis forward from that moment read very much like an account of a flower child of the 1960s, but the difference becomes evident as the story progresses: Francis does not return to his "senses" but devotes his life entirely to his religion, attracting a large group of followers, achieving papal recognition for the Order, and, eventually, sainthood two years after his death in 1226.

This is a story worth reading no matter what one's philosophies. It is an uncomplicated account which reports both the miracles and the public skepticism without comment, bringing Francis to life in a way that helps the reader to understand something of the flavor of all great obsessions. De Paola has been careful to avoid all pietistic sog both in text and pictures, and the latter are quite wonderful, I think: strong outline, soft colors, no fussy detail anywhere, a nice feeling for the countryside and architecture of the

place and time. All of the things that are positive about his style work well for him here, including the fixed serenity of his faces. Only once in the book is a face shown open-mouthed, giving it the emphasis it needs: a picture of Francis near death, leading his companions in song. De Paola is to be congratulated for a beautiful piece of work. (p. 17)

Natalie Babbitt, "Fairy Tales and Far-Flung Places," in Book World—The Washington Post, *May 9, 1982, pp. 16-17.*

De Paola retells the well-known stories of the young man from Assisi: Francis rebelling against his father, taming the wolf of Gubbio, creating the first Christmas crèche. He has also included much on the life of Clare Scifi, in her own right an interesting saint, and a beloved friend of Brother Francis. Some source notes and a chronology are included, but no index. Text and illustrations face each other on double pages of picture-book size. These illustrations are among the most thoughtful de Paola has done recently, with monumental figures and rich, varied coloring. Yet one might have difficulty reconciling his drawings of an unsmiling, ascetic saint with the Franciscan quality he has identified as "simplicity, joy, the love of nature, and the love of Lady Poverty."

Anna Biagioni Hart, in a review of "Francis: The Poor Man of Assisi," in School Library Journal, *Vol. 28, No. 10, August, 1982, p. 114.*

If you are going to write a saint's life for children, St. Francis, already associated in the popular mind with birds, flowers and animals, is the logical place to begin. In *Francis: The Poor Man of Assisi* Tomie de Paola captures the sweetness and the gentleness of St. Francis, particularly in the illustrations, whose flattened perspective and muted earth, green and rust tones are obviously inspired by Giotto.

Mr. de Paola recounts Francis' journey from self-indulgent young playboy to begging ascetic. He reminds us of the well-known conversion of the wolf and recalls the appearance of the Christ Child to Francis in the cave on Christmas Eve. It is particularly in the author's favor that he does not forget to include the women who had an important place in Francis' life; St. Clare, who gets attention as a serious spiritual force; and a charming character, Jacopa de Settesoli, a wealthy religious matron whom St. Francis called "Brother" Jacopa and who provided his only physical indulgence—home-baked honey cakes.

The author mentions Francis' stigmata, without making clear to the child reader the exact nature of the phenomenon or the fact that others before and after Francis experienced the same thing. But the inclusion of the text of Francis' "Song to the Sun" makes a charming conclusion for the book. It demonstrates many of the less-than-pleasant aspects of Franciscan thought that Mr. de Paola simply airbrushes out of the rest of his text.

Only after reading "Song to the Sun" did I feel somewhat dissatisfied by the narrative that preceded it. The tale is too sweetly told; this is Francis of Assisi according to Mister Rogers. We ought to have learned from Bruno Bettelheim that children need not be spared the contradictory, the unpleasant, the frightening. It is not, I think, a service to children to make them believe that saints are just nicer guys than the rest of us. The parent or friend who gives a child the life of a saint is clearly doing this to expose the child to a heroism distinctly eccentric; it is an introduction to another world, perhaps less familiar to the modern child than outer space. I wish that Tomie de Paola's Francis were a bit more ragged, a bit wilder, that the wolf looked a little less tame, the stigmata a bit more bloody.

But this is a book of quiet charm, and a kind of serenity floats from the pages. In an era of video games and of stimulus bombardment, *Francis* can provide the serious child with soothing, nourishing refreshment.

> *Mary Gordon, in a review of "Francis: The Poor Man of Assisi," in* The New York Times Book Review, *August 22, 1982, p. 33.*

Giorgio's Village   (1982)

Indefatigable de Paola's latest creation is a pop-up with extras, vitalized by his hallmark, a blend of understated comic touches and rich paintings of memorable places. Here the boy Giorgio invites us to untie the ribbons that open the gates to his Italian-Renaissance village, where he is sweeping the square in the morning, accompanied by his cat Puffino. Pulled tabs get a long, loaded clothesline from the window of a house and, in following scenes produced in three dimensions, activate things and people throughout the day: the church bells ring the Angelus at noon; Giorgio drops a coin in the wishing well; puppets perform in the late afternoon, etc. Finally, the moon sails high in the sky, a flock of birds and the villagers make for home and so do Giorgio and Puffino. The book is spectacular, amusing as well as educational, and a very likely gift item.

> *A review of "Giorgio's Village," in* Publishers Weekly, *Vol. 221, No. 25, June 18, 1982, p. 74.*

A pop-up book opens from the center; with the divided cover forming side panels, each page is pulled down to show a scene in a medieval Italian village, with foreground details that pop up, some movement within the page (via pull-tab or a door-flap) and a brief sentence or two of text. . . . This is not as ingenious technically as some pop-up books, in that the moving parts do not change the scene, as happens, for example, in the books by Lothar Meggendorfer, but it's attractive; the colors of the painting are soft and bright, the stiffness of the figures relieved by comic details.

> *Zena Sutherland, in a review of "Giorgio's Village," in* Bulletin of the Center for Children's Books, *Vol. 36, No. 1, September, 1982, p. 7.*

Giorgio is a street sweeper; Puffino is a cat who pants after fish. They spring up in an Italian Renaissance town with a predominance of pink tile roofs in *Giorgio's Village,* the prolific Tomie de Paola's umpteenth production.

Production? Well, it is rather theatrical, a pop-up book with six scenes that fold down into three-dimensional stagelike settings of the village square throughout the day. . . . And then there's the supporting cast. You open

shutters and doors to reveal Strega Nona, Mona Lisa, Romeo and Juliet, others. The text, printed stage front, is minimal and unimportant. All of this is clever, of course, but more show than book.

> *George A. Woods, in a review of "Giorgio's Village," in* The New York Times Book Review, *September 26, 1982, p. 30.*

Sharp eyes will . . . find Romeo and Juliet, Strega Nona, a wash line that retracts, cats who dream of fish, and dozens of other surprises hidden behind folding doors and tucked into pictures. A wonderful story-hour introduction to de Paola's other books (especially those with Italian settings) and a joy to pore over on its own. The look and feel of another country comes magically alive. (p. 244)

> *Barbara Elleman, in a review of "Giorgio's Village: A Pop-Up Book," in* Booklist, *Vol. 10, No. 1, October 1, 1982, pp. 243-44.*

Strega Nona's Magic Lessons   (1982)

Some people never learn—to quote an old adage—and Big Anthony seems to be one of them. His dabbling in magic brought him only trouble in *Strega Nona*; in *Big Anthony and the Magic Ring* he fared no better; but here, once again, the fates tempt him. When Bambolona, the baker's girl, quits her job to become Strega Nona's apprentice, Anthony decides he would like lessons too. Turned down the first time, he reappears at Strega Nona's door disguised as a girl. Strega Nona takes "her" in, but Antonia's spells continually go awry and one day Strega Nona disappears in a puff of smoke, leaving a frog behind. Alarmed by what he thinks he's done, Big Anthony promises never to play with magic again. Sharp-eyed viewers will see Strega Nona peeking around the corner and know that she and Bambolona had the upper hand all along. De Paola's familiar, well-rounded figures and dot-and-line faces appropriately return here to accentuate the humor, extending the style of the other two Strega Nona tales. Illustrations vary from several sequential, rectangular frames per page to two-page spreads, all of which flow in harmony with the story. Details evoke the Italian setting, and pleasing, well-chosen colors tone down the foolishness of the plot. Played for laughs—successfully.

> *Barbara Elleman, in a review of "Strega Nona's Magic Lessons," in* Booklist, *Vol. 79, No. 8, December 15, 1982, p. 563.*

Big Anthony's episode at the baker's seems superfluous to the plot but the story flows along nicely, ending with Big Anthony's comeuppance but untrustworthy (most likely) repentance. DePaola's irrepressible illustrations add vibrancy and humor.

> *Craighton Hippenhammer, in a review of "Strega Nona's Magic Lessons," in* School Library Journal, *Vol. 29, No. 5, January, 1983, p. 58.*

The Legend of the Bluebonnet: An Old Tale of Texas (1983)

DePaola retells the Comanche Indian tale that explains

the origin of the Texas bluebonnet flower. The shaman announces the people must burn their most valued possession as a sacrifice to the Great Spirits and scatter the ashes to the four points of the earth to bring an end to the drought and famine. She-who-is-alone offers her warrior doll, her only link with her family who died from the famine, as a sacrifice. The next morning the hills are covered with bluebonnets, a sign from the Great Spirits; soon rain comes and saves the people from more suffering. This is a solemn, simply-told tale and the concept of an unselfish parting with a prized possession is one to which children will readily relate. Although the figures appear wooden and flat, the full-color paintings in tableau-like settings are nicely staged with well-executed design and color.

> *Anne McKeithen Goodman, in a review of "The Legend of the Bluebonnet," in* School Library Journal, *Vol. 30, No. 1, September, 1983, p. 104.*

Tomie de Paolo [is] one of the great masters of the picture-book. There is none of his characteristic humour in **The Legend of the Bluebonnet,** but plenty of his sincerity and his feeling for folk-motifs. The simple story tells how a Red Indian child's sacrifice saves her tribe and gives Texas its state flower. The text is masterly in its directness and brevity, the pictures exquisitely drawn, gravely formal—as befits the theme—and richly atmospheric. This quiet book approaches perfection.

> *M. Crouch, in a review of "The Legend of the Bluebonnet," in* The Junior Bookshelf, *Vol. 47, No. 5, October, 1983, p. 197.*

Tomie dePaola is an author and illustrator of no small talent, with an obvious liking for his young audience, so it was with some interest that I opened **The Legend of the Bluebonnet.** The book is less than perfect, but its positive aspects outweigh the flaws. (p. 17)

The courage of children is always very moving, and the illustrations are among the loveliest dePaola has ever done. The sequence of evening sky, shading from lavender to blue to star-flecked night, has a luminosity rarely seen. The emotional impact of the book is strong.

Some of the book's flaws are trivial. (Do Commanche bluejays really say "jay-jay-jay"?) Others, more serious. In the long author's note, dePaola says that "the Commanche People did not have a concept of one God or a Great Spirit. They worshipped many spirits equally. . . ." It is a truism that Native American beliefs have become unrecognizable in translation, but the Christian sweetness of **The Legend of the Bluebonnet** seems far enough from the spirit of the people from whom it supposedly came to cause one to speculate upon its original form. Of this, we are told only that a friend kept him supplied "with as many versions as she could locate" of the folktales about the origins of the bluebonnet, the state flower of Texas.

In the context of tribal life, the little girl's complete isolation seems a bit unconvincing. Clearly *someone* takes care of her. When night came, she "returned to the tipi, where she slept, to wait. . . . Soon everyone in the tipi was asleep." Who are they?

A further word about the illustrations. Although dePaola's people do not have quite the hieratic quality of those in the illustrations he did for [Jean Fritz's] **The Good Giants and the Bad Pukwudgies** (what one reviewer, meaning it as praise, called "calm-eyed noble savages"), still they are not, with the exception of She-Who-Is-Alone, drawn as individuals. They have a homogeneous set of features; they are "Indians." This is particularly noticeable if comparison is made to some of the author's other books, where the people have very different kinds of faces—and are not all identically dressed, either.

While it is disappointing that dePaola did not manage to avoid some of the more common pitfalls, I would not hesitate to use this book with small children. I do not think that Anglo children can pick up any unfortunate attitudes from it; there is nothing here to shame or hurt an Indian child. Whatever else, the author does not condescend to his material, and his portrayal of She-Who-Is-Alone is not demeaning. He is not writing about "primitive" people. This story is animated by the same love and respect for children that lie behind all his other work. (p. 18)

> *Doris Seale, in a review of "The Legend of the Bluebonnet," in* Interracial Books for Children Bulletin, *Vol. 15, No. 4, 1984, pp. 17-18.*

The Story of the Three Wise Kings   (1983)

DePaola proves once again that a book with a religious theme can be reverent without being dull. In a brief introduction that cites sources, he explains how he has drawn on legends, the Bible, tradition and art for the story. The succinct text recounts how the three kings studied the stars and traveled to Bethlehem to honor the child King. The pink and blue tones of the background provide warmth while people, animals and angels are treated in a highly stylized manner. The Christmas star is shown as a large pink sphere containing petal-shaped rays from which pink stripes stream. DePaola's illustrations are not simply pictures designed to expand the text: his illustrations *are* the text. DePaola uses the influence of Byzantine and Romanesque art to depict and enlarge our understanding of character and humanity. This book is a good example of the richness of genuine simplicity. (pp. 175-76)

> *Jean Hammond Zimmerman, in a review of "The Story of the Three Wise Kings," in* School Library Journal, *Vol. 30, No. 2, October, 1983, pp. 175-76.*

De Paola's toy-like, sculptural figures and his conventionalized, spun-sugar landscapes do have a certain Near Eastern look—and his pinky-red, floret-centered star, trailing streamers in a mottled white sky, is certainly different. So, for that matter, are Mary and the Babe as the three kings find them: seated, Byzantine-painting-like, on a throne, with no signs of the manger present at all. Pictorial novelty is the book's one yes-and-no attraction; there is almost no expression, or expressiveness.

> *A review of "The Story of the Three Wise Kings," in* Kirkus Reviews, *Vol. LI, No. 21, November 1, 1983, p. J184.*

From Sing, Pierrot, Sing: A Picture Book in Mime, *written and illustrated by Tomie de-Paola.*

The Christmas story of the three kings, which has grown through tale and legend since its brief mention in the Gospel of St. Matthew (noted in author's preface), is extended here in a splendid full-color interpretation. De Paola's stylized approach, which he uses consistently throughout, solves what could be an awkward depiction—the coming together of the three men from three different places. The opening spread shows old Melchior of Arabia, young Gaspar from Tharsis, and black Balthazar of Saba each in his own home, distinguished by architectural motifs, against a simply patterned, aquamarine background that smoothly sets the stage. Costume details differentiate characters as they each begin their journeys, come together, meet with Herod, follow the star, and offer gifts to the Christ Child at the inn in Bethlehem. Riding high over the travelers is a beribboned, red-orange star with a five-pointed flower at its center, which gloriously streams across one double-page spread to herald the joyous occasion. Textured backgrounds in subtle shades of pink, blue, and green lend an appropriate Mediterranean ambience and provide quiet space for the cherry-robed angels, green palm trees, and white-pink birds as well as for the spare,

dignified text. A truly memorable addition to any Christmas shelf—or collection of fine picture-book art.

Barbara Elleman, in a review of "The Story of the Three Wise Kings," in Booklist, *Vol. 80, No. 6, November 15, 1983, p. 495.*

Marianna May and Nursey (1983)

Tomi de Paola is a prolific picture book artist whose popular work is often said to be childlike. In de Paola's case, the epithet readily calls to mind the artist's kindly amiability as a storyteller and the uncomplicated (if at times cloying) prettiness of his softly outlined, pastel graphics. A typical de Paola creation, *Marianna May and Nursey* is mildly whimsical, comfortably rather than adventurously plotted. Its characters are stock types wistfully retrieved from an earlier, more "innocent" day: a poor little rich girl and her overattentive Victorian nanny, a friendly ice man and a friendly cook. Its colors are the artifical dye colors of ice cream. *Marianna* reminds one of the visiting relation who, anxious to please the little folk, arrives with bulging pockets overladen with sweets. (p. 18)

Leonard S. Marcus, "The Look of the Story,"
in Book World—The Washington Post, November 6, 1983, pp. 15, 18.

There was Kay Thompson's *Eloise* (S. & S., 1969) and
Edith Hurd's *Hurry, Hurry* (Harper, 1960). Now dePaola
creates another rich but winning little girl with a strict but
affectionate nurse. In the present neo-Edwardian case,
Nursey doesn't let Marianna May do anything that would
get her "white, white, white" dress dirty. It takes an entire
staff of servants to solve the problem in a fashionable way.
Deliberately repetitive for the first half of the book, the
text abandons this mannerism—and with it its implicit appeal
to pre-reading children—in its later pages. There are
full-color drawings on every pretty page and if they aren't
exactly new, they are certainly very nice.

Joan W. Blos, in a review of "Marianna May
and Nursey," in School Library Journal, Vol.
30, No. 5, January, 1984, p. 63.

Marianna May is a poor little rich girl, whose main affliction
is that she cannot do what she likes because Nursey
insists she keep her beautiful white dresses clean. The iceman
notices her melancholy, and the servants join together
to solve the problem by dyeing Marianna May's dresses
a rainbow of useful colors, such as green for grass and pink
for strawberry ice cream. This solution to the problem has
two advantages: Not only can Marianna May eat orange
ice to her heart's content in the orange dress, but the illustrator
also has the opportunity to picture a series of colorful
Edwardian outfits. Even Nursey, a good sort at heart,
bursts forth—in a glorious pink and violet ensemble, eating
pink cotton candy. The story is a triumph of practicality
over prissiness, and the illustrations are a vehicle for a
splendid display of color.

Ann A. Flowers, in a review of "Marianna May
and Nursey," in The Horn Book Magazine,
Vol. LX, No. 2, April, 1984, p. 182.

Sing, Pierrot, Sing: A Picture Book in Mime   (1983)

In a wordless picture book a love-struck Pierrot goes to
woo the beautiful Columbine with a rose from his rose
bush and a love song of his own devising. An audience
gathers as Pierrot sings under Columbine's balcony, only
to laugh in ridicule as Harlequin smugly appears with the
scornful Columbine. The wistful Pierrot then climbs a ladder
to the moon and broods, but a group of sympathetic
children retrieve his rose, his music, and his instrument.
They coax him down to play for them; then they all sit
companionably, silhouetted against the moon. Told entirely
in pictures, the charming tale follows the European
tradition of Harlequin and Columbine presented as a pantomime.
Unusually pleasing illustrations in glowing colors
show to perfection a pensive Pierrot usually accompanied
by a cat, a dog, and a rabbit as well as by a Botticelli-like
Columbine and an enormous brilliant moon. (pp. 697-98)

Ann A. Flowers, in a review of "Sing, Pierrot,
Sing: A Picture Book in Mime," in The Horn
Book Magazine, Vol. LIX, No. 6, December,
1983, pp. 697-98.

In traditional Italian improvisational touring theatre,
commedia dell'arte, stock characters play out stock roles.
Clever Arlecchino (Harlequin) clowns and wins the equally
clever Columbine, while sweet, sad Pierrot (an addition
from the romantic but cynical French) always woos and
loses. Here is Pierrot in white clown suit and clown white
mime face wordlessly courting Columbine with rose and
mandolin in moonlight beneath her balcony. . . . This silent
paean to mime is one of dePaola's best, obviously a
labor of love, profuse with rich double-page spreads.
Where picture order might be confusing, dePaola incorporates
circled numbers into the design.

Helen Gregory, in a review of "Sing, Pierrot,
Sing: A Picture Book in Mime," in School Library
Journal, Vol. 30, No. 4, December, 1983,
p. 54.

Sadness and gaiety are shown as facets of human affections
in fine, mannered pictures, varied by the subdued humour
suggested by the dog, cat and rabbit who join in the
action. Muted colours and firm ink line combine to create
a serene and beautiful gloss on the *Commedia del arte* tradition.

Margery Fisher, in a review of "Sing, Pierrot,
Sing," in Growing Point, Vol. 22, No. 6,
March, 1984, p. 4221.

Noah and the Ark   (1983)

Tomie dePaola has pared the story of Noah down to its
essentials and given it simple illustrations in warm, soft
colors. His use of shape and pattern, his solemn olive-eyed
people and animals and cozy little ark make for a comforting
tale of divine retribution and redemption. Hutton's
Noah and the Great Flood (Atheneum, 1977) is closer to
the Old Testament while Lorimer chose a modern vernacular
for his retelling of *Noah's Ark* (Random, 1978). Both
versions are more sophisticated in language and richer in
illustrative detail. Max Bolliger's *Noah and the Rainbow*
(Harper, 1972) has a more poetic, impressionistic quality.
In *Noah's Ark* (Doubleday, 1977), Peter Spier tells a witty
and expressive version solely through his minutely detailed
drawings. This one, with its repetition and simplicity,
is appropriate for very young children.

Robin Fenn Elbot, in a review of "Noah and
the Ark," in School Library Journal, Vol. 30,
No. 8, April, 1984, p. 100.

In an unadorned retelling of the Noah story, de Paola provides
an ark and set of animals that resemble a carefully
carved wooden-toy set and places them in a stylized,
small-format setting. Colors are mostly earth tones, relieved
by the red tile of the ark's roof and the deep blue-green
of the water. This is not as humorous as Peter
Spier's *Noah's Ark* nor as elegant as Warwick Hutton's
Noah and the Great Flood but a simple version that makes
smooth reading aloud for the very young. (pp. 1113-14)

Barbara Elleman, in a review of "Noah and
the Ark," in Booklist, Vol. 80, No. 15, April 1,
1984, pp. 1113-14.

The Mysterious Giant of Barletta: An Italian Folktale (1984)

A statue of a giant boy stands in Barletta, enjoying the children and lovers at his feet, the sleeping doves on his shoulders, until word comes that an enormous army is coming to invade the town. The Mysterious Giant comes to life, and, with the aid of old Zia Conchetta, concocts a scheme to turn the army away. He meets the army, crying about the other boys in town: "They say I'm too small. They call me names, like *minusculo* and *debole*—'tiny' and 'weakling . . . ' " Of course, the army retreats from the prospect of even bigger giants. The illustrations are among DePaola's best: vigorous line and expressive movement against an atmospheric background of rich golds, blues, and reds. The last wordless page—*Colosso* at rest again, surrounded by the sleeping city—is beautiful. A fluent retelling and large-scale paintings make this ideal for story hour.

> *Zena Sutherland, in a review of "The Mysterious Giant of Barletta," in* Bulletin of the Center for Children's Books, *Vol. 37, No. 10, June, 1984, p. 184.*

The fantasy of the small child defeating a large, threatening force is understandably popular with children. The Italian folktale retold here by dePaola manages to provide a hero who is both Goliath and David at once. . . . If dePaola's chubby, round-eyed little-boy giant doesn't look much like an antique image of a noble young man, well, most children won't mind. And if the first half of the book is a trifle slow, the climactic trick is satisfyingly successful. In the age of "He-Man" and other superheroes, we might all be grateful for a story celebrating a small boy's brains rather than a giant's brawn.

> *Patricia Dooley, in a review of "The Mysterious Giant of Barletta: An Italian Folktale," in* School Library Journal, *Vol. 31, No. 4, December, 1984, p. 69.*

[This] is a lively, bright, funny Italian folktale, . . . enshrining an ancient but still satisfying joke about a giant who scares an invading army away from his home town by claiming to be just the runt of the family. It is the anti-Rambo of fairy-tales and should inspire that reverence for cowardice that is the beginning of wisdom. If a young person may not learn such ancient verities from these antique tales, there is little point in keeping them going.

> *Angela Carter, "Told and Re-Told: Picture Books 2," in* The Times Literary Supplement, *No. 4313, November 29, 1985, p.1360.*

The First Christmas (1984)

Probably destined for a conspicuous place among home Yuletide decorations, dePaola's pop-up Nativity radiates universal feelings of peace and goodwill. The artist tells the ages-old story simply but he illustrates events with lushly hued paintings in his instantly recognizable fashion. Gabriel's announcement to Mary and what follows are celebrated in three-dimensional scenes with many inspired details that catch the eye. The journey of Joseph and Mary from Galilee to Bethlehem and the birth of Jesus in the stable are heralded by angels that bring shepherds from the hills while the three kings are guided to the manger by the star in the east. Doves, sheep and other animals, as well as the human figures, possess the childlike innocence that dePaola renders so disarmingly. (pp. 78-9)

> *A review of "The First Christmas," in* Publishers Weekly, *Vol. 226, No. 10, September 7, 1984, pp. 78-9.*

Center-tied hard covers open to form the wings of a backdrop for a series of pull-down, papercut pages that serve as a medieval setting for the abbreviated text (half-a-dozen sentences) that tells the Nativity story. The illustrations are attractive, but this seems a trivial pursuit when there are more poetic versions, some of them handsomely illustrated and using or paraphasing the beautiful language of the Bible. Here there is, on the title page, a slightly longer version of the Christmas story than is contained on the cut-paper pages, but it is also truncated.

> *Zena Sutherland, in a review of "The First Christmas," in* Bulletin of the Center for Children's Books, *Vol. 38, No. 2, October, 1984, p. 23.*

DePaola's triptych book, with six tableaus, is a three-dimensional celebration of the story of Christ's birth in the style of **Giorgio's Village.** When the three panels are opened, there is a brief retelling of the gospel. As succeeding pages are folded down, parts of the story are illustrated, with moving panels: the angel Gabriel tells Mary that she will be the mother of Jesus; Mary and Joseph arrive in Bethlehem; an innkeeper points out the way to his stable. The most impressive movement is the kaleidoscope star, which can open up as the wise men approach. This is an unusual presentation of the Christmas story, whose most obvious use would be in a Christmas display or in a holiday story hour.

> *Elizabeth M. Simmons, in a review of "The First Christmas," in* School Library Journal, *Vol. 31, No. 2, October, 1984, p. 173.*

Tomie dePaola's Mother Goose (1985)

[This new edition of **Mother Goose**] is a mutedly colorful, well-designed and rich sampling of 200-plus rhymes and songs of childhood. Its selections, leaning heavily toward those emphasizing domestic animals—cows, pigs, ducks, hens, geese, cats and dogs—make this a Mother Goose decidedly aimed at the younger range of listeners. (It also results in an unavoidable sameness to some of the pictures, particularly in the early part.)

The rhymes are told complete in most instances, with the texts taken from Iona and Peter Opie, the folklore specialists in Britain. The book includes such nontraditional rhymes as "Three little ghostesses, / Sitting on postesses" and " 'I went up one pair of stairs.' 'Just like me.' " (This ends with, " 'And there I saw a monkey.' 'Just like me.' ")

Here, as elsewhere in a markedly successful 20-year career

in children's picture books, Mr. dePaola provides ingratiating, cheerful and intelligent illustrations, albeit perhaps too bland. His *Mother Goose* cuts a commendably wide ethnic swath with black, Hispanic, Oriental and gypsy characters taking full part in the verse happenings. Rhymes about time and weather are illustrated together inventively.

Mr. dePaola often depicts his *Mother Goose* in what might be called tableau style. In his **"Old King Cole,"** for example, all the necessary characters and props are set out on the page, but they are not in action. The text must supply every bit of that. He follows the same course in **"Sing a Song of Sixpence"** and countless others. While this illustrative approach is defensible—certainly it encourages close listening—it sometimes looks like a failure of nerve and an unwillingness to come to grips with an event full of graphic possibilities. It does, in the end, also make for a static quality that palls. We yearn for a Keystone Kops approach.

When Mr. dePaola does go out for the action—as in his inspired 26-frame animation for **"Old Mother Hubbard,"** in which we never see more than her head and shoulders yet are fully aware of what is going on—he is first-rate. His **"Jack and Jill,"** in which the rhyme's action takes place on a puppet stage, and his **"Hey Diddle, Diddle,"** with an infectiously laughing dog, are also noteworthy.

Where he excels, however, is as a decorator rather than as an illustrator of action. His **"Sally Go Round the Sun"** and his full-page **"Dance to Your Daddy"** are lovely embellishments of the verses' ingredients, as is his balletlike **"Jack Be Nimble."** Mr. dePaola is at his best when his illustration catches the music of a given rhyme, and he can do this with a vignette or a full-page picture. In the book's final section, about Christmas and bedtime, the artist provides full-page, richly painted settings for such snippets of verse as **"Twinkle, Twinkle, Little Star"** and **"Matthew, Mark, Luke, and John."** Just on the outer verges of sentimentality, still they work.

If Mr. dePaola's *Mother Goose* is not as wide-ranging and varied as Raymond Briggs's distinguished 1966 edition, he has certainly managed to give the old Dame a most tasteful and affectionate valentine.

> *Selma Lanes, in a review of "Tomie dePaola's Mother Goose," in* The New York Times Book Review, *December 22, 1985, p. 24.*

Destined to become a classic, *Tomie dePaola's Mother Goose* is a large, ample, unfussy edition of every child's first staple of literature. On the cover Mother Goose herself, placidly waving, is garbed de rigueur in a countrywoman's dress, a large white apron, and a black hat and mitts, with a basket over her arm, and is affectionately stroking her fine, substantial white goose. The neat, flat illustrations are darkly outlined and colored generally in the illustrator's favorite palette of clear pinks, blues, and violets and surrounded with a lot of white space. Each verse is pictured in a simple and unmistakable interpretation, easy to see and understandable to a young child. Some are strikingly beautiful: "Matthew, Mark, Luke and John / Bless the bed that I lie on" depicts four hovering

angels, and two facing pages of domestic fowl—a goose, black hen, and rooster—are graphic art at its best. The rhymes are the familiar ones, **"Humpty Dumpty," "Simple Simon," "Old Mother Hubbard"**; usually the Opie versions are used. Roughly similar rhymes are grouped together—rhymes about going to bed, love, birds, animals, weather, the sea. The very last selections are children's prayers, ending with **"Now I lay me down to sleep."** A perfectly basic and lovely Mother Goose, lavish yet simple, and a splendid beginning for the youngest listener.

> *Ann A. Flowers, in a review of "Tomie dePaola's Mother Goose," in* The Horn Book Magazine, *Vol. LXII, No. 1, January-February, 1986, p. 66.*

Every good children's illustrator comes sooner or later to Mother Goose. Here, for the most part in good traditional Opie versions, Tomie de Paola has arranged by unobtrusive thematic links some 200 nursery rhymes, with gloriously funny illustrations. They owe much to earlier woodcut chapbook style (come to think of it, that must always have been one source of his inspiration), but among the very varied formats, there is something of Kate Greenaway's early verse books and, in the solider pages of illustration, of Walter Crane. The clarity of line and colour, the economy of background, with a strong use of plain white, the chunky figures with such telling expressions (my favourite is Crosspatch, but Georgy-Porgy takes some beating) are a joy. There is no doubt that this is not only, arguably, this American illustrator's best work to date, but that it will become a classic of nursery illustration.

> *M. Hobbs, in a review of "Mother Goose," in* The Junior Bookshelf, *Vol. 50, No. 1, February, 1986, p. 14.*

Merry Christmas, Strega Nona   (1986)

Strega Nona is busily preparing for her annual feast for the whole town of Calabria, a place readers will remember from the Caldecott Honor-winning *Strega Nona.* Because "Christmas has a magic of its own," Strega Nona and her bumbling assistant Big Anthony have to do everything the hard way—this is the one time each year that "Grandma Witch" abandons her potions and spells. On the day before Christmas, Strega Nona sends Big Anthony to town with a shopping list, which he promptly forgets. For the first time ever, there will be no chance for her to prepare anything; Strega Nona will be alone on Christmas. But it's not to be—the townspeople bring their own feast, thanks to Big Anthony's plans. DePaola shows a master's touch for twisting readers' emotions, first when Strega Nona waits futilely for Big Anthony to arrive with supplies, then when she trudges up the hill toward her darkened, lonely looking home. The joyful ending and sparkling illustrations make this one of the most warmhearted selections of the season.

> *A review of "Merry Christmas, Strega Nona," in* Publishers Weekly, *Vol. 230, No. 13, September 26, 1986, p. 74.*

In this fourth story featuring Strega Nona and her bumbling helper, Big Anthony, the pair are hard at work preparing for the traditional Christmas feast. . . . DePaola continues with his softly hued pictures of landscapes and costume and with his subtle lines to create very funny expressions. Here, he uses to advantage the opportunity to introduce some Italian customs and words. Anthony is still a gangling, oafish, but good-natured helper. It's nice to see him do something right for a change. *Buon Natale!* (p. 109)

Judith Gloyer, "Celebrate the Season!" in School Library Journal, *Vol. 33, No. 2, October, 1986, pp. 109-13.*

Vibrancy echoes through both story and graphics in dePaola's affectionate portrayal of these old friends. Drawings, done in pencil, colored inks, and watercolors, are nicely shaded, accentuating the comedic tones with proper punch. It's especially satisfying to see a bona fide story centered on Christmas that is funny, accessible, and contains a gentle message tucked neatly inside. (p. 408)

Ilene Cooper, in a review of "Merry Christmas, Strega Nona," in Booklist, *Vol. 83, No. 5, November 1, 1986, pp. 407-08.*

Tomie dePaola's Favorite Nursery Tales (1986)

This collection of favorite stories for the youngest appears

From Tomie dePaola's Favorite Nursery Tales, *written and illustrated by Tomie dePaola.*

as a companion to the author/illustrator's **Mother Goose,** which was published last year.

Liberally padded with Aesop, it contains most of the expected stories: **"Little Red Hen," "The Three Bears,"** and so forth. Also included are a few familiar verses from Stevenson and Longfellow. The retellings are the most nonviolent possible, while retaining fidelity to the story (the troll in **"The Three Billy Goats Gruff "** is tossed into the water, for example), which should satisfy parents, if not purists. The prose style usefully takes the stories from beginning to end in a straightforward manner, with few pauses for interesting language or description along the way. DePaola's brightly colored illustrations liberally decorate the pages and suit the nature of the text, both in their pragmatic carrying out of story themes and their lack of distinction.

Enormously useful as a gift book and as an added collection for libraries. For memorable storytelling, however, it will never replace the collections done by Rockwell and Rojankovsky.

A review of "Tomie dePaola's Favorite Nursery Tales," in Kirkus Reviews, *Vol. LIV, No. 22, November 15, 1986, p. 1720.*

An irrepressible sense of humor permeates the selections and illustrations for **Tomie dePaola's Favorite Nursery Tales.** This attractive companion volume to last season's **Tomie dePaola's Mother Goose** has a similarly large, handsome format with vivid colors and many of the same comical characters who always inhabit dePaola's enchanted world. To the seventeen tales from traditional sources, such as Grimm, Andersen, Asbjørnsen, and Joseph Jacobs, have been added some poems and several of Aesop's fables. Only a few of the best-known stories overlap with the stories in *The Helen Oxenbury Nursery Story Book.* Among the cumulative tales are **"Chicken Licken"** and **"The Little Red Hen"** and the less familiar **"How Jack Went to Seek His Fortune"** and **"The Cat and the Mouse."** Though **"The Three Little Pigs"** is attributed to Joseph Jacobs, it has been substantially changed. At the end of this version, the chimney is too hot, so the wolf goes away, and the pig fetches his mother to live with him. While this ending is unfamiliar, the beribboned mother pig posing for a portrait in front of the brick house is another of dePaola's unforgettable creations. Some of the other memorable characters are the ornate, foppish puppy in **"The Emperor's New Clothes,"** the friendly animals marching across the pages in **"The House on the Hill,"** and a Woody Allen type of owl dancing by the light of the moon with a vamp of a pussycat. Tomie dePaola's illustrations have given children so much pleasure, his artwork has acquired the instant recognition of a trademark.

Hanna B. Zeiger, in a review of "Tomie dePaola's Favorite Nursery Tales," in The Horn Book Magazine, *Vol. LXIII, No. 2, March-April, 1987, p. 228.*

This is a book that will last for three generations or more. . . . (p. 125)

Tomie de Paola, most endearing of modern illustrators on the world scene, has gathered a couple of dozen folk-tales, all in familiar and lively versions, added a small handful of rhymes, and explored, adorned and enriched them all with his inimitable drawings in excellent colour on every page. I could wish no better first storybook for a very special child, and it would do much good to less special children too.

De Paola's is a world of wise innocence. There is not a hint of sophistication in his drawings. Here is a child's fresh and timeless view. Witness the spoilt-child of a princess in **'The Frog Prince'** and the jolly little boy prince recently transmogrified from frog, and the equal innocence of Andersen's **'Real Princess'**. De Paola is one of those rare artists who are as good and amusing with human subjects as with animals. His cocky resilient fox crops up perkily in several stories, always a wild creature even when he has added human characteristics, whereas the three Bears are obviously animated teddy-bears manipulated by Goldilocks. Every page offers its delights to be shared between reader and hearer. (pp. 125-26)

> *M. Crouch, in a review of "Favourite Nursery Tales," in* The Junior Bookshelf, *Vol. 51, No. 3, June, 1987, pp. 125-26.*

Katie and Kit at the Beach; Katie, Kit and Cousin Tom; Katie's Good Idea; Pajamas for Kit   (1986)

In these sturdy board books for older toddlers, dePaola presents Katie and Kit, two kitten children whose everyday experiences have a familiar ring. The stories concern a day at the beach, getting along with nasty cousin Tom, Kit learning to ride his tricycle, and Grandpa figuring out what to do when Kit forgets to bring pajamas for an overnight visit. Pictures are scaled to fit the small format; the kitten figures appear in simple compositions placed against a plain, white backdrop. Considering the age level for which these books are designed, their stories are strong, with recognizable structure and plot elements. They will be welcome additions to the board-book shelves.

> *Denise M. Wilms, in a review of "Katie & Kit at the Beach," "Katie, Kit & Cousin Tom," "Katie's Good Idea," and "Pajamas for Kit," in* Booklist, *Vol. 83, No. 17, May 1, 1987, p. 1366.*

This series of board books is sure to give children and adults alike more than just a few chuckles. Illustrated in dePaola's delightful style, the books show child-like features on kittens, from a disappointed kitten whose day at the beach is rained on (*Katie & Kit at the Beach*) to the demanding look of a bully (*Katie, Kit, and Cousin Tom*). In *Katie's Good Idea,* Kit has a common problem—his legs are not long enough to reach the pedals of his new tricycle (which is said to be red but is really orange and pink). In *Pajamas for Kit,* the toddler-kittens are all ready to spend the night at Grandma and Grandpa's house, when Kit decides to repack his bag with more of his precious belongings, only to find once he arrives that he has left out one very important item—his pajamas. Preschoolers and early readers will easily relate to all of the themes that dePaola has chosen, and will relish the appealing personalities of the kitten kids, but it is *Katie, Kit, &*

Cousin Tom that is sure to hit home with any child who has ever faced a bully. These four board books will take their place along side those by Rosemary Wells and Helen Oxenbury.

> *Blair Christolon, in a review of "Katie & Kit at the Beach," "Katie, Kit, & Cousin Tom," "Katie's Good Idea," and "Pajamas for Kit," in* School Library Journal, *Vol. 33, No. 11, August, 1987, p. 66.*

Bill and Pete Go Down the Nile   (1987)

Bill, the little lime-green crocodile, is back with Pete, his magenta, living-toothbrush bird, in another humorous adventure.

This time Ms. Ibis is taking the class on a trip to the Royal Museum to see the Sacred Eye of Isis. "OOOOOOOO," say all the little crocodiles, suitably impressed by the treasures. But Bill and Pete are quick to notice "The Bad Guy" about to steal the treasure. Working together, they foil the thief; and as a reward all the little crocodiles are sent home on the "Nile Queen." "And so, Mama, that's what happened on our first class trip," says Bill. "My goodness," says Mama. "What an adventure." Indeed. A warm and funny picture-book that should find a wide audience.

This is also a visual delight, with simplified shapes, Egyptian motifs, and soft, stucco-like colors.

> *A review of "Bill and Pete Go Down the Nile," in* Kirkus Reviews, *Vol. LV, No. 8, April 15, 1987, p. 635.*

Fresh and funny, this will not only amuse little ones (and teach them a bit of Egyptology), but will also provide plenty of laughs for the adults who are reading this aloud—as when the Bad Guy calls the crocodile a walking suitcase. Pure blues, greens, and pinks are the dominant colors dePaola uses to punctuate his continually amusing pictures. Whether focusing on the class of crocodiles moving in a straight line up the side of the pyramid, or on teacher Ms. Ibis, safari hat on head, umbrella in hand, the story has laughs aplenty. More Bill and Pete, please. (p. 1366)

> *Ilene Cooper, in a review of "Bill and Pete Go Down the Nile," in* Booklist, *Vol. 83, No. 17, May 1, 1987, pp. 1365-66.*

DePaola turns his gaze from the beloved hills of Italy to return to the fertile shores of Egypt's Nile River. . . . The humor is gentle, and a bit of mystery and adventure is woven in as Bill and Pete capture a couple of bad guys during a class trip down the Nile. Egyptian motifs and warm colors accompany the full-page drawings that show Mama's ever-present gaze, always full of loving hearts for her dear son Bill. Humor, adventure, even a bit of Egyptian history and lore—who could ask for anything more, except for more "Bill and Pete" adventures.

> *Judith Gloyer, in a review of "Bill and Pete Go Down the Nile," in* School Library Journal, *Vol. 34, No. 1, September, 1987, p. 162.*

An Early American Christmas   (1987)

DePaola begins with a historical note that surely will intrigue children: in Colonial New England, the celebration of Christmas was shunned in many villages. He depicts the arrival of a German family into one such town, showing their careful, loving preparations. Their efforts begin in autumn, when bayberries are picked and candles made; they continue throughout the fall, until apples are dried and strung, cookies and pretzels are baked, "hearts of man" and other paper ornaments are snipped and, finally, candles are lit in every window. This provides a fascinating look at Christmas as it once was: a holiday whose customs were entwined with the season's natural bounty. The emphasis is on the joys of preparation and of quiet, heartfelt observance; refreshingly, gift-giving is not a concern. This is a warm and beautifully realized tribute to the spirit and traditions of the season.

> *A review of "An Early American Christmas," in* Publishers Weekly, *Vol. 232, No. 11, September 11, 1987, p. 93.*

Using an imagined New England family of Germanic roots, dePaola personalizes and traces the arrival of what we think of now as traditional American Christmas customs. . . . The artist's palette is more muted, borders less bold than in earlier books, but present are his signature cats, hearts and stars, flat people, and framed illustrations. A good book for talking about other Christmas customs children may celebrate in their own homes and the origins of these family traditions.

> *Susan Hepler, in a review of "An Early American Christmas," in* School Library Journal, *Vol. 34, No. 2, October, 1987, p. 31.*

DePaola shows us each traditional preparation in gleeful detail, from gold-painted walnuts and papercut decorations for the tree to Christmas cookies in the shapes of tulips, lovebirds, and "hearts in hand." His brightly colored, folk-art style nicely complements his story of one family's way of celebrating Christmas. Avoiding holiday sentimentality without sacrificing joy in the season, this is a nice addition to holiday book collections.

> *A review of "An Early American Christmas," in* Kirkus Reviews, *Vol. LV, No. 19, October 1, 1987, p. 1460.*

The Miracles of Jesus; The Parables of Jesus   (1987)

Decorative Romanesque-inspired illustrations illuminate familiar Bible stories in a masterful blend of art and idea. DePaola uses soft, chalklike colors and repetitive geometric shapes to create a rich and satisfying tapestry. The rhythm of waves, wind, fabric folds, and rich patterns of leaves, animals, and people provide a feast for the eyes.

In *Miracles*, a double-page layout is used for each story, creating a unit with a distinct mood and thought. **"The Wedding at Cana," "The Ten Lepers,"** and **"The Loaves and Fishes"** are among the 12 miracles adapted from the New Testament.

Parables presents 17 brief stories, including **"The Good Samaritan," "The Prodigal Son,"** and **"The Mustard Seed."** Children without exposure to Bible stories may have difficulty with the vocabulary: Pharisee, publican, leaven, sower. The illustrations are more complex, often several to a page, and require careful reading, sometimes in sequences from left to right or top to bottom. In **"The Laborers in the Vineyard,"** the scenes form a tapestry with narrow lines of color used to indicate the time sequence from early morning to evening.

Striking and evocative creations by a master craftsman.

> *A review of "The Miracles of Jesus" and "The Parables of Jesus," in* Kirkus Reviews, *Vol. LV, No. 18, September 15, 1987, p. 1391.*

Seventeen of the best-known parables and thirteen miracles, with the Biblical texts only slightly shortened and simplified, are retold with the beauty and dignity of the original. The artist's typical stylized, flat, highly decorative illustrations of sturdy, pensive figures, their faces often expressing awe, in soft, warm tones, have a still, timeless quality particularly appropriate to the spirituality and eternity of the subject. Birds, animals, plants, and buildings, arranged with dynamic symmetry, enhance the pleasing harmony of line, shape, and color. No attempt has been made to portray historically accurate scenes. Inspiration for the artwork has come from the ornamental, geometric, and earthy Romanesque period of the 11th Century of Europe, giving a universality in keeping with the perennial Biblical themes. A clear, attractive typeface completes the handsome large format. The miracle stories are more straightforward and easier to understand than the parables, but both books would need some previous background knowledge or adult input. While the parables of the sowers and the weeds in the wheat are included, Jesus' explanations of them are not, so the stories lack clarity. The rest of the material is presented in its entirety, without addition or comment. Although there are many acceptable Bible story collections available, these companion volumes, with their masterful integration of text and fine art, would make a valuable addition to any library.

> *Patricia Pearl, in a review of "The Miracles of Jesus" and "The Parables of Jesus," in* School Library Journal, *Vol. 34, No. 2, October, 1987, p. 121.*

[In *The Parables of Jesus*] dePaola retells New Testament parables, many of which invite further discussion about their messages (some of the parables will require a bit of puzzling through for picture book readers). The palette of the illustrations has an intense, hand-mixed look; the pictures reveal clues about the stories' meanings. **"The Good Samaritan"** is included, as is **"The Mustard Seed," "The Prodigal Son"** and other pieces from the books of Matthew, Mark and Luke, parables that dePaola makes into entertaining, thought-provoking material for young readers. A luminous collection.

> *A review of "The Parables of Jesus," in* Publishers Weekly, *Vol. 232, No. 15, October 9, 1987, p. 87.*

Tomie dePaola's Book of Christmas Carols (1987)

Unlike dePaola's recent *An Early American Christmas,* which shows the dawn of holiday jubilance in a New England village, this book portrays the more serene aspects of Christmas, of reverance and religious imagery. The selections are mostly familiar—**"O, Come All Ye Faithful,"** **"I Saw Three Ships," "Good King Wenceslas," "Bring a Torch, Jeannette, Isabella!"**—with some lesser-known songs as well: **"The Cherry Tree Carol"** and **" 'Twas in the Moon of Wintertime."** But well-known or not, the carols are lovingly placed among pictures with varied settings: Victorian and biblical, some on gatefold pages. DePaola's intense hues—slate blues, rich burgundies and mossy greens—reflect the way colors show up in a wintry background. His Christmas spirit, here of subdued joy, is infectious.

> *A review of "Tomie dePaola's Book of Christmas Carols," in* Publishers Weekly, *Vol. 232, No. 14, September 25, 1987, p. 105.*

A perfect collection of 32 carols, mostly familiar, with words and music printed large enough for sharing around the piano and with simple arrangements suitable for accompaniment or part singing. Serene full-page illustrations (plus several triple-page fold-outs) and rhythmically arranged decorations on every page make this a handsome, well-designed volume. Certain to be one of the prolific author-illustrator's most popular.

> *A review of "Tomie dePaola's Book of Christmas Carols," in* Kirkus Reviews, *Vol. LV, No. 20, October 15, 1987, p. 1514.*

A handsomely produced book of carols lavishly illustrated by the artist in his distinctive style. Angels, Christmas trees, holly and snow abound and there are magnificent double spreads with a Christmas theme. As usual, children are shown as pleasant, solid and down-to-earth.

The first verse of the carol sung by mice in *The Wind in the Willows,* sets the scene. It is followed by thirty-two carols. Here are the familiar hymns typified by **'Once in Royal David's city'** and **'Hark the Herald angels sing',** the traditional Coventry Carol and **'Silent night',** and less familiar carols from other countries. Very suitably the last carol is the familiar 'We wish you a merry Christmas'.

The tunes are the familiar ones with the exception of that to **'Away in a manger'** which has a tune which, although not the usual one, is pleasant and simple. Accompaniments are reasonably uncomplicated.

A seasonable and representative collection delightfully illustrated. Such a carol book is always good to have as a family possession.

> *E. Colwell, in a review of "Book of Christmas Carols," in* The Junior Bookshelf, *Vol. 52, No. 1, February, 1988, p. 29.*

Tomie dePaola's Kitten Kids and the Big Camp-Out;
Tomie dePaola's Kitten Kids and the Haunted House;
Tomie dePaola's Kitten Kids and the Missing Dinosaur;
Tomie dePaola's Kitten Kids and the Treasure Hunt
(1988)

DePaola fans who expect delightful sequels to the Kitten Kids board books are in for a disappointment. Although these new tales are based on characters he created, they are fairly successful imitations [by D & R Animation] of the author/artist's bold line drawings and color washes. The design and format of the books seem to be intended for the younger preschool set, yet the text in each tale is overlong, appearing dense and dark against the page; in addition, the dialogue is rather wooden, and the stories are convoluted. Rather self-consciously "cute" and slick, the collection has a certain undeniable appeal: the illustrations are in bright pastels and the price is affordable. But discerning dePaola fans should beware. (pp. 272-73)

> *A review of "Tomie dePaola's Kitten Kids and the Big Camp Out," "Tomie dePaola's Kitten Kids and the Haunted House," "Tomie dePaola's Kitten Kids and the Missing Dinosaur," and "Tomie dePaola's Kitten Kids and the Treasure Hunt," in* Publishers Weekly, *Vol. 233, No. 19, May 13, 1988, pp. 272–73.*

The Legend of the Indian Paintbrush (1988)

Little Gopher can't keep up with the other Indian boys; he prefers making and decorating small figures. When it's his turn to go out into the hills "to think about being a man," a vision tells him to become a painter, using colors "as pure as . . . the evening sky." But though he works hard, Little Gopher is dissatisfied with his dull, dark paintings. Patiently, he gazes at the sunset each evening till at last he is rewarded: brushes with sunset colors spring up for his use, returning next day—and each spring thereafter—as flowers.

In a full-page note, dePaola traces this story to *Texas Wildflowers, Stories and Legends,* a collection of newspaper articles by Ruth D. Isely—which doesn't really give much clue to its Native American source. The retelling is pleasantly cadenced, even though it tells us more about the artist's need for self-expression within any society than about Plains Indians. And dePaola's somber tones burst forth into satisfyingly brilliant sunsets. This should do well at picture-book tour.

> *A review of "The Legend of the Indian Paintbrush," in* Kirkus Reviews, *Vol. LVI, No. 10, May 15, 1988, p. 759.*

This book will inevitably be compared with *The Legend of the Bluebonnet,* but the pivotal elements are very different. The humanity expressed in this story illustrates the value of perseverance, and of endurance of effort that will bring its reward. DePaola's softly rounded shapes and his hero's diminutive stature, downcast eyes, and sober mien breathe attitudes of acceptance, of quiet waiting, of diligent persistence. The picture of the boy gazing mutely, patiently, into the western sky is ineffably moving. And dePaola must have had a wonderful time painting the gloriously uplifting skies depicted here. (p. 97)

Ruth Semrau, in a review of "The Legend of the Indian Paintbrush," in School Library Journal, *Vol. 35, No. 9, June-July, 1988, pp. 96-7.*

How a young Indian boy, Little Gopher, becomes a man, He-Who-Brought-the-Sunset-to-the-Earth, is an engaging tale of strength, perserverance, reverence, and obedience. DePaola's familiar style is as ideal for this tale as it was for **The Legend of the Bluebonnet** and **Mary Had a Little Lamb.** The native American motifs are rendered simply and authentically; the night sky and glorious sunset spreads are truly beautiful with line, color, and form perfectly balanced to capture the text.

Elizabeth S. Watson, in a review of "The Legend of the Indian Paintbrush," in The Horn Book Magazine, *Vol. LXIV, No. 4, July-August, 1988, p. 505.*

Baby's First Christmas   (1988)

This excellent holiday board book for toddlers features simple declarative sentences, one per page, about the many symbols of Christmas. "This is the wreath that hangs on the door" is followed by words about the candle, holly, manger scene, candy and ornaments, stockings, cookies, Santa Claus, and finally the Christmas tree "with presents for you to open." No people are shown. The slightly larger-than-usual size of this sturdy board book and the colorful, uncluttered pages make it a natural for preschool story groups as well as a satisfying lap reader for the pointer set.

Susan Hepler, in a review of "Baby's First Christmas," in School Library Journal, *Vol. 35, No. 2, October, 1988, p. 33.*

Sturdy board pages, brightened with the images of Christmas, make up a catalog of Christmas symbols to share with little ones anticipating the holiday. "This is the wreath that hangs on the door . . . This is the holly that goes all around. This is the manger scene that sits on the mantle." DePaola's simple, stylized drawings illustrate each item in its setting. Slight in concept, but the artist's accomplished sense of design and color make it a nice introduction to the season.

Denise M. Wilms, in a review of "Baby's First Christmas," in Booklist, *Vol. 85, No. 4, October 15, 1988, p. 406.*

Tomie dePaola's Book of Poems   (1988)

A pleasant, undemanding collection of 86 poems, most of them already familiar, in large format with generous use of white space. The arrangement is rather loose—there are some morning poems to begin with, and both the end of the year and the end of the day come at the end of the book—but there's no real subject access. While his illustrations are decorative and accessible, dePaola has not ex-

From The Art Lesson, *written and illustrated by Tomie dePaola.*

tended the poems' meanings; in many cases, he is content merely to picture a pensive speaker—at least he can't be faulted for intruding on the listener's imagination! These *are* good, popular poems from the usual obvious sources, and this makes an attractive collection for browsing or sharing with a young child. Table of contents; index of first lines; no author index.

A review of "Tomie dePaola's Book of Poems," in Kirkus Reviews, *Vol. LVI, No. 20, October 15, 1988, p. 1525.*

Like **Tomie dePaola's Mother Goose,** this most recent addition to the dePaola anthologies is thoughtfully compiled and organized. The opening poem, **"There is no frigate like a book"** by Emily Dickinson, prepares the way for the entries that follow, which take readers from the beginning of the day to the end, and all around the world. The first poems are morning poems such as **"The Way to Start a Day"** by Byrd Baylor and **"Time to Rise"** by Robert Louis Stevenson; these are followed by more general poems such as **"Bananas and Cream"** by David McCord and **"Mother to Son"** by Langston Hughes; at the end of the volume are evening or ending poems, which include **"Cat in Moonlight"** by Douglas Gibson, **"Autumn Leaves"** by Aileen Fisher and **"Stopping by the Woods on a Snowy Evening"** by Robert Frost. While dePaola's characteristic illustrations are beautifully executed, this collection lacks the luminescent quality so pervasive in both his earlier **Favorite Nursery Tales** and **Christmas Carols.** The theme of a day's passing doesn't prove, at least in this book, to be as compelling a basis on which to build a collection of poems.

A review of "Tomie dePaola's Book of Poems,"

in Publishers Weekly, *Vol. 234, No. 18, October 28, 1988, p. 76.*

The companion volume to **Tomie dePaola's Mother Goose, Tomie dePaola's Favorite Nursery Tales,** and **Tomie dePaola's Book of Christmas Carols** is a handsomely produced anthology, designed to encourage browsing and read-aloud sessions. The selections, chosen for their vigor, imagery, and child appeal, offer ample possibilities for visual interpretation—possibilities which the illustrator has generously explored in an array of vividly colored, exuberantly limned pictures. There are witty details recalling earlier works, for dePaola's distinctive style is immediately recognizable. What is not always so obvious, however, is the amazing range of that style and its comfortable compatibility with the requirements and limitations of bookmaking. Such an anthology affords opportunity for fuller appreciation. There are individual portraits, including that of the self-satisfied baseball player in Tony Johnston's **"Overdog,"** which combine elegant use of color with the fluid line of the cartoonist to capture a specific personality: a wonderfully crowded full-page spread conveys the humor in the folk rhyme **"Old Noah's Ark"**; a masterfully executed double-page spread underscores the ups and downs of life in a department store, as recounted in Eve Merriam's jaunty **"Alligator on the Escalator"**; and a simple line of stylized trees is an effective visual translation of Dorothy Aldis's metaphor "Tall trees are brooms/Sweeping the sky." The selection of poems is equally generous, ranging from William Blake to Mark Van Doren, from Lewis Carroll to Jack Prelutsky, from Langston Hughes to Nikki Giovanni, from Robert Louis Stevenson to Margaret Wise Brown, with a delightful lagniappe—the confessions of a young artist in **"The Secret Place"** by Tomie dePaola. While poems on similar topics are frequently juxtaposed, there is no explicitly stated subject arrangement.

Mary M. Burns, in a review of "Tomie dePaola's Book of Poems," in The Horn Book Magazine, *Vol. LXV, No. 1, January-February, 1989, p. 85.*

Haircuts for the Woolseys; Too Many Hopkins   (1989)

In his new Friendly Families of Fiddle-Dee-Dee Farms series, dePaola tells a brief story about a family of sheep called the Woolseys and a family of rabbits known as the Hopkins. These enticing books feature thick, sturdy paper and bright, cheerful pictures. As winter is ending, the Woolseys get their annual "haircuts," but when a cold snap hits, they can't play outside until Grandma comes to the rescue with warm new sweaters knitted from the cuttings. The large Hopkins family sets out to do the spring planting, which should go smoothly because Mommy and Daddy have left specific instructions as to what each should do. But 15 little rabbits manage to get in an unproductive jumble anyway, until Mommy and Daddy Hopkins sort them out. The latter story has a clear sense of childlike behavior, and both books display the kind of humorous warmth children readily respond to. Both of these are appealing picks for toddlers.

Denise M. Wilms, in a review of "Haircuts for the Woolseys" and "Too Many Hopkins," in Booklist, *Vol. 85, No. 12, February 15, 1989, p. 1001.*

[In **Haircuts for the Woolseys** just] the right note of old fashioned cozy plumpness is displayed in the warm, muted drawings and the pleasant "togetherness" expressed by each of the Woolseys. Delightful illustrations and finely tuned whimsy in a simple story make this a winner with preschoolers. . . . [In **Too Many Hopkins** the] soft, warm colors of dePaola's ink and watercolor drawings quietly capture the comfortable feeling of the story, and each bunny is so carefully delineated that this book can also be used as a counting book—up to 15 little bunnies and 2 big bunnies.

Louise M. Zuckerman, in a review of "Haircuts for the Woolseys" and "Too Many Hopkins," in School Library Journal, *Vol. 35, No. 8, April, 1989, p. 80.*

The Art Lesson   (1989)

Budding artist Tommy knows from his grown-up cousins that art's two main credos are "don't copy" and "practice, practice, practice." It's a real blow, then, when Tommy finally gets to first grade and a real art teacher, that she tells the children to *copy* the Pilgrim she's drawn on the board, and allows them only one piece of paper. Tommy goes on strike, but an agreeable compromise is struck, and Tommy goes on drawing, "and he still does," with the last illustration showing a gray-haired Tommy (Tomie?) surrounded by familiar dePaola motifs. While the illustrations hold few surprises, the story has the kind of specificity that characterizes the best dePaola texts, such as **Nana Upstairs and Nana Downstairs.** Here, for example, is kindergarten art time: "It wasn't much fun. The paint was awful and the paper got all wrinkly . . . If it was windy when Tommy carried his picture home, the paint blew right off the paper." And Miss Landers' announcement that everyone must use SCHOOL CRAYONS will strike a chord of remembered dismay in anyone who has ever treasured the Crayola box of sixty-four. (pp. 168-69)

Roger Sutton, in a review of "The Art Lesson," in Bulletin of the Center for Children's Books, *Vol. 42, No. 7, March, 1989, pp. 168-69.*

The perennial conflict between Individual and Authority, or between Artist and Society, lies behind this anecdote, and it's gratifying to see the small non-conformist accomodated. Everyone can enjoy dePaola's gentle autobiographical evocation of a loving family and a happy obsession. But most kids *like* to copy, and copying is essential to the discipline of learning. All great artists did it. DePaola's own style is eminently copyable, and this entertaining book shouldn't discourage young artists from drawing a few dePaolas on their way to copying Rubens.

Patricia Dooley, in a review of "The Art Lesson," in School Library Journal, *Vol. 35, No. 8, April, 1989, p. 80.*

In the first half of **The Art Lesson** we meet young Tommy, who loves to draw, does it all the time and is encouraged by every member of his family. His twin cousins, who are in art school, tell him not to copy and to practice, practice, practice. In the second half the boy discovers that his eagerly anticipated art lessons and his self-expression do not automatically go hand in hand—at his very first art lesson he is asked to COPY! . . .

That's the story, but without the inflection and chuckles inherent in an oral telling (not to mention the implied and, I think, very real affection for family and teachers), it is at best mediocre and at worst self-indulgent. The typically flat, pseudo-childlike pictures don't help. Almost without exception, they simply repeat what the words tell us.

Given the pictorial similarity of all of Mr. dePaola's books, regardless of subject matter, it is hard not to recall those twin cousins' advice. Perhaps when one has become an artist, copying is perfectly acceptable as long as you copy yourself. But isn't that the wrong art lesson?

> *David Macaulay, "Portraits of the Artists," in* The New York Times Book Review, *May 21, 1989, p. 44.*

Tony's Bread: An Italian Folktale (1989)

In this retelling, the prolific dePaola says he has taken great liberties with one of several explanations for the origin of *panettone,* the Italian Christmas bread. Tony the baker has a lovely daughter grown plump because he keeps her sequestered; she has nothing to do but console herself with *dolci.* Fortunately, a nobleman spies her and concocts a clever way to win her for his bride: he sets her father up in a Milanese bakery, where the three devise the famous bread in order to vie with the fine local bakers. The illustrations here are in the artist's familiar, best-selling style: decorative, but with nothing new to say. And *why* must his characters keep their eyes demurely closed? Like the bread, this incorporates some good flavors; but the result is oversweet.

> *A review of "Tony's Bread: An Italian Folktale," in* Kirkus Reviews, *Vol. LVII, No. 17, September 15, 1989, p. 1402.*

The story, which dePaola states he has "taken great liberties with," is one of several alleged to explain how the famous Milanese, fruit-laced *panettone* bread developed. Lighthearted pictures in the artist's familiar style back the text, which heartily celebrates the setting with a liberal sprinkling of Italian phrases and such characters as the three meddling aunties. Occasionally the dialogue is jarringly contemporary ("But please, call me Tony. All my friends do"); overall however, this blend of humor, folklore, and history works.

> *Denise Wilms, in a review of "Tony's Bread," in* Booklist, *Vol. 86, No. 3, October 1, 1989, p. 347.*

The tale is a typically charming dePaolian effort, and the illustrations abound with his trademark coziness. Another nice touch: like Tony's currant-filled buns, the story is sprinkled with Italian words and phrases, translations of which are cleverly woven into the text.

> *A review of "Tony's Bread," in* Publishers Weekly, *Vol. 236, No. 14, October 13, 1989, p. 53.*

My First Chanukah (1989)

In board book format, dePaola introduces young children to the customs and symbols of Chanukah. Unfortunately, dePaola's overuse of the menorah (which is the focal point of six of the interior illustrations and appears on two others as well) makes this visually monotonous. Also mentioned are potato latkes, the dreidel, and Chanukah gelt. While not as successful as dePaola's **Baby's First Christmas,** this is an adequate presentation of this holiday for preschoolers.

> *Susan Hepler, in a review of "My First Chanukah," in* School Library Journal, *Vol. 35, No. 14, October, 1989, p. 41.*

With simple text and clear cheerful illustrations, dePaola has created a board-book introduction to Chanukah. The opening spread depicts an inviting primary landscape, with menorahs glowing in a window of each house. Following pages identify the traditional holiday accompaniments, such as the dreidel and latkes—complete with applesauce and sour cream. The progression of lighting the menorah is explained briefly, and the book closes with a nice sense of continuity for youngsters: "We will celebrate Chanukah again next year." The book's tone is geared to a very young audience, which provides parents with a good opportunity to elaborate on the story each year.

> *A review of "My First Chanukah," in* Publishers Weekly, *Vol. 236, No. 17, October 27, 1989, p. 63.*

In the gentle lines and soft pastel hues synonymous with his distinctive style, dePaola paints the symbols and customs of Hanukkah. From the menorah in the window and the latkes on the table to the spinning dreidels on the floor, he compresses simply phrased definitions and traditions into two lines of text on each uncluttered, colorful page. The result is a pleasing and much-needed board book constructed to withstand its certain demand and conveying a perfect measure of information for the very young. A must for holiday collections.

> *Ellen Mandel, in a review of "My First Chanukah," in* Booklist, *Vol. 86, No. 5, November 1, 1989, p. 544.*

Little Grunt and the Big Egg: A Prehistoric Fairy Tale (1989)

The popular author sets a predictable story among cavemen, adds dinosaurs, and terms the result a fairy tale—certainly a loose term at the best of times. The Grunts are expecting the Ugga-Wugga tribe for brunch, but what to feed them? Little Grunt brings home a giant egg, which won't do because it hatches. The resulting dinosaur,

"George," doesn't make a good pet; but after being banished for being inconveniently huge, "he" returns to save the Grunts from an erupting volcano—and proves to be not George but Georgina. The illustrations are typical dePaola. The kids will lap it up, as they do TV cartoons of the same undemanding quality.

A review of "Little Grunt and the Big Egg: A Prehistoric Fairy Tale," in Kirkus Reviews, *Vol. LVIII, No. 6, March 15, 1990, p. 421.*

With his irrepressible, childlike approach, dePaola creates a chuckle-filled spoof, with, he admits, more inspiration from the comic strip "Alley-Oop" and the characters in "The Flintstones" than from the Museum of Natural History. Children will be tickled by the likes of Unca Grunt, Granny Grunt, and Chief Rockhead Grunt, as they vociferously express their opinions of George, the baby dinosaur that Little Grunt adopts as a pet. When the lovable beast (with the typical dePaola enigmatic smile) grows to normal colossal proportions, Chief Rockhead sends the dinosaur away. But, as in any good fairy tale, when disaster strikes—here, a lava-spewing volcano—the hero (George, of course) comes to the rescue. But, just before the "happily ever after," George is discovered sitting on a pile of eggs, and soon Little Grunt has "Georgina's" new family to play with. DePaola's soft earth-toned palette contrasts nicely with his boldly proportioned blue-green dinosaur. A winning crowd-pleaser, start to finish.

Phillis Wilson, in a review of "Little Grunt and the Big Egg: A Prehistoric Fairy Tale," in Booklist, *Vol. 86, No. 15, April 1, 1990, p. 1545.*

DePaola's books possess his inimitable stamp, and this prehistoric romp is no exception: the round-faced Grunt clan is unmistakably his, as are the many comical touches such as Chief Rockhead's green banana headdress and the ladies' costume jewelry. This lively twist on the familiar tale of a boy and his pet is sure to provoke giggles.

A review of "Little Grunt and the Big Egg: A Prehistoric Fairy Tale," in Publishers Weekly, *Vol. 237, No. 15, April 13, 1990, p. 63.*

David Kherdian

1931-

American author of nonfiction, fiction, and picture books; poet; and editor.

Major works include *Settling America: The Ethnic Expression of Fourteen Contemporary Poets* (1974), *The Dog Writes on the Window with His Nose and Other Poems* (1977), *Country, Cat, City, Cat* (1978), *It Started with Old Man Bean* (1980), *The Road from Home: The Story of an Armenian Girl* (1979), *Root River Run* (1984).

Kherdian is well known as a writer and editor of works for children and young adults which characteristically reflect his exploration of ethnic heritage and personal identity, interest in contemporary poetry, and affection for nature. An American of Armenian descent, he is the creator of prose and poetry based on his related experience and on that of his family; he often presents these works in the form of autobiographical fiction. Kherdian is perhaps best known as the author of *The Road from Home,* a novel for middle graders written from the perspective of his mother, Veron Dumehjian, which describes her life from her childhood in the Armenian sector of Azizya, Turkey, to her decision at the age of fifteen to depart for the United States as a mail-order bride. Outlining the sufferings endured by Veron and the other Armenian Christians who were deported to Syria in 1915 as well as the loss of Veron's family, her injury during a bombing, and her escape to a refugee camp in Greece, Kherdian balances his narrative with warm details of Armenian family life and information about Armenian customs. With his sequel, *Finding Home* (1981), Kherdian narrates Veron's arrival in America, her adjustment to her new country, and her acceptance of life as a married woman in his own voice. Both novels are praised for their portrayal of Veron as a vital, determined person whose faith enables her to survive and to build a new life for herself. With *Root River Run,* Kherdian focuses on his own childhood and adolescence in a young adult novel which evokes the pleasures and pains of growing up Armenian in Racine, Wisconsin; *A Song for Uncle Harry* (1989), a story for middle graders, is a fictionalized memoir about Kherdian's uncle, a disabled Armenian immigrant who teaches his nephew about life and prepares him for a closer relationship with his father. Kherdian is also the creator of two stories for middle graders, *It Started with Old Man Bean* (1980) and *Beyond Two Rivers* (1981), which are set in the Midwest in the early 1940s and are reminiscent of Kherdian's experiences of the time; the books feature the best friends Ted and Joe, whose adventures in the Wisconsin wilderness provide them with insights both into nature and themselves.

A respected poet and anthologist for adults who is also the founder of several small presses, Kherdian began his career as a creator of juvenile literature with several poetry collections for young adults which represent a variety of recent American poets and also include personal contribu-

tions. The anthologies, which feature works by such poets as Allen Ginsburg, Jack Kerouac, Denise Levertov, Richard Brautigan, Lucille Clifton, Lawrence Ferlinghetti, Anne Sexton, Al Young, and William Carlos Williams, are organized thematically and cover such subjects as poetic assessments of America, autobiographical reflections, and cultural perspectives on a variety of ethnic experiences; *The Dog Writes on the Window with His Nose and Other Poems* and *If Dragon Flies Made Honey: Poems* (1977) are similar introductions to contemporary poetry for younger readers. With *Country, Cat, City, Cat* (1978), Kherdian created a book of original poems for elementary grade readers which celebrates cats and other animals in urban and rural settings while outlining the cycle of the seasons. Among Kherdian's additional works are several picture books and a fantasy for middle graders which feature animals as well as a mystery story for preteens and a fictionalized biography of American explorer Jim Bridger. Many of Kherdian's works are illustrated by his wife, Nonny Hogrogian, who is also a distinguished creator of children's books. *The Road from Home* received the *Boston Globe-Horn Book* Award for nonfiction and the Lewis Carroll Shelf Award in 1979 as well as the Jane Addams Children's Book Award in 1980; it was also named a Newbery Award honor book and nominated for an American Book Award in the latter year.

(See also *Contemporary Literary Criticism,* Vols. 6, 9; *Something about the Author,* Vol. 16; *Contemporary Authors,* Vols. 21-24, rev. ed.; and *Contemporary Authors Autobiography Series,* Vol. 2.)

TITLE COMMENTARY

Visions of America, by the Poets of Our Time (1973)

"All that comin back to America" done by the literary descendants of William Carlos Williams and their post-'50's peers is compressed here into a remarkably workable anthology that introduces Corso, Amiri Baraka, Creeley, Kerouac, O'Hara, Patchen and others. Some of the poems are literally "visions of America," like Ignatow's struggle to "get the gasworks into a poem" and Ginsberg's "A Supermarket in California," and a few are overtly political visions, notably Diane di Prima's cry "we are eating up the planet." Others specifically recall American childhoods—Stafford's "Mine was a Midwest home," Koch's "You were wearing your Edgar Allan Poe printed cotton blouse," and Patchen's memories of his "orange bears with their coats all stunk up with soft coal." In all, the selections have been intelligently chosen to present experiences to which young people can easily relate without sacrificing the poet's individuality. Unfortunately, Nonny Hogrogian, who has illustrated her husband's selections, seems out of her element here. Otherwise, a neat first step towards bringing poetry back home.

> *A review of "Visions of America," in* Kirkus Reviews, *Vol. XLI, No. 8, April 15, 1973, p. 465.*

Sixty poems by 35 of America's best contemporary poets constitute this fine collection. Ammons, Brautigan, Corso, Creeley, di Prima, Ferlinghetti, Ginsberg, Kerouac, Levertov, Patchen, Rexroth, Stafford, and Wakoski are among the poets whose works are included. Grouped in only three sections—"Growing Up," "In America," "And Its Cities"—the pieces cover a wide range of topics from nature to poetry itself to child-parent relationships to first love to fantasy and surrealism. Only the three poems by William Carlos Williams—to whom this volume is dedicated—are likely to be duplicated in other collections for young teens. The brief preface explains Williams' important role in the development of American poetry; short, critical biographical notes on each poet completes the book. Both preface and notes are written clearly and simply and touch on points of interest to young people, even to those who are not already poetry buffs. Unfortunately, Hogrogian's four black-and-white drawings are for a younger audience than the rest of this otherwise clearly excellent collection.

> *Margaret A. Dorsey, in a review of "Visions of America," in* School Library Journal, *Vol. 20, No. 1, September, 1973, p. 143.*

David Kherdian has put together a tasteful selection of some contemporary poets who trace their lineage through Williams and Olsen back to Whitman. Most appeared in Donald Allen's *The New American Poetry.* . . . What these various talents have in common is the supple, colloquial voice, a penchant for making direct statements with oblique humor, and the presence in their poems of America's tin can Eden, a place of gaseous rivers, hydrant summers and back lot baseball. These poems lie open to the reader. They go a long way toward presenting the new movement in American poetry, as well as suggesting how immediate and unfussy a poem can be. They are poems not to analyze, but to emulate. (p. 209)

> *Kim Kurt Waller, "Poems for and by Children, and How to Pass Them Around," in* Children's Literature: Annual of the Modern Language Association Seminar on Children's Literature and The Children's Literature Association, *Vol. 3, 1974, pp. 206-10.*

Settling America: The Ethnic Expression of Fourteen Contemporary Poets (1974)

Immediacy rather than excellence is the watchword here, and though some may object to the uneven quality and rough language of the selections, something is demonstrated that young people rarely have the opportunity to learn—that poetry is a living enterprise as well as a high art. In "ethnicity," the selections range from the scathing social commentary of Al Young's "Dance to Militant Dilettante" and Carolyn Rodgers' polemics to the more subtle concerns of half-Chinese Mei Berssenbrugge, who confesses, "I wonder what being an ethnic writer means, and if that is what I am, I've given up telling stories about my Chinese relatives." With a few exceptions (notably Gregory Corso and Charles Reznikoff) these poets are likely to be unfamiliar to the general public. But while the bigger names (and especially Kherdian himself) disappoint, the lesser are happy discoveries—surely 23-year-old Joy Harjo's singing economy in "Creek Mother Poem" and "Snake Poem I" is something to get excited about. Many features of this volume—the spacious typesetting, the generous number of pages alloted to each contributor, the manageable size—could well be copied by other juvenile anthologies; yet this is another animal entirely—straight talk and strong emotions aimed at young people who may have found nothing of themselves in the old standbys.

> *A review of "Settling America: The Ethnic Expression of Fourteen Contemporary Poets," in* Kirkus Reviews, *Vol. XLII, No. 21, November 1, 1974, p. 1165.*

In spite of its inviting contents David Kherdian's *Settling America* never quite delivers what the subtitle promises: "The Ethnic Expression of 14 Contemporary Poets." Victor Hernández Cruz writes out of his Puerto Rican experiences, Nicholas Flocos out of his Greek background, Lawson Inada as a third generation of Japanese ancestry and so on. Their poetry and the poetry of others in the book are full of ethnic detail; yet it is not quite clear how their ethnic grounding has informed their work or marked their verse. Flocos's poem about his grandmother Eleni, for example, is no more intense than James Merrill's "After the Fire," which is about the Greeks he knows. And the editor's portrait of his Armenian father is no more effective than Robert Lowell's portrait of his New England grandfather in "Dunbarton." Only the black poets Carolyn Rodgers and Al Young and the original and exciting James Welch, a Blackfoot Indian, live up to the purpose of the book. And there is not enough of their work to fill the intention of the title. Ideology aside, *Settling America* has a decent quota of poetic virtues.

> *Thomas Lask, "Getting Them While They're Young," in* The New York Times Book Review, *December 29, 1974, p. 8.*

A [broad] selection of ethnic voices appears in *Settling America.* Fourteen young poets from various cultural backgrounds, among them Japanese-American Lawson Fusao Inada, American-Indian Joy Harjo, Lebanese-Muslim Sam Hamod, and Puerto Rican Victor Cruz, write about their families, their neighborhoods, their loves, their memories, their disappointments, hopes, angers, and celebrations. Although some of these poems are weak in diction, bland in imagery, or peter out at the end, most of them give a good sense of the coming together of two cultures in the life and thought of the various poets, as in Armenian David Kherdian's:

> Years later, reading the solemn and bittersweet
> stories of our Armenian writer in California,
> who visited as a paperboy coffee houses in
> Fresno, I came to understand that in these
> cafes were contained the suffering and
> shattered hopes of my orphaned people.

The best feature of this book is that it combines one hundred poems reflecting different ethnic experiences in sufficient number from each culture so that the uniqueness of each way of life can be caught and savored and compared with the others. (pp. 197-98)

> *Alethea K. Helbig, "Trends in Poetry for Children," in* Children's Literature: Annual of the Modern Language Association Seminar on Children's Literature and The Children's Literature Association, *Vol. 6, 1977, pp. 195-201.*

Left to right, Kherdian's father Melkon, Uncle Haigan, mother Veron, and Uncle Aram in 1924.

Poems Here and Now   (1976)

Kherdian has edited two previous anthologies, *Visions of America* and *Settling America,* both notably at home with the contemporary scene. This collection of very short poems lacks the breadth and spaciousness of those anthologies, but its emphasis on "laughter, amazement, delight, and surprise" accomplishes something and has a lot of fun doing so. Kherdian teases our notions of what's appropriate to poetry—whether through subject matter (Frank O'Hara's "Poem" on the headline "Lana Turner has collapsed!," Jack Anderson's self-destruct instructions to "Please note / You are reading a poem . . ."), playful tone (Brautigan's in "The Chinese Checker Players," and Victor Hernandez Cruz' in "Business"), or simply the kinetic energy and free line breaks of Paul Blackburn and Sam Hamrod. In the same spirit a lot more might have been done with experimental forms and concrete poetry, but there are examples of these too, especially Gerard Malanga's "Pure Poetry" in which every word but the last is crossed out. Not aggressively here and now, but an enjoyable setting-up-exercise for today's poetry. (pp. 333-34)

> *A review of "Poems Here and Now," in* Kirkus Reviews, *Vol. XLIV, No. 6, March 15, 1976, pp. 333-34.*

The 41 poems in this collection are meant, according to the editor's preface, to represent examples of his favorite "kinds of poems being written now . . . poems of laughter, amazement, delight, and surprise." That seems an extravagant description for some of the thoughtful and mildly ironic selections here. Almost all the poems were written in the last ten years; however, there are two poems by William Carlos Williams, with only the Biographical Note at the end hinting that Williams's influence was the reason for his inclusion in a sampling of contemporary poems. Most of the other poems, though, are new to children's anthologies. . . . Relatively short, generally simple, the poems which are attractively packaged, will attract, rather than intimidate, young readers.

> *Margaret A. Dorsey, in a review of "Poems Here and Now," in* School Library Journal, *Vol. 22, No. 9, May, 1976, p. 70.*

Traveling America with Today's Poets   (1977)

It must be said that this is a large, sprawling anthology with no more than a handful of really distinguished entries. Nevertheless, the contributions—many from young, still maturing poets and all geographically arranged by state and city—add up to a fresh, likable, and often provocative view of regional America. At worst, some of the selections are merely ingenuous: a number of Kherdian's poets seem to be just passing through, their reactions often inspired more by professional angst than by the localities themselves. ("A man can specialize in loneliness," notes William Heath aptly in his elegy on "Cold Feet in Columbus.") Yet these are balanced by the well-grounded statements of such as Lucille Clifton, Dave Etter, Philip Levine, Millen Brand, and Al Young. In these, and in such differing landscapes as Jack Anderson's staccato, sardonic "Invention of New Jersey" and Cleopatra Mathis' quick-sand-like dream of Louisiana, readers are sure to encounter something they can call home.

A review of "Traveling America with Today's Poets," in Kirkus Reviews, *Vol. XLV, No. 1, January 1, 1977, p. 7.*

This collection of over 140 poems by over 100 contemporary poets is a state-by-state trip through America of the 60's and 70's in the vagabond poet tradition of Whitman and Sandburg. In a conversational style that will appeal to adolescent readers, these poems record a deep-felt loss of natural beauty, cultural heritage, and community. Unfortunately, there is no biographical material on the poets and the poems are crammed together. The book is too packed with print for a poetry collection aimed at young people. Both D. Kherdian's *Visions of America: By the Poets of Our Time* and Stephen Dunning *Reflections on a Gift of Watermelon Pickle and Other Modern Verse* (Lothrop, 1967), which are divided thematically and are smaller and more selective collections, are better choices for a teenage audience.

Joan Stern, in a review of "Traveling America with Today's Poets," in School Library Journal, *Vol. 23, No. 9, May, 1977, p. 70.*

The Dog Writes on the Window with His Nose and Other Poems (1977)

Twenty-two small poems, most by big names—among them Gregory Corso, Lawrence Ferlinghetti, William Stafford, William Carlos Williams, and Theodore Roethke. None is more complicated than a single image, the haiku scale is typical, and some are even slighter: the book's title is not a poem's title but a complete entry (it's by Philip Whalen); the title of Jim Gibbons' "Poem for Cat Haters" is longer than the work itself (which reads, in toto, "catscat"); and Aram Saroyan's column of crickets—the word repeated 25 times, once to a line, until the 26th runs off the page—will leave you wondering whether Kherdian's definition of poetry has a floor. More felicitous is Roy Drew's "While I write these / Fat little birds / type upon the snow"; Brautigan contributes some playful quirks with his views of a "xerox candy bar" and of "thousands of pumpkins . . . floating in on the tide"; and there are enough such quizzical conceits to make this an auspicious first brush with poetry. The small format (5 x 7¼) helps, and Nonny Hogrogian's watercolors are pleasant and unassuming, though they tend to reduce whatever is odd or individual in the observations to a uniform, comfortable level.

A review of "The Dog Writes on the Window with His Nose and Other Poems," in Kirkus Reviews, *Vol. XLV, No. 4, February 15, 1977, p. 167.*

The Dog Writes on the Window with His Nose seems to strive for very young as well as older readers. It has 22 brief poems, small pages, touching little watercolor pictures by Nonny Hogrogian. . . . Our 4-year-old was much taken with its looks, but a literate 7-year-old and another lad of 10 found the ironies of the selections too sub-

tle for them. Richard Brautigan's "Xerox Candy Bar" ("Ah, / you're just a copy / of all the candy bars / I've ever eaten") left them blank; while Gregory Corso's "In the Mexican Zoo / they have ordinary / American cows" drew the reaction, "Why shouldn't they?" (p. 33)

X. J. Kennedy, "The Flat, Fat Blatt," in The New York Times Book Review, *May 1, 1977, pp. 31, 33.*

Hogrogian's watercolors set in frames decorate the white spaces in this small (5″ × 7¼″) collection of 22 haiku-type poems plus bits of neat imagery and nicely-put phrases from contemporary adult poetry by Kerouac, Brautigan, Corso, Ferlinghetti, Saroyan, Roethke, etc. The clues to the sources are not given except in the reprint permission page and in the table of contents where the titles of the excerpts are italicized and those of the complete poems are not. While more geared toward making readers appreciate a bon mot than think about what is being said in a poem, this anthology is still bright and attractive; young readers will find in it pleasant browsing and a spicey-sweet taste—but only a taste—of poetic artistry.

Marjorie Lewis, in a review of "The Dog Writes on the Window with His Nose and Other Poems," in School Library Journal, *Vol. 24, No. 1, September, 1977, p. 110.*

If Dragon Flies Made Honey: Poems (1977)

An even less imposing and younger-looking poetry collection than *The Dog Writes on the Window with His Nose*—and all the better for it. Of the 25 selections, very few contain more than 25 words; one, by James Minor, consists solely of the word *giddyup* repeated sixteen times, but like several of the concrete bits included, it's the words' arrangement on the page that makes the image. (That, and the illustrators' extension—which also adds to Minor's "OVO ovo," the entire text of a poem titled "Pine at Night / Cry of the Owls.") A. R. Ammons leads the list, numerically and lyrically, with four "Small Songs"—for example, "The reeds give / way to the // wind and give / the wind away." And [Jose] Aruego and [Ariane] Dewey surpass their recent self-imitation in the witty illustrations; unlike the best of the poems, they don't quite take that last inspired step off the edge of the earth, but they do bounce the images about in a joyful demonstration of creative play.

A review of "If Dragon Flies Made Honey," in Kirkus Reviews, *Vol. XLV, No. 19, October 1, 1977, p. 1044.*

Although all of these 25 contemporary poems are short and simple, some of them, like "Zounds" ("But an old stone / That gathers moss / Moans in the woodlands") and several others, are not apt to be easily understood or found appealing by young readers. Since the text only partially fulfills the jacket copy's claim that this is "a first poetry book to . . . treasure," it is an unnecessary purchase despite the unqualified success of the animated illustrations.

Margaret A. Dorsey, in a review of "If Dragon

Flies Made Honey," in School Library Journal, *Vol. 24, No. 3, November, 1977, p. 48.*

Country, Cat, City, Cat (1978)

The woodcuts [Nonny Hogrogian] created to illustrate the new collection of poems by Kherdian (her husband) are stark, graphic and full of life. . . . The poems are brief, musical creations that put the reader into events throughout the seasons in a bucolic setting, then in a tenement section of a city. City and country, both celebrate the spunkiness of wild, free creatures as perceived by Missak, the Kherdians' cherished cat, to which they dedicate this feast for lovers of felines, poetry and art.

A review of "Country, Cat, City, Cat," in Publishers Weekly, *Vol. 213, No. 4, January 23, 1978, p. 373.*

Twenty-one tiny, mostly vertical, unrhymed poems, only a few short lines or a few words each, offer fleeting glimpses of cats and other, smaller animals. There is little if any reductive cuteness or straining after imagery ("butterflies roost / on the new flowers—/ Swedish maidens basking in the sun" is the most obtrusively "poetic" selection); Kherdian's one failing lies in a shortage of the sharp, fresh vision that is evident, for example, in Valerie Worth's *Small Poems* (1972). Sometimes his flatness of manner adds to the picture ("the flea-bitten dog / in front of the / ramshackle garage / in the aging New / England village / [on the last day / of March] // sits alone in the / new dust of spring"); more often it just misses delivering: "OPENING THE DOOR / ON THE 18TH OF JANUARY, / LATE IN THE EVENING, / TO LET THE CAT IN" (that's the title) reads "as the moon glides through / streaking clouds // the cat with frightened / tail // sniffs and enters / his only home." But this is always appropriately scaled, direct, and uncondescending.

A review of "Country, Cat, City, Cat," in Kirkus Reviews, *Vol. XLVI, No. 5, March 1, 1978, p. 239.*

Singular moments of a season's cycle are the stuff of these brief poems, linked loosely by the title's city-country cat. Truly striking images are few: "the sparrows have / been ice-skating / on the bird bath again" is one; "the white daisies / above the sleeping cat / inhale the night" is another. More often there's just a simple gracefulness in making the ordinary seem special: "Missak on his / rocktop moss / covered throne / (in our fern & / flower garden) / sits & catches / flies and keeps / his belly warm." With less of the pristine clarity that sparked *The Dog Writes on the Window with his Nose* but nice nonetheless. . . . (p. 1191)

Denise M. Wilms, in a review of "Country, Cat, City, Cat," in Booklist, *Vol. 74, No. 14, March 15, 1978, pp. 1190-91.*

I Sing the Song of Myself: An Anthology of Autobiographical Poems (1978)

Kherdian's latest anthology contains 58 mostly contemporary, intensely personal (rather than strictly autobiographical) works. Sexton, Snodgrass, Blackburn, Dugan, Corso, and Ammons are among those whose works are represented along with those of younger poets. Biographical notes are included, along with a table of contents and indexes. The selections here are generally longer than those in Kherdian's other recent collections, and many lack the crisp and immediate images that create new poetry fans among teen-agers. Nor will the narrow-margined format and stodgy jacket attract a browser's eye. Some sophisticated readers will enjoy the thoughtful, musing quality of this book, but it's not a must purchase for those who must satisfy the greatest number of readers for the price.

Margaret A. Dorsey, in a review of "I Sing the Song of Myself:" An Anthology of Autobiographical Poems," in School Library Journal, *Vol. 25, No. 3, November, 1978, p. 76.*

Never intimidating but seldom invigorating, these personal memories and reflections are drawn largely from the hang-loose school, with some impressively crafted exceptions. Several of the selections are of childhood memories when "many things were new, fresh" (though that poem isn't particularly) and of parents (mostly fathers, as in Charles Bukowski's easily shared reactions in "The Twins"); but there are also many musings about being a poet of 30 or more, in tones too tired for strong YA appeal. Typically, Alan Dugan calls himself an aging phony, while Marvin Bell totes up life's mundane expenses in terms of the lines of poetry they cost him. And the more memorable selections—for example, W. D. Snodgrass' muted, affecting "April Inventory" and Anne Sexton's strong "Ambition Bird," of an insomniac "laying poems away" in an "immortality box," are undeniably mature in sensibility. As always, Kherdian gets across the impression that poetry is related to real life, but these lives have less relation than usual to his target reader.

A review of "I Sing the Song of Myself," in Kirkus Reviews, *Vol. XLVII, No. 1, January 1, 1979, p. 14.*

The Road from Home: The Story of an Armenian Girl (1979)

Writing from the perspective of his mother, Veron Dumehjian, Kherdian retells with simple honesty the story of her childhood—beginning with her early years in the Armenian quarter of Azizya, Turkey, and ending in 1924, the year she emigrated to the U.S. to become the mail-order bride of Melkon Kherdian. The sufferings endured by Veron and the Armenians living in Turkey during the early twentieth century become evident as Veron tells of the Turkish government's continuous efforts to destroy the Armenian Christian minority, her family's deportation, their deaths, her own injury during a bombing, and finally her escape to a refugee camp in Greece after a murderous Turkish rampage at Smyrna in 1922. Deliberately rather than smoothly crafted, with occasionally awkward interweavings of customs and terminology, Kherdian's account projects only a hazy notion of the actual history involved (an expanded preface might have helped here).

Nevertheless, the drama and import of his unusual first-person narrative are unmistakable.

> *A review of "The Road from Home: The Story of an Armenian Childhood," in* Booklist, *Vol. 75, No. 13, March 1, 1979, p. 1049.*

In the recent past we have been reminded, by way of *Roots* and information about the Holocaust, of the sufferings and planned genocide of Blacks and Jews. A less well-known atrocity story is related here—the attempt by the Turks to annihilate the Armenian people. Interwoven into the telling of this tragic history are warm, intimate details of family life, relationships and customs (including pre-scribed marriage). Veron, high spirited mother of the author of this fictionalized biography, tells her story of grow-ing up as a member of a persecuted minority. The contrast between a secure and happy life, sometimes enjoyed by Veron and her neighbors, and the precariousness of their flight as refugees or the starkness of existence in intern-ment camps are described without bitterness, and there is evidence of the strength lent by deep faith in religion. The narrative of trials, tribulations and close escapes from death by fire, bombing, disease, starvation, etc. ends on an upbeat note with the information that Veron arrived in the United States in 1924, seven years before the birth of the author, as a mail order bride!

> *Lillian L. Shapiro, in a review of "The Road from Home: The Story of an Armenian Child-hood," in* School Library Journal, *Vol. 25, No. 8, April, 1979, p. 69.*

Kherdian well captures the voice of a basically optimistic and very likable young girl, and whether the scene is a gar-den picnic or mass death and panic at the harbor where everyone is fleeing the Turks, it is seen through her eyes and reported as if from vivid memory.

> *A review of "The Road from Home: The Story of an Armenian Childhood," in* Kirkus Re-views, *Vol. XLVII, No. 11, June 1, 1979, p. 644.*

Veron's story is more than a record of tragedies, horrors, and escapes. There is also dignity, simplicity, and a haunt-ing view of Veron's people, which reminds us of the strength and the vulnerability of any minority at any place or time.

> *Faith McNulty, in a review of "The Road from Home: The Story of an Armenian Girl," in* The New Yorker, *Vol. LV, No. 42, December 3, 1979, p. 212.*

For the reader who is expecting dramatic adventures, the book may disappoint for it is not a novel, but real life. Its sincerity and very lack of overemphasis on horrors, con-vinces the reader and gains sympathy for the girl who en-dured such terrors with courage and even cheerfulness. A worthwhile book for young people.

> *E. Colwell, in a review of "The Road from Home: The Story of an Armenian Girl," in* The Junior Bookshelf, *Vol. 44, No. 5, October, 1980, p. 251.*

It Started with Old Man Bean (1980)

"How many kids do you know our age who are sitting on a knoll above a wild river about to hunker down to coffee and Old Golds?" Too few, in real life. This adventure story is for boys who dream of "camping secret-like."

David Kherdian draws the reader right into Ted and Joe's conspiracy. The only trouble is with Old Man Bean. The tale starts with Old Man Bean and it stays with him far too long—through 25 pages of leafing through the L. L. Bean catalogue, choosing the right tent, towel, pack, etc., and rustling up the money. Then "There was nothing to do but wait for our stuff to arrive," and the reader waits, too, until the adventure finally starts on page 74.

From this point the reader is hooked as surely as Ted's Big Fish. "A glorious week stretched out before us, and no one . . . not anyone at all to tell us no." The boys have lied to their parents about their destination. They travel well beyond the relatively safe Snake River to the wild McCable, where they live off the land, watch bear and deer and explore. Here, the style becomes almost poetic.

Portrait of Kherdian as a young adult. From Root River Run, *written by David Kherdian. Illustrated by Nonny Hogrogian.*

But fickle nature throws a tantrum. Joe is injured, and no one knows were the boys are.

David Kherdian, poet and anthologist, is known as an ethnic writer. . . . Ted and Joe, however, are American kids engaged in an experience that will illumine their lives. "We want to be men when we grow up." They seem to be well headed in that direction.

> *Anne Crompton, "Camping Out," in* The New York Times Book Review, *April 27, 1980, p. 63.*

Although this nostalgia piece is set in the midwest in the 1940's, there is little—save for some references to prices or to current sports figures—to identify time or place; Ted tells the story of a camping trip he and his friend Joe took, and their isolation focuses the reader's attention on the joys or problems of the trip, which could be any place, and almost any time. For readers who enjoy camping or the outdoors, this may have strong appeal, but for the general reader it may seem long and painstakingly detailed. There is some variation: Joe suffers a multiple fracture of the elbow and it's a struggle to get back home, and the two almost drown in the last episode. Basically, however, it's a record of fishing, cooking, talking, and hiking, all a bit drawn out.

> *Zena Sutherland, in a review of "It Started with Old Man Bean," in* Bulletin of the Center for Children's Books, *Vol. 34, No. 1, September, 1980, p. 13.*

The adventures and revelations shared by two thirteen-year-old boys during their long awaited and secretly planned camping trip sound like promising material for the young adult fiction shelf. Unfortunately in the hands of last year's Horn Book award winner for non-fiction, David Kherdian, the story of Ted and Joe's trip is awkward, slow moving, and dated.

Kherdian has chosen first-person narration by Ted presumably because of the immediacy and involvement of the technique. But too often his early adolescent slang or code contributes to a superficial and cliche-ridden account. For instance, we find the friends both berating the articles in *Sports Afield* and *Outdoor Life* as "pretty phony" and stating flatly that their mutual hatred of rules is the reason "why we stink at school." . . . Huck Finn's awkwardness as a narrator was explained by his ignorance of the chore of writing; Ted, however, is the bookish member of the camping party. While Twain allowed his pioneering hero to wander through the labyrinth of conscience and its awesome demands, poet Kherdian grants Ted few observations beyond the ordinary. After an unsuccessful attempt at landing a magnificent black bass, Ted ponders in this expansive though pedestrian fashion: "If kings are happy in their castles, if angels are happy in their heavens, then I was in bliss on that elm tree trunk, in the middle of the wilderness, with grasshoppers and frogs my chorus, and in the presence of a noble, uncatchable but somehow, someday, catchable black bass." The real promise in Ted's account comes a sentence later when he muses, "I would like to be water myself someday, . . . or wind blowing over it, or fish deep within it." Lest his narrator become

too cerebral, Kherdian brings such musings to an abrupt halt as Ted returns to the concern of the healthy outdoorsman, food gathering.

The novel is set in the American Midwest of the 1940s. As a result, the two "buddies" use expressions like "okay by me," "no foolin' " and "Holy Toledo!" They listen to "The Green Hornet" and "Inner Sanctum," idolize Johnny Weissmuller and puff manfully on Old Golds; sports heroes are Stan the Man Musical and Andy Pafko; a Three Musketeers bar costs a nickel and so does a package of beef liver from the neighbourhood butcher. It is not the passage of forty years which leaves the reader nonplussed. What is questionable here is the pristine comradeship of these blood brothers and their calm untormented lives which Kherdian presents glowingly. The circle of family acquaintances for Ted Stavros and Joe Sokol is Graeco-Slavic. Grocer Markopoulos bids farewell to his young customer with this otiose immigrant paean to the new land: " 'You growing boy, this big country, anything can happen you. Go try luck!' " Although Ted is supposed to have inherited his father's quick temper, the reader sees little, if any, evidence of it. Instead, the narrator remains placid and cool-headed—when plans go awry, when fish are not caught, when rain continues to pour down and even when Joe injures his wrist and elbow. As first-time campers the boys do a lot of talking about where they are, what they have seen, and how they have changed. As Joe comments, " 'You betcha. This is the wilderness, buddy—when you get away from civilization, you take your chances with the rest of 'em.' " Ted is ever anxious to chart their progress: " 'We're growing up, wouldn't ya say?' "

I was not searching for a Juniors' *Deliverance* in **It Started with Old Man Bean.** But I do think that young readers will find its narrative line, which only abandons the idyll for the reality of camping in the last quarter of the book, forced and uninvolving. (pp. 78-9)

> *Patricia Demers, in a review of "It Started with Old Man Bean," in* The World of Children's Books, *Vol. VI, 1981, pp. 78-9.*

Finding Home (1981)

This sequel to **The Road from Home** is not as good as that deeply felt, courageous "autobiography" of Kherdian's Armenian mother, a survivor of Turkish atrocities prior to W.W.I. and the very prototype of the strong immigrant mother. This time, Kherdian's own voice as narrator tells the story of his mother's arrival in America and her marriage, at 16, to a man she'd never met and would not have chosen herself. The awesome experience of a new country, the strange customs, the tight-knit Armenian community that monitored her every move, all combined to make Veron's new life a most difficult one. The story is of Veron's adjustment and acceptance, of her longings, fears and small triumphs. There is neither much internal conflict nor external adventure—and little sense of a historical time frame (Kherdian clearly assumes that readers will have read the first book). Confusion arises, too, when Armenian terms, family nicknames and proper names send readers scurrying to the glossary for information that might have been clarified in context.

> *Marjorie Lewis, in a review of "Finding Home," in* School Library Journal, *Vol. 27, No. 9, May, 1981, p. 74.*

In *Finding Home* David Kherdian illuminates the immigrants' experience in America with his story of an Armenian girl who settles in Wisconsin. . . .

Veron's situation and feelings mirror those of the other Armenians in Racine. [Her husband's] friend Vartan, separated from his wife and child during the massacres, does not know if he will find them again. Lucy, Veron's friend, also married to an older man, is melancholy although he is kind and generous. Everyone has lost family and friends. Many of the women are orphans and mail-order brides, brought to America to help rebuild an Armenian community. Kherdian shows that their life as immigrants is not easy. He describes the crowded discomfort and uncertainty about the future for those held at Ellis Island, the strangeness of arrival in new cities, the long hours at hard work, often two jobs for those who must save to bring their families over. He also conveys his characters' strength and resilience and the promise America holds. Because Kherdian does not sentimentalize the immigrants' experience in this "land of opportunity," the moments of courage, beauty and hope shine with an extra brightness.

Finding Home is a plain and honest book, the style and tone reflecting the condition of its characters. It is not as dramatic, gripping, or glittering with images as *The Road From Home,* but it deals with a different time and situation, and explores the human heart in quieter ways. The two books stand separately, but together they enrich each other greatly. They show the heroism needed to survive violence and catastrophe, and the heroism that helps us face life and rebuild.

> *Linda Barrett Osborne, "Mail-Order Bride," in* Book World—The Washington Post, *May 10, 1981, p. 19.*

A lyrical, simply written, biographical account of 16 year old, orphaned Veron Dumehjian's painful immigration and assimilation into an American community from her native Armenia. . . .

[This novel has] the outline for a potentially strong and enduring tale. The reader is lured to continue reading in anticipation of a climax; yet the implied action is never attained. The author has refused to take the poetic license necessary to raise the book from the prosaic level of a family biography to that of a universal quest for roots and acceptance in a foreign land. Rather than speculate on or even embroider events of which he has no knowledge, Kherdian instead sketches only a framework, leaving the reader hungry and unsatisfied. The result is a novel which might appeal to those related to Kherdian, to those of Armenian descent, or to students interested in immigration. Most YAs, however, will find the novel sadly lacking.

> *Brooke Dillon, in a review of "Finding Home," in* Voice of Youth Advocates, *Vol. 4, No. 4, October, 1981, p. 34.*

Beyond Two Rivers (1981)

Ted and Joe, introduced in Kherdian's *It Started with Old Man Bean,* are about 12 years old and the best of friends. It is 1940. They have returned from a camping trip near their Wisconsin town that almost ended in disaster for Joe. They are anxious to go back because they spotted a man who, in their imagination, might be an escaped Japanese soldier. The mysterious stranger turns out to be a Mr. Matsu, who lives in the woods that he loves and who is a font of nature lore and wisdom. He both intrigues and baffles the boys, who return home knowing little more about the man than before (we may well see a third novel with the same characters). Kherdian is a poet, a good writer and, obviously, a nature lover. His wartime setting is necessary only because it allows him to create two bright, old-fashioned children who seem very quaint today (and maybe did then, too). They say things like: "What say we mosey along the bank and see if we can't rely on our intuition." Mr. Matsu sounds like an early guru.

> *Robert Unsworth, in a review of "Beyond Two Rivers," in* School Library Journal, *Vol. 28, No. 1, September, 1981, p. 126.*

[The] story's atmosphere derives from the boys' fascination with their wild surroundings. The crucial—and unlikely—figure of Mr. Matsu is never explained, something that will bother thoughtful readers. Nevertheless, he is a forceful presence whose knowledge will penetrate readers as deeply as it does the boys.

> *Denise M. Wilms, in a review of "Beyond Two Rivers," in* Booklist, *Vol. 78, No. 4, October 15, 1981, p. 307.*

As in *. . . Old Man Bean,* Kherdian conveys a feeling for the wilderness and the time of his youth, but overdoes the boys' callow savoring of their experience. (Their airy references to their "java and Old Golds" would be enough without Ted's repeated explicitness about the "manly feeling" of camping out on their own.) They also ooh and ah excessively, at first over a sports' reporter's trout-fishing skills (a mere prelude to Mr. Matsu's); and Matsu's freeze-dried guru wisdom is laid on especially thick.

> *A review of "Beyond Two Rivers," in* Kirkus Reviews, *Vol. XLIX, No. 24, December 15, 1981, p. 1520.*

The Song in the Walnut Grove (1982)

To ask questions without expecting ever to get to the end of things, to make a friend of a "genealogy" shunned by one's family, to share an adventure, to return home only to find that you "can't get into" the family ritual, to question the meaning of life and experience and friendship, and, finally, to become aware that you "can't go home again" and don't want to: All these rites of passage are experienced by Kherdian's little cricket Ben, a curious youngster who goes off to see the world in the daytime and takes up with a similarly nonconforming grasshopper named Charlie. The two are covered by grain pitched by two boys working in a barn. Later Ben takes Charlie to a clinic where the firefly doctor fixes his wing with bees' wax and extract of acanthus leaf, and pops him into the infirmary overnight. (That's when Ben returns home.) In the process of his seeking, Ben discusses purpose (and the purpose of happiness) with an oregano leaf, chirrups ultimate questions to the moon and the stars and the wind, and finds that most creatures are as unquestioning and as contented with their old ways as is his own family. On occasion Ben becomes a tad too earnest, but overall he and Charlie turn in a creditably charming performance.

> *A review of "The Song in the Walnut Grove,"* in Kirkus Reviews, *Vol. L, No. 19, October 1, 1982, p. 1106.*

Talking animals do not necessarily make a fantasy. Anthropomorphism must be written with words so delicate and so true that every thought or action strikes readers as just right. Kherdian's talking cricket, Ben, is not lightly anthropomorphised, but lumpily. Ben is too much the stereotyped little boy asking questions in a human family, too much the vehicle for this obvious message: Friendship (capital F) can be wonderful, and if we were all friends we should all live together happy as clams. What should please us in this book, such as the insect hospital to which Ben's grasshopper buddy goes to have his rumpled wing repaired, is merely heavy-handed incredibility.

> *George Gleason, in a review of "The Song in the Walnut Grove,"* in School Library Journal, *Vol. 29, No. 3, November, 1982, p. 86.*

This short, lyrical tale is not as cohesive as it might be. It lacks the focus of a true fable, the real adventure of a quest. Sometimes its insect heroes move unsteadily toward an anthropomorphic portrayal, and at other times they behave as real animals. But saints be praised, the book does contain ideas.

Some are original: "A friend is someone you've had an experience with." Many are worth repeating: "Once you understand something, it's yours, and no one can take it from you." And Mr. Kherdian's characters, like the friendly oregano leaf and the riddling katydid, witty descendants of Lewis Carroll's, weave the book's major theme out of the interrelatedness of all things: insects, humans, plants, the Earth, even stars.

This is a story for a parent or teacher to share aloud with a child. Like Carroll and William Steig, Mr. Kherdian delights in "big words," and perhaps because he is a poet, there is a wonderful auditory quality in his writing, particularly in dialogues.

> *Patricia Lee Gauch, in a review of "The Song in the Walnut Grove,"* in The New York Times Book Review, *December 19, 1982, p. 26.*

The Mystery of the Diamond in the Wood (1983)

While illegally hunting squirrels in Taylor's Woods, Sam and his friend Howie discover a diamond ring hidden inside a dead log. Sam, whose groping hand actually snags the ring, knows there's more loot inside, but the sound of footsteps sends the nervous boys fleeing. When they return later, the log is empty. The boys' suspicions about the loot and who may have put it there center on Jeb Taylor, brother of the mayor, lately an ex-con, and secretly in town. They approach the police, who won't listen, and then set out to keep an eye on Taylor themselves. Ultimately, their detective work pays off, making them heroes of the hour while the police are red-faced. In the meantime, there is the excitement of the boys' catching Jeb in the act of robbing a store and then the suspense of their becoming his prisoner. Kherdian's mystery-adventure has lots of boyish appeal; smooth writing and a well-characterized friendship allow the escapist, good-guy-bad-guy fancy to remain credible throughout. An entertaining adventure with special appeal for boys.

> *Denise M. Wilms, in a review of "The Mystery of the Diamond in the Wood,"* in Booklist, *Vol. 80, No. 3, October 1, 1983, p. 297.*

David Kherdian, in **The Mystery of the Diamond in the Wood,** has the words but not the music. He has constructed a nice little puzzle, and unravels it in an appropriate way, but he seems so busy looking over his shoulder to be certain that he inserts the right words and phrases—a caper, casing the joint, etc.—that there really is no tension to the plot. I rather think children like tension when they read a book, while it is adults who think of reading as relaxation, and I cannot see that this mystery will whiten any knuckles.

> *Robin W. Winks, "The Detective Wore Sneakers," in* Book World—The Washington Post, *November 6, 1983, p. 16.*

The real mystery of Kherdian's new novel is why he appears so painfully insensitive, so different from the author of superbly human stories that have earned him numerous prizes. Sam Svoboda, 12, tells about events involving him and his friend Howie Baker, starting when they shoot a squirrel. The squirrel is wounded and hides in a dead tree stump that the boys set afire. The animal comes "wobbling and scrambling out with smoke pouring off its back." The sportsmen shoot again and the squirrel lies still, but then "suddenly comes alive again, thrashing madly" before it will die. All this has little to do with ensuing events except that the boys find stolen diamonds in the hollow stump, the squirrel's refuge, and embark on the adventure of tracking the thief. Readers may feel more sympathy for the hunters' victim than for them, when they land in a trap set by the robber.

> *A review of "The Mystery of the Diamond in the Wood,"* in Publishers Weekly, *Vol. 224, No. 26, December 23, 1983, p. 59.*

Right Now (1983)

Alternations—mostly from down to up (quarrel/reconciliation, lost/found) but also, oddly, from yesterday or tomorrow to "right now." The present moment, pictured [by Nonny Hogrogian] in color, is contrasted with both past miseries and coming felicities, pictured in black-and-white. The very pattern is confusing. First: "Yesterday a daisy died"; "But right now a whole field is bloom-

Kherdian with his cat Missak in front of the rented house in Eugene, Oregon where he wrote The Road from Home *(1979). He dedicated* Country, Cat, City, Cat *(1978) to Missak.*

ing." Then: "Tomorrow I'm going to the zoo"; "But right now the rain is falling." Several of the examples are hackneyed and babyish: "Yesterday I lost my shoe in the pond" (weeping); my-mother-wouldn't-let-me-help-with-the-pie, but I-am-making-mud-cake. And one might really wonder at the wisdom of exalting "right now" as an outlook on life, even for quite small children.

A review of "Right Now," in Kirkus Reviews, *Vol. LI, No. 21, November 1, 1983, p. J-186.*

A delightfully warm picture of the joys and trials of childhood. A little girl tells what she is looking forward to or what bad thing has happened to her followed by the contrast of "right now." The past and future events, such as a fight with a brother, a lost cat or a trip to the zoo, are illustrated with black-and-white drawings of the girl expressing her feelings, such as sticking out her tongue. The opposite page depicts present events, like weeding the garden with her brother, making up with a best friend or feeding the cat, in warm pastel colors. The little girl seems old-fashioned and is reminiscent of a Tasha Tudor or Marguerite de Angeli character. A soothing lap story to share

with a child who may have just had a disappointment, this is a gentle, quiet book. . . .

Margaret C. Howell, in a review of "Right Now," in School Library Journal, *Vol. 30, No. 5, January, 1984, p. 65.*

Root River Run   (1984)

Kherdian chronicled his mother's childhood and marriage, her path from Turkey to Wisconsin, in **The Road from Home** and **Finding Home.** Here, in an undramatic but evocative series of vignettes, he recalls his own childhood and adolescence in Racine, 1935-1947. Veron, the mother, now retreats into the background, while father Mike becomes a central figure: helping David to catch his first perch; embarrassing him with his broken English; bargaining over the price of a grand red Schwinn; and yearning to work as a chef—but limited to part-time short-order cooking because of his English-language illiteracy. David is also attached to his joyous Uncle Jack, who rhapsodizes about the Armenian "soul"—only to drift away from the family after marrying Aunt Blanche, an unpleasant surprise for possessive little David. And the sense of growing-up-Armenian is also vivid in the schoolyard: David's friends Garabed, Khatchik, and Esahag decide to choose American names (Chuck, Harry, and "Ees"); a fourth-grade teacher nicknamed "Old Kidney Beans" seems to discriminate against Armenian kids—leading to one powerful moment of confrontation between Kidney Bean and a magisterial Armenian mother. Otherwise, however, David's youth has the familiar highlights of the place and time: the glories of radio-listening; the fear and excitement of a part-time shoeshine career, venturing even into Armenian coffee houses; first conquests in hunting, dancing, and backseat sex. ("I kept thinking of Alice and wondering who she was and why she had taken all of us on . . . I felt cheated, but I still wasn't sure what I had been cheated of.") Gentle, understated, plain-spoken nuggets of recollection—with more appeal for nostalgic adult readers, perhaps, than for a general YA audience.

A review of "Root River Run," in Kirkus Reviews, *Juvenile Issue, Vol. LII, Nos. 18-21, November 1, 1984, p. J-111.*

Because of its fragmented nature and the lack of adequate transition, this simply written, matter-of-fact account misses the dramatic tension which made **Road from Home** such an effective and moving narrative. The book ends with the author making a declaration to himself to be a success and to be true to himself. Of interest primarily to those readers who followed the author's life story through the first two books.

Jack Forman, in a review of "Root River Run," in School Library Journal, *Vol. 31, No. 5, January, 1985, p. 86.*

The Animal   (1984)

The Animal is a strange, harmless extraterrestrial visitor to this animal kingdom. He smiles at flowers, examines dandelions and chases butterflies. The other creatures ask why the animal is so full of wonder. Will he eat the flower, or, as Fox suggests, does he love it? Fox concludes that the animal loves everything because he sees everything through new eyes, and "seeing is loving." Despite elegantly simple language and luminous pastel illustrations [by Nonny Hogrogian] which combine to portray infinite serenity, *The Animal* fails as a story. The book's language and look will appeal to children much younger than those who can grasp the sophisticated concept they express. However, as an element of continuing ethical or religious instruction, *The Animal* may find a niche.

> *Carolyn Noah, in a review of "The Animal,"* in School Library Journal, *Vol. 31, No. 4, December, 1984, p. 72.*

The gentle, touching illustrations—such as the noble but bemused lion, the thoughtful elephant—are rendered with delicate line and color that emphasize the nature and loveliness of all beasts. Almost a fable in form, simple and beautiful in design, the book is a paean to the peaceable kingdom. (p. 47)

> *Ann A. Flowers, in a review of "The Animal,"* in The Horn Book Magazine, *Vol. LXI, No. 1, January-February, 1985, pp. 46-7.*

The Kheridans have blended their talents together into a multileveled tale. As the veneer is peeled away from a simplistic telling the underneath reveals and requires perception and understanding, fashioning a book that can be shared with many different ages. . . . Definitely a special book.

> *S. A. T., in a review of "The Animal,"* in Catholic Library World, *Vol. 56, No. 8, March, 1985, p. 341.*

Bridger: The Story of a Mountain Man   (1987)

Kherdian fictionalizes an account of 18-year-old Jim Bridger's journey up the Missouri, initiation into the life of a trapper, relations with Crow Indians, and "discovery" of the Great Salt Lake (long known, of course, to Native Americans). The first-person narrative is smooth and interesting, though the dialogue is sometimes awkward and the dialect uneven. Source notes would have been helpful, too, or some afterword as to what portion of the account is documented and what invented. As it is, this reflects a somewhat romanticized view of Bridger's adventure; there are also a few vague time lapses between vivid scenes; and, as often as not, the commonly held prejudices against "Injuns" (to which Bridger did not subscribe) prevail. The setting, however, is strong. On balance, readers will come away with a sense of the excitement and hardship of opening up a wild, beautiful country. (pp. 148-49)

> *Betsy Hearne, in a review of "Bridger: The Story of a Mountain Man,"* in Bulletin of the Center for Children's Books, *Vol. 40, No. 8, April, 1987, pp. 148-49.*

This could be a useful update to biographies about the most famous of the legendary mountain men. Fictionalizing tends to be limited to dialogue, although there is also an invented, if likely, romantic involvement with Whippoorwill, an Indian girl; whether the romance is consummated is hard to tell. Occasional want of transition, a handful of sexual references, and the use of some undefined period words (a five-term glossary is nearly worthless) may daunt some readers. Kherdian's style is a mixture of fact and poetic rendition. He is more inclined to go for a striking, if not always appropriate, simile than to settle for a more prosaic, factual explanation or observation. *Jim Bridger* (Houghton, 1952; o.p.) by Doris Shannon Garst is a more interesting book and is superior to Kherdian's.

> *George Gleason, in a review of "Bridger: The Story of a Mountain Man,"* in School Library Journal, *Vol. 33, No. 7, April, 1987, p. 111.*

Although a fascinating account of the first two years of Bridger's mountain man life, there are gaps in the storyline that may confuse the reader. It seemed sometimes that some adventures were started and then never allowed to conclude. A list of characters would have been helpful as they are referred to by both first and last names at different points in the book. A short glossary was included in the front of the book, but a more detailed one would help because of the mountain man dialect used. Maps were indicated but not included in the advance proof and will be a useful addition so that Bridger's travels may be followed. Well researched and easily read, this book fills a gap in most collections especially when it's time to study the U.S. Westward expansion period.

> *Kathryn L. Havris, in a review of "Bridger: The Story of a Mountain Man,"* in Voice of Youth Advocates, *Vol. 10, No. 2, June, 1987, p. 79.*

A Song for Uncle Harry   (1989)

Twelve-year-old Pete reminisces about his treasured Uncle Harry, who always has time for him and who teaches him some important lessons about life. Harry is an Armenian immigrant who is disabled, having being gassed while serving as a U.S. serviceman in World War I. Pete's recollections focus on special times he's had with Harry: riding in his Model-T car on a fishing trip to the country; carrying news of Harry's sister's death; and eating chestnuts by the fire. The boy also remembers the encouragement he got to pursue his art work. Though the events themselves are unexceptional, Harry's presence makes them special. Kherdian makes clear just how Harry had his own way of seeing and appreciating the world around him—something he imparted successfully to his beloved nephew. Though the story is set in the 1930s, the relationship between Pete and Harry is timeless. Every kid needs an Uncle Harry; those who don't can find one between these carefully phrased pages.

> *Denise Wilms, in a review of "A Song for Uncle Harry,"* in Booklist, *Vol. 86, No. 2, September 15, 1989, p. 184.*

A fictionalized memoir, warm and sweet, of growing up Armenian in Wisconsin between the two World Wars. . . . The brevity and simplicity of these remembrances make this appropriate for middle-elementary readers, while older readers may better appreciate Kherdian's autobiographical *Root River Run,* which includes slightly different versions of several of the same incidents and an account of his initiation to sex.

Joel Shoemaker, in a review of "A Song for Uncle Harry," in School Library Journal, *Vol. 36, No. 1, January, 1990, p. 104.*

The Cat's Midsummer Jamboree (1990)

This mandolin-strumming, singing cat has an extraordinary ear for music and a boundless enthusiasm that soon extends to encompass a toad with a harmonica, then a fox with a flute. The felicitous feline proves adept at encouraging each musician to give up a solo career, as the trio soon becomes a country band, with members joining in a lyrical chain reaction. First they form a parade, then climb into tree branches to create their own colorful symphony. The music takes over "until the world of that place was filled with the happiness that all began with a cat who loved to sing." Soft-as-velvet illustrations from . . . [Nonny] Hogrogian seem to spring out of the clean white pages. A diverse collection of wildflowers provides a gentle backdrop for the forest folk. Kherdian's rhapsodic story will make

readers and listeners want to reach for an instrument and burst into song.

A review of "The Cat's Midsummer Jamboree," in Publishers Weekly, *Vol. 237, No. 13, March 30, 1990, p. 61.*

As a story, this is thin, but there's no denying the simple pleasure of its celebratory mood; Hogrogian fans will relish her play of woodland colors and the unaffected anthropomorphism that cements the animals' charm. Light but nonetheless engaging.

Denise Wilms, in a review of "The Cat's Midsummer Jamboree," in Booklist, *Vol. 86, No. 17, May 1, 1990, p. 1706.*

In this simple, low-key story, a singing, mandolin-playing cat comes upon a variety of other animal musicians and persuades each in turn to join in and travel along. . . . Kherdian's stylized telling has the quality of a folktale as the players progress from a duet to a trio, to a quartet, and so on, introducing a new animal and instrument each time. The text is slightly more formal than Hogrogian's familiar soft, whimsical colored-pencil and wash drawings, set unfettered against white backgrounds or enclosed in a lush forest backdrop. A pleasant enough stroll, although rather tame stuff for midsummer madness.

Corinne Camarata, in a review of "The Cat's Midsummer Jamboree," in School Library Journal, *Vol. 36, No. 7, July, 1990, p. 61.*

Christobel Mattingley

1931-

Australian author of fiction and picture books and journalist.

Major works include *The Windmill at Magpie Creek* (1971), *The Battle of the Galah Trees* (1973), *New Patches for Old* (1977), *Rummage* (1981), *The Miracle Tree* (1985).

One of Australia's most respected writers, Mattingley is celebrated for creating a variety of works for readers in the early grades through high school that reflect her social and environmental concerns as well as her understanding of her audience. The author of realistic fiction, fantasy, comedy, and picture books acknowledged for their depth, insight, lack of sentimentality or condescension, and superior prose style, Mattingley is perhaps best known for the stories she has written for middle graders, a type of book she is credited with pioneering in Australian children's literature. Mattingley's early works characteristically describe the attempts of their young male or female protagonists to save endangered animals or trees or to conquer personal fears, actions which bring out their resourcefulness and lead to independence, maturity, or self-assurance. Influenced by her childhood reminiscences and observations of her own family, the stories share an Australian setting and roots in everyday experience. In 1974, Mattingley took her children to Europe, a trip noted for initiating the broadening of setting, subject, and theme that characterizes her more recent works.

Mattingley is perhaps best known for her award-winning picture book *Rummage,* the story of how a merchant who runs a junk stall in an English street market strikes a blow for individuality, and for *The Miracle Tree,* a novel for middle graders that is often praised for its dignity and moving quality. In this work, Mattingley describes how Taro, a Japanese gardener and former soldier, his wife Honako, and her mother are separated during the Second World War by the bombing of Nagasaki; after a search that lasts twenty years, they are reunited around a pine tree that has kept their hope alive. Among her other works, Mattingley is the author of several books for early readers that are considered especially substantial for their audience; young adult novels that deal with change, growth, and the acceptance of self and others; the poignant reminiscences of a German woman who describes her experience as a refugee during World War II; and a black comedy about a schoolboy who exorcises a ghost. She is also the editor of an adult work that considers the aboriginal experience from the nineteenth century through the present. Both *The Windmill at Magpie Creek* and *Worm Weather* were highly commended for the Book of the Year by the Children's Book Council of Australia in 1972, while *Rummage* was named the Australian Junior Book of the Year and commended for the Australian Book of the Year in 1982.

(See also *Something about the Author,* Vol. 37; *Contemporary Authors New Revision Series,* Vol. 20; and *Contemporary Authors,* Vols. 97-100.)

GENERAL COMMENTARY

John Gough

Although Christobel Mattingley is well-known as a writer of picture story books and illustrated novellas, her two full-length novels have received little attention. The shorter stories range from simple tales of everyday life to historical realism, fantasy, and larger-than-life comedy. Almost all of her stories are concerned with a central character coming to terms with some problem. In the recent picture story book *Brave With Ben*, a small boy finds the courage to explore his grandmother's intimidatingly overgrown backyard. In the early short novel *Windmill at Magpie Creek*, a young boy finds an ingenious way to deal with the dive-bombing magpies that are nesting on the old windmill. In *Rummage*, the rather eccentric Mr. Portwine must defend his market junk stall and himself against the disapproving criticisms of his fellow stall-holders, who are purveyors, with conceited superiority, of exclusive antiques and collectors' items. Even her very first published story, *The Picnic Dog*, concerns the father of a family coming to terms with a boisterous young puppy.

Both of Mattingley's two full-length novels, *New Patches For Old* and *Southerly Buster*, are also concerned with coming to terms with problems. But these problems are essentially different from aggressive magpies, critical colleagues, or nasty-looking trees. More importantly, there is room to explore character in considerable depth, exploiting a richness of imagery and significance which is not possible in the shorter stories.

There are other differences between the two full-length novels and Mattingley's picture stories and novellas. The central characters are teenagers, considerably older than the young children of most of the other books. Consequently, both novels are concerned with problems of adolescence.

It is also notable that these two novels have no illustrations. In these novels, Mattingley's language frequently attains the power of poetry, where heightened imagination far exceeds the confines of a specific picture. (pp. 97-8)

Even *The Picnic Dog*, Christobel Mattingley's first story, showed an ear and eye for language.

> "No, we can't take Piccolo [the dog]," the children's father said. "There isn't room. Bassinet and baby, barbecue and butterfly net, baskets and billies, boots and bags for blackberrying. We can't take Piccolo." He scratched his head as he looked at the pile beside the car. "Quite a conglomeration to cram in! We need a caravan!"

Alliteration, assonance, and choral patterning suggest that Mattingley has a talent for verse which has otherwise gone unrevealed.

But in her novels Christobel Mattingley shows a subtler kind of poetics. At the very start of *New Patches For Old* the teenage heroine of the story watches her mother making a pastry tart:

> she began crimping the edge between her finger and thumb, "as if her life depended upon it," Patricia said afterwards when she was telling her brother Mark about it. Her mother finished the tart crust to the last pinch before she looked at Patricia again, and then before she said a word, Patricia knew something was wrong.

She is told that her father's job is finishing and they will have to emigrate to Australia:

> Patricia had the sensation that the familiar room was dissolving like a bubble, that her life was shattering into fragments. For an instant she experienced a sense of nothingness, as if her heart had stopped beating, and she lost all feeling. Then she remembered her mother's hands gathering up the pastry scraps, gently kneading them together, rolling a new piece from what was left over, cutting out a new shape.

Patricia's unhappy feelings of disintegration, expressed in images of a bursting bubble and a stopped heart, are further echoed and implicitly resolved in the image of pastry scraps, cut off, gathered, and reformed. Lives, indeed, depend on a mature ability to cope with drastic change. It is this maturity which Patricia must learn through the rest of the book.

Again and again, images of disintegration, change, growth, and renewal occur as natural elements in the literal narrative and as poetic elements in the implicit emotional narrative. Even before the upheaval in her life, the heroine is not wholly integrated as a person. She is Patricia, to herself, but her school friends call her Tricia, and her father calls her Paddy. But in her new school in Australia, she must wear a second-hand schooldress that is patched, and an unpleasant girl in her class, who is also called Patricia, humiliates her by refusing to accept "Patricia," "Tricia," "Paddy," or even "Pat." Instead she is given the nickname "Patches" . . . . (pp. 98-9)

Memories, feelings, images, and related events link Patricia's old life and Patches' new life. Her Grandpa's absorption in his English garden is matched by her efforts to grow wattletrees, marigolds, petunias, and daffodils in the parched bare soil of her family's rented house. Patched dress, Patch name, good patches and bad patches of experience, cross-patch and garden-patch. Then the kind school nurse shows her patch-work, remaking scraps of other people's lives into new, rich materials, echoing her mother and the pastry scraps. Patricia takes a step forward in making an Australian life by choosing to use the previously hurtful nickname with a new-found sense of pride: "She had lost the battle for her name, but indirectly the victory was hers".

Images of patches, and the significance of the title of the novel, are further extended by an encounter with an upholsterer who makes "new chairs for old" and who "dealt in change," passing "treasures from one cherished keeping into other caring hands and kept the lustre of past loves, past lives, burnished in the chain of change". This echoes the wisdom of Patches' Grandma at the start of the book: "Losing is part of living and letting go is part of loving," and "You can't have people or pets for ever. The parting hurts, but then you can be glad because you have known them and in a way they have become part of you".

Echoes, reflections, correspondence of images, correlations between objects and emotions: in *New Patches For Old* these are threads running through and across the whole book. (pp. 99-100)

As well as the main problem of coping with emigration, *New Patches For Old* is also concerned with the adolescent problem of first love. This is very sensibly and sensitively handled, without emotional excess. Although Patches' friends speak of her as being "wrapped" in the young man, she does not label her feelings. The word "love" is not applied to the special friendship that blossoms between Patches and Geoff, even though they do hold hands, and kiss, and long to see each other when they are apart. Their feelings may be recognised as love, but Mattingley is careful not to overstate this or exaggerate its seriousness, and avoids the gushiness or debasement of romance novels and pop-songs. Patches and Geoff are people in their own right, neither idealised nor sentimentalised. Both have problems thrust upon them which they must deal with. Incidentally, the way Mattingley, through her characters, describes Patches having her first unexpected period is a model of simplicity. On a beach picnic, Geoff is the first to notice, but he and his friends respond so kindly that Patches' first feelings of shame and embarrassment are completely lost in the pleasure of "The day to make you glad you came to Australia." Accepted with a minimum of fuss as a natural part of life, her period is part of the day, something to be glad about.

Slowly, through the novel, Patricia-Patches finds there are decisions and choices she can make. She is not a pawn in a game, the helpless victim of inexorable external forces. Nonetheless, the central narrative thrust of *New Patches For Old* derives from the problem of migration from England to Australia. This problem is essentially outside of the heroine, although the narrative interest is on Patricia and how she and her family will respond.

Southerly Buster is also concerned with a teenage heroine responding to a problem. But, perhaps because the problem is essentially psychological, the book does not make this problem explicit. Julie Jeffrey's mother, at the late age of forty-two, is expecting a baby. Julie is upset and confused. The problem, which is internal rather than external, lies with Julie's response to her mother and father. She is forced into an awareness of their sexuality, a recognition that they are human beings who have natural sexual appetites and are in fact sexually active—with obvious consequences. Equally, Julie is forced into a new awareness of herself and her peers as sexual beings. She is challenged, by her mother's pregnancy and her own experience and maturing, to grow from the preadolescent Freudian latency period into adult sexuality. All of this sounds very heavy and potentially sordid. It is actually beautifully handled by Mattingley, and, as in *New Patches For Old*, it is the poetic use of imagery that achieves this.

In *New Patches For Old* one marvellous image captures the heart of the book. Walking on a winter beach, Patches' friend Geoff finds a rare and delicate paper nautilus sea shell, and gives it to her:

> Patches took the delicate gift, as lustrous white as the stone egg [an earlier gift] but so fragile, curved and tipped with a row of tiny black spikes . . .
>
> Patches gazed at its transluscent beauty and stroked its rippled surface. "How did it survive through all this?" she asked. She looked at the surging sea and felt the surge rising within her as Geoff looked at her.
>
> "You should know", he said.

The symbolism is powerful: beauty, fragility, hazardous travel, wild sea, surging emotion, finding, sharing, giving, understanding. Similar use of imagery occurs throughout *Southerly Buster*, which begins with a family beachside holiday.

A sea shell also provides an image for Julie. A delicate, hollow sea-urchin shell is given to Julie at the end of the holiday by Bob, a medical student who works during the holidays as a lifesaver.

> She looked at its intricate pattern, tracing the ridges and dots lightly with her finger. "It's beautiful."
> "It's there all the time under the prickles," Bob said.
> Julie said, "I haven't enjoyed being an adolescent little fool."
> "Do you think I don't understand that, Urchin?"
> There was a moment of sunlight, the scent of eucalyptus, the sound of cicadas and surf.

Later, Julie feels "as hollow, empty as the sea-urchin shell", and when the baby is born, Bob points out that the baby cries when Julie holds it, because it is like "being held by a sea urchin . . . All spikes and prickles of antagonism and resentment". Just as Bob saved Julie from half-intentionally drowning herself when she had first heard that her mother was pregnant, so now Bob's metaphor triggers a change in Julie's feelings, "a rush of emotion which almost stopped her breathing," and she loses the prickles.

Bob, the lifesaver, restores Julie with butterscotch Lifesavers. This kind of punning imagery recurs through the book. Milk shakes and milk-like moonlight remind Julie of breast milk; jelly babies naturally connect with the idea of babies; jelly beans are coloured, red for stop, green for go, yellow for caution, purple for passion, green for jealousy. Even as she knits baby bootees, Julie counts stitches, thinking "One into one makes one more . . . Two together make one". Sexual imagery flows through the whole book. It is not just that Julie is jealous of the baby. . . . (pp. 100-02)

Rather she resents being forced to recognise that her parents have an adult part of their relationship that does not include her.

All of this becomes resolved when Julie finds and accepts her own sexuality. Other writers might do this kind of thing with explicit sexual experiment and experience and overwrought emotions. Mattingley simply describes Julie feeling suddenly "overwhelmed" with longing as she dances with Damon. "Her whole body, her whole being vibrated for him". Then in his car,

> He leaned towards her. Julie felt the hot longing sweep through her again. His lips were on her, his hands.
>
> *No, no. Not a baby. O, God, not a baby. Yes, yes . . . Don't stop, don't stop. Oh Damon, don't stop now.*

Fortunately Damon does stop, and Julie, recognising and accepting her own passion, is glad—glad about her parents, and the baby, and about herself and Damon. The book ends on a great affirmation of adult love.

Happening within the last page and a half, this might seem rather sudden. But Mattingley has subtly prepared for it. Julie's images of knitting; her warm, womanly response to the baby; her thoughts of sharing a bed, of "sexing," as she makes her parents' bed; her talk with a schoolgirl friend who is happily on the pill; her caring for a stray pregnant cat; her enjoyment of taking a shower and of swimming naked in a rock pool; talking with other pregnant parents in the hospital where Bob works. These simple, unlurid events all help build a new maturity and establish adult connections that rescue Julie from feeling "like kelp in the sea, torn from its safe anchorage on the rocks, at the mercy of the tides".

Images echo and reecho, related events reflecting the themes of the book. Even something as simple as the colour pink runs like a thread through a range of images: rose-pink sunglasses for seeing the world optimistically, pink sea shell, pink baby wool, stale pink iced cake in the threatening milk bar, pink with embarrassment, pink toy teddy and bunny, pink raw sausage, pink cupids (!) and rose buds on a gift card, pink examination question paper. All of these echo the pink of the newborn baby, and, implicitly, the sensual pink of adult nakedness. The title, also, "Southerly Buster," works in several ways as an image: literally, it is a sudden storm from the sea, fierce and brief, bringing cool and violent relief after a summer hotspell; for Julie it is her emotional stormy response to news of the coming baby, but it is also literally a real storm that nearly drowns her; for her family, the baby is a Southerly Buster, bringing turmoil to settled routines, and indeed the baby is born on the night of a southerly storm, and then is nicknamed Buster. It is an image of sudden change, of crisis, which soon blows over and leads to a new resolution.

By the end of the book Julie is captured in another brief image by Damon:

> pink for girls and all that is corny. . . . People can be any colour. You're an opal. All flash and fire. Never the same for two minutes. I'm never quite sure. . . . You're much more interesting than pink. Pink is a prawn. Pink is icing on a cake. Pink is a sausage.
> "Oh, shut up," Julie said.
> Damon looked at her. "Like I said. An opal. Embers and sparks. Never know when you'll flare up next."

Like Julie, **Southerly Buster** and **New Patches For Old** also flash fire, shimmering with a mosaic richness of imagery which is remarkable in children's books. We can hope for many more books of this poetic subtlety from Christobel Mattingley, books whose intricate weaving of threads of imagery reveal something of the dazzling tapestried complexity of life. (pp. 102-04)

> *John Gough, "Tapestries of Image and Emotion: The Novels of Christobel Mattingley," in* Children's Literature in Education, *Vol. 18, No. 2, Summer, 1987, pp. 97-104.*

Stephen Matthews

It is my contention that Christobel Mattingley has been a pathfinder certainly in two and arguably in more areas of Australian children's literature: first, in the writing of books especially appropriate for seven to nine year olds in the sometimes difficult traditional period between picture books for young children and novels: second, in the use of such books to tell stories presenting a clear moral viewpoint on such matters of social concern as the protection of the environment and the effects of war. A look at just a few of Christobel's books will support these assertions.

Windmill at Magpie Creek, Christobel's second book . . . offers clear grounds for the first assertion. . . . It is the story of Tim, a boy beset by two fears which are alluded to in the title and are inescapable from the fact of living on the small farm his parents own: first, there are the magpies who seem always to choose him to attack; and second, there is the windmill, which Tim has climbed once and thereafter dreads. The book describes how, following an accident to his father, Tim has to confront and eventually to overcome his fears by climbing the windmill with his own anti-magpie device, because if the mill does not get proper maintenance his incapacitated father will have to replace it with a more manageable diesel-operated one.

Tim's triumph at reaching the top is succinctly drawn out on the last page when he tells his friend Barney: 'It's a stiff climb . . . and it's a bit scary the first time you do it. But it's worth it to get to the top'. Heart-warming is an overworked epithet, but there is no better one to describe the effect on the reader of this conclusion to a deceptively simple book which is perfectly suited to its seven to nine year old readership. They are years when fears similar to Tim's loom large, and the book achieves its effect by showing, very accessibly, how they may be overcome. Note especially however that the reader is not encouraged to believe that it is an achievement which can occur without sustained effort and heart searching.

The whole theme is so plainly an effective one that Christobel has reworked it in other books, as have other writers, notably in recent times Ivy Baker, in *The Monday sheepdog*. Christobel herself returned to the theme in **The long walk, The big swim, The jetty** and **Brave with Ben.** Without question the theme is what gives those, of all her books, the power to evoke the greatest response among young readers. **The big swim** in particular strikes a very deep chord. . . . (pp. 74-5)

The assertion that Christobel Mattingley has contributed greatly to the provision of top quality reading for young people is further validated by **Rummage**. . . . Undoubtedly enhanced by Patricia Mullins' illustrations (which, though extremely evocative, are regrettably inconsistent in execution), it is a story of individuality triumphant. Mr. Septimus Portwine's street market stall is too untidy for the tastes of some of his fellow stallholders who try to improve his appearance and upgrade his clientele. He becomes ill and pines for his former self, which he finally reasserts with good-humoured defiance. All the book's readers recognise and respond to those aspects of Mr. Portwine's character and behaviour which they share, and they immediately reject the snobbism and intolerance of his critics. There is no question that **Rummage** was in the forefront of the move, which has gained momentum in the 1980s, towards copiously illustrated books for young readers making the transition between picture books and novels.

It is worth noting here that Christobel's **The great Ballagundi damper bake**, published in 1975 and similar to **Rummage** in presentation as well as underlying themes, was an even earlier part in the same trend. One may also speculate about how Christobel's first book, *The picnic dog*, would have been presented had it appeared after the trend was under way, for it certainly appeals to a similar readership and would be enhanced by more expansive illustrations.

The second of my assertions about Christobel Mattingley's work is that she led the way in the creation of stories for young readers which have serious (though not solemn) social messages. *The battle of the galah trees* demonstrates the author's commitment to environmental conservation. Somewhat longer than most of her books, but still intended for and readable by younger readers, it tells how a boy called Matt determines to prevent the destruction of two big gum trees in a neighbourhood park, initially because they are home to a galah which he has nursed back to health after a fall from its nest. It's no easy task however, for as Matt discovers, the protection of the environment means little to some people in responsible positions. For example, there is Mr. Cain, a nouveau-riche local councillor and father of a boy in Matt's class at school—'Mr. Cain and his car were like an ant and a beetle under the huge trees but Mr. Cain had power. Matt was disquieted'. With the help of his friends, especially Janey, a hitherto meek and retiring girl new to the school, Matt leads a fight which culminates in the saving of one of the trees at least.

The destruction of the other tree gives the writer the opportunity for an impassioned and exceptionally moving account of its dismemberment and uprooting, which is a model of committed writing. The book is noteworthy too for its characterisation of Matt; without contrivance, it portrays a caring, sensitive boy unafraid to step out of the more traditionally masculine mould of most of his schoolmates. Yet the book came out in 1974, before publications such as the first Sugar and Snails non-sexist book guide began drawing attention to the need to break down traditional stereotypes in children's books.

The characterisation of Janey is also of interest, both with regard to the fact that it is she who becomes the decisive participant in the battle to save the galah trees, and also that in so becoming, she ceases to be the class misfit and achieves acceptance by her fellow pupils. (The plight of the misfit is a recurrent subtheme in Christobel Mattingley's work, featuring for example in *Rummage*, *The great Ballagundi damper bake* and *New patches for old*, among others.) (pp. 75-6)

If additional evidence is sought of Christobel's contribution to environmental awareness in young readers, there is no need to look further than *Lizard log,* in which a boy on a camping holiday finds himself saving lizards from an unsavoury pair of illicit dealers who trap and sell their ill-gotten reptilian prey. Understated in Christobel's typical style, the book offers another portrayal of a caring, sensitive boy who shares an affinity with the bush creatures (especially the lizards) he loves to observe and to feed. The story is told within an unobtrusive structure which allows the attentive reader to notice that despite contrary appearances the boy's mother has observed his removal of various items of food for his beloved lizards. Sadly, to modern

eyes, the first (1975) edition of the book is very much in need of the new illustrations planned to replace the muddy originals. Nevertheless, children of six and seven upwards still respond enthusiastically to this satisfying simple story.

In discussing Christobel Mattingley's contribution to the creation of stories for young readers which reflect social concerns, attention must be given to the two books which are arguably her finest achievements, namely *The angel with a mouth-organ* and *The miracle tree*. Both are heart-rending, but ultimately optimistic accounts of war-ravaged families. . . . These books are very different from Christobel's other children's books in that they are also read by adults for their own interest. It may even be that the depth of emotion and concern these books contain can only be fully discerned and felt by adults, with their fuller experience and insight. Certainly they have the power to leave adults in tears on first and subsequent readings. It is probably no coincidence that both books are based on collections of real incidents, told to or observed by the writer, which involved adults rather than the children whose experiences underpin her earlier books.

The angel with a mouth-organ begins and ends with scenes of a present day family in which two children resolve their argument about which of them should complete the decoration of their Christmas tree by the family tradition of placing a glass angel at its top. In between, we hear from the children's mother the story of how the angel came to belong to the family. It is a sombre and harrowing story, given alleviating counterpoint by the richly-coloured illustrations of Astra Lacis (whose father's wartime experiences were among those incorporated in the story), and by the contrast with the present day Christmas scene.

The storyteller describes how, as refugees towards the end of World War II, she and her sister and mother become separated from her father and undergo a series of horrifying experiences, having to confront death, hunger and destitution before being reunited with him. The story is told in simple, spare prose using repetition to great effect in conveying the wearying trudge towards safety and peace. It also has a tight structure which allows incidents like the death and burial of an accompanying refugee's baby to find telling resonances in the furtive concealment of the shattered remains of a representation of Jesus. In an especially shocking scene this is taken from its crib by the narrator's sister, unable to contain her rage at the crib's appearance of peace and tranquillity amidst her own experience of the turmoil of war.

It is, however, the sequence where her father returns which brings readers to tears. In the space of five short lines the word 'hugged' is repeated six times, and the reader's spine tingles. Then the father brings out the glass angel which he found in a ruined church and which has sustained him during the separation from his family. It is a richly crafted story.

The miracle tree, on the face of it, is a less subtle story, based not so much on a gifted retelling of actual experiences as on a wishfully imaginative (but finely wrought) reassembly of unconnected incidents, albeit still actual.

Again it is a story of a family separated by war; but this time there are no young children, but instead, a husband and wife and her mother (who was alienated from them by their hasty and unannounced marriage before the war). Taro, the husband, and Hanako, the wife, are parted by the war and after its end Taro discovers that Hanako was in Nagasaki when the atom bomb was dropped. He goes there in search of her but eventually presumes her dead and concentrates on his new occupation of gardening, caring in particular for the pine tree of the title, which he has planted himself. Unbeknown to him his work on the tree, and the tree's growth, are observed by his wife's mother, who had also come to Nagasaki in search of her daughter; never having met, neither knows the identity of the other. The daughter meanwhile, alive but disfigured by the bomb, lives in seclusion in sight of the tree and fills her time writing poetry. Years pass and the tree grows until one Christmas when, all unknown to one another, Taro comes to tend the tree; his wife struggles against worsening illness to write one more poem, about the tree; and his mother-in-law watches his work on the tree. Hanako finishes her poem, folds it and launches it from her window. It lands on Taro's tree and, accompanied by his still unrecognised mother-in-law, he goes to look for its author. Despite her disfigurement, Hanako is recognised by Taro and the family of course is reunited, thanks to their shared interest in the tree, just in time to celebrate the miracle of their first (and, it is implied, probably their last) Christmas together.

Though seen by some as contrived, the story has, rather, the inexorable quality of a folk tale, in which the reader almost wills it to as happy an end as the circumstances allow. It certainly makes the horrific subject of nuclear war and its effects accessible to young readers, while not comprising poignancy or emotional power. And the Christmas message of peace has probably never been more forcefully conveyed in a book for younger readers.

This has merely scratched the surface of Christobel Mattingley's work. I have looked at only six of her books; I have not discussed the breadth of range in her writing, yet in addition to her books for younger readers there are the picture books, like *Lexl and the lion party* and *Black dog*; and the longer novels like *The jetty* and the inexplicably little known and now out of print *Southerly buster* (a moving book for young teens). In addition to the stories of social concern, there is the comedy of *The ghost sitter* and *McGruer and the goat*; the fantasy of *The magic saddle*; and the good natured everyday incident of *The surprise mouse*. There are others as well, yet the central puzzle remains—why has such an extensive contribution to Australian children's literature been so little understood and so sadly unremarked by the Children's Book Council of Australia.

Christobel herself realises that some critics consider her style and themes a little old-fashioned—not sensational enough for today's television-stimulated readers. To some extent that may be true, but it surely does not diminish the quality of her writing and many young readers will be surprised to discover that they are not supposed to respond to her books. Certainly Christobel Mattingley does not

write about (and by so doing celebrate and encourage) 'spoilt brats'. She writes with a moral purpose, though never in a preachy or didactic way. She wants her readers to aspire to, and recognise the need to strive for, better things. She knows that that involves struggle and requires fortitude, but she writes stories which show that the effort and persistence bring worthwhile and satisfying rewards, as we saw Tim tell us at the end of *Windmill at Magpie Creek.* Christobel consistently invents characters who embody models of behaviour which affirm and encourage moral conduct, characters who do what we all know to be the right thing and what we want for each other; characters who persist even when the going gets tough. Sometimes criticised for not being realistic enough in her fictions, Christobel Mattingley in fact exalts a truer reality: that it is effort, fortitude and perseverance which win out in the face of adversity, rather than the adoption of the easy way out. She writes books which sow seeds, eventually to grow and blossom in their readers' minds. Her books are never contrived, coming rather (even the simplest ones) from deep inside her soul and so born of integrity that she will never have to repudiate any of them as unworthy of her vision and purpose. (pp. 76-8)

Stephen Matthews, "A Truer Reality: The Work of Christobel Mattingley," in ORANA, *Vol. 24, No. 2, May, 1988, pp. 73-8.*

TITLE COMMENTARY

The Picnic Dog (1970)

The children's beloved pet finally wins the favour of the intolerant adult—in this case, birdwatching father whose camera is constantly endangered by the excitable puppy. There is nothing original in the plot, and the Australian setting is barely noticeable, yet the book should find favour with young children alive to the excitement of language and appreciative of the shape of the story. The framework of repetition gives a spice of the expected to each new disaster, and pleasure in words is evident throughout. Children will delight in the alliterative lists of picnic gear to be crammed into the little car, leaving—Father says hopefully—no room for Piccolo.

Iris Wilcox, in a review of "The Picnic Dog," in The School Librarian, *Vol. 19, No. 1, March, 1971, p. 85.*

The Windmill at Magpie Creek (1971)

[Tim] is afraid of heights and after one climb up the open structure of the wind-tower that raises their water, he refuses to help his father again with the twice-yearly servicing, especially as the magpies round the house seem to regard him as an enemy only fit to be dive-bombed. When his father has an accident, Tim realises he must conquer his fear; determination, and a Ned Kelly hood made from an ice-cream tin, help him to make his climb and even to move the nest which the magpies have built on the windmill. There is plenty of local colour in this short book, and an understanding of the way fear, fun and confidence can jostle in a boy's mind.

Mattingley in 1947 as a prefect at the Friends' School, Hobart, Tasmania; she had already begun to publish her works in the children's pages of magazines and newspapers at this time.

> *Margery Fisher, in a review of "The Windmill at Magpie Creek," in* Growing Point, *Vol. 10, No. 2, July, 1971, p. 1758.*

The limitations imposed on an author writing stories for the young reader from 7–9 years are considerable. Mrs. Mattingley has confined herself to a simple, brief style while retaining a fresh and imaginative expression.

The daily life on an Australian farm is shown with clarity and attention to those details which doubtless will appeal to most young children, but boys in particular will respond to the descriptions of catching yabbies and other outdoor activities.

> *A review of "The Windmill at Magpie Creek," in* Bookbird, *Vol. XI, No. 1, March 15, 1973, p. 42.*

Worm Weather (1971)

[The] brief anecdote **Worm weather** gives us a complete picture in everyday terms. There is a close companionship between Wendy and her grandfather; he is teaching her a good deal of natural history but he is also learning from her, and each is conscious, though in differing ways, of their lines of communication. Such a story offers a young reader the stimulus of new ways of doing things (looking after worms, for example), new reasons, new technical terms, and at the same time it calms him with the domestic intimacy that warms it.

> *Margery Fisher, in a review of "Worm Weather," in* Growing Point, *Vol. 10, No. 2, July, 1971, p. 1763.*

Queen of the Wheat Castles (1973)

Mrs. Tabbs was known to be fond of cats, so strays and unwanted cats were often dumped near her house. The situation became quite out of hand when she found herself with thirty-six cats, and no one seemed to want one. Cathy determined to help Mrs. Tabbs and tried everything she knew. At one stage she rode the wheat train and was almost killed, at another she persuaded the local nurse to say, in the paper, that every family with very young children needed a cat to protect the children from mice. In the end Cathy managed to find homes for all thirty-six cats, and then, on top of everything, she was crowned Queen of the Wheat Castles. This book conveys a warm, quiet and gentle atmosphere but interest is never lost. The reader is taken from one incident to the next in the smoothest fashion and all the time identifies with Cathy for whom nothing seems to go right at first, and for whom everything turns out well in the end.

> *G. L. Hughes, in a review of "Queen of the Wheat Castles," in* The Junior Bookshelf, *Vol. 37, No. 6, December, 1973, p. 393.*

The heat of an Australian summer hangs over this story of red-haired Cathy who tries to find homes for an ever increasing number of stray cats. Having satisfied all demands in the small town where she lives, Cathy, with the cats, stows away on an empty wheat train in search of new territory, and almost comes to grief. Once again Christobel Mattingley has produced a convincing little story which will appeal to a wide range of readers. Cathy moves in a world of adults, and although in a book of this length there is no time to develop minor characters the vignettes do ring true and the reader feels acquainted with a cross section of the population of the little Australian town.

> *Joyce Taylor, in a review of "Queen of the Wheat Castles," in* The School Librarian, *Vol. 22, No. 2, June, 1974, p. 199.*

The Battle of the Galah Trees (1973)

The battle of the galah trees has a firm conservation point which is pressed strongly, perhaps now and then a little too strongly for a short book with a branching plot. Matt's affinity with animals involves him in a community problem. At first he is only concerned with a particular bird, a part-fledged parrakeet which he has rescued from a nest smashed by a falling branch. But when he learns that this gum tree is threatened he is anxious about the galahs that use it each year on passage, and boldly starts a campaign to save the tree. Various adults enter the affair—Barry's domineering father, who hopes the scheme for a new car park will be a vote-catcher in the Council elections; Matt's form master, an enthusiastic conservator; the corporation gardener who finds the sprawling tree hardly fits his tidy layout; an elderly artist who started his career in the locality. Christobel Mattingley is well capable of quickening a story with a true feeling for community matters; there is a sense here, behind the simple sequence of events, of where and how people live, and this gives this relatively short book a feeling of space. It is a good example of what can be done with books for the middle-stage reader, given an author who deploys words pleasingly and is properly selective with scenes and details. (pp. 2426-27)

> *Margery Fisher, in a review of "The Battle of the Galah Trees," in* Growing Point, *Vol. 13, No. 2, July, 1974, pp. 2426-27.*

The writer of this book is an Australian, and the story has an Australian setting. Matt finds a young Galah bird and rescues it from his schoolmates who intend to use it as bait. His caring and concern for the bird lead him to a greater concern for the gum trees on the recreation ground, which the local council propose and commence to remove, considering them a public danger. After initial and somewhat hesitant support from classmates, Matt gradually engages the interest of an artist, a museum director, a botanic garden specialist, the local M.P. and school staff. This, together with the very active help of one school friend—who, with Matt, actually obstructs the work of the tree destroyers—and the co-operation of his family, finally arrests any further felling.

The story has no great originality or inspiration and the chain of events seems at times to run too predictably to a close, while only the liveliness of Gareth Floyd's illustrations enliven the rather poor production. The writing however, to some extent, redeems the theme and conception by flashes of insight in the choice of word and expression. What could have been a very pedestrian piece of work is highlighted by intermittent gleams of imagination and perception, while the story itself has sufficient interest and excitement to hold the young reader's attention. (pp. 215-16)

> *E. A. Astbury, in a review of "The Battle of the Galah Trees," in* The Junior Bookshelf, *Vol. 38, No. 4, August, 1974, pp. 215-16.*

The Surprise Mouse   (1974)

Nicky gives **The Surprise Mouse** to his mother for her birthday. His ingenuousness may be more appealing to an adult than to a child, though the incident has been taken from life, as the dedication reveals: **The Surprise Mouse** is written from the heart and does communicate the warmth of feeling between mother and son.

> *"Much in Little," in* The Times Literary Supplement, *No. 3760, March 29, 1974, p. 333.*

Tiger's Milk   (1974)

Antony could not really understand why his name was always shortened to Ant, he would so much rather have been called Tony or Tiger. Of course he was small for his age, and his mother had always coddled him, with the result that he was never allowed to walk to school, walk down the stairs or play with other children. It was only when he went to stay with his grandmother in the country that he really began to learn what life was all about. At first everything scared him, especially the cows and the bigger boys but gradually under Granny's administrations, and with some help from Mr. Benny, the farmer, he started to grow up. Any child who has felt uncomfortable in strange surroundings, has been the weakling of his year or who has been transported into an alien world will feel every sympathy with Antony. The author has sympathetically put herself in his place with the result that one lives Antony's fears, shares his joys and feels bigger and stronger just for reading the story. An excellent book with a simple plot which, nevertheless, grips the attention from beginning to end.

> *G. L. Hughes, in a review of "Tiger's Milk," in* The Junior Bookshelf, *Vol. 38, No. 6, December, 1974, p. 352.*

The Great Ballagundi Damper Bake   (1975)

[This] story is unlikely to interest any child outside Australia as it is so localised as to mean very little to any reader other than perhaps an adult devotee of Arthur Upfield or similar writer about the Outback. There is insufficient general interest in the story to make it acceptable to young children. Phrases such as 'and there was a wheat glut. For the past three years farmers all around had had bumper crops' or 'it's not just proper damper if the flour's store bought' do not help to produce a strong story line.

> *M. R. Hewitt, in a review of "The Great Ballagundi Damper Bake," in* The Junior Bookshelf, *Vol. 40, No. 1, February, 1976, p. 28.*

The Special Present   (1976)

In this thoroughly delightful story of ordinary, everyday life in Southern Australia, four little girls and their families share happy adventures together such as picnics in the garden, holidays beside the sea, and sailing boats, and the less happy times like feeling too ill with the measles to finish a jigsaw puzzle. One of the best stories is **"Saturday Sailor"** in which Janey submits a crossword competition entry which wins her brother a new boat. Excellent tales of family life. . . .

> *B. Clark, in a review of "The Special Present," in* The Junior Bookshelf, *Vol. 41, No. 6, December, 1977, p. 337.*

The Long Walk   (1976)

In the persuasive format of a picture-book with an extended text, here is a symmetrical, pleasantly detailed account of how a schoolboy solves the problem of walking home alone from school when his elder brother stays behind for football practice. Each possible route has a disadvantage (teasing girls, bully-boys, a noisy dog): each provides minor incidents to enliven Michael's journeys into independence in a book short enough for an unpractised reader but with plenty of substance in style and thought. (pp. 3274-75)

> *Margery Fisher, in a review of "The Long Walk," in* Growing Point, *Vol. 16, No. 8, March, 1978, pp. 3274-75.*

New Patches for Old   (1977)

Patricia Morgan has to leave her English home and the school where she is known and admired, for an Australian transit-settlement and a school where she is laughed at for her accent and for the second-hand dress which is as near as her parents can afford to get at first to the correct uniform. Another Patricia—rich, fat and malicious—decides the new girl is to be called Patches and, home-sick and resentful though she is, Patricia realises she has to make the name her own. Almost by accident she finds a way, when the school nurse, helping her to adjust to the heat of an Australian summer, introduces her to the craft of patchwork. The hobby becomes fashionable at school, and provides a way to new friends and to a new, assured self. The story, perhaps a little too tidy and optimistic, nonetheless contains much that is shrewd and searching in its picture of girls and boys in the middle 'teens exploring the possibilities ahead of them in the day-to-day life of school and home.

> *Margery Fisher, in a review of "New Patches for Old," in* Growing Point, *Vol. 16, No. 3, September, 1977, p. 3167.*

A story of the experiences of an English schoolgirl and her family as emigrants to Australia, in which Pat finds it very hard to adapt to the Australian way of life with its differing values. At school she is at a disadvantage for she is shabby, her background knowledge is of little use in Australia, and her home circumstances are not very happy as her father is out of work. She needs a long period of adjustment before she is ready to admit that she is glad she came to Australia. It is only through friendship—particularly one boy's friendship—that she begins to be happy again.

Patches (as her schoolmates christen her) is not a very appealing heroine for she indulges in a great deal of self-pity and harbours resentment against her parents far longer than is kind or reasonable. Incidentally an episode is introduced, possibly to give an impression of contemporary frankness, which seems unnecessary and rather distasteful. Except for this the story is acceptable and interesting as a picture of contemporary Australia. It may prove helpful as an introduction for potential emigrants to a progressive and unfamiliar country. (pp. 362-63)

> *E. Colwell, in a review of "New Patches for Old," in* The Junior Bookshelf, *Vol. 41, No. 6, December, 1977, pp. 362-63.*

Budgerigar Blue   (1977)

This sequel to **Surprise Mouse** is produced not in the small format of that book but in picture-book size. This gives the artist [Tony Oliver] a chance to establish, as he does most effectively, the proper atmosphere of an Australian local fair. Stallholders, weather, the movement and colour of crowds, provide a brash, vigorous impression that enlivens a rather soft-centred family tale of a boy's search for a present for his mother. This is an interesting example of the way illustration can extend the range of a slight story.

> *Margery Fisher, in a review of "Budgerigar Blue," in* Growing Point, *Vol. 17, No. 3, September, 1978, p. 3395.*

The Jetty   (1978)

Australian children's books are [stern] stuff, and **The Jetty** is no exception. The jetty of the title is the one outstanding feature and tourist attraction of a declining small-town port in South Australia, the pride and joy of all its inhabitants except the young hero Brad, who fears and loathes it. Forced by community feeling to hide his fears, he simply avoids the jetty as far as possible and hopes that the visiting government inspectors will condemn it as unsafe. When the inspectors come, Brad befriends one of them who camps in the town over the weekend, and with the tactful help of this man, a substitute figure for his own drowned father, the boy as last defeats his fears.

The rest of the town is rather less friendly to the visitors. The adults cold-shoulder them in the pub and obstruct their access to the jetty, while two of Brad's schoolmates vandalize the camp of his new-found friend with exploding cans of putrefying mullet-gut. It is acknowledged that the men are "only doing their job", but this does not protect them from spiteful persecution.

The tribulations of the young loner, at odds with his society, and the sour force of communal adult prejudice, are familiar and important themes in Australian children's books, classically treated in Ivan Southall's *Josh*. In **The Jetty** Brad's lonely and secret troubles are sensitively presented, but the book is half-hearted and evasive in its verdict on public delinquencies. Nevertheless it has the strengths we associate with good Australian writing: it respects the child reader, and is not afraid to face him honestly with the facts of injustice and moral blindness in children and adults alike.

> *Peter Hollindale, "Lone Rangers," in* The Times Literary Supplement, *No. 3991, September 28, 1978, p. 1090.*

Black Dog   (1979)

The change from misery to relief provides the shape of **Black Dog**, a brisk tale of Kerry's first day at a new school. Lost in endless passages, the small girl consoles herself in the library with some of her favourite books, but when she has to leave its security she is followed by a large dog who terrifies her but who proves to be a guide to the way out and to future confidence. The prose, low-keyed and simple enough for newly fledged readers, is enhanced by the artist [Craig Smith], who has chosen to show children and interiors in a slightly formalised way, using composition to underline the mood and feeling of Kerry's progress through the day. Skill in the presentation of images and the choice of words has made a vivid particularisation out of an ordinary combination of circumstances. (pp. 3809-10)

> *Margery Fisher, in a review of "Black Dog," in* Growing Point, *Vol. 19, No. 5, January, 1981, pp. 3809-10.*

Rummage (1981)

Elegance ('tasteful correctness' or 'ingenious simplicity', as the dictionary has it) is not a virtue often attributed to books for the young: all the more reason why it should be sought after on their behalf, so that they come to recognise that style and content are not two separate things but partners in the quest for excellence. (p. 3990)

'Ingenious simplicity' certainly describes **Rummage,** a picture/story book that draws a firm conclusion about individuality, . . . through a careful arrangement of opposites. On one side we have Mr. Septimus Portwine, whose twice-weekly market stall is stocked on a system; but though 'On Wednesday he never put the same boxes in his cart that he had taken on Saturday. And on Saturday he never took Wednesday's boxes', even so 'he had forgotten what was in most of them', so his stall provided a glorious treasure hunt for his customers, who would rummage through piles of broken china, buttonless coats, odd earrings, and never fail to find something they wanted. Everyone was happy—except his market neighbours, specialists who turned up their noses at his untidy heap. In the end, Miss Sarah Snodgrass who sold antique dolls, Mrs. Coralie Clinkett who stocked antique jewellery and Major Martindale who went in for military souvenirs 'which he organised in regiments', took their neighbour in hand. But his newly tidied stall, labelled 'Bric-a-Brac', remained unvisited on the Wednesday morning, for his customers did not recognise Mr. Portwine in his new suit and bowler hat. Rescue came unexpectedly. After two days in bed with a cold, due to a wet day without his shabby greatcoat, 'his face was bristly grey and whiskery, and his new clothes were still in a sodden heap in the corner'; and when thankfully he returned to his old ways, his customers flocked back to the stall now once more 'Rummage'. Literal children might possibly express some doubt that his beard could have grown so luxuriantly in so short a time, but they are likely to pick up the message. . . . [The author] always invites her readers to share her relish for words, and there are some splendid moments to pause over—like the comments of Miss Sarah Snodgrass ('You have a most undistinguished stock, Mr. Portwine. And a disreputable clientèle') and of Mrs. Coralie Clinkett, who calls his stall 'A dirty grimy higgledy-piggledy hotch-potch'. There are passages written to please the author:

. . . all the world coming to look—young and old, rich and poor, boys and dads, girls and grannies, sailors and sweethearts, tourists and tramps, debutantes and dowagers, academics and unionists.

and passages to please children, like the resounding list of the sales Septimus made when he returned to his old, slovenly ways. Riotous and exuberant, wise and warm, this picture/story book from Australia deserves, perhaps unexpectedly but justly, the label of elegance. (pp. 3990-91)

> *Margery Fisher, in a review of "Rummage," in* Growing Point, *Vol. 20, No. 5, January, 1982, pp. 3990-91.*

There is not much nostalgia in Christobel Mattingley and her illustrator, Patricia Mullins. These two Australians give us, surprisingly, a bit of the Portobello Road in uncompromising realism. Mr Portwine lowers the tone of the market with his junk stall, and is bullied by his neighbours into becoming a specialist. It is a failure, and he goes back to his old scruffy ways. There is a sharp satirical eye at work in this moral tale. Perhaps, like Mr Portwine, the presentation is a little crude, but it is lively and spirited and should give a great deal of soundly-based pleasure, especially to city children.

> *M. Crouch, in a review of "Rummage," in* The Junior Bookshelf, *Vol. 46, No. 3, June, 1982, p. 93.*

Duck Boy (1983)

The challenge that faces young Adam in **Duck Boy** seems at first unremarkable to his elder siblings, Kate and Steve, preoccupied as they are with the horse and the boat available to them for their country holiday, but the brother they patronise impresses them finally by his resolve to make a shelter for a pair of ducks he has found in a secret inlet of the river and to help them to rear a clutch of eggs in spite of the danger from fox, goanna and other predators. In fact, when accident interrupts their usual activities, Kate and Steve are glad to help in the campaign and to acknowledge something of a new status in the family for the younger brother. The confident, vivid background of New South Wales countryside gives substance to a story which is as much about relationships as it is about those holiday hours of freedom which are the staple of so many books for the middle years. Readers as young as eight could enjoy this one, partly because they could feel close to the central character and, as well, because there are delicately-accurate drawings [by Patricia Mullins] to punctuate the narrative and echo its serenely, precisely detailed scenes.

> *Margery Fisher, in a review of "Duck Boy," in* Growing Point, *Vol. 22, No. 3, September, 1983, p. 4132.*

Here is a book to add to those likely to attract eight-year-olds. It is in largish print and well written. The Australian idiom might present a few puzzling moments ('Adam kicked off his thongs'), but not enough to hinder understanding. The story builds up to a quiet victory for the youngest of a family of three, sent off on holiday into the country. Adam is left to his own devices while the others claim the plum pursuits, like riding and canoeing. He comes upon a duck and drake, Lucy and the General, defending their brood rather hopelessly against goannas, rats, and finally foxes. The steady realism with which these enemies are dispatched makes this a different animal story. There is some brief reflection on the fine, dead fox, but not much. The main concern is the vulnerable brood of ducklings, 'swimming on the pool behind their mother, like little spoonfuls of lemon meringue'. The old convention of children away from their parents is freshened by the robust reality of the widow, Mrs Perry, who maintains both house and holding in the absence of her son. Things happen. Adam helps his brother at a dangerous moment and proves to be a better shot, a neat and resourceful hand with wood and wire, in fact the one to whom Mrs Perry turns as a reliable assistant—not just a boy on holiday capers. This book would make a good pair with Betsy Byars's *Midnight fox*.

> *Dorothy Atkinson, in a review of "Duck Boy,"* in The School Librarian, *Vol. 32, No. 1, March, 1984, p. 51.*

The plot and the style are simple enough to pull in readers just tackling "chapter books" independently. The characterization of Adam is solid, that of his siblings a bit cliched. Readers will enjoy the adult character's appreciation of "the least child's" courage, aptitude, and pride in achievement even though the relationship between them—and the outcome of the story—are a bit pat.

> *Betsy Hearne, in a review of "Duck Boy," in* Bulletin of the Center for Children's Books, *Vol. 40, No. 1, September, 1986, p. 14.*

Southerly Buster   (1983)

Mum is pregnant, and ahead of both her and the reader lies a long summer during which daughter Julie wallows in a self-centred, self-pitying reaction to this situation.

The almost unbelievable thing is that so many people try to befriend her. Mum endures uncomplainingly comments which would try the patience of a saint whilst Dad, genuinely pleased by the prospect of unplanned fatherhood, is treated with contempt and dislike. Two agreeable young men vie for Julie's attention, and in the interests of the plot suffer tragedies beside which her situation cannot be regarded as more than a minor embarrassment. Only in the final chapters, after the baby has been born, is this heroine allowed to mellow into slightly less unappealing behaviour.

Christobel Mattingley understands well how arrogantly selfish young people can be but seems not to realise the unattractiveness of this characteristic, especially when overdramatised as in this book.

> *R. Baines, in a review of "Southerly Buster,"* in The Junior Bookshelf, *Vol. 48, No. 3, June, 1984, p. 148.*

Christobel Mattingley's writing has strong physical impact. One shares from inside the heroine's sensations: the feel of sand and sea, hunger, the taste and texture of food, the revulsion of a sudden vomiting attack. Her emotions, too, are immediate, whether it's the distress so total that she walks into the sea with her clothes on and swims out beyond the point of safety, or the sense of reassurance that follows her rescue, when she has been wrapped in a warm jersey and given sweets to suck. To empathise is easy; to sympathise rather harder. I also doubt whether a teenage girl would react with quite such dismay and disgust to the news of her mother's unexpected pregnancy. Julie's friends, however, treat her with great kindness and forbearance, and in the second half of the book she awaits the baby's arrival with slightly better grace. I like the scene where she sits up waiting for news from the hospital, gripped by anxiety and working at some belated knitting in the superstitious belief that completing it will avert disaster; and I wryly appreciate the later fate of the bootees, thrown away by Julie because the baby has managed to dirty them so thoroughly. Eventually Julie is reconciled to the baby after a wise friend points out that it cries because it senses her dislike. She is at once able to switch to warmer feelings, and it falls asleep in her arms. Not very convincing, but Julie's relationship with an aspiring boyfriend is well done, and once she has worked through her initial over-reaction to the pregnancy she is easier to like.

> *Rodie Sudbery, in a review of "Southerly Buster," in* The School Librarian, *Vol. 32, No. 4, December, 1984, p. 373.*

The Magic Saddle   (1983)

Chosen as Picture Book of the Year by the Children's Book Council of Australia, this nursery drama fully deserves its award for [Patricia Mullins's] superb use of varying depths of paint and the celebration of fancy in the extended text. Jonnie's longing for a rocking-horse is hardly satisfied by the tiny Christmas tree figure bought at St. Nicholas Fair so he offers it as a present for the Christ Child in the family crêche; nor does the gingerbread rocking-horse fulfil his hopes—until it offers him a ride on its edible saddle and away over the rooftops they go, over the sea and through the jungle and back home with the promise of more journeys in the future. For inspired paint and quiet, well-selected prose, a real winner.

> *Margery Fisher, in a review of "The Magic Saddle," in* Growing Point, *Vol. 23, No. 4, November, 1984, p. 4348.*

Ghost Sitter   (1984)

Lavatories, toilet-paper and gastric 'flu balance supernatural appearances in a coarsely comic tale of school with a bitter undertone. The ex-headmaster's widow, a secret witch, is opposed by Mr. Jones the caretaker and the school secretary, a middle-aged lady whose past knowledge of the sinister Effie helps her to discover the evil intentions behind the hideous toilet-roll dollies contributed to successive school fêtes. A schoolboy impressively named Claudius Imperator Hobbs plays a leading part in

Mattingley in her study, 1983.

a black comedy of accident and malice whose undercurrent of marital hostility may make some young readers uneasy but, equally, may be overlooked by others.

> *Margery Fisher, in a review of "Ghost Sitter," in* Growing Point, *Vol. 23, No. 6, March, 1985, p. 4406.*

The plot of this unusual book concerns a boy named Claudius Imperator Hobbs, who encounters in school the ghost of F. Art Smith, a past headmaster. After unwittingly contributing to the death of the headmaster's widow, Hobbs exorcises the ghost.

This brief outline does not do justice to the running joke which threads its way through the story. The lavatory provides the basis for most of the humour, pathos and progress of fate. Mrs Smith (who is a witch) strikes her enemies down with diarrhoea; Mr Smith has his first heart attack in a school lavatory and his second at the local sewage works where he drowns in the sewage; Mrs Smith is submerged in cartons of toilet rolls then crushed to death by the water tank from the old headmaster's lavatory as it falls through rotten floorboards on to the woman below.

Despite these preoccupations, there is nothing offensive about the book. The slight story is well told, if a little dated in expression, and is sometimes very funny.

> *Gill Vickery, in a review of "Ghost Sitter," in* The School Librarian, *Vol. 33, No. 1, March, 1985, p. 39.*

This is a mystery cum supernatural school story which contains all the elements which should appeal to readers from ten years and up—secret doors, toilet paper rolls, mystery, a talking parrot, someone called F. Art Smith and much more. Somehow, however, it does not quite come off. The story is at times hard to follow, and Christobel Mattingley, who has a marvellous way with the English language, sometimes lets her love of playing with words take over from the story. It is almost as though she has tried too hard to include all the elements which should be in a good school story, and at the same time has attempted to inculcate the reader with a love of the English language. This is not one of Christobel Mattingley's best books by any means, and it is basically just a reasonable read for senior primary and junior secondary readers.

> *Stephanie Owen Reeder, in a review of "Ghost Sitter," in* Reading Time, *Vol. XXXI, No. III, 1987, p. 64.*

The Angel with a Mouth Organ (1984)

Of several recent picture books about war, this has the strongest story and clearest child's perspective. It follows a refugee family from the first bombing of their village through a long march, seven moves, and their last camp, where the narrator and her older sister and mother wait hopefully for Father's return. The years are telescoped into several moving incidents: the loss of a neighbor's baby, the death of Grandma, the rounding up of Father and other male civilians to replace soldiers shot down in the road, the children's endless search for food, shelter, and coal. The narrator recalls moments of beauty—a pattern of frost crystals, the song of a cuckoo—as well as the toll her experiences take on her childhood. Characterizations are adeptly suggested through brief scenes, as when the narrator's sister angrily smashes a chubby plaster baby in its creche and the narrator replaces it with her one-armed doll. The father's return is a triumph of family warmth. Vivid pen-and-wash illustrations [by Astra Lacis] surround the text, giving it a sensitive immediacy; artist Lacis manages to express the family's circle of strength and sense of play amidst the devastation around them. Without diluting the truth, her pastel colors and delicate hatching soften it to the tone of a manageable memory. Although basically a story for elementary-grade readers, this could also be shared aloud with second graders or younger children with one-on-one discussion. (pp. 132-33)

> *A review of "The Angel with a Mouth Organ," in* Bulletin of the Center for Children's Books, *Vol. 39, No. 7, March, 1986, pp. 132-33.*

Losing one's home and being a refugee going in fear and hunger, are matters which are very much in the forefront of people's thoughts at the present time. *The angel with a mouth organ* is set in Europe in the Second World War; and the emotions portrayed—fear, loss, sadness, fortitude, grief, anger, despair, bravery, and above all love—are all part of this moving story, which goes some way towards giving readers an insight into what it was like to suffer then, as now. Prompted by a squabble about just who should hang the little glass angel on top of the tree, a mother tells her children of her experiences as a child in war-stricken Europe. This is a beautifully constructed and illustrated story for older readers and listeners. Its poignancy is underscored in the sombre water-colour pictures.

Jill Bennett, in a review of "The Angel with a Mouth Organ," in The School Librarian, *Vol. 34, No. 1, March, 1986, p. 34.*

This war-time experience would be a searing one for any child, but the horror is made tedious by the author's recitation. This happened, then this happened, then this happened. The family is never personalized. Only near the very end are the children's names even given. Only one incident—when the older sister smashes the Christ child in a nativity set, crying "It's not fair"—has any emotional impact. Her younger sister picks up the pieces and leaves her doll in its place. This one moment has all the drama and emotion of a full story that is lacking in the rest of the text. Lacis' illustrations are similarly low key and restrained. This is a very personal family story, but Mattingley has failed to ground it in individuals with whom readers can identify. (pp. 112-13)

Judith Gloyer, in a review of "The Angel with a Mouth-Organ," in School Library Journal, *Vol. 33, No. 2, October, 1986, pp. 112-13.*

The Miracle Tree   (1985)

A story of three lives tragically altered by the bombing of Nagasaki, this traces the separate paths of an ex-soldier, his bride, and her mother as they search and mourn each other for twenty years, to meet finally because of a pine tree that has nourished hope in all of them. The author of ***The Angel with a Mouth-Organ*** has once again caught the sufferings of families victimized by war, but the tone here is more tragic in keeping with the ultimate threat of nuclear holocaust. In spite of its picture-book format, this is a story for older readers. The illustrations [by Marianne Yamaguchi], subdued charcoal drawings with a green pine-bough motif, underscore the overall tone of sadness tempered with hope for peace. A thought-provoking Christmas story that will draw tears as the dying girl, bending over a nativity scene with her new-found husband and mother, yearns for the baby she can never have and places her paper cranes on the manger as a prayer for the future.

Betsy Hearne, in a review of "The Miracle Tree," in Bulletin of the Center for Children's Books, *Vol. 40, No. 4, December, 1986, p. 72.*

An exceptionally elegant and dignified production from Australia. At first it may seem that the matter of the story is at odds with the format, for this is a story about the Nagasaki bomb, not a subject for elegant treatment. But, quite apart from the Japanese spirit, which brings dignity and restraint to the most ghastly of tragedies, this is a story about endurance and enduring love. . . .

Christobel Mattingley miraculously realizes the potential of her tale, steering its course clear of sentimentality, and working its sentiment to the limit. In this she has a fine collaborator in Marianne Yamaguchi, whose soft charcoal drawings are deployed with true Japanese economy. Add to this book-design and typography of the highest order, and you have a book of rare quality, not perhaps a book for children but certainly one in which the whole family can be united.

M. Crouch, in a review of "The Miracle Tree," in The Junior Bookshelf, *Vol. 50, No. 6, December, 1986, p. 226.*

Stories written with a purpose all too often are simply polemics. They are worthy but not necessarily remarkable, the emotional equivalent of hot gruel—nourishing but hardly inspiring. It takes a rare kind of genius to turn purpose into passion, to transform coincidence into logic, to convince even the most constant of reviewers that miracles do happen. Christobel Mattingly is that rare genius. Perhaps the secret of her art is the spare introduction: "In the city of Nagasaki on the Japanese island of Kyushu three people lived for twenty years hoping for a miracle." Perhaps it is the skillful use of the quest motif: three people separated by the horrors of war who are seeking one another—Taro, the gardener; his once lovely bride, Hanako; and the mother. Perhaps it is the lovely rhythmic prose—which, like poetry, uses repetition to build tension—or the ending with its miracle of recognition, reunion, and reconciliation despite the underlying mood of sorrow. Or perhaps it is the concluding line, Hanako's unspoken prayer as she stands with her husband and mother on Christmas Eve in the church which has risen from the rubble of war: " 'Let peace prevail on earth.' " Whatever it is, the story—like *The Birds' Christmas Carol, The Other Wise Man,* or "The Gift of the Magi"—elicits suppressed sentiments and touches subdued emotions. As the nineteenth-century novelist might say, "It leaves the reader with a suspicious moisture about the eyes." And perhaps that is why the book is so effective: it is genuine, not manipulative, written from love and commitment to humanity. Fortunately, it has been published in a format which both complements the text and underscores its resemblance to a time when fine bindings, handsome artwork, and thoughtful design endowed a book with permanence beyond its possible seasonal appeal. The illustrations, like the story, are particularly noteworthy as being both decorative and interpretive. Executed in charcoal, they develop the characters and reveal the passage of time with extraordinary sensitivity to the idiom of Japanese art as well as to the text. An inspired production, this book is one of the few which spans generations as well as seasons. (pp. 210-11)

Mary M. Burns, in a review of "The Miracle Tree," in The Horn Book Magazine, *Vol. LXIII, No. 2, March-April, 1987, pp. 210-11.*

McGruer and the Goat   (1987)

A whimsical fantasy, but set realistically in New Zealand, this is also a love story with a few cheerful differences. The protagonists are Mrs. Dumpling and Captain Duff. Their pets, Mrs. Dumpling's goat McElliot, and Captain Duff's octopus, McGruer, eventually reach a warm companionable understanding as well.

The tale is set in the hills of Otago where Mrs. Dumpling kept black sheep and had an apple tree with the juiciest apples. Captain Duff had returned to his home after years of travel and seafaring. Though they had so many stories to exchange they felt obliged to argue instead of chatting in a neighbourly way.

Christobel Mattingly has a wonderful technique of creating stories for young audiences around adult characters. This one would be informative and fun for older primary children to read but even better shared aloud with adults.

> *Elspeth Cameron, in a review of "McGruer and the Goat," in* Reading Time, *Vol. XXXII, No. I, 1988, p. 33.*

Joan Lowery Nixon

1927-

(Also writes as Jaye Ellen) American author of fiction, nonfiction, and picture books.

Major works include *The Kidnapping of Christina Lattimore* (1979), *The Seance* (1980), *If You Say So, Claude* (1980), *The Other Side of Dark* (1986), *A Family Apart* (1988).

Called "the *grande dame* of mysteries for young readers" by *School Library Journal,* Nixon is a prolific, popular author who is perhaps best known for the stories of suspense she has written for readers in the early, middle, and upper grades which comprise approximately half of her works. The first author to win the Edgar Allan Poe Award three times, she is considered a skillful creator of plot and character who invests her mysteries with action, humor, optimism, and a sympathetic understanding of the young. Nixon began her career with mysteries for middle graders which feature the Nickson sisters, Kathy and Maureen, who are modeled on two of her children; she sets these books in New Orleans, Mexico, and her home state of Texas, a background Nixon uses frequently in her works. With *The Kidnapping of Christina Lattimore,* Nixon introduced the first of her well-received psychological thrillers for young adults: in this story, a wealthy teenage oil heiress learns self-reliance as she tries to convince her family that she was not an accomplice in her own kidnapping. Nixon characteristically couples both mystery and psychology in these novels: often centering around murder, theft, and suicide and underscored by elements of the occult, the books feature teenage female protagonists who gain maturity by solving personal problems as well as crimes. Nixon has also written several mysteries for beginning readers, most notably the "Holiday Mystery" series in which she uses major holidays as the background for stories which involve the Connally siblings Susan, Mike, and Barney in a group of domestic adventures.

In addition to her mystery tales, Nixon is the creator of several volumes of realistic fiction with both historical and contemporary settings. Among her most popular contributions is the "Orphan Train" series, a projected quartet of stories for middle graders set in the mid-nineteenth century. Based on an actual placement program sponsored by the Children's Aid Society, the stories highlight the often suspenseful adventures of the Kelley family, six siblings who are sent from New York to the West for adoption. Nixon is also the author of two series with show business backgrounds; in a projected trilogy for young adults entitled "Hollywood Daughters" which spans the early 1940s through the early 1970s, she explores personal individuality and the relationships between mothers and daughters, while in the "Maggie" series of contemporary stories for middle graders she describes how the only child of a movie-director father who marries a twenty-year-old starlet surmounts self-doubts, accepts her father, his wife, and

their eccentric family, finds romance, and discovers her talent as an actress. Nixon is also well known for her "Claude" series, humorous tall tales for early and middle graders about a pioneer couple which are characterized by their colorful, fast-paced style and the tag lines represented in the title of each volume. Also a writer of nonfiction for adults, Nixon has contributed several additional works to a variety of genres in the field of juvenile literature; among them are collaborations with her husband, geologist Hershell H. Nixon, on a series of basic introductions to such subjects as volcanoes, earthquakes, glaciers, and marine biology; a series of science fiction books featuring two friends and a protective robot; picture books about both realistic characters and anthropomorphic animals; adaptations of stories from the Old and New Testaments as well as fiction and nonfiction with religious subjects and themes; and an informational book which teaches the fundamentals of creative writing in story form to early graders. Nixon won the Edgar Allan Poe Award for *The Kidnapping of Christina Lattimore* in 1980, for *The Seance* in 1981, and for *The Other Side of Dark* in 1987, and was named an Edgar runner-up for *The Mysterious Red Tape Gang* in 1975 and *The Ghost of Now* in 1985. She also received the Golden Spur Award for best juvenile Western for *A Family Apart* in 1988 and for *In the Face of Danger* in 1989 and has won many child-selected awards.

(See also *Something about the Author,* Vols. 8, 44; *Something about the Author Autobiography Series,* Vol. 9; and *Contemporary Authors,* Vols. 9-12, rev. ed.)

AUTHOR'S COMMENTARY

What are the magic ingredients of a mystery novel for the eight-to-twelve age group that draw young readers to it? What does a writer need to include in his story so that his readers won't be able to put the book down until they have come to the last page?

In a mystery story the idea is often the starting point. Sometimes this idea can come from a magazine article or news item. I once read an article about artifacts being smuggled out of Mexico that led to research on the subject and eventually to a juvenile mystery novel.

Sometimes the idea can come from experience. When we moved to Corpus Christi, Texas, we found ourselves in the middle of a hurricane. The eye of the storm missed our city, but the force of the rain, wind, and waves caused tremendous damage. The area had been evacuated, but I wondered what someone would have done who couldn't leave—who, for some reason, had been left behind in the confusion. The beach houses could not withstand the force of the storm, or stay intact, but what if high on the hill there stood a stone "castle," strong enough to survive the storm and to shelter its occupants? And what if this castle were known to have as its only occupant a ghost? Out of these questions came my book *The Mystery of Hurricane Castle.* (p. 23)

A mystery novel should give the reader an interesting background that will expand the child's horizons. Phyllis A. Whitney, in her excellent mystery novels for children, has taken her readers to many exciting and unusual foreign settings. But even the author who cannot travel can make a small town on the coast of Maine, or a truck stop in the middle of the Arizona desert, colorful and interesting to the child for whom this too is a new experience.

Deciding upon the main character is the next step in developing the mystery novel. It is his story. He (or she) will have to solve the mystery, and he will go about it in his own, individual way.

It is important to make the main characters well-rounded, interesting, and actively alive. The children who read the novel will want to identify closely with them and eagerly follow their adventures to the last page. They should have a minor fault or two—something with which children feel familiar. Maybe the boy's in trouble because he can't seem to remember to keep his room tidy, or perhaps the girl's impatient and plunges into things without thinking.

The main character preferably should be twelve or thirteen years old—at the top of this age group. Eight-year-olds will read about older children, but older children do not want to identify with younger children. Plots featuring boys and stories with girls as main characters are equally popular.

Once an editor told me, "Most of the mysteries I get take place during the summer vacation. I'd like to see one in which the main character was going to school." So in *The Mysterious Red Tape Gang,* I place my main character right in the middle of the school year. His problem with turning in homework on time gave him a character flaw and added some humor to the story.

A little light humor can be a good ingredient in a mystery novel. I learned this lesson when I was writing my first mystery. I read chapters to my children, and my fifth-grade daughter would sometimes say, "It's scary for too long. Put in something funny." What she was telling me, in essence, was to break the mood of suspense occasionally. The author can't, and shouldn't, sustain tension in the story from beginning to end. It should have peaks of suspense and valleys—breathing space, one might say, and natural humor is a good ingredient to use for this purpose.

In order to make the main character more of a "real person," I think it's good to give him a personal problem to handle along with the mystery to solve. For example, in one story I let my character's fear of a neighborhood bully turn to compassion and a tentative attempt at friendship as he began to realize what made this boy behave like a bully. In another, I matched two girls as friends—one who thinks her younger brothers and sisters are a burden, and the other an only child who lives in an adult world. Each girl learns from the other, and each learns to appreciate her own family life.

The story must be told from the main character's viewpoint only, although if there are two characters traveling this mysterious road together—friends, brothers, or sisters—the viewpoint can include them both. You are telling the story through your main character's eyes, and it's important not to have anything happen of which he or she isn't aware. She may see an obvious clue and overlook it, thinking it's not important; or he may sidetrack his efforts, and thereby come closer to danger, thinking something is important that is not; but in either case, it is the main character's story alone, and the author of the juvenile mystery must keep this in mind.

As to clues, children love the puzzle in a mystery. They love to find obvious clues which the main character seems to miss. They love to search for clues which the main character has discovered, but the readers haven't figured out. Both types of clues are needed in a mystery, but the hidden clues shouldn't be too well hidden. After the solution of the mystery is reached, at the end of the story, the reader should think, "Of course! I remember that! I should have known it all along!"

Sub-mysteries, which are complications, unexpected scary situations, or new questions raised, should be used throughout the story. They all tie into the main mystery, although some of them can be solved along the way. Each chapter, through action and suspense, moves the mystery closer to its solution, and each chapter should end with something tense or a little frightening—a cliff-hanger ending—so that the reader cannot stop at the end of the chapter, but must read on to see what happens. An example is this chapter ending for *The Mysterious Red Tape Gang:*

Linda Jean grabbed my arm and squeezed so tightly that the pressure of her fingers was painful. "Mike," she whispered, "those men might hurt my father!"

The same thought had occurred to me. I wanted to answer her; but my mouth was dry, and I tried to swallow.

Mr. Hartwell's face looked awful. He was like a trapped animal.

"Mike!" Linda Jean whispered. "You've got to do something!"

Children read for pleasure, not for all the reasons for which adults read—because the book is a best seller, or because one received it as a Christmas present. If a child doesn't like a book, after the first page or two, he puts it down and looks for something else to read.

Therefore, the story should immediately introduce the main character, lead into the mystery as soon as possible, and grab the reader. In the opening paragraphs of *The Mysterious Red Tape Gang,* I set the scene, established the mood of the story, introduced my main character, told something about the other characters who would be important, and gave the first hint of the mystery to come:

My father gets excited when he reads the newspaper at the breakfast table. Sometimes a story makes him mad, and he reads it out loud to my mother. And all the time he reads, he keeps pounding his fist on the table.

Once, when his fist was thumping up and down, my little brother, Terry, carefully slid the butter dish over next to my father just to see what would happen. Terry had to clean up the mess, but he said it was worth it.

Sometimes my father reads a story to me, because he says a twelve-year-old boy ought to be aware of what could happen if he fell in with bad companions.

At first I tried to tell him that Jimmy and Tommy Scardino and Leroy Parker weren't bad companions, but I found out it was just better to keep quiet and listen.

"Michael," he said one morning, "listen to this! The crime rate in Los Angeles is rising again! People being mugged, cars being stolen! A lot of it is being done by kids! Watch out, Michael!"

I nodded. What I had planned to do after school was work on the clubhouse we were building behind our garage, along with Tommy and Jimmy and Leroy. None of us wanted to steal cars. In the first place, it's a crime, and in the second place, we can't drive.

The mystery novel should have plenty of action. The old-fashioned mental detection type of story, with lots of conversation and little action, is out of date even with adult readers. With children it's doubly important to include a great deal of action and excitement in mystery stories.

However, dialogue is important, too. Dialogue not only breaks up a page and makes the story look more inviting in print, but it draws the reader into the story in a way narrative description cannot do. A careful mix of dialogue with lots of action usually results in a fast-paced, suspenseful story.

The ending of a mystery novel is important to the writer, because it's one of the first things he must think about in planning his book. After he has mentally worked out the idea of the mystery, who his main character will be, and how the story will begin, he should decide how it will end. Once this is established, the middle will fit into place, with the clues planted and the direction of the action set. I find it helpful to make an outline, chapter by chapter, so vital clues and important bits of planted information won't be omitted.

A good mystery should always be logical, and the ending should be satisfying. It should never depend on coincidence. The main character must solve the mystery. If it's necessary to bring in adults to help out—such as the police or someone who could give advice—it must be the decision of the main character to do so.

The ending of a mystery novel should satisfy the reader, because it should present an exciting climax. The solution of the mystery should contain all the answers, so a drawn-out explanation of who-did-what-and-why isn't needed. Throughout the story the reader must be given reference points he can remember—well-planted clues. Just a page or two should be used to end the story and tie up all the loose ends concerning the main character's relationship with others in the book.

Stories for the reader of eight to twelve shouldn't be gory or horrifying: Characters can be captured or threatened, but description should be kept within the bounds of good sense. The occult can be used in stories for this age, and can be left unexplained, if the author wishes, as in the witchcraft in Scott Corbett's *Here Lies the Body.* At the author's whim, ghosts can be explained, or left forever to haunt future generations.

As for the title: Writers should remember the key words for which librarians look and make their titles mysterious or frightening. Some child who wants the pleasure of following a character through a scary adventure will reach for that book. (pp. 23-6)

Joan Lowery Nixon, "Clues to the Juvenile Mystery," in The Writer, *Vol. 90, No. 2, February, 1977, pp. 23-6.*

TITLE COMMENTARY

Mystery of Hurricane Castle   (1964)

The Nicksons, Kathy 13, Maureen, 11, and Danny, 4, go to spend a holiday at the Gulf of Texas where their young fears and fancies respond to an abandoned castle on a hill and the ghost (or is it a live presence?) on the dunes known as the Sea Witch. A hurricane blows up and, in the evacuation to follow, the children are left behind. They take refuge in the castle where they discover not only many paintings, just like Kathy's, but a lonely recluse . . . Quivers and shivers, not too menacing, for the youngsters whose taste for terror is still at the peanut butter and jam level. Easily told, . . . a very friendly, spooky story. (pp. 452-53)

> *A review of "The Mystery of Hurricane Castle," in* Virginia Kirkus' Service, *Vol. XXXII, No. 9, May 1, 1964, pp. 452-53.*

[Three children take refuge from a hurricane] in an old house—the "castle." There are sounds and signs indicating an unseen resident, and the three finally discover that an artist lives there; the shy inhabitant is a recluse who keeps to herself since she knows that she frightens local children because of her scarred face and her odd ways. Some of the outdoor scenes are vividly described, and there is some appeal in Kathy's interest in painting; the characters seem flat, and the plot is contrived and very much drawn out.

> *Zena Sutherland, in a review of "Mystery of Hurricane Castle," in* Bulletin of the Center for Children's Books, *Vol. XVIII, No. 6, February, 1965, p. 90.*

Mystery of the Grinning Idol   (1965)

When 13-year-old Eileen Harrigan comes to visit her Mexican relatives at the motel that they run, one of her first reactions concerns a guest. After a brief and apparently very superficial view of him, she immediately decides that "he acts like someone who has something to hide." Whenever events can't be jammed together to make a cohesive mystery the girl comes through with her sixth sense. With all her sensitivity it seems odd that she, along with her two cousins and a member of the Mexican customs bureau should mistake for so long the real culprit trying to smuggle out an ancient clay statue. He comes posing as the stereotype American tourist, price tag waving from his shoes and all, acts completely dense until he glimpses the statue, when he becomes very knowledgeable. Mexican scenery is incidental—of course it's fiesta time. . . . The statue is primitive, so is the plot. (pp. 311-12)

> *A review of "Mystery of the Grinning Idol," in* Virginia Kirkus' Service, *Vol. XXXIII, No. 6, March 15, 1965, pp. 311-12.*

[*The Mystery of the Watching Eyes* by Jeanette Brown MacKenzie, *The Mystery of Hard Luck House* by Teri Martini, *The Mystery of the Chinatown Pearls* by Betty Antoncich, and *The Mystery of the Grinning Idol*] are trite books, not recommended for library purchase. . . . [Stolen] Mexican artifacts are being spirited into the United States from a motel across the border in *The Mystery of the Grinning Idol,* a clumsily written book which is the weakest of the lot. In all four of these the writing is not good enough to compensate for tired plots and stereotyped characters. (pp. 123-24)

> *Sarah Law Kennerly, in a review of "Mystery of the Grinning Idol," in* School Library Journal, *Vol. 11, No. 9, May, 1965, pp. 123-24.*

Mystery of the Hidden Cockatoo   (1966)

Eventually, of course, that hidden cockatoo does come creeping out of the woodwork of this creaky little mystery. But first you have to get a full dosage of Atmosphere: romantic New Orleans (at least it isn't Mardi Gras time), a fortuneteller named Madame Lala and her pet crow which is apt to quote "Watch out," a presumed ghost, a session at the wax works—all swallowed up by the heroine Pam Peters with ponderous, humorless seriousness. Pam is visiting her New Orleans aunt because she wants to get away from her four younger brothers and sisters but her friend Felicity, who is all too completely alone, points up Pam's dependence on her family—and the Author's Message is stridently inserted. The jeweled cockatoo pin, which the girls know has to be hidden in the house where Pam's aunt lives, turns out to have been stashed in the fireplace—not very surprising since the fireplace was known to be the only part of the house which hadn't been rebuilt, and the mystery is why the competing sleuths are so stupid about it all. Even mystery-addicted girls should give *Cockatoo* the bird. (pp. 1105-06)

> *A review of "Mystery of the Hidden Cockatoo," in* Virginia Kirkus' Service, *Vol. XXXIV, No. 21, October 15, 1966, pp. 1105-06.*

[*Mystery of the Hidden Cockatoo*] is another mediocre mystery for girls. Pam (13) visits her aunt, who lives in the romantic French Quarter of New Orleans, and finds a diamond pin in the shape of a cockatoo that had been hidden in the house generations ago. The characters are wooden and the exotic, eerie atmosphere rings false. Not recommended.

> *A review of "Mystery of the Hidden Cockatoo," in* School Library Journal, *Vol. 13, No. 3, November, 1966, p. 112.*

Mystery of the Haunted Woods   (1967)

Mystery of the Haunted Woods [is a] trite story too stereotyped to merit serious consideration. Kathy and Maureen Nickson, and their four-year-old brother Danny (whom we met in the *Mystery of Hurricane Castle*) are left alone in their Aunt Julia's New Mexico ranch home with only a 16-year-old Indian girl for protection. Frightened by tales that the neighboring forest is haunted, the children, unable to sleep, notice mysterious comings and goings during the night, strange footprints in the snow, etc. Everything has a simple explanation, and the mystery is all in the minds of the children.

> *A review of "Mystery of the Haunted Woods," in* School Library Journal, *Vol. 14, No. 20, November, 1967, p. 86.*

Mystery of the Secret Stowaway   (1968)

This one, as told by eleven-year-old cut-up Joe Riley (who sounds like Damon Runyon out of Art Linkletter) follows activities aboard a ship en route to Mexico . . . with night club singer Dodi Doll . . . with Harriet Handy, one of a large clutch of children which makes it possible for him to be dubbed in as her brother—handily seasick . . . and further enabling the exposure of a Mr. Riggle who disappears and reappears under the wig of a Miss Stanhope. . . . Sheer bunk-um.

> *A review of "Mystery of the Secret Stowaway,"*
> *in* Kirkus Service, *Vol. XXXVI, No. 12, June*
> *15, 1968, p. 643.*

Delbert, the Plainclothes Detective   (1971)

[Although] once he gets the sleuthing bug in his head he's a worthy observer, Delbert's awfully slow on the uptake and doesn't learn until the end what we know from the first. When he finds a self-proclaimed "plainclothesman" in the closet just after Mrs. Crilly next door has been robbed, he importantly agrees that mum shall be the word like the man says; not only won't he jeopardize the police investigation, but he and friend Andy will help out. They assume that older bully Tiger dunnit and they do some spying at his kitchen window, where Delbert pointedly perceives that "Tiger's mama didn't look as warm and kind and loving as his own mama and that Tiger's father acted almost as mean as Tiger himself did when he was after somebody"—this in inescapable apposition to Delbert's fatherless, poor-but-proud black household, delineated deliberately with what might be called overt casualness (" . . . sometimes the lady Mama worked for would give her some clothes her children had outgrown. He hoped the oldest boy had outgrown his coat . . . "). The prototype is a cliche and the lack of suspense or surprise is an insult—not to mention the unbridled ill-disguised moralizing. (pp. 501-02)

> *A review of "Delbert the Plainclothes Detec-*
> *tive," in* Kirkus Reviews, *Vol. XXXIX, No. 9,*
> *May 1, 1971, pp. 501-02.*

[*Delbert, the Plainclothes Detective*] has the virtue of being a simple, commonplace little story with which inner-city children can identify. . . . [In the closet Delbert finds] a strange man who quickly explains that he is a plainclothes detective looking for the burglar. Delbert wants to help and, in return for his silence, the detective promises to make him a junior partner. Of course he is the burglar himself, and young readers who figure this out will enjoy feeling smarter than Delbert.

> *Sarah Law Kennerly, in a review of "Delbert,*
> *the Plainclothes Detective," in* School Library
> Journal, *Vol. 17, No. 10, May, 1971, p. 83.*

Delbert is a small black boy whose trusting nature interferes with his common sense. . . . The child's naivete is the weakest point of the story, and the writing style is undistinguished, but the setting, a middle class black neighborhood, is realistic and the relationships within Delbert's family are warm and natural.

> *Zena Sutherland, in a review of "Delbert: The*
> *Plainclothes Detective," in* Bulletin of the Cen-
> ter for Children's Books, *Vol. 25, No. 1, Sep-*
> *tember, 1971, p. 13.*

The Secret Box Mystery   (1974)

Michael John walks carefully to school with his secret in a shoe box, but when it's time to show his science project, the secret has disappeared. Wilma, who has brought in her grandfather's false teeth for her science project, pushes past the others to look at the box ("Wilma was like that" we're told not once but four times in the 1000 word story) but it is Paul, the new boy from Arizona without a project of his own, who helps Michael John retrieve his secret. For Paul has guessed that Michael John's project is a desert elf owl who can be lured by meat from Wilma's sandwich, and as "Paul knows more about owls than I do," Michael John suggests that the two boys share the science project. Innocuous—but then first readers tend to be like that.

> *A review of "The Secret Box Mystery," in*
> Kirkus Reviews, *Vol. XLII, No. 11, June 1,*
> *1974, p. 579.*

Not a suspense tale, Joan Lowery Nixon's **Secret Box Mystery** is misleadingly titled. Michael John wants his science project to be a surprise but, returning from recess, he discovers that the "project" has escaped from its shoe box. A new boy, an Indian from Arizona, not only guesses that a baby owl is on the loose but devises a way to entice it out of hiding. The two boys then decide to work on the project together. Touches of humor and appealing illustrations by Leigh Grant make this a better-than-average science book for beginning readers.

> *Alice Ehlert, in a review of "Secret Box Mys-*
> *tery," in* School Library Journal, *Vol. 21, No.*
> *4, December, 1974, p. 49.*

The Mysterious Red Tape Gang   (1974)

This is one of those fast reading trifles that summer readers consume at the rate of three or so a day—where a neighborhood gang of children habitually sneak out to their clubhouse at midnight (eleven here) and end up dodging police and crooks as well as parents; where one persistent girl is reluctantly admitted, then at last really accepted, into the gang; where for one reason or another the hero is unable to tell his parents about the illegal activity he spies out just around the corner. Here it is the respectable father of the girl, Linda Jean, who is involved in a car theft racket, and the club members conspire to "help" him turn state's evidence. That's about what does happen, with a vacant house, threatening notes and gunmen for excitement and for humor scenes like the one where "It sure looked funny with those two guys all dripping wet slowly going ker-thump, ker-thump down the street in a car with four flat tires."

> *A review of "The Mysterious Red Tape Gang,"*
> *in* Kirkus Reviews, *Vol. XLII, No. 14, July 15,*
> *1974, p. 744.*

The Alligator under the Bed   (1974)

The focus in this latest picture tale of wild things in the nursery is neither Jill nor her imaginary alligator but understanding Uncle Harry who solves the little girl's problem by—as therapists say—participating in her fantasy. Though both Mama and Daddy pooh-pooh her claim that there's an alligator under her bed, Uncle Harry sits down and chats casually about the unusual visitor, finally talking the alligator into following him down the hall and out the front door. This is really less a child's view of those common bedtime fears than an object lesson for grownups on how to handle them, but Uncle Harry does make an entertaining game of the occasion.

> *A review of "The Alligator under the Bed," in* Kirkus Reviews, *Vol. XLII, No. 16, August 15, 1974, p. 874.*

An experience common to many children is treated here with both humor and understanding. The illustrations [by Jan Hughes] are a delight—from the endearing alligator with its derby and a pink rose on its tail to the two mice that skitter about, appearing here and there throughout the pictures. An excellent choice for all imaginative children who have, at one time or another, had an alligator under the bed, as well as for those who have, or wish they had, an Uncle Harry. (pp. 240-41)

> *Barbara Dill, in a review of "The Alligator under the Bed," in* Wilson Library Bulletin, *Vol. 49, No. 3, November, 1974, pp. 240-41.*

The illustrations do not distinguish between reality and fantasy (Uncle Harry is shown, for example, collapsed under the alligator's weight in one picture) and the writing lacks the humor that makes a similar situation more pointed in Barbara Williams' *Albert's Toothache* in which it is a grandmother who understands how to handle a child's apprehension when parents take a no-nonsense stand.

> *Zena Sutherland, in a review of "The Alligator under the Bed," in* Bulletin of the Center for Children's Books, *Vol. 28, No. 6, February, 1975, p. 97.*

The Mysterious Prowler (1976)

Jonathan is sure he sees a shadow on the porch, he certainly sees hand-prints on the outer side of the window and bicycle tracks on the lawn. The telephone rings and nobody speaks. Determined to track down the prowler, Jonathan looks for a bicycle with treads that match the marks; he finds it and follows a boy who proves to be a new neighbor, Pat. Pat has wanted to make friendly overtures, but each time was overwhelmed by shyness. Jonathan had known there was a "Pat" moving in next door, but his mother had heard that Pat was a girl. The ending of the story is anticlimactic and the behavior of Pat seems overdrawn, but the story is simply written for the beginning reader . . . and the book has a modicum of suspense and should, therefore, be useful to fill the demand for easy-to-read mystery stories.

> *Zena Sutherland, in a review of "The Mysterious Prowler," in* Bulletin of the Center for Children's Books, *Vol. 29, No. 11, July-August, 1976, p. 180.*

Oil and Gas: From Fossils to Fuels (with Hershell H. Nixon, 1977)

To aid the young reader, the authors use fairly simple vocabulary, large print and short sentence segments. About two-thirds of the book deals with the nature, origin, and accumulation of oil and gas. The remainder of the book contains discussions of exploring, drilling and refining, as well as uses of oil and gas, the location of U. S. oil-producing states, and the relative contributions of different countries to world oil and gas production. Other sources of energy, and the need for conservation and the development of alternate energy sources are mentioned briefly. The book is illustrated [by Jean Day Zallinger] with drawings on virtually every page. Although they contain a few errors or confusing relationships, the illustrations are generally well drawn and very helpful in making the concepts understandable to the intended audience. Since the topic is so complex, it is important that the teacher be prepared to explain and expand on the material. (p. 181)

> *R. McGehee, in a review of "Oil and Gas: From Fossils to Fuels," in* Science Books & Films, *Vol. XIV, No. 3, December, 1978, pp. 180-81.*

Danger in Dinosaur Valley (1978)

The **Danger in Dinosaur Valley** stems from a flesh-eating tyrannosaurus. It takes an encounter with the modern world—in the form of tourists who, via satellite, return to prehistoric times bearing with them a T.V. tuned to the World Series—to teach little herbivore Dip(lodocus) how to bat his carnivore adversary around. The glaring flaw in Joan Lowery Nixon's story is the lack of correlation between text and picture on a page which is crucial to understanding what's going on. The text describes the landing of a flying saucer, but Marc Simont's cartoon shows a monster called Tyrannosaurus Rex. Incidentally, beginning readers are expected to toss off such names with the ease of sounding out "Pterodactyl." (pp. 81-2)

> *Kathy Coffey, in a review of "The Danger in Dinosaur Valley," in* School Library Journal, *Vol. 24, No. 9, May, 1978, pp. 81-2.*

A time-shift story for young independent readers should have added appeal because of the dinosaur characters and because of the humor of the concept and writing. If readers also get a glimmer of how different things look to someone from another culture and time, so much the better, but this isn't didactic. Little Diplodocus, gentle and herbivorous, knows that his family's biggest enemy is Tyrannosaurus Rex. With a skill that is newly acquired from another culture, he and his parents fight the terrible carnivore. What's the skill? Well, some space-age time travellers had brought along a "something," and one of the two-legged creatures had watched something called "Giants" who hit a round thing with a stick. (Television set; baseball game.) Practicing hurling rocks held in their mouths, Dip and his parents drive off their enemy. Dip does wonder if the tiny "Giants" have driven off *their* Tyrannosaurus Rex, too. (pp. 181-82)

> *Zena Sutherland, in a review of "Danger in Dinosaur Valley," in* Bulletin of the Center for Children's Books, *Vol. 31, No. 11, July-August, 1978, pp. 181-82.*

Volcanoes: Nature's Fireworks (with Hershell H. Nixon, 1978)

This introduction to volcanoes describes their formation and cause and tells about famous eruptions. Photographs are used to illustrate the many types of volcanoes and the land forms caused by volcanic eruptions. Technical terms are well explained in the text. However, *The Story of Volcanoes and Earthquakes* by William H. Matthews (Harvey, 1969) presents the same information in more detail and also includes many color photographs.

> *JoAnn Carr, in a review of "Volcanoes: Nature's Fireworks," in* School Library Journal, *Vol. 25, No. 4, December, 1978, p. 55.*

This is a modest introduction to a fascinating subject. The authors provide a simple review of the fundamental scientific ideas involved in the study of volcanoes. It is by no means an exhaustive review of the topic, but it should stimulate the interest of many boys and girls who pick it up. I think a more thorough treatment of the idea of plate tectonics would have been very useful, and that subject is certainly within the grasp of students of this age. My major concern is that the writing level is sometimes difficult. Convoluted sentences such as: "So the inhabitants of the towns beneath the towering mountain, which was 4,000 feet high (1200 meters), were taken by surprise when a large cloud rose from the summit, accompanied by quakes and rumblings from within the earth" occur just a bit more often than they should. Also, a couple of the authors' explanations of scientific phenomena (the seismograph and the formation of water in the atmosphere) are just badly enough written to be misleading or outright wrong. The photographs are wonderful and add a great deal to the pleasures of the book.

> *David E. Newton, in a review of "Volcanoes: Nature's Fireworks," in* Appraisal: Children's Science Books, *Vol. 12, No. 2, Spring, 1979, p. 43.*

Muffie Mouse and the Busy Birthday (1978)

Four short episodes center around Muffie's attempts, frustrations, and resulting victories in making her mother's birthday a happy one. A surprise breakfast in bed (cold root beer and a peppermint candy sandwich) delivered too quickly lands on the floor; visits from greedy Tommy Mouse and obnoxious Harry Mouse motivate Muffie to teach them each a lesson (Tommy gets cookies frosted with mustard and hot peppers), and Muffie's plans to make table decorations are continually interrupted with the complaint that she is in the way. The gentle yet effective manner in which Muffie handles each incident will

evoke empathy from young readers, while [Geoffrey] Hayes' gray-shaded drawings underscore the gemütlichkeit. (p. 617)

> *Barbara Elleman, in a review of "Muffie Mouse and the Busy Birthday," in* Booklist, *Vol. 75, No. 7, December 1, 1978, pp. 617-18.*

Muffie wants Mother Mouse's birthday to be the best ever. Four brief episodes chronicle the peppermint sandwich and root beer breakfast she makes, her moral for a non-sharer and would-be scarer, and her mother's lesson in loving. Serviceable for second and third grade proficient readers who will enjoy the varied vocabulary and Muffie's antics. Less proficient readers will quit; and older readers will not be interested.

> *Dana Whitney Pinizzotto, in a review of "Muffie Mouse and the Busy Birthday," in* School Library Journal, *Vol. 25, No. 5, January, 1979, p. 45.*

Four linked episodes, set on Mother Mouse's birthday, put Muffie Mouse's ingenuity to the test—but only one takes her through more than a comedy routine. . . . [It's] the last chapter that gives Muffie something to really feel uncomfortable about as, trying to make party decorations, she keeps getting in the way. Her solution, taking refuge under the kitchen table (with a sign claiming this as her "special place"), is not original but it is a mite poignant; the rest is not only unoriginal, it's crude.

> *A review of "Muffie Mouse and the Busy Birthday," in* Kirkus Reviews, *Vol. XLVII, No. 2, January 15, 1979, p. 63.*

The Boy Who Could Find Anything (1978)

David is definitely **The Boy Who Could Find Anything,** mostly by stumbling into it (e.g., he finds lost false teeth when they chomp on his derrière). Despite cartoons by Syd Hoff, David still limps through this one, and would seem more at home with the three stooges.

> *Kathy Coffey, in a review of "The Boy Who Could Find Anything," in* School Library Journal, *Vol. 25, No. 8, April, 1979, p. 46.*

The Kidnapping of Christina Lattimore (1979)

It was inevitable that the Patricia Hearst story would find fictional form. **The Kidnapping of Christina Lattimore** is an early example. The scene is shifted to Texas, but the trappings are familiar—an oil-wealthy family, a flinty matriarch running the business, a pious but distant father, and Christina, who as a schoolgirl is introverted, more or less unhappy with her lot and herself, and keeps "things all bottled up . . . and I don't really know what I want or where I'm going."

When at length Christina is kidnapped, matters are set for a tale of both detection and self-discovery, and that is what we get—in the currently fashionable vein of "Who am I?" books depicting all adolescents as emotionally puzzled searchers after the truth about themselves. The detection is better than the introspection, however, for Christina's inability to persuade the authorities or her family that she was not an accomplice in the crime makes for good narrative, though her growth and self-enlightenment along the way seem merely trite. Surely Patricia Hearst's case, if Christina's is supposed to echo it, touched depths of human personality murkier and more troubling to understand—and thus touched us all in a way *The Kidnapping of Christina Lattimore* never does.

> *Paxton Davis, in a review of "The Kidnapping of Christina Lattimore," in* The New York Times Book Review, *May 13, 1979, p. 27.*

A brittle (*not* brutal) kidnapping with a Sam Bronfman-inflection and, belatedly, a modicum of mystery. Houston heiress Christina Lattimore, granddaughter of tyrannical oil mogul Christabel, is seized and held by—it will be apparent to any sluggard—the proprietors of a local greasy spoon; but when the police close in, the guilty pair claim that Christina conspired with them to extract money from her grandmother. . . . The moral is stand on your own, like Christabel, even if it means saying good-by to her millions. But none of this plastic cast including Christina, is worth a second thought.

> *A review of "The Kidnapping of Christina Lattimore," in* Kirkus Reviews, *Vol. XLVII, No. 10, May 15, 1979, p. 580.*

This is a very hip teenage novel written from the egocentric point-of-view, and it works. The interior monologue is not strictly adhered to; not only does the voice subdivide but it moves beyond interior or dramatic monologue to subjective narration. All of this is skillfully handled by the author and the reader is ever increasingly enticed deeper within the story.

The Kidnapping of Christina Lattimore is a mystery focused on how to identify the third person responsible for the abduction and captivity of Christina. The complication is that when the teenager is rescued by police her captors claim that the youth herself is the brains behind the scheme—a ploy to extort thousands from a rich, domineering, and attractive oil executive grandmother.

Everyone, it seems, believes the two kidnapper/accomplices—probably because they have the moral integrity and accomplished genius of selfish three-year-olds. They simply aren't clever enough to set up the job; certainly they were not clever enough to carry it off. Whereas, Christina is brusque, self-sufficient—save for money locked up in a trust fund controlled by Gram—and *very* independent.

The family abandons her. Mom and Dad, plaster statuary, come crashing to the ground. The independent skills of Gram are seen in a new light. And the child discovers how suspicion breeds itself. But out of this jungle of human frailties, a new young woman is formed, one who can rebuild in herself and in those around her a new life motive that is not dependent upon recrimination.

> *Russ Williams, in a review of "The Kidnapping of Christina Lattimore," in* Best Sellers, *Vol. 39, No. 6, September, 1979, p. 230.*

Set in modern day Houston, Texas, this readable mystery about the kidnapping of Christina, a teenage oil heiress, is an above-average addition to young adult collections. . . . The heroine grows in strength and maturity through the experience of being accused of plotting her own abduction. Not a typical poor little rich girl story, however, readers are kept in suspense right up to the final pages as to the identity of the criminals.

> *Linda E. Morrell, in a review of "The Kidnapping of Christina Lattimore," in* School Library Journal, *Vol. 26, No. 1, September, 1979, p. 160.*

Bigfoot Makes a Movie (1979)

Cartoon-comedy yuks, just about on the Flintstone level. A dopey young humanoid, Bigfoot, who can't understand why his parents are wary of people, stumbles onto a woodland movie set—and is taken for the film's shaggy-suited star, Bigfoot. He pursues the heroine properly, and even saves her from a rockslide; but when the truth outs, nobody wants to be his friend. Funny people, he thinks, heading home with an abandoned hat. Reading this book, you might have doubts too.

> *A review of "Bigfoot Makes a Movie," in* Kirkus Reviews, *Vol. XLVII, No. 17, September 1, 1979, p. 999.*

Well, assume there IS a creature called Bigfoot. How would it act if it were young, friendly, and had a confrontation with people? In this unlikely but entertaining tale, a young Bigfoot sees another like himself and reaches out for an amicable hug. The other creature slides out of its skin and emerges as one of those human beings Bigfoot's parents have told him to avoid. Then a girl comes along and talks to him; he doesn't understand that there's a filming going on and that he is supposed to chase her, but he does run after her to save her from danger. And that's how Bigfoot gets into a movie, makeup and all. Everyone thinks he's the actor in a Bigfoot skin; at least they think so until the actor shows up, costume over his arm. Then they all run. Young Bigfoot is disappointed, but he has a good story for his parents. Monster stories are seldom as cheery as this, and Hoff's cartoon style fits nicely.

> *Zena Sutherland, in a review of "Bigfoot Makes a Movie," in* Bulletin of the Center for Children's Books, *Vol. 33, No. 4, December, 1979, p. 76.*

The New Year's Mystery (1979)

Mike and Susan's mother tells them she has called on several neighbors and invited them to a New Year's party; these are the people the two children turn to when they learn that an ingredient for holiday chocolate chip cookies is missing. Each place they go, the neighbor also reports a missing food. The solution: their two-year-old brother has put all the goodies in his toy moving van, having taken them when he was at the neighbors' homes with his mother. Easy to read . . . and adequately written, the story is

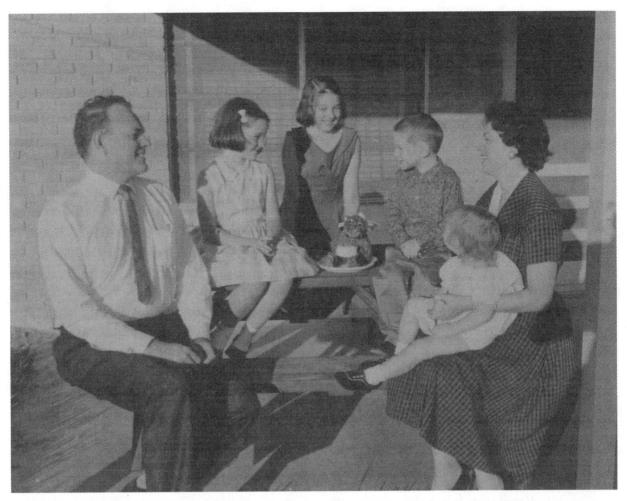

Nixon with her family in 1960: from left, husband and collaborator Hershell (Nick), daughters Maureen and Kathleen, son Joseph, and daughter Eileen.

weakened by the slight plot and by an irrelevant episode in which Mike and Susan call on a dithery neighbor who keeps misinterpreting what the children are saying and insisting they are asking purple elephant riddles. Silly.

> *Zena Sutherland, in a review of "The New Year's Mystery," in* Bulletin of the Center for Children's Books, *Vol. 33, No. 4, December, 1979, p. 77.*

The Valentine Mystery (1979)

Nixon's latest mystery for beginning readers once again stars Susan Connally and her brothers Mike and Barney. In *The Valentine Mystery* Susan receives an anonymous valentine and sets out to find the sender. Her only clue comes from two-year-old Barney who tells her the sender had "watches on his tennis shoes." Barney's crazy clue sends Susan and Mike off in search of someone answering that description and leads to several run-ins with the wacky Mrs. Pickett. Eventually, the children figure out that Susan's secret admirer is Pete, the new boy in their apartment building. (Pete was wearing boots with buckles when he delivered the valentine.) Nixon's characters have

always been fun, but *The Halloween Mystery* and *The New Year's Mystery* were greatly weakened by average plots. Fortunately, *The Valentine Mystery* hits the mark with a clever story while even [Jim] Cummins' ordinary drawings have their moments.

> *Drew Stevenson, in a review of "The Valentine Mystery," in* School Library Journal, *Vol. 26, No. 8, April, 1980, p. 96.*

The Happy Birthday Mystery (1980)

Mike and Susan plan to surprise kooky Mrs. Pickett by presenting her with an angel food cake in *The Happy Birthday Mystery.* But it is the children who are surprised when Mrs. Pickett opens the box and finds not a cake but a kitten. It turns out that a boy switched boxes with them while everyone was watching a sidewalk magician. As with others in this series, both Joan Lowery Nixon's plot and the line drawings by Jim Cummins are unexceptional.

> *Drew Stevenson, in a review of "The Happy Birthday Mystery," in* School Library Journal, *Vol. 26, No. 9, May, 1980, p. 85.*

The Séance (1980)

The seance never takes place. Conducted by a high school outcast hoping thereby to make friends, it's just beginning when one of the girls freaks out, falls on the candle, and in the ensuing darkness and confusion, disappears. Days afterwards her body is found in an out-of-town thicket. But one of the girls must have bolted the door behind Sara, and no one is talking. Roberta, who held the seance, is the next to turn up dead in the thicket—no doubt killed by the same man who killed Sara, perhaps in fear that Roberta knew too much. This is told by Lauren, who also attended the seance, and who now fears that she will be the next victim. Because Sara had been staying at Lauren's house as a state ward, the man might think that she had told Lauren who it was she planned to meet that night. In building up Lauren's fear, Nixon breaks one major rule: though readers believe they are getting Lauren's view of the incident, it is not until toward the end that she reveals—to the sheriff and to us—that it was she who conspired with Sara and locked the door behind her. Otherwise this is a standard mystery with some diversionary false leads, a surprise villain, and the obligatory climactic fright scene.

> *A review of "The Seance," in* Kirkus Reviews, *Vol. XLVIII, No. 10, May 15, 1980, p. 651.*

Lauren's character is developed well enough that the reader cares about her and follows the mystery to its suspenseful conclusion. While experienced mystery fans may be able to pick out the killer before the end and some English teachers will wish for more rounded portraits of the other characters, most junior high readers will read this for what it is—a fast action who-done-it with a touch of the occult.

> *Dick Abrahamson, in a review of "The Seance," in* English Journal, *Vol. 70, No. 7, November, 1981, p. 95.*

Gloria Chipmunk, Star! (1980)

"Today you will be a star!" Gloria Chipmunk confidently tells herself while preparing for her part in the school play. Suddenly, her mother is called away, the baby sitter fails to show, and Gloria finds herself stuck caring for her younger brother, Tippy. Undaunted, she takes Tippy to school, where, despite admonitions from her teacher, the school secretary, and the kindergarten lady that he must be taken home, Gloria persists. Determined not to miss her part in "Sleeping Beauty," she ingeniously finds a way to meet her sisterly responsibilities and still be in the play, becoming a bigger star than she had ever dreamed. Nixon's heroine is commendable, and the combination of humor and verve makes this a lively tale for young readers wanting chapter books.

> *Barbara Elleman, in a review of "Gloria Chipmunk, Star!" in* Booklist, *Vol. 76, No. 21, July 1, 1980, p. 1609.*

This little number pounds home, in an easy-reading format, several noxious concepts unneeded by the average second-grader. . . . The lessons, in effect, are: 1) parents will saddle you with responsibilities which you are ill- (or un-) equipped to handle, all promises to the contrary; 2) adults think rules are all-important and are incapable of any solutions which do not involve obeying them; 3) the female of the species is solely responsible for child-care and must juggle, not abandon, the responsibility in pursuing any independent success; and 4) "looks" and or a little flashy footwork will make you a star. . . . [Because] this is aimed at an independent-reading audience, the questions that ought to be raised will likely go unasked and the assumptions undiscussed.

> *Kristi L. Thomas, in a review of "Gloria Chipmunk, Star!" in* School Library Journal, *Vol. 27, No. 1, September, 1980, p. 62.*

Casey and the Great Idea (1980)

All sixth-grader Casey's ideas go awry. An ardent feminist, she involves her principal in a widely publicized discrimination against women news story. Her aunt, the role model for Casey's involvements, seems in danger of actually falling in love with a young newsman who's been covering Casey's escapades. Casey's mother is unenthusiastic about Casey's plans for her to go out into the business world. And her best friend is much more interested in meeting a dreamy television star than in fighting for women's rights. However, an idea to reinstate an aging ex-stewardess in her former job leads to the capture of a black market baby ring and Casey learns that true liberation is the freedom to choose what one wants to do rather than being forced into a mold. This thin, silly novel has neither the characterization nor the plot to make it at all memorable.

> *Marjorie Lewis, in a review of "Casey and the Great Idea," in* School Library Journal, *Vol. 26, No. 10, August, 1980, p. 68.*

The premise that a television reporter would spend so much time with two 12-year-olds strains believability, and the concluding events are not only contrived but also pointed in their message—that true liberation is being able to make your own choices (Casey's mother decides not to have a career). Nevertheless, Casey is a spunky character, her spirited approach is commendable, and the story contains elements of humor and suspense—ones that nondemanding readers readily latch on to. (p. 461)

> *Barbara Elleman, in a review of "Casey and the Great Idea," in* Booklist, *Vol. 77, No. 6, November 15, 1980, pp. 460-61.*

Glaciers: Nature's Frozen Rivers (with Hershell H. Nixon, 1980)

This sparse, brief introduction to glaciers and the study of them is very worthwhile. Black-and-white photographs amply illustrate the concepts which are clearly, concisely, and accurately described. What glaciers are, how they move and where they are found are discussed at the outset. Specific features such as crevasses, and icebergs are covered. Most concentration is applied to the effect of glaciers upon the land both in the past as well as their continuing effects presently and presumably in the future. This is a utilitarian book which should satisfy the needs of the student who wants to write a paragraph about glaciers or the neophyte glaciologist.

> *Deborah Robinson, in a review of "Glaciers: Nature's Frozen Rivers," in* Appraisal: Children's Science Books, *Vol. 13, No. 3, Fall, 1980, p. 50.*

This little book is a very good introduction to glaciers, their origin, dynamics, and effects. Assisted by some thirty black-and-white photographs, some very striking, and almost all helpful, the reader learns about various kinds of glaciers, cirques, horsn, tarns, fjords, till, drumlins, kames and kettles, and other details about the remarkable rivers of ice. For the most part the information is conveyed simply and clearly. There are some weaknesses which, although not sufficiently serious to detract from the generally successful treatment, need to be pointed out. During the period when large portions of the Earth were covered with ice sheets, did only "some" of the frozen water come from the oceans? (pp. 52-53) Where did the rest of the water come from? The authors imply that icebergs from Antarctica and Greenland are equally numerous in the shipping lanes (p. 31). The fact is that most antarctic icebergs are trapped in the antarctic waters. The explanation under the temperature graph (p. 54) can mislead the reader into thinking that Krakatoa and Mount Agung are in the Northern Hemisphere. The map of the Pleistocene ice sheet (p. 49) would have been more helpful if place names had been inserted at the edge of the ice sheet. The description of recrystallization in the formation of glaciers (p. 11) is, in itself, accurate and clear. The difficulty for the reader is that the process is not compared with similar processes with which the reader may be familiar. It would have been helpful if, instead of presenting the recrystallization of snow to small ice crystals and then to larger ones as though this were a unique event, the process were compared with the metamorphosis of sandstone to quartzite and limestone to marble. (pp. 50-1)

> *Layar Goldberg, in a review of "Glaciers: Nature's Frozen Rivers," in* Appraisal: Children's Science Books, *Vol. 13, No. 3, Fall, 1980, pp. 50-1.*

Glaciers: Nature's Frozen Rivers is a very informative book with abundant, striking black-and-white photographs. The book describes physical features and locations of glaciers with emphasis on valley glaciers. There are also short sections on continental glaciers and "ice ages." Basic questions such as "What is a glacier," and "How do glaciers move," are answered and many definitions of the specialized terms for glacial features are provided. The book's strengths are the beautiful photographs of glaciers, short and clear definitions and accurate information. This would be a good book for a young person to read for a class book report or for a teacher to use as a supplement to an earth science textbook. There are two shortcomings, however. The book is unimaginative and perhaps too "dry," although the photographs appearing on almost every page may motivate a young reader who tires of all

the definitions. Also, the book provides no references for an interested reader to pursue.

> *Dale E. Ingmanson, in a review of "Glaciers: Nature's Frozen Rivers," in* Science Books & Films, *Vol. 16, No. 2, November/December, 1980, p. 92.*

The Thanksgiving Mystery (1980)

Susan and Mike don't understand why their friend Pete, who lives in the same apartment building, is so cross and refuses to help them hunt the white "thing" that has been seen and heard on the steps of the building. They secretly watch, and they discover that the "ghost" is Pete, reluctantly going to rehearsals of a Thanksgiving play. His mother had insisted he be in a play her club was putting on; dressed as a turkey, he had gone in and out draped in a white sheet. End of a feeble mystery. The story has action, it's easy to read, and it has two riddles (awkwardly interpolated, but the kinds that appeal to lower-grades readers) but it is slight in structure and has no feeling of suspense.

> *Zena Sutherland, in a review of "The Thanksgiving Mystery," in* Bulletin of the Center for Children's Books, *Vol. 34, No. 2, October, 1980, p. 39.*

What sets **The Thanksgiving Mystery** apart from others in the often disappointing series [First Read-Alone Mystery Books] is that here Joan Lowery Nixon manages to create an atmosphere of suspense. The explanation might have been a letdown if not for Jim Cummins' picture of Pete in costume, at once quite funny and a little frightening.

> *Drew Stevenson, in a review of "The Thanksgiving Mystery," in* School Library Journal, *Vol. 27, No. 4, December, 1980, p. 72.*

If You Say So, Claude (1980)

Jauntily paced pioneer tall tale with built-in patterns and action that will make it fun to tell or read alone. Claude leaves the rough mining towns for "that great state of Texas," seeking peace and quiet. Each time he thinks he's found it, in northern canyons or scrub desert, with "sun . . . mean enough to sizzle lizards," he orders camp—to wife Shirley's dismay. But each time, her bad aim and good luck in encounters with wildlife ends with their moving on and her relieved, "If you say so, Claude." Finally, her firmness—plus her wildest encounter—wins her settlement in fertile meadowland. Humorous cartoons [by Lorinda Bryan Cauley], alternately in browns and full color, are framed with the text, whose colorful prose and large print third and fourth graders could read with ease.

> *Ruth M. McConnell, in a review of "If You Say So, Claude," in* School Library Journal, *Vol. 27, No. 3, November, 1980, p. 66.*

Like most pioneer women, Shirley meekly answers, "If you say so Claude," when her scruffy white-bearded mate decides to leave their Colorado Territory mining town and seek peace and quiet in Texas. . . . [When] Shirley finds a likely spot—so pretty Claude fears it will soon fill up with people—she covers up a bobcat's appearance and talks Claude into staying. When he comes round, she's all demure: "If you say so, Claude." This is intended perhaps as a sly demonstration of a rifle-totin' woman's underhanded power play. But Cauley's crassly obvious style is about as sly as a charging hog; Nixon's telling is also short on surprise and nuance; and though Shirley's indirect tactics were a necessary resort in her day, they'll only make today's young feminists' blood boil. (pp. 1461-62)

> *A review of "If You Say So, Claude," in* Kirkus Reviews, *Vol. XLVIII, No. 22, November 15, 1980, pp. 1461-62.*

The Christmas Eve Mystery (1981)

An old Irish legend that says horses speak on Christmas Eve prompts Susan and Mike to go with two of their neighbors, Mr. O'Bryan and Mrs. Pickett, down to the old stables to see if the legend is true. The children hide in the hayloft, where they overhear two men discussing a place to stash some stolen cash. Afterwards, the skittish behavior of one of the mares signals the group that the money might be near, and Mike finds it in her hay box. Though the story holds no real surprises, it is easily manageable, with just enough tension to keep beginning readers on board till the finish.

> *Denise M. Wilms, in a review of "The Christmas Eve Mystery," in* Booklist, *Vol. 77, No. 21, July 1, 1981, p. 1395.*

Kidnapped on Astarr; Mysterious Queen of Magic (1981)

A lightweight yet involving series that blends science fiction and fantasy into fast-action hero stories. Set on a distant planet in a futuristic universe, the books center around Kleep and her friend Till who, accompanied by Kleep's protective robot, Zibbit, manage to avert cosmic disasters. Nixon offers an odd mixture of imaginative ideas and tired gimmickry, solid characterization and unsupported plot twists. The stories draw one in, nevertheless, and the genre is a lure in itself.

> *Judith Goldberger, in a review of "Kidnapped on Astarr" and "Mysterious Queen of Magic," in* Booklist, *Vol. 78, No. 6, November 15, 1981, p. 446.*

Earthquakes: Nature in Motion (with Hershell H. Nixon, 1981)

This is a good summary of current earthquake knowledge and theory. On the scientific side, there is little new; several recent books on plate tectonics have been similar. However, the questions of research into possibilities of earthquake prediction, especially in this country and China, are well described; and advice on what to do during such a phenomenon seems unusually good—at least, it contains

points which had not occurred to me on a straight logic basis, and which I have not read elsewhere.

My own preference in books for this age is to go more deeply into causes, however theoretical they may be; but the Nixons have formed their own judgement on this point, and built a very good book around it. (p. 51)

> *Harry C. Stubbs, in a review of "Earthquakes: Nature in Motion," in* Appraisal: Children's Science Books, *Vol. 15, No. 1, Winter, 1982, pp. 50-1.*

Earthquakes tries to acquaint the reader with causes and effects of this old earthly affliction. The nature of earthquakes, where they occur, their causes and signs or precursors, their measurement and prediction, and what to do before, during, and after an earthquake is discussed. However, the presentation fails due to superficiality and generalization. The subjects of earthquake prevention and control could be dealt with in greater depth, and I was disappointed in the section "Can an Earthquake be 'Turned Off'?" There are many good black-and-white photographs and an index, but a table of contents and suggestions for further reading are not included. A subject this spectacular should be more exciting reading. Because many readers will experience an earthquake somewhere in the United States in their lifetime, why not provide greater understanding for that exciting experience?

> *Robert E. Riecker, in a review of "Earthquakes: Nature in Motion," in* Science Books & Films, *Vol. 17, No. 4, March/April, 1982, p. 214.*

The Easter Mystery (1981)

[This] is a story that incorporates a few facts about Easter customs and a slight story line. Susan and Mike gossip about the Easter "treasure" a neighbor's said she is bringing home from the bank, and their voluble concern in alerting other neighbors helps the police catch two thieves. The treasure proves to be a beautiful old hand-painted egg. Not a very mysterious situation, and rather plodding in its development, this has little information about Easter that isn't easily found elsewhere. It's timely, and it provides practice for the beginning independent reader. (pp. 135-36)

> *Zena Sutherland, in a review of "The Easter Mystery," in* Bulletin of the Center for Children's Books, *Vol. 35, No. 7, March, 1982, pp. 135-36.*

The Trouble with Charlie (as Jaye Ellen, 1982)

A plot built around the unlikely conflict between a 15-year-old girl entering the dating world and her overprotective older brothers is the underlying premise of **The Trouble with Charlie.** The result is a contrived teenage romance with no real surprises. During her father's overseas work assignment, Charlie's older twin brothers, Rick and Adam, appoint themselves her surrogate father. Each of her first dates ends in an absurd situation from which she is rescued by Rick and Adam. Eventually, Mark Potter, the handsome new boy in school, catches Charlie's eye. Andy, the boy next door and her brothers' close friend, offers kindly advice on how to pursue Mark and avoid her brothers' close scrutiny. That he has "ulterior motives" is blatantly clear to the reader, but Andy doesn't announce his love for Charlie until the end of the book. Her realization that Andy, not Mark, should be her boyfriend is also painfully slow in surfacing but no less obvious. Flat characters muddle through the programmed, episodic plot. Comparative brevity is the book's only redeeming quality. It is difficult to imagine that even those basically "hooked" on teenage romances could fall for this one.

> *Reneé Steinberg, in a review of "The Trouble with Charlie," in* School Library Journal, *Vol. 29, No. 6, February, 1983, p. 88.*

Charlene's father is out of the country, and her older twin brothers—senior varsity football—have decided to step in for him and monitor Charlie's fledgling dating life. . . . Humorous to the point of delightful, this has booktalk potential that most romances lose because of their sappiness. Charlie's a real girl with real problems who finds in her own assertiveness a real solution.

> *Jorja Perkins Davis, in a review of "Trouble with Charlie," in* Voice of Youth Advocates, *Vol. 5, No. 6, February, 1983, p. 35.*

The Specter (1982)

The story is relentlessly told in the present tense: "The whisper strikes through the darkness, and I struggle to meet it, clutching at the sound." Two girls lie side by side in hospital beds. Dina, 17, is physically ill with Hodgkin's disease. Julie, 9, after surviving an accident that killed her parents, seems a little crazy. Is she raving when she claims that a man named Sikes wants to kill her?

The scary beginning of this psychological puzzle is neatly balanced by the surprise in the last chapter. But in the middle of the book, during an interlude in which the two girls adjust comfortably to a foster home, readers will have to forge ahead patiently to discover the startling climax.

> *Jane Langton, in a review of "The Specter," in* The New York Times Book Review, *February 27, 1983, p. 37.*

This slim novel has ingredients for success: friendship, illness, death, life in an orphanage, first love, the will to live, a psychotic killer. Despite these ingredients, however, **The Specter** is slim stuff indeed. Nothing or no one is sufficiently developed to grip a reader's imagination and, by the end of the novel, the surprise ending is really not much of a surprise. Readers thirteen and older will probably find the story a mild yawn.

> *Leila Christenbury, in a review of "The Specter," in* The ALAN Review, *Vol. 10, No. 3, Spring, 1983, p. 19.*

When [Julie and Dina] are discharged to the same foster home, Julie's attachment to Dina seems almost obsessive; the little girl attempts to thwart anything or anybody who

might come between them while continuing to talk about the ominous presence of a mysterious stranger. Then Dina senses that Julie's behavior could be linked to the accident—a suspicion confirmed in the stunning climax of a psychological thriller that derives much of its impact from the three-dimensional delineation of the central character and from the skillful crafting of the plot. Told from Dina's perspective, the novel becomes more than an engrossing mystery; it is also a revealing picture of the anguish afflicting a young adult whose future is jeopardized by chronic disease and who must also cope with dramatic physical changes. At the end Dina opts for hope rather than despair; no miracles are promised, but she has decided to look beyond her anger and concentrate on living. The change is believable; the effect is moving without being manipulative.

> *Mary M. Burns, in a review of "The Specter," in* The Horn Book Magazine, *Vol. LIX, No. 2, April, 1983, p. 173.*

The Gift (1983)

Brian, an 11-year-old American boy, spends the summer with Irish relatives while his parents attend meetings in Dublin. At first unhappy about leaving baseball, swimming and friends, he soon realizes that salmon fishing, farm animals, and Grandad's tales of "little people" will more than compensate for what he is missing. Brian becomes determined to catch a leprechaun as a gift for his grandfather, not just to please him but mainly to prove to impatient Aunt Nora that he is not just a foolish old man telling fanciful stories. He does, in fact, catch one and takes him home in triumph. Grandad's eyes sparkle, but Aunt Nora, still unconvinced, says, "Anyone can see that you are holding a very large cat!" Readers must decide the reality of the situation, guided by Grandad's observation that people see what they want to see and hear what they want to hear. Nixon writes a delightful story set in the Irish countryside. Skillfully drawn characterizations give the story substance. The visual description of mornings in the Irish mist, of the bucolic countryside, transports readers; all of these elements come together around the theme: if you have the eyes to see, magic can be found anywhere. (pp. 74-5)

> *Doris E. Weber, in a review of "The Gift," in* School Library Journal, *Vol. 29, No. 9, May, 1983, pp. 74-5.*

The author delights in presenting contrasting characters. The staunchly realistic aunt is an effective foil for the story-telling grandfather, yet her warm concern and caring permeates the story. The friendship between the boy and his great grandfather matures because their mutual gift of seeing the wee folk is subtly but powerfully developed.

> *Ronald A. Jobe, in a review of "The Gift," in* Language Arts, *Vol. 60, No. 8, November-December, 1983, p. 1022.*

Magnolia's Mixed-Up Magic (1983)

Described unaccountably as a beginning reader, this is the

serviceable but unoriginal story of Magnolia Possum (to rhyme with blossom?), whose grandmother finds a dusty old magic book at Mrs. Fox's store. Though Grandma is all for progressing slowly, Magnolia goes right to the disappearing trick, making postman Mr. Beaver invisible with a two-line ditty and a closing *Abracadabra*. Then she gets Grandma to make her (Magnolia) float on the ceiling, and only then do they discover that the back pages on undoing the tricks are missing. So it's back to Mrs. Fox's store where the floating Magnolia and the invisible postman surprise a robber . . . and Magnolia, from her vantage point near the ceiling, finds the missing pages stuffed into a mouse hole. Then with an *Alakazam* it's back to normal for Mr. Beaver and Magnolia, who will settle henceforth for making ice cream disappear. This pretty ordinary picture-book business is illustrated [by Linda Buckholtz-Ross] with agreeably loose and mildly amusing line-and-wash cartoons. . . .

> *A review of "Magnolia's Mixed-Up Magic," in* Kirkus Reviews, *Vol. LI, No. 11, June 1, 1983, p. 618.*

This brisk little story has several elements that appeal to children: magic, animal characters, justice meted out, a problem that has a happy ending. . . . The style is direct, the action well-paced, and the length and humor of the story are just right for the read-aloud audience or those primary-grades readers who can manage independently.

> *Zena Sutherland, in a review of "Magnolia's Mixed-Up Magic," in* Bulletin of the Center for Children's Books, *Vol. 37, No. 1, September, 1983, p. 14.*

The language is lyrical and smooth. Vivid pictures pop to mind as when [postman Bernard Beaver] states, "My throat couldn't feel any more dry and scratchy if I were eating stale potato chips in a sandstorm." The amusing illustrations in shades of gray highlight the story line: the colorful jacket illustration is an attention-getter. The characters, somewhat reminiscent of Rosemary Wells' *Benjamin and Tulip* (Dial, 1973), provide delightful entertainment.

> *Terri M. Roth, in a review of "Magnolia's Mixed-Up Magic," in* School Library Journal, *Vol. 30, No. 2, October, 1983, p. 152.*

Days of Fear (1983)

Although Eddie recognizes the armed, masked man who robs him as the elder of two teenage brothers who are terrorizing the neighborhood, he is afraid to turn the young man in to the police and hides the truth from his family. His secret makes him miserable and his fear makes his trips home from his nightshift job almost unbearable, but it isn't until his wife's friend disappears that he can muster enough courage to go to the authorities. Few characters, a limited time span, and straightforward plot aimed directly at older teenagers (with carry-over for some adults with reading difficulties), plus a very low reading level, make this a choice item for the high school high-low shelf.

> *Stephanie Zvirin, in a review of "Days of*

> *Fear," in* Booklist, *Vol. 79, No. 22, August, 1983, p. 1458.*

The theme of being courageous is obvious and heavy-handed and both plot and characters are poorly developed. The story lacks appeal and readers will have little sympathy for the protagonist. Stick with Patricia R. Giff's *Suspect* (Dutton, 1982).

> *Myra Seab, in a review of "Days of Fear," in* School Library Journal, *Vol. 30, No. 1, September, 1983, p. 138.*

A Deadly Game of Magic (1983)

When their car breaks down during a storm, Lisa and her three classmates seek refuge and a telephone at a secluded house, where they are greeted by a strange couple who hurriedly depart the premises. It isn't long before some creepy things begin to happen, and the young people come to realize that someone in the house is putting on a bizarre and deadly magic show for their benefit. Characters are limp, and Nixon falls disappointingly short of real edge-of-the-chair suspense, relying instead on obvious magic gimmickry to keep the story moving. But teenagers familiar with her previous novels will want to read this anyway, since books involving magic and the occult still seem to have great YA appeal.

> *Stephanie Zvirin, in a review of "A Deadly Game of Magic," in* Booklist, *Vol. 80, No. 3, October 1, 1983, p. 234.*

Four teenagers, returning from a speech and drama tournament, find themselves unwilling participants in *A Deadly Game of Magic* when they are caught in a Texas monsoon with a dead car. Seeking shelter in a sprawling isolated house, the four soon realize that they are not alone. . . . As the web of terror tightens it is Lisa who persistently seeks to find out more about the house and its owner in an effort to learn the identity of their hidden tormentor. Eventually it is her knowledge of magic which enables them to outwit him. Nixon keeps the suspense cooking on all burners and the result is an original heart-pounding thriller. The chills begin almost immediately and never let up right through the book's last sentence, which is a final deliciously wicked touch of the macabre.

> *Drew Stevenson, in a review of "A Deadly Game of Magic," in* School Library Journal, *Vol. 30, No. 4, December, 1983, p. 86.*

For me, Ms. Nixon's latest was a tedious game of hokum. The plot stretched credulity, the suspense, what there was of it, relied on exclamation points and cliff-hanger chapter endings, and the characters were flat on the one hand and overblown on the other, alternately gushing their fears and making half sense. The author's attempts to make her book "more than just a mystery" (you see, each of the kids must live with illusions of one kind or another, and stage magic too is based on illusion—get it?) are obvious and unsuccessful.

I'm sure Joan Lowery Nixon has written far better books than this one, but to say so is not exactly a compliment.

Jim Brewbaker, in a review of "A Deadly Game of Magic," in The ALAN Review, *Vol. 11, No. 2, Winter, 1984, p. 23.*

The Ghosts of Now (1984)

Seventeen-year-old Angie agonizes over her brother's near-fatal hit-and-run accident which has left him in a coma. Angie's investigation does not sit well with her new classmates or the new town she has recently moved to. Anonymous phone threats, lies and secrets encourage Angie's questions. The suspense builds slowly with a psychological twist involving family relationships, bored teenagers, trust and love. Although the writing is stiff and the psychological theme explored superficially, undemanding readers will find a story here akin to Nancy Drew with a heroine as undaunted in her quest for the truth. (p. 10)

J. C., in a review of "The Ghosts of Now," in Children's Book Review Service, *Vol. 13, No. 1, September, 1984, pp. 9-10.*

Not only does [Angie] uncover the truth about Jeremy's accident but she also comes to understand the real emotions beneath the surface of her family and **The Ghosts of Now** they have all become. Nixon knows this town and these people as she places readers squarely in the heart of Angie's private hell. Although the final answers are not well developed and carried through, it is not the solution that is the backbone of this novel but the agonizing search.

A review of "The Ghosts of Now," in School Library Journal, *Vol. 31, No. 4, December, 1984, p. 102.*

A boy is badly injured under mysterious circumstances by a hit-and-run driver, and the only clues to the incident are pathetic entries in his private journal. His sister, the narrator of the mystery, searches for answers in an atmosphere of suspicion and hostility. "The ghosts of now," a phrase from the journal (and title of the book), provides not only a key to the puzzle, but helps explain what drove the boy towards his misfortune in the first place.

Indeed, the events leading to the injury and the working out of the mystery are only effects of a deeper problem. They are symptoms of an illness of sorts, a social condition with which many young readers can identify.

The sister and brother live in a world where their elders cannot hear them, and do not care to. Their father, a corporate nomad, will not acknowledge his wife's alcoholism,

Nixon with her three Edgar Allan Poe awards.

145

a disability caused in part by his cyclical uprooting of the family. Their mother, even when sober, can address her children only in formulaic questions designed not to elicit significant responses or even warm small talk, but to fill the uncomfortable minutes of the children's hour between home-from-school and off-to-bed. The children deal with the situation by retreating to their peers (the generation gap) or to their fantasies (the reality gap). Even the older sister, ironically, while lamenting the gap between herself and her parents, cannot communicate with her brother.

Eventually, communication bridges these gaps, and helps to solve the mystery as well. They talk, they touch. Reality returns, and the ghosts disappear.

> *D. V. O'Brien, in a review of "The Ghosts of Now," in* Best Sellers, *Vol. 44, No. 10, January, 1985, p. 399.*

The Stalker   (1985)

Nixon keeps her string of thrillers intact with **The Stalker.** Set in Corpus Christi, Texas, this is the story of 17-year-old Jennifer Lee Wilcox and her efforts to help prove the innocence of her best friend, Bobbie Trax, who has been jailed for the murder of her mother. Jennifer cannot afford to hire a professional detective so she enlists the aid of a recently retired police detective. Their relentless digging eventually pays off, but not before Jennifer has several brushes with death. Although Bobbie's innocence is proven, Nixon's ending offers no easy answers for Jennifer. Since Bobbie remains a shadowy one-dimensional figure, it is sometimes hard to fathom Jennifer's fierce loyalty toward her. It is Jennifer's relationship with her family and boyfriend and her uneasy partnership with Lucas that is the backbone of the story. The plot has several unbelievable moments, but the few weaknesses aside, Nixon is an old pro at suspense and readers will not be disappointed.

> *Drew Stevenson, in a review of "The Stalker," in* School Library Journal, *Vol. 31, No. 9, May, 1985, p. 111.*

Suspense is maintained by means of short passages of internal monologue interpolated between chapters of third-person narration. Gradually, this unidentified voice—clearly that of the murderer—acknowledges awareness of Jennifer's efforts to uncover his identity. The book's pace increases as the "Stalker" menaces Jennifer's life. Potential culprits abound, though readers are likely to guess the murderer's identity. A skillful handling of subplots and a vivid depiction of Jennifer's working-class milieu give the novel more depth than is usual for thrillers. (p. 319)

> *Charlotte W. Draper, in a review of "The Stalker," in* The Horn Book Magazine, *Vol. LXI, No. 3, May-June, 1985, pp. 318-19.*

The storyline moves at an accelerating pace and slickly covers the subject areas expected of a thriller—hard drugs, credit card swindles, multiple murders—with the tried and tested red herring thrown in for good measure. It begins to grip the reader—probably an average or less able third-, fourth- or fifth-year pupil—about half

way through. It offers fast-paced entertainment without tears—literary merit is there none.

> *V. R., in a review of "The Stalker," in* Books for Keeps, *No. 47, November, 1987, p. 22.*

Maggie, Too   (1985)

When Margaret was two, her mother died, and her movie director-father's parenting style can best be described as benign neglect. Now he is about to marry a 20-year-old starlet, and he decides the best place for 12-year-old Margaret is with her maternal grandmother, whom she does not know. She goes—filled with hostility—but before she can show her displeasure, all kinds of things start happening. Within hours of her arrival, a gunman arrives at the house next door. Margaret assists in his capture and appears on the news. Grandma Landrey's adult children see the story and show up to protect her. One daughter comes with her children, another daughter comes with her problems, and the son shows up with a huge, slobbering guard dog named Flower Pot. In addition, the neighbor whom the gunman terrorized moves in along with her two little children. Margaret finds this madhouse hard to comprehend after her lonely existence; yet her grandmother's sincerity shines through all the hubbub, and before long Margaret's plan for an escape turns into a way for her grandmother to get a vacation. Nixon's amusing mélange of characters may remind readers of the frenetic Bagthorpe family. Eminently readable, this will hook readers right from the first paragraph, and their page-turning will be punctuated by giggles.

> *Ilene Cooper, in a review of "Maggie, Too," in* Booklist, *Vol. 81, No. 17, May 1, 1985, p. 1256.*

For readers who can accept the vague background around which this story develops, the characters will win them over. . . . The ending is as predictable as the rest of the story is not. [Margaret's grandmother] Maggie is a high-school librarian who really cares about and understands young people; Margaret is a gruff, sensitive, struggling 12 year old who has a lot with which to deal. Readers will wish that Margaret and Maggie had gotten together sooner. Nixon brings them both to life, and young people will enjoy meeting them. (pp. 137-38)

> *Rebekah Ray, in a review of "Maggie, Too," in* School Library Journal, *Vol. 32, No. 1, September, 1985, pp. 137-38.*

Land under the Sea   (with Hershell H. Nixon, 1985)

Although rather dry in its prose and disappointing in its dull black-and-white illustrations (especially after the enticing full-color jacket showing Cousteau's *Calypso* anchored in a very blue blue hole), the book is a coherent introduction to marine geology. No charming dolphins here, nor luminescent creatures, but the abyssal plains, the canyons, ridges, seamounts, drowned rivers and lava flows themselves—how they were formed and how they have been mapped, and the technology used in the process. In a brief 62 pages, the Nixons wisely do not try to provide in depth (no pun intended) information, but they give a glimpse of a secret world where not only budding geologists, but chemists, biologists, cartographers and others may discover new, undreamed of horizons.

> *Patricia Manning, in a review of "Land under the Sea," in* School Library Journal, *Vol. 32, No. 4, December, 1985, p. 92.*

This is an excellent, general introduction to the discovery and exploration of the unique lands beneath the sea. With appropriate language, the authors relate our ever-increasing knowledge of the trenches and mountains, shelves and shores, plates and plateaus of the underwater world. The early explorers and their contributions as well as modern scientists and their most recent discoveries are discussed. The tools of the oceanographers are explained and their uses are delineated in an understandable fashion. Scientific concepts and terminology are clearly defined and then carefully developed. Plate tectonics, underwater volcanism, ocean floor spreading and fracturing, and mineral formation are explained in the context of the physical forms they create. Numerous black-and-white photographs, diagrams, and charts further elucidate the material discussed. (Two depth-sounder diagrams, however, have no point of reference and would have been better placed horizontally.) Much information is presented, but the spacing of the text and the variety of illustrations make the book approachable for the young reader. This book seems particularly appropriate for the motivated third or fourth grader or as an accessible subject overview for upper elementary grade-level students.

> *Peter Roop, in a review of "Land under the Sea," in* Science Books & Films, *Vol. 21, No. 4, March-April, 1986, p. 227.*

Joan Nixon is a skilled writer indeed, and when she teams up with her geologist husband to write a science book, the result is excellent.

In this discussion of the ocean floors, readers are led smoothly from the water's surface through history and growing technology to the very depths of the seas. Along the way words such as "seismic troughs" and "shelf breaks" are unobtrusively introduced and succinctly defined so that the prose flows uninterrupted. Black and white photographs are carefully integrated into the text and provide lucid examples of the kind of discoveries which have been made by geologists, biologists and other scientists who work as oceanographers.

There are clear explanations of how the surfaces of the ocean floors form and how they shift, of how cores of rock are taken from different spots in the world's oceans and used to determine the age of specific sea floors, and of how instruments measure the depths of the sea.

This is the kind of book children will look to for answers; it will also evoke wonder and encourage future study. (p. 35)

> *Norma Bagnall, in a review of "Land under the Sea," in* Appraisal: Science Books for Young People, *Vol. 19, No. 2, Spring, 1986, pp. 34-5.*

The House on Hackman's Hill   (1985)

After Jeff and Debbie hear Mr. Karsten's spine-tingling tale about some weird long-ago happenings in a nearby, now-deserted house, they decide to investigate the place. Snow begins to fall on their way to the mansion where they plan to search for the supposedly stolen Egyptian mummy, and soon a blizzard traps them overnight. Tension builds swiftly to a riveting climax before simmering down to a credible ending. The book is divided into two parts: Mr. Karsten's story of his experience as the young son of the housekeeper for the Egyptologist Dr. Hackman and Jeff and Debbie's exploration today. Nixon uses this two-in-one combination well, which helps make this original paperback a quick and enjoyable read.

> *Barbara Elleman, in a review of "The House on Hackman's Hill," in* Booklist, *Vol. 82, No. 20, June 15, 1986, p. 1543.*

And Maggie Makes Three   (1986)

This lively, humorous sequel to **Maggie, Too** continues the adventures of Maggie Ledoux, now a seventh-grader.

Maggie, motherless child of famous film director Roger Ledoux, is spending the school year with her grandmother in Houston. She has an uneasy relationship with her hard-to-please father and is dreading the prospect of having to meet his new wife, a beautiful actress. Maggie also worries about starting a new school, making friends, staying out of trouble. The last seems impossible—the first day, she punches a wise guy named Jerico after he demands her seat and calls her Fatso. Still, Maggie makes a friend, Lisa. Both join the drama club, where Maggie wins a role in a production of *The Sound of Music*. Maggie develops a crush on the lead, handsome, ambitious Alex, but she feels left out when her friends rehearse a musical review without her. Alex leaves school, and her friendship with Lisa is threatened when the newspaper reports plans by Roger and his wife to see "their daughter" in "her" school musical review. Surprisingly, it's Jerico who offers comfort and insights on the up-and-down nature of friendships. Various mishaps occur on opening night, but Maggie manages to impress everybody with her performance, including Roger. Happily, her stepmother also turns out to be a warm, unpretentious young woman.

Nixon is a real pro at delivering likable, true-to-life characters and intriguing plots. Readers will sympathize with Maggie from the first and will rejoice at the story's happy ending.

> *A review of "And Maggie Makes Three," in* Kirkus Reviews, *Vol. LIV, No. 7, April, 1, 1986, p. 548.*

Maggie was first introduced in **Maggie, Too;** here she seems a more self-aware person. Readers meeting her for the first time will find her and her grandmother well-developed and easy to understand characters, but the same cannot be said for Maggie's extended family, introduced in *Maggie, Too* but too quickly thrown at readers here. Also difficult to accept are Maggie's two classmates who give her a hard time; the fact that they are black is revealed only through their dialect and their depiction on the homely jacket. The novel closes with loose ends so suddenly and neatly tied up in the last chapter that readers will have a difficult time believing it.

> *Ellen Fader, in a review of "And Maggie Makes Three," in* School Library Journal, *Vol. 33, No. 1, September, 1986, p. 138.*

The Other Side of Dark (1986)

Awakening from a four-year coma, Stacy learns that the intruder who shot her also killed her mother, and that she was the only witness. Stacy has to come to terms with her new identity: physically a 17 year old, yet mentally still a 13 year old, she has missed four years of growing up and of popular culture. At the same time, she realizes that she has to identify the killer before he can silence her. Stacy is a vivid character whose need to be brought up to date provides some comic moments, such as her confusion at new hair styles and her unfamiliarity with pasta salad. While this mystery is generally tense and dramatic, the first-person narrative does remove the edge from some of the suspense. One other weakness is Stacy's love interest, a narcotics officer masquerading as a high-school senior. Nixon does not convince readers that this 23-year-old man would fall in love with someone who in so many ways thinks and acts like a 13 year old. Yet the clever premise, the quick pace, and the determined protagonist should attract and hold readers. (pp. 145-46)

> *David Gale, in a review of "The Other Side of Dark," in* School Library Journal, *Vol. 33, No. 1, September, 1986, pp. 145-46.*

Nixon has written another compelling page-turner, though the suspense flags near the end once the mystery of the killer's identity has been solved. Until then, almost everyone seems suspect, especially handsome Jeff who has been paying Stacy a great deal of attention. In a neat touch, her simple, childlike desire for revenge on the killer gives way to a more mature and complex attitude about justice as she grows up to fit her body.

> *Hazel Rochman, in a review of "The Other Side of Dark," in* Booklist, *Vol. 83, No. 2, September 15, 1986, p. 121.*

Nixon is a master of taking a what if situation and creating a good story around it. What happens after a 13 year old is shot and remains in a zombie-like coma for four years? What is it like to resume life as a 17 year old beautiful girl who remembers the man who shot her and killed her mother? Nixon develops the plot well, with only a few rough spots where the reader's credibility is stretched. *The Other Side of Dark* has believable characters, suspense, mystery, a little romance, and will make its readers want to read Nixon's other books. The main criticism is that by making such a big deal out of the four year time lapse, Nixon includes many fads and events that may date this

book sooner than many other titles. But the book should be worn out by then.

> *Mary L. Adams, in a review of "The Other Side of Dark," in* Voice of Youth Advocates, *Vol. 9, No. 5, December, 1986, p. 221.*

Beats Me, Claude (1986)

In this sequel to *If You Say So, Claude,* Shirley and Claude continue to enjoy their newfound peace in the cabin in the great state of Texas. When Shirley, who has never been a very good cook, tries her hand at baking an apple pie, the result is a surprise for her and for readers. . . . At times the text is forced, but the exaggerated humor will still tickle readers' funny bones. Reminicent of the "McBroom" series by Sid Fleischman, this is corny, silly, but, oh what fun.

> *Orvella Fields, in a review of "Beats Me, Claude," in* School Library Journal, *Vol. 33, No. 4, December, 1986, p. 107.*

A sequel to *If You Say So, Claude,* this is a three-chapter picture book in which a couple starts out admiring the peace and quiet of their Texas homestead. For Shirley, the only thing lacking is someone else to talk to; for Claude, it's a juicy apple pie. They both get what they want—in a very roundabout way. While Claude is out in the fields, Shirley has three visitors: the first is a shyster who leaves behind an orphan; the second is a bank robber, and the third a group of army deserters. Shirley does them all in with her horrible apple pies, along with convincing Claude to keep the orphan, who bakes like an angel. This has tall-tale humor, nonstop action, and satisfying lines. Shirley tells Claude she needs to go into town to pick up some of the orphan's things. "What things?" Claude asks. "Just some clothes, some books, and a sister," says Shirley. [Tracey Campbell] Pearson's sassy art work has helter-skelter lines highlighting the slapstick, as well as inventive details; the armadillo that pokes through every riotous scene makes a funny contrast to the moose head, which observes it all through the spectacles of one of Shirley's victims. Chaotic and colorful, this is a sure-fire read-aloud to younger listeners as well as a tall tale for those who can read it independently.

> *Betsy Hearne, in a review of "Beats Me, Claude," in* Bulletin of the Center for Children's Books, *Vol. 40, No. 5, January, 1987, p. 94.*

The three short chapters relate Shirley's culinary disasters with a lilt and swing that resembles, in exaggeration and humor, the fanciful absurdity of an American tall tale. Children will be able to gloat over their ability to name the pies' missing ingredients. Scribbly, cartoonlike illustrations of the delightful messes and hoodwinked outlaws add even more amusement to the lively but unpretentious story.

> *Ethel R. Twichell, in a review of "Beats Me, Claude," in* The Horn Book Magazine, *Vol. LXIII, No. 2, March-April, 1987, p. 205.*

Maggie Forevermore (1987)

Thirteen-year-old Maggie from *Maggie, Too* and *And Maggie Makes Three* returns in this story of family problems. Maggie resents her father's demand that she leave her grandmother's Houston home and spend Christmas with him and his new young wife in California. Although she is upset about leaving her friends behind, it is not long before Maggie has made new friends. Nixon incorporates an exotic Malibu setting, a handsome young television star, a budding romance, and a mystery into this fairly fast moving coming-of-age teen novel. Characters border on the one-dimensional, and it's not very realistic that in one short week Maggie should discover that she has lost weight, is pretty, can act mature, loves her stepmother, and has a handsome new boyfriend. However, the likable characters and the action-filled plot should make this book popular.

> *Susan McCord, in a review of "Maggie Forevermore," in* School Library Journal, *Vol. 33, No. 7, March, 1987, p. 164.*

While this is a light story, mostly focused on Maggie's detective work to trap an unscrupulous talent agent, Maggie's problems with her irritable dad remain, and the problems of youthful stars (and would-be stars) add depth and texture. The characterization of Kiki, the young wife, is refreshingly free of cliches: while beautiful, she's no bubblehead, and the affection and respect between her and Maggie is rewarding for them both.

> *Roger Sutton, in a review of "Maggie Forevermore," in* Bulletin of the Center for Children's Books, *Vol. 40, No. 8, April, 1987, p. 152.*

Readers will readily identify with Maggie's frustration over adults who make all the decisions without asking a child's opinion and the problem of where to spend holidays in divided families. Young readers should enjoy the movie world story line although TV characters named Doc and Dick Dackery are a turn-off.

The plot is somewhat simplistic. It includes a dose of glamour, mystery and adventure. Maggie and Kiki are the strongest characters. Maggie's father is at times insensitive toward his daughter, but he means well, and like Maggie he learns a lot during her visit.

> *Irene Close, in a review of "Maggie Forevermore," in* Voice of Youth Advocates, *Vol. 10, No. 4, October, 1987, p. 204.*

Haunted Island (1987)

Chris Holt, 13, and his family are assisting a relative in repairing a recently purchased inn on an island, when they hear that the island is haunted by Amos Corley, who died 175 years ago. In fact, they hear the story from Corley himself. Chris eliminates the hauntings forever by using a tinder box, an old journal, a chest of clothing, and information he learned from a school report on pioneers. The story is quickly paced and well plotted. It is similar to but easier than Mollie Hunter's *A Stranger Came Ashore*

(Harper, 1975) and should be popular with mystery fans. (pp. 102-03)

> *Kristine Johnson, in a review of "Haunted Island," in* School Library Journal, *Vol. 33, No. 8, May, 1987, pp. 102-03.*

Fat Chance, Claude (1987)

Backing up a bit from the time frame of *Beats Me, Claude,* this tells the story of Shirley and Claude's childhoods and courtship. Ever the individual, Shirley has an independent disposition that scares away most suitors—the last one runs after he sees her riding a bull—until she sets out for Colorado to pan for gold and finds herself parked next to Claude in the wagon train west. After saving him from a rattlesnake and later staking out the same claim as Claude, she agrees to go partners all the way. This represents endearing characters, adroit writing, and an action-packed feminist pioneer tall tale all at once ("Shirley was born long and lean, with hair the color of prairie dust and a mouth wide enough to hold a couple of smiles at the same time"). To enjoy—north, south, and east as well as west.

> *Betsy Hearne, in a review of "Fat Chance, Claude," in* Bulletin of the Center for Children's Books, *Vol. 41, No. 1, September, 1987, p. 15.*

In crisp, sure language laced with delightfully outrageous exaggeration, Nixon has spun a rib-tickling yarn with an underlying message about the value of friendship. [Tracey Campbell] Pearson's spirited illustrations double the hilarity and silly good fun: the picture of Claude proposing is worth a pan of gold.

> *A review of "Fat Chance, Claude," in* Publishers Weekly, *Vol. 232, No. 14, September 25, 1987, p. 107.*

Transitional readers will relish the exaggerated humor of the "Colorado or Bust" shenanigans, and they will share the joy of the couple's first hug. (From the sequels, we know that Shirley remains a spirited, liberated female after the wedding.) Nixon blends Western drawlin' with contemporary tale spinning, giving Shirley a new trademark response: "Fat chance, Claude." Pearson's colorful yet sketchy cartoons again illustrate. They match the folksy spirit of the text, although characters lack detailed facial expressions. This new yarn will entertain followers of the frontier pair, and it should tantalize them to try the more complex tall tales of Pecos Bill and Paul Bunyan.

> *Charlene Strickland, in a review of "Fat Chance, Claude," in* School Library Journal, *Vol. 34, No. 4, December, 1987, p. 75.*

A Family Apart (1987)

Announced as the first volume in the **"Orphan Train"** quartet, this is based on a real program, the Children's Aid Society's placement of orphans who travelled from New York City to the West to be adopted by residents there. In this story, set in 1860, widowed Mrs. Kelley realizes she cannot support her six children and gives them up for adoption. The protagonist is the oldest girl, Frances, who disguises herself as a boy so that she can be paired with her baby brother for adoption, and they are indeed taken together by a very nice family. "Frankie" is rather quickly discovered to be Frances, and everyone is happy about it. This tale is framed (to no advantage) by a contemporary setting and a grandmother who tells the whole-book story. This has sentimental appeal, sympathetic if not subtly-drawn characters, and historical interest. It suffers, albeit not gravely, from a predictability that is based in part on stock situations (clearly, the story of brother Mike, planned as the second book, is going to be one about an adoptive family as unpleasant as his sister's is pleasant) and from an aura of must-get-those-facts-about-slave-markets-and-the-Underground-Railroad-in-there. (pp. 35-6)

> *Zena Sutherland, in a review of "A Family Apart," in* Bulletin of the Center for Children's Books, *Vol. 41, No. 2, October, 1987, pp. 35-36.*

At the end [of *A Family Apart*] Frankie becomes Frances again, as much loved by the Swensons for being a daughter as she was as a son. The second volume will be Mike's story and the kicker sentence at the end, "Why, Mike even began to wonder if Mr. Friedrich [his adopted father] had committed a murder!" will leave young and old alike breathlessly waiting for Mike's tale.

This is as close to a perfect book as you'll buy this year. The plot is rational and well paced; the characters are real and believable; the time setting important to U.S. history, and the values all that anyone could ask for. Buy it, book-talk it, push it.

> *Dorothy M. Broderick, in a review of "A Family Apart," in* Voice of Youth Advocates, *Vol. 10, No. 4, October, 1987, p. 204.*

A kind of period piece, circa 1860, **A Family Apart** has a distinct Horatio Alger tone. Well constructed incidents, including the widowed mother giving up her children so they can be sent west to find a better life, a grass fire set by sparks from the train, and a holdup of the train contribute to fast action and considerable suspense—particularly about the oldest girl, Frances, who disguises herself as a boy so she can better help her brothers and sisters. *An Orphan for Nebraska* (Atheneum, 1979) by Charlene Joy Talbot is a similar orphan train story, but about one boy. Patricia Beatty's *That's One Ornery Orphan* (Morrow, 1980) is more humorous but less of a saga. What happened to orphans and street children of the last century may well appeal to many of today's children who hear so much about street children and abducted and deserted kids.

> *George Gleason, in a review of "A Family Apart," in* School Library Journal, *Vol. 34, No. 3, November, 1987, p. 106.*

The Dark and Deadly Pool (1987)

The thefts from the posh Houston hotel where narrator Mary Elizabeth has her first summer job seem unrelated at first—how could the pickpocket, the purloiner of two ten-foot sofas, and the person snitching meat from the kitchen be the same? But, with the help of a new friend Fran (whose only drawback is that he's four inches shorter than Mary Elizabeth), clues are cleverly assembled—and less cleverly communicated to characters whom the reader will suspect before the overtrusting heroine does. Meanwhile, two murders heighten the tension; and the obligatory near-murder of the amateur girl sleuth and resolution of the mystery are quickly followed by Mary Elizabeth's realization that being taller than a boy is not the worst thing.

Patterned, predictable, and not always plausible (the police are ingenuously ready to confide the progress of their case to a 16-year-old), this is not the popular author's best, yet it reads smoothly and is adequate as light suspense fiction.

> *A review of "The Dark and Deadly Pool," in* Kirkus Reviews, *Vol. LV, No. 22, November 15, 1987, p. 1632.*

This has neither the terror nor suspense of Nixon's best mysteries, but it's a neatly worked out procedure as Mary Elizabeth, Francis, her budding beau, and Tina, a young security guard *cum* Dr. Freud, piece together a pattern out of what appear to be disparate crimes. There's humor here in the characters of two garrulous and competitive (but sharp eyed) old dowagers, and Mary Elizabeth's slightly caustic narration adds a bit of texture.

> *Roger Sutton, in a review of "The Dark and Deadly Pool," in* Bulletin of the Center for Children's Books, *Vol. 41, No. 4, December, 1987, p. 72.*

After the initial terrifying scene in the pool, the pace slackens somewhat. Many suspects appear, but readers may find it difficult to sort them out. Some important details are hard to picture—such as a semi-fake plant by the pool in which money is hidden and the security system used to check the identification of guests. The romance between Mary Elizabeth and Fran will appeal to readers, but they may wonder why Mary Elizabeth trusted him so quickly in view of all the sinister events taking place. However, there is lots of action and a sympathetic heroine to compensate. (p. 86)

> *Judy Greenfield, in a review of "The Dark and Deadly Pool," in* School Library Journal, *Vol. 34, No. 6, February, 1988, pp. 85-6.*

Caught in the Act (1988)

In this second book of the **Orphan Train Quartet,** the story of the six Kelly children continues with 11-year-old Mike's experiences on a Missouri farm.

From the beginning, Mike believes his new family has left a secret in their native Germany, and although the tricks plotted by the Friedrichs' loutish son earn Mike severe beatings, Mike suspects that Mr. Friedrich is really whipping someone from the past—Ulrich, his eldest son. Mrs. Friedrich is glad to fill Mike with delicious food, but cowers when her husband demands her silence. When the hired man disappears without a word, Mike accuses Mr. Friedrich of murder and then discovers the secret: Ulrich died in a German prison, accused of stealing to feed the family. Mike helps to clear Mr. Friedrich, but then decides to live with an army captain and his wife at Fort Leavenworth.

Unfortunately, Mike's story suffers from one-dimensional characters and unimaginative plotting. The Friedrich family embodies a plethora of German stereotypes; their son's tricks would fool no one. Newly independent readers may need the story's cliffhangers, but they also deserve unhackneyed plot twists, interesting characters, and a richer sense of time and place.

> *A review of "Caught in the Act," in* Kirkus Reviews, *Vol. LVI, No. 5, March 1, 1988, p. 367.*

The plot is attenuated, a situation stretched into a story and given some suspense by Mike's suspicion, aroused by overheard conversation, that Friedrich has committed a serious crime and is in hiding (he isn't) and by Mike's need to change his home (he does). Period details are adequately handled; none of the characters or events of the story are historically based beyond the fact of the agency's work. The writing style is pedestrian and the characters seem overdrawn. (p. 164)

> *Zena Sutherland, in a review of "Caught in the Act," in* Bulletin of the Center for Children's Books, *Vol. 41, No. 8, April, 1988, pp. 163-64.*

The puzzle is believably pieced together as the motivations of father and son are revealed at story's end. Unfortunately, this revelation does little to extend the dimension of these two flat characters who approach ethnic stereotypes. The industry and discipline required by agrarians of the period, along with their isolation (an element which contributes to the book's suspenseful, at times melodramatic, tone), is adequately conveyed. On the other hand, information about slavery and immigration is presented in a contrived manner. Flaws outweigh attributes. Events referred to which occured in the first installment are unclear, plot threads are unresolved, and the dialogue is weak. In the final analysis, this is more of a suspense novel with a historical setting than a solid historical novel with a suspenseful storyline.

> *Julie Corsaro, in a review of "Caught in the Act," in* School Library Journal, *Vol. 34, No. 11, August, 1988, p. 97.*

If You Were a Writer (1988)

When Melia begins to ask her mother questions about what she does, her mother has all the answers. "A writer doesn't work just with a typewriter. A writer works with words. If you were a writer, you would think of words that make pictures." Later, Melia discovers that her mother asks, "what if," when she sees a scene, how she might expand on the story ideas around her, how she gets readers to want to keep reading more, and how she begins with a character and a problem to solve, and then thinks of interesting ways for that to happen. The fundamentals of

creative writing are passed along, even the adage to "show, not tell" the story, but much of this is wordy. And using the girl and her mother to stage a discussion still has all the trappings of didacticism. [Bruce] Degen's pictures lighten the atmosphere of learning, offering neighborhood scenes of a writer's life at home. The work, despite shortcomings, will be of value to readers, for it gives serious answers to the question of what a writer does. (pp. 133-34)

> *A review of "If You Were a Writer," in* Publishers Weekly, *Vol. 234, No. 11, September 9, 1988, pp. 133-34.*

Melia's mother is a writer and Melia thinks she might like to be one as well. In this perceptive re-creation of what goes on in a writer's mind, Nixon tells Melia that one must think of words that make pictures. Melia tries—a pie's fragrance is spicy, a silk blouse is slithery and soft. But there are other secrets to writing, too. "Where does a writer get ideas?" Melia asks. So her mother suggests she think about "what if." What kind of a mystery story might result from a boy seeing a diamond necklace getting caught on his dog's collar. And what if the boy were a detective in disguise? Through the continuing conversation, Melia—and readers—will learn about the creative process in an insightful and natural way. . . . There should be infinite uses for this unique offering in libraries and in English and creative writing classes as well; young writers will find it a source of inspiration, written right at their level.

> *Ilene Cooper, in a review of "If You Were a Writer," in* Booklist, *Vol. 85, No. 3, October 1, 1988, p. 324.*

I approached this book with a certain suspicion, largely because I have an inflated sense of my profession and didn't think anyone could make it understandable to children. That Bruce Degen's illustrations have such an engaging domestic warmth only increased my skepticism.

As it happens, I was wrong. This story of a young girl learning to put her imagination into words and form her words into stories is as accurate an introduction to writing as a practitioner could hope for. The instruction is tucked unobtrusively into a charming evocation of family life. Nixon's explanation of how stories are born is engaging enough to make a child take up pen and paper.

> *Jim Naughton, in a review of "If You Were a Writer," in* Book World—The Washington Post, *July 9, 1989, p. 10.*

Secret, Silent Screams (1988)

Everyone believes that the death of high school senior Barry was a copycat suicide, but his best friend Marti is convinced he was murdered. No one believes her: not his parents, nor hers; not his friends, who hide a guilty secret; not the minister, who's crusading against pro-suicide rock lyrics; not the counselors, who believe she's experiencing the classic denial stage of grief. Only Karen, a young police officer, is prepared to listen. As Marti slowly gathers evidence, she realizes that other lives, including her own, are in danger. This isn't as tight as Nixon's best. Some of

Nixon and her husband in 1989.

the clues are clumsy, and readers will be well ahead of Marti in unraveling the mystery; even the spooky terror of being alone in an empty house or of being followed by a car in a lonely street is exploited too often. But the suspense is taut, and Marti is a determined, independent hero who tracks the killer and then fights him off alone. The information about suicide causes and prevention is unobtrusive and unglamorized, especially the need for parents and friends to listen to a depressed teen's call for help.

> *Hazel Rochman, in a review of "Secret, Silent Screams," in* Booklist, *Vol. 85, No. 2, September 15, 1988, p. 151.*

The book goes in two directions—one dealing with the problem of teen suicide and the other with Marti's murder investigation. It goes astray on both counts. There is some factual and theoretical thought on the symptoms and causes of teen suicide smattered throughout the story, but not enough to be helpful or informative to readers curious about the subject. Nixon also masterfully denigrates any person who might be considered as a source of help or accurate information. The guidance counselor is condescending and incompetent; the suicide psychologist pompous and self-serving; the police, except Karen, bungling

and insensitive; the clergyman preoccupied with his campaign against rock music lyrics; and the parents well-meaning but ineffective. And since she doesn't provide any alternatives, Nixon makes the message clear that for young people in need of answers about suicide, there is no suitable confidant. As for the mystery aspect, readers who even dabble in the genre will find many flaws. The identity of the murderer leaps out within the early chapters of the book, and the heinousness of the crimes he commits far outweigh his motive. The inefficiency of police forces has long been fair game in mystery stories, but this group's disregard for the most elementary forensic data will grate on readers. Readers will find both the mystery and the discussion of teen suicide very run of the mill.

> *Joanne Aswell, in a review of "Secret, Silent Screams," in* School Library Journal, *Vol. 35, No. 3, November, 1988, p. 128.*

Nixon has done it again—written a mystery YAs will love. Based on a contemporary problem facing all teens, suicide adds an element of danger to a plot that moves along smoothly to a satisfying conclusion. The problem in the novel is the addition of the two adult viewpoints as to why Barry committed suicide, either the evil of rock music or copycat suicide. They don't add any suspense and it seems their addition only shows two reasons why young people commit suicide, like teaching a lesson inside the story. This aspect of the story was not resolved except to allow the young adult of the story to show that "she was right and the adults were wrong," as the YA I gave it to joyfully explained. This YA loved the book, and in fact, it was scary enough for her that the night she finished it, she slept on the floor of her sister's room. Don't expect to see it on your shelves once word gets around!

> *Kathryn Havris, in a review of "Secret, Silent Screams," in* Voice of Youth Advocates, *Vol. 11, No. 6, February, 1989, p. 288.*

In the Face of Danger   (1988)

The third volume in the projected "Orphan Train Quartet" tells the story of 12-year-old Megan Kelly after Emma and Benjamin Browder take her to live with them on the Kansas prairie. This exciting and touching novel projects an aura of historical reality. Megan believes that she brings bad luck to herself and those around her because of a gypsy curse. This image of herself as a "bad-luck penny" colors her perceptions of everything that happens to her and her loved ones until her kind foster mother helps her to understand that life can be what she makes it. Slowly she gains confidence in herself and is instrumental in saving her family from a killer on the run. The historical aspects of **In the Face of Danger** will have particular interest and appeal to this generation of children who hear so much about the problems of today's foster, abandoned, and street children that they will be able to relate to and understand the problems of the Kelly children and others like them 130-some odd years ago.

> *Janet E. Gelfand, in a review of "In the Face of Danger," in* School Library Journal, *Vol. 35, No. 4, December, 1988, p. 110.*

Whispers from the Dead   (1989)

Nixon's reputation as the *grande dame* of mysteries for young readers remains solidly intact with this thriller. After a swimming accident, 16-year-old Sarah Darnell had a near-death experience and begins to hear voices. Labeled as weird by her old friends, she hopes for a fresh start when she and her parents move to Houston. However, as soon as she enters her new home, Sarah feels uneasy. She's the only one who hears the frantic cries for help in Spanish, and no one in the neighborhood wants to talk about the murder which took place in the house two years earlier. When Sarah begins to have visions of the crime scene and finds previously undiscovered evidence of a second murder, her parents, refusing to believe she has psychic abilities, decide that Sarah should see a psychiatrist. Slowly, and reluctantly aided by two new friends, Sarah pieces the puzzle together, and her life almost comes to an end for a second time. Most readers will easily anticipate the outcome, but knowing what is about to happen only intensifies the suspense, and Sarah's first-person narration

adds to the intimacy of the danger and tension. A top-notch choice for all collections. (pp. 275-76)

> *Jeanette Larson, in a review of "Whispers from the Dead," in* School Library Journal, *Vol. 35, No. 13, September, 1989, pp. 275-6.*

Even die-hard Nixon fans will find this a little overblown and predictable, with one-dimensional characters, constant shivers wiggling up and down the heroine's spine, and heavy hints that the seductive, mustachioed guy with "a voice as soft as dark silk" is not what he seems. But the pace is fast, with language accessible to reluctant readers, and the haunted house is a pleasant brush with the occult.

> *Hazel Rochman, in a review of "Whispers from the Dead," in* Booklist, *Vol. 86, No. 2, September 15, 1989, p. 164.*

It's a credit to Nixon's skillful suspense-building that readers will race through the book despite its many contrivances. No one (except Sarah, who's dating him) will fail to spot the identity of the murderer early on, but this kind of one-step-ahead reading has its own appeal: our eye rolling at the heroine's gullibility is combined with a protective instinct that shudders at knowing just who is hiding behind the door.

> *Roger Sutton, in a review of "Whispers from the Dead," in* Bulletin of the Center for Children's Books, *Vol. 43, No. 2, October, 1989, p. 40.*

Star Baby   (1989)

From the dedication, it sounds as if Nixon spent her teenage years in Hollywood. **Star Baby** is the first in the new series **"Hollywood Daughters: A Family Trilogy."** The year is 1942, defense plants are springing up all over and 17 year old Abby, a once-famous child star, is trying to show her mother that she is growing up. Her pushy mother, formerly part of an unsuccessful vaudeville act, keeps trying to force Abby into childish clothes and book her into clubs where she sings the little songs from her childhood movies. When Abby discovers her agent and her mother are having an affair, she finally breaks free of her mother. She realizes she can be a successful comedienne, and leaves on a USO tour as the book ends.

Unfortunately, the writing is wooden, the characters are very stereotyped (a very strong mother, a weak father who doesn't notice how nasty his wife is, and a submissive daughter), and more soap-opera dialogue than the *action* teens look for. This is disappointing from a popular author who is usually very enjoyable.

> *Andrea Davidson, in a review of "Star Baby," in* Voice of Youth Advocates, *Vol. 12, No. 4, October, 1989, p. 215.*

Set in 1942, this story follows Abby through a few important months in her life as she, with the help of a friend, gradually gains confidence in her abilities and own wishes. Although readers may become frustrated with Abby's compliance and her too-sweet attitude towards her brother, those who enjoyed Myers' *Crystal* (Viking, 1987) will be interested in reading about another teen's venture into stardom as well as her self-examination and resolution of complicated situations.

> *Dana McDougald, in a review of "Star Baby,"* in School Library Journal, *Vol. 35, No. 15, November, 1989, p. 128.*

A popular writer of YA suspense novels tries something different here with mixed results. Instead of contemporary teenagers caught up in eerie adventures, Nixon harks back to the early 1940s, re-creating a colorful era of fabulous Hollywood stars and increasing public anxiety over war in Europe. . . . Whether Nixon has purposefully larded her plot with clichés and caricatures is not really clear, and savvy readers will probably lose patience with wishy-washy Abby, her obnoxious parent, and the relationship that never gets beyond stereotype. But younger readers unfamiliar with the 1940s Hollywood mystique might be lured by the author's broadly stroked view of glamorous days gone by, dig right into Abby's coming-of-age struggle, and look forward to successive episodes in the planned trilogy.

> *Stephanie Zvirin, in a review of "Star Baby,"* in Booklist, *Vol. 86, No. 5, November 1, 1989, p. 541.*

You Bet Your Britches, Claude   (1989)

Shirley and Claude, the pioneer odd couple from Texas, come back for a fourth go-around. Looking to settle down with their adopted son, Tom, Shirley and Claude start wrangling about the boy's sister, Bessie. Shirley wants to adopt her, too, but Claude thinks there will be no peace with a chattering girl around. That doesn't stop Shirley and Bessie from scheming to wrest the girl away from where she's working, to capture a cowboy who is trying to clean out the general store, and, finally, to catch a bank thief. Bessie's eyes are so sharp and her detection skills so honed that the sheriff makes her a full-fledged deputy. Now Claude changes his mind about having her around—things would be peaceful, he's sure, with a deputy sheriff in the house—and he agrees to the adoption. Nixon's telling, slightly less exaggerated here than in the other books, is enticing, and Bessie, stepping center stage, breathes new life into the series. As usual, [Tracey Campbell] Pearson's zesty watercolors are right on target, roping in all the fun.

> *Ilene Cooper, in a review of "You Bet Your*

Britches, Claude," in Booklist, *Vol. 86, No. 4, October 15, 1989, p. 462.*

Another zany tale about Nixon's silly pioneer couple from Texas, Shirley and Claude. The strength of the story is not in its plot, which is entertaining and warmly predictable, but in the extraordinary use of language. Nixon writes with vigor and charm, using a down-home Texas style that is hilarious. The story as a whole has a rhythm and flow that make it ideal for reading aloud. Characters are clearly drawn, mostly through dialogue, and the central conflict, convincing Claude to let chatty little Bessie join their family when all he yearns for is "peace and quiet," is nicely resolved. Pearson's fluid cartoon-style illustrations complement the mood of the story well, mirroring the vitality of the tale, but drawing readers deeper into the book with details and funny visual subplots.

> *Lee Bock Pulaski, in a review of "You Bet Your Britches, Claude,"* in School Library Journal, *Vol. 36, No. 1, January, 1990, p. 87.*

Overnight Sensation   (1990)

Like its predecessor, **Star Baby,** set in the 1940s, the latest installment in Nixon's show-biz trilogy also explores mother-daughter relationships as they evolve against a background of Hollywood glamour. It's 20 years, four husbands, and one 16-year-old daughter since Abby Grant first made her comedy debut. And while she's learned a lot about being a star, she still has much to learn about being a parent. That's certainly the opinion of her daughter, Cassie, who, as narrator, relates her struggle to step out of mother Abby's shadow. There aren't any real villains here—even Abby, stubborn, insecure, selfish, obviously means well—and Cassie's endeavors to get mom's attention are generally as tepid as the novel's late 1960s-early 1970s Hollywood backdrop. But there's very little question that nice Cassie will make good at whatever she tries, whether its rounding up funds for her boyfriend's movie or convincing Abby she's an individual as well as a daughter. For lightweight entertainment, that's just fine. (pp. 1693-94)

> *Stephanie Zvirin, in a review of "Overnight Sensation,"* in Booklist, *Vol. 86, No. 17, May 1, 1990, pp. 1693-94.*

Maud (Fuller) Petersham

1889-1971

Miska Petersham

1888-1960

Maud—American author and illustrator of picture books, nonfiction, and fiction; reteller; and editor.

Miska—(Born Petrezselyem Mikaly) Hungarian-born American author and illustrator of picture books, nonfiction, and fiction; reteller; and editor.

Major works include *Miki* (1929), *The Christ Child, as Told by Matthew and Luke* (1931), *The Story Book of Foods from the Fields: Wheat, Corn, Rice, Sugar* (1936), *An American ABC* (1941), *The Rooster Crows: A Book of American Rhymes and Jingles* (1945).

Considered among the most distinguished American authors and artists for children of this century, the Petershams are lauded for their innovation in subject matter, approach, and artistic style. Combining their interests, talents, and backgrounds to create works acknowledged for their beauty, richness, variety, and appeal, the husband and wife team is credited with introducing an international scope to the American picture book, for developing informational books that are attractive as well as informative, and for setting a standard in book illustration through their mastery of the lithographic method, experimentation with printing processes, and emphasis on total book design. They directed their works, many of which have a patriotic or religious theme and are inspired by personal experience, to children and young people from preschool through the middle grades. Enhancing the descriptions of their subjects with pictures that elaborate on the texts, the Petershams wrote simple but lively narratives and provided illustrations for their works which ranged from brilliant multicolor lithographs and stylized art deco designs to delicate watercolors and Hungarian folk motifs taken from those of Miska's birthplace. Trained as artists in their respective countries of origin, the Petershams usually worked together on their books: Maud handled the rough dummies and the writing of the texts while Miska planned the page layouts and finalized the illustrations.

The Petershams began their career as illustrators of fiction and anthologies by such writers as Charles and Mary Lamb, Carlo Collodi, Washington Irving, Kenneth Grahame, Johanna Spyri, and Carl Sandburg; they also contributed illustrations to the popular series My Book House and My Travelship as well as to textbooks and children's magazines. In 1924, they provided illustrations for *The Poppy Seed Cakes,* written by Mary Elizabeth Clark and Margery Closely Quigley under the joint pseudonym Margery Clark; this book, a story about young Andrewshek, his relatives, and his talking animal friends which is illustrated with glowing colors and peasant details, is considered a pivotal work in the development of the picture

book. The Petershams's first collaborative work, *Miki,* describes the adventures of a small American boy who goes to visit his grandparents in Budapest. Based on the boyhood experiences that Miska shared with the Petershams's son, Miki, it is often considered the first American picture book to be set in a foreign country and is credited with stimulating other writers and artists to portray international settings in their works. The Petershams later wrote and illustrated two additional *Miki* stories that incorporate Maud's childhood memories and introduce Miki's cousin Mary. The daughter of a Baptist minister, Maud reflected her interest in the Bible in several of the works she composed with her husband, the most notable being *The Christ Child, as Told by Matthew and Luke,* a reverent and authentic interpretation of the birth and childhood of Jesus. The Petershams are also respected for their six series of nonfiction titles on such topics as food, clothing, homes, utensils, and transportation which were published between 1933 and 1939 in omnibus volumes and twenty-four single editions. Following their subjects from their invention through the present, the books are noted as clear and interesting overviews which integrate illustrations featuring child protagonists, animals, and toys as well as examples of historical art for educational purposes. With the advent of World War II, the Petershams concentrated on works with a national theme that are known collectively as the "This Is America" series and include an alphabet book; a collection of games, rhymes, and riddles; and histories of American presidents from Washington through Eisenhower, American postage stamps, and the Virginia colony of Williamsburg. Although *An American ABC* and its companion volume *The Rooster Crows: A Book of American Rhymes and Jingles* were initially noted for expressing a positive view of historical and contemporary America in their sincere evocation of great individuals, landmarks, symbols, and principles, the books were later criticized for their inclusion of stereotypical illustrations of ethnic groups and rhymes in black dialect; a revised edition of *The Rooster Crows* was published in 1969 that deleted the offensive material. The Petershams were also the creators of picture books for very young children of which *Get-a-way and Háry János* (1933), the adventures of a loyal stuffed horse and his boastful toy soldier friend, and *The Circus Baby* (1950), the story of how a mother elephant learns to appreciate her baby for what he is, are among the most well-received. *An American ABC* was named a Caldecott honor book in 1942, and *The Rooster Crows* received the Caldecott Medal in 1946. In addition, the American Institute of Graphic Arts held a thirty-year retrospective of the Petershams's works in 1953.

(See also *Something about the Author,* Vol. 17; *Contemporary Authors New Revision Series,* Vol. 29; *Contemporary Authors,* Vols. 33-36, rev. ed. [obituary for Maud Petersham] and Vols. 73-76; and *Dictionary of Literary Biography,* Vol. 22.)

AUTHORS' COMMENTARY

Each day Miska and I are working, making pictures for children; and when I say "for children" I mean just that. In some ways we do not much care whether grown-ups like our pictures or not; but we do care whether children like them. The highest compliment we can have is to hold some child's happy interest and attention with one of our pictures. It is only fair, we believe, to make a child's book for the child and not for the grown-up who gives it to him. There are many reasons why a child may not like pictures made for grown-ups.

There is no reason, though, why a grown-up should not like pictures made for children, unless, of course, he is very badly petrified. We, I must admit, get an immense amount of pleasure from a child's book with good illustrations. . . . One must be partially grown-up, I believe, to appreciate the beautiful illustrations of Rackham and Dulac, but even a little child can love the pictures of Boutet de Monvel.

We have a bad habit (perhaps it is odd rather than bad) of picking up a book, looking carefully over the illustrations and make-up, and judging it from these. This, we

must admit, is not showing a proper respect for the content. (pp. 85-6)

People with regard for good illustrations wonder why children are sometimes delighted with pictures that are in most respects very poor; but any picture that has a strong appeal for a child is worthy of some consideration, for there must be something in it that holds and interests him. It may be that the illustration tells a story very obviously and clearly, or it may be clear bright color that attracts the child or very decided action in the picture, or perhaps a certain kind of humor or fun which the child especially appreciates. (It is easy for grown people to forget that what a small child thinks is very funny is rather different from what a grown-up thinks is very funny, unless the grown-up is considering the situation from a child's point of view.) A good illustration should have the qualities that I have mentioned—story, color, action, and fun—but it should also be beautiful in design and line and should have feeling. The design should be simple and the line sensitive. A good illustration does not grow old-fashioned because of treatment. Today one can get no better illustrations for the stories of Dickens than those originally made by Cruikshank. This is true also of the drawings of Tenniel for the first edition of *Alice in Wonderland*. When I say there should be color in an illustration I do not mean color as one ordinarily used the term. The making of color plates is now so costly that in many cases it is prohibitive, but even a black and white drawing can be full of "color," this "color" being given by the different grays. What I mean by the other requirements—story, action, and fun—is obvious from the terms.

The pictures a small child looks at are perhaps going to mean as much to him as the text he struggles to read. Of course he may not appreciate the difference between a book with badly drawn pictures and a poor layout and the one with good pictures, good type, and suitable make-up, but it is certain that the taste of the grown-up child has been influenced by all that was about him when he was small—so by all means give him beautiful books when he is little. All the beauty we have the power to grasp we want and need, and the child who is not learning to see beauty is losing an inestimable source of happiness.

It is more fun to make pictures for children than to make them for grown-ups. One has much greater freedom. The child is not restricted by hard facts. When you make pictures for him he understands the fanciful things you draw quite as well as the pictures of things that appear as they really are in life. Although on some points the child is a severe critic—and objects seriously if we put three buttons on Alice's coat in one picture and two in the next—on the other hand there is nothing that cannot seem real to him. In fact, he *wants* to exercise his imagination. He wants his animals sometimes to act as he would, not just to walk on four feet in their own fur clothes, but to sleep in real beds, eat from real bowls, and wear coats or skirts. Another reason why we like to make pictures for children is because we can put into the pictures things that please ourselves without any fear of being criticized by the author; for if an author writes children's books well he has imagination and likes to let us exercise ours in the pictures. We draw houses we think it would be fun to live in, furniture that pleases us, and special kinds of clothes that suit us too. You may not agree with us that the house we planned for the Three Bears is much to be preferred to an ordinary, suburban, lace-curtained domicile, but we think so and have built a home like it under the pines. (pp. 86-7, 89)

This sounds as if making illustrations for children were all fun. We wish this were true, but it is not. Sometimes a picture does not come out at all as we want it to. When you have put all your heart and time into the work and are not satisfied with results there is no fun in that. Suppose you have a new story or poem to make a picture for. You have a beautiful, clean, white paper and a soft pencil (it is impossible to think with a hard pencil). The story or poem tells of a little girl picking oranges in southern France. You cannot remember exactly what an orange tree looks like, and you can't find a good picture of one in your files. If you try to make up one the drawing will almost certainly be wrong. Then the little girl must be dressed correctly—another search through the files for the correct costume, with unsatisfactory results. However, after a time orange tree and costume are made right. At this point the girl refuses to stand properly on the ladder in the position you want, so you hunt up a ladder, Miska poses or Maud poses, and at last you get really started on the picture. But by this time you have lost all your feeling for the little girl, and this gets into the picture. There is no use trying to make a picture one does not feel. We often work at tables facing each other, as we are a right-handed, left-handed combination, and Miska sometimes asks why I am making such funny faces. Then I realize that I have been thinking out the feeling and expression of the character that I am trying to put on paper. . . .

Miska came from Hungary and had his instruction in a Budapest art school—a school that gave him a thorough training in all branches of art work and a good technical knowledge. I studied in an art school where I learned little, and Miska has been my severe and thorough teacher. I, too, have become very critical as time has gone on; and when we can make a picture that passes and pleases us both we are happy. (p. 89)

> *Maud Petersham, "Illustrating Books for Children," in* The Elementary English Review, *Vol. 2, No. 3, March, 1925, pp. 85-9.*

GENERAL COMMENTARY

May Massee

I met [the Petershams] in Chicago when they were working on the drawings for Carl Sandburg's ***Rootabaga Stories.*** Miska wanted to travel in the Middle West to get the feeling for that book. Then they did the pictures and they are delightfully true to the spirit of the book. But Miska was still so close to his European upbringing that many of the pictures seemed to have come straight from Central Europe rather than from the United States. If Miska should make those pictures today, they would have absolutely the American feel, because, with the versatility of a true artist, and with the close association with his own

very American little boy, and Mary, their niece, he has absorbed the American scene. Miki and Mary in their latest picture book are unmistakably little Americans in any country of the globe or in any costume they adopt.

Then came ***The Poppy Seed Cakes,*** stories that Margery Clark wrote from association with a nice old peasant woman after she came to America. And that was just the right medium for Miska to give the best of his experience. Miska said that he wanted to do something he had never done: use very rich flat colors, and have colored borders on the pages. And so that book was made, glowing with color, with all the richness of peasant embroidery—a genuine art contribution brought from Central Europe to this country to stay. Of course the children loved it, and for ten years it has been one of the most popular children's books, as it *is* one of the best. (p. 1468)

People often ask what part Maud does and what part Miska does in a book. Maud does the writing after they talk over what they are going to put into the book. Before they made the ***Miki*** book, they went on a pilgrimage to Hungary, so that Maud could see the reality of what Miska was talking about, and so that Maud could help choose what material would be most effective in the book. They plan their books together that way, and Maud makes a great many of the sketches and plans the layouts; that is, what pictures to make and where to put them. When it comes to the actual drawing in the book, they decided a long time ago that it would be better to have Miska do that, because it is important to have unity throughout in the pictures of a book. Their instinct for what children will like is a gift they both have, and it is a combination of the European and the American love for children that makes their books so fascinating.

The Poppy Seed Cakes and ***Miki*** give Miska's background. ***The Ark of Father Noah*** was a bit of Maud's, and ***Auntie,*** of course, is as full of Maud's own childhood as ***Miki*** is of Miska's.

When Maud was a little girl, her father was a minister in Kingston, N.Y., and she used to sit in church and draw pictures of the Bible stories, of which her favorite was Noah's Ark. She had always wanted to make a picture book of it, and one day she went to see "Green Pastures" here in New York, and called me up after she got back from the theater, and said, "We just *have* to make that Noah's Ark book! I have been to see 'Green Pastures' and have been making sketches on my program all the way home." So they made Father and Mother Noah and all the amusing animals in a thoroughly child-like version.

Then came ***Auntie.*** "Auntie" is really Maud's Auntie, and the story about the little girl who hid in the barn when the others went off so that she could stay with "Auntie" is true, and that is how Maud stayed with Auntie for two years when she was a little girl, and how she knew all about the Quaker school and the stern grandfather who meant to be kind. And the part about Auntie and Miki is true, too, because Auntie has been Miki's best friend from the time when he was a baby and, although now she is very old and not quite as strong as she was, she still is a great and beloved power in all their lives.

From Miki, *written and illustrated by Maud and Miska Petersham.*

Next came **The Christ Child,** for which they traveled to Jerusalem to get their pictures. They say that, while they could have made some of the pictures from photographs, they never could have known really how the country looks from description or from photographs. They had to see the almond trees in blossom around Nazareth to get that lovely black and white picture of the little child shepherd with the lamb on the hill outside the city. And so with all the other pictures that are so human and yet so beautiful that they add to the beauty of the text. It took a long quiet sojourn in Palestine to be able to make them. Probably, back of them all, is the influence of the Italian primitives on Miska when he spent months in Italy as a very young man, drinking in all the beauty that the museums could show him.

Then came the toy book. Wherever they go, they collect toys. Toys mean to them the evidence of a civilization as well as its art. So they made the lovely **Get-a-way and Háry János;** taking an American toy and a Hungarian toy and putting them into a toyland which could exist nowhere but in America, and yet which has touches of color and design from many other countries. All the toys in that book are really toys, and children who love it are storing up pictures that will help make history vivid to them later, although they won't know it at the time, and don't know it now.

That same year **The Story of Things We Use** series grew out of a desire to make attractive books of information for young children with pictures as an integral part of the text. Their immediate popularity in schools and in the trade shows that they fill a need. (pp. 1469-70)

The modern Russian picture books undoubtedly gave some of the inspiration for these books. Those Russians know the value of pictorial representation of facts and we all have a long way to go in that direction.

And now comes **Miki and Mary.** Mary is Miki's little cousin, and she lived with the Petershams for two or three years when they were both small. Of course, the trip they take is really a trip that Maud and Miska took a number of years ago when they saw the country as children would see it. The children have perfectly natural adventures in each of the famous places they visit, but the backgrounds are beautiful travel pictures, which every child will absorb and acquire without knowing, a background of beauty and appreciation of other lands besides his own.

It is easy to write about the books—they have set a new standard for book making.

But it is frightfully difficult to put into a few words what the Petershams mean to children's books today. Maud with her American background of New England and New York and Vassar College, Miska with his European background of years in Hungary, Italy, and England, have contrived between them to translate much of the beauty of the old world into terms of the new. This they have done so vividly and so simply that their books have a life-long value for the children who absorb them. And this doesn't half tell the story. (p. 1470)

May Massee, "The Petershams: The Story of Two Favorite Artists for Children," in Publishers Weekly, *Vol. 126, No. 16, October 20, 1934, pp. 1467-70.*

Irene Smith Green

For two full decades the name (rather than names) of Maud and Miska Petersham has been known constantly to all whose experience with children's books goes back to the 1920's. This old and rich acquaintance is deeply rooted in our picture book literature. It is interwoven with the growth of better illustration in books for the young. It stands the test of years because it is planted in the bedrock of good work, work that is sound, informed, and enduring. . . .

When *Miki* was published . . . in 1929, a wave of fresh air breezed through the current picture book modes. At once we knew that our immediate borders included far-off Hungary, stretched there by a book that was honest and gaily childlike. That year we saw how the children loved it. *Miki* has never faltered in their regard. It is still asked for, slept with, worn to tatters in growing families, and replaced continually in public library children's rooms. (p. 248)

[The Petershams'] lovely illustrations for *The Christ Child* were inspired during three months which Maud and Miska Petersham spent in Palestine. There they made the sketches, then completed the drawings in Leipzig. Today, as fifteen years ago, it is the Bible picture book which children and their elders cherish first. (p. 249)

In 1941 we were all more aware of America than we had been since 1917, and we welcomed *An American ABC* with its spirited interpretations of The Liberty Bell, The Declaration of Independence, The Mayflower, Yankee Doodle, and other symbols of our national life. The artists offered it as an expression of their own vital creed. Which brings us to *The Rooster Crows, A Book of American Rhymes and Jingles*. . . . Designed as companion to *An American ABC,* this is Americana highly appealing to the young. The beautiful pictures in soft, airy colors are full of humorous, homely details which confirm the rhymes' origins in American soil. These seventy-seven jingles, finger games, and rhymes for skipping rope and counting out are a part of our language: "Bushels of wheat . . .", "This little pig . . .", "Roses are red . . .", "The bear went over the mountain. . . ."

Maud and Miska Petersham work together on the same pictures. Theirs has been called "a perfect collaboration." Miska is right-handed, Maud left; surely a partnership by destiny. Their texts come off the same way, from both, although Maud does most of the actual writing. (pp. 251-52)

They thank their son for serving not only as a frequent model, but also as touchstone. They learned wisdom, in reaching children's tastes by watching Miki's reactions to their drawings. As long as he remained unmoved they worked to find the missing spark. Their approach therefore is always lifelike and vigorous. They tackle their stories *pictorially:* places for the pictures first, the text to be adjusted.

These artists came in when our present picture-book era was young. *Miki* set a standard. They took their responsibility seriously, in a period when too often children's illustration was, for lesser workmen, no more than a casual interlude. From the start they made complete layout dummies, worked closely with their engraver, guarded each step toward the book. With infinite painstaking, free from hurry and from avarice, Maud and Miska Petersham have cared only to give their best. In this they have had their true reward. (p. 255)

Irene Smith Green, "Maud and Miska Petersham," in The Horn Book Magazine, *Vol. XXII, No. 4, July-August, 1946, pp. 248-55.*

May Massee

[In 1924] the Petershams used Miska's understanding of frank gay color in the beautiful old-gold, vermilion, bright blue and black of the pictures for *The Poppy Seed Cakes* by Margery Clark. Before this they had been doing excellent illustration of the more conventional type. This was the first time that they had made a book just the way they wanted to make it. Here was a text that brought the old world into the new and the chance to express the beauty that came with Miska and his knowledge of the traditional peasant art of Europe.

The Petershams have always been innovators. Their *Miki* with its delightful Hungarian pictures ushered in a long line of other artists' children from every quarter of the world. In the school field they illustrated a set of readers that charmed the children so that other publishers scurried around to find artists to create rival sets. They were very much attracted to the Russian educational picture books that showed various phases of Soviet life in revealing and, at the same time, imaginative color lithographs. The best artists have worked on these books—they often have real beauty and humor, they are paperbound, distributed by the millions, and make a unique and thrilling experiment in education.

From the Petershams' interest in these books grew a whole series of picture books of the arts and industries. Here are some of their best drawings and the pictures show their mastery of the lithographer's craft. No one surpasses Miska in his color and in his use of beautiful gray. These books are a monument to their own art and industry and the series would have flowered to more use and beauty if the publishers had not been so insistent on speed and the desire for "one more series this year." Artists do their best work when they can set their own time and pace and do not have to conform too much to a set pattern.

When they planned *The Christ Child* they had the perfect text in the King James Version. For the pictures they wanted to make the color drawings just as they would appear in the book. They wanted to forget all the toilsome processes of color separations necessitated by the costs of bookmaking and just make beautiful finished water-color drawings for illustrations. But . . . there was no printer here who could undertake such a task of platemaking and printing. So they went to Germany, where they found the three-generations-old firm of Meissner and Buch in Leipzig. These printers were artists as keen as the Petershams to get just the right colors from their plates.

That book was sheer joy in the making from start to finish. A trip to Palestine gave them their inspiration, the costumes, characters and the contours of the country. Add to all these their own great reverence and love for their subject and you have one of the most beautiful books ever made for children. (pp. 234-36)

> *May Massee, "Developments of the Twentieth Century," in* Illustrators of Children's Books: 1744-1945, *Bertha E. Mahony, Louise Payson Latimer, and Beulah Folmsbee, eds., The Horn Book Inc., 1947. pp. 215-46.*

Barbara Bader

When the first systematic study of children's preferences in book illustration was made in 1922, it was 'discovered' that youngsters respond to storytelling quality, humor and action. A 1929-30 investigation, confirming and extending these findings, identified realistic presentation and familiarity of subject matter as determinants. Such studies, still being conducted, have to be viewed with a certain bemusement—one 'discovered' no interest among fourth-graders in a picture of toilet articles—and no uncertain skepticism (as testing the obvious by the available); but in the field of textbooks they make a limited kind of sense. If Tom, Dick and Harry take to a funny, lively picture of a bear making pancakes, in its own way realistic and familiar, they will want to read what goes with it. So went the reasoning, and such were the results that the Petershams were the leading illustrators of readers in the Twenties. *The Poppy Seed Cakes* aside and *Miki* as yet unseen, they are represented in the 1929 compilation *Realms of Gold* by more entries, all told, than any other illustrator(s) except Rackham.

With *The Poppy Seed Cakes* and *Miki,* however, they came to be identified with the colorful treatment of highly flavored subjects, whether foreign, religious, patriotic or "things we use." But the nature of a book does not compel interest in it, and this the Petershams seem to have realized instinctively. (pp. 38-9)

This is not to deny that *Miki* was 'the first of the international picture books,' as May Massee liked to say, and in fact it was roundly welcomed for its depiction of "everyday life in a picture book country." That Hungary should, in a picturebook, become a "picture book country" is a curious inversion accounted for by the fact that the Petershams tacitly propelled their sneakered son Miki into the high-booted childhood of his father Miska. Many of their successors did likewise, and to a generation growing up on 'foreign dolls' and peasant party costumes it made no difference. Among their elders as well, thinking of the Old Country as old-fashioned was commonplace, while thinking of it as picturesque was encouraged by the relative plainness of American life.

Going abroad means, moreover, the disruption of routine, shucking responsibility, following impulse—for Miki, wanting to be in Hungary and, without a by-your-leave, being there; knocking at a strange door, sitting at a strange fire, sleeping in a strange bed; taking the family goose to find grass, staying overnight at a shepherds' camp, going off with the goose and the shepherds' dog to Budapest: all highly irregular and at home unthinkable.

Far from being an everyday story of Hungary or anywhere, *Miki* is a cheerful flight of fancy colored by its setting. Boy and dog and goose sit around talking, that's how they decide to go to Budapest, and once there they have a high old time running back and forth across the bridges between Buda and Pest, comforting a tearful, tongue-less lion, riding and riding on the merry-go-round. Detail, incident and improvisation keep it going without a point or a plot, on the assurance that children would love to be in Miki's new boots—as who wouldn't?

The best of the pictures, the big curtained bed piled high with pillows, boxes in the flat color and surface patterns, and with them Miki's energy—his jersey half off, his sneakers askew. The color and design are organic to the material, the composition achieves a kinetic balance. But go outdoors and the color becomes raw, its tints crude, the effect stagey: there is no less energy in the drawing—the three vagabonds dash across the bridges with a gusto that is contagious—only less finesse in the ensemble. (pp. 39-40)

In the fall of [1930] the first of the Petershams' Bible stories, *The Christ Child,* came out: soft and comparatively delicate, done in watercolors, printed in Germany. The illustrations are no less anecdotal, however, which accounts at least equally for the book's popular success.

Given the freedom to work as they would, in watercolors, and a subject that was eminently theirs, the Petershams produced in *Miki and Mary: Their Search for Treasures* a more perfect synthesis and a vicarious experience hard to top. *Miki and Mary* is all make-believe, the jaunt of two American children through a Europe composed unabashedly of picturebook places. Adventure is what they're after but children is what they are, and if their ocean liner isn't boarded by pirates, well, it does have a bang-up Punch and Judy show. At Mont-Saint-Michel they decide against dungeons and exchange their swords for an omelet pan, on the Grand Canal proud, haughty "Maria" gets dunked and comes out just plain Mary. Still, they stride about in wooden shoes (Brittany) and Turkish slippers (Rhodes) and bare feet (Jerusalem), and there's no end of treasures to fill their crossbone chest.

For those children, the great majority, to whom a trip is only as good as what can be brought back, there is no better picture in the book, and the Petershams, alert to children's interests, don't omit an item. In the suggestive rendering of the Piazza San Marco, however, they merge immediacy and movement with air and space and architectural splendor for a prime evocation of place. The wave border, ingeniously worked—see how the fishes come out of the white stripe, how one seems to grin, another to gasp—supplies a bond, a base, a rhythmic surge and, when there's no picture to look at, a bridging distraction.

Four years had passed since *The Christ Child,* and *Miki and Mary* was printed here, from plates made by a special method known as the Knudsen process. It is very much the product of its manufacture. Capitalizing on offset lithography's way with fade-ins and fade-outs, the Petershams eschewed their usual strong outlines and contrasts and designed instead for thin films of ink and graduated color tones, sometimes with real sensitivity.

Later, in the group of books picturing Early American stanzas and sayings which includes the Caldecott winner *The Rooster Crows,* the lithographic effects become a mannerism, essentially meaningless, and what would better have been broad and robust is finicky and fussy. As historic recreations, they have the slick quaintness of a wax-museum Williamsburg.

The Box with Red Wheels and *Circus Baby,* on the other hand, brought the Petershams back to where they began, portraying animals for the delight of small children. What can be inside the box with red wheels, the animals wonder, and one by one they look in, call out ("Moo-oo-oo-oo-oo-oo . . . Q-U-A-C-K"), shake their heads or flop in. The dog, looking wise, knows the answer; "It was a baby"—who pops up and won't be comforted until her mother lets the animals return. Repetition, suspense, surprise, satisfaction; barnyard animals, their sounds, their friendly presence; and a baby, wondering too, a fuzzy-haired fat baby: for a three-year-old, it is ideal. So is the look of the book, bright and solid and amply spaced, what is obvious about the drawing softened by the warm beige contours.

The Circus Baby is not without its lapses into the conveniently cute or comical but the spectacle of elephants playing house, of mother elephant trying to bring up baby after the fashion of the clown family, is inherently endearing and funny and, "after all, *you* are an ELEPHANT" concludes the futile attempt with a nice plug for the natural order of things. When the Petershams addressed themselves to children and what they enjoy (or don't), their work has a sturdiness that sustains it irrespective of the subject. (pp. 41-2)

> *Barbara Bader, "Foreign Backgrounds," in her* American Picturebooks from Noah's Ark to the Beast Within, *Macmillan Publishing Co., Inc., 1976, pp. 38-59.*

TITLE COMMENTARY

Miki (1929)

[*Miki*] is the story of a little boy who heard his father talking about Hungary and who managed to get there himself. Maud and Miska Petersham have brought to this book all the brightness of atmosphere and character of illustration for which they have long been known. The story itself was first told to their own small son, chiefly about Mr. Petersham's own boyhood experiences in Hungary—adventures with Sari, the goose, with Matyi, the shepherd's dog, stories of the gypsy camp on the road to Budapest. And because of the manner of its inception, there is about it the intimate touch of verity to which children so quickly respond.

> *Helen Ferris, in a review of "Miki," in The*

From The Christ Child, as told by Matthew and Luke, *written and illustrated by Maud and Miska Petersham.*

> Bookman, *New York, Vol. LXX, No. 3, November, 1929, p. 308.*

Picture books with gaily patterned borders and quaint foreign designs have been increasingly popular abroad since the war, and their beautiful, colored pictures have been, I think, instrumental in raising our own standards of color printing. . . . [*Miki* belongs in this class]. . . . The Petershams, already well loved for their other picture books, have made a gay and altogether delightful volume about the surprising things a small American boy did and saw when he returned to visit his grandparents in Budapest. Undoubtedly this is the ideal way to acquaint young readers with geography and racial differences.

> *Rachel Field, in a review of "Miki," in* The Saturday Review of Literature, *Vol. 6, No. 17, November 16, 1929, p. 403.*

[*Miki*] is a gay book, and for better or worse Hungary will seem an incredibly gay and romantic place to those who meet it first with Miki.

This book has, above all, the quality of exuberant childhood. The bright color for which the Petershams are known is there too and, though one may wish for a hint of something beyond what is on the surface, there is undeniable attraction in their pages. It is indicative of the way your artist is going to note that the Petershams wrote the text for their book. Innumerable advantages are inherent in this way of working, and one hopes that in later books these artists will solve more successfully the relation of words to pictures; a drawing can have a greater share in recording the story in addition to delineating background detail and stating color.

Lynd Ward, in a review of "Miki," in New York Herald Tribune Books, *November 17, 1929, p. 9.*

The Ark of Father Noah and Mother Noah   (1930)

[In *The Ark of Father Noah and Mother Noah*] the pictures are gay in color and delightfully whimsical and toy-like in design—a book that has gaiety and charm. A little streamlet of text goes along the pictures—it tells of the doings of Noah and Mrs. Noah and Shem and Ham and Japheth and the animals. But the real joy of this book is in the beholding of Noah and Mrs. Noah stepping joyously out of the ark, and Mrs. Noah stooping down to fondle the large bright flowers that are before them, or in the colored and large-beaked birds who are stretching their wings on the top of the ark, or in Mrs. Noah trying to remember stories that will win the animals out of the tedium that has fallen on them—the animals getting glummer and glummer and the rabbits not even pretending to listen!

Padraic Colum, in a review of "The Ark of Father Noah and Mother Noah," in The New Republic, *Vol. LXV, No. 833, November 19, 1930, p. 24.*

This flat, square, highly colored volume is certain to delight any infant beyond the age of four. No children who have suffered the mingled joys and deprivations of rainy days have ever in my experience failed to respond to any tolerably exciting account of the great rain, with Noah and his family and all the animals, two by two, tucked snugly away in that incredible ark. And the Petersham version is a much more than tolerable account of the fabulous flood. It is unaffected, moves crisply and unselfconsciously, and smacks far less than most stories for children of the will to amuse and instruct. The diction is simple and colorful and comprehensible to the veriest babes; and the pictures are delectable, clear in color and gayly conceived. Here is not the conventional march of the carnivora, the hippopotami, etc. Instead we have Father Noah, in his blue robe and curly white patriarchal beard, down on his knees counting the endless procession of bright-colored bugs and insects. "This took a long time. Mother Noah helped him."

The tribulations of the Noah family with that heterogeneous herd of animals during the course of those forty days of rain make a poignant story. "It was gloomy, gloomy. Rain, rain! Forty days it rained. The rain made the animals gloomy. His Majesty the Lion . . . sulked, and the giraffes were most unhappy." Whereupon follows some whimsical data in the vein of the "Just So Stories" of Mr. Rudyard Kipling, as to where the giraffe got his long neck, the camel his thirstlessness; and for budding anthropologists there is a deliciously plausible account of what happened, alas! to the poor dinosaurs. . . .

I should like, though, if I may, to take the Petershams to task for their little preface, "The Characters in the Story."

In it they explain that "there were some other people in the story, but they were more bad than good. They were not important, so we won't make any pictures of them." Whereupon follows a space with "NO PICTURES" in large letters arched across it. Which is no adequate compensation for the absence of any picture of the wicked ones which have, I believe, a legitimate place in any child's story of the ark. And isn't the juxtaposition of "people more bad than good and not important" a slightly smug *non sequitur?*

If *The Ark of Father Noah and Mother Noah* has not quite the freshness of the authors' earlier *Miki,* it is perhaps not only because the story of the flood is an oft-told tale, but also because it is to be presumed that neither of the Petershams has ever seen the ark with his or her own eyes. Whereas one of them, at least, actually grew up in Hungary, where the Miki of their earlier volume bounces about in huge Hungarian feather beds, participates in the herding of geese and the making of strudel and the building of a Christmas manger for Jesus. Nevertheless, both volumes are certainly indicated for the 1930 library of the well-booked child.

Florence Haxton Britten, "It Ain't Gonna Rain No Mo'," in New York Herald Tribune Books, *November 30, 1930, p. 8.*

The writing and the illustrating of *The Ark of Father Noah and Mother Noah* must be credited to two heads and hearts rather than one. Published in 1930, this version has some significant stylistic traits. Every page contains a humorous lithograph of Noah, his family, or the animals. Throughout the book humor and optimism are reflected in both the illustrations and the text. (p. 54)

The Petershams opted to divide the story into four chapters. Each segment is short; the first chapter is the longest, and each of the other three is progressively shorter. For youngsters the two beginning chapters would be most fascinating since they deal with the preparations of the ark and the time spent on the ark. Using a straightforward narration that could be easily read by third graders, Maud and Miska intertwined the Biblical story along with their own commonplace episodic details. In the first chapter, after they related [the Biblical story] . . . , they extended the happenings to include the day to day progress of Noah and his family in building the ark, finding the animals, and loading the ark. In the beginning of this narrative they wrote:

> So Noah had built the Ark just as he had been told. He had made a little mistake in the size of the door, but he felt that would not matter. He knew the rest of the building was all correct.

Toward the end of the chapter it says:

> Poor Father Noah! He had made a mistake. The door of the Ark was a little too small for some of the very, very large animals to go in. It was raining harder now and there was no time nor chance to enlarge the opening.

The following narrative concerning those left behind has continual appeal. Children have a real fascination with prehistoric animals. Somehow the Petershams were aware of this interest, and were able to humanize the formal scripture by adding:

> The Dinosaurs wept. The Mammoths and the Baluchitheres, the Thunder Lizards and the Caronivores and the "Dippys" all wept because they could not go with Noah.

The second chapter, "The Rain", is more like charming folklore, the story contains enough detail to keep the narrative alive, and to maintain the interest of the intended audience—in this case young children—with the progress of this floating menage. The reader finds out that the animals are unhappy with their living quarters, their food, and the weather. (pp. 54-5)

The real climax of the story comes in chapter three, "The Sun". This chapter has a lulling effect. The animals and the humans surmount their frustrations, and bask in the promise of a new land. The animals have all been illustrated in happy, positive poses, and when at last the dove brings back the message of land, the people and animals rejoice together. The story's mundane realism is reflected at the chapter's end, when the reader is informed that the sun and the wind "dried up the water slowly."

In the conclusion, "The Rainbow", the story returns to the Biblical, and explains God's promise and his sign of the promise rainbow. Even in the final pages however, the personal feelings of Noah and his family become an integral part of the narrative. And while the story is in large that of God's commands to Noah and Noah's belief in God, the story ends with a reminder to the reader of man's promise to the animals, saying:

> It was hard for Ham to say goodbye to some of his favorite animals. He had learned to love them deeply. They stood together and looked at the rainbow. They promised always to be friends.

Like the original Biblical story, it is a hopeful tale that contains a warning of God's power to punish man if he forgets his promises to the land, to the animals, to other human beings and to God himself. . . .

Although their drawings are not simplistic, they are bold in line and are bright with amusing character portrayals. Stylistically similar to the twentieth century pop art of Peter Max, these bold graphics are symmetrically balanced. They underscore the folktale quality of this retelling without detracting from the greatness of the events. (p. 55)

> *Jill P. May, "Looking at the Twentieth Century: Three Picture Book Adaptations of Noah's Ark," in* Catholic Library World, *Vol. 51, No. 2, September, 1979, pp. 54-7.*

The Christ Child, as Told by Matthew and Luke   (1931)

Here is a picture book that in its reverent and childlike beauty has captured the very spirit of Christmas. Before making the pictures Maud and Miska Petersham went to Palestine, with the result that the characters of the Christmas story move across a background both beautiful and authentic. The text, which tells of the Child Jesus as He grows from infancy to boyhood, is taken unchanged from Matthew and Luke. The pictures themselves, however, in their clearness and dramatic simplicity suffice to tell the story to the child too young to read. Unerringly the artists have put into their illustrations just the details which appeal to a child. The animals, from the small lamb that the shepherd is sheltering beneath his cloak, to the splendid camels of the Wise Men, interest and please children. Lambs especially, as these artists draw them, have a gentle humor that is very winning, and the tiny, exquisite flowers that are often found with them in the drawings have the same youthful quality. The manger scene suggests the reverent and poetic imagination of the legends of animals in the stable, speaking and worshiping on Christmas Eve. The deep-blue cover, with its golden stars, carries with it the feeling of Christmas, and the illustrations, which were printed in Germany, under the supervision of the artists, are remarkably fine examples of color-printing. The book makes a wide appeal for older boys and girls, and adults as well seem to enjoy it as much as do the six and seven year olds.

> *Anne T. Eaton, in a review of "The Christ Child as Told by Matthew and Luke," in* The New York Times Book Review, *December 13, 1931, p. 12.*

This book is an illumination of the life of the little Jesus. The text is by Matthew and Luke; it is that part of their gospels which deals with His birth and childhood. There is no lesser comment; the story flows on unbroken in beautiful print on a beautiful page. The illustrations are simple and in many instances they are beautiful; they are beautifully printed. The publishers announce that Maud and Miska Petersham visited Palestine to make their pictures. Thus the child who looks at them may believe them to be true in detail—a matter of satisfaction to children. Doubtless Joseph's tools were like these pictured tools, and Mary ground her meal on such a stone. In this the book approaches, in a modest fashion, certain of the realities so arduously assembled by Tissot, and this is good. But the virtue of the pictures is in a kind of atmosphere; they are flooded with a delicious light and gaiety.

It is said that the Petershams are much appreciated by children. Certainly there are no complexities in these pictures, none of the adult implications: Mary and Joseph, like many other parents, keep their own counsel. The desperate nature of their adventures, their anxious journeys and their solicitudes, are not suggested. The shepherds having heard the angels are entirely uninspired; the wise men who travel under the most gorgeous of stars, and upon the best dressed of camels, are without perceptible religious fervor. True, Herod the king is caught in a bad half-hour; and Simeon with his hat on, is obviously uplifted after the manner of grandparents; but in general the adults pictured here are without the faculty of communication.

With the animals and the flowers it is otherwise—these are informed by living ardors. The lambs, so tender, so irresistible and amusing—they know well who made them. The flowers so eager and springing—they know well who approved them. The donkeys, so pious and dutiful, adore the little Jesus as every Christian beast has done in every Christmas crèche, and the heart melts to look at them. Their innocent and modest piety should be, I think, very contagious. A child will know them, and the so friendly birds, for his own brethren as the Christ child does. This insistence on a universal peace between the creatures, and upon an immanent present love in the world, is the climate of the book—the holy child, surrounded by so much benignity is entirely reassured and much at his ease. For those parents who are concerned that their children should early know that irresistible fascination, this picture book will be a means. And for those parents who are hard put to it that their children shall be told a perfect story which they themselves cannot tell them—here is the story in its immortal words a book to their hand. It is the Story of the Christ Child for children, told in all its beauty and without any mutilation whatever.

Jean Kenyon Mackenzie, "The Little Lord Jesus," in New York Herald Tribune Books, December 20, 1931, p. 8.

During my years of bookselling I suppose I showed **The Christ Child** to thousands of people, and I never opened it without a thrill of pleasure in its *rightness* and gracious beauty. If there is anything the matter with it I still don't know what it is. In my opinion no shop that sells real books for children should ever be without it. (p. 3205)

Lena Barksdale, "The Petershams—Caldecott Medal Winners for 1946," in Publishers Weekly, Vol. 149, No. 25, June 22, 1946, pp. 3203-05.

For all of their illustrations for Biblical stories, the Petershams did painstaking research in the country where the stories took place. But authenticity is only one of their virtues as illustrators. They catch the spirit of these matchless tales and picture them with grace and understanding. This will always be a favorite edition of the Nativity. The text has never been surpassed, and the pictures have tenderness and beauty. (p. 338)

May Hill Arbuthnot, "Religion, Ethics, and the Arts," in her Children's Reading in the Home, Scott, Foresman and Company, 1969, pp. 309-41.

Auntie and Celia Jane and Miki (1932)

There have been books for children in which the special affection between the very young and the very old sets up its glow; there have been books celebrating the special pleasure of having an aunt; but so far as I have found, no book until now with an inherited aunt, passed on from one generation to another with delight undimmed. Such is the new picture-book of the Petershams. Celia Jane, in the days when motor-cars were first making their way in Quaker circles of Philadelphia, loved and was loved by Auntie. There was something of the goddess in Auntie, for she kept a school in her own home; she was of a warm domestic Olympus, of which Grandfather was Jove. Auntie was sheltering Demeter, one fancies, to a little girl who

had a perfectly good family of her own, yet had also Auntie. So this is the first half of the book, with its own prologue and pictures in the rich detail of the turn of the century. Then Celia Jane, grown up, has a little boy of her own—familiar to American children as "Miki"—and that makes the second half, prologue, pictures and all. Auntie is a very old lady now, by the calendar, but Miki knows better than that. Every one grown up is old to Miki, as to any little boy; Auntie is just immortal—immortal love and understanding and tenderness.

There is even a chance that in the book she may last like that from one generation of readers to another.

May Lamberton Becker, in a review of "Auntie," in New York Herald Tribune Books, December 11, 1932, p. 9.

A very attractive picture book dealing with every-day happenings and situations that children enjoy. Auntie is a real character and so is Miki, so also is Celia Jane, the little girl who once went to live with Auntie. . . . A true story of three generations and the record of a sympathetic friendship between children and a grown-up. The lithographs, in soft colors, have a life and charm and humor that will delight both children and adults.

Anne T. Eaton, in a review of "Auntie and Celia Jane and Miki," in The New York Times Book Review, December 18, 1932, p. 11.

Get-a-Way and Háry János (1933)

Háry János was once a Hungarian soldier; they still make soldiers like him, and this is one of them. Get-A-Way is a stuffed horse, loved into the plastic state in which alone a stuffed toy can be completely responsive. What becomes of old, forgotten toys? You will be glad to learn—and I hope it will be with a sort of catch in the throat—that toys know all the time they are toys; that when the time comes they will go to a country where the Governor has but to say One-two-three and a battered toy begins to grow back to beauty. Beyond into a greater beauty, perhaps, for when it has recovered all its lost legs and buttons it need not stop—it can say "Enough" at any point, and be like that to stay. One of the painted-pig money-boxes waited too long to say it and burst into bits. It was necessary to start One-two-three all over again with the pieces.

The trouble with being a toy is that it comes alive only by long loving, the very thing that wears off the paint. Háry János the boastful and the kind resourceful Get-A-Way now at last have life and beauty, too—a beauty that takes all the colors of the palette to do it justice. A happy four-year-old here may see Get-A-Way making the first use of four complete legs to jump the fence into a meadow full of toy horses; some of them come from prehistoric Rhodes and some from the Black Forest, but they all have a family look because the spirit back of every toy horse makes it a distant cousin of Pegasus. Here is the gay kitchen of their house, with a smug china cat on the mat; here is a house-warming with Hopi Indian dolls and ladies from the Victoria and Albert Museum, and a Kathe Kruse baby. The

THE PUEBLO

Near the cliff dwellings in our Southwest, there are Indians living today. Their houses are something like the old cliff dwellings. These people are called Pueblo Indians. "Pueblo" is the Spanish word for village. Every village looks like a big apartment house, because these Indians build their dwellings one above another, against the side of a cliff.

The houses are made of a clay called adobe. Often they are painted over with yellow mud. The inside walls are whitewashed. There is a great deal of sunshine in our Southwest, and the sunshine, together with the light-colored houses, makes a gay, bright scene. Indian children play on the flat roofs of the houses and climb up and down the ladders.

From The Story Book of Things We Use, *written and illustrated by Maud and Miska Petersham.*

two Hungarian heroes make friends with them all—all, that is, but the toys in the Annex, where the Woolworth toys come for repairs. These never quite belong, somehow. Nobody has really treasured them in the way a toy must be to come alive; nobody made them to be treasured. Even the iron ones come apart. Better the wooden Russians with red kerchiefs, better even the Nutcracker taken from his work to be made into a toy.

I know of but one scene in a story-book for little children that moves me in the same way as this book: the moment in Margery Bianco's deathless *Velveteen Rabbit,* when the rabbit, having helped a little boy through scarlet fever, rises released by purifying flame and goes leaping gladly toward some paradise well earned by good toys. Here, in the Petershams' best book, is that rainbow paradise complete.

> *May Lamberton Becker, in a review of "Get-a-Way and Háry János," in* New York Herald Tribune Books, *October 22, 1933, p. 9.*

Get-a-way and Háry János is a very gay picture story book, but it reaches farther than that. It places an importance on the quality of interest imparted to children concerning the life of a toy and its place in civilization that we have not had in a child's book before. (p. 9)

> *Anne Carroll Moore, "What Keeps a Child's Book Alive for Years," in* New York Herald Tribune Books, *November 12, 1933, pp. 8-9.*

Perhaps the love for stories about toys goes back as far as the love for the toys themselves. Richard Horne's *Memoirs of a London Doll,* first published in 1852, is still read. *Polly Cologne,* by Mrs. Diaz, has delighted two generations of children; Rachel Field's *Hitty* has won an estab-

lished place among the favorite books of boys and girls, while in *Floating Island* Anne Parrish described a family of dolls in a fashion nothing short of inspired. Mrs. Bianco's *Velveteen Rabbit* and her *Poor Cecco,* A. A. Milne's *Winnie-the-Pooh* and *The House at Pooh Corner* are stories about toys that young readers have promptly taken to their hearts.

Get-A-Way, that most faithful of stuffed cloth horses, and Háry János, the Hungarian soldier doll, give the title to a book which in the form of a story suggests the history of toys through the ages all over the world, from the Egyptian bread mixer of 2000 B. C. and the bronze horse of the fifth century Greece to the mid-Victorian lady of the nineteenth century and the Kathe Kruse little-girl doll of today. (pp. 12, 18)

The lithographs in six colors and black and white are fine examples of color printing. Some of the toys they picture are in Mr. and Mrs. Petersham's own collection, others were sketched in shops and museums in many different countries. The drawings have more than beauty and historic accuracy, however; they suggest the affection and imaginative sympathy that are part of the child's attitude toward his best loved toys. (p. 18)

> *Anne T. Eaton, in a review of "Get-a-Way and Háry János," in* The New York Times Book Review, *December 17, 1933, pp. 12, 18.*

The Story Book of Things We Use (also published separately as *The Story Book of Clothes, The Story Book of Food, The Story Book of Houses,* and *The Story Book of Transportation,* 1933)

The Petersham's latest example of close harmony begins

to charm with the jacket, on which the four subjects it treats—houses, food, clothes and transportation—appear, respectively, as a tepee, an appealing cow, a gray-silk lady at a spinning wheel and an old-fashioned locomotive, each in a colored picture bright as a Valentine. The house section begins with two children in a Cro-Magnon cave-dwelling with bison pictures on the wall; their conveniences may be few, but one sees by the picture that they have tamed the blue bird. Then come lake-dwellers; here the red-headed son of the house has a pet wolf-dog. Then follow tree-houses, cliff dwellings, pueblos, igloos, grass-thatched huts like Younghill Kang's, a tent (with an irresistible camel-colt convincing a reluctant Arab baby that he must have that bun), a tepee, a log cabin complete with settlers, a Hungarian peasant house painted like a jewel box where even the little girl's pet pig has decorative quality; a castle, a Chinese junk, Dutch houses with gable fronts and tulip beds, and an American suburban cottage, tidy and multi-colored, past which a little girl in gingham is leading a family of miscellaneous kittens. In each of these houses children are living, usually with a pet animal of some kind, almost always in action. This process is repeated with food stuffs from all over the world, with clothes, and again with means of transport, in each case beginning with primitive man. The fourth set of pictures is the most dramatic, for all the sleds and stage coaches and Egyptian rollers and chariots are busily going somewhere and taking people in costume.

Every brilliant lithograph is detailed and explicit; the Egyptian scenes suggest wall-paintings and the medieval wagon, more faintly, the Luttrell Psalter, but for the most part the characters have the wholesome red-cheeked plumpness and bright garments characteristic of Petersham people. There is such variety that each picture has the unexpectedness that holds attention. For the text there is by no means so much to be said. The style does not suggest **Get-Away and Hary Janos,** the other Petersham offering of the season, so much as it does a school reader—which is the same as to say that there is more merit than pleasure to be acquired from reading it.

This, however, makes less difference than one might think with the book's special public—children, especially boys, just old enough to read for themselves, and delighted to find their world enlarging with each new word. Such an audience is not exigent in regard to literary style. I have just heard of a seven-year-old boy who entertained a group of younger companions all the way to a school one morning in the recent cold spell with an account, based on three pages of this book, of how houses are made at the North Pole, out of bricks made of snow. On the other hand, the mother of a five-year-old, reading it aloud, found that the child's attention strayed from what was heard to what was seen. The inference is that it had better be kept till a child can read it for himself under the stimulus of the pictures.

> *May Lamberton Becker, in a review of "The Story Book of Things We Use," in* New York Herald Tribune Books, *February 25, 1934, p. 9.*

An attractive picture book by two artists who know how to make pictures for children. These illustrations have life

and charm, and the colors are gay and pleasing. . . . [The text] is a highly miscellaneous collection of information, for on turning the page we jump from ancient Egypt to a Western wheat field and in following the pictures it is constantly necessary to bridge long intervals of time. For children of the age for which the book is evidently intended, this is confusing; a different arrangement of material—for example, all the information about food, houses, clothing and transportation—grouped together according to the different countries or climates, would be easier for the young child to follow. The book, however, will be useful, for we have few attractive volumes that give information in a fashion simple enough for 7 and 8 year olds to read for themselves, and many boys and girls will enjoy these charming pictures, whether or not they are interested in the text.

> *Anne T. Eaton, in a review of "The Story Book of Things We Use," in* The New York Times Book Review, *March 18, 1934, p. 11.*

It doesn't seem possible that we really have a book, well written and admirably illustrated on Houses, Clothes, Food and Transportation. But it is true. This book with its simple text and illustrations which in themselves tell a story and that with touches of humor, has so many uses that one scarce knows where it is most essential. The young "question box" of four will enjoy having it read to him and the second and third "graders" who are learning how other people live and what they do, will read it with delight.

> *Mary R. Lucas, in a review of "The Story Book of Things We Use," in* Library Journal, *Vol. 59, No. 9, May 1, 1934, p. 403.*

Miki and Mary: Their Search for Treasures   (1934)

In this third book about Miki he has a small companion of his own age, Mary, and together they sail away on an ocean liner. After their happy voyage is over they explore Mont Saint Michel, Concarneau, the Canary Islands, Venice, Athens, Rhodes and Jerusalem; and finally they see a fairylike city of tall towers in the distance and land once more in their own New York. The pictures of the ship, of Mont Saint Michel, of Venice, Rhodes, Jerusalem and the rest are beautiful in drawing and in color and so imaginative and understanding that they express the spirit of the places they represent much more truly than it could be interpreted by photographs. In the same way the text is not a literal account of an actual trip; it is more nearly a description of the way imaginative children make believe whether they are abroad or at home. At each new stopping place Miki and Mary took delight in recalling a bit of the past, a legend of ancient Greece, a tale of fine ladies in Venice, or of crusading knights at Rhodes. Into their "treasure chest," as reminders of their travels, went just such treasures as children would collect on a journey if they could—a long-handled omelet pan from Mont Saint Michel, pigeons from St. Mark's in Venice, lava from a real volcano, canaries from the Canary Islands and a donkey from Jerusalem. Child readers, whether they have ever traveled abroad or not, will enjoy these pictures and in them may find the same kind of treasure that Miki and Mary discovered on their journey.

Anne T. Eaton, in a review of "Miki and Mary: Their Search for Treasure," in The New York Times Book Review, *November 11, 1934, p. 10.*

This method of imaginary traveling in historical faraway lands is a worn-out romantic experience. No doubt it has great allure for children, but personally, I feel that it always leaves in them a mood of false nostalgia. The publishers of this book point out that "to the Petershams the search for beauty is the important thing in travel." That is a worthwhile thing to look for, and a noble idea to instil in children. Its lasting effect depends, however, on the point of departure. Certainly, beauty can always be found on the old beaten paths in foreign lands, yet for the American child who "comes from Missouri" that kind of search for beauty strikes him as "sort of fishy."

The illustrations in this book are a combination of affected realism, idealism, and visual platitudes.

Peppino Mangravite, in a review of "Miki and Mary," in The Saturday Review of Literature, *Vol. 11, No. 18, November 17, 1934, p. 286.*

The little boy whose adventures in Hungary in full color made him familiar to American children, and Mary who shares his travels, visit in the new Petersham book countries seldom touched by traveling children. . . .

This travelling is accomplished as much in large full color lithographs as by the fanciful text. A child will not find this as fanciful as an older person may. For though eight-year-old Miki and Mary travel quite alone, and through a world as much dream as reality, that is the way imaginative children do travel. There may be a dozen adults in the party, but you may be sure that so far as two children in it are concerned, they are carrying on the journey quite by themselves through scenes they alone can see. As for the treasure chest, whose contents amused the customs men, were these so different from the things we all bring back from foreign parts, amulets through which we still control treasure far away? One of the first lessons a wise person learns is to respect other people's junk; it is likely enough to be their treasure.

May Lamberton Becker, in a review of "Miki and Mary: Their Search for Treasures," in New York Herald Tribune Books, *November 18, 1934, p. 11.*

The Story Book of Wheels, Ships, Trains, Aircraft (also published separately as The Story Book of Aircraft, The Story Book of Ships, The Story Book of Trains, and The Story Book of Wheels, 1935)

The series of story-picture-books [which includes *The Story Book of Things We Use* and *The Story Book of Earth's Treasures*] by the Petershams has already put children in touch with "earth's treasures," and "things we use" was good when it started and has been getting steadily better. In the beginning the pictures were much better

than the text: the next book brought the stories into line with the unusual excellence of the colored illustrations, and now the present one, improving the pictures to the highest pitch of the series, has swung into brief but rousing narrative with genuine human interest, about how men have gone about on the surface of earth and sea, and in the air, since history began.

The result is a book that may be confidently given to any child who can read, trusting it to hold his attention like a story book and delight his eye as well. The research involved must have been great; the drawings are exact, the colored plates—128 of them—reflect art methods of the time. Thus, the glowing Egyptian colors; the magnificent Assyrian king hunting lions in his chariot to a blaze of red, green and gold against a ceramic blue; the whirling spray cleft by the Viking ship; the equally thrilling progress of a modern liner with a bone in her teeth. It is hard not to get at least a little excited over such pictures, in which the human element is always not only present but predominant. The modern dirigible standing out metallic against the page as if seen through a telescope, is quite as picturesque as the Montgolfiers' emblazoned balloon; the streamline train scudding under the aerial expanse of the Hell Gate Bridge is as beautiful and as personal as the loaded stagecoach churning up eighteenth century snow.

Beginning with rollers under Egyptian monoliths, the wheel develops under a child's eyes; the Scythian car and Chinese conveyances give way to medieval litters and the coach of Queen Elizabeth, the bicycle, the automobile, the wheels of modern industry. The story runs with the pictures. Beginning again with rude log boats, types develop to the trans-Atlantic flier; trains begin before the Rocket, and aircraft—after a picture of Icarus and his determined papa—shows first in the flyers of legend and the Darius Greens of early experimentation, then Lilienthal with a great white bird balancing near by, and so on to the present.

May Lamberton Becker, in a review of "The Story Book of Wheels, Ships, Trains, Aircraft," in New York Herald Tribune Books, *January 5, 1936, p. 8.*

Even in this day of innumerable finely illustrated books for children, **Wheels, Ships, Trains, Aircraft** stands out as a beautiful and thrilling volume. It is still better than the author's two preceding volumes, **The Earth's Treasures** and **The Things We Use.** The text succeeds in giving considerable information in readable fashion and includes an astonishing amount of human interest. As for the pictures, they are little masterpieces in their way, proving that an artist's drawing is more stimulating to a child's imagination than is the finest photograph.

Here is history actually told by pictures; the drawing of the Assyrian king hunting lions from his chariot conveys a sense of the ancient world that pages of print might not succeed in giving. So, too, with the primitive boats and with the great galleys that the Crusaders and their steeds stand ready to board. These drawings are dramatic, something is happening in every one, which is the reason that boys and girls are taking them to their hearts at once. The drawings are printed by offset lithography in six clear and attractive colors.

The four sections of the book, rollers turning into wheels, early wagons and carts, the wheels of industry, from tread-mills to the great wheels of modern machinery; trains, from Stephenson's little Rocket down to the great passenger locomotives of today; flying, beginning with the legend of Icarus and ending with the stratosphere balloon, contain much material of value that is well within the comprehension of 7 and 8 year olds, while boys and girls considerably older will enjoy this book for its lively illustrations.

Anne T. Eaton, in a review of "The Story Book of Wheels, Ships, Trains, Aircraft," in The New York Times Book Review, *February 9, 1936, p. 11.*

The Story Book of Foods from the Field (also published separately as *The Story Book of Corn, The Story Book of Rice, The Story Book of Sugar,* and *The Story Book of Wheat,* 1936)

The new Petersham book is a positive blaze of color. Not a page goes without a picture; where one might expect an occasional wash drawing one gets a spirited scene in at least two colors, and at every possible point a many-hued double-page spread bursts upon the beholder like a fire-works show. The effect is not at all "modernistic," not at all confusing; these colors belong there; this is a book about things we eat that grow for us in the fields, and a large proportion of these foods, we here discover, grow under gleaming skies and are garnered by people in bright raiment.

Take rice, for instance, a food we sometimes have trouble in getting children to take. What child could think it a pallid vegetable who sees it sown by ancient Chinese courtiers in orange and green and scarlet, harvested by peasants in what looks like an Oriental illumination, or cultivated in the Philippines by brown workpeople with parrot-tinted shorts and gold rings in their ears, standing in terraced slopes of bright blue water? Here is sugar in 1530 being rolled by Indians under the eye of a glittering conquistador, in a canefield crowded with turbaned Negroes, in a mill to which fat little donkeys draw red-wheeled carts, in beetfields under towering mountains, in the kettle of a charming Vermont sugar-house. Here is wheat and corn in the same sort of gay yet realistic pictures, with honest, straightforward text trotting alongside and giving the facts.

Facts of this sort used in my day to be found in small "supplementary readers" with slick, shiny pages and smudged

The Petershams in their studio.

half-tones. The generation before me got them from the less important pages of heavy geographies with minute and perfunctory woodcuts in the text. This is the way children get them now if they go to schools that reinforce textbooks after this fashion—and I find it a mighty good way.

May Lamberton Becker, in a review of "The Story Book of Foods from the Field," in New York Herald Tribune Books, *January 24, 1937, p. 8.*

The Petershams have a way of lifting the common facts of living far above the commonplace. To their series of informational books, which have removed much of the onerous implication of that term, they have added a fourth book, a story book of the basic foods from the large and diversified grass family: wheat, corn, rice and sugar. When the creators of this book have finished with their pen and brush bread emerges from its cellophane wrappings as a heritage of the ages. Corn is recognizable as a gift of the gods, itself a divinity and a medium of exchange among the Indians, a life-saver to the first settlers of America. Rice becomes an object or romance and sugar a precious commodity, the sweetness of which is not to be lightly regarded. Legends and folklore about these foods are interspersed with the history of their use and development from primitive man's first discovery of them to the great grain elevators and the sugar-beet fields of today. Facts about their cultivation and harvesting, even their transformation into food are discussed in phrases which younger children can readily understand, but which convey also a sense of the picturesque.

The pictures are superb. Glowing on every page, they almost tell the story by themselves in brilliant hues of soft-toned wash drawings. We see wheat traveling halfway around the world, carried by sad-eyed Russian emigrants, ground in Palestine by ancient millstones and harvested on the Great Plains of America. Tawny-skinned Indians dance in the corn festival and American pioneers make merry at a husking bee. A soldier in Alexander's army discovers sugar cane in India and in sixteenth-century Venice merchants barter shrewdly for huge sugar loafs brought from the Orient. A Chinese Emperor, in raiment as gorgeously colored as a hummingbird's, scatters the first precious seed in the rice festival and a few pages later we see the wonderful rice terraces of the Philippine Islands. The styles of the illustrations change with each period and country described and an infinite variety of facial expression adds character and life to each picture. Education becomes a practically painless matter for 7 and 8 year olds when it is supplemented by books of this imaginative and artistic quality.

Ellen Lewis Buell, in a review of "The Story Book of Foods from the Field: Wheat, Corn, Rice, Sugar," in The New York Times Book Review, *February 14, 1937, p. 10.*

[*Updated material from* The Story Book of Foods from the Field *was published in 1969 as* Let's Learn about Sugar. *The following excerpt is from a review of that book.*]

[This] is a good factual account of the history of sugar from the time of primitive man to the present day. Included are clear descriptions of the growing and processing of cane, beet, and maple sugar, along with some details about sugar substitutes. The illustrations, all new to this edition and some of which are copies of old prints and engravings, are informative; and the type is large and easy to read. A welcome addition in an area of social studies requiring good supplementary trade books.

Ruth Berman, in a review of "Let's Learn about Sugar," in School Library Journal, *Vol. 16, No. 1, September, 1969, p. 159.*

Stories from the Old Testament: Joseph, Moses, Ruth, David (also published separately as **David: From the Story Told in the First Book of Samuel and the First Book of Kings; Joseph and His Brothers: From the Story Told in the Book of Genesis; Moses: From the Story Told in the Old Testament; and Ruth: From the Story Told in the Book of Ruth,** 1938)

AUTHORS' COMMENTARY

I always think of Miska and myself as being rather lucky. Some people long to do things but it never quite seems to work out. This happens to us, too, but many of the things we have wished for very much we have been able to do. One of these things has been the making of a picture book of Bible stories as we wanted it.

As a child I had all kinds of Bible story books with pictures good and bad. But there was only one of these books that I really loved and felt satisfied with. Then one day my father, who was a minister, took this special book to a little child—a child who was very sick in hospital. The book was lost. Father promised to get me another like it, but we were never able to find another copy. So perhaps in making the Petersham Bible Story Books there was a feeling of making a book which would take the place of the one I lost when I was a child.

We have never had more joy in making pictures than with these. We have been slow and careful of details. We have tried, in the details of the pictures, to use only designs and objects which are known to have been possible in those Bible days.

The thing that helped us most of all with our pictures was our three months' visit to Palestine. From the stormy day we left the steamer and were rowed between the black rocks of Jaffa to the shore, each day was exciting. (p. 67)

Even the short time we had in Palestine gave us a little understanding of the country and of the people. And we have tried to put this feeling into the pictures of these Stories from the Old Testament. We have drawn and painted the pictures hoping they make the stories of Joseph, of Moses, of Ruth and of David, more real to you. (p. 68)

Maud Petersham, "A Dream Comes True," in The Junior Bookshelf, *Vol. 3, No. 2, December, 1938, pp. 67-8.*

The Petershams have once more risen to the occasion, and the mark was set high. Here are the histories of four Old Testament worthies, retold from the Bible in dignified contemporary English, accompanied by beautiful and distinguished pictures. They come, as in preceding Petersham publications, either all together in one big book or in four little ones, with the stories of Joseph, Moses, Ruth and David told separately. One way or another, they should all be in a child's own library.

These thoroughly satisfactory pictures are full-page in six colors with wash drawings interspersed; though bright, they are mellow and glowing rather than striking. That quality is left to the vigor of their designs; all their scenes are at great moments and in none is it possible to forget these are people of sinew and purpose, men who make destiny. They are more like the wiry tribesmen of Tissot's paintings than those in the plump Teutonic pictures of so many family Bibles; they have a wild charm. The pictures for Ruth are the most romantic, for Joseph the most sympathetic, for Moses the most powerful—the mass scenes are expertly handled—and for David the most dramatic; the child is shown the ravaged face and tense figure of Saul as the little harper tries to recall the troubled spirit, the instinctive recoil of David at the thought of attacking the sleeping king, the combat with Goliath, the stages of the tragedy of Absalom. I have waited a good while for a book that would do all this, and have passed over with a sigh more than one that tried to do what this has done so well.

> *May Lamberton Becker, in a review of "Stories from the Old Testament," in* New York Herald Tribune Books, *October 16, 1938, p. 8.*

For these four stories retold from the Old Testament Maud and Miska Petersham have made many full-page pictures in color and some in black and white. The retellings are simple and unpretentious; they will be easy for 9 and 10 year olds to read to themselves. Adults, however, should see to it that boys and girls do not miss the experience of hearing these same stories read aloud from the Bible itself.

The pictures are arresting; they are dramatic and accurate in detail, like all the work of these artists. Nevertheless, both the drawings and the reproduction of the drawings lack something of the exquisite quality of imagination and workmanship which make the Petersham's *The Christ Child as Told by Matthew and Luke,* published a few years ago, one of the loveliest and most satisfying of children's books.

> *Anne T. Eaton, "Old Testament Tales," in* The New York Times Book Review, *December 11, 1938, p. 10.*

The Story Book of Things We Wear (also published separately as *The Story Book of Cotton, The Story Book of Rayon, The Story Book of Silk* and *The Story Book of Wool,* 1939)

Like earlier issues of these excellent picture-information stories, the four little books of this group may also be obtained in one volume. . . . They follow the pattern of their predecessors: if the pictures cannot be so brilliant as those, for example, in the food series where landscapes were so glowing, the information, both in word and pic-

ture, has often the charm of the unexpected. At least I feel sure many children will find out for the first time how fascinating a background rayon has, from the bits about it given here. *Silk* is, as might be guessed, the prettiest book.

> *May Lamberton Becker, in a review of "The Story Books of Things We Wear: Rayon, Cotton, Silk, Wool," in* New York Herald Tribune Books, *December 24, 1939, p. 7.*

[*Story Book of Cotton, Story Book of Rayon, Story Book of Silk,* and *Story Book of Wool*] give excellent factual material on the subjects for children of fourth and fifth grade reading ability. Each subject follows a general outline covering its discovery and history, its development in manufacturing, its general uses and the countries which raise crops or manufacture it as a major industry. On rayon there is little material available for children elsewhere and this, as well as each of the other subjects, is clearly and concisely presented. The books are the same in format as the others in this series by the Petershams, and the numerous illustrations clarify the text and make an interesting and attractive page.

> *Eunice G. Mullan, in a review of "Story Book of Cotton," "Story Book of Rayon," "Story Book of Silk," and "Story Book of Wool," in* Library Journal, *Vol. 65, No. 3, February 1, 1940, p. 123.*

An American ABC (1941)

A patriotic picture book which aims to show something of the background of our country; Many quiet scenes, such as two Quaker children tending a wounded deer and a little Colonial girl praying beside her bed, are included. The most dramatic pictures are those illustrating the landing of the Pilgrims and Yankee Doodle. One wishes that more of the pictures showed the strength of character and virility which these two display. The text is simple, yet written with feeling. The book could be used with children from five to eight. Its artistic format will appeal to adults.

> *Elsie T. Dobbins, in a review of "An American ABC," in* Library Journal, *Vol. 66, No. 18, October 15, 1941, p. 908.*

Patriotism of the kind that counts is not only the keynote but the melodic scheme of this beautiful picture book with accompanying text. As authors and as artists the Petershams have set out to show children something about the America into which they were born or to which they have come, awakening thereby a sense that there is something beautiful and glorious about America, something worth living for. There is for every letter of the alphabet a page of simple, sincere text and a full-page picture in colors—chiefly tones of the national colors, though softened and blended so that this patriotic feature is not overemphasized. A dreaming boy, guarded by an eagle, is on the page for "America, land that I love." Then follow the ringing of Liberty Bell, Columbus at Palos, Daniel Boone, emigrants on their way (a lovely family group), a touching design for Freedom, George Washington as a boy, Henry Hudson and his son, Independence Hall, Jamestown, the

Knickerbockers, Lincoln, and so on to Valley Forge, the White House, Christmas and Yankee Doodle with the eagle soaring over the last page for Zeal.

It would be hard to go through this book without a thrill.

> *May Lamberton Becker, in a review of "An American ABC," in* New York Herald Tribune Books, *November 2, 1941, p. 7.*

A book whose form and title suggest a picture-book for the very young only is Maud and Miska Petersham's **An American A B C,** but there is a message for all Americans in this timely book. These two favorite author-illustrators have put into it their love for America and for the people, qualities and spirit that have had a part in the making of America. From "A is for America, the land I love," to "Z is for Zeal, an American trait," in brief, dramatic stories with beautiful full-page pictures in color—the tale of America's heritage of freedom is unfolded. Here is a first history for boys' and girls' own reading, a gay picture book for young and old to enjoy together, an inspiration for Americans "to keep America a great land and a land of liberty and freedom."

> *Florence Bethune Sloan, in a review of "An American ABC," in* The Christian Science Monitor, *November 3, 1941, p. 11.*

Maud and Miska Petersham's **An American ABC** utilizes the alphabet to retell the history of the United States of America, from "A is for America/The land I love." Each letter deals with an individual or location of historical importance, the principles upon which America was founded, or the symbols of American freedom.

It is this spirit of patriotism, which the illustrations and text espouse, that no doubt won it a 1942 Honor Book position. The predominantly red and blue illustrations and the embellishment of the alphabet reinforce the sense of pride the audience should feel in the United States. Unfortunately, in retrospect, the book's illustrations portray many stereotypical elements that greatly affect the durability of the book over the years. American Indians, blacks, and South Americans are illustrated in ways that today seem offensive. The presentation of "X is for Xmas" might also be deemed a less than appropriate designation for the letter and seems out of place, especially in a book dealing with a country founded on diverse religious beliefs.

The strength and courage it took to mold the United States into the nation it is shines through in the illustrations of early heroes and explorers who risked their lives for freedom. The detailed figures, in their historical clothes and settings, reflect a compassion for the suffering the characters had to endure. The Petershams' style helps make these characters more real to the audience and brings both closer together. (pp. 248-49)

> *Linda Kauffman Peterson, in a review of "An American ABC," in* Newbery and Caldecott Medal and Honor Books: An Annotated Bibliography, *by Linda Kauffman Peterson and Marilyn Leathers Solt, G. K. Hall & Co., 1982, pp. 248-49.*

The Rooster Crows: A Book of American Rhymes and Jingles (1945)

AUTHORS' COMMENTARY

[*The following excerpt is from the Petershams' Caldecott acceptance speech, originally delivered in 1946.*]

For us the idea of preparing a speech was difficult but the making of a book comparatively simple, so today, instead of a speech, we have made for you a book.

[The title page] reads:

> *A SHORT TALE OF THE*
> *DEPRESSIONS AND THE PEAKS*
> *THAT OCCUR IN THE MAKING OF THE*
> *LITTLE PRETTY PICTURE BOOK*
> *WRITTEN AND ILLUSTRATED BY*
> MAUD AND MISKA PETERSHAM
> *BUFFALO, 1946*

The next page is the Contents and here there are three chapters.

> *Chapter* I. MAUD'S chapter
> *Chapter* II. MISKA'S chapter
> *Chapter* III. MAUD AND MISKA'S chapter

(p. 133)

From An American ABC, *written and illustrated by Maud and Miska Petersham.*

Chapter I

Once upon a time, long, long ago, after we respectively said good-bye to the advertising studio where we were both working, Miska and I started making children's books together. Miska solemnly told me that a picture wasn't worth making unless you were willing to suffer over it. At the time that seemed to me a strange and dreary statement. Now I understand, although I must say it has been on the whole "pleasant suffering." But it does mean that we have put our hearts and all our efforts into the pictures and books we have made. We always try to tell a story in our pictures and often we put a little unimportant story within a story. We have the satisfaction of believing that some children discover these—which are not for everyone, but something between us and certain children.

We have committed some grave offenses in our work. Once we proudly sent off some animal drawings. These were some of the first we had ever made. The editor slipped. The drawings went through and when the books were published, letters from children poured in. Why had we given the big bear, the middle-sized bear and the little bear, hands instead of paws? Why did the wicked, still-hungry wolf in Grandmother's nightcap and nightdress reach out a hand to Red Ridinghood?

I suddenly realized that while we were making the drawings we were thinking of the animals as behaving like people (perhaps Miska even posed for that big bear). We made them smile, we made them frown like people (even making faces ourselves as we were drawing) and so—we just gave them hands.

Again and again we are justly called to account by children. In our *Story of Trains* it passed unnoticed for a couple of years that we had drawn a locomotive gaily pulling a string of cars that were not even coupled to it. It took a small boy to find that.

A biology professor was once greatly upset because we placed the wrong number of legs on a wee little butterfly in the corner of some drawing.

And now in *The Rooster Crows* again we have gone wrong. In the **"Bye Baby Bunting"** picture, Father's gone a-hunting, Mother's gone to milk a cow—but alas our critic tells us Mother is sitting on the wrong side of the cow and at the wrong end of her anatomy. I can't claim to having ever achieved the art of milking, but I have seen cows—and something, I admit, *is* wrong with that picture.

We learn many things from the children who write us. I am continually surprised how much color means to them, for they speak of it so often. They are always very definite in their ideas. One child gave us a hard question to answer when he wrote that he had definitely decided to become an author and would we please give him all the facts on how to be one. We were put in our place by another child, who told us that he liked our books very much but he had a bike and he loved that best because that had a speedometer. I should like to know the little girl who wrote that she had just read our *Bible Stories* and the *Story of Ruth.* She said, "I forgot to tell you that I thought Ruth was very

loyal not to leave Naomi. I would have done the same. Thank you very much."

I wish all critics were as truthful as children, even if indirect. A long letter from a western boy ended by telling us that he liked the *Story of Joseph* and the *Story of Moses* very much indeed but would we *please* write a book about boys and girls having fun. The happiest compliment we ever had was from a little pig-tailed girl who was very disappointed when she met us and said, "Oh! I didn't know you were just real people. I always believed you were magic."

There was a sad time a few years ago when, for the first time, working on children's books brought us no pleasure. In fact it seemed almost impossible. Half-heartedly we tried this and that and a book failed to materialize. (We also have books turned down, you know.) Red Cross work, a garden, standing on the post watching for planes that never appeared, even listening to the news, all seemed far more important. There were plenty of good books for children, so why waste our time trying to make another?

Then just at that lowest moment it was the simple, happy things we had known and felt as children that seemed the only truths worth hanging on to. I realized that books for children were still important and that any truth or beauty, which even in a small way we could give a child, could be a vital influence. One night at that time, while trying to forget the eleven o'clock news which we had just heard, and while trying to put away the worry that so many weeks had passed since we had heard from our child [who was serving in the war], I played a childish game with myself. Instead of counting sheep I tried to recall the foolish little rhymes and jingles I had not thought of for so many years. In the morning I went to my desk and wrote them down and then naturally they had to have illustrations. It was purely an escape move on our part but while we were working on those pictures we found we could live in a little world which was decidedly more sane than the real world was at that moment.

We worried our friends and their friends for different versions of the jingles and they grew and grew in number. When we decided to put them into a book the task of selection was difficult. It was surprising how many of the jingles involved problems and prejudices. Here are a few and you will understand that they could not be included.

"Eenie, Meenie, Minie, Mo." I know we would have been in trouble with parents and teachers if we had given the next two lines. Another we didn't use was this:—

> Republican Rat take off your hat
> And make way for the Democrat.

From the father of a friend in the Deep South came a rhyme that when a small boy he and other children of the town had shouted.

> Jeff. Davis rode the big white horse
> Lincoln rode the mule
> Jeff. Davis was our President
> Lincoln was a fool. . . .

You can see we had to make a selection and there were many jingles we found which we did not include in *The Rooster Crows.*

Now I turn this book over to Miska and to his chapter.

Chapter II

I left Hungary in 1911 soon after I finished art school. When I arrived in England, the customs official asked me if I had anything to declare. I answered in French that I was a painter, meaning that no painter would have any luxury articles. The customs man looked at me, marked my strange assortment of luggage "free" and asked no further questions and I was in England where I had long wanted to be. (pp. 134-38)

Then a rich friend of mine turned up in London. I knew he must be rich, for although he had left Hungary for America but a few years before, here he was with two months vacation, traveling and visiting back home, and now seeing London. One day he asked me what success I had had in England and I told him that success was not remotely possible. Then he asked why I didn't go to America. I was very much surprised, for I couldn't understand who there could be in America who would appreciate art. I could see no opportunity for an artist in a land inhabited by Indians and cowboys.

As a boy I had read eagerly stories by Fenimore Cooper and books about America by the German writer with a fanciful mind, Karl May, who, although he had never been in America, outdid any American author with his exciting tales of Indians and pale-faces. In Europe we thought him a marvel, as he himself was the hero of all the tales he wrote. My friend then told me that he would pay my passage back to England if in America, within six months, I could not make a living. In five minutes I had made my decision.

In a short time I was on a boat coming into New York harbor. (p. 138)

This friendly, open country was amazing and unbelievable to me. The language was to my liking. If I could not make myself understood right away, people would listen and help and in many cases "yes" or "no" was enough without any frills. My friend was right. In six months I was working. I had an apartment with another friend. I owned a new suit of clothes from Wanamaker's and a pair of American-made shoes that all Europeans longed for, and I had extra money in my pocket for a glass of beer with which I was presented a roast-beef sandwich. I had misjudged America and no doubt about it. (p. 139)

I found here a country that I had dreamed of, but never thought could really exist; I found ideals and principles that I had always believed in. I don't think any American-born can appreciate this country as I do.

In the books we make I am happy when we can picture some of those wonderful things which American children can claim as their heritage. Working on **An American ABC** book meant a great deal to me aside from the making of the pictures. In **The Rooster Crows** we have tried to put into the hands of children little snatches of story that are rightfully theirs. And now we are working on a book of United States postage stamps, those small squares of paper commemorating events of which American children can

be so proud. We are trying to put before the children of this country those things which are theirs for the taking.

Now comes the last chapter, our chapter, Maud's and mine.

Chapter III

The climax of this tale is short but exciting. Today, June 18, 1946, we have received the Caldecott Award. We are proud and happy because it comes to us as an assurance that the love, the hard work, and any skill we may possess, which we have put into our work, have been considered worthy. If we have given any child real joy or have made him a little more appreciative of the beautiful in this world, we are satisfied. (pp. 140-41)

> *Maud Petersham and Miska Petersham, "Acceptance Paper," in* Caldecott Medal Books: 1938-1957, with the Artist's Acceptance Papers & Related Material Chiefly From the Horn Book Magazine, *edited by Bertha Mahony Miller and Elinor Whitney Field, The Horn Book Incorporated, 1957, pp. 132-141.*

Here are the "counting-out" rhymes, the words for the singing games and the rhymed riddles that American boys and girls have said and sung for generations. The illustrations, in color, are the most important part. Their details are varied and amusing, and they often give an original interpretation to the old words.

In almost every one the Petershams manage to put some of their delightful baby animals. (p. 41)

> *Mary Gould Davis, "In Color and Rhyme," in* The Saturday Review of Literature, *Vol. XXIX, No. 10, March 9, 1946, pp. 41-2.*

Counting-out and rope-skipping rhymes bring up visions of generations of American children, in the playground and the street; familiar finger-plays and folk-jingles recall the nursery and the home. **"Mother may I go out to swim?"** and **"Star Light, Star Bright,"** come back to the memory as easily as **"Yankee Doodle."** The Petershams have made delightful pictures, in soft harmonious colors, with plenty of humor for these and many other rhymes that American children chant freely. They have made a beautiful book. . . . (pp. 131-32)

> *Alice M. Jordan, in a review of "The Rooster Crows," in* The Horn Book Magazine, *Vol. XXII, No. 2, March-April, 1946, pp. 131-32.*

Apparently the librarians who selected this book as "the most distinguished American Picture Book for Children published in the United States" in 1945 were not bothered by four pages showing Negro children with great buniony feet, coal black skin, and bulging eyes (in the distance, a dilapidated cabin with a black, gun-toting, barefoot adult). White children in this book are nothing less than cherubic, with dainty little bare feet or well-made shoes. After eighteen years enough complaints had been received to convince the publisher that the book would be improved by deleting the illustrations of Negro children. In the new edition of **The Rooster Crows** (1964) only white children appear. (p. 160)

Nancy Larrick, "The All-White World of Children's Books," in The Black American in Books for Children: Readings in Racism, edited by Donnarae MacCann and Gloria Woodard, The Scarecrow Press, Inc., 1972, pp. 156-68.

This collection of American rhymes and jingles of childhood recounts many familiar words of the forgotten days of youth. It is the nostalgia of these chants of youth and the Petershams' ability to capture the essence of these games in their illustrations that made the book a popular choice for the Caldecott Medal.

The fifty-eight illustrations, some in full color, others in one or two colors with black and white, capture the humor, rhythm, and all-around fun that are contained in the words. Nothing but compassion can be felt for **"Fuzzy Wuzzy,"** who loses his hair, as he sits forlornly staring out from the page. The humor of **"Engine, Engine, Number Nine,"** the locomotive so shiny a cow cannot take her eyes off her own reflection (much to the dismay of the train's conductor), brings a new meaning to those words of rote so often recited in childhood.

The illustrations of the Finger Games help guide the child with the proper hand positions and give the book a kinesthetic extension beyond its pages. The predominantly blue, brown, and pink illustrations add variety to the book's format, and the interjection of full-color pictures adds more interest. There are only two pictures, since removed in a revised edition, that detract from the book's illustrations, both of which negatively depict blacks.

But aside from these illustrations, the reception of which has changed from the time of the book's publication, the work would have interest for today's audience, especially were an adult to demonstrate how some of these games were played "in the olden days." (p. 263)

Linda Kauffman Peterson, in a review of "The Rooster Crows," in Newbery and Caldecott Medal and Honor Books: An Annotated Bibliography, by Linda Kauffman Peterson and Marilyn Leathers Solt, G. K. Hall & Co., 1982, pp. 262-63.

[Few] Caldecott-winning artists are more easily recognized as having reflected the political climate during certain periods of American history than . . . Maud and Miska Petersham in their pictures for *The Rooster Crows.* [This] book exemplifies the ethnocentrism and patriotism that swept the United States immediately following World War II. . . . (p. 64)

Inspiration for *The Rooster Crows* was said by Maud to have come from a sleepless night during World War II, when she eased her concern about young Miki, then a navigator on a B-24 in the Pacific, by reciting to herself rhymes remembered from her own childhood. The authors later decided to collect these verses in a book, and the illustrations that followed reflected the pride in the American way of life that was prevalent during and after the war. Although other collectors of folk verse, such as Ray Wood in *American Mother Goose* and *Fun in American Folk Rhymes,* may present a better sampling of pure American invention, the Petershams' illustrations give

their volume a superior American flair. Colonial boys and pioneer girls, small-town kids and 1940s city kids, farm boys or sailor boys or Yankee Doodle boys, all are there for children of today to find. At their best (and many are quite charming), the pictures are reminiscent of Norman Rockwell's sentimental portrait of Americans.

Romanticism regarding childhood and portrayal of an idealized child with prettiness, good health, and cheerful disposition—in the case of *The Rooster Crows* the perfect white American youth—had artistic roots in the nineteenth century. The bourgeois sentimentality in much of Victorian English art itself followed Eastern, primitive, and Renaissance traditions of idealized form. No penetration of character is shown in the Petershams' depictions of children—Lazy Mary is as easily seen to be "the darling daughter" who's gone out to swim or Tuesday's child "full of grace." Just as George Washington is pictorially glorified frozen as a statue on his horse, so are all these childish characters basically frozen in time as one child, "blythe and bonny and good and gay." Rockwell could imbue his characterizations with some complexity and humor, but the Petershams did not exhibit psychological insight in their work. They are seen today as folk artists to whom face and figure were primarily decoration on the page.

Mother Goose and other children's rhymes, however, are known for their portrayal of action without introspection, so the Petershams' lack of individuality for their characters does not in itself detract from children's pleasure in the beauty and fun found in *The Rooster Crows.* Girl characters are not pictured in any dominant roles; this point may be discussed with students as sexist stereotyping prevalent in many children's books of the 1940s. Generally speaking, though, the parts played in the various illustrations are acceptable as befitting the rhymes. Throughout the history of children's literature, the best illustrators of Mother Goose rhymes have recognized that the challenge in picturing these short nonsense verses lies in the ability to present art that has a life of its own; the Petershams' book has a lasting quality due to its touches of Americana.

One reason these verses continue to attract children is the age-old appeal of learning something "by heart" (one of the loveliest phrases in the English language). The Petershams have collected some of the most popular old rhymes to have come down to us over the years. A Mother Goose or calling-out rhyme is for the very young one of the first exercises of language, and the brevity, repetition, and surprises inherent in them appeal to youngsters' limited attention span. These light-hearted introductions to poetry are unburdened by the bewildering formalities of instruction. Once children get the idea of onomatopoeia and other sound patterns in words, they usually demand the opportunity to immediately recite the whole piece on their own. The strong cadence and dependable rhythm of Mother Goose rhymes entrance children and speak to their sense of movement, dance, and music, inviting them to participate. Although they may sit quietly at the beginning, they will spontaneously join in as the rhyming helps to record the sequence of characters and/or events necessary to get through the verse. For the very young, learning by heart a favorite rhyme in *The Rooster Crows* is a large part of the fun, and for older children an additional benefit lies in the bits of weather lore and the early versions of verses they may know in more modern forms.

Of interest also to older students is the history behind some verses; this may be pursued in *The Annotated Mother Goose* by William and Ceil Baring-Gould. Finding background information for some of the Petershams' patriotic scenes often indicates the care with which these two artists researched their pictures. For instance, the **"Yankee Doodle"** rhyme reprinted here was originally written by a British army doctor to mock the ragged American colonialists as silly Yankee "do-littles" during the French and Indian Wars, and it is this militiaman rather than the more commonly pictured Revolutionary soldier that the Petershams' illustration depicts. In the verse George Washington is referred to as a captain, the rank he held during the French and Indian Wars, and he is portrayed as such rather than the general he later became. And on page 31 appears the best-known verse for the song with picture of an indisputably ragtag Yankee "do-little," complete with his outlandish feather "Macaroni" (an eighteenth-century slang term for an English dandy who put on Continental airs). Such is the historical precision with which illustrations were fashioned in *The Rooster Crows* by Maud and Miska Petersham, American patriots and beloved artists for America's children. (pp. 65-8)

The nine full-color illustrations in *The Rooster Crows*

From The Rooster Crows: A Book of American Rhymes and Jingles, *written and illustrated by Maud and Miska Petersham.*

present good examples of how the continuous-tone artwork afforded by lithography can simulate reality. The modeling of shapes and figures by gradations of hues implies contour and texture. The naturalistic distribution of shades and highlights implies some source of illumination for many scenes. This modeling, shading, and highlighting is achieved through use of lines both visible and invisible and through use of color *tone.* (p. 86)

[For this book the] Petershams' choices are not pure primaries but are instead tones of these same hues. They are used as the predominant colors throughout *The Rooster Crows.* Every hue has its tone, produced by mixing the hue with its complementary color, and every tone has its shade, produced by adding black, and its tint, containing white. The gradation of a hue from its tone into its tints or shades can subtly model a figure, for example in the illustration of the girl and the mountains in **"I have a little sister"** on page 37 of the hardbound. In this picture are no visible lines for the mountains as they stretch out "high, high, high"; rather, line effects are created as the cyan tone meets its tint or shade, the lighter or darker version of the same hue. The results lend contour to the mountains and shade those areas not highlighted by the moon shining overhead. The child's nightgown and even her hair are also modeled in this manner, with very little use of visible lines at all.

Gray is naturally created through a combination of black and white; it is seen in various gradations along with black and white themselves throughout *The Rooster Crows,* often with the striking addition of just one of the color tones. Since variations of gray contain the elements black and white, considered by artists to be lacking in hue as such, gray has come to be thought of as the antithesis of pure color; in fact, it seems to clash or appear garish when used with pure color. However, tones, tints, shades, grays, black, and white are called *color forms* and in combination may result in pleasing combinations. This effect is called the *harmony of color forms.* In addition to the full-color illustrations easily recognized for use of all these color forms, many of the other illustrations stand out for their creative use of a more limited selection, such as the shade of brown with black and gray in **"Wake up, Jacob"** on page 14 or with black and white in **"Entry, kentry, cutry, corn"** on page 47. Once the children begin to train their eyes to seek out such harmonies, they can better appreciate the tinting and shading of a single hue that implies contour and texture and lends a sense of balance when many other hues are used as well.

Sometimes one color form can be felt to control a picture's effect on the audience, as exampled by the still serenity unmistakable in **"I see the moon"** on page 29. A gentle wash of blue tint imposes a lovely sense of quiet as the entire scene is flooded with moonlight, an unearthly cast over wagons and canvas tops and the little girl's gown, face, and hair. Even the slight addition of pink has a blue tinge. This ability of a tint to envelop a scene with one pervading visual sensation is called the *harmony of a dominant tint.* A dominant tint draws all other colors or color forms together and mellows them. The Petershams use the technique most appropriately for several illustrations in *The Rooster Crows.* (pp. 87-8)

Use of color forms throughout *The Rooster Crows* elicits a [quiet, calm] response, which is appropriate for a compilation of many rhymes. . . . For children of today the book provides a glimpse into the past, not only because of its historical figures and scenes but also because of the illustrators' coloring itself. Some of this artwork can have an effect on the audience that may or may not have been intended by the Petershams forty years ago. For example, of the different color schemes used for major illustrations occupying half- or full-page layouts, the harmony of color forms in which tone of brown is combined with gray and black is by far the most common. The dominance of brown in these pictures is reminiscent of the daguerreotype, rather a dull color usage in a picture book even in the most pleasing compositions. In these cases, the activity depicted in the scene itself is usually all that truly engages the attention of modern-day young viewers accustomed to brighter hues. Of the illustrations in which blue plays a major role, by far the most effective still today are those that exhibit harmony of a dominant tint to create atmospheres for weeping Sally Waters, baby bunting wrapped up on a blue-cold frosty day, seeing the moon and the moon sees me, or climbing up the mountain high, high, high. Addition of red or green to combinations of blue and gray results in a bit more appeal for youngsters in illustrations that are less than full color.

The eight full-color pictures, however, have survived the years to remain understandably the most attractive to children of today. Whether of historical, commemorative, imaginative, or 1940s contemporary significance, each stands out in *The Rooster Crows* as a prime example of the Petershams' abilities to create exquisite tonal variations when, despite high costs of color reproduction in the forties, they were allowed to work with a full spectrum. Addition of green to the triadic harmony of magenta, cyan, and yellow tones along with black, gray, and brown lends just the right richness to the color scheme for such classic representational art from the period. Many children today react most favorably to this straightforward, simple, and idealized portrayal of color as well as of figure.

As a final observation, one cannot help noticing that, in all the full-color illustrations, important figures for storytelling purposes are colored red and blue, and an area of white space is always included to provide a pleasing contrast and sense of balance. Children now might not think this a particularly significant or intentional detail in picture composition until one turns to the book jacket design and points out also the frame of red, white, and blue that surrounds the "rooster crows" illustration. In the historical context given this book, the patriotic effect was surely not a total accident on the part of Maud and Miska Petersham in 1945. (pp. 89-90)

Lyn Ellen Lacy, "Color: 'Drummer Hoff' and 'The Rooster Crows'," in her Art and Design in Children's Picture Books: An Analysis of Caldecott Award-Winning Illustrations, *American Library Association, 1986, pp. 64-103.*

America's Stamps: The Story of One Hundred Years of U.S. Postage Stamps (1947)

Once more the Petershams ring the bell. Judging from my experience as Reader's Guide, from comments of adults who passed my desk while an advance copy of *America's Stamps* was open there, and from what I hear of the nature of the demand for it before publication, I am convinced that many adults will be as glad to get it as the children will—indeed, the Philatelic Foundation endorses it as presenting the attractions of stamp collecting to all ages." But for young folks in particular, its brilliant color plates, beautifully reproduced stamps, and running narrative combining history with philately combine to present the subject as an intelligent beginner might ask to have it presented.

One hundred years of U.S. postage stamps unroll from the days of Coffee House Mail, Postmasters' Provisionals, and the first government issue in 1847. These opening pages have shown a large color plate of a ship captain navigating a crowded street of old New York, hugging his leather pouch; several photographs of early letter-sheets: a portrait of an old Penny Postman of Albany; four Provisionals in facsimile, and reproductions of the five and ten cent adhesives of 1947, also a picture of a ten-center cut in half to carry five-cent mail. This pictorial arrangement carries through: occasional color plates, many incidental drawings, and a complete display of issues up to the present day. This is, as the authors say, not a stamp catalogue, but a picture-book of American stamps; each is shown with gratifying clarity, on a scale larger than life, and along with each goes information on the historic event commemorated or the achievement honored.

To those who have never been stamp-collectors this display may be an eye-opener. The table of contents, naming issues in alphabetical order and arranging them in double-columns, takes up two of these large pages, and at the other end of the book come all the air mail stamps and a round-up of special deliveries.

May Lamberton Becker, in a review of "America's Stamps: The Story of One Hundred Years," in New York Herald Tribune Weekly Book Review, *March 23, 1947, p. 8.*

One hundred years ago an Act of Congress authorized the first issue of adhesive stamps. In recognition of this fact, the authors of this book have undertaken to tell the history of our nation in terms of its postage. The volume contains a good deal of philatelic information—including some for the period of stampless covers and provisional stamps—and carries an endorsement of general accuracy from the Philatelic Foundation. There are a large number of illustrations, many in color. Some of the imaginative ones are especially fine and should be fascinating to children. The reproductions of the various stamp issues are full size; thus the volume could be used as a stamp album.

It is unfortunate that the book contains many historical inaccuracies. Some involve new interpretations, as in the cause of Braddock's defeat; but altogether too many are errors of elementary fact, such as calling Benjamin Harrison a two-term President, or continuing McKinley in the White House for three years after his death. In general, the narrative that accompanies the pictures is too brief and dull to arouse much interest in either the stamps or their history.

> *Ralph Adams Brown, in a review of "America's Stamps: The Story of One Hundred Years of U.S. Postage," in* The New York Times Book Review, *April 20, 1947, p. 33.*

This picture album, which is not a stamp catalogue, contains reproductions of the stamps used during the hundred years since the founding of the Federal postal system. Stampless covers are shown, together with the early issues, cancellation marks and special stamps of many kinds. Interspersed among the reproductions, the Petershams have scattered pictures which indicate the period when certain stamps were in use, and brief pertinent text. History and romance lie behind these profusely illustrated pages which hold interest for philatelists of any age.

> *Alice M. Jordan, in a review of "America's Stamps," in* The Horn Book Magazine, *Vol. XXIII, No. 3, May-June, 1947, p. 220.*

My Very First Book   (1948)

6 pages in full color—2 colors on almost every other page—48 pages in all—but even that isn't enough to redeem the disappointment in this too blatantly obvious, dated baby book—or scrap book for baby's first year—or whatever you call it. This sort of book is sold in layette departments—for young parents who haven't learned that the diaper services give one free. Here is a chance missed to incorporate the best in charts, in the findings of experts today. The form followed was the form used two generations back:—date and place of birth, name of doctor and nurse, birth certificate and footprints, family tree, birthstone, lullabies, christening date, first time out, vaccination, illnesses, first tooth, first words, first steps, weight, Christmases, pictures, etc. etc. Oh yes—a few changes and additions and omissions. But it's expensive merchandise for people who expect more from this gifted couple.

> *A review of "My Very First Book," in* Virginia Kirkus' Bookshop Service, *Vol. XVI, No. 3, February 1, 1948, p. 55.*

The authors of this book are announced on the title page as "in collaboration with," and then two lines for the names of the child's parents. It is indeed a happy example of the "baby record" book, of which it may truly be said, as they say of this one, that "when it is finished there will be no other book like it in the whole wide world." Everything from the names of the officiating doctors in the first chapter to the fifth birthday party with which it concludes is accompanied by bright, lovely pictures that will not lose by being often seen. It will make in the end a sort of scrapbook, as many photographs can be pasted in at appropriate spots.

> *May Lamberton Becker, in a review of "My Very First Book," in* New York Herald Tri-

bune Weekly Book Review, *April 4, 1948, p. 10.*

The Box with Red Wheels   (1949)

It was with a feeling of exhilaration that this reviewer turned the pages of the *Box with Red Wheels.* Here was a new book by Maud and Miska Petersham done in their own lively manner and in a style reminiscent of their early use of color; a bold and imaginative use of red, orange and yellow. The pictures of the animals' amazement at the baby in the box and the child's delight in the animals are an expressive projection of mood. (pp. 1531-32)

> *Avis Gregory Zebker, in a review of "Box with Red Wheels," in* Library Journal, *Vol. 74, October 15, 1949, pp. 1531-32.*

It is good to have a new picture book by Maud and Miska Petersham. It is a simple story that tells how the cow, the pony, the rabbit, the kitten, the little dog, and the ducks were curious about the box with red wheels that stood on the other side of the garden gate. They found that the gate would open, so they investigated—and in the box with red wheels they found a baby! The color printing is unusual and deeply satisfying. Deep, bright red and gold outline the pages and the animals are printed in soft gray and black, with the red box and the golden duck bringing a touch of color to every page. Little children will surely take this picture book for their own. Like *Miki,* it will be a favorite for many years.

> *Mary Gould Davis, in a review of "The Box with Red Wheels," in* The Saturday Review of Literature, *Vol. XXXII, No. 46, November 12, 1949, p. 21.*

A picture book with a real surprise ending that will delight both adults who are reading the story and the youngsters listening. . . . The animals are pictured realistically in such a gentle, friendly manner that even a child who is afraid of one or all of them might be persuaded to overcome his feelings. The warm reds, yellows and black make the illustrations glow. Pictures and text combine to make a truly beautiful, outstanding book.

> *A review of "The Box with Red Wheels," in* Bulletin of the Children's Book Center, *Vol. 3, No. 1, December, 1949, p. 9.*

The Circus Baby   (1950)

Although really a sensible sort of pachyderm, Mother Elephant does have one ambition that even her best-of-all-babies can't quite satisfy. She would like him to eat at the table, like Mr., Mrs. and Baby Clown, whom she loves best of all the circus people. Like many a maternal whim, this one goes sadly awry. Baby's nature wins out, and Mother wisely concludes that he doesn't have to adopt spoon and dish, because, "after all, *you* are an ELEPHANT."

Maud and Miska Petersham have combined talents again to make a delightful picture book. The four-color circus scenes are bright and simple. Mother and Baby are wonderfully expressive but still quite real elephants, rather than the stuffed-toy variety so familiar in the nursery books.

> *Miriam James, "Etiquette for Elephants," in* The New York Times Book Review, *October 1, 1950, p. 24.*

With the Petersham reds, yellows, and grays so exactly right, one wonders how these illustrators could have so long resisted the circus theme. This is a simple story of a baby elephant whose mother's desire to have him eat nicely like the clown's baby brings on the kind of catastrophe that small children love. (pp. 1835-36)

> *Florence W. Butler, in a review of "The Circus Baby," in* Library Journal, *Vol. 75, No. 18, October 15, 1950, pp. 1835-36.*

The new title by the Petershams is a merry picture book for small children, those a little older than the audience for last year's **The Box With Red Wheels** . . . . It is a simple tale, whose joy is mostly in the lovely pictures, the wonderful poses and expressions of the two elephants, the charming colors. Little children all love baby animals, and the troubles of this irresistible small elephant will give them great joy.

> *"An Elephant, a Scotty, a Cuckoo Clock," in* New York Herald Tribune Book Review, *November 12, 1950, p. 9.*

The Story of the Presidents of the United States of America (1953)

Short biographies of the Presidents from Washington to Eisenhower, which give only brief factual accounts and yet manage to convey very definitely the character and personality of each man. Illustrations (on every page) are in black, blue, and white; format resembles the authors' **American ABC.** Certainly, every school and children's library will want this for its attractive format, subject appeal, simplicity, and brevity.

> *Emma Jean Bowland, in a review of "Story of the Presidents of the United States of America," in* Library Journal, *Vol. 78, No. 9, May 1, 1953, p. 818.*

Because the Petershams are beloved illustrators, and because this is a most attractive two-color book . . . , it will be widely welcomed. Each brief biography has at the head, the president's name, nickname, party and dates. The one, two or three pictures do not attempt to offer exact portraits, but give varied bits of significant action, in pleasantly decorative style. The frontispiece of old Federal Hall, New York, is most attractive. On the way through, we see the White House in 1800 and 1841, the Capitol in 1825.

The text is excellent, considering the space limitations. Great events are well selected. Personalities are described neatly. There is no room for generalizing on politics or the flow of social history, yet readers of about 11 to 14 would gather much history from the pages. At the end, the presidential portrait stamps are beautifully shown, tying the book in with that fine one by the same author-artists, **America's Stamps.**

> *"To 'Rouse the Lincoln in You All'," in* New York Herald Tribune Book Review, *May 17, 1953, p. 22.*

Off to Bed: Seven Stories for Wide-Awakes (1954)

A real answer to a mother's prayer! Seven short drowsy little stories for your very own "wide-awakes." They are *very* short, just perfect for that last minute before tucking in the covers and saying good-night. The little animals sleep in different ways. The turtle in his shell, the bears in their cave, the poor greedy duckling *not at all,* because HE had gobbled up a BUMBLE BEE.

Charming illustrations. Just right stories. Save them, if you can, for bedtime. (pp. 5, 9)

> *E. S. D., in a review of "Off to Bed," in* Chicago Tribune, *November 14, 1954, pp. 5, 9.*

A first picture-story book to read to small children, this tells how bear cubs, chickens, possums, ducklings, rabbits, penguins and coons go to bed. Each little story has action and humor, and is just the right length for four-year-old listeners. There are gentle, real, beautifully colored pictures on every page. It is an appealing addition to the group of books for the nursery by these popular artists.

> *A review of "Off to Bed: Seven Stories for Wide-Awakes," in* New York Herald Tribune Book Review, *November 14, 1954, p. 4.*

Weary parents who find the bedtime-story hour the longest part of the day will welcome these seven brief tales of the animal world. Each story requires only five minutes for reading aloud and contains the simple but important moral that "it's best to follow mother's advice." The little chick who didn't come when his mother called and had to spend a miserable night in the rain wished he had listened. So did the greedy duckling who insisted on having just one more grasshopper and got a bumble bee instead.

The stories also emphasize a basic trait or activity of each animal, such as the fact that raccoons wash their food and paws before eating—and this tale merits re-reading! The illustrations, while not distinguished, are numerous and certainly adequate for tired eyes to focus on.

> *George A. Woods, "Tales with Morals," in* The New York Times Book Review, *November 14, 1954, p. 42.*

The Boy Who Had No Heart (1955)

The doctor found that John had no heart and advised him to try to get one, somehow. He tried to buy one, to get one made—then he bought a big candy heart and ate it up. How did he get a real heart at last? On this moral tale, **The Boy Who Had No Heart,** Maud and Miska Petersham expend their beautifully drawn, handsomely colored pictures. The sad clown on the cover is alluring, but we doubt the wide appeal of the story.

Louise S. Bechtel, in a review of "The Boy Who Had No Heart," in New York Herald Tribune Book Review, *July 17, 1955, p. 8.*

Johnny had become so unpleasant that his parents sent him to their wise old doctor to learn what was wrong. On being told that he had no heart, Johnny at first felt very superior. But as time passed and his difference made him more and more lonely, he decided he needed a heart like other people. So he set out to buy one, but everywhere he was told that hearts are not for sale. It was a sad-faced clown at the carnival who finally taught him how to find his own heart.

A new book by this distinguished author-illustrator team is always welcome. The theme of this one seems somewhat mature for the recommended age level, but fourteen good full-page pictures help carry the direct teaching message to younger and older children.

C. E. Van Norman, "Not for Sale," in The New York Times Book Review, *August 7, 1955, p. 16.*

The Silver Mace: A Story of Williamsburg (1956)

[*The Silver Mace*] tells the story of Williamsburg from its early 17th century beginnings thru its period as capital of the Virginia colony to the day in 1776 when its church bell proclaimed liberty and the silver mace no longer symbolized the authority of the British crown. Stirring events and famous names are here. So, too, is the town itself—the craftsmen's shops, the crowded streets used by sea captain and backwoodsman, elegant lady and painted Indian alike, the lovely buildings. A lively story, its pictures aglow with color and authentic in detail, this is a book for all the family to enjoy.

Polly Goodwin, in a review of "The Silver Mace," in Chicago Tribune, *July 1, 1956, p. 7.*

If you do not know what a "mace" is, and if you are interested in Williamsburg, Va., you should welcome this book. Perhaps you are one of the many families at large this vacation season who may be visiting this authentic colonial village restored by the Rockefeller Foundation. For, although it is designed for small children, it is a book all the family will enjoy—from the early beginnings of the village, to the great day when the bell of Bruton Parish church rings out exultantly proclaiming that Virginians are free. Yes, Thomas Jefferson appears. And, of course, Patrick Henry.

Fifth in their series of books on early America—all quite

independent of each other—the reader is lured on always by the delightful Petersham pictures—endpapers included. In the course of the story we visit the printer, the apothecary, the wigmaker—who also pulls teeth—and the bootmaker, among others, and learn much of colonial ways. (Incidentally, a mace is the colonial emblem of authority—topped by the king's crown.)

Olive Deane Hormel, in a review of "The Silver Mace," in The Christian Science Monitor, *July 19, 1956, p. 11.*

In this charming picture-story book about Colonial Williamsburg the Petershams tell us that the modern restoration was made in order that "we Americans may better understand the precious heritage of Liberty and Freedom which is ours today." We wish they had also spoken of another gift of the restoration, which as artists they must have revelled in, the respect for the beauty of handicrafts. Nine and ten year olds, and older readers too, will be attracted by the lovely cover and the handsome end papers showing a picture map with the brilliant blue waters of the James and York rivers setting off the sites of Jamestown and Williamsburg. They will learn much from the short chapters with wise use of detail and pictures, either touched with blue or in full color, on every page.

Margaret Sherwood Libby, in a review of "The Silver Mace: A Story of Williamsburg," in New York Herald Tribune Book Review, *September 9, 1956, p. 6.*

The Peppernuts (1958)

The Peppernuts, a delightful invention of those whimsical Petershams, are a happy, vaguely Bohemian family. There is Flitter, and her brother Captain, the twins Tua I and Tua II, Mother Peppernut, and of course, Father. Father reads books, typewrites, and wears a hat. He is an author. At least he thinks that he is until his publisher ignores his latest book, and it begins to look as though the happy Peppernuts are going to have to be happy without a roof over their heads. But nothing goes wrong too long for the Peppernuts, and in the end things are as they were at the beginning. Safe, cozy, and just a little bit zany. Fantasy, balanced by enthusiastic sanity, underlie this domestic circus. Not too much of a story, but such a nice family!

A review of "The Peppernuts," in Virginia Kirkus' Service, *Vol. XXVII, No. 15, August 1, 1958, p. 546.*

Alf Prøysen

1914-1970

Norwegian author of fiction, short stories, and picture books.

Major works include *Little Old Mrs. Pepperpot and Other Stories* (1959), *The Town That Forgot It Was Christmas* (1966), *Mrs. Pepperpot's Busy Day* (1970), *Mrs. Pepperpot's Outing and Other Stories* (1971).

Often considered the best known Norwegian author of literature for children, Prøysen is the creator of the popular series of comic fantasies for early graders about Mrs. Pepperpot, an elderly housewife who lives on a Norwegian farm and suddenly and unexpectedly shrinks to the size of a pepperpot or teaspoon. A shrewd and resilient woman characterized by her friendliness, mischievousness, and love of adventure, Mrs. Pepperpot (who is called the Teaspoon Woman in Norwegian and Granny Teaspoon in other translations) finds that when she is small she can understand the language of animals, a gift that, when combined with her adaptability and common sense, helps her to triumph in a variety of situations. Mrs. Pepperpot, who shrinks at inconvenient yet useful moments and helps the deserving animals and humans she encounters, becomes involved in adventures ranging from being swept downstream on a soap packet and almost being burned on a bonfire to protecting a family of kittens and assisting a little girl with her schoolwork by whispering in her ear. Although Mrs. Pepperpot is benevolent and cheerful, Prøysen places her directly in the trickster tradition by giving her a wily quality which she uses to persuade her husband, her neighbors, and the animals she meets into doing her will; due to their earthiness and wry humor, the stories, which are called *Teskjekjerringa* in Norway, are often compared to Norwegian *eventyr* or folktales. Prøysen, a former radio entertainer for children, writes his episodic books about Mrs. Pepperpot in a straightforward yet rhythmic style and fills them with invention, attention to detail, and droll humor. Critic Vivien Jennings has written of Mrs. Pepperpot, "Here is a character whose adventures will be remembered by future generations as a 'classic of our time.'"

In addition to the six collections of stories and two picture books centering on Mrs. Pepperpot that have been translated into English, Prøysen is the author of *The Town That Forgot It Was Christmas,* a nonsense story for early graders that incorporates several Norwegian customs, as well as a group of fantasies that are as yet untranslated; several of the Mrs. Pepperpot books also contain short stories about other human, animal, and supernatural characters. Prøysen won the Kirke- og undervisningsdepartements premier for boker skikket for skolebiblioteker, the Norwegian children's literature award, on five occasions: third prize for *Kjerringa som ble så lita som ei teskje* (*The Old Woman Who Became as Small as a Teaspoon*) in 1958, first prize for *Sirkus Mikkelikski* (*Mikkelikski Circus*) in

1964, second prize for *Den grønne votten* (*The Green Mitten*) in 1965, second prize for *Teskjekjerringa på camping* (*The Teaspoon Woman Goes Camping*) in 1968, and posthumously for his body of work in 1971; the same award was also given to the illustrators of several of Prøysen's works for the best picture book of the year.

GENERAL COMMENTARY

Ingrid Bozanic

More directly than most, Norwegian children's literature has its origins in an oral tradition of folktales and songs, and its written beginnings in a collection of folk-tales. The definitive collection of Norwegian folk-tales, *Norske Folkeeventyr,* assembled by Peter Christen Asbjörnsen and Jörgen Moe, appeared about 1850. The work was directly inspired by the great success of the Grimm brothers' collection of German folktales called *Kinder und Hausmärchen;* in its retention of local dialect it was undoubtedly also influenced by a current upsurge of romantic nationalism in Norway.

Asbjörnsen and Moe's collections consists of *sagn* or legends connected with historical events or specific places, and of *eventyr* which are the completely fictional stories sometimes called *märchen* or fairy tales. It is the *eventyr* with its trolls, princesses and treasures that has made the Norwegian folktales popular all over the world.

Besides the obvious trolls it is difficult to identify the peculiarly Norwegian elements in an *eventyr* that make it differ from variants in other countries. George Webbe Dasent, who translated Asbjörnsen and Moe's tales into English as *Popular Tales from the Norse* in 1858, made the following observations in his introductory essay:

> These Norse Tales we may characterize as bold, outspoken, and humorous, in the true sense of humor. In the midst of every difficulty and danger arises that old Norse feeling of making the best of everything, and keeping a good face to the foe. The language and tone are perhaps rather lower than in some other collections, but it must be remembered that these are the tales of "hempen homespuns. . . . "

Dasent has mentioned the major characteristics of the tone of Norwegian folktales: sharp objectivity, commonsense, a basic or earthy quality, and a keen sense of humor. (p. 61)

Alf Pröysen is probably the Norwegian children's author most well-known abroad. In addition to many excellent collections of songs, Alf Pröysen is the author of the Teskjekjerringa series which is called **Mrs. Pepperpot** in English. These are stories about the adventures of a little old lady who often shrinks to the size of a teaspoon or a pepperpot in the English version. In many ways they resemble the Norwegian *eventyr* more than they do other modern children's fantasies about miniature people, such as Mary Norton's *The Borrowers* or T. H. White's *Mistress Masham's Repose*. To begin with, Mrs. Pepperpot is a rather unorthodox main character or heroine for a children's book; but a wily old hag who tricks her husband, neighbors, and animals is traditional *eventyr* material. The tale "Kjerringa mot Strömmen" (The Women Against the Current) is only one example of an obstinate or willful wife in Norwegian folk-tales. Also typical is the lawless and amoral tone of the stories where anything goes as long as it benefits Mrs. Pepperpot. Mrs. Pepperpot's miniature size brings to mind the *eventyr* "Tommeliten" (Thumbkin) and "Dukken i Gresset" (Doll in the Grass). Her ability to understand the language of the animals is common in many Norwegian folk-tales. The books do not have one continuous plot but are episodic, and at the end of each episode Mrs. Pepperpot emerges triumphant and laughing. The stories tend to be wry and satirical.

Alf Pröysen's other stories for children include **Den Grönne Votten** which is the history of the adventures of a green mitten and **Sirkus Mikkelikski** in which the mistreated animals in a small circus revolt and decide to train the circus keepers. (pp. 62-3)

> *Ingrid Bozanic, "Contemporary Children's Literature in Norway," in* Children's Literature: Annual of the Modern Language Association Seminar on Children's Literature and The Children's Literature Association, *Vol. 3, 1974, pp. 61-5.*

Margery Fisher

Mrs Pepperpot is a pleasant, normal Norwegian housewife. But one morning she wakes to find herself shrunk to the size of a pepperpot, 'and old women don't usually do that'. Mrs Pepperpot is not the kind of person to lie in bed and brood over her dilemma. Instead, she cleverly persuades the mouse to clean the house ('or I'll tell the cat about you'), the cat to lick the dishes clean ('or I'll tell the dog about you') and the dog to air the bed, with a bone as reward. With similar threats and promises she induces the rain to wash the clothes, the wind to blow them on to the line and the sun to dry them, while with apt flattery she manages bowl, frying pan and pancake mixture so that Mr Pepperpot's supper is on the table when he comes home; and 'just as he opened the door, Mrs Pepperpot turned back to her usual size'.

This first story about the unusual Norwegian housewife sets the pattern for many more, while Björn Berg, as illustrator, comically confirms the impression of sharp features and forthright personality which we receive from the text. A capable and experienced housewife, Mrs Pepperpot knows how to improvise. She is fond of animals and her care of various foundlings, together with her friendly approach to wild creatures, amply repay her when she is in difficulties. Above all, her sense of humour and love of adventure ensure that she enjoys the most bizarre experiences—acting the Sleeping Beauty in a puppet show, playing horse and cart with a family of mice, carried by a crow to its nest. The ingenious detail in the stories, their meticulous attention to size and setting and their inventive fancy, culminate in the lively personality of the central character. Alf Pröysen and Björn Berg have together created an endearing and believable little woman who may claim to be included among the classic characters of nursery-rhyme and nursery tale. (pp. 249-50)

> *Margery Fisher, "Who's Who in Children's Books: Mrs. Pepperpot," in her* Who's Who in Children's Books: A Treasury of the Familiar Characters of Childhood, *Holt, Rinehart and Winston, 1975, pp. 249-50.*

TITLE COMMENTARY

Little Old Mrs. Pepperpot and Other Stories   (1959)

This spring, a promising character is Mrs. Pepperpot. She makes her appearance in a translation by Marianne Helweg of Alf Pröysen's **Little Old Mrs. Pepperpot,** a book roughly for five-to-seven-year-olds.

> There was once an old woman who went to bed at night as old women usually do, and in the morning she woke up as old women usually do. But on this particular morning she found herself shrunk to the size of a pepperpot, and old women don't usually do that. The odd thing was, her name really was Mrs. Pepperpot.
>
> "Well, as I'm now the size of a pepperpot, I shall have to make the best of it," she said to herself,

for she had no one else to talk to; her husband was out in the fields and all her children were grown up and gone away.

Now she happened to have a great deal to do that day. First of all she had to clean the house, then there was all the washing which was lying in soak and waiting to be done, and lastly she had to make pancakes for supper.

"I must get out of bed somehow," she thought, and, taking hold of a corner of the eiderdown, she started rolling herself up in it. She rolled and rolled until the eiderdown was like a huge sausage, which fell softly on the floor. Mrs. Pepperpot crawled out and she hadn't hurt herself a bit.

The style is right—economical, exact, matter-of-fact, and, being for small children, rhythmic; and the insistent details of reality are there all the time. Even though only some of the stories in the book are about Mrs. Pepperpot, and even though sometimes even these are occasionally slightly spoilt by indulgence—welcome to Mrs. Pepperpot!

> *"The Rules of Magic," in* The Times Literary Supplement, *No. 2987, May 29, 1959, p. xiii.*

Five of the stories in this quite delightful collection concern the adventures of the little old woman who finds one morning that she has shrunk to the size of a pepperpot. She accepts the phenomenon with a cheerful optimism and quietly sets about reorganizing her life to meet the unexpected situation. She is equally undaunted when, just as her husband comes in for supper, she returns to normal size. In Mrs. Pepperpot the author has created a shrewd and very amusing character whose warmth and friendliness will appeal to children. The actual adventures are imaginative and full of fun. The other stories in the collection are short, light and quite entertaining but not as good as those about Mrs. Pepperpot.

> *F. P. Parrott, in a review of "Little Old Mrs. Pepperpot," in* The School Librarian and School Library Review, *Vol. 9, No. 6, December, 1959, p. 516.*

Just as quaint, and much more plucky than Tom Thumb or Stuart Little, the resilient Mrs. Pepperpot may become a permanent member in the repertoire of children's book people. The other stories here are also uniquely imaginative, revealing the author's gift for bringing the familiar and the fantastic together in a completely entertaining fashion.

> *A review of "Little Old Mrs. Pepperpot," in* Virginia Kirkus' Service, *Vol. XXVIII, No. 6, March 15, 1960, p. 235.*

Mrs. Pepperpot Again and Other Stories   (1960)

As in the first book about Mrs. Pepperpot, that comical Norwegian housewife, strange things are still happening in her house chiefly as a result of her habit of shrinking to the size of a pepperpot at the most inconvenient moments. This, of course, keeps her in a constant flutter—and her young audience on the verge of gasps and giggles.

Here are more of her curious misadventures that will appeal directly to the younger child's sense of humor in stories that are first choice for reading aloud.

The vigorous story-teller's style has not been lost in Marianne Helweg's translation but there is one drawback to this volume. Seven stories about Mrs. Pepperpot are followed by five other stories about ogres, lady-bugs and people who live in Topsy Turvy Town. They're not bad stories, but they belong between different covers. Mrs. Pepperpot is in a class by herself as are Mary Poppins, the Peterkins and Mr. Popper.

> *Barbara Nolen, "Shrinking Lady," in* The New York Times Book Review, *July 30, 1961, p. 16.*

[The] elegantly simple alteration of ordinary domestic processes . . . makes the tales of Mrs. Pepperpot so engaging. **Mrs. Pepperpot again** should certainly be kept in print, like others in the sequence, for the sake of the droll absurdity and neat shape of the stories. The Norwegian housewife who shrinks to pepperpot size at inconvenient moments is seen making the most of her curious disability as she picks bilberries, minds a neighbour's baby and protects a family of kittens, enlisting help from cat, mouse, fox, wolf and other animals in turn. Among six additional stories of a more generally folk-lore type, **'Father Christmas and the Carpenter'** is especially intriguing with its alert, warm-hearted view of a Scandinavian festival. (pp. 4152-53)

> *Margery Fisher, in a review of "Mrs. Pepperpot Again," in* Growing Point, *Vol. 22, No. 4, November, 1983, pp. 4152-53.*

Mrs. Pepperpot to the Rescue   (1963)

Some readers of the under ten group will be familiar already with these Scandinavian stories of a little woman who at unexpected but useful moments becomes the size of a pepperpot and is thus enabled to do good turns to those she feels deserve them. If the situations in which the author places her are by now fairly stock ones this does not detract from the pleasing and jolly tone of the book and the real sense of humour that underlies the stories of the reducing lady and others in this collection. It goes further at times with a fine touch of the ridiculous but the writing and [Marianne Helweg's] translation are always attractive and apt.

> *A review of "Mrs. Pepperpot to the Rescue," in* The Junior Bookshelf, *Vol. 27, No. 3, July, 1963, p. 136.*

The heroine of these seven short stories is the now well-known and always enjoyable Mrs. Pepperpot. She is, by turns, spunky, meddlesome, and teasing, but always kind. She still, to the distress of her husband, shrinks without warning to the size of a pepperpot. This enables her to go to class with a little girl and slip her the answers to her school work. In the next story she decides it's the teacher who needs a lesson, but learns that she hasn't got a corner of kindness. Her methods of transportation, when suddenly shrunk, are always part of the fun—sometimes she goes by cat-back and in others she whirls on the wind. In the last story she scares the wits out of a steer by hiding and chattering in his cap, but she steers him to victory. It's the best nonsense out of Scandinavia.

> *A review of "Mrs. Pepperpot to the Rescue," in* Virginia Kirkus' Service, *Vol. XXXII, No. 5, March 1, 1964, p. 235.*

The Town That Forgot It Was Christmas   (1966)

I liked Alf Prøysen's nonsense tale, **The town that forgot it was Christmas,** for its spontaneous fun and for the shapely way the story develops. Here is a town in Norway where everyone is forgetful and everyone relies on chance to get back to normal—for instance, a small boy notices a blacksmith shoeing a horse and realises nobody is wearing shoes. The application to Christmas Day gives the author the chance to bring in Norwegian customs and an attractive background of food, furniture and cheerful merry-makers . . . [in] a story which is well on the way to giving readers not 'easy reading' but just—good reading. (pp. 716-17)

> *Margery Fisher, in a review of "The Town That Forgot It Was Christmas," in* Growing Point, *Vol. 5, No. 1, May, 1966, pp. 716-17.*

Mrs. Pepperpot in the Magic Wood   (1968)

Further unrelated adventures of Mrs. Pepperpot, the old lady who shrinks unpredictably and often inconveniently to pocket size. Small, she's mistaken for Betty Bodkin (from the finger rhyme "Here is Thumbkin . . . ") and for a talking 'tato (by a baby-talker), learns to swim from a frog and parrots for a parakeet; full-size, she promotes her husband into the presidency of the Society for the Protection of Helpless Animals, and from then on he has to be kind to *all* animals, whether he likes them or not (he doesn't). The last episode is the funniest: playing Sleeping Beauty in a puppet show, Mrs. Pepperpot injects commercials into her dialogue, to the delight of the audience and the dismay of the bossy puppeteer. Some of the situations are labored, to say the least, but there's a *do unto others* reminder from a captive crow that's apt and extra amusement from the discomfiture of much-put-upon Mr. Pepperpot.

> *A review of "Mrs. Pepperpot in the Magic Wood," in* Kirkus Service, *Vol. XXXVI, No. 5, March 1, 1968, p. 262.*

There is something particularly appealing about miniatures in a natural-sized world; look at the success of *The Twelve and the Genii* and *The Borrowers.* Here is the third in a series of story-books about the incredible shrinking housewife, whose enchanting appearance with skewered bun atop her head and sharply tip-tilted nose is familiar to many children of five and up. I find her essentially adult common-sense her most endearing quality: she is never coy, and the situations in which she becomes involved are always within the realms of possibility, a fact which helps to reinforce the fantasy of her size.

> *G. Maunder, in a review of "Mrs. Pepperpot in the Magic Wood," in* Children's Book News, *London, Vol. 3, No. 3, May-June, 1968, p. 139.*

The fiery lady who shrinks in size when she leasts expects it is back with further adventures. By this time, devotees may find the climaxes predictable but they will probably continue to enjoy Mrs. Pepperpot. Outstanding among the stories in this title are Mrs. P.'s attempts at learning how to swim with a frog as teacher, her collaboration with a misused parakeet, and her participation as a member of the cast of a puppet show.

> *Dorothy Gunzenhauser, in a review of "Mrs. Pepperpot in the Magic Wood," in* School Library Journal, *Vol. 15, No. 1, September, 1968, p. 194.*

Mrs. Pepperpot's Busy Day   (1970)

The first story about Mrs. Pepperpot has now been made into a picture book. The text has been very slightly modified in two or three places and the number of illustrations [by Björn Berg] has been increased. The result is a large and quite attractive picture book in strong colour with the diminutive Mrs. Pepperpot set against a colourful background.

Presumably more of the stories will be presented in this way, so introducing Mrs. Pepperpot to a younger generation. Her liability to shrink at inconvenient moments, requires no 'suspension of disbelief' on the part of children and her astringent personality is wholly convincing.

> *E. Colwell, in a review of "Mrs. Pepperpot's Busy Day," in* The Junior Bookshelf, *Vol. 35, No. 2, April, 1971, p. 100.*

Mrs. Pepperpot's Outing and Other Stories   (1971)

> [*The following excerpt is from a review of the original Norwegian edition of* Mrs. Pepperpot's Outing *published in 1968.*]

[Prøysen] deserves a feather in his cap and a flower in his buttonhole, because he has actually managed to make the fourth volume even funnier and better than its predecessors. He has thus disposed of the theory that a series must steadily deteriorate.

Prøysen again has many home truths to tell, for instance how stupid it is to be impressed by new-fangled junk and flipperies. It is obvious that he is particularly concerned about the fact that there will soon be few animals even on farms. Perhaps he is also thinking of those city flats where one may keep neither cats nor dogs.

Mrs. Pepperpot and her husband have no pets any longer. The husband is only interested in his car and in competitions of all sorts: gymkhanas and rallies, marching competitions and fishing competitions. During the summer holidays he must of course go camping with Mrs. Pepperpot just like everyone else. This trip is the framework of the new Pepperpot-stories and despite all modern gadgets the whole is a fairy-tale in the good old tradition. Every time the wife shrinks to the size of a pepperpot, the fairy-tale atmosphere engrosses us and it seems perfectly natural that she can speak with all the animals she meets. She finally crowds the back seat of the car with sick or deserted animals which she wants to take home without her husband noticing anything—a kitten, a piglet, a puppy and a hen. The fox, however, has to stay in the woods.

And then everything happens as before. The husband gives in and recognizes that there must be animals on a farm for everyone's benefit. But before we have reached that far, young and old have been captivated once more by the excitement of the story, which is only right and proper if the book is to be equally delightful for adults and children. This is a book which even beginning readers will master, . . . and there are so many wonderful maxims and verses which split up the story for the children. Here again as in the earlier books Prøysen weaves in a number of funny songs and we find ourselves agreeing with the husband in the book that we "have heard the melody before, only the text is new." (pp. 38-9)

Astrid Feydt, "The Best Norwegian Children's Books," in Bookbird, *Vol. VI, No. 3, September 15, 1968, pp. 34-40.*

The little old lady who shrinks without warning to the size of a pepperpot in a story that is consistently slight. The outing occurs in Mr. Pepperpot's car, and during the course of the afternoon jaunt Mrs. Pepperpot shrinks five times—*and* collects a cat, a pig, a dog and a hen, which she must smuggle home without her husband's knowledge. The complications result from her attempts to keep all of this a secret from her husband, though he is solicitous throughout about her affliction and agreeable to keeping the animals once they are revealed to him, back home—which makes what little plot there is seem arbitrary. Mrs. Pepperpot's friends will want to join her excursion, but there's just too much shrinking and swelling with too little point.

A review of "Mrs. Pepperpot's Outing," in Kirkus Reviews, *Vol. XXXIX, No. 21, November 1, 1971, p. 1157.*

These new stories are as fresh and original as ever. The late Alf Proysen's talent for his own brand of situation comedy is conveyed within a sense of warmth and homeliness. In the first story in this collection, the longest that Proysen has written about Mrs. Pepperpot, there is plenty of opportunity for Mrs. P. to display the two unusual qualities which single her out from the general populace; the first of shrinking at the most inopportune moments and the second of, once having shrunk being able to communicate with the animals in their own language. Too often books which purport to be humorous are stilted and lack awareness of a child's sense of humour, neither criticisms could be levelled in this direction for very truly the 'liveliest effusions of wit and humour are conveyed to the world in the best chosen language'. Here is a character whose adventures will be remembered by future generations as a 'classic of our time'. There is, as usual, one story in the collection about the ogre with the insatiable appetite, Gaby Gob.

Vivien Jennings, in a review of "Mrs. Pepperpot's Outing and Other Stories," in Children's Book Review, *Vol. I, No. 6, December, 1971, p. 192.*

The crisp, trim, ebullient tales about the shrinking Swedish housewife strike a responsive chord in children all over the world. *Mrs. Pepperpot's outing* is a long story with a repetitive plan, admirably planned, in which Mrs. Pepperpot talks herself out of difficulties with a kitten, a piglet, a puppy and a hen and makes it impossible for her long-suffering husband to refuse their adoption into the household. Besides this disarmingly nonsensical tale there are three shorter ones which are not quite up to standard. Two are about Mrs. Pepperpot, one crediting her with a smart sister who comes on a visit from America; the entertaining social satire of this particular story doesn't altogether subdue in me certain serious genetic doubts.

Margery Fisher, in a review of "Mrs. Pepperpot's Outing," in Growing Point, *Vol. 10, No. 6, December, 1971, p. 1846.*

One for older or more mature children, this. Personally, I can take Mrs Pepperpot or leave her; she has never seemed very lovable to me. But she is liked by children, usually girls who are young but fluent readers, and this collection is inventive and entertaining. The situations in which Mrs Pepperpot finds herself as a result of her predilection for suddenly shrinking to the size of a pepperpot make lively introductions to 'big, thick books' for children who are gaining stamina but not yet ready for a novel format.

Liz Waterland, in a review of "Mrs. Pepperpot's Outing," in Books for Keeps, *No. 50, May, 1988, p. 10.*

Mrs. Pepperpot's Christmas (1972)

Mrs. Pepperpot is quite a character, and one who in recent years has endeared herself to the hearts of many young readers. Her contemporaries include *Paddington* and *My Naughty Little Sister* and similarly a whole series of stories have been written about her and each new one is eagerly awaited. Her latest adventure is in picture-book format and adds the extra dimension of colour to Mrs. Pepperpot. As previously, Alf Proysen's illustrator is Björn Berg who has projected the visual image of Mrs. Pepperpot so well in all her adventures to date. For new readers, suffice to say that Mrs. Pepperpot shrinks from time to time to the size of a pepperpot and thus finds herself in all kinds of predicaments. She uses this facility for her own ends in the latest story, hiding herself in her husband's knapsack on his way to market to make sure that he buys a sheaf of corn, a little bird-house and a wreath of mistletoe from the Christmas market. By threatening to reveal to the shoppers at each stall that he has a wife who shrinks, she manoeuvres her husband into doing as she wishes. Taking flight on a balloon given to her husband, she enlists the aid of the birds in guiding her homewards where returning to her normal size, she welcomes her husband home with a kiss. As enchanting and warm hearted as Mrs. Pepperpot herself, this is a picture story book which should please many four to eight-year-olds. (pp. 180-81)

Edward Hudson, in a review of "Mrs. Pepperpot's Christmas," in Children's Book Review, *Vol. II, No. 6, December, 1972, pp. 180-81.*

Mrs. Pepperpot's Year (1973)

Mrs Pepperpot might have stepped straight out of folklore; she is shrewd, benevolent, with a mischievous sense of fun. . . . Sometimes she is herself as vulnerable as a small child: a mother hen insists on treating her as one of its chicks, and another time she is swept dangerously downstream on a packet of soap powder. **Mrs. Pepperpot's Year** has a story for each month, all short but substantial; they make an excellent collection.

"New Growth," in The Times Literary Supplement, *No. 3742, November 23, 1973, p. 1439.*

[In] **Mrs. Pepperpot's Year,** Alf Proysen tells twelve new tales about Norway's most unusual housewife. . . . Mrs Pepperpot does her spring cleaning, saves her friend the moose from being hunted, and ends up in hospital. It is all straightforward and wacky in that peculiar combination we have come to expect of the Pepperpot saga. I think

it is charm and good-heartedness which makes it memorable.

Robert Nye, "Tell Me a Story," in The Spectator, *Vol. 231, No. 7591, December 22, 1973, p. 823.*

Stories for Summer (1990)

There is no special reason why these stories should be for summer; in fact, in the case of one, **'Mrs. Pepperpot is Taken for a Witch',** it would be more appropriate for 5th November. It's also a very confusing story, perhaps due to translation problems. Mrs Pepperpot is not 'taken for a witch', nor even *mistaken* for a witch, but is nearly burnt on the bonfire, as witches once were, because nobody knew she was there. This is puzzling, as is the end of the story where we have to take it for granted that she has got home safely without any explanation of how she did so. This one story apart, however, the rest in the collection are very entertaining. They're not all about Mrs Pepperpot, which pleases me since she's not my favourite person, and they have a pleasant, folk-tale air about them. The children especially enjoyed **'The Kid That Could Count to Ten'.**

Liz Waterland, in a review of "Stories for Summer," in Books for Keeps, *No. 63, July, 1990, p. 9.*

Lynne Reid Banks

1929-

English author of fiction.

Major works include *The Farthest-Away Mountain* (1976), *The Indian in the Cupboard* (1980), *The Writing on the Wall* (1982), *Return of the Indian* (1986).

A writer praised for her versatility, insight, and skill as a literary stylist, Reid Banks is the creator of both fantasy and realistic fiction for readers in the early, middle, and upper grades. Respected as a novelist, playwright, and writer of nonfiction for adults, she is best known in the field of children's literature for the popular trilogy *The Indian in the Cupboard, Return of the Indian,* and *The Secret of the Indian* (1989), fantasies for middle graders that describe how ten-year-old Omri, his best friend Patrick, and Patrick's sister Emma are placed in exciting situations when they discover that Omri's miniature toy figures can be transformed into tiny human beings by being placed in a magic cupboard. Through his experiences with the toys in both contemporary and historical times, Omri learns that, as real people, they deserve respect despite their size. Beginning these works as oral tales told to her youngest son Omri, Reid Banks is acknowledged for creating original and believable stories that are often considered modern classics. She is also the author of several other books that rework or extend elements from traditional fairy tales, myths, and legends; in her fantasy *The Farthest-Away Mountain,* for example, Reid Banks gives a feminist spin to the familiar quest story by portraying a determined young woman who refuses to marry until she travels to her mountain destination, and in *Melusine: A Mystery* (1988), she uses the old French legend of a woman who is both human and snake as the basis for a modern psychological thriller for young adults. Reid Banks is also noted for the deft blend of fantasy and reality she brings to several of her works of this type; for example, in *Maura's Angel* (1984) she weaves the problems of modern Belfast into the story of a Catholic child who meets her guardian angel after a bomb explodes.

Reid Banks is also the author of several realistic novels for young adults that consider such themes as class conflict and the establishment of personal independence. In both *My Darling Villain* (1977) and *The Writing on the Wall* (1981), she places her teenage protagonists and their parents in opposition over the boyfriends of each girl; however, Kate and Tracy resolve their problems and unite with their families at the end of their respective stories. In addition, Reid Banks is the creator of works that reflect her interest in the Jewish people. Her first book for children, *One More River* (1973), is the story of the transformation of a spoiled Canadian girl forced to emigrate to Israel just before the Six-Day War that Reid Banks wrote after spending eight years as an English teacher on an Israeli kibbutz; she followed it with *Sarah and After: The Matri-*

archs (1975), a fictionalized account of the lives and viewpoints of five Biblical women.

(See also *Contemporary Literary Criticism,* Vol. 23; *Something about the Author,* Vol. 22; *Contemporary Authors New Revision Series,* Vols. 6, 22; and *Contemporary Authors,* Vol. 1, rev. ed.)

AUTHOR'S COMMENTARY

[The following excerpt is from an interview by Amanda Smith.]

In her native England, Lynne Reid Banks is known as an author of adult fiction, most especially of ***The L-Shaped Room,*** which was adapted into a successful movie. But in the U.S., she is known as an author of children's books. . . . Her interests—ranging from the fantastic to the grittily realistic—are well represented by works appearing this fall. There is ***The Secret of the Indian*** the final volume in a trilogy about a boy whose cupboard magically transforms plastic figures into living beings. There is also ***Melusine,*** in which a British boy travels on holiday with his family to a mysterious French chateau. And finally, there is the paperback edition of *The Fairy Rebel* Reid Banks's charming story of a couple helped from their childless state by a fairy. (p. 30)

Reid Banks was born in London 60 years ago to a Scottish doctor and an Irish actress. "I was the only child of parents devoted to each other and to me," she says. "It was a rather typical middle-class English childhood, with cousins in the country and holidays by the sea."

War broke out when Reid Banks was 11, and she, her mother and cousin were evacuated to Canada—at first a difficult, but finally a happy time. "I was extremely self-centered and interested in my own life and not doing madly well at school," she recalls, "but [I was] the star of the drama club."

Reid Banks returned to a country devastated by wartime bombing and to a changed family. "We had a lot of trouble getting all together again; our experiences had been so different. And then having to get down to being English again from being Canadian. I had a Canadian accent, all my friends were there, and no way was I going to be sent back to school even though I was only 15."

Reid Banks wanted to "study for the stage," but her mother wisely insisted that she learn shorthand and typing first. "I was dragged out of bed and dispatched to this bomb-blasted, freezing-cold building to learn shorthand and typing through numbed fingers, which I eventually, reluctantly, did, and of course it's been the mainstay of my life."

According to Reid Banks, her mother's being an actress was one of the major influences of her life. "I grew up surrounded by evidences of theater and acting," she says, "and I had no idea of being anything but an actress from the time I could think. I went to drama school, then I did act for about five years." She found some of the plays she was in "pretty awful" and decided she could do better. Her first play, a comedy, was performed by a local repertory company, and later by the BBC. "It was quite something to have a play on BBC when you were only 24. Even though it got the most terrible notices that any play has ever got and certainly the worst notices I've ever had in my life, that kind of set me up. I thought then, well, I would be a playwright."

Reid Banks's acting career "kind of petered out" and she became a journalist and then one of the first two women television reporters in England. Her first novel, *The L-Shaped Room,* published as she was "going on 30," established her as a novelist; it has never been out of print.

After completing her second novel, she lived in Israel for the next eight years. "I was very attracted by the idea of Israel, and had been following its fortunes since 1947." During those years, she married an Englishman—a Liverpudlian she met in London through Israeli connections—had three sons and began a new career—teaching English. "It was one of the most exciting discoveries of my life—that I'm a good teacher," she says. "I did that for eight years. And then we came home. Since then I've been a full-time writer."

Reid Banks wrote her first children's book, *The Adven-*

tures of King Midas before she had written any other book. "There was a little boy who used to wander home with me from walks with my dog," she says. "He couldn't read well, so I started to write a story in big print to teach him to read. I told him the story of King Midas and the Golden Touch. When I got to the end of the legend, where poor Midas realizes that he's made a right tat out of himself, and his daughter's turned to gold and he can't eat, this little boy said, "This is awful, it's not fair, he's sorry now, can't leave him like that.' I thought, that's right, so I continued so that the story develops into a quest to have the magic annulled and his daughter brought back to life. Years later, some publisher asked me if I had ever written for children. And I said, 'Oh yes, I've got this little manuscript.' "

Reid Banks's next children's book was *The Farthest-Away Mountain* "another kind of fabulous story. I was ahead of my time in this, because I made the heroine a very gutsy girl, very feminine, not a tomboy, but gutsy. I was at this time writing adult books at the rate of one a year, and every now and then I'd get bogged down in all this turgid soul-searching or research or whatever, and I'd write another children's book. By this time my kids were old enough so that I was keeping my brain active telling them stories. One of the stories I told my youngest son was about this little plastic Indian." That eventually became *The Indian in the Cupboard,* which has sold over 50,000 copies in hardcover and more than a million in paperback.

"Apart from *The L-Shaped Room,* I have never had a success like it," she says. "My books have been successful, but this is a blockbuster. I didn't have any idea of continuing [*The Indian in the Cupboard*]. It was just that there was so much demand from children for another one. There were so many good ideas in their letters . . . that it really started my imagination ticking off again."

Plans are afoot to make a film of *The Indian in the Cupboard;* however, Reid Banks says, "They're going to make the boys American, and it's going to ruin it. It will be a tragedy, because so many American kids have absorbed something of the British way of life from reading these books, and the contrast between the American little people and [the British] Omri and his chums give the story its creative bite."

The more somber *Melusine* has its origin in a vacation when Reid Banks's family went to France and stayed at a ramshackle chateau, where she heard about Melusine, a local legendary figure. "At first when I mapped the story out it was just about this boy and his family who go there, and there's this mystery about the girl [who transforms herself into a snake]. It wasn't enough that she was a legend, or that there was some myth come to life. There had to be some reason that she made this horrendous change. . . . I gradually realized that I'd been laying the ground for myself with this solitary, sinister, lonely, depraved old father. And I realized what it had to be. . . ."

The issue she chose to explore was sexual abuse, one that presented problems of its own. "In America, you get terribly worried if you mix good and evil up," she continued.

"The father had to be a villain because people who do that to their children have got to be absolutely wicked. And if it was said that she missed him and was sad that he died, it would look as if she loved him, as if she had been complicitious in her own seduction. But ask any child who's been seduced by her father—they still love them. That's the terrible difficulty that social services face."

Reid Banks terms the **The Fairy Rebel** "a very intimate story for me." The book is dedicated to "Bindi and her mother," and Reid Banks says, "I think I'm the only writer who ever dedicated a book to herself. . . . Bindi was actually my name when I was a little girl. The story about the woman who wanted a baby and couldn't have one and met a fairy who arranged it was the story my mother told me about how I was born. The thing that I loved best about the adventures my cousin and I had with fairies was that unlike every other fairy story I ever read, the parents were in on it. I was simply unsatisfied as a child by the explanation, 'Well, grown-ups don't see fairies because they don't believe in them.' I *always* make it true in my fantasies."

She believes **The Fairy Rebel** is original in that the real adventure happens to the woman, not to a child. "But of course my publisher was quite worried about that. Can children identify with a grown-up heroine? And I said the *fairy* is the one—she's a child fairy who grows up during the course of the book. It's a story of birth and regeneration, which is a lot nicer than the cabbage patch and the gooseberry bush and the stork and all that."

Reid Banks clearly enjoys writing stories that find imaginative resolutions to even the oldest legends. In doing so, she gives delight to even her youngest readers. (pp. 30, 32)

Amanda Smith, "Lynne Reid Banks," in Publishers Weekly, *Vol. 236, No. 17, October 27, 1989, pp. 30, 32.*

GENERAL COMMENTARY

Michele Landsberg

[**The Indian in the Cupboard**] is a good example of a story so captivating, so exciting, that the moral choices facing the main character seem to be just a more wrenching part of the action. Omri is the youngest of three brothers in an ordinary London family; we are catapulted into the action from the first line, when Omri's best friend, Patrick, gives him a disappointing birthday present—a used plastic Indian figurine, just like the dozens of plastic figures Omri already owns. His older brother gives him a tin medicine cabinet that he found in an alley. And that night, when Omri puts the Indian in the cupboard and locks it with an old curly-topped key given him by his mother, the Indian comes to life.

Of course, it is an old fantasy—the nursery toys coming alive—but Banks gives it a wonderful fresh immediacy by using a modern toy, and one that turns into a real person, though admittedly stereotyped. The transformation makes your pulse leap:

He was crouching in the darkest corner . . . And he was alive . . . though he was trying to keep still, he was breathing heavily. His bare bronze shoulders rose and fell, and were shiny with sweat. The single feather sticking out of the back of his headband quivered, as if the Indian were trembling . . . As Omri peered close, and his breath fell on the tiny huddled figure, he saw it jump to its feet; its minute hand made a sudden, darting movement toward its belt and came to rest clutching the handle of a knife smaller than the shaft of a drawing pin.

The medicine cupboard is a true Pandora's box. Even before Omri can savor the miracle to its full, he finds himself caught up in the difficulties of having created life. The Indian is imperious, demanding: He asks for a horse, a longhouse, a fire, food, and tools, and Omri must use all his wits to keep an Iroquois brave properly equipped from the scroungings of a modern suburban house. Almost at once, Omri is made to realize that a live person, no matter how small or powerless, can't be a toy. When he picks up Little Bull against his will ("his body was heavier now, warm and firm and full of life . . . through Omri's thumb, on the Indian's left side, he could feel his heart beating wildly, like a bird's") he senses Little Bull's humanity—and in the same instant, is struck by the insulting cruelty of handling him.

Life gets more complicated when Patrick insists on being let into the secret. Horses, a cowboy, and an old chief are brought to life, sometimes with disastrous consequences. The small creatures weep, fight, wound each other, stab Omri, shoot at Patrick. The pony, a wonderful creation, has to be taken outside for exercise and real grass; Omri desperately warns Little Bull against "mountain lions big enough to swallow the pony." He has learned to see the world, and the neighbor's cat, through Little Bull's eyes.

Children, who are the bottom of the pecking order, are naturally fascinated with miniatures; all the more enthralling when the miniatures breathe and ride horses; all the more shocking and sobering when they assume a life of their own, and small as they are, are no longer totally in the child's power. There is humor in **The Indian in the Cupboard,** and excitement to spare, but it has another, more difficult but enriching dimension that makes Omri a changed person. (pp. 120-22)

One More River by Lynne Reid Banks is not nearly so accomplished as her later **Indian in the Cupboard,** but it is a curiously convincing coming-of-age story about a spoiled Canadian fourteen-year-old Jewish girl who finds herself transplanted to an Israeli kibbutz. The most poignant aspect of Leslie Shelby's "enlargement of self" is her tenuous, fragile, wounded friendship with a Palestinian boy who lives on the other side of the Jordan River. The wound of disillusionment—"the complete realizing that not any one can believe" just what you believe—is delicately probed in this book; it touches not only on Leslie and the Arab boy, but on Leslie's difficulties with the Israeli teenagers and on the many inevitable rifts within her family. The adult task of remaking wounded relationships after the ruptures of disillusionment is one of the book's encouraging themes. (pp. 218-19)

Michele Landsberg, "The Quest for Identity" and "Growing Up," in her Reading for the Love of It: Best Books for Young Readers, *Prentice Hall Press, 1987, pp. 99-128, 201-28.*

Opal Moore and Donnarae MacCann

Banks has created two novels, **The Indian in the Cupboard** and **The Return of the Indian,** that make deliberate use of the favorite American cinematic combination—the cowboy and the Indian. (p. 27)

In these technically well-crafted novels, Omri and his friend Patrick are plausible in their responses to the magical transformations. But Little Bear's portrayal is in no way creative. He is presented as savage and childish, volatile and irascible. He is designed to incorporate all of the assumptions that attach to the cinematic Indian. In fact, Little Bear makes his dramatic entrance in **The Indian in the Cupboard** with an act of bravado: he stabs Omri with a "knife smaller than the shaft of a tack." As the surprised Omri nurses his wound, "the Indian stood there . . . chest heaving, knife ready, black eyes wild. Omri thought he was magnificent". Immediately, Omri expresses concern that the Indian might not speak English: "All the Indians in films spoke a sort of English; it would be terrible if his Indian couldn't." But of course Little Bear obliges as expected: " 'I speak,' he grunted." And, true to the movies, the Indian rarely just speaks—he grunts, growls, snarls, barks, and shouts his broken caveman-style dialogue. He also seems to require a daily quotient of killing, like a vitamin, and is unhappy when there is nothing around for him to shoot.

Of course, it's all in fun, or so we are to assume, as Banks makes use of these traits of the stereotypical Indian and plays them for laughs. Because the Indian is miniscule, his inhuman attributes are supposed to be viewed as amusing, like his diminutive acts of violence. Only Boone breaks the constraints of stereotype and, of the little people, he is the only one permitted to undergo change. (In **The Return,** we are told he no longer hates Indians.) Rather than the hard-jawed, fast-on-the-draw cowboy familiar in the American western, Boone is a sensitive type who cries when he is lonely and draws lovely pictures in Omri's art class. He is stereotypical only in his hard drinking, his refusal to bathe, and his disdain for "them dirty savages." But these "flaws" do not impair his portrayal as a good-hearted, reasonable man who, unlike Little Bear, does not like to pick a fight. This contrasts with the Indian character who stuns Omri with his brag of having taken thirty scalps.

Even as stereotypes, the white characters tend towards competence and humaneness. A miniature nurse, medic, or company of white soldiers are trotted out routinely to patch up the havoc created by the Indians and "their warring." The climactic aggression in the first book is Little Bear's shooting of Boone, an act provoked by Boone's open display of hatred for the Indians being mowed down in a typical television western. Distressed by the seemingly real scene, Little Bear joins the fray by shooting Boone with an arrow. As Boone lies deathly still, Omri, like a stern parent, instructs Little Bear to remove the shaft and save Boone's life. He warns the Indian that, "if [Boone] dies, it'll be doubly your fault."

This is the bottom line of these novels. Little Bear is portrayed, with tongue in cheek, as a stereotype not to be taken seriously, and yet he remains a symbol of American Indians, a group cast as a self-destructive rather than a persecuted people. Little Bear's protest against the crimes of the whites who "move onto land! Use water! Kill animals!" is presented in inarticulate and unconvincing language, and it is then belittled as petulance and temper. Both Omri and the author choose to ignore the legitimacy of his protest, especially since the soft, harmless Boone never effectively evokes the image of the evil white men whom Little Bear refers to. In a display of remorse, Little Bear deliberately tramples a beautiful ceremonial headdress—a symbol of his heritage. The meaning is clear: Little Bear must accept the blame for the novel's distortion of history. He alone is required to repent his actions. Boone is not required to recant his attitudes about Little Bear. This failure to repudiate his attitudes is a fictional parallel for the tendency of the white writers to avoid responsibility for the role their predecessors have played in the havoc of the past. Instead, Boone magnanimously allows that he holds no grudge for his injury because "that there's a Injun's natural nature. Pore simple critter c'd no more help himself than Ah kin keep away from mah horse and mah bottle!"

In **The Return of the Indian,** the miscasting of history continues. Omri decides to help the Iroquois fight the French, but Banks obscures the "told" facts about the European contingent by providing vivid images that contradict them. Specifically, the French are *mentioned* as enemies of the Iroquois, but when Omri climbs into the magic trunk and goes back in time to look at the historical moment, he does not see the French soldiers the way Little Bear has gaspingly described them: " . . . come burn village! Burn corn! . . . break—burn—steal—kill . . . kill . . . " He *sees* the Algonquins, "their faces . . . wild, distorted, terrifying masks of hatred and rage". He sees Indians destroying each other. Banks is, of course, technically safe. The Algonquins were allied with the French, but the point here is that the author is willing to mention the French involvement for the sake of correctness, but is unwilling to place them in the plot action as the enemy, or state the nature of the conflict. The Indians appear to be fighting each other for no apparent reason other than their "Injun's natural nature." As a result, the near-obliteration of the American Indian nations through the aggression of whites is neatly avoided.

Because these two novels are fanciful, questions of "reality" may appear out of place. Fantasy aside, ample opportunity exists for the parodying of stereotypes without validating them. . . . Banks provides openings in the novels' structure for more sensitive renderings, as we see to some extent in Boone's characterization. But, at the moment of truth, she refuses to alter the "model" of the stereotypical savage. Ironically, Omri chides his friend Patrick for his irresponsible use of the miniature people: "They're not safe with you. You *use* them. They're people. You can't use people. The same admonition could be made to the author. Banks makes free use of the Indian and of historical situations with little regard for their reality or ours. She uses fantasy as a license to manufacture a history. (pp. 27-8)

> *Opal Moore and Donnarae MacCann, "The Ignoble Savage: Amerind Images in the Mainstream Mind," in* Children's Literature Association Quarterly, *Vol. 13, No. 1, Spring, 1988, pp. 26-30.*

TITLE COMMENTARY

One More River (1973)

[Lynne Reid Banks] takes as the subject of her first children's book the ordeal of a Canadian Jewish girl whose rich parents suddenly decide to emigrate to Israel, just before the six-day war. Unfortunately, the not uninteresting reckoning of value between individualist and communal living has been ludicrously fudged by making the heroine a caricature of spoilt and obstinate shallowness, so that any change in her is necessarily for the better, and there is no loss, it seems, to set against the gain.

The central theme of the book is provided by a friendship between the girl and an Arab boy she sees across the Jordan. There are some very fine scenes in the book; notably the reunion between the girl's father and her estranged brother, and the conversation when she finally meets her Arab friend face to face. But for the most part the tale unfolds with a wearisome slackness of technique. A kindly adult is wheeled on for the first time two paragraphs before her likely disapproval occurs to the girl; the six-day war kills people of whose existence we have only just been told. History lessons come in hectoring letters from the brother. Visiting Jerusalem for the first time makes no impression upon the Canadian girl; it is all being saved up for the second time, which makes the climax of the book. And one cannot help wondering how the writer of that moving reunion could possibly append to it a sentence like: "You did the trick, Sis. We're a family again."

Children do not lack either memory or sensitivity; it is a sad spectacle to see a fine writer underestimating her readers.

> *"Pawns of War," in* The Times Literary Supplement, *No. 3709, April 6, 1973, p. 380.*

Though the author herself once immigrated to Israel, her harsh condemnation of Lesley's difficulties in accepting the change from decadent wealth as a department store owner's daughter in Saskatoon, Canada, to kibbutz poverty results in a strange lack of empathy. Lesley, in her clothesmad Canadian days, is analyzed with clinical cruelty ("what 'spoiled' really means is that your character is too weak, too petted . . . "). And though both parents are permitted some doubts about the wisdom of their decision, Lesley—after initial stubborn rebellion—embraces her new life with fervent intensity and almost utopian results; her brother Noah, who had been disowned because of his marriage to a Catholic, rediscovers his Jewishness and comes from Canada to volunteer during the Six Days War, and an Arab boy is so overwhelmed by Lesley's con-

cern for his mistreated donkey that he unlearns the lesson of hate. Many scenes of the warmth and vigor of kibbutz life do communicate a feeling of joyous affirmation of the Israeli experience, but certain readers—particularly those quick enough to realize that the author must regard *them* as Lesleys of a sort—will be discouraged by her moralistic stance.

> *A review of "One More River," in* Kirkus Reviews, *Vol. XLI, No. 9, May 1, 1973, p. 521.*

After the realism of **The L-Shaped Room,** I found **One More River** a great disappointment. . . .

The plot may sound reasonable but the treatment is a mixture of sentimentality and morality worthy of the worst of the Victorians. There is no subtlety in either the characterization or the philosophy and I think the author has been so carried away by the wish to convey a 'message' that the novel is merely a vehicle for this. It may be read for its picture of kibbutz life but otherwise I could not recommend it for young adults.

> *Aileen M. McNamara, in a review of "One More River," in* The School Librarian, *Vol. 21, No. 2, June, 1973, p. 142.*

It is pleasant to read a new novel for young people that really tries to be a novel. . . .

Miss Banks uses the length of the book to explore several characters and relationships, and the society of the kibbutz is convincingly presented.

Unfortunately the book is written too much to a moralising plan: Lesley, spoilt in materialist Saskatoon, is bound to become unselfish in the communal socialism of Israel. But the way in which this happens is convincing, and reflects much real experience. Young readers will find enrichment in the portrayal of this Jewish family and the struggles of a dedicated people.

> *M. H. Miller, in a review of "One More River," in* Children's Book Review, *Vol. III, No. 3, June, 1973, p. 80.*

Sarah and After: The Matriarchs (1975)

Gradually I became disappointed as I read through Lynne Reid Banks's chronicle of four generations of the tribe of Abraham. The first section dealing with Sarah, Abraham's wife, destined to become the founder of a race 'chosen by God', I found hauntingly beautiful, but page by page the spell was broken. Too much was tragedy, too much on the same key. Retelling the Old Testament is indeed a formidable task, but here I think it has been done in a strange way too literally. There are however many beautiful parts; the descriptions of the desert at night and before dawn are some. On a more practical note I would have liked a map, I like to know where my characters are going. On one point however I did feel the author had excelled: that was the dialogue. She has spent some time in Israel and this shows clearly in her turn of phrase, as for example when Jacob says to Esau 'Without food, we lose our strength.' This may seem a small point but it does give authenticity to the book. (pp. 242-43)

Joan Murphy, in a review of "Sarah and After," in The School Librarian, Vol. 23, No. 3, September, 1975, pp. 242-43.

In Banks' retelling of their stories, five Old Testament heroines—Sarah, Rebecca, Leah, Rachel, and Dinah—emerge as real, believable, and very contemporary. And there's the rub. The intricate psychological interpretation of each woman's thoughts, feelings, and actions does not mesh with the ancient simplicity of the original tales. For example, there is no way for Banks to know that Sarah and Abraham's relationship "remained strained for some time" since it is not mentioned in the Old Testament (there is also an error concerning Sarah's death). As a group of fictionalized biblical tales with the emphasis on the woman's point of view, this is lively enough and Banks often captures the mood and phrasing of the biblical text, but readers who interpret the Bible literally will not be comfortable with it. (pp. 60-1)

Eleanor Tandowsky, in a review of "Sarah and After," in School Library Journal, Vol. 23, No. 6, February, 1977, pp. 60-1.

With imagination and skill, the author has created a deeply human drama based on the Biblical history of the five generations from Abraham to Joseph. Focusing on the lives of Sarah, Rebecca, Leah, Rachel, and Dinah, the story begins in the third person and shifts to the first when Leah is introduced. The innermost thoughts, burdens, and fears of these women—and of the men they bore—are convincingly portrayed. Similarly, the relationships between the men and the women and between the people and God are sensitively drawn. The central role of God in their lives, in their view of the world, and in the fate of their nation is the awesome force behind the drama. By dedicating the book to her goddaughters "lest they, like many of their contemporaries, grow up believing that the Christian religion sprang up without roots in the year 1," the author has set a goal for her writing which she admirably achieves.

Karen M. Klockner, in a review of "Sarah and After: Five Women Who Founded a Nation," in The Horn Book Magazine, Vol. LIII, No. 4, August, 1977, p. 448.

The Adventures of King Midas (1976)

The adventures of King Midas is hard to define and impossible to like. It can hardly be described as a re-telling of the legend, since this merely provides the start of a facetious sequence of dotty adventures endured by the King while, following the advice of "the little man" who grants his rash desire for the golden touch, he searches for a certain Old Gollop, a river-god who alone can break the spell. The King's wanderings are as absurd and tasteless as his given character, petulant and whimsical, and the self-consciously slangy dialogue. This astonishing vulgarisation has totally obliterated the meaning of the legend and its antique elements without putting anything of value in their place; even George Him's wry, spry illustrations cannot help enough.

Margery Fisher, in a review of "The Adven-

tures of King Midas," in Growing Point, Vol. 15, No. 4, October, 1976, p. 2962.

A very amusingly told extension of the familiar Greek myth when everything King Midas touches turns to gold—in this version, even his precious young daughter. Here this retelling departs from the traditional mythical story, and the King goes on a series of mysterious adventures on his quest to find someone or something who will rid him of this dreadful predicament. . . . The dialogue between the various folk Midas encounters and Midas himself is very witty. (pp. 267-68)

B. Clark, in a review of "The Adventures of King Midas," in The Junior Bookshelf, Vol. 40, No. 5, October, 1976, pp. 267-68.

As story-telling ***The Adventures of King Midas*** . . . is in a tradition best forgotten: as myth it is a travesty. Tricked out with a hotch-potch of irrelevant incident, spurious characters—"Biffpot", "Mumbo", "Old Gollop" to name only a few—facetious jokes, and slangy dialogue, the book trivializes beyond meaning and beneath words a powerful story. Like Midas himself in this version, the myth loses dignity, and both are truly demeaned. Nothing of value has been substituted and it is hard to see what the author's intention was. If to provide children with a jolly book, then the children too are demeaned.

It is hard to like this book even with its addition of George Him's pictures, which themselves lose in stature by association with such remorseless vulgarity and lack of feeling. If Lynne Reid Banks hopes to add children to her audience she will have to offer them something a good deal better than this.

Judith Vidal Hall, "The Myth Is the Message," in The Times Literary Supplement, No. 3900, December 10, 1976, p. 1554.

The Farthest-Away Mountain (1976)

All the ingredients for a fairy story are here—a pretty and innocent girl, her head full of dreams, an enchanted prince, a witch, a giant and three trolls who have been turned into gargoyles. And a quest for a magic ring and who could wish for more! Out of these elements, the author has woven an exciting adventure story which, at the moment of success, constantly meets unexpected setbacks, thus prolonging the suspense.

An enjoyable story—almost too full of action—but a 'good read' for children of 8-10.

E. Colwell, in a review of "The Farthest-Away Mountain," in The Junior Bookshelf, Vol. 41, No. 2, April, 1977, p. 84.

The essential roughage that is so conspicuously lacking in Lynne Reid Banks's writing for adolescents is supplied in ***The Farthest-away Mountain*** by particularly well-conceived magical characters. The little brass troll which Dakin finds soon after she has set out on her urgent but somewhat vague journey to the horizon, the pterodactyl who serves the sinister Master on the mountain and the melancholic gargoyles whom the heroine helps—all the creatures she meets are sharply defined. The setting, too, is firmly visualised and is skillfully used to assist both plot and atmosphere—the witch's trap of coloured snow is a good example. To clarify the relation of her fanciful fiction to true fairy-tale the author concludes on an ironic note. When Dakin has, through a mixture of intuition, warm-hearted sympathy and happy accident, fulfilled the conditions of her quest and freed the Prince from enchantment, she finds him far too self-absorbed and dreary to be accepted as her due reward and turns to Croak the frog, conveniently transmogrified as Ravik, once an inhabitant of her own village. I have a suspicion that the story is offered at least in part as an allegory of youth seeking independence, but I hope it will be enjoyed as a deft and attractive neo-fairy-tale.

> *Margery Fisher, in a review of "The Farthest-Away Mountain," in* Growing Point, *Vol. 16, No. 2, July, 1977, p. 3142.*

Though almost fifteen and sought after by most of the lads in the village, Dakin refuses to marry until she has been to the farthest-away mountain and met a gargoyle—and then she will only marry a prince. But no one has ever been to the farthest-away mountain because no matter how far you travel it never gets any closer. And everyone knows that Prince Rally, the only prince hereabouts, can't marry without the ring of kings which disappeared at his christening seventeen years ago. Just the same, the mountain nods one morning and Dakin goes—into a mechanical sequence of setbacks and progressions. . . . Dakin, being wise and brave as well as good, frees the mountain from a two-hundred-year-old spell and, in the process, finds the missing ring. Fortunately for the story it isn't picky Rally that she marries but Croak the frog himself, now a handsome young man and Dakin's prince of the mountain. But a board game could be more compelling, and just as significant.

> *A review of "The Farthest-Away Mountain," in* Kirkus Reviews, *Vol. XLVI, No. 1, January 1, 1978, p. 2.*

My Darling Villain (1977)

[The following excerpt is from a letter from Lance Salway to Nancy Chambers dated 8 March 1977; Chambers's reply appears below.]

A party plays an important part in Lynne Reid Banks' **My Darling Villain**. . . . It's a very different party though: a decorous teenage affair with some rather daring punch to drink but, never mind, mummy and daddy are upstairs to keep an eye on things. But Lynne Reid Banks would have us believe that mummy and daddy would sleep soundly through all the noise that comes from downstairs and that they would remain undisturbed when the party is invaded by a gang of nasty gatecrashers who start to smooch in the bedrooms and end up by throwing trifle at the walls. One of the gatecrashers is mysterious and moody Mark for whom Kate falls heavily and he for her—though goodness knows she's a dull enough creature, forever giggling with her friends and being rude to the much more interesting Pamela Wilton who, of all the teenage characters in this

book, shows signs of life below the waist. Mark has the wrong accent and rides a motorcycle and—oh my God!—thought he'd "knocked a girl up last year." Not a very suitable companion for nice Kate Dunhill. But, despite the opposition of her family, Kate and Mark fall in love and, after a totally gratuitous near-fatal accident at the end, find that both sets of parents quite approve of them both. Despite an attempt at a conventional setting and ordinary characters, **My Darling Villain** is a completely unreal confection. Compared with this, the strange worlds of Benjamin Lee [in his *It Can't Be Helped*] and Paul Zindel [in his *Pardon Me, You're Stepping on My Eyeball*] are as homely as apple-pie. But, whereas Lee and Zindel are writing about teenagers today, Lynne Reid Banks seems to be firmly rooted in the fifties when books like this were fairly shocking, when people were still convinced by the old plot of the nice girl and the unsuitable boy making it together, and when Anna Neagle was a wow at the Odeon in *My Teenage Daughter*. If teenagers today really do like to find their own anxieties reflected in books, they are more likely to find this achieved in *It Can't Be Helped* and *Pardon Me* than in the weak and woeful **My Darling Villain**. (pp. 94-5)

> *Lance Salway, in a letter to Nancy Chambers on March 8, 1977, in* Signal, *No. 23, May, 1977, pp. 93-7.*

[The following excerpt is from a letter from Nancy Chambers to Lance Salway dated 16 March 1977.]

My Darling Villain is, largely, wet and unlikely and strangely dated in atmosphere. But Banks does sound, throughout her books, the kind of doleful note which every girl at some (perhaps fleeting) moment in her life likes to hear. Banks has never been anything other than what she is here—**L-Shaped Room** is just as unramified (that's what we are really not liking) as **MDV**—and I find I can't rake up too great a rage against perfectly competent *Woman's Own* writing. It's not easy to do, for a start. What I do miss, I guess, is any sense of commitment to her material. That's a quality you can find in the least accomplished writing ("writing" in the sense of "word-wielding"), and while it doesn't necessarily redeem bad writing completely, without commitment, good—even the best—writing is so much empty spinning. End of homily. (pp. 101-02)

> *Nancy Chambers, in a letter to Lance Salway on March 16, 1977, in* Signal, *No. 23, May, 1977, pp. 100-03.*

This is a very readable story conveyed in lively realistic teenage style—all the questions and interests which absorb teenagers seem to find a place in the romance of middle-class Kate from the Comprehensive (with all the class-consciousness which that seems to entail here) and working-class Tom. Sadly, in pressing her arguments against class and race-consciousness, private education, and a number of other issues the modern teenager encounters, the author manages to undercut her message. The story is certainly in character with its narrator: teenagers see things in black and white, and echo their parents' opinions while imagining they see more clearly. The examination of Kate's difficulties with Tom, however, seems to intensify rather than smooth away the gap between them, while begging several important questions by making him untypically middle-class in attitude (if we *must* be so aware of differences) in essential areas of behaviour. Still, sophisticated gatecrashers at innocent schoolgirl parties, the problems of the Jewish family next door, disobeying parental ruling over riding on a motorbike, even a schoolfriend's Lesbian godmother, are ingredients which make up an absorbing story, if one can forget its palpable designs upon us. (pp. 187-88)

> *M. Hobbs, in a review of "My Darling Villain," in* The Junior Bookshelf, *Vol. 41, No. 3, June, 1977, pp. 187-88.*

Smooth and tailored, **My darling villain** misses the chance of saying something honest and truly contemporary about adolescent love and its attendant miseries and glories. Here are several of the crises which seem obligatory in novels for the 'teens—unwanted pregnancy, class differences, social violence—any of which, handled by writers of the calibre of John Rowe Townsend or Jane Gardam, could have been both serious and particularised. Expertly but with a deadly blandness the author has steered her heroine, fifteen-year-old Kate Dunhill, through the shoals of her first real love affair, with the older and more experienced Mark Collins, who is not only socially different (his father works in a factory, hers is a television actor) but also alarmingly anarchic. With more acerbity and less optimism this could have been a better story—that is, more specific, truer to the contemporary scene and tougher as a literary experience; as it is, both character-drawing and story-line leave one with a feeling of dissatisfaction.

> *Margery Fisher, in a review of "My Darling Villain," in* Growing Point, *Vol. 16, No. 2, July, 1977, p. 3146.*

[*My Darling Villain*] shows craft and competence. The story is a first-person narrative by a fifteen-year-old girl who turns sixteen in the course of the novel and who describes the process of becoming an adult via her first sexual involvement. At the beginning of the book Kate is an adolescent who goggles at the mysteries of dating and having a boyfriend. By the end she has found a boyfriend and on the way described the emotional growth involved in committing herself to him.

To an adult reader the emotional stages sound convincing; for example, the herd instinct of the immature Kate and her friends at the very British girls school, Lady Mary Engels. The girls giggle and gossip and are suitably hateful to a sexually mature classmate for whom they plan a party so that they can ogle her boyfriend. But "the dreaded Pamela" neatly sabotages the party and later justifies herself with the perspicacious remark that, after all, she had only been invited "out of spite and curiosity".

The central action involves Kate's relationship with an uninvited boy she meets at the party, Mark Collins, who is seventeen, moody, and working-class. The shifting perspective of her evaluation of him according to context and social pressure is nicely done.

Kate's growth centers on resolving class conflicts between the values of her working-class boyfriend and of her par-

ents. Kate's father is an actor who has climbed from a working-class Lancashire background. Her mother is gentry. They and Kate are part of that great, fuzzy blanket, the middle class, and the plot mechanism revolves around class differences. In spite of his sentimental socialism, her father has rejected his working-class background, but the father of Kate's boyfriend sentimentally clings to his. Kate's older brother has failed his eleven-plus and in the course of the narrative defies his father by becoming an auto mechanic. By the end of the book class conflict is resolved as the families of Mark and Kate unify as if they were holding hands at an encounter session. (pp. 74-5)

My Darling Villain is a fast-paced and intelligent novel. Still, something in it doesn't ring true even beyond the pat resolutions of plot and conflict. In spite of occasional explosions for the sake of believability, Kate's parents are remarkably liberated and understanding, even to a reader who does not hold with theories of generational conflict. Kate's parents are paragons, just as Mark Collins is a paradigm of Ideal Boyfriend, a knight in working-class armor resolved to preserve Kate's sexual virtue while he initiates her to the hard facts of a socially stratified society. Because she is a teenager, Kate defies her parents a bit by riding on Mark's motorbike. But the wisdom of parental admonitions is carefully illustrated when Mark skids on a patch of grease and smashes himself up. Earlier Mark has delivered an evaluation of exploitative rock bands by commenting that "seeing your kid come back from a session like that just once'd be enough for any parent with a grain of sense". Even though Mark is likely to follow Kate's father in rejecting his working-class background, he is too much a Knightly or Darcy to be accepted realistically. In his fluctuation between lower-class intruder and moralistic voice of the author he reflects the same division as the style which isn't always comfortable in its dual role of mouthing teeny jargon and presenting a moralistic program.

Style and boyfriend reflect the technical problem of an author who wants to illustrate realistic facts of existence for modern teenagers and at the same time lead them not into temptation. Thus Jackson Burgess's review of **The L-Shaped Room** is pertinent to this book, because after remarking upon Miss Banks's novelistic skill, he comments that it takes a while to realize that the novel "might better be titled *Elsie Dinsmore Gets Pregnant.*" That Kate doesn't is an illustration that this book is intended to appease the fears of parents more than the curiosity of its teenage readers. (pp. 75-6)

> *Sara Stambaugh, in a review of "My Darling Villain," in* The World of Children's Books, *Vol. III, No. 1, Spring, 1978, pp. 74-6.*

I, Houdini: The Autobiography of a Self-Educated Hamster (1978)

Anyone of any age who has ever kept or thought of keeping hamsters should undoubtedly be given *I, Houdini*. It is hamster life from within and any of us who have ever crawled under sofas after our loved ones, will recognise that it might well be like this from the other side—although, as he himself is the first to recognise, Houdini is a somewhat exceptional hamster. This witty and delightful book . . . will have bits read aloud all Christmas afternoon, while the rest of the family try to grab it.

> *Naomi Mitchison, in a review of "I, Houdini," in* The Times Educational Supplement, *No. 3308, November 24, 1978, p. 50.*

The secret of writing a successful animal story is to invest the creature with some of our own foibles. Remember the impossible Mr. Toad? Houdini, this escapologist hamster, has a certain vanity, verging on self-importance which one expects from denizens of the best clubs in St. James'. Fortunately he does not meet other hamsters which he would have bored to tears with his self-centred anecdotes. Well, he does have the chance to mix it with a doe hamster who provides him with an Evening to Remember. He escapes on every possible opportunity and even ventures into the outside where he meets enemies fiercer than his gentlemanly character can tolerate.

Needless to say what makes the book a success is the skill and experience of the authoress whose wit, lightness of touch and way with words ensure that once started it will not be laid aside until finished.

> *D. A. Y., in a review of "I, Houdini—The Autobiography of a Self-Educated Hamster," in* The Junior Bookshelf, *Vol. 43, No. 2, April, 1979, p. 111.*

What Houdini does is accurate and naturalistic: he escapes with fiendish ingenuity to make nests in the piano, gnaw holes in the water-pipes under the floor, get shut in the fridge; he narrowly escapes the cat and fails to fancy the mate provided for him. What he says is somehow less appealing. He is arrogant, complacent and thoroughly middle-aged, and his prose style, slightly ponderous and long-winded, caricatures all those adventurous chaps who win out with self-deprecating modesty against incredible odds. Children who have hamsters will be harmlessly entertained if they can take the style.

> *Dorothy Nimmo, in a review of "I, Houdini: The Autobiography of a Self-Educated Hamster," in* The School Librarian, *Vol. 27, No. 2, June, 1979, p. 132.*

The Indian in the Cupboard (1980)

[Lynne Reid Banks's story] certainly uses some of the strengths she has shown in the best of her adult novels. Her new book *The Indian in the Cupboard* is a real children's book: original, lively, compulsive reading. There is no fine writing, but the children in the story are real children and the results of the boy Omri's bringing to life of one of his plastic Red Indians appallingly convincing. The impressive thing is that, having thought of this good idea, Ms Banks is able to develop and sustain her invention and, while remaining entirely within the appreciation of her young readers, to touch on basic problems of human relationships. The plastic men *become* human and the problems go far beyond the obvious one that the Indian may shoot the cowboy with his minuscule arrows. The story

will well stand that repeated reading children often give to books that seize their imaginations.

> *Ann Thwaite, "Dickensian Christmas," in* The Times Literary Supplement, *No. 4051, November 21, 1980, p. 1326.*

Lynne Reid Banks treads sure-footed along the knife-edge between reality and fantasy, between the day-to-day world of a family and the plastic toy figures that change into human beings and rapidly make their needs, personalities and idiosyncrasies felt. The two owners of the models, Omri and Patrick, are typical noisy boys, somewhat perplexed by the prospect of coping with a live Indian seven centimetres high and a live cowboy who is a near alcoholic . . . particularly when they are put together in the magic bathroom cupboard. The traditional enemies fight with miniature guns and arrows; wounds are healed by a First World War medical orderly and quarrels are diplomatically smoothed by Omri, who persuades Little Bull and Boohoo Boone to become blood-brothers.

Ms Banks is remarkably and consistently successful in scaling everything down to exactly the right size and in sustaining the illusion of reality: a crumb of cheese, a kernel of sweetcorn, a bullet big as a bee's sting. Speech, actions and reactions are convincing, as are the problems crowding in on Omri and Patrick—keeping the living toys out of sight of family and friends, protecting them from a resident rat, finding the lost vital key to the cupboard.

The final resolution is wholly acceptable and unforced, an appropriate conclusion to a captivating story, enlivened throughout with tension, conflict, imaginative vision and credible characterisation of both normal size and miniature human beings. (pp. 111-12)

> *G. Bott, in a review of "The Indian in the Cupboard," in* The Junior Bookshelf, *Vol. 45, No. 3, June, 1981, pp. 111-12.*

The various adventures of Gulliver and Alice enable children to tease out the problem of size. In this book, a magic medicine cupboard turns plastic models into living miniature people. It is brilliantly written so that it touches precisely on the nerve-ends of children's fantasy and the lives with which they invest their toys. But it is more: there is a subtle interplay of relationships and feelings through which a sense of responsibility is established towards other forms of life.

> *Ralph Lavender, in a review of "The Indian in the Cupboard," in* Children's literature in education, *Vol. 12, No. 3, Autumn, 1981, p. 147.*

In a fresh and vivacious fantasy, two English boys have the exciting and disturbing experience of seeing some toys come to life. . . . There are many minor adventures (taking the Indian and the cowboy to school, with dire results) before Omri decides that he cannot play with the lives of human beings, and that these are human beings who have traveled in time, and he sadly puts all of them in the cupboard and turns them back into plastic, presumably releasing the real Little Bear, Bright Stars, Boone, and two wee horses to return to their own times. This is an adroit mix of realism and fantasy, written with an ingenuously serious acceptance of the miraculous, and quickly building characters and relationships so that the miniature people seem real.

Zena Sutherland, in a review of "The Indian in the Cupboard," in Bulletin of the Center for Children's Books, *Vol. 35, No. 2, October, 1981, p. 22.*

Two qualities make this book a delight. First, there is the particularity—the tiny pile of manure left by [Little Bear's] tiny horse, and the distinct, spiky character of the Indian. Little Bear is no mere dummy to be manipulated. He is fiercely independent, uncommonly courageous, imperious, sometimes just a bit greedy. You have to like him, and you have to worry about him as he guides his horse through grass blades tall as trees, past gigantic, monstrous ants.

Second, the story has much to say about responsibility. Omri is a sensible boy who quickly realizes what it means to be totally in charge of another person's welfare; but his best friend, Patrick, is more impulsive. Patrick thinks nothing of bringing to life a plastic cowboy, natural enemy to Little Bear—a cowboy with a working revolver. In fact, why not bring *all* Omri's figures to life, whole regiments? It's lucky Omri knows what's what. "They're people," he tells Patrick. "You can't use people." . . .

As for the proper age to read this book—why, any age, any age at all. A toddler could follow the story with ease. Grown-ups will be equally spellbound, especially if they can remember how it once felt to dream a doll alive.

Anne Tyler, in a review of "The Indian in the Cupboard," in The New York Times Book Review, *October 11, 1981, p. 38.*

The Writing on the Wall (1981)

The Writing on the Wall is a substantial novel, both in domestic and social details and in the nuances in dialogue and description which establish [sixteen-year-old Tracy], her parents and teachers, her friends and neighbours. For Tracy the bicycling trip to Holland represents a major victory in the struggle for independence, since she has persuaded her shrewd Irish mother and her protective Polish father that she is old enough to make her own decisions and that Kev, with his spiky hair and punk outfit, is a suitable boy-friend. The fortnight in Holland convinces her, painfully, that she has made a mistake, in a way that parental warnings could never have done. Kev proves to be devious and without scruples, while the older Michael, whose care for the rest of the party had seemed irritating if not downright square, proves to have the qualities Tracy needs and desires. The perils of the journey are as believable as the pleasures, for the London school-fellows, of a new country and an intoxicating freedom from social conventions. Scenes and events are skilfully chosen and arranged so that the view of events comes to us through Tracy but extends, subtly, beyond her to suggest the attitudes and needs of the other characters, in an accomplished and satisfying piece of fiction.

Margery Fisher, in a review of "The Writing on

the Wall," in Growing Point, *Vol. 20, No. 1, May, 1981, p. 3887.*

There's just one flawless Y. A. performance in all the seven books I read [for this review]: Lynne Reid Banks's ***The Writing on the Wall.*** Mrs. Banks is English, and so is her slang ("copper," "daft," "rows"), but no matter. American young adults will identify with her perfectly pitched story of a 16-year-old pulled between her Polish survivor father's steady, anchoring love and the temptations and dares of her "Punk" peers.

Maybe because Tracy Just comes from a solid family (a vanishing species in Y. A. fiction these days), she brings a healthy skepticism to the risks her father knows every teenager must take: visiting a dance hall with her Punk friend Connie (a gallant character, whose mother is battered by her father and who movingly explains the hurt idealism underlying Punk); tentatively necking with her broody boyfriend, Kev; joining a group trip to Holland led by Michael, a schoolmate's older brother. In Holland, Tracy almost goes to bed with Kev . . . , unknowingly gets her bicycle pump packed with contraband heroin and falls in love with Michael. It could be sensational; it isn't. It's a tightly crafted novel, which is true to the awareness of a 16-year-old, without any behind-the-scenes preaching.

Anne Gottlieb, "Young but Not Innocent," in The New York Times Book Review, *April 25, 1982, p. 44.*

The author writes with a sure hand, creating convincing characters and a lively plot with unexpected twists and turns. . . . As in ***My Darling Villain,*** the author has pitted daughter against parents over a romantic affair and the question of independence and responsibility. Tracy's struggle to break free of her protective family and to establish herself as her own person is perceptively portrayed. The language is contemporary, and the situations the girl finds herself in are often perplexing. Although she plays the role of rebel in behavior and in dress, she is inwardly striving to maintain a sense of personal integrity. The book is yet another example of the author's strong writing and versatility.

Karen M. Klockner, in a review of "The Writing on the Wall," in The Horn Book Magazine, *Vol. LVIII, No. 3, June, 1982, p. 296.*

Maura's Angel (1984)

The novels of James Stephens, especially *The Demi-Gods,* set a fashion in Irish fiction for precipitating some supernatural being into an ordinary setting, and making a comedy of manners out of his inability to make sense of everyday matters there. It wasn't only in Ireland, however, that the supernaturally alien character became a colourful fictional device: we remember the queen in E. Nesbit's *The Story of the Amulet,* transported from Ancient Babylon to Edwardian London, and other examples, from which Lynne Reid Banks seems to have learnt very little, show how this particular literary conceit can be used to good effect.

Maura's angel is conjured up by a bomb blast. The book is set in present-day Belfast, with a typically disaffected family at the centre of the theme: father on the run, son in the Maze, eldest daughter retarded, mother exhausted, younger daughter put-upon. The last is Maura, who comes to after an explosion to find a beautiful replica of herself lying naked beside her on the pavement. This strange girl, whom Maura introduces into her own home without exciting undue comment from the rest of the family, answers to the name of Angela. Angela doesn't understand about eating, sleeping or blowing her nose, but she's quick to pick up these skills once their purpose is explained to her. She's adept, on the other hand, at sensing holiness, and quickly locates this quality in Maura's defective sister Colleen. "She is bright in the soul", is the comment Angela offers when Maura explains that Colleen isn't bright in the head.

There are other embarrassing moments. "Are you—an angel?" Maura inquires when the truth dawns on her, sounding for all the world like an awestruck infant in a Sunday School tract of the mid-Victorian period. Lynne Reid Banks isn't good at conveying the oddity of the situation—"Fancy being homesick—for heaven! It'd take more than a taste of fish-fingers to make up for that!"—and she doesn't show any ingenuity at all in the way she causes it to develop. There is some solemn talk about souls, but very little actually happens in the book.

Lynne Reid Banks, we learn from an article published last August in the *Sunday Telegraph,* spent five days in Belfast with an ordinary Catholic family, observing social conditions and local peculiarities. It wasn't enough. The dialogue of *Maura's Angel* at times recalls Irish amateur theatricals at their most highly coloured: "Why did your da have to go off with the boyos, with never a thought or a backward look at his family? . . . What do I care for all his high-flown words when it's himself I'm needin' to help and support me." Plot inadequate, dialect inaccurate, grasp of political complexities not exactly in evidence—this novel illustrates very clearly the dangers of tackling a large theme in a loose way.

Patricia Craig, "A Little Learning," in The Times Literary Supplement, *No. 4233, May 18, 1984, p. 558.*

Not for the first time I find myself wishing that a story developed as fantasy could have been presented as a straight piece of contemporary reporting. However that is the author's business, and Lynne Reid Banks, whose previous books have, I believe, been fantasies, has made a conscious choice in interpreting the ills of Northern Ireland in this manner. . . .

As befits the subject, this is a strong story, which offers no easy solutions to Northern Ireland's problems. Mrs. Banks faces the agony without ducking any of the issues, and she is particularly successful in showing so much of the action through the eyes of a little girl who has never known peace and security. Maura may repeat all the Catholic slogans parrot-fashion, but she continues to fight a way through her bewilderment towards the vision of something 'bright and beautiful' which Angela has made clear to her.

Mrs. Banks stayed with a Belfast family while she was preparing her book, and she has clearly taken great pains to be faithful to the partial view that the Cuddy family represents. The only part of her clever and moving book that I find a little less than convincing is her attempt at the catch-phrases and the lilt of the Belfast accent, but that is something that even her keen ear cannot master at such brief acquaintance.

M. Crouch, in a review of "Maura's Angel," in The Junior Bookshelf, *Vol. 48, No. 4, August, 1984, p. 173.*

The most admirable qualities of this fine novel are those which will not be immediately apparent to young readers. How do you 'explain' the situation in Belfast—its causes, its daily difficulties—to a reader who has little knowledge of it and for whom Northern Ireland has always been a news story so familiar that it is scarcely taken note of ? . . . [Into Maura's] life comes a 'guardian angel', straight from heaven, as friend and helpmate. She could be Maura's twin but she is unmarked, unused by experience, an innocent. In this way the angel becomes a convenient device for raising questions which readers outside Northern Ireland may need to have answered. She can ask about the Maze prison, about Provos, about soldiers, and be given the necessary information by a child. It is a child's view throughout—demonstrating imperfect understanding but marked by the intensity of actual experience. The guardian angel becomes the agent of small and happy miracles but her innocence cannot survive in an imperfect world. The novel's ending, tragic in one way, helps to confirm Maura in her own sense of what is important in her world and renews and deepens her relationship with her mother.

Maura's relationship with her handicapped adult sister, Colleen, is described with a sensitivity that rings especially true. Colleen is a never-ending responsibility faced with a mixture of affection and irritated exasperation. There is a memorable scene in a supermarket where Maura predicts with the accuracy of long experience exactly how Colleen will react when the guardian angel fails to fulfil a promise.

My twelve-year-old test reader 'quite enjoyed' the book but found difficulty in accepting an angel from heaven in a book so clearly rooted in the recognisable here and now, and the end of the novel left her unsatisfied too. I fear this may be the reaction of many young readers, which would be a pity as it is a book full of compassion, as well as a fast-moving narrative.

Sandra Hann, in a review of "Maura's Angel," in The School Librarian, *Vol. 32, No. 3, September, 1984, p. 256.*

The Fairy Rebel   (1985)

This author's stories are never the product of a limited imagination and *The fairy rebel* is no exception. Fairy characters, some good (notably Tiki in forbidden jeans) and some remarkably evil, blend with three middle-class earthlings: parents and daughter Bindi, whose transformation from her magically-induced conception eight years before to a wholly human condition provides the climax.

Occasionally one is conscious of an excess of ideas in such a relatively short book. There is no shortage of emotion either: the pain of childlessness and the guilt of theft are only two of the complex feelings which different characters have to face, and both are tackled with sensitivity. The grimmer scenes are set against a somewhat over-sentimental ending, but it is the magical incidents which remain in the mind.

> *Jane Woodley, in a review of "The Fairy Rebel," in* The School Librarian, *Vol. 33, No. 3, September, 1985, p. 233.*

Rose-petal fairies are, currently, rather less in fashion as literary bait for 8 to 12-year-olds than more aggressive stuff like Fighting Fantasies. Yet Fairyland too has its share of tyranny, torture, imprisonment. And all reduced from recognizable dimensions to something so teeny-weeny you can scarcely see it. Lynne Reid Banks has explored this before in **The Indian in the Cupboard,** her moving and entirely credible account of a two-inch plastic Red Indian who becomes real. . . .

For all her idiosyncratic ways, tiny Tiki, rebellious fairy, isn't half as charismatic a characterette as the plastic Indian. Her human contact is not a child but a lame, lonely doctor's wife. Fairy and woman are both too sweet-natured and understanding of one another's problems for their relationship to develop an interesting edge. However, Lynne Reid Banks always writes so clearly and compellingly that one really does want to find out if, in the vicious dictatorship of Fairyland, Tiki will fade away from a deficiency of nectar, will be tormented to death by trained killer wasps, or whether Right will triumph.

> *Rachel Anderson, in a review of "The Fairy Rebel," in* The Times Educational Supplement, *No. 3619, November 8, 1985, p. 33.*

A lighter-weight story than Banks' **Indian in the Cupboard,** with the details lending the story its appeal: Tiki, who continually uses magic to change her clothing from one mod outfit to another; the evil wasps who play a number of parts in the queen's mischief; Bindi's hidden blue hairs, which turn out to hold the power of a few good deeds. Charlie's Victorian protectiveness toward Jan is plausible, but feminists will wish Banks took it less for granted. Still, she tells her story with such charm and wit that it would be curmudgeonly to fault it for that.

> *A review of "The Fairy Rebel," in* Kirkus Reviews, *Vol. LVI, No. 1, September 1, 1988, p. 1319.*

Return of the Indian (1986)

In a sequel to **The Indian in the Cupboard,** Omri and Patrick again invoke miniature people from the past by bringing plastic figures to life, and return with Little Bear to the French and Indian War.

The first book had a fine balance between childish desire to play with the tiny figures and awareness that, though small, they were real people who ought not to be so manipulated. This is darker, the problems grimmer. Patrick and his mother have moved away from an abusive father, Omri to a neighborhood threatened by bullies and thieves. Little Bear is now a chief, embroiled in war, for which he seeks weapons to save his village. Patrick is still the enthusiast barging ahead in a good cause; more cautious, Omri helps gather an army of braves. The rescue mission is a tragic partial success: riding in a circle, many of the new recruits accidentally wound and kill one another. Meanwhile Little Bear's son is born; the return of the little family to their own time without the modern guns is a gesture toward life and peace.

Feisty, likable characters and the precise logic by which Banks evolves events from her premises make this one of the better recent fantasies. Readers, enjoying the action and adventure, may also ponder its moral dilemmas. (pp. 1367-68)

> *A review of "The Return of the Indian," in* Kirkus Reviews, *Vol. LIV, No. 17, September 1, 1986, pp. 1367-68.*

Lynne Reid Banks's popular **The Indian in the Cupboard** told the story of Omri and his friend Patrick whose magic cupboard brought to life any toy plastic figures they put in it. The boys soon found themselves embroiled in the lives of the miniature people they snatched out of the past: the Iroquois Little Bull, his squaw Twin Stars, and Boone the cowboy. In this sequel the characters and the magic principles are revived, but changes have occurred in the boys' lives and there are enough surprises to refresh the original idea, in particular the boys' discovery that the magic properties they thought the cupboard held are in fact invested in the key. An old chest in Omri's room, one large enough for the boys to climb into, becomes a time-and-place machine.

In the earlier book, Patrick and Omri found that bringing their miniature friends to life led to all kinds of difficulties and dangers, and they wisely brought their experiments to a halt. In the intervening year, Omri has drawn on these adventures to write a story for a competition.

When he learns he has won a prize, he is tempted to check that all the fantastic events really did happen. But the moment he brings Little Bull to life, his hopes of simply satisfying his curiosity vanish: "his" Indian has just been wounded in battle and now lies there helpless, dying perhaps. To leave him thus would be to shrug off all responsibility. Omri and Patrick conjure up medical assistance; then they call on the services of a toy soldier, Royal Marine Corporal Fickits, to train Indians in the use of modern weapons. With this help, Little Bull is sent back to save his people. The central adventure makes enthralling and hair-raising reading. Keeping all these goings-on secret from Omri's family is a feat and there are practical problems such as how to feed forty tiny Iroquois braves and their horses in an attic bedroom.

One aspect of the novel is handled less successfully. In the opening pages, we learn that Omri's family have moved to a large house in a rough area. The boy has to contend with a group of bullying skinheads on his way home from school. Omri's opportunity to get his own back comes when the skinheads burgle his family's house: he and Patrick are alone and make use of Fickits, their loyal and efficient Royal Marine, to attack the skinheads with a miniature army. All this is fair enough. What is questionable is the portrayal of the skinheads. We accept that the corporal or the hospital matron should be comic stock characters. But there is a strong identification (and it must be said, a complacently negative one) between the working-class area and the aggressive, thieving louts. The only point of contact between our nice little heroes and these young thugs is fighting and the balance is tipped in favour of the better-off children to whom this book perhaps unwittingly addresses itself.

> *Nicole Irving, "A Small Battalion," in* The Times Literary Supplement, *No. 4359, October 17, 1986, p. 1175.*

The adventure of *The Indian in the Cupboard* gave young Omri a glimpse of the responsibility anyone incurs when he experiments with magic. Now in the sequel, *The Return of the Indian,* the point is made more strongly. . . . There is humour in this vigorous fantasy-adventure, especially in the activities of a formidable hospital Matron from World War I brought to life to help wounded Little Bull, but behind the meticulous detail and racy action there is a serious message which any perceptive young reader will appreciate, a message carried as much through the relationship of the two schoolboys and their growing awareness of other people's rights as through any general implications of an anti-war philosophy.

> *Margery Fisher, in a review of "The Return of the Indian," in* Growing Point, *Vol. 25, No. 4, November, 1986, p. 4705.*

I like the way Comanche Indians speak of love. When a Comanche wants to say "I love you," he says, "My mind cries for you." When a Comanche wants to say something is "lovable" or "beautiful," he says it is "mind-cry-able."

Which is how I feel about the characters in Lynne Reid Banks's new children's novel, *The Return of the Indian.* My mind cries for Omri, the contemporary English boy who has the power to bring small plastic figures to life. My mind cries for Little Bear, the two-inch plastic Indian who is transformed into two inches of flesh and blood. My mind cries for Bright Stars, Little Bear's mind-cry-able wife, who is the size of a pinkie, and for Boone, an 1890's Texas cowboy, who is no bigger than a .45-caliber bullet.

I first fell in mind-cry with these characters when I read *The Indian in the Cupboard*. . . . In that almost perfect children's book, Omri accidentally learned to bring plastic models to life by placing them in a cupboard and then turning a magic key. Soon Little Bear and Bright Stars and Boone were riding mouse-sized horses all over his bedroom. But Omri was frightened by the magic and so reduced his little friends to plastic once again—thereby sending them into the midget past from which they came.

In *The Return of the Indian*—a sequel almost as good as the original—Omri cannot resist bringing the little folk back to life to tell some good news. He has won first place in a writing contest with a story about them. Everyone

thinks it is fiction. Soon he finds himself once again mesmerized by his living toys. And who can blame him?

Little Bear and company appeal to children—and the child in us all—because they are a welcome addition to what I call the Micro World. They share this world with many other smaller-than-life characters such as E.T. and Yoda, Hobbits and Muppets, Strawberry Shortcake and the Smurfs, Stuart Little and the Borrowers, Tom Thumb and Thumbelina. Small children, who often feel overwhelmed by the great big world around them, are drawn to the Micro World where they are bigger than life.

In the Micro World, children are big enough to be the bosses. In the Micro World, children are the equivalent of adults. They are giants, sometimes even gods, bringing their toys to life at will. In *The Return of the Indian,* Omri, who seems to be about 12 years old, is bullied by big boys—"skinheads" in leather jackets—in the tough London neighborhood where he lives. So he is naturally attracted to the little people who come alive in his upstairs bedroom. In this magical world, he isn't a bully, but he is the final authority.

In the end, Omri enlists his little men in a war against the bullying skinheads. He brings to life a whole platoon of contemporary toy soldiers—armed with machine guns the size of safety pins—and orders them to open fire on skinheads who are attempting to burglarize his home. So the Micro World becomes not just a means of escaping from the Macro World but also a way of defeating it.

Omri also brings to life an army of Indian braves and sends them back in time to fight in the French and Indian War. But he wonders if he is doing the right thing. "Omri felt a cold shiver," writes Lynne Reid Banks. "He didn't like the idea of playing God. But it was too late to back out now."

Nine of Omri's Indians get killed and many others wounded. He learns that it isn't so easy being a god—or a boss—or even an adult. Being the biggest is also being the most responsible for what happens. With power comes guilt. Like the best Micro World stories, this one shrinks people but not moral issues.

The Micro World is a more mind-cry-able place for the addition of Little Bear and little Boone—and even the little platoon and the little Indian army. Anyone from 10 to at least 43 (my age) should enjoy it.

> *Aaron Latham, "Small Is Mind-Cry-Able," in* The New York Times Book Review, *November 9, 1986, p. 40.*

[*Return of the Indian*] a stunning sequel to *The Indian in the Cupboard.* With a force too strong to resist, the magic key draws Omri to open up his secret world of miniature people in a classic adventure of magic and childhood ingenuity which leaves the reader dangling over a precipice of excitement. Will Little Bull save his tribe? Will Boone, the wayward cowboy, escape death? . . .

Lynne Reid Banks hurls us from past to present in such excitement and delight that the reader can not put down this lovely book. It is full of seat-edge story-telling and spot-on characterisation that is everything a children's book should be. It will become a firm favourite with teachers and parents who enjoy a good book to read aloud and will no doubt appear on recommended book lists.

L. A. S., in a review of "Return of the Indian," in The Junior Bookshelf, *Vol. 50, No. 6, December, 1986, p. 221.*

Melusine: A Mystery **(1988)**

A decayed château in the sultriest depths of France, picked from a holiday brochure by a hatchback-sized English family, provides Lynne Reid Banks with all the ingredients for an old-fashioned foreign-parts mystery, where things go *mal* in the night. Pubescent hero Roger, spoiled twins Polly and Emma, historically minded Dad and slightly edgy Mum find themselves lodged in a renovated wing, where the comforts are plush and ornate; but the rest of Château de Bois Serpe is a crumbling rural Gothic domain, vaguely reminiscent of Cold Comfort Farm, where the sinister Monsieur Serpe oils his shotgun in a fly-blown kitchen, and wields a surly tyranny over his shy goatherd-daughter Melusine.

There is evidently more to this *ménage* than meets the holidaymakers' eye; and when Roger strikes up a haltingly bilingual friendship with Melusine over the morning milking-pail, his nose is soon bothered by more than the rank smell of goats. What lies behind the locked door of the semi-ruined tower, for instance, where her secretly conducted tour stops abruptly short? And what is the rustling presence in the dark of his bedroom, which lays its horrifying weight across his feet? When Melusine rescues Polly from drowning on a canal-exploring trip, and emerges dry, we know that she holds the key to a whole hoard of questions; but it is clear to Roger that this melancholy creature, with her queer skin and inscrutable eyes, is imprisoned in more ways than one.

Reid Banks holds a delicate balance between the daylight of English normality and the more improbable, doom-laden elements of **Melusine** in which the vital clues emerge from a deep *oubliette* of legend and superstition. Midnight storms, collapsing gateposts and underground passageways are handled as realistically as parental scepticism, and Roger's own frightened incredulity in the face of the girl's supernatural character. His feelings of pity and protective sympathy, steadily intensified by the menace that surrounds her, turn into a rather touching study of adolescent arousal, in which echoes from the Garden of Eden resound without too much sense of contrivance. Readers over French-learning age will appreciate it best; and it's assumed that they will not be mystified, nowadays, by the unsavoury thread of incest that comes to light.

Gerald Mangan, "The Pains of Growing," in The Times Literary Supplement, *No. 4469, November 25-December 1, 1988, p. 1322.*

On vacation with his family in a great decaying French château, British teenager Roger hears strange noises and glimpses terrible secrets connected to the mansion's hideous owner, Serpe, and his compelling daughter, Melu-

sine. As Roger explores the remote area with his parents and his bickering twin sisters, he learns of a local legendary Melusine, who is both woman and snake, embodiment of good and evil. Then he faces what he has resisted knowing: Serpe sexually abuses his daughter, and she changes into a huge snake to escape. The working out of the symbolism is a little purposive (though, fortunately, not heavily Freudian), and some of the plot-legend parallels seem too neat, especially in the slaying of the monstrous Serpe. But the story smoothly integrates fantasy with mundane reality, drawing widely on myth and fairy tale while revealing the strangeness in ordinary life. The characterization of Roger and his family is sharp and surprising, and readers will be fascinated not only by the gothic mystery of dark passageway, squalid kitchen, and fabulous splendor, but also by Roger's inner transformation. As he struggles with his cowardice, violence, and sexual shame, his voice begins to break, and he finds the power to imagine the struggle of others.

Hazel Rockman, in a review of "Melusine," in Booklist, *Vol. 86, No. 3, October 1, 1989, p. 273.*

There are several questionable plot elements here. Melusine's name is explained as a "regional" one connected to the figurehead on the old church. The ancient Melusine "was an embodiment of both good and evil, being a woman—Eve herself, perhaps—by day and a snake by night." While this explains the origin of Melusine Serpe's first name, it does not explain the origin of her power to shape change, for Banks establishes no link between the ancient Melusine and the present one except their names. The ambivalence of Roger's father and other authorities toward the possibility that Melusine is being sexually abused is unbelievable here, as is the juxtaposition of the fantasy/shape-changing elements with the horrendously real possibility of incest. Banks maintains an eerie, almost gothic feeling throughout, but the revelation that the coffin in the tower contains the remains of Melusine's older sister (who committed suicide rather than continue being sexually abused by her father) is nothing short of sensational. There are moments when Banks is too visible, usually when Roger is having a "heart to heart" with his father, and the use of sexual abuse as a plot device requires something more than a willing suspension of disbelief. (pp. 124-25)

Janice M. Del Negro, in a review of "Melusine: A Mystery," in School Library Journal, *Vol. 35, No. 15, November, 1989, pp. 124-25.*

This absorbing book shows the author at the height of her powers, weaving elements together with a deftness which defies their disparate and sometimes unlikely nature. . . . There's something of the fairy tale at first: the castle, the beautiful daughter who tends the goats and the brutish ogre-like father. But, with incest at its heart, the novel anchors transmutation and fantasy in a rich psychological reality.

Adrian Jackson, in a review of "Melusine," in Books for Keeps, *No. 63, July, 1990, p. 16.*

The Secret of the Indian (1989)

This sequel to *The Indian in the Cupboard* and *The Return of the Indian,* follows so closely on the heels of its predecessor that it could be labeled a continuation. At the end of *Return,* friends Omri and Patrick wonder how to explain to Omri's parents the weird property damage resulting from the all-out battle that occurred when some tiny figures (brought to life in Omri's magic cupboard) built fires, waged war, and fought off the malevolent neighborhood skinheads. At the beginning of *Secret* the parents return, and unlikely explanations ensue. Soon Patrick uses the magic to travel back in time to the Old West, where as a tiny figure he makes his way by his wits and the help of friends. He returns, bringing a tornado with him, which devastates part of southeast England, causing Omri to decide, tentatively, to have the magic key locked up in a bank vault for safety, as a dubious inheritance for his children. Readers unfamiliar with the first two books will find the third confusing, despite the interwoven explanations. However, the many who have enjoyed the Indian books will want to follow these exciting escapades as well. While not as well plotted as its predecessors, this story nevertheless displays Banks' own magical gift for creating sympathetic characters, believable elements of fantasy, and an irresistible narrative flow.

Carolyn Phelan, in a review of "The Secret of the Indian," in Booklist, Vol. 86, No. 2, September 15, 1989, p. 170.

[*The Secret of the Indian* is the] third volume in the excellent series. . . .

Though the first pages make an attention-seizing beginning, they actually refer back to the previous book. Few new ideas are introduced here. The kids (with Patrick's cousin, a girl, now included) are still engaged in keeping their toy-sized visitors from other centuries a secret from the adults. Patrick does pay an exciting visit to Boone's 19th-century Texas, meeting Boone's scarlet-satin-clad lady love in a saloon. Led by Omri's school headmaster, the suspicious adults are finally closing in when Patrick's return from Texas pulls along a cyclone—diverting adult attention so that the friends can work out what to do with their small visitors, clearly unsafe in 20th-century London.

Banks' style is pungent; her kids are resourceful and witty. She takes this opportunity to point out that "Native Americans" may be the preferred nomenclature, and that "Red Indians" is not acceptable. The final scene, Boone's wedding, which serves also as a curtain call/reunion, is an unabashed revel in the pleasures of the diminutive. Afterwards, with Omri and Pat reiterating that meddling with the past, or with other's lives, does harm and is wrong, everyone returns to his or her own time. Not so strong as its predecessors, this is mostly a mop-up operation, of interest to previous fans—but deserves a hearty welcome nonetheless.

A review of "The Secret of the Indian," in Kirkus Reviews, Vol. LVII, No. 17, September 15, 1989, p. 1398.

The Secret of the Indian is careful to emphasize respect for other cultures and mores: "Send the dead brave back," Little Bull tells Omri. "Own people find, know what to do, obey customs for the dead." But women don't do too well in this book: Patrick's prissy sister Emma and the cowboy's lodger Ruby Lou fit both ends of the stereotype (the one good, the other bad). In terms of realism, there is also something peculiar about the treatment of the unfortunate headmaster, Mr Johnson, in this story. He is apparently to be punished equally for having a Porsche and discovering the secret of the magicked alive miniature figures. . . .

It is as if in struggling to chart the fall from innocence to experience, *The Secret of the Indian* has lost the assurance of Lynne Reid Banks's earlier Indian books. In terms of its double structure (alternating between Omri and the Indian's, and Patrick and the cowboy's adventures) and cleverly handled time travel, this novel represents an advance. The allegorical intention is too clearly signalled however: "He realizes he couldn't treat him just as a toy—he was a person to be respected, despite his tiny size and relative helplessness."

Sandra Kemp, in a review of, "The Secret of the Indian," in The Times Educational Supplement, No. 3835, December 29, 1989, p. 18.

Lynne Reid Banks, whose fiction cannot be mistaken for fact, has been writing plays and novels successfully for over thirty years, and her latest book can be strongly recommended for school libraries. . . . Any illusion of reality depends upon the reader's capacity to fantasise: the story is fantastic but it is not fantasy in the fairy tale sense. The unusual aspect of the story is the reality of life in which the toys live, and the dangers and responsibilities up to which their child owners must face.

There have been many famous stories in which children's toys come alive: this book is in the same great tradition.

Jill Warren, in a review of "The Secret of the Indian," in The School Librarian, Vol. 38, No. 1, February, 1990, p. 17.

Gianni Rodari

1920-1980

Italian author of fiction, short stories, and poetry; journalist; and editor.

Major works include *Telephone Tales* (1965), *A Pie in the Sky* (1971), *Tales Told by a Machine* (1976).

Often called Italy's leading contemporary writer for children, Rodari is celebrated as an original, versatile, and especially creative author who is credited with changing the direction of Italian juvenile literature by blending elements of traditional fantasy into the realistic characteristics of modern society, especially those relating to technology. He is also noted for using his fantasies, short story collections, and poetry to address current social and political ills in an amusing, enthusiastic, and affirming manner that simultaneously reflects his deep concern for the world and its future. Although his works address such harsh subjects as political tyranny and social abuse and ruthlessly satirize pompous adults, Rodari is often credited for his playfulness and optimistic viewpoint. Rodari believed that children are integral to the betterment of society; in many of his stories, only the child characters are able to view situations with clarity. A former teacher who often received ideas for his books from his discussions with students, Rodari intended his works to increase the awareness and inspire the creativity and critical thinking of his young readers. Viewing fairy tales as an especially useful tool in developing the child's ability to evaluate the world, he promotes such values as peace, freedom, solidarity, understanding, and respect for individuality while underscoring his stories and poems with a profound affection for humanity. Rodari's works also promote the child's imagination and decision-making abilities; several of his books include created words, inverted proverbs, inventive dialogue, and such brain-teasers as offering young readers the choice of three endings for a story.

An active member of the Italian Communist Party at the end of World War II, Rodari became a writer for children when he began using nursery rhymes, verse, and short poems to comment on the events affecting the readers of *L'Unità,* the Party newspaper for which he was a columnist. Rodari was later appointed director of *Il Pioniere,* the organ of the association of the Italian Pioneers, a general organization for children with parents who belonged to or sympathized with leftist parties. Rodari's first book *Il libro delle filastrocche* (*The Book of Nonsense Rhymes*) was published in 1950; as yet untranslated into English, both this work and Rodari's second collection of poetry *Il treno delle filastrocche* (*The Train of Nonsense Rhymes*) (1952) are composed of poems first published in *Il Pioniere* and are noted for accurately mirroring the Italian social climate of the time; later works are considered more subtle, with increased emphasis on surreal plots and dynamic use of language. Rodari's first book to be published in English was *Favole al telefono* (translation as *Telephone Tales*),

short bedtime stories for middle graders told by a traveling father to his daughter over the telephone; other outstanding translated titles include *La torta in cielo* (translation as *A Pie in the Sky*), a comic fantasy for middle graders that describes how a radioactive mushroom from a test atom bomb is transformed into a giant cake, and *Tales Told by a Machine,* seven stories that answer the question "What would happen if . . . ?" Although most of Rodari's books are as yet untranslated, they have received coverage in English-language publications. Among the most notable are *Gip nel televisore* (*Gip in the Television Set*) (1962), a humorous contemporary story about the adventures of a small boy with televisionitis, a disease that affects children who sit too long before their television screens, and *Il libro degli errori* (*The Book of Mistakes*) (1964), a tale in which Rodari uses the Italian school system for correcting papers to present his opinion on social injustice. Rodari is also the author of a third poetry collection as well as several other fantasies and short story collections; he is also the editor of the Italian edition of Stanovsky and Vladislav's *Enciclopedia della favola* (*Encyclopedia of Fairy Tales*). Rodari received several Italian awards for his works, including the Premio Prato for *Filastrocche in cielo e in terra* (*Nonsense Rhymes in Heaven and on Earth*) in 1960, the Premio Castello for *Gip nel televisore* in 1963 and *La torta in cielo* in 1968, the Premio Rubino for *Il libro degli errori* in 1965, and the Premio Europa Dralon for *La torta in cielo* in 1967; *Gip nel televisore* was placed on the International Board on Books for Young People (IBBY) Honour List in 1964, a designation also given to *La torta in cielo* in 1968. In 1966, Rodari was named a highly commended author for the Hans Christian Andersen Award; he received the Andersen Medal in 1970 for his body of work.

AUTHOR'S COMMENTARY

[*The following excerpt is from Rodari's Hans Christian Andersen Award acceptance speech, originally delivered in 1970.*]

[My father] was a baker and loved cats very much. We always had cats at home. Maybe that is why I am always thinking up cat stories. Like the story of a cat who was very efficient in business and ran a grocery store. The cat sold canned mice. Anyhow, that was her intention. For this purpose, she bought a lot of nice milk cans and made a sign that read: "A can opener free with the purchase of three cans!" The dumb thing was, however, that the mice did not want to sleep in the cans. The cat finally had to find another line of work.

Then there is the story about a cat called Milan. Her master was the station master in Bologna. Once when a train came, the cat ran out of the house to watch—and the station master ran anxiously after her in fear that she would run under the wheels. Loudly he yelled, "Milan, Milan!" and all the passengers jumped out of the train and rubbed their hands together, thinking they had already arrived in Milan. Of course, all kinds of confusion and adventures resulted.

I really think that the Andersen Prize instilled a great desire in me to write cat stories. And I hope no one will mistake this intention for a threat or tell me that such stories would hinder the child's development into a serious adult. One can certainly talk about people when talking about cats, and one can even talk about serious and important things while telling a happy story.

And what is more—what is a serious person anyhow? Take the case of Mr. Isaac Newton. In my opinion, an overly-serious man. Once—if what they say about him is true—he sat underneath an apple tree and an apple fell on his head.

Anyone else in his place would have said a few not exactly polite words and looked for another place in the shade. But Mr. Newton asked himself: why did this apple fall down? Why not up? Why not left or right, but straight down to the ground? What mysterious power pulls it down?

An unimaginative person would say hearing this: This Mr. Newton cannot be taken seriously. He believes in magic powers; he probably even thinks there is a magician in the ground; he thinks that apples can fly about like magic carpets. He believes in fairy tales—at his age!

Contrary to this, I think that this Mr. Newton discovered the law of gravity because he had a mind open to every direction, because he could, provided with lots of fantasy that he knew how to use, imagine unknown things.

It takes a lot of fantasy and a lively imagination to be a real scientist, to be able to imagine things that do not yet exist and then to discover them, to imagine a better world than ours and to work towards it.

I think fairy tales—both old and new—can help in the development of the mind. Fairy tales are the place of all hypotheses—they can give us the keys and help us find new ways to reality; they can help the child learn about the world and give him the ability to evaluate it.

For this reason, I think that writing fantastic stories is useful work. I must say that it is entertaining work—and from one point of view, it seldom happens that one finds a type of work which is all at once entertaining, profitable and even worthy of prizes.

It would really be great if everyone had a job which suited, interested and entertained him. However, that is a Utopia right now, a fairy tale. But fairy tales often come true. For example, in fairy tales there are flying carpets, flying ships—and today we have supersonic jets. Although we cannot say "Table, set yourself!" like in the fairy tale, we can say "Laundry, wash yourself!" and "Dishes, dry yourselves!"

Things we *say* can come true. The big problem is to want the *right things* to come true. No one alone has the magic word. We must all seek it together, in every language, with discretion, with passion, with sincerity and with fantasy—one way we can do this is by writing stories which make children laugh. There is nothing more beautiful in the world than a child's smile. And if one day all the children in the world could laugh together, all of them, with no exceptions, then that would be a great day—let it come! (pp. 3-4)

Gianni Rodari, "Acceptance Speeches," in Bookbird, *Vol. VIII, No. 2, June 15, 1970, pp. 3-5.*

GENERAL COMMENTARY

Carla Poesio

In the field of Italian literature for young people Rodari clearly presents a new trend. It is, however, necessary to underline that this novelty is not empty virtuosity, but a continuous attempt by the writer to adapt his pages to the needs of contemporary readers, while remaining faithful to the eternal categories of children's mythology.

In fact, the best pages of Rodari are intimately bound to an inextinguishable tradition, that of the *fantastic* and of the *wonderful*.

These traditional elements are inserted into the frame of current reality. The *wonderful* is seen by the eyes of the present-day reader who is accustomed to live in a technological world, a world of machines. But machines too have their magic life where the coldness of the scientific side is enlivened by a human warmth.

Usually in Rodari's books, all of a sudden we find an unexpected twist to the course of events belonging within normal reality, a surrealistic prance transporting the action in an imaginary sphere free from reality while still referring to it.

Gip nel televisore (Gip in the television set) is a clear example of this. Gip is a little boy watching—as normal boys do—the children's television-programme with his brother. He is watching it so intently and fixedly that he is literally absorbed into the television screen just in the middle of an Indian fight he was looking at and he disturbs the sight of his little brother who has remained outside the screen and who begs him to move aside a little. The efforts of the members of the family to draw Gip out of the television set are quite useless and at one point Gip disappears from the national programme and starts a series of adventures in those of other countries, causing an amusing succession of events full of humour and of gentle social criticism.

Along the same lines we find reality and fantasy equally mixed in *Il pianeta degli alberi di Natale* (The planet of Christmas trees). When we say "mixed", however, we always mean a basic equilibrium of the two elements with a constant reference of the fantastic world to the real one.

Marco, the hero, is a boy in Rome who is given a rocking horse by his grandfather. The boy is a little disappointed (a rocking horse is a present for a little child!) but as he is absent-mindedly rocking without being amused and feeling rather bored, all of a sudden the rocking horse starts flying and Marco is mysteriously kidnapped and taken to a strange planet. There the atmosphere of Christmas Day is always present and Christmas trees spring up everywhere, everything is easy, violence is unknown, evil does not exist and life flows pleasantly with the help of robots. A new existence, full of unexpected details, is opened up in front of Marco who gradually comes to appreciate all of it by the original and meaningful conclusion of the story.

In *La torta in cielo* (The cake in the sky) the radioactive mushroom cloud from an atom bomb test is transformed through the enormous blunder of a scientist into a big cake descending slowly from the sky on a hill near Rome. The authorities think of an invasion from Mars and only the children very soon become aware that this is a wonderful chance to eat as much cake as they want. Their joy rewards the scientist (hidden inside the cake and full of shame at his blunder) and persuades him that it is much better to put his science at the disposal of cake manufacturers than to use it for atom bombs.

As we can see, facts and characters are tightly bound to the atmosphere and to the problems of our time. Rodari never tries to evade reality though it may often appear arid and painful. On the contrary, he lets us see how to live in it without losing the charge of humanity which exists in each of us. Most of his pages are born from a kind of "running in" which takes place in the schools as a consequence of his conversations with pupils in the classroom. This does not mean that Rodari wishes to indulge the easy-

going taste of children: on the contrary, it means that the writer's poetic invention and creative strength is suited to the topography and the myths of the child's psyche. He expects his readers to reflect, to meditate and to participate in an intense way. As a result his books have a certain and pedagogically deep influence in the formation of the mental attitudes of the child.

Let us examine—in support of this statement—one of the main features of Rodari's books: humour.

His is a type of humour which keeps its roots in reality. It does not attempt to escape from it, but tries to free it from empty conventions, dogmas, lazy customs, and false rules of good behaviour.

Let us remember, for instance, the blind society (in *The cake in the sky*) which does not see the difference between an atomic cloud and a big cake (only children do) and insists by autosuggestion on the necessity for police measures and military defence preparations, or the strange Government ruling the planet of Christmas trees (the name of which runs: *The Government-which-does-not-exist*). What is, in fact, the use of a Government—says the author—in a country where everything is all right?

Or let us remember the strange atmosphere created by a dictatorial king in *Gelsomino nel paese dei bugiardi* (Gelsomino in the land of the liars) where lies are law, bread is called "ink", cats must bark and dogs must mew, where the doors of the lunatic-asylum are opened for those who want to tell the truth and the highest posts in the Government go to those who can best tell falsehoods.

Like every form of genuine humour, this one requests a form of detachment from the object under consideration. It is a mental operation which can be learnt little by little and accustoms one to the critical spirit as well as to sincerity and the courage of one's own convictions. It is not bitter satire, because it lets the young reader think and believe that some errors of our reality can and must be modified.

There is nothing didactic, however, no form of utilitarianism in this reading matter. Spontaneity, desire to amuse, enthusiasm for living, for seeing and discovering: such feelings enliven his prose and are the spirit of his poems.

Poetry, too, has an original, personal form in Rodari's work. In *Filastrocche in cielo e in terra* (Nonsense rhymes in heaven and on earth), in *Il libro degli errori* (The book of mistakes) and the poems in the Appendix to *The planet of Christmas trees* we feel a certain link with nonsense or nursery rhymes: the reader enjoys them as little songs or like some brief musical motifs, but, as happens with every single line of true poetry, many of Rodari's motifs leave an echo in the mind of the reader and with it some new words, some new ideas spring out so that it is not only mere amusement. They exist as an invitation to sincerity, to faith in justice, to brothership and understanding between all human beings. We could speak—if we wanted to—about Rodari's "message" but that might lead one to suspect that Rodari wrote his pages just to spread his message. Nothing could be more wrong. What Rodari can teach his reader is implied artistically and does not appear openly. The reader *feels* it and discovers it in his *personal* reading, as something he has received personally. We all—as educators—know how great is the importance of the personal discovery of the deeper meaning of some page for the mental formation of the young reader. Nothing is more essential than the moment when he grasps for himself the central theme of the book.

Let me quote again, as an example, the last pages of *The planet of Christmas trees.* Marco, after a period of disagreement, finds himself quite at ease in the new planet. The only thing he does not understand is why he has been "kidnapped" and taken there. He will learn it from other boys like him when the members of the "Government-which-does-not-exist" decide that he is "mature", that is, he has passed the test he has been subjected to. Which test? Which trial?

To ward off the possibility of future landings by hostile invaders of the planet (the progress of space navigation is increasing so fast, especially in the planet which is called "Earth"!), the Government has accepted the suggestion of some special advisers, the pupils of an elementary class, to let some children from Earth spend some time on the planet of Christmas trees and make friends out of them. It is to be a kind of experiment in understanding with those children who will be the generals, astronauts, scientists and politicians of tomorrow, in a word, those *responsible* for the pacific or hostile attitude towards the inhabitants of the planet of Christmas trees.

Marco does not think he will be one of those responsible tomorrow: but he has one aim on coming back to Earth: to create there a new planet like the one he has visited. The reader will appreciate Marco's adventure for its unexpected and fantastic facets and will not think—at the moment—of the future life of the hero or of the future destiny of the strange planet. In his mind, however, or, better, in his heart, a strong feeling will remain, a feeling which is perhaps a certainty that in every country, in every place something like the strange planet, where evil and violence do not exist, ought to be created.

Rodari's language . . . is such that the value of the word, the mechanism of the sentence and of the paragraph offer the possibility of understanding at different levels.

The elementary school pupil will seize on the rhythm and the immediate brilliant images in Rodari's poems and the verve and originality of the facts in his prose; older boys will also accept the invitation to critical observation and will appreciate the way Rodari affirms some social values; the adults will find in these pages what a man is or should be when heart and brain work in a harmonious partnership. (pp. 19-22)

Carla Poesio, "Gianni Rodari," in Bookbird, *Vol. VI, No. 3, September 15, 1968, pp. 19-23.*

Lucia Binder

Gianni Rodari was one of the most noted contemporary Italian authors for children whose works have also met with wide acclaim abroad. His books for children truly reflect his personality; they show that—even though he gave

up his teaching career—he never stopped concerning himself with pedagogics and that he ascribed a great importance to fantasy and humor in the educational process. He was also a zealous advocate of the role of imaginative children's literature in activating children to use their own creative potentials.

Rodari never had any difficulty in finding subjects for his children's books. In one of his stories for children he says: "Where are the stories? You can find them everywhere—in the wood the table is made of, in the glass, in the rose . . . " This assertion characterizes all of his books. He wrote stories "on foot and from the car" and "stories on the telephone"; he described the experiences of a child who came under the spell of the television set, of people who landed on the Christmas tree planet and the adventures of a boy who ended up in the land of liars.

His stories are full of surprises, yet they are clearly and deliberately constructed. They develop according to their own natural laws even though these may not always coincide with outer reality. They are truly fantastic stories rooted in our modern world which, through their very playfulness, often take a very critical view of it.

Diverse though the colorful backgrounds of Rodari's stories may be, the ideas behind them are quite similar. Gianni Rodari wanted to sharpen his young readers' visions, so that they will learn to distinguish between essentials and non-essentials. He wanted to open their eyes to all the things they meet with less and less in the world around them—to true humanness (the life of one single child is more valuable than all rockets put together in *Gip nel televisore* [Gip in the television], for example, to tolerance and international understanding (e.g. the stories **"The war of the bells"** or **"The young crab"** or **"One and seven"** from *Favole al Telefono* [Stories on the telephone]), to social justice (e.g. **"The blue arrow"**) and to mental and personal individuality. His depictions of social abuses are not charged with indignation or with condemnation, but simply express sadness, silent accusation and deep feelings, which in themselves solicit a posture. The last story in the volume *Favole al Telefono* perhaps shows the author's intention most clearly. According to this story, the world is imperfect and it takes a lot of effort to improve it. Mankind is far from being finished with the task and all must work together in order to make the world the way it should be.

Gianni Rodari never becomes didactic, however, his stories are much too fantastic and playful. His prose stories hint of the fact that the author also wrote several volumes of nonsense verse—they are so light, so amusing and yet meaningful. After reading only a few sentences, the characters of the stories—whether a small stuffed dog who has come to life (Spicciola), or an upright lawyer who has his "very favorite programs" on television or on old lady who feeds birds—become as alive for the reader as if he were seeing them in a film. At the same time the author also makes their emotions and thoughts manifest. Especially his short stories—and Rodari wrote a great many short stories!—demonstrate his mastery of verse, at times caricatured, but always vivid and memorable depictions.

Rodari often calls upon children to make use of their own powers of imagination. As the title of one of his books, *Tante storie per giocare* (Play stories) suggests, the collected stories in this volume are intended to animate readers to take an active part. Each story has three different endings to choose from; after having selected the ending he likes best, the reader can look up the preferred ending of the author in an appendix and compare it with his own. In spite of such playful elements, most of the fantastic stories in this book have a deeper meaning than at first appears. In one story, for example, we become acquainted with a magician who tries to show people his magic tricks; he finally comes to the realization that he has become superfluous, however, because through modern technology everyone has become so inured to magic—at the push of a button darkness turns to light, at another push of a button people who are miles away become visible, and much more. Another story in this volume describes the experiences of **"Dr. Frightful"** who has stolen the moon and demands a large ransom for its return; his plan is foiled when people simply substitute a series of satellites for the moon. The third ending to the story about the **"Adventures with the TV Set"** can be taken as a kind of résumé of what Gianni Rodari tried to tell people: "That it isn't enough to close the door of one's house in order to shut out the world, the people, their sorrows and their problems. That no one can really enjoy the pleasures of life, when he knows—and a television set is enough to tell him this— that someone else is crying, suffering, dying, either near or far, but always on this earth, the common home of all of us."

Another very essential element in Gianni Rodari's work is humor. A characteristic example for this is *Gip nel televisore,* a whimsical, modern tale having a subject which is of present interest not only in Italy, i.e. "televisionitis" caused by constant television watching. The comical main effect is based on an interchange of what is real and what is unreal—Gip becomes absorbed by television not only symbolically but actually. This book is also reminiscent of ancient situation comedies with which we became familiar through Pinocchio. The reader knows that Gip has been pulled into the television set but Gip's mother doesn't and so she scolds her youngster as though he were only up to his ordinary mischief.

Rodari's descriptions are not only spiced with southern temperament but also contain elements of understatement—deliberately ordinary portrayals of extraordinary situations. Another very obvious characteristic of his style is that his characters often seem to take their own actions very seriously, but in reality this is based on self-irony.

As in many fantastic stories of world literature, in Rodari's stories it is also usually the children—who as yet have few prejudices—who are able to see an extraordinary situation for what it really is. In *La torta in cielo,* for example, the adults are alarmed and believe in the appearance of flying saucers, while the children have already found out that the thing in the sky is really a giant pie. Rodari likes to poke fun at officious and pompous behaviour which makes people blind to their surroundings.

Their themes and subjects predestine Gianni Rodari's

books for translation, but his subtle use of language makes this difficult. His writing style is simple and straightforward, but he loved to play with words and expressions. In fact, he often invented his own words, which have very lucid meanings but which also call for a translator who is as inventive and creative with language as the author. In addition Rodari makes quite a bit of use of dialogues, whereby he often achieves comical effects, as for example in the story about "the little mouse from the picture stories", who can only speak in the language of comics and cannot therefore make itself understood by the other mice. This also demands a great deal of penetration and creativity from a translator. Notwithstanding, Gianni Rodari's stories have become known in many countries and it can only be hoped that his works are published internationally even more in the future. (pp. 28-30)

Lucia Binder, "Gianni Rodari—In Memory of the Renowned Italian Writer and Andersen Award Winner," in Bookbird, *No. 3, September 15, 1980, pp. 28-30.*

Carla Poesio and Pino Boero

Italian literature for children in the 1950s felt the general effects of the cold war. On the one hand we found the Catholic world represented by the Christian Democrats, and on the other, the forces of the "Left" represented by the Communist and Socialist Parties.

Gianni Rodari, an active member of the (Italian) Communist Party at the close of World War II, was a political columnist for the Party's paper *L'Unità.* He started to write for children almost by chance: commenting through nursery rhymes, verses, short simple poems on the events which touched the feelings of the readers of *L'Unità.*

Later Rodari was appointed by his party to direct the weekly newspaper *Il Pioniere* (The pioneer), the organ of the association of the Italian Pioneers, a general organization for the children of those who belonged to the leftist parties or sympathized with them.

Rodari's *Filastrocche* (Nursery rhymes) appeared in *Il Pioniere* and then were collected in *Il libro delle filastrocche* (The book of nursery rhymes) and *Il treno delle filastrocche* (The nursery rhyme train). They openly reflect the social climate of that time.

Many workers, for instance, had scanty wages; Rodari wrote the famous *Filastrocca del sabato sera* (Saturday evening nursery rhyme):

> Saturday evening rhyme,
> Father says: The envelope is light.
> Mother says: It is not enough:
> I have to pay for rice and pasta.
> Father says: Wages are measly.
> His voice is low and hoarse.
> Mother says: Girls and boys,
> No movies tomorrow.
> Father says: The envelope is light
> Tomorrow no merry-go-round.
> The white envelope lies on the table,
> Father is sad, Mother is tired.

(p. 20)

Rodari handed his reader a message of accusation and introduced some new themes to Italian poetry for children: the world of labor, social differences, the fight for freedom, anti-militarism, the solidarity among the weakest—not in a tendentious way but through a poetic language and very often with a light sense of humor.

His first two novels: *Il romanzo di Cipollino* (Little onion's novel) and *Gelsomino nel paese dei Bugiardi* (Gelsomino in the liar's country) appear openly revolutionary, especially if one considers their publication dates [1952 and 1957, respectively] and the themes which until then had been common in our literature for young people. In fact they deal with the motif of revolt against tyranny, using the genre of fantasy.

Later the political message of Rodari gradually takes a different direction. In the 1970s it seems to diminish, so much so that some critics speak of a lack of renewal, in a revolutionary sense.

I think that Rodari from the very beginning of the 1960s chose other ways of injecting a renewed spirit into Italian children's literature and increasingly focused this renewal on the fantastic and linguistic elements.

Filastrocche in cielo e in terra (Nursery rhymes in heaven and on earth), is a selection of his nursery rhymes published in 1950 and 1952 and some new ones, emphasizing, above all, the verbal power of association and the extreme flexibility of the imagination. *Favole al telefono* (Fables by telephone) contains very short stories which a father—a travelling salesman—tells his little girl on the telephone every night. The themes are drawn from everyday life: a touch of humor lifts them to a surrealistic plane with some linguistic play, some inverting of common proverbs, some paradoxes in our every day reality, which create another dimension of the reality itself. For example, there are bells manufactured from melted down guns which toll instead of shooting and let the peace break out instead of war.

Another example: a traffic light decides to turn blue. The traffic becomes angry and does not know what to do. A policeman, with the turn of a switch, brings everything back to normal. "What a shame!" says the traffic light, "I gave them the blue light for heaven: they could have flown away but they did not understand."

In *Il libro degli errori* (The book of mistakes), Rodari shows through prose and poetry children's mistakes, such as misspelling or grammar, in red and adult's mistakes, usually due to social injustice, in blue. [In Italy the teacher corrects small mistake by underlining them with a red pencil and indicates large errors with a blue pencil.]

These last two books presume a silent dialogue with the young reader who is stimulated to elaborate on Rodari's tricks and to use words with extreme liberty, reversing stated orders, overturning old cliches and predictable structures and creating new ones, since language (as Rodari insists) is not an absolute reality but an historical product, a human product, and its law can always be changed and manipulated.

Rodari places full faith in the intervention of the reader in the writer's game. The reader always has some propos-al, some solution of his own: and so it must be, because the reader must be not only a consumer of culture but also its producer.

Such participation in the plot's action on the part of the reader is implied for instance in *La torta in cielo* (The cake in the sky). This is a novel which Rodari wrote together with the children in a Roman school. He presented them with the plotline: a strange object, like a flying saucer, slowly lands in the suburbs, keeping the authorities on the alert because they are convinced they are dealing with an invasion from another planet. The elaboration of this hypothesis continues: the children run toward this mysterious object in spite of the adults' alarm. They discover that it is a gigantic cake, the result of a blunder by a scientist who wanted to create an atomic bomb but confused the formula. The plot appeals to the critical spirit and to the creative participation of the child reader.

The same happens in *Tante storie per giocare* (Many stories to play with). For each of these tales Rodari proposes three solutions, inviting his reader to choose one and give the reasons for the choice.

In Rodari's books the word and the plot are always the starting point to alter the situations as a free product of imagination.

In 1973 *La grammatica della fantasia* (The grammar of the imagination) appeared, with this subtitle: *An introduction to the art of inventing stories.* Here Rodari presents the nature and use of the writer's tools, inviting everyone to employ them. He begins with an uncommon combination of words which provides the point of departure for a tale, and he arrives at the dismantling of the fundamental elements of the fairy tales in order to create new ones.

Even the plot of his last novel, *C'era due volte il barone Lamberto* (Twice upon a time there lived the Baron Lamberto), insists on the value of the word. Its end stimulates the reader toward a creative intervention: "Each reader," insists Rodari, "if he is not happy with my ending, can change it, adding to this book one chapter or two. Or thirteen, if he likes. One should never be scared by the words 'The End.' "

The appeal of Rodari to the unlimited imagination, to the critical spirit of the reader, to the reader's sense of humor, the ability to take a position—what else can it be but a political message? Reading is—according to him—the starting point for a personal creativity, but it means, above all, refusing passive acceptance. In this sense the short poem **"Lettera ai bambini"** (Letter to the children) which Rodari included in *Parole per giocare* (Words to play with), is a vibrant political message:

> It is difficult
> To do difficult things:
> To speak to the deaf,
> To show the rose to the blind.
> Children, learn
> To do difficult things:
> To give your hand to the blind,
> To sing for the deaf,
> To free the slaves
> Who think they are free.

There is also a strong political message in the invitation to handle the word in different ways. The word is a continuous vehicle for knowledge, according to Rodari, and, as a consequence, a way to achieve liberty for everyone. From the earliest age on everyone can learn that the word is a powerful tool. Mastering words means in fact having the ability not only to build messages but also to dismantle the messages one receives from the mass media, from those in power.

Such a concept is reflected in these lines which Rodari wrote in **Grammatica della fantasia:** "All the uses of the word to all. Not in order that all may be artists, but in order that no one may be a slave." (pp. 20-1)

> Carla Poesio and Pino Boero, "Gianni Rodari: An Appreciation," in Phaedrus: An International Annual of Children's Literature Research, Vol. 8, 1981, pp. 20-1.

TITLE COMMENTARY

Gip in the Television Set   (1962)

[*The following excerpts are from reviews of the original Italian edition of* Gip in the Television Set, *published in Italian as* Gip nel televisore.]

In the age of technical progress in which children take a lively part a new disease, Televisionitis, suddenly occurs. It can happen to children who sit too often and too long motionless before their television set that they are suddenly seized by it and turned into an electro-magnetic wave. This happens to little Gip who thus suddenly finds himself in the clutches of the wave-lengths and is pushed from one television programme to the other. In Sweden he suddenly finds himself in the stomach of a patient who is being examined by a famous doctor with the help of a television camera and in Germany he causes much confusion during the pursuit of a thief. In many other countries, too, Gip's unexpected appearance on the television screen causes much astonishment, it being indeed amazing when a small boy suddenly emerges at the bottom of the sea, in the flames of a furnace, or between the rings that encircle the planet Saturn.

Gip himself does not know what is the matter, he only feels that he is caught and cannot do anything about it.

Of course this extraordinary case is taken up by the newspapers and the most sensational reports are published, so that everyone is soon interested in the fate of the little Italian boy.

His parents are particularly worried as no one has any idea how to rescue the child. Fortunately a Japanese scientist at last finds a way to extricate Gip from this vicious circle. Three valuable space ships, however, must be sacrificed for this, in order to unite all the television networks of the world. "Is not a child more precious than three rockets, than 300, than 300,000 rockets?"

The rockets are gladly given and the experiment succeeds. Gip can now be seen on all television screens all over the world simultaneously and is soon freed. This fantastic story is told with much verve and humour.

> "Translation Service: Fantasy from All Over the World," in Bookbird, No. 3, September 15, 1964, p. 100.

The great breakthrough of humour in children's literature occured after the Second World War.

At first there was a wave of mutual introductions. The most popular books travelled from country to country in translation. The North conquered the South, and it became clear that "typically English" humour, the whimsical and twisted, as well as serene chortling found a lively echo in other countries, too.

Equally victorious was Pippi Longstocking's progress from Sweden to the south, and in her wake came *Karlsson, The Children of Noisy Village, Rasmus* and *Lotta.* The Moomins with their part whimsical, part genial gaiety set forth from Finland.

And very soon the situation of humorous children's books—viewed internationally—was much rosier. Rich indigenous creation set in everywhere, as well as translating. It is most interesting that the new books were not mere imitations of foreign models but rather the result of the new impulses being taken up and individually fashioned. This means that themes and motifs became international while treatment and presentation followed native tradition in many cases. The humorous stories by the Italian author Gianni Rodari . . . are an excellent example.

His book **Gip nel televisore** (Gip in the television set) is a whimsical modern tale dealing with a topical theme that does not only concern Italy: the "television disease" or "televisionitis" caused by constant staring at the television screen.

The main comic effect lies in the alternation between reality and irreality: Gip is not only symbolically but literally sucked up by the television set.

Something of the old traditional comedy of situation which had stamped Pinocchio keeps cropping up: the readers know that Gip has been pulled into the television set, Gip's mother, however, does not known this and admonishes her boys as if they had just been up to one of their usual tricks.

Further elements of situational comedy are Gip's trials in the television set, where he disappears in lather, acquires a ballpoint pen beard or escapes from powder clouds with great difficulty. In addition there are satirical side-stabs at the neighbour who is reluctant to lend his television set, at the electrician who promises to come within ten minutes and only turns up long after Gip has disappeared and so on. Following the Italian tradition, admonition is combined with humour: one must not stare uncritically at television, etc. (pp. 19-20)

It is one of the most striking characteristics of humorous Italian children's books that actions and irrelevant details are taken seriously on the surface, but this seriousness is really based on self-satire. Despite all comedy of situation, modern Italian humour is rather intellectual. (p. 20)

> Lucia Binder, "Humour in Children's Books,"

in Bookbird, *Vol. IX, No. 2, June 15, 1971, pp. 19-23.*

Telephone Tales   (1965)

I do not know what to make of Gianni Rodari's short stories. The publisher tells us that he has won awards and is highly thought of in Italy and indeed some of the stories show a highly imaginative talent. Perhaps Italian children are different from British ones or perhaps the stories have lost in the translation, but I can not see many of this collection appealing to young children. All of them start off very well, the imagination is stirred immediately but as often as not there is a rapid let down. There is no climax to the story, the ending just fades away without any real meaning. This may do with nonsense stories but these are not funny enough to come into this category, not crazy enough. One is left feeling disappointed because obviously the author has talent, it is rather like hearing an untrained singing voice, the notes are there but something is lacking all the time. (pp. 283-84)

> *A review of "Telephone Tales," in* The Junior Bookshelf, *Vol. 29, No. 5, October, 1965, pp. 283-84.*

The Befana's Toyshop: A Twelfth Night Story   (1970)

An Italian animated toy story must raise the ghost of *Pinocchio;* Gianni Rodari's new story **The Befana's Toyshop** is similarly a tale with a moral. The Befana is a kind of Italian Father Christmas whose toys run away from her in order to give themselves to Francesco, a poor boy who never gets presents on twelfth night. A crotchety old lady, the Befana saves Francesco in the end and after frightening adventures the toys find worthy homes.

> *"Off to a Flying Start," in* The Times Literary Supplement, *October 30, 1970, p. 1252.*

The Befana's Toyshop is a Twelfth Night story. . . . In his native land Signor Rodari's fun is as well known as that of Lewis Carroll in England. The Befana is a female edition of Father Christmas, according to herself 'nearly a baroness', and though ultimately benevolent, not at all to be trifled with. She rides on a broomstick on Twelfth Night attended by her downtrodden maid, Teresa, to distribute to suitable children the toys displayed in her wonderful store. Francesco, who is a very poor member of a large family and who gets steadily poorer, spends all his free time pressing his nose against that window. The toys get to know him and like him, and wish they could help him, for they are quite sure he is not going to get anything from the Befana this year. Luckily, the toys are no ordinary toys. Rag, the dog, leads them to find Francesco, who has, in fact, been taken away by the police. There is an important toy soldier, the General, and a sailor, Captain Halfbeard, and an Indian Chief, Silver Feather (who has cowboys with lassoes waiting for him) and the most splendid toy of all, the Blue Train, complete with rails and level-crossing and station-master, driver and guard. There is the Seated Pilot, in his aircraft, and a box of crayons, every colour full of personality, and a dozen dolls of which the Hawaiian never takes her eyes off the Seated Pilot. The Teddy Bear has a very small head for his size, and it is stuffed with sawdust, but although very shy he can dance. All these characters have their own views on how to find and help Francesco. In the end it is the Befana who 'wasn't such a bad old bird after all,' who got him out of the police station, and here she was, leading him through the streets, like an affectionate slightly severe old grandma. She never knew that all her toys had escaped to join Francesco. But she did know that the boy, intimidated by two of the worst gangsters of the town, who had made him crawl into her store-room, had refused to open up to them and had raised the alarm. The very happy ending is that Francesco and his now-widowed mother and all his brothers and sisters move in to protect the Befana's shop, attended by Rag, who has become Francesco's own. But he is so much changed for the better that she does not recognise him.

'The Befana put her head out of the room behind the shop and peered over her glasses. "What has that wretch got to bark about?" she demanded. "He's happy, m'lady. He's happy to be alive. Isn't that right?" And Rag barked "Yup! Yup".' (pp. v-vii)

> *Carola Oman, "Two from Italy," in* The Spectator, *Vol. 225, No. 7432, December 5, 1970, pp. v-vii.*

The Befana's toyshop has plenty of the crisp detail that seems proper to toys and which I certainly associate with Gianni Rodari's writings; it has also a swingeing do-good point in the Pinocchio tradition. This is a journey-story with plenty of stops on the way for minor adventures. The journey is undertaken by a group of toys led apparently by two irascible officers, an army General and the naval Captain Halfbeard, but in fact kept together by the sense and the sensitive nose of Rag the dog. These and the other toys, including indispensable transport in the shape of a toy train and an aeroplane, sneak out of the shop at night because the old witch has not put aside any toys for the street urchin Francesco who has so often been seen gazing longingly at the shop window. Children will be glad that the poor boy finds a home but I think it will matter more to them that he finds a boon companion in the toy dog who so well deserves to come to life.

> *Margery Fisher, in a review of "The Befana's Toyshop," in* Growing Point, *Vol. 9, No. 7, January, 1971, p. 1658.*

A Pie in the Sky   (1971)

[*The following excerpt is from a review of the original Italian edition of* A Pie in the Sky *published in 1966.*]

Through a scientist's mistake the radioactive mushroom of a test atom bomb is transformed into a gigantic cake suspended from a hill near Rome. The competent authorities take it for a spaceship from Mars. The two sons of a guard, however, do not let the others' fear influence them and recognize the true nature of the mysterious object. The desperate scientist finds himself faced with sweets and cream and cries for his damaged reputation. And yet making cakes gives more satisfaction than making atomic bombs. This is demonstrated by throngs of happy children who attack the cake at the bat of an eyelid as soon as they hear the good news. In view of this great joy the scientist retains his equilibrium. Sooner or later he will put himself at the service of the fine art of pastry-making.

The content of this delightful story is in favour of pacifism and international understanding and demonstrates the power of innocence and non-conformism.—A story full of happy humour, poetry and felicitous concentration. Highly original drawings by Munari. (pp. 39-40)

> *A review of "The Cake in the Sky," in* Bookbird, *Vol. 6, No. 1, March 15, 1968, pp. 39-40.*

As might be expected from a Hans Christian Andersen Prize winner, this story of a peculiar shape which appeared over the suburb of Trullo in Rome is really a delightful frolic. The police are alerted, the army is called out, and the citizens suspect that this strange thing in the sky heralds a visit from the inhabitants of another planet. It is only the children—and first of all the local police constable's children—who realise that this whole grotesque flying object is one glorious creamy chocolate cake. How they prove this, and how they make friends with the solitary occupier of the cake makes a delicious piece of nonsense told with a verve and a sharp sense of humour. The dialogue and fast-moving pace of the story make it very suitable for children of eight years upwards who are able to read for themselves.

> *B. Clark, in a review of "A Pie in the Sky," in* The Junior Bookshelf, *Vol. 35, No. 6, December, 1971, p. 383.*

Among the main features of contemporary Italian children's literature one may note the continuous presence of antinomies and conflicts typical of mankind at large. This also characterized the literature of earlier periods, but with a substantial difference in presentation. Though such conflicts, which are so difficult to solve or overcome, may be considered an educational liability rather than as an asset in books for children, deeper analysis will show them in another light, for they provide an effective way to build up a dialogue, a possibility of communication. An evaluation of differences and conflicts existing between individuals or social and ethnic groups can be made, in fact, not to any discriminatory purpose, but with a view to acquiring in depth some data which will enable any reader to define for himself the terms of the different problems—and maybe solve them. Of course to understand does not mean to consent, to accept does not mean to approve. Differences, antinomies, conflicts *do* remain, in great part. However, the way to any form of dialogue passes through the knowledge of differences. The problem is, in our field, how to choose the tools (that is, the narrative language) which will let young people seize and know these differences, not in a traumatic way or, still worse, in a sweetened form, but in a dynamic, constructive process.

Italian children's literature from its inception (about the second half of the last century) is an exhaustive fresco of differences of all kinds: economic, social, ethnic, psychological, philosophical; they reflect the historical situation of a country which reached its unity as a state in a slow and gradual movement from 1848 onward. But the achievement of this unity has not cancelled, not even to this day, the unpleasant consequences of the previous situation, the frictions and contrasting attitudes connected with it. (pp. 180-81)

It pays to compare the aims of past writers with contemporary ones as regards the depiction of the world around them and around their heroes, in every country's literature. As concerns the Italian, here are the main questions: How do contemporary writers introduce to young readers the conflicts and antinomies typical of our time? What conflicts do they choose to show? Do they lead the reader to the solution of problems or do they not? In the best books the main point is the provocative strength of their statements, which do not suggest a solution but rather stir up the reader to look for it, to weigh its necessity, to shape a personal proposal. In other words, the problem is, for the writer, how to induce his reader to meditation and, afterward, to participation and engagement.

In the best books of the past . . . situations were communicated to the reader without the aim of stirring up in him anything more than sympathy. On the contrary, in [some] authors writing after 1945 . . . , we find a more provocative expression and an invitation to initiative (sometimes even an initiative of rebellion, of revolt) as if the writers themselves would admit that young people better than adults are able to change a world which is on the way to dehumanization. (pp. 181-82)

Gianni Rodari, the best known of our contemporary writers, was awarded the H. C. Andersen Prize in 1970. He employs humor and fancy to point out some of the oppositions which cause conflicts and wars: poor and rich; people of good will and people of bad will; oppressive people and peaceful people; exploiters and exploited. He believes in children as the ones who are not overwhelmed by prejudices, stereotypes, and ideologies which would prevent them from building a better world.

In his book *La torta in cielo* (The Cake in the Sky), a strange space ship lands in the outskirts of Rome. Authorities, army, police, are in fighting trim. Only children escape such a hostile attitude; they approach the space ship and discover . . . it is an enormous cake! They taste it, or better, they eat it up, until they discover, well hidden inside, a scientist full of shame for what has happened to him. In fact he was to prepare an atomic bomb, but, by an incredible mistake in the mixture of the different elements, his bomb became a cake. A great blow to the prestige of a scientist, indeed! But when he sees the enthusiasm of the Roman children for his cake he makes up his mind: he will always prepare cakes instead of bombs. (pp. 183-84)

> *Carla Poesio, "Some Features of the Modern Italian Literature for Young People," in* Children's Literature: Annual of the Modern Language Association Seminar on Children's Literature and The Children's Literature Association, *Vol. 5, 1976, pp. 180-88.*

Mr. Cat in Business (1975)

Mr. Cat in business is a satire on modern methods, smart in style and clear in its application. Mr. Cat decides to make his fortune by selling tinned mice and pays a kitten to stick labels on the tins in spite of the reluctance of the mice to fall in with the plan. When the would-be tycoon is taken to court for fraud, his defence is couched in familiar terms:

> Mice lead mean, inglorious lives . . . I want to give them a better future, put them in the shop window where everyone can see them. At my own expense I provide solid, well-sealed tins with labels designed by a leading artist on which the mice look better than they really are. I give away a tin opener and free coupons, fix a popular price within the reach of every purse. And what is the result? They sabotage me in the most cunning way and bribe the judge with cheese to get me fined. There is no honesty left in this world. There is no such thing as religion any more. I'd do much better to become a bandit.

In the end one of the putative victims earns a fortune himself, selling tickets to watch the matrimonial spats of Mr. Cat and his kitten assistant. Eight-year-olds who expect an animal story on the usual pattern will have to enjoy the slapstick: older boys and girls who like to feel they can see through advertising techniques should appreciate the sardonic humour. . . .

> *Margery Fisher, in a review of "Mr. Cat in Business," in* Growing Point, *Vol. 14, No. 7, January, 1976, p. 2786.*

This is a really funny story of a cat who tries to become a business tycoon—I was really not sure if he made the grade or not—but his intended victims certainly did. Shrewd, sharp but essentially kindly wit has created a character to enjoy and remember; a story which many adults will enjoy reading aloud as much as the young listener will enjoy the hearing. The young reader will require fluency to keep up with the momentum of the style, too halting an approach might well spoil the effect.

> *M. R. Hewitt, in a review of "Mr. Cat in Business," in* The Junior Bookshelf, *Vol. 40, No. 1, February, 1976, p. 29.*

Tales Told by a Machine (1976)

Humour does not always travel well but one country's jokes are more easily understood by another when satire is in question. The almost universal problem of hiding the detritus of civilisation (so neatly aired in the Wombles books) is stated with freakish humour in **"A Tinned World"**, one of seven stories taken from **"Novelle Fatte a Macchina"**. . . . The story opens with a small shock of ambiguity. Signor Zerbini exhorts his family to leave their picnic place on the Tolfa Mountains tidy; "There, doesn't that look better?' he remarks, when each bush has been adorned with a paper cup and the empty bottles are arranged under a chestnut tree. The bottles, however, have other ideas. As the family drives towards Rome the children (who wish there had been time to use the "charming

tableau" as a "target for throwing stones") notice that the discarded glassware is following the car. They are not alone in observing this strange happening:

> A long procession of cars was now moving along Via Aurelia, each with its own tail of empties— glass bottles, plastic bottles and milk bottles. Each empty had its own particular clicking sound and its own personal rhythm. They jumped along with tiny steps or great leaps, skidding violently on the hairpin bends. The spectacle was enough to put joy into your heart. Signor Zerbini remembered his boyhood when he had played the plates in the Crash Clatter Band.

The trick is to distract attention from the absurdity of the situation by entirely matter-of-fact elaboration. So the bottles, accepted into the household, grow on the scientific principles explained by Professor Boxford, "world expert in containers and packaging", and reveal new possibilities in domestic comfort. The children's room, now wholly contained in a coffee tin, is wildly suitable for the game of sardines, and husband and wife sleep cosily in bottles— "Signora Octavia chose the orange bottle because she couldn't stand the smell of beer". Speed and a dizzily mounting recital of plausible detail keep the nightmarish aspect of the story in check, and the same balance can be seen in **"Off with the Cats"**, although the escape of Signor Antonio the retired stationmaster has an unusually strong undercurrent of unease in spite of the cheerfully explicit satire of the dénouement, when he joins scores of cats, animal or transmogrified humans, in a sit-in in the Colosseum, to demand that a "Cat Star" be added to the constellations.

In almost all the stories the theme of identity—lost, changed, threatened or achieved—provides a key to meaning and adds gravity to the nonsense. The dexterity of the method is seen especially well in **"The Fisherman of Garibaldi Bridge"**, an escalation almost unbearably stretched out to a melancholy conclusion. The question "Who am I?" is asked more than once, though less searchingly, in a set of bizarre anecdotes labelled **"One for each month"**. The odd structure of this "chapter" is not immediately appealing but there are good things here, particularly **"August on the Train"**. This acid little piece describes a man who after recording on tape, over a period of thirty years and entirely in his own voice, all the voice and orchestral parts of "Aïda", puts on a performance in the town theatre and "It sounded exactly like a gramophone record".

These are stories which, one way or another, get under your skin. . . . If I have any doubts about how far the tales will be appreciated by young English readers, they have been provoked by the last story, **"Piano Bill and the mystery of the Scarecrows"**. Not because the parody of cowboy films and television ads is not topical and obvious enough to transcend national frontiers, but because behind the verbal and situation humour there is an unusually strong affirmation of belief. I hope the deepening of the satirical voice will be heard as the author intended. (pp. 3010-11)

> *Margery Fisher, in a review of "Tales Told by*

a Machine," in Growing Point, *Vol. 15, No. 6, December, 1976, pp. 3010-11.*

Seven stories have been selected from a series written by this versatile Italian author. They try to answer the question "What would happen if ?" . . . and as may be imagined many impossible situations arise: the canals in Venice so envelop the town that the inhabitants have to live entirely under water; all the rubbish tins and empty bottles become so numerous that whole cities are engulfed. Such propositions sound like a kind of science fiction, but as they increase in improbability, so the humour becomes semi-adult in style. All children may not appreciate this, but for those who do, the books will prove a feast of enjoyment.

B. Clark, in a review of "Tales Told by a Machine," in The Junior Bookshelf, *Vol. 41, No. 4, August, 1977, p. 226.*

Helen Roney Sattler

1921-

American author and illustrator of nonfiction, author of fiction, and journalist.

Major works include *Recipes for Art and Craft Materials* (1973), *Dinosaurs of North America* (1981), *The Illustrated Dinosaur Dictionary* (1983), *Sharks, the Super Fish* (1986).

Respected as a writer of informational books acknowledged for their thoroughness, accuracy, clarity and fascination to young readers in the early grades through junior high, Sattler is especially well known for creating introductions to dinosaurs and other animals as well as for a series of craft books which present directions for making toys, games, furniture, and presents with inexpensive and easily accessible materials. Praised for providing her audience with sound advice and reliable information not represented in other sources, she is also the writer of several works considered authoritative on their subjects. Sattler began her career by writing craft and puzzle books which outline instructions for creating both familiar and unusual items in simple language and include her own black-and-white illustrations and diagrams. With *Dinosaurs of North America,* a book for middle graders and junior high school students prompted by the request of her grandson, she introduced the subject that now comprises the majority of her works: studies of animals both living and extinct, notably dinosaurs. In the well-received *Dinosaurs of North America,* she describes every type of dinosaur thus far discovered on this continent, explaining technical information about the creatures as well as their relationship to the changes of the earth and the most popular theories regarding their extinction. Sattler is also the author of *The Illustrated Dinosaur Dictionary,* another popular title on its subject for middle graders in which she defines the characteristics of over three hundred kinds of dinosaurs, as well as books on flying reptiles, Tyrannosaurus Rex and its relations, the evolution of the human race as traced from fossil remains, and, for younger readers, a title on baby dinosaurs; her books of this type also include an abundance of additional material, such as indexes, bibliographies, time and species charts, maps, and pronunciation guides. In addition to her works on prehistoric subjects, Sattler is the author of informational books for middle graders on sharks, whales, eagles, and giraffes which define the general characteristics of these mammals along with specific facts covered in extensive glossaries as well as books on animal anatomy and intelligence, the weather, and train signals. Among her other books, Sattler has written a job guide for middle graders and two works of fiction, a humorous realistic story and a fantasy for readers in the early grades. *The Illustrated Dinosaur Dictionary* received the Golden Kite Award for nonfiction in 1983, while *Dinosaurs of North America* was named a nonfiction honor book by the committees for both the Golden Kite Award in 1981 and the *Boston Globe-Horn Book* Award in 1982.

In addition, eight of Sattler's books, including *Dinosaurs of North America, Whales, the Nomads of the Sea,* and *Hominids: A Look Back at Our Ancestors,* were named Notable Books of the Year by the American Library Association.

(See also *Something about the Author,* Vol. 4; *Contemporary Authors New Revised Edition,* Vol. 14; and *Contemporary Authors,* Vols. 33-36, rev. ed.)

TITLE COMMENTARY

Kitchen Carton Crafts (1970)

A teacher-librarian-mother-den mother demonstrates that containers can be as versatile as they are various—and who has not wanted to dismember a pressed-cardboard egg carton as Mrs. Sattler does to good purpose here? Out of it she makes now A Kneeling Camel, now A Totem, now a Bottle Cap Toss, while a plastic bubble and tray (the kind cold cuts come in) is almost ready-made for a roll-in-the-hole Bead Game. Among the most ingenious *and* useful in the large gift department are plant pots from plastic scouring powder containers (upside down, the top is decorative and has drain holes; the bottom is handy for a saucer) and a litter box designed to rest securely on the center floor hump of a car (as well as put worn-out jeans, among other things, to new use). Then there are party hats, masks and party ornaments—enough to keep children busy from one holiday to the next. For this is painstaking puttering for a purpose, not Creative Activity. The succinct directions are clear and simple, as are the accompanying line drawings, and the whole, if not inspired, is eminently practicable.

> *A review of "Kitchen Carton Crafts," in* Kirkus Reviews, *Vol. XXXVIII, No. 3, February 1, 1970, p. 109.*

This is a book which instantly appeals to the eye. . . . [The author's] excellent diagrams . . . please and, more important, . . . encourage a child to make something himself—the somewhat bossy Martian and the placid turkey both proved favourites with young children. Further delight—these crafts can be practised fairly painlessly, as all the materials used are readily obtainable in any family home, as the title suggests, and Mrs. Sattler's instructions are very easy to follow. The book is divided into sections, which include toys, games, presents, and party hats, and should provide entertaining occupations for young readers, who could make the tug boat for instance, and for their older brothers and sisters who would enjoy the challenge of making a pilgrim boy from cardboard, or a wolf mask from a cereal box and a carton. Mrs. Sattler dedicates her book to her family, who have encouraged her. I imagine that many other families will be glad they did so.

> *Barbara Sherrard-Smith, in a review of "Kitchen Carton Crafts," in* Children's Book Review, *Vol. II, No. 1, February, 1972, p. 21.*

Holiday Gifts, Favors and Decorations That You Can Make   (1971)

Beginning impartially in spring with a Purim rattle and a St. Patrick's day blarney stone, Mrs. Sattler proceeds through the year with clearly illustrated, step-by-step directions for making a Passover scroll, Easter bunny, 4th of July cannon, Columbus day ship, and so on through a "patriotic diorama" for February. For December there's a soda straw Christmas angel and a Hanukkah menorah made of a broomstick and spools. Most of the finished products are table decorations—centerpieces, nut cups, place cards—and, as in the author's **Kitchen Carton Crafts,** most of the projects start with food packages such as egg cartons, cottage cheese or oatmeal containers, plastic meat trays, etc. Also like its predecessor, this offers no new ideas or prods to creativity, but the suggestions supplement the somewhat fussier ones in Leeming's *Holiday Craft and Fun* (1950), and there's a predictable seasonal demand. (pp. 1076-77)

> *A review of "Holiday Gifts, Favors, and Decorations," in* Kirkus Reviews, *Vol. XXXIX, No. 19, October 1, 1971, pp. 1076-77.*

The directions, coupled with simple, clear line drawings,

are easy to follow and suggested materials are readily obtainable. Unfortunately, the projects outlined lack variety, e.g., there's a drum nut cup for the Fourth of July, a Scroll nut cup for Passover, a Shamrock nut cup for St. Patrick's day, etc. Purdy's *Christmas Decorations for You to Make* (Lippincott, 1965), though limited in scope to that one holiday, offers a wide range of imaginative projects and Jordan's *Holiday Handicrafts* (Harcourt, 1938) is a good source of craft ideas linked to major holidays.

> *Estelle Schulman, in a review of "Holiday Gifts, Favors, and Decorations That You Can Make," in* School Library Journal, *Vol. 18, No. 5, January, 1972, p. 61.*

Ideas for making holiday table decorations and favors and a few gifts out of throwaway and inexpensive materials are contained in a book which, though not particularly imaginative, will be useful for scout and church groups, clubs, classroom, and home. Both the textual and pictorial directions are clear and easy to follow and only basic designs are given.

> *A review of "Holiday Gifts, Favors, and Decorations That You Can Make," in* The Booklist, *Vol. 68, No. 12, February 15, 1972, p. 507.*

Sock Craft: Toys, Gifts, and Other Things to Make (1972)

Easy-to-follow directions, accompanied by clear line drawings, for making 25 toys, 13 gifts, and several accessories, pet accessories, and decorations out of old socks. Although the book was written for young children it will be useful to others including scouts, club groups, and anyone wishing to make items for gifts or possibly for sale.

> *A review of "Sock Craft: Toys, Gifts, and Other Things to Make," in* The Booklist, *Vol. 69, No. 8, December 15, 1972, p. 406.*

Through clear, simple instructions and diagrams, Sattler shows how to use socks (any size, shape, color, or type), old nylons (for stuffing), and scraps of material, buttons, etc. to make many items. Add tracing paper, needles and thread, plus a minimum of sewing know-how (only two stitches are needed). The result is an imaginative variety of stuffed toys, bags, doll's clothing, etc. The projects are fun for children, and this makes a good addition to craft book collections. (pp. 74-5)

> *Dorothy S. Jones, in a review of "Sock Craft: Toys, Gifts, and Other Things to Make," in* School Library Journal, *Vol. 19, No. 9, May, 1973, pp. 1684-85.*

Jewelry from Junk   (1973)

The problem is that most of the end results are pretty junky too. Sattler turns dough (a slice of bread kneaded with glue and food coloring) into rose petals for pins and earrings and uses chicken neck and spine bones and leather to make silly little animals she calls Weird Willies, Hot Dogs and Monsters, when the bones would be more decorative as natural forms undisturbed by dangling puppy tongues, etc. Most of the projects are quite simple but it's questionable whether the final products are worth even the trouble of flattening and drilling holes in bottle caps (to make a Roman belt) or sawing ball point pen barrels into one inch lengths (for bracelets). The low point is reached with a tie clip made from plastic toys (animals, airplanes "or something similar") found in cereal boxes or gum machines. Perhaps the author of **Kitchen Carton Crafts** is at last running out of convertible trash.

> *A review of "Jewelry from Junk," in* Kirkus Reviews, *Vol. 41, No. 4, February 15, 1973, p. 192.*

Tin cans, bottle caps, and watermelon seeds emerge from the garbage to get a new lease on life here. One project, a "Dinosaur Bone Tie Clip," is made from a chicken wing bone, a hair clip, plus standard household supplies. The book is well organized according to type of junk used, and the index is arranged by name of article made. This will be especially useful since the materials suggested are free or inexpensive.

> *Mary E. Decker, in a review of "Jewelry from Junk," in* School Library Journal, *Vol. 20, No. 1, September, 1973, p. 133.*

Recipes for Art and Craft Materials   (1973)

A particularly useful sourcebook for all who work with crafts, whether as hobbyists or as teachers. It contains directions for making a great variety of pastes, modeling and casting compounds, paints and paint mediums, inks, and flower preservatives. Materials needed are inexpensive and easily procured. Directions are succinct, clear, and illustrated [by Sattler] with simple, explanatory line drawings.

> *Beryl Robinson, in a review of "Recipes for Art and Craft Materials," in* The Horn Book Magazine, *Vol. L, No. 3, June, 1974, p. 293.*

[The following excerpts are from reviews of the revised edition published in 1987.]

A welcome addition to libraries when the first edition was published in 1973, Sattler's collection of recipes has become useful in both circulating and reference collections for adults and children. The revised edition is similar to the first in most respects. Among the fourteen new additions are formulas for nutty putty, silk screen or poster paint, oil pastel crayons, colorful burning pinecones, and homemade coloring for paints and modeling clays. As well as stating in the introduction that the concoctions are "not for human consumption," Sattler has added numerous notes within the recipes warning when a mixture or ingredient is toxic. Where possible, she suggests a safer ingredient if the material is to be used by small children. Although the illustrations [by Marti Shohet] were not available in galley for review, the new dust jacket is promising—looking more handsome and professional than that of the earlier book. A worthwhile new edition of a dependable old standby. (p. 72)

> *Carolyn Phelan, in a review of "Recipes for Art*

and Craft Materials," in Booklist, *Vol. 84, No. 1, September 1, 1987, pp. 71-2.*

Anyone who has ever worked with crafts and children will want to add this recipe book to their collection. Concoctions include a variety of pastes and glues, modeling compounds, different types of papier-mâché paints, inks, and even flower preservation. All ingredients may be found easily in grocery, drug-or hardware stores; many already will be in the kitchen. "Helpful hints" identify where less common items may be found as well as other important considerations. Safety tips are presented in a preface and are repeated at the end of a recipe when a potentially harmful ingredient is used. Other craft books, such as Ann Wiseman's *Making Things: the Hand Book of Creative Discovery, Book 2* (Little, 1975) and Phyllis Fiarotta's *Sticks and Stones and Ice Cream Cones* (Workman, 1973) sometimes include a similar recipe or two, but it's quite handy to have a number of these recipes under one cover. This revision of the 1973 edition includes more than 12 new recipes, many of which do have warning notes accompanying them, making this edition more appropriate for adult use or adult supervised activities with young children. For young children, the best book is still Chernoff's *Clay Dough, Play Dough* (Walker, 1974; o.p.).

> *Maria B. Salvadore, in a review of "Recipes for Art and Craft Materials," in* School Library Journal, *Vol. 34, No. 6, February, 1988, p. 81.*

Jar and Bottle Craft   (1974)

Numerous ideas for recycling used glass jars and bottles are assembled by the author of **Kitchen Carton Crafts.** Tips and directions are copiously illustrated with line drawings. Safety is stressed (especially with glues), and no projects involve cutting the glass. All finished products have a practical use and many would be useful for scout troops. Children will be delighted with the simple bird waterer or cat bookends, and older crafters will enjoy making canister sets and lamps. Suggestions for this type of project can be found in such handicraft compendiums as Tina Lee's *Things To Do* (Doubleday, 1965), but Sattler's is the only title for children composed entirely of bottle and jar crafts.

> *Janet M. Bohl, in a review of "Jar and Bottle Craft," in* School Library Journal, *Vol. 20, No. 8, April, 1974, p. 61.*

Train Whistles: A Language in Code   (1977)

"On modern railroads, train crews also talk to each other by radio or telephone," Sattler allows toward the end of this illustrated glossary of *toots* and *woooos*. But if you have the chance to watch trains go by you can still hear that whistle blow—and now you'll know how to read the different combinations of blasts. Sattler takes a typical train through a number of situations that call for whistled messages, and for convenience she repeats them all in an appended list: three short blasts mean the train is backing up, one long means the train is coming to the station, and there are others warning people off the track, dispatching the flagman or calling him back, etc. Indispensable knowledge for the train buff, even if (s)he only applies it on the toy track at home.

> *A review of "Train Whistles: A Language in Code," in* Kirkus Reviews, *Vol. 45, No. 20, October 15, 1977, p. 1095.*

How whistle codes function to communicate with the train's crew, with animals, people, and with other trains is explained in this different approach to the ever-popular subject of trains. Along with the meaning of the signals (two longs, one short, and another long indicates that a train is coming down the track), interesting facts about railroad personnel and procedures are included. [Tom] Funk's yellow, red, and black drawings of trains en route and amiable children, pets, and adults will attract and hold pre-schoolers' attention. Informative and entertaining.

> *Michele Woggon, in a review of "Train Whistles: A Language in Code," in* School Library Journal, *Vol. 24, No. 3, November, 1977, p. 51.*

[*The following excerpts are from reviews of the revised edition published in 1985.*]

[Guilio] Maestro's watercolor illustrations are the highlight of a revised edition of Sattler's 1977 book. Through most of the story, readers follow a freight train on its run. This sensible device provides continuity while allowing for a variety of situations to arise in which the engineer must use the standardized code of signal whistles to which the title refers. . . . Sattler's text flows well, imparting information about the language of train whistles in a lightly fictionalized mode wholly appropriate for this age level. Young train buffs can actually learn the code, while others will enjoy the trip without feeling overloaded with technical details. A beautiful picture book on an ever-popular subject.

> *Carolyn Phelan, in a review of "Train Whistles: A Language in Code," in* Booklist, *Vol. 81, No. 18, May 15, 1985, p. 1338.*

Featuring a text that has been updated to reflect the railroad's increasing reliance on electronics, this revision reads somewhat more clearly than the original due to some subtle reorganization and smoother transitional passages. Sattler describes the meaning of several audible train signals and demonstrates their use in the course of a typical freight train journey. An addendum lists the signals covered in the book as well as a few additional signals. . . . Its attractive illustrative material, more contemporary typeface and cover graphics coupled with pre-schoolers' chronic interest in trains should make *Train Whistles* an essential purchase for most libraries.

> *Jeffrey A. French, in a review of "Train Whistles," in* School Library Journal, *Vol. 32, No. 1, September, 1985, p. 125.*

Nature's Weather Forecasters (1978)

This is the most detailed title for the age group on observing and interpreting weather signs. Readers are alerted to signs that reveal changes in humidity, temperature, winds, and clouds and to what those signs portend. Attempts are also made to illustrate the effects of weather on people and their social environment. Unfortunately, Sattler's writing is marred by a plethora of anecdotes which distract from rather than illuminate the concepts discussed. The fictionalized dialogue in these anecdotes will turn off young scientists who want their facts presented straightforwardly.

> *JoAnn Carr, in a review of "Nature's Weather Forecasters," in* School Library Journal, *Vol. 25, No. 1, September, 1978, p. 148.*

Weather as indicated by natural phenomena is the subject of Sattler's brisk, sometimes overly dramatic examination. If you subtract scenes such as the opener (" 'Shep tried to warn us, but we wouldn't listen,' sobbed a fourteen-year-old girl from her hospital bed after a tornado struck her home.") and concentrate on how factors such as atmospheric pressure, humidity, temperature, or wind and cloud patterns leave their mark, there's a good deal of interesting information to be had. Beginning chapters on animal signals sometimes come (rightfully) with advice to check other signs as well; some pointers seem too vague or meaningless ("Perhaps you have noticed that fleas bite harder after a dog has had a bath."), but later portions point out the more easily observable atmospheric signs and explain how weather systems operate. Weather rhymes are quoted extensively ("When dew is on the grass, / Rain will never come to pass.") and sometimes seem awkward or made up; still, the curious can find plenty of pointers among literary lapses.

> *Denise M. Wilms, in a review of "Nature's Weather Forecasters," in* Booklist, *Vol. 75, No. 1, September 1, 1978, p. 53.*

While I am still not completely convinced about animal behavior as evidence of coming weather, Mrs. Sattler puts up a very good argument. She presents plausible reasons why barometric pressure changes or low-frequency sound waves which may travel ahead of storms could be detected by animals which then seek shelter, though I am not convinced that they are driven by a conscious "fear of death." I don't see why smaller animals should be more responsive to pressure changes because of their size alone, as Mrs. Sattler claims, and I fear she is not basing phrases such as "most farmers will say . . . " or "most animals become uneasy . . . " on actual statistical studies. There are a few statements which must be called really inaccurate, notably the claim that dust particles in the earth's atmosphere cause the stars to twinkle. However, in spite of these reservations, I have to admit that she has put the whole matter of animal behavior well beyond the point where it can be laughed off casually, and her challenging of the reader to check things for himself is certainly in the scientific spirit.

> *Harry C. Stubbs in a review of "Nature's Weather Forecasters," in* Appraisal: Children's Science Books, *Vol. 12, No. 2, Spring, 1979, p. 55.*

Dollars from Dandelions: 101 Ways to Earn Money (1979)

Anyone wanting to earn extra cash will find here not only

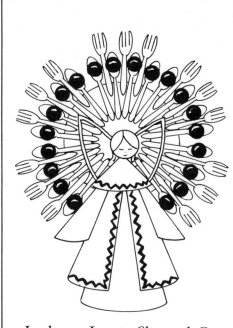

Holiday Gifts, Favors, and Decorations
THAT YOU CAN MAKE

Lothrop, Lee & Shepard Company
New York

Written and illustrated by
HELEN RONEY SATTLER

From Holdiay Gifts, Favors, and Decorations That You Can Make, *written and illustrated by Helen Roney Sattler.*

ideas but also worthwhile tips on their successful execution. Sattler arranges her job guide into categories such as outdoor services, farm work, cleaning, pet and plant care, apprenticeships, recycling, cash from the kitchen, and starting your own business. Both individual and group efforts are covered. Advice on getting jobs, gimmicks for advertising, guidelines on good business sense, and how-to information (growing seedlings, making compost bins, and painting house numbers on curbs) based on actual experiences of young people is written in a lively and motivating style. (pp. 1629-30)

> *Barbara Elleman, in a review of "Dollars from Dandelions: 101 Ways to Earn Money," in* Booklist, *Vol. 75, No. 22, July 15, 1979, pp. 1629-30.*

As usual with such roundups, most of these ideas will be useless to most kids. Few teenagers qualify as manuscript typists, tutors, lawn-mower repairers, or newspaper reporters; few will make a success of a mail order or animal-breeding business ("Donald sells his rabbits live to a local meat market"); and few will find much work as doll doctors, horse exercisers, gift wrappers, or office sitters. Most of Sattler's other suggestions are already well-aired: newspaper or bottle recycling, car or window washing, housework, plant sitting. True, it only takes one idea to launch a business, and who's to say a kid won't find one here that didn't turn up in The Amazing Life Games Company's *Good Cents* (1974) or in Horn's *Dozens of Ways to Make*

Money (1977)—both similar, but breezier-looking compilations.

> *A review of "Dollars from Dandelions: 101 Ways to Earn Money," in* Kirkus Reviews, *Vol. 47, No. 14, July 15, 1979, p. 801.*

Here are 110—by actual count—suggestions for young people wanting to earn money. . . . Lots of good advice is included—always do a good job, have a clear understanding of wages to be paid for work to be performed, never enter a stranger's house alone, don't get discouraged by refusals when job-hunting. Practical, specific, upbeat, . . . this will prove useful to young workers and would-be workers.

> *Phyllis Ingram, in a review of "Dollars from Dandelions: 101 Ways to Earn Money," in* School Library Journal, *Vol. 26, No. 7, March, 1980, p. 136.*

Dinosaurs of North America   (1981)

Considering that they are on the same subject, [*Dinosaurs* by Mary Packard and ***Dinosaurs of North America***] could hardly be more different. Mary Packard's *Dinosaurs* is, as befits its younger audience, bright (in fact, nearly Disneyesque) in color and brief in text. . . .

A very much more meticulous, more complete, and more elaborate book is Helen Roney Sattler's. Handsomely designed and illustrated in sepia [by Anthony Rao], it takes on the ambitious project of describing and placing in its environmental and phylogenetic context every genus of dinosaur so far discovered in North America. This is hardly a book to read at one sitting, but for the advanced secondary-school student, for the dinosaur buff and for school and library collections, it may well become the authoritative reference.

Mrs. Sattler is at home with much else besides paleontology, and one of the book's greatest virtues is that it will stimulate interest in such matters as geology, ecology and climatology. Her five-page discussion of the extinction mystery is a model of clarity and completeness, and her prose is superbly understandable, with never a hint of condescension. It is not, all in all, an easy book, but a rewarding one, nevertheless.

> *Georgess McHargue, "Giants of the Earth," in* The New York Times Book Review, *November 15, 1981, p. 64.*

This is truly an outstanding addition for any library no matter how many dinosaur books are already on the shelves. The text is well-organized and very readable, with a brief introduction as to "What is a dinosaur?" and how we learn from fossils about these creatures no one has ever seen. The individual types are presented chronologically with explanations about their development and probable life styles. A fascinating final chapter entitled, "The Mystery of Dinosaur Extinction" presents a myriad of theories, some of which are refuted and some supported. A bibliography, a reference by location, and an index are included. Although Ms. Sattler has concentrated on the dinosaur findings of North America, she also refers to studies done in other parts of the world and their relationship before the continents became divided. Throughout the volume are beautiful brown tone illustrations by Anthony Rao. There are both small sketches to explain some point in the text and full page drawings showing the animals in their natural settings. At no time is there any confusion between what is scientifically known from actual remains and what might be surmised for theatrical effect. (pp. 57-8)

> *Sallie Hope Erhard, in a review of "Dinosaurs of North America," in* Appraisal: Science Books for Young People, *Vol. 15, No. 1, Winter, 1982, pp. 57-8.*

Dinosaurs of North America is a large and handsome volume that is special in two ways: It mentions every kind of dinosaur found in North America, usually in some detail, and it also tells in what geographic locations these creatures have been discovered. This information gives the reader a chance to develop a special interest in the dinosaurs listed for his own state—or, at least, a neighboring one. Introductory pages to each section of the book are exceptional for their graphic view of drifting continents and changing climates over three geologic ages. Following these are descriptions, which average one page each, of over eighty genera of dinosaurs of North America. The wording varies, but the information usually includes length, weight, unusual body features, leg type, geographic location and, of course, whether the creature is a plant or an animal eater. In addition, the correct pronunciation of the scientific name is given, along with the meaning of the Latin name. Accompanying each dinosaur is a carefully made color-washed line drawing, sometimes with a background sketched in. The last chapter offers a comprehensive assortment of theories on the reasons for dinosaur extinction. While few readers will read the book from cover to cover, it is an outstanding reference work for those who want more technical information than is often available on specific dinosaurs. Attractive illustrations and generous spacing keep the book from being overbearing. To discuss only North American dinosaurs is to set up artificial boundaries; dinosaurs equally worthy of note existed on other continents, which were joined together at the start of dinosaur evolution. A purist would prefer to see them also included. Occasionally, however, the author refers to fossils elsewhere. If we had a similar book on dinosaurs of other continents, it would be difficult to imagine needing another book on dinosaurs for the same reading level.

> *Sarah Gagné, in a review of "Dinosaurs of North America," in* The Horn Book Magazine, *Vol. LVIII, No. 1, February, 1982, p. 77.*

Most people have been fascinated by the exotic and spectacular dinosaurs of Earth's Mesozoic Era, and they will delight in this charming book which, to my knowledge, is the only one that exclusively covers the Saurians native to North America. Sattler thoughtfully mentions, in many cases, the other global locations where significant fossil remains have been found. The book begins with a discussion, "What is a Dinosaur?" All Dinosaurs fall into only two orders and are classified according to the shape of the hip: Saurischia (lizard-hipped) and Ornithischia (bird-hipped). Within these two orders, however, an immense variety of forms evolved, and more than 80 kinds of dinosaurs are described here. The chapters proceed with a chronological discussion of all forms known during the Triassic, Jurassic and Cretaceous periods. We all yearn to know what could have caused the dinosaurs to disappear from Earth and the book concludes with a surprisingly complete review of the most popular theories of dinosaur extinction. Throughout the text, Sattler focuses on the relationship of dinosaurs to the Earth's changing geography, climate, and plant life. Rao's superb line drawings vividly bring these animals to life, and the book's simple language and uncomplicated format make this a good choice for a high school level class text as well as a general reference. It will be a welcome addition to the current literature and a delight to young and old.

> *David M. Drucker, in a review of "Dinosaurs of North America," in* Science Books & Films, *Vol. 17, No. 4, March/April, 1982, p. 199.*

No Place for a Goat (1981)

Joey's pet goat, Sam, both curious and persevering, awaits a chance to get into the house. Finding a hole in the screen door, he watches until everyone has left and chews his way inside. Sam enjoys climbing on the table and jumping on the sofa, but when Joey's mother returns home, Sam panics and causes considerable damage before he finally concludes that, "a house is no place for a goat." Children in the primary grades will enjoy the incongruity of a goat in the house, and the simple vocabulary and short sentences will enable them to read the story on their own. . . . Not unique, but lots of fun.

> *Nancy Westlake, in a review of "No Place for a Goat," in* School Library Journal, *Vol. 28, No. 5, January, 1982, p. 69.*

The Smallest Witch (1981)

Wendy Witch keeps being told she is too young to participate in the annual cobweb harvest. She waits for her turn to arrive and finally becomes a harvester. At first it is fun, but soon it becomes hard work, and she finds distraction in joining a group of trick-or-treaters. Wendy's white cat disappears into an old farm building that contains a large number of cobwebs; Wendy harvests them, proving to the other witches that she can complete an assigned task. Children will enjoy a real witch taking part in the Halloween parade; the moral of finishing what we start is very gentle. . . . It's a reasonably good additional title for reading aloud at Halloween.

> *Shaaron Girty, in a review of "The Smallest Witch," in* School Library Journal, *Vol. 28, No. 6, February, 1982, p. 70.*

Noses Are Special (1982)

An easy-to-read text describes the noses of 12 animals and one bird. Following brief background information, each nose is introduced by making reference to a nose it is not, which is confusing. Although Sattler appears to have intended to present concepts of adaptation and structure and function, the concise information regarding each kind of nose is framed by empty reference to unnecessary comparisons. . . . A good idea, containing factual information, but confusing in presentation.

> *Catherine Wood, in a review of "Noses Are Special," in* School Library Journal, *Vol. 29, No. 6, February, 1983, p. 70.*

The Illustrated Dinosaur Dictionary (1983)

[The Illustrated Dinosaur Dictionary *has black-and-white illustrations by Pamela Carroll and color illustrations by Anthony Rao and Christopher Santoro.*]

The *magnum opus* of this lot is unquestionably Helen Roney Sattler's **Illustrated Dinosaur Dictionary.** Its elegant artwork is as attractive as it is informative, and the entries display the lucidity and succinctness that marked the same author's distinguished **Dinosaurs of North America.** From "Acanthopholis" to "Zigongosaurus," this present volume is likely to become the premier reference work on the subject.

> *Georgess McHargue, "Dinosaurs Galore," in*

The New York Times Book Review, *November 13, 1983, p. 46.*

This very readable reference source is likely to receive more steady use than many conventional treatments of the subject. It might better have been titled *The Paleontological Dictionary* since the terms it defines include not only the names of nearly every known dinosaur and prehistoric creature, but also many words associated with paleontology such as *extinction, coloration* and *omnivore*. The entry for each creature includes a pronunciation guide, source of name, brief description of physical characteristics, mention of its feeding habits and its specific classification in terms of infraorder, suborder and order. Many also specify the fossil remains from which the animal's appearance has been deduced, whether whole skeletons or merely footprints. Approximately half of the name entries are accompanied by clear black-and-white drawings [by Pamela Carroll] which emphasize the distinctive characteristics of the animal under discussion. Names and terms in the dictionary listing are capitalized when they appear in the body of another entry. Supplementary sections include maps of continent formation, a simplified evolutionary chart, a 27-entry bibliography and a geographical listing of fossil finds divided by continent, country and state and referring to name entries in the dictionary. This title far surpasses the much briefer *Dictionary of Dinosaurs* (Messner, 1980) by Joseph Rosenbloom in scope and is similar in quality to Sattler's excellent **Dinosaurs of North America.**

> *Ann G. Brouse, in a review of "The Illustrated Dinosaur Dictionary," in* School Library Journal, *Vol. 30, No. 4, December, 1983, p. 69.*

The Illustrated Dinosaur Dictionary is a fascinating mini-encyclopedia for any dinosaur buff. It is less technical than Donald Glut's *Dinosaur Dictionary* and contains helpful pronunciations. Terms such as herding, diet, and intelligence are also listed providing a rich source of material on the physiology, behavior, ecology, etc. of this vast assemblage of prehistoric creatures. It is unfortunate, however, that several of this book's illustrations are of such poor quality that they often detract from the written material. Photographs of fossils would also have been helpful. I noticed only one error on page 285, the labelling of the sauropod titanosaurus as a meateater. Unless there is some recent finding unknown to me, titanosaurus should be classified as a planteater.

> *Bertrand Gary Hoyle, in a review of "The Illustrated Dinosaur Dictionary," in* Appraisal: Science Books for Young People, *Vol. 17, No. 2, Spring-Summer, 1984, p. 41.*

This illustrated dictionary is strong in its dictionary aspects and weak in its illustrations. As a dictionary, it includes terms related to dinosaurs as well as terms used in general paleontology and the names of animals often confused with dinosaurs. Each animal's name is accompanied by a pronunciation guide, an etymology, and a description of the animal's probable appearance and life style. Of particular interest is the author's frequent note on the amount of fossil material from which the taxon has been described. Two addenda provide a list of further readings and the

11. Turn it wrong-side out and stitch, as in Figure 11. Sew patches on the drab fabric, both skirt and blouse. Decorate the ball gown with lace, buttons, bows, or sequins. Use your imagination to create a handsome gown with whatever you have on hand.

12. Put blouses on dolls and whipstitch them closed. Turn under cut edges and whipstitch ends of blouses together (Figure 12).

13. Pull skirts over the blouses and turn raw edges to the inside. Tie a cord between the skirts (Figure 13). Cover the seam on top with ribbon if desired.

14. Turn ball gown skirt down and tie a scrap of drab fabric around Cinderella's head. Flip her over, and she is ready for the ball (Figure 14).

From Sock Craft: Toys, Gifts, and Other Things to Make, *written and illustrated by Helen Roney Sattler.*

geographical locations of fossils, but the latter addendum is somewhat uneven as some fossils are listed by state while others are given under more general categories, such as by continent or country. The illustrations include several color plates of habitus showing animals that don't look as if they were ever alive, a simplified diagram of past continental drift activities, and a chart indicating major dinosaur groups and their relation to modern animal forms. The text also sporadically includes line drawings. The writing is clear and relatively simple. However, the format of this book as a dictionary restricts its use to that of a reference for young readers.

> *Veronica Dougherty, in a review of "The Illustrated Dinosaur Dictionary," in* Science Books & Films, *Vol. 20, No. 1, September/October, 1984, p. 33.*

Baby Dinosaurs (1984)

Little is known about the reproductive and family behavior of dinosaurs, but with the discovery of nests, eggs and rare skeletons of younger animals at several sites, scientists are piecing together a fuller picture of the dinosaur life cycle. Sattler surveys approximately a dozen species, describing the eggs which have been found, the probable

size and physical characteristics of the baby dinosaurs and the likely dangers encountered by each. She explains the general prinicples and the actual information which have been established and states clearly what is still speculative. Because the body of knowledge is still limited, the text becomes somewhat repetitive as it moves from species to species. . . . Although general material on dinosaur species is abundant in most collections, the focus on newly-developing information expands the coverage of this universally popular subject.

> *Margaret Bush, in a review of "Baby Dinosaurs," in* School Library Journal, *Vol. 31, No. 3, November, 1984, p. 117.*

[Sattler] offers a proficient discussion of infant dinosaurs based on fossil findings worldwide. Lengthy for a picture-book text, this tends more toward description than analysis, with many helpful comparisons enabling youngsters to comprehend the relative sizes of dinosaur hatchlings and their parents ("Huge plant-eating dinosaurs . . . hatched from eggs just a little larger than basketballs"). Resplendent color-pencil drawings [by Jean Day Zallinger] on every page exert eye-catching appeal, but their scale is frequently misleading: the aforementioned basketball-sized baby comes halfway up the foreleg of an adult Camarasaurus. Furthermore, since all but one of the scenes are uncaptioned, it is sometimes impossible to identify the dinosaurs pictured. Overall, this is a less cohesive presentation than Freedman's *Dinosaurs and Their Young,* but dinosaur enthusiasts are sure to pounce on the book for ts storehouse of information as well as its lovely artwork.

> *Karen Stang Hanley, in a review of "Baby Dinosaurs," in* Booklist, *Vol. 81, No. 6, November 15, 1984, p. 450.*

Once again Mrs. Sattler has written a fine book about dinosaurs, but in a very different mode from her early large volumes. This slim little account is aimed at a younger audience and is limited in scope to just one aspect of the subject. The author states on the first page, "Hundreds of dinosaur fossils have been found, but not many of them were babies." She goes on to describe the few findings and what they mean to scientists. As before she is very clear to explain what is known from the fossils and what can only be surmised to be true. (pp. 33-4)

> *Sallie Hope Erhard, in a review of "Baby Dinosaurs," in* Appraisal: Science Books for Young People, *Vol. 18, No. 2, Spring, 1985, pp. 33-4.*

Fish Facts and Bird Brains: Animal Intelligence (1984)

This is a generalized, pseudoserious treatment of animal intelligence in a browsing book format. The information is so general with such scanty entries on specific animals that it would not be of much help to students writing reports. The chapter on testing a pet's intelligence concentrates on dogs with a few tests thrown in for cats and very few for hamsters, gerbils, mice, turtles and worms. Sattler does cats a disservice by stating that although they are about as intelligent as dogs, they don't do as well on tests as dogs because they aren't anxious to please. This reasoning completely overlooks the differing psychologies of pack animals (dogs) and individual hunters (cats). Animal intelligence is a topic of continuing and growing interest that deserves a less trivial treatment.

> *Frances E. Millhouser, in a review of "Fish Facts & Bird Brains: Animal Intelligence," in* School Library Journal, *Vol. 31, No. 3, November, 1984, p. 128.*

In the first eight chapters, Sattler presents anecdotal gleanings from ethologists' previously published accounts of scientific studies of animal behavior and intelligence. A bit humdrum, these chapters could have been enlivened by a discussion of some of the benefits of the studies. However, amazing studies of chimpanzees, crows, elephants, and planarians (flatworms) are included. (A reading list cites articles and books by many of the scientists involved.) Chapter nine gives details on how to test one's own pet for intelligence, and chapter ten, perhaps the most interesting, links the benefits of animal studies to human learning. Overall, this book will be of interest to many youngsters.

> *Sharron McElmeel, in a review of "Fish Facts & Bird Brains: Animal Intelligence," in* Science Books & Films, *Vol. 20, No. 4, March/April, 1985, p. 220.*

The basic problem with *Fish Facts* . . . is that cramming so many stories about so many different kinds of animals into one book results in a much too shallow presentation. Readers wanting to test their pets' intelligence might be interested in the chapter with simple (some time-consuming) tests for verbal comprehension, attention span, curiosity, reasoning and memory which might prove useful for a behavioral science project.

Although narrower in scope than *Fish Facts* . . . both Ann Michel's *The Story of Nim* (Knopf, 1980) and Eleanor Coerr's *Jane Goodall* (Putnam, 1976) provide full, well-written accounts of animal adaptability and intelligence, as does Ronald Fisher's *Namu: Making Friends with a Killer Whale* (National Geographic Society, 1973). *Fish Facts and Bird Brains* is a featherweight by comparison.

> *Mary Johnson-Lally, in a review of "Fish Facts and Bird Brains," in* Appraisal: Science Books for Young People, *Vol. 18, No. 4, Autumn, 1985, p. 34.*

Pterosaurs, the Flying Reptiles (1985)

Flying reptiles are usually mentioned only briefly in treatments of prehistoric life. This handsome book describes and illustrates nearly two dozen species of these creatures which, the text explains, were not related to the dinosaurs with whom they existed. The book also clearly distinguishes between the two main types of pterosaurs: rhamphorhynchoids and pterodactyloids. As in her earlier books, Sattler details the clues which have led paleontologists to startling conclusions about the habits of specific pterosaurs. . . . Smoothly written text is followed by a time chart listing species of pterosaurs in the specific time period in which they first appeared. A combined pronunciation guide and index translates each dinosaur's and pterosaur's name into English and indicates pages on which pictures and text appear. This is more current and colorful than John Kaufmann's *Flying Reptiles in the Age of Dinosaurs* (Morrow, 1976; o.p.).

> *Ann G. Brouse, in a review of "Pterosaurs, the Flying Reptiles," in* School Library Journal, *Vol. 32, No. 5, January, 1986, p. 70.*

The acquisitions librarian who is searching for a big, beautiful book on flying reptiles may find this one difficult to resist. Every page bears large, color illustrations [by Christopher Santoro] which are dynamic enough to be engaging, yet detailed enough to be informative. The text flows easily and correlates well with accompanying illustrations.

For the most part, the flying reptiles are depicted as they appeared in life. There is, however, one illustration of an archaeologist at work unearthing a skeleton. A full page illustration gives a useful picture of the skeletal remains unearthed by the archaeologist. Interested readers, therefore, can see for themselves the meager archaeological evidence upon which the color illustrations are based.

After examining the archaeological evidence, in the form of skeleton illustrations, the reader easily grasps the importance of skeleton diagrams when they appear side by side with the probable appearance of the animal when it was alive. By this technique, the illustrator draws the reader into the process of making inferences from fragmentary data. An important point because, as the book progresses, some of the animal forms are incredible. The skeptical reader may look for more evidence, and that could lead to the direct use of reference materials. If that happens, this beautiful picture book will have served the reader well.

Georgia L. Bartlett, in a review of "Pterosaurs, the Flying Reptiles," in Appraisal: Science Books for Young People, *Vol. 19, No. 3, Summer, 1986, p. 62.*

This is a comprehensive look at pterosaurs, the flying reptiles that commanded the skies during much of the reign of the dinosaurs. After a clear examination of why pterosaurs are classified as reptiles (and why some scientists think they shouldn't be), the book identifies characteristics of all pterosaurs, then details individual species. Each species is described through easily recognizable attributes, and its name is highlighted and explained. Probable habitats are discussed in light of fossil location as well as species characteristics. The color illustrations are outstanding, depicting the various pterosaurs soaring, feeding, and nesting in their individual habitats. The illustrations complement and expand the text, creating an attractive unity. Bone structure, fossils, and "close-ups" of individual pterosaurs further delineate the uniqueness of these animals. The book concludes with a brief discussion of the possible causes of pterosaur extinction. A clear, easy-to-read time scale is provided as well as a pronunciation guide and index. The integration of concise writing and detailed illustrations makes this an exceptionally fine book for elementary students. Like the pterosaurs themselves, this book soars. (pp. 111-12)

Peter Roop, in a review of "Pterosaurs, the Flying Reptiles," in Science Books & Films, *Vol. 22, No. 2, November/December, 1986, pp. 111-12.*

Sharks, the Super Fish   (1986)

In a readable, accurate text, Sattler supplies straightforward information on shark physiology and behavior. Strangely, her chapter on shark attacks neglects the hammerhead and the Australian nurse shark, authenticated as "man-eaters," but she does comment on the dangerous propensities of the lemon shark and the oceanic whitetip in the "Glossary of Sharks." This glossary will probably be the main focus of reader attention. Arranged alphabetically, it gives information on 20 families of sharks and over 100 varieties. Unfortunately, this format leads to many "See" and "See Also" references which can be annoying and is not as clear as a grouping by family. There is an excellent list of further readings—including a number of juvenile titles. All this is superbly accompanied by [Jean Day] Zallinger's glorious illustrations in soft grays, accurate and non-sensational. While McGowen's *Album of Sharks* (Rand McNally, 1977) has color illustrations, it does not have as much information as Sattler's book.

Freedman's *Sharks* (Holiday, 1985) has less to offer, too, but it still presents its information in a most gripping way, while Dingerkus' *Shark Watcher's Guide* (Messner, 1985) is less well organized, although more compact in size. A most welcome addition. (pp. 96-7)

Patricia Manning, in a review of "Sharks, the Super Fish," in School Library Journal, *Vol. 32, No. 10, August, 1986, pp. 96-7.*

What is most admirable about Sattler's book is the amount of information on the shark coupled with the sense of how much is *not* known about this incredibly wide-ranging and widely varied creature. The dual organization—general coverage of shark characteristics and an encyclopedia glossary (more than half the book) covering specific species and families, with a drawing for each—broadens the book's scope beyond that of Freedman's *Sharks* which was aimed at a younger audience in format as well as in tone. . . . A list of sharks, organized by family, and of books for further reading rounds off the presentation, which is indexed for students bent on reports. Browsers, however, will get hooked as well; who can resist a 5-inch shark called tsuranagakobitozame, found near Japan, or for that matter, the wobbegong shark (looking woebegone) that lives near the shores of New Zealand?

Betsy Hearne, in a review of "Sharks, the Super Fish," in Bulletin of the Center for Children's Books, *Vol. 40, No. 1, September, 1986, p. 18.*

Ms. Sattler does less well by sharks than she has for dinosaurs in three previous books for young readers, but this is still a thorough survey of shark species, physiology and behavior. The writing is a bit hyperbolic at times, and one might quarrel with her assertions of shark intelligence and predatory skills: "They have the best hunting tools on earth", she writes of shark teeth.

The book is informed by several well-told anecdotes. Wisely, though, Sattler treads lightly on man-eating escapades, perhaps a disappointment to bloodthirsty young readers.

Don Lessem, in a review of "Sharks: The Super Fish," in Appraisal: Science Books for Young People, *Vol. 20, No. 1, Winter, 1987, p. 60.*

Whales, the Nomads of the Sea   (1987)

[*Whales, the Nomads of the Sea*] packs a lot of information into an inviting format for middle and older readers. As the book opens, the author is getting acquainted with a pod of gray whales in San Ignacio Lagoon in Baja California. The whales breach, and she follows in her inflatable skiff. They nudge the boat, and she gives them a tentative pat or two. They beat the water with their tails, leaving smooth "footprints" on the surface, and she becomes convinced that they, indeed, have come to play.

The opening welcome is carried forward in an engaging text, with chapters titled "Amazing Mammals" and "Sea Soup and Sonar." . . . After learning about whale talk and the world's biggest babies, readers can dive into an illustrated 60-page glossary of whale species—more than enough to satisfy a demanding science teacher, plenty to fill a rainy afternoon.

> *Diane Manuel, "Whale Tales Take Kids 'Deep Down Where Seaweed Grows and Fishes Hide',"* in The Christian Science Monitor, *December 3, 1987, p. 26.*

Using the same format as their successful **Sharks, the Super Fish** Sattler and [illustrator Jean Day] Zallinger continue to explore the oceans, this time discussing the perennially fascinating whale, porpoise, and dolphin. Seven introductory chapters, often with titles more cute than descriptive, investigate the behavior and general characteristics of these intelligent mammals. The text is packed with accurate and intriguing information and is enlivened with accounts of Sattler's experiences while watching whales. Because the size of some whales is so immense, the author helps readers with comparisons; the blue whale, for example, is as long as two diesel locomotives and weighs as much as thirty elephants. A glossary of the known whale species offers straightforward information on each, including common and scientific names, geographical range, and physical descriptions. Numerous shaded drawings and diagrams of varying sizes amplify the text; each species in the glossary is illustrated and labeled to avoid confusion about relative size. Whale enthusiasts will find more information in this attractive volume than in many other children's books. Great for browsing, report writing, or reading from cover to cover, the book would make a wonderful gift and is a valuable selection for all libraries. Bibliography and index.

> *Ellen Fader, in a review of "Whales, the Nomads of the Sea,"* in The Horn Book Magazine, *Vol. LXIV, No. 1, January-February, 1988, p. 88.*

The first part of this book consists of seven essays on the biology of whales and dolphins in general and on our relationship to these large aquatic mammals. . . . The essays are very readable, yet at times they are preachy and pedantic. The author seems mesmerized by numbers (length of animal, length of flippers, number of teeth, and the like, all of which are subject to variation) and prone to using a scientific convention of abbreviated nomenclature (such as *B. musculus*) without appropriate introduction. This latter tendency certainly will cause problems for young (or nonbiologist) readers. However, the book is redeemed by its magnificent illustrations—numerous pencil drawings executed by Jean Day Zallinger. Deceptively simple, these drawings are often works of art, yet are scientifically precise as well as full of motion and grace. The drawings make this book. The artist deserves an "A"; the writer, a "B."

> *George R. Bernard, in a review of "Whales: The Nomads of the Sea,"* in Science Books & Films, *Vol. 23, No. 5, May/June, 1988, p. 301.*

Hominids: A Look Back at Our Ancestors (1988)

Hominids is a fascinating and well-organized account of the complicated process of piecing together prehistory from fragmentary remains. Sattler meticulously describes

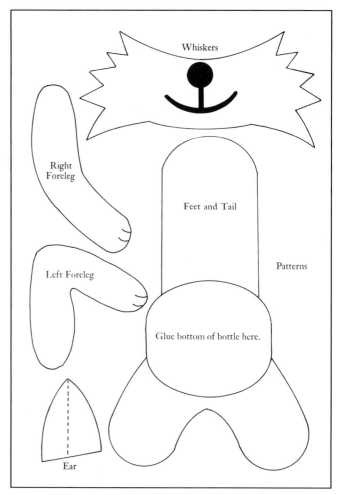

From Jar and Bottle Craft, *written and illustrated by Helen Roney Sattler.*

the changes of human evolution, always cognizant of the hypothetical nature of what is stated as archaeological fact. Along with the linear development of humans, she provides a wealth of information about the climate, food, tools, fauna, and flora that played a role in the development of mankind. Despite the difficulty of the subject matter, the succinct and clear style of both artist and writer make this book accessible to young readers. Sources cited include a plethora of recent adult science articles—sources far more recent than those cited in other children's books on the topic. Although *The Search for Early Man* (American Heritage, 1968; o.p.) by John E. Pfeiffer and F. Clark Howell's *Early Man* (Time-Life Books, 1973; o.p.) cover more material, both are for an older audience. True, these two volumes include color pictures and photos, and are more comprehensive in their coverage of archaeology, but Sattler's book is more current and more child-oriented. Tom McGowen's *Album of Prehistoric Man* (Macmillan, 1979) is closer in format to Sattler's book, but it lacks the scientific detail (for example, species and detailed time charts) that Sattler includes. Ironically, it's this attention to detail which ultimately conveys to readers a sense of the precarious nature of our own evolution. That, along with superlative writing, illustration, and research make this book an essential resource that no children's library should lack.

Cathryn A. Camper, in a review of "Hominids: A Look Back at Our Ancestors," in School Library Journal, *Vol. 35, No. 9, June-July, 1988, p. 112.*

From the expressive cover of an early australopithecine to the comprehensive time and species charts, the complete integration of clear, succinct text and definitive, evocative illustrations captures the reader's attention and offers a rewarding experience. *Hominids* is a book for all libraries.

Ms. Sattler discusses the complex concepts of the development of the human race based on scientists' evaluation of fossil discoveries; stating what is accepted as fact, where there are disagreements, what is not known but may be surmised, and areas where little or nothing is known. Information is included, not only on the evidence of the existence of hominids as man's earliest ancestors, but also on the accompanying climate, food, plants and animals. Emphasis is placed on the importance of cooperative behavior and on the use and making of tools in human development.

This is an extremely well-organized book. Each chapter leads logically and easily into the next: comparisons are made between species and continually with modern man both in text and in line drawings. Conveyed throughout is a sense of awe and respect not only for how much has been learned from the scarcity of available evidence but also for our early ancestors. (pp. 71-2)

Nancy R. Spence, in a review of "Hominids: A Look Back at Our Ancestors," in Appraisal: Science Books for Young People, *Vol. 22, Nos. 1 & 2, Winter & Spring, 1989, pp. 71-2.*

Because I believe that *Hominids* attempts to convey an understanding of our species' evolution at a time when strong organized and well-financed forces are hard at work to prevent such understanding, it is important that *Hominids* be more than *A Look Back at Our Ancestors.* It is, after all, a guide to our evolutionary history; it is not a guide in the sense of a field guide to the birds. *Hominids* intends to help readers understand how we have arrived at our present form. It does not intend to help the reader identify Lucy's sister should the reader come across her remains. To convey that history persuasively and to make all the examples of change coherent, requires an introductory chapter on evolution, from Darwin's revolutionary discovery to evidence of kinship from molecular biology. I hope that a second edition will include such a chapter.

I recommend one other change. In the present edition the growth of the brain is given prominent attention. Undoubtedly, the consequences of a growing brain are immense. However, from the point of view of complexity of origin, it is more surprising that ape-like creatures began to stand on two feet than that their brain grew larger. More attention should be given to this remarkable structural change.

I hope that children will find *Hominids* at hand along with

Human Origins by Richard E. Leakey, *Darwin for Beginners* by Jonathan Miller, and *Charles Darwin* by Roy A. Gallant. The combination will help children withstand the onslaught of obscurantis and pseudo-science. (pp. 72-3)

Lazer Goldberg, in a review of "Hominids: A Look Back at Our Ancestors," in Appraisal: Science Books for Young People, *Vol. 22, Nos. 1 & 2, Winter & Spring, 1989, pp. 72-3.*

Tyrannosaurus Rex and Its Kin: The Mesozoic Monsters (1989)

Tyrannosaurus Rex is probably the most popular dinosaur among children, and now Sattler attempts to do for it and its relatives what her book *Pterosaurs: the Flying Reptiles* did for flying dinosaurs. Ironically, despite the carnivores' popularity, this book makes for less interesting reading that *Pterosaurs,* partly because much of the information given on these creatures is fragmentary, and partly because Sattler limits her coverage to only those predatory dinosaurs related to T. Rex. Too, Sattler's book, while informative, lacks the imaginative hypothesizing found in Bakker's *Dinosaur Heresies* (Morrow, 1986) or *Predatory Dinosaurs of the World* (S. & S., 1988) by Gregory S. Paul, a book which covers a much wider spectrum of predatory beasts in a more creative fashion. Although these two volumes were written for adults, they are full of wonder and creative speculation, elements which which attract children to read more about dinosaurs in the first place. As usual, Sattler does a superb job of presenting factual material in an appealing and accessible manner, but while her book is an excellent dinosaur reference, her failure to indulge in more speculative storytelling makes the text drier than its subject matter would imply.

Cathryn A. Camper, in a review of "Tyrannosaurus Rex and Its Kin: The Mesozoic Monsters," in School Library Journal, *Vol. 35, No. 7, March, 1989, p. 196.*

Forty relatives of Tyrannosaurus rex are described in this attractive book, with information on fossil remains plus speculation on habitat and eating habits—the author (with her usual care) distinguishing carefully between fact and conjecture. Most of the relatives look remarkably like the familiar Tyrannosaurus, with upright stance, small front arms, powerful hind legs and tail, and enormous, razor-sharp teeth. A variety of nose bumps, head crests, skin patterns, and spine ridges distinguish these huge carnivores from one another, as depicted by [Joyce] Powzyk—an admirably precise, much experienced illustrator of wildlife; her illustrations here are realistic and dramatic without being sensational, adding interest by varying activities (imagine a dinosaur trying to get up from a prone position). Young fans are sure to enjoy this look at a popular family's more obscure branches. Sattler includes a location guide, time line, pronunciation guide, list for further reading, and index. (pp. 769-70)

A review of "Tyrannosaurus Rex and Its Kin: The Mesozoic Monsters," in Kirkus Reviews, *Vol. LVII, No. 10, May 15, 1989, pp. 769-70.*

A book on the meat-eating dinosaurs should be exciting, informative, and realistic. This book fills the bill only to a point. Although most of the information is good and reasonably accurate, the book is a curious mix of fact and hype. The facts are precisely stated, although with new discoveries constantly revising current beliefs, some of these facts may become obsolete. The major types of carnosaurs are individually described, and full scientific names are used. Related animals are described, and lesser-known types are included. Unfortunately, the author repeatedly calls the carnosaurs "monsters," as though this word had meaning outside of nightmares and Hollywood movies. Their vicious habits are overly stressed. Also, tyrannosaurids are described as having pillar-like legs (a common dinosaur catch phrase), yet the illustrations all show the more angular and flexed leg stance now considered to be correct. The illustrations are interesting and lively and will be enjoyed by young readers. Sattler states that the carnosaurs' coloration probably consisted of dull hues like most big animals of today; this restricts the choice of dinosaurs included in the book, and I would hardly call today's tiger dull in color. Taken with a grain of salt, or a dose of reality, this book is a summary of the most fascinating of the dinosaurs, the carnosaurs. It will probably delight the new generation of dinosaur lovers. Teacher and parents should remember, however, that science is not a recital of facts but a search for evidence and underlying principles. How we have come to know what we know about dinosaurs is not explained here. This omission and the repeated hype of the "monster" aspect of carnosaurs make this book only acceptable.

> *Jo Ann Coburn, in a review of "Tyrannosaurus Rex and Its Kin: The Mesozoic Monsters," in* Science Books & Films, *Vol. 25, No. 1, September/October, 1989, p. 36.*

The Book of Eagles   (1989)

Using the same format, and displaying the same impeccable regard for accuracy and detail found in *Sharks, the Super Fish* and *Whales, the Nomads of the Sea* Sattler and [illustrator Jean Day] Zallinger offer a book that is a must-buy for every library seeking clear, logically organized information about the more than 60 species of eagle that inhabit the world. The eagles' life cycle is described, as well as their physical characteristics and typical patterns of flight and hunting. Sattler's style is lively and packed with many intriguing tidbits such as the fact that a Bald Eagle's 7,000 feathers weigh less than 1.5 pounds. Children will appreciate the volume's emphasis on our natives, the Bald Eagle and the Golden Eagle. The "Glossary of Eagles" devotes a paragraph to each of the 60 species discussed, and, for each, Zallinger includes a range map as well as illustrations of the birds in flight, at rest, and in various plumages. The watercolor illustrations are painstakingly accurate, and the small sketches scattered throughout amplify and enlarge upon the text. . . . Ryden's *America's Bald Eagle* (Putnam, 1985) and Patent's *Where the Bald Eagles Gather* (Clarion, 1984) devote more space to our national bird, but *The Book of Eagles* is clearly the one to choose for current, complete, and authoritative worldwide coverage.

> *Ellen Fader, in a review of "The Book of Eagles," in* School Library Journal, *Vol. 35, No. 13, September, 1989, p. 268.*

Following a pattern established in her attractive oversize handbooks on dinosaurs, sharks, and whales, Helen Roney Sattler combines several short thematic chapters on physical and behavioral characteristics of four types of eagles with a long illustrated glossary describing the sixty species of eagles found worldwide. The text emphasizes how little is known about some of the birds and the difficulty in studying them due to their speed and remote nesting sites. Topics include hunting, courting, nesting, rearing of the young, human dangers, and conservation efforts. Unlike earlier volumes, this book is illustrated with color paintings that are both an asset and a liability. The jacket portrait, a head-on view of an eagle in flight, is garish, emphasizing the large open beak, and suggests a highly dramatized treatment. Some full-page pictures are slightly indistinct and softened in tone, highlighting foreground details. The glossary portraits showing the distinctive colors, markings, and open wingspan of each bird are very useful, as are the small maps locating each eagle's range of habitation. Though visually less successful than some work by these collaborators, the book is highly appealing in its subject matter and invaluable in bringing together all of the species related to the Golden Eagle and Bald Eagle of the United States. Sattler continues to be unerring in her choice of subject and reliably thorough in her arrangement and treatment of information. (pp. 643-44)

> *Margaret A. Bush, in a review of "The Book of Eagles," in* The Horn Book Magazine, *Vol. LXV, No. 5, September-October, 1989, pp. 643-44.*

Giraffes, the Sentinels of the Savannas   (1990)

Calling them "walking watchtowers," Sattler draws on her usual keen observational skills and fine writing ability to provide a fascinating picture of giraffes. She begins with a dynamic you-are-there scenario—"I could tell we had entered giraffe country; the huge, twelve-inch-long hoofprints in the mud beside the road couldn't have been made by anything but a giraffe"—and interlaces specific facts with general information in a pleasing commentary. In addition to physical descriptions of these majestic animals, Sattler discusses their habitats, food, child rearing, behavior, and relationship to humans. This last area is of obvious interest to the author, who stresses the need to appreciate, understand, and even learn from these unique beasts of the African plains. Twelve pages are dedicated to an illustrated glossary, which is followed by a geological timetable, a classification table, and a list of further reading.

> *Barbara Elleman, in a review of "Giraffes, the Sentinels of the Savannas," in* Booklist, *Vol. 86, No. 16, April 15, 1990, p. 1638.*

A thoroughly detailed, affectionate look at these appealing oddities, describing giraffes' unusual evolution, anatomy, and habits as well as efforts to keep them from extinction—extended and enhanced by soft brown drawings [by Christopher Santoro] that focus on unique features of hoof, teeth, skin patterning, and skeletal structure while capturing the giraffe's charm in its many unlikely-looking attitudes (including a sequence showing the difficult feat of arising from a recumbent position.

Like Sattler's excellent ***The Book of Eagles, Giraffes*** skillfully fuses a lucid, well-organized, carefully researched text with outstanding illustration and handsome format. Illustrated glossary of giraffes and their close relatives, past and present; further reading; geological timetable; classification chart; index including both scientific and common names. Outstanding. (pp. 654-55)

> *A review of "Giraffes, the Sentinels of the Savannas," in* Kirkus Reviews, *Vol. LVIII, No. 9, May 1, 1990, pp. 654-55.*

Julian F(rancis) Thompson

1927-

American author of fiction.

Major works include *The Grounding of Group 6* (1983), *A Question of Survival* (1984), *A Band of Angels* (1986), *Simon Pure* (1987).

Perhaps the most controversial writer for young adults to emerge in the last decade, Thompson is the creator of realistic fiction, comic novels, and psychological thrillers which are underscored by his belief in young people and desire for them to question the values and mores of adults in order to improve the world. Considered an iconoclastic and irreverent author who challenges his readers with lengthy, sophisticated novels characterized by intricate plots, experimentation with language, and inclusion of contemporary social concerns, Thompson is often celebrated as an original and remarkably inventive writer whose works reflect both his understanding of adolescents and his honest evaluation of their lives. Several observers, however, are equally adamant about Thompson as a pretentious and sophomoric author whose work is crude, violent, convoluted, and overly sarcastic.

Thompson began his career with *The Grounding of Group 6,* a thriller that takes place in Vermont, the setting for several of his works and the state where he currently resides. Often considered his best book, the novel describes how five teenage students at a private school survive the attempt to "ground" or eliminate them, a plan initiated by their parents. Written after his experiences as a teacher, counselor, and director in private and alternative schools, *Group 6* introduces several features that have become standard in Thompson's books: the presentation of his adolescent protagonists as responsible, loving, intelligent, and outspoken citizens who survive the situations foisted on them by adults; his characterization of most grownups as eccentric, ridiculous, uncaring, or evil individuals who attempt to take away the personal freedom, and even the lives, of the teenagers who threaten them; and the inclusion of explicit sex, graphic language, and violent images, including death. Thompson addresses such themes as relationships with parents and peers, academic independence and the defense of basic rights, the development of identity, and the importance of love and friendship, and provides realistic backgrounds that reflect such contemporary social elements as drug use, venereal disease, cults, and the threat of nuclear war. Although many of his books are darkly satiric, Thompson is consistently sympathetic to his young adult characters and often playful in approach, writing in a distinctive style that incorporates such characteristics as colloquial speech, asides and quips, symbolic names, invented words, puns, and doublespeak. *A Band of Angels* was selected as a Best Book for Young Adults by the American Library Association in 1986 and *Simon Pure* received the Editor's Choice from *Booklist* in 1987.

(See also *Something about the Author,* Vols. 40, 55; *Con-*

temporary Authors New Revision Series, Vol. 30; and *Contemporary Authors,* Vol. 111.)

AUTHOR'S COMMENTARY

[The following excerpt is from a speech delivered by Thompson to the Assembly on Literature for Adolescents which was presented by the National Teachers of English in 1987. It was quoted by Dave Jenkinson as part of an interview he conducted with Thompson for Emergency Librarian.*]*

There are three things I think most Americans believe. They believe children are a precious gift, adorable and tender. They believe art can be uplifting, insightful, exciting, and often beautiful. And I think an awful lot of Americans believe that 15-year-old people are none of the above, and that they are instead a royal, and tasteless, and peculiar pain. Books that 15-year-olds perceive to be about themselves will, therefore, be anathema to many of their elders. Why 'anathema' I ask myself? Why are my books, which are seen by me to be sweet texts, anathema to people my own age? I think the first thing has to do with 'tone,' which is a main ingredient of 'atmosphere.' There is a tone in my books that affects some people like the passing of long nails across a blackboard. It's a tone they'd describe as being 'fresh' or 'rude' or 'wiseguy.' If that tone is used when writing about adults, it sets off alarms in some adult readers' minds because, I think, they perceive it to be an invitation to kids to go and do likewise. I don't think this is true. I think kids read it differently. I think kids read it as something they call 'goofing on.' Kids goof on things a lot; it's one of their main lines of defense in situations where they feel defenseless. They perceive my adult villains not as serious attempts to describe teachers or parents, but just as people that I'm goofing on, and that aren't to be taken literally. They know these adults are unbelievable.

Now 'unbelievable' is a word that's also used sometimes to talk about my work by people who dislike it. Why must fiction be believable? I know my books are unbelievable. I know my books have stuff in them that's unbelievable. I know my premises are unbelievable sometimes. When I have a group of kids set off in their parents' car to think about life and discover whether they want to go to college or not, I'm not describing an event that is likely to happen or even should happen to everyone. I'm describing an event which almost all of us would have loved to have happen to us at some point in our lives, but which, for one reason or another, never did. But it frees me up to put these kids in a situation where they are by themselves and can talk about things which are very much their own concerns. In this case, the concern was nuclear war and the book was *A band of angels.* The kids I wrote about, in this and all my other books, are also 'unbelievable', I guess, in that they tend to be unbelievable because they tend to be good students, loving and kind, athletic, non-manipulative, chemical free, reverent, honest, egalitarian, virginal and hopeful. But that's intentional as well. I choose to write about the hopeful side of my young characters. (p. 64)

Dave Jenkinson, "Julian F. Thompson," in Emergency Librarian, *Vol. 16, No. 2, November-December, 1988, pp. 60-4.*

TITLE COMMENTARY

The Grounding of Group 6   (1983)

Introducing an author with a remarkable literary style and frightening inventiveness, this psychological novel is set in an isolated Vermont area. Nat Rittenhouse leads five 16-year-olds into a wilderness in order to kill them, which he has been paid to do by Dr. Simms, headmaster of the private school the three girls and two boys believe they will attend. Their parents, disgusted with kids they consider losers, have given Simms a huge sum to "ground" the group permanently. Nat, however, discovers his conscience and realizes he likes the children, and he confesses the plot and his part in it to them. That means that Simms and his armed cohorts go after Nat and his charges, the point where Thompson's story reaches a tremendous pitch of suspense and ends in a smashing surprise. Everyone will be looking for more feats by the talented author.

A review of "The Grounding of Group 6," in Publishers Weekly, *Vol. 223, No. 4, January 28, 1983, p. 86.*

Even with Thompson's abundance of bad language, sex and supposed teen values, this is a boring book. The six main characters and the secondary cast all have stories to tell, and *tell,* and TELL. . . . The parents' reasons for no longer wanting their teens are as unbelievable as the basic premise. Nat, of course, immediately sees potential in the youngsters, and joins them in hiding out from the villainous school staff and Arn the Barn, a hired killer. In the end, the three girls pair with the two student boys and Nat, and they all go off in the woods to live happily ever after. No matter what age, people deserve quality writing. This isn't.

Judi Porter, in a review of "The Grounding of Group 6," in School Library Journal, *Vol. 29, No. 10, August, 1983, p. 81.*

A satiric thriller—not for squeamish teenagers—intensifies the age-old adolescent-adult battle. . . . Obviously conversant with teenagers' attitudes and language, the author develops his premise convincingly. Writing fluently about adolescents in one key (romantic realism) and about adults in another (surrealistic black comedy), he doesn't even pretend to play fair. The adolescents, once away from their parents, are all remarkably responsible, good citizens; the lunatic adults are all ridiculous, discordant, and heinously wicked. Humorously antiestablishment and slick, the book is pure, page-turning entertainment. (pp. 586-87)

Nancy C. Hammond, in a review of "The Grounding of Group 6," in The Horn Book Magazine, *Vol. LIX, No. 5, October, 1983, pp. 586-87.*

Facing It   (1983)

After the tragic loss of three fingers puts an end to his promising pro-ball career, a young man hires on as a boys' camp counselor and baseball coach, hoping to escape images of the life he might have had. Among the kids and fellow counselors he encounters, two stand out—12-year-old David Taliaferro, a talented soprano whose voice is changing, and professional dancer Kelly Carnevale, who is coping with emotional devastation following a recent hysterectomy. A special affinity gradually grows up among the three as they help one another make the difficult transition from past loss to future promise. Though the knack for strong characterization Thompson evidenced in *The Grounding of Group Six* is not as apparent in this convoluted endeavor, the author effectively maintains a difficult narrative device; his dialogue and situation display both freshness and realism; and he combines humor and poignancy in equal proportions.

Stephanie Zvirin, in a review of "Facing It," in Booklist, *Vol. 80, No. 1, September, 1983, p. 76.*

Coming after Thompson's debut in the meaty, original *The Grounding of Group 6,* his second novel should be even more exciting. It isn't. The narrator Jonathan is an egotist, a puerile youth who will, however, appeal to adolescents who find that his views on his adopted parents and other adults jibe with theirs: grownups are to be tolerated, at best, as less intelligent and less understanding than teenagers.

A review of "Facing It," in Publishers Weekly, *Vol. 224, No. 24, December 9, 1983, p. 51.*

Ingredients of adolescent difficulties abound but not the convincing element needed to make style and character come fully alive. Topics and themes covered in the action and through the hero's introspection are contemporary and often controversial: grass at seventh-grade parties, sex by grade nine, casual affairs at college, the often awkward and painful encounters with the opposite sex in a serious relationship, the positive connotation of peer-group friendships, venereal disease, problems with personal identity, painful relations with parents and language sprinkled with four-letter words and swearing. There is also an emphasis on a code of ethics: it is not manly to kiss and tell, adolescent physical and emotional handicaps require human sympathy and understanding, honesty is essential in committed relationships while deception is anathema and, even though pain and loneliness often constitute a part of adolescence, they can be lessened by paying attention to true love and friendship. While at times dealing honestly with adolescent life, Thompson at other times loses readers' attention by too much verbosity and ineffective asides. Unfortunately, brief passages of excellence do not fully compensate for the general flatness of mood, style and characterization. Only those libraries who need a wide selection of hard-hitting teenage novels will wish to purchase this one.

Hope Bridgewater, in a review of "Facing It," in School Library Journal, *Vol. 30, No. 5, January, 1984, p. 90.*

This is far from the usual camping story; although counselors and campers have problems, they are not camp-induced but intrinsic to the array of well-differentiated characters. It is, oddly, almost a three-way love story, since Randy and his girl both love one of the children who returns their affection and who helps Randy in his search. The happy ending is believable, the writing style sparkles with intellectual sophistication, and the story is imbued with a persuasive warmth.

Zena Sutherland, in a review of "Facing It," in Bulletin of the Center for Children's Books, *Vol. 37, No. 6, February, 1984, p. 119.*

A Question of Survival (1984)

The literary style is so grindingly cute, the smart-aleck, pun-laden style so heavy and the numerous sarcastic digressions so interminable that **A Question of Survival** is almost impossible to plow through. When Toby and Zack attend a teen survival session, they are completely cut off from the outside world and at the mercy of stupid JB, sadistic Willis Rensselaer and leering Bobo Bodine. Toby and Zack free the alley cats whose recapture was to be the session's culminating activity; they are caged, to be hunted in place of the cats. They escape this fate, and the book ends with the recapture of the camp by seven men wearing Sammy Davis masks. The plot does fit together like an intricate puzzle, and some of the comic scenes are truly funny. However, the story doesn't start moving until the last 100 pages. Worst of all, the book is drenched in sex, foul language, images of violence and sexual fantasy to an extent seldom encountered in young adult fiction. Joseph Heller managed a blend of violence and black humor to powerful effect in *Catch 22*. In **A Question of Survival,** it merely comes off as slick. It is difficult to imagine many teens wading through 293 pages of turgid prose and cute philosophizing, unless propelled by an interest in the sex and obscene language.

Kathy Fritts, in a review of "A Question of Survival," in School Library Journal, *Vol. 31, No. 2, October, 1984, p. 171.*

Unlike the parents in **The Grounding of Group Six** who knowingly sent their children on what they hoped would be a one-way trip to camp, Mr. Ayer wants Toby to go to survival camp so she will have the skills to survive when the bomb lands on Hartford, Connecticut, and "they" (read blacks) flee to the countryside and will be attacking all the nice white suburban folks. Zack Plummer goes along because his relationship with Toby is moving from casual friendship to hot passion. What neither Toby nor Zack know is that the death of Oke, the town eccentric (read truthsayer) was caused by vandals invading his home and burning it down with him in it. But Louie Ledbetter knows, and believes Toby and Zack can identify him as one of the vandals and is determined to kill them both. . . .

What is so interesting about Thompson's adult characters is that there isn't a one of them, except Oke, who holds an opinion left of Jessie Helms, but all are painted as decent, well-meaning folks. Weird maybe, but likable. And when the directors of the Frances Marion Survival Camp decide to go find out why Toby and Zack have called for help, they dress up in black face and decide to test the camp's security arrangements by staging an invasion. It sounds terribly racist, and it is, but that's how these folks think. The miracle, of course, is that their kids don't think as they do, and that is the hope of the world. Thompson has done a masterful job in creating two very interesting teenage characters while giving life to the adults as well. That makes this something special, and there isn't even room here to tell you about how funny it is, and how tender it is in describing the growing sexual attraction between Toby and Zack.

Dorothy M. Broderick, in a review of "A Question of Survival," in Voice of Youth Advocates, *Vol. 7, No. 6, February, 1985, p. 333.*

Literature or entertainment? How often are you involved in a debate with colleagues or an argument with yourself about the merits or demerits of a popular title as literature? I differentiate between entertainment and literature on the basis of meaning or intent in a work. Entertainment frequently conforms to a clearly recognizable type or genre with the primary intent of diversion. Literature intends to enlighten and enrich, to explore some aspect of the human experience for the reader. Both should be well written; both are appropriate and necessary for young adult readers. (p. 47)

[*A Question of Survival*] deals with fears—the fear of a nuclear war and fear as a psychological motivator. The treatment of the subject and style of narrative . . . place this novel for mature high school students largely into the area of entertainment. As in the author's *The Grounding of Group 6,* teens are placed in the far from tender care of apparently qualified adults by parents who, in this case, are concerned about their offsprings' abilities to survive a nuclear war. The kids, by and large, handle the physical demands of their month long survival course at the Francis Marion Institute in northern Connecticut with more success than their parents would have expected. Only Zack and Toby, however, have the self-confidence to put a stop to their instructors' planned final exercise of tracking and hunting feral cats. Their "civilized" behavior is rewarded by making them the prey that the others must track and "kill". "Incredible!" you say? Not in Thompson's novels where typical attitudes, actions and situations are exaggerated just enough to make the apparently bizarre a chilling possibility. Teens will love the innuendo-laden dialogue and enjoy the ridicule heaped on adults and adult institutions. Some—the real Tobys and Zacks—may appreciate the writer's deeper purpose and realize that teens are not exempt from the paranoia, stupidity, greed, and cruelty ascribed to adults in this novel. (pp. 47-8)

> *Christine Dewar, in a review of "A Question of Survival," in* Emergency Librarian, *Vol. 12, No. 4, March-April, 1985, pp. 47-8.*

Discontinued (1985)

After Thompson's debut in *The Grounding of Group 6,* readers have the right to expect equally remarkable adventures, not such an uncontrolled novel as this. The author's intrusions sit like boulders in the way of readers tracking the narrative, which is a shame. Without all its pretensions, the story could be terrific. The protagonist is Duncan (Dunc) Banigan, 17. When a bomb kills his older brother and divorced mother, Dunc leaves his girl Terry, school and his empty house to hitch to Vermont in hopes of decoding a clue to the murderer in a note written by Brian. The investigator meets Abraham Fetish, his gorgeous daughter Caitlin and the devout members of Nukismetic Humanism who have an unusual slant on nuclear war. Dunc takes a job at the shop where the group sells at large profits, NU HU cosmetics, food, etc. Caitlin and Dunc become lovers and the days pass until the novel's critical point strains Thompson's ability to balance buffoonery and frights. The author's genuinely inspired humor and the story's thrills are lost in wordiness, and the book poses another problem. There are sure to be complaints about the sexual episodes which are explicit and will be attacked as unsuitable for subteens.

> *A review of "Discontinued," in* Publishers Weekly, *Vol. 228, No. 7, August 16, 1985, p. 70.*

Discontinued is written with tongue-in-cheek humor and an economical use of words and phrases verging on a somewhat stiff tone. While this style can be effective, especially in satirical works, *Discontinued* is not successful. . . . Characterizations are weak and two-dimensional, making it difficult for readers to remain interested. As well, the plot is superficial, lacking the depth which would again maintain interest and sympathy. The ending is flat and disappointing. Throughout, the novel is dry, dull and seems half-finished.

> *Nancy E. Black, in a review of "Discontinued," in* School Library Journal, *Vol. 32, No. 2, October, 1985, p. 188.*

Thompson's unusual style makes for enjoyable rhythmic reading. Like his *Grounding of Group Six,* the mystery carries the story without dominating the atmosphere to the extinguishing of his more important ideas. Thompson does not like adults in their destructive thinking and amoral actions. And he makes a very strong case.

Young adults will enjoy the story but will need to be sold. The cover art is not eye-catching and contains too much text to grab commercial addicted eyes. A title that should be considered for YASD's Best Books list.

> *Janet G. Polacheck, in a review of "Discontinued," in* Voice of Youth Advocates, *Vol. 8, No. 5, December, 1985, p. 322.*

There's nothing in this serio-comic story that *couldn't* happen; few readers are likely to believe that it does, although they will probably find themselves intermittently touched and frequently amused by the characters. . . . It's fun, but the farcical ending is disappointing, moving the story from funny to inane. (pp. 97-8)

> *A review of "Discontinued," in* Bulletin of the Center for Children's Books, *Vol. 39, No. 5, January, 1986, pp. 97-8.*

A Band of Angels (1986)

As in *Discontinued*, Thompson begins *A Band of Angels* with a death. Jordan Paradise's lifelong companion/ guardian is a victim of a hit and run driver leaving Jordan alone with a station wagon and a suitcase full of money. Neither will do him any good if the people who want to kill him locate him. Riley Roux, daughter of a wealthy family, witnesses the accident and goes to comfort Jordan who has fled the scene without acknowledging knowing the dead woman. Riley takes Jordan home and soon the two of them in company with Riley's best friend Michael are on the road.

The story of Jordan, Riley, and Michael alternates with scenes of Eric and Sweets, two government agents searching for Jordan and his now dead companion, Karen/ Dorothy. Years earlier Jordan's parents, two research scientists, had discovered a deadly virus that held too much potential for disaster in the hands of our government or any other. To avoid handing over their discovery, the Goodspeeds committed suicide after liquidating their considerable resources and handing over Jordan (nee Amos) and the money to their good friend Karen. Eric will kill Jordan if he can; Sweets will save Jordan, if he can.

As the youthful trio makes it way across the country, there are tensions between Michael and Jordan because it is clear Riley considers Michael a friend and Jordan a potential lover. They pick up two runaways, Lisa and David, in separate encounters and the five travel together while trying to figure out ways in which they, the young of America, can put an end to the mindless threat of nuclear war. What would happen if the young took a vow to NEVER be a part of any operation or activity that could lead to nuclear war? Is a 20th century Children's Crusade possible?

There is the usual Thompson irony in all this: five young people devoting their energy to thinking about worldwide peace while two government agents pursue them to end their lives. Julian Thompson is a unique voice among the new male YA authors: his male-female relationships are loving, caring without any of the phoniness found in the series romances; his males do not need to win a big game to be sure of their maleness; his females are strong, independent without being males-in-disguise (reverse stereotyping is the literary phrase); his faith in the young to build a better world is unbounded, and while it is true he does not think much of adults in general, he always offers us a couple decent adult characters who are supportive of the young. All these qualities plus a gorgeous cover painting by Edwin Herder should make it possible for mature YA librarians to sell this outstanding author to the outstanding young.

> *Dorothy M. Broderick, in a review of "A Band of Angels," in* Voice of Youth Advocates, *Vol. 9, No. 2, June, 1986, p. 84.*

The conversations among the teenagers are long and repetitive, with cliched points often the outcome ("Loving is accepting everything. And every*one*, I guess"). The plot itself has some thriller appeal, in spite of unlikely elements, and there's a love story involved. But both the style and humor are self-consciously hip, and the messages heavily pervasive.

> *R. S., in a review of "A Band of Angels," in* Bulletin of the Center for Children's Books, *Vol. 40, No. 2, October, 1986, p. 39.*

Sentimental self-absorption is . . . a hallmark of adolescence, and frequently of the young adult novel as well. But until what Julian F. Thompson in *A Band of Angels* calls "this whole thing, this nuclear deal," writers of the genre tended to stay away from anything remotely political (Robert Cormier's novels are an important exception), confining themselves to issues of personal development and adjustment to the adult world. In *A Band of Angels,* Mr. Thompson flips these conventions, finding the solution to the nuclear threat in a refusal to grow up. "How about . . . if some kids, some day, could make it to adulthood still unflawed . . . and simply turn this rotten world around." The teen-age angels of the title hit on a plan to stop the arms race: buttons. "That'd just say NEVER on them. Wouldn't that be neat?" All the kids in the world, "even ones who may not know exactly what a nuclear

weapon is at this point," will wear these buttons, and sign an antinuclear pledge.

Clap your hands together, three times. My problem here is not just with this Peter Pan approach to world tensions; my problem is that the youngsters in this book don't do anything but talk.

> *Roger Sutton, "Yooks, Zooks and the Bomb," in* The New York Times Book Review, *February 22, 1987, p. 22.*

Simon Pure (1987)

At Riddle University, Vermont, gifted 15-year-old Simon Storm rapidly changes from a self-described "sociosexual island" into a romantic hero and defender of academic freedom. Thompson embroils Simon in an outrageous plot: a secret society of power-hungry business students are using subterfuge and scandal to reorganize the university to their liking. Simon and the wacky psychology professor Grebe recognize the perpetrators and their motives just in time to thwart unjust resignations and Simon's expulsion for cheating. This tongue-in-cheek novel mocks the competitive psyche of business majors. Thompson's informal, parenthetical style works better with this zany plot than in his more suspenseful books like *A Band of Angels.* Nevertheless, many will find the writing to be coy, sarcastic, and patronizing and the crude sexual innuendos offensive. The absurdites of "everyday" life at Riddle University will probably bewilder most pre-college readers. Wit is not a successful substitute for literary craftsmanship.

> *Gerry Larson, in a review of "Simon Pure," in* School Library Journal, *Vol. 33, No. 7, March, 1987, p. 177.*

The arch, know-it-all style of this YA novel is likely to irritate most readers. They may not have the patience to follow the book's meandering path to its tiresome conclusion 324 pages later. Simon Storm is a genius and, at 15, the youngest freshman in the class of 1990 at prestigious Riddle University. Although Simon is obviously modeled on Thompson who was also a precocious student, it's difficult to empathize with him—or any other character—because of the author's snide and supercilious stance. Most of the dialogue echoes Thompson's intrusive narrative style—Noël Coward-cum-Me Generation—making the characters, from a 14-year-old girl to a bearded psychology professor, all too similar. Nothing much seems to occur in the story either, due to Thompson's writing *around* the action, rather than writing about it. (pp. 86-7)

> *A review of "Simon Pure," in* Publishers Weekly, *Vol. 231, No. 8, March 13, 1987, pp. 86-7.*

There are several features one can count on in any book written by Julian Thompson, and his latest offers no exceptions. First, it is lengthy; . . . second, there are an abundance of commas and parenthetical expressions and third, the young adults will love it! *Simon Pure* is pure delight to read—it's clever, inventive and funny.

Take one 15-year-old prodigy, our college freshman, Simon Pure; add an ambitious, conniving economics professor, Greg Holt; an "elite" select economics fraternity, A-CHOIR, bent on upsetting the college hierarchy; an "older" woman, Amanda, a college sophomore who takes Simon under her wing; and the 14-year-old daughter of the college president, Kate, who offers a love interest for Simon. Put all this together and you have the main ingredients for a slapstick tale of misadventure and intrigue on the campus of Riddle University. Some scenes have the reader convulsed in laughter, especially when Amanda sets out to get Professor Greg Holt drunk on martinis, an episode that calls up all the machoness in Greg as he tries to hold his own against "a little thing" who just happens to be swilling those martinis in her boot.

The author blurb would have you consider that the book might be autobiographical—but when a book is funny, witty and suspenseful, who cares? And if it is autobiographical, it merely illustrates that Thompson excels at writing about those things familiar to him, for this work is even better than *The Grounding of Group Six.* A must purchase for libraries.

> *Pam Spencer, in a review of "Simon Pure," in* Voice of Youth Advocates, *Vol. 10, No. 1, April, 1987, p. 34.*

The Taking of Mariasburg (1988)

Who hasn't wondered and daydreamed about what to do with a million dollars? In *Uneasy Money,* Robin Brancato's hero bought townhouses and a car, much to his father's dismay. But Thompson's heroine, Maria (pronounced Muh-rye-a), has done the ultimate in teen freedom and independence with her inheritance of millions. She's bought a town, the little town of Jacks-'r-better, now renamed Mariasburg. This is a town where, as Maria said, ". . . we'd get to have some time that wasn't any of their business," a place away from "All the ones with scorecards." But that idea of a town is difficult for adults to accept and the cast of characters includes authoritative adults such as the father who wants the town investigated; Omar, the local sheriff of Hupee County, and Sledge, the leader of a religious cult awaiting Armageddon. Maria is aided in her town settlement by her boyfriend Seppy, her best friend Mimimi and more than 20 other teen inhabitants.

The author's advocacy of young adults is well known, and he continues that support in this book. He allows his characters to do "grown-up" tasks, accepting and expecting that they can; certainly his plot of a town for teens reinforces his belief in them. While all that is wonderful, there is some unevenness in his writing; instead of flowing, the story ebbs and floods, leaving the reader alternately reading enthusiastically to barely plowing through. Some of the dialogue is curiously abstruse, which causes some frustration and confusion. But, for all that, the book has a "knock-your-socks-off" ending that redeems any and all weaknesses, real or imagined, one encounters in the writing; it's an ending that will keep you busy for weeks writing mental sequels to the book. Julian Thompson is characterized by wonderfully creative, inventive plots; a demonstrated caring for and advocacy of young adults and a writing style that is sometimes cryptic—but boy is he worth reading!

> *Pam Spencer, in a review of "The Taking of Mariasburg," in* Voice of Youth Advocates, *Vol. 11, No. 1, April, 1988, p. 30.*

This begins with a typical Thompson flourish: 17-year-old Maria . . . inherits untold millions from a father she's never known (or even heard about) and decides to buy a town for teenagers. It's to be a "space to put the time in," namely, time not spent pleasing and obeying *them,* namely, grownups. This, too, is a familiar Thompson never-land, and most of the adults in the story are stereotypically silly, patronizing, or, like, *evil.* The teens, of course, are cherubs, so the conflict is clear if not terribly interesting. Maria herself is meant to be an admirably Modern Woman, but she's really a post-feminism male fantasy: beautiful, rich, intelligent, aggressive—*and* she hems the tablecloths, *and* she has a tattoo on her butt. Thompson has a vigorous voice that can be sly and joyful in turn, but it is too easily distracted by its own sound, wasted on coy and pointless asides, sacrificing complexity for cuteness. Like the two sympathetic teachers in his novel who tell the kids "*We are the exceptions, please believe me,*" Thompson sets himself up as an advocate for youth and its attendant innocence, but he is underestimating his audience, who (one hopes) knows better.

> *Roger Sutton, in a review of "The Taking of Mariasburg," in* Bulletin of the Center for Children's Books, *Vol. 41, No. 9, May, 1988, p. 190.*

Maria, an altruistic type, decides to use some of the funds [she received from her father] to buy a town to be lived in by teenagers, where they can be free of parental and other adult interference. Here in Mariasburg they can prove to all that they can be responsible. From this low point the novel moves steadily down hill to the final scene, which features a fascist guru who is bombarding the town with mortar shells while the sheriff is relieving himself in the main square. In between there's lots of talk about the importance of the project and how Maria and her boyfriend have some sort of truth and wisdom denied to all others. There's lots of talk, and it's in some sort of jargon that is reminiscent of the old Valley-Girl talk. The dialogue is often difficult to follow. The whole novel, in fact, is difficult to swallow. None of the adults has any values, and all of the men are lecherous no-goods, and stupid besides. None of the characters is developed to any extent, including Maria. Despite its humorous tone, the novel comes off as sarcastic and sophomoric.

> *Robert E. Unsworth, in a review of "The Taking of Mariasburg," in* School Library Journal, *Vol. 35, No. 8, May, 1988, p. 113.*

Feminists may detect inadvertent ironies: Maria's administrative talents come from her father, and the kinky sheriff is slightly titillating as well as abhorrent. The conclusion is abrupt—why not revel just a bit in the final triumph? Still, Thompson—who is as witty as Zindel but somewhat less frantic—provides a lively plot, engaging characters, and sure entertainment.

A review of "The Taking of Mariasburg," in Kirkus Reviews, Vol. LVI, No. 11, June 1, 1988, p. 834.

Goofbang Value Daze   (1989)

A lively satire about a Texas town in which the rights of teenagers are threatened. After a weather dome is built over Dustin, three moral extremists are elected school directors, and life in Dustin changes. Gabriel Podesta, a witty and perceptive 16 year old, speculates on the social impact of the dome and rebels against the school directors who mandate a values course and try to control teen behavior and sex mores both inside and outside school. His parents; girlfriend, Dori Fabb; and her father side with Gabriel. In the end Mr. Fabb tries single-handedly to destroy the dome and the "ideologues" who live under it. His tragic end arouses the social conscience of the town and serves as a reminder that the "little guy" can make a difference. Thompson trademarks abound: symbolic names, self-deprecating asides and quips by the narrator, outspoken teenagers, and a backdrop of contemporary social concerns. Characters range from fanatics to ardent freedom fighters to diplomats. Gabriel and Dori are well-adjusted adolescents who value parental wisdom, question injustice, and respect and care for each other. Nonetheless, the frequent use of slang, and Gabriel and Dori's open but cautious sexual attraction, make this book a better choice for older readers. The flippant title of this novel belies the deeper message: basic rights must be protected and defended.

Gerry Larson, in a review of "Goofbang Value Daze," in School Library Journal, Vol. 35, No. 6, February, 1989, p. 103.

Thompson's latest novel [is a] a tragicomedy of sorts that pits the "little guy" against big, bad Authority. . . . There's sure-fire teen appeal in the scenario, and the characters are a generally colorful, if similar-sounding lot. But Thompson's plot is overloaded with 1980s issues (from unauthorized drug testing to free speech), and his humor comes uncomfortably close to trivializing them at times. Still, Gabe is cut from a popular Thompson mold: he is clever, intelligent, and bold, and the author's following will undoubtedly revel in Gabe's perseverance and enthusiasm, even as they puzzle out what he's trying to say.

Stephanie Zvirin, in a review of "Goofbang Value Daze," in Booklist, Vol. 85, No. 13, March 1, 1989, p. 1130.

Thompson knits plot threads into a convincing whole, despite a cumulation of almost-stock characters: Dori's father for one, Gabe the activist-nonconformist for another, and several of the censorious adults (the school directors; the ranting and militant congressman, Mr. Orrifice). Amongst the issues that arise are the abuse of testing for AIDS, student behavior regulations, pressure on school athletes. Gabe protests, volubly and repeatedly; as Dori's father says when the authorities respond in hostile fashion,

"This Gabe, he seems to think he's free to practice all the liberties our laws allow him to, and use all their protections, too. Well, they can't stand it." To some extent, the forces of reason are vindicated in this tart examination of values education. The book is often funny, despite a somber ending (Dori's father commits suicide, Dori leaves town), and the humor may make the theme more provocative, but the writing is weakened by the typecasting, the determined comedy-script aura of the dialogue, and the improbability of some of the incidents.

Zena Sutherland, in a review of "Goofbang Value Daze," in Bulletin of the Center for Children's Books, Vol. 42, No. 11, July-August, 1989, p. 285.

Herb Seasoning   (1990)

[*Herb Seasoning* is] a wacky, challenging story in which a high-school senior wondering what to do with his life gets to preview some choices.

Referred by his guidance counselor to "Castles in the Air," Herbie Hertzman meets the more-than-mortal Sesame DeBarque, who invites him to spin a wheel of career fields. When the wheel stops on "Crime," she packs him into her "Upwardlimobile" and dispatches him to Prince Edward Island, where he joins a merry gang turning Mexicans into *faux* yuppies and inserting them into US corporations. Not sneaky enough to succeed here, Herbie returns to the castle to spin the wheel again—and again. Though Thompson leaves plenty of ambiguity, unfinished business, and unexploited conceits (e.g., Private Road, who complains about his superiors Corporal Punishment and General Nuisance), he salts his narrative with entertaining word- and horse-play and creates in Herbie a decent-hearted, cleareyed character, fortunate enough to have options and wise enough not to limit them. In the end, after rejecting a spiritual leader's happiness drug, Herbie returns, virginity lost but sense of humor intact, to find himself with the girlfriend whose alter egos have guided him along the way—literally and metaphorically approaching a crossroads.

Readers may find this hard to swallow, but they'll enjoy chewing on it first.

A review of "Herb Seasoning," in Kirkus Reviews, Vol. LVIII, No. 4, February 15, 1990, p. 271.

Thompson writes with verve and originality, and one can be caught up in his narrative, especially the hilarious scenes in Herb's second journey to Hometown, a place that has the Big Red Chicken as mayor. But, although there is some very funny content here, the writing lacks discipline. And one wonders why Thompson consistently uses "like" in its current slang manner. Does he consider it, "like," trendy and appealing? One can't but believe that much of his humor will go right by nearly all adolescent readers, although there will also be much that they will get, and there's some powerful wish-fulfillment for boys.

Ronald A. Van De Voorde, in a review of

"Herb Seasoning," in School Library Journal, *Vol. 36, No. 3, March, 1990, p. 240.*

Entrenched somewhere between zanies Paul Zindel and Daniel Pinkwater and the irreverently clever Aidan Chambers, Julian Thompson is one of the most original and humorous of today's YA writers. While his books will either enchant you or make you furious with their sexism, wholesale stereotyping, and smart-aleck characters, you shouldn't ignore him.

His first novel, *The Grounding of Group Six,* surprised readers with its premise: parents would pay to have their teenagers "lost" forever in the wilderness. *Goofbang Value Daze,* set in a dome-topped city of the not-too-distant future, further stretched the boundaries of realistic fiction. Thompson's books resonate with figurative language and colloquial speech, and he shows a real talent for writing humorous fiction, the best example being *Simon Pure,* a marvelous spoof that cleverly blends sophisticated wit and sophomoric hijinks with a host of solid, eccentric characters.

In *Herb Seasoning* the same kind of linguistic acrobatics and comedy are used to treat two common YA concerns. The results are mixed. Herbie (of the title) Hertzman has "a mind awash in negativity." He can't decide what to do after high school graduation: "mixed nude synchronized swimming" is out, as is selling hair care products for his strange Uncle Babbo, and Hampshire College doesn't seem right either. On top of that, Herbie's still a virgin, another bothersome detail he doesn't know how to fix. It's "seasoning" he seems to want, and he finds that Castles in the Air, a most unusual counseling concern, is the place where he can get it. There, under the nurturing direction of chatty Sesame deBarque (open Sesame?), Herbie whirls a giant wheel of fortune, then slips through time and space to investigate the unusual destinies he has spun.

From this wacky setup comes a string of loosely knit comic situations: in pursuit of a future in "Health Care," Herbie takes a trek by yak to find a formula called Bummer Balm; while investigating "Public Service," he's charged with opening Hometown's safe, the combination for which is tattooed on a local prostitute's derriere. Predictibility and surprise balance out in each strange scene: we never doubt that beleaguered Herbie will get the combination he needs; we just can't imagine how he'll do it.

YA's are bound to chortle at Thompson's parody of familiar graduation woes. They'll spot the novel's strong roots in American popular culture and a Wizard-of-Oz-like fantasy—Big Red Chickens become mayors, magic ointments create bliss. But there's a good deal of distracting silliness, too: conversations with painters, fence posts, and people in Yeti costumes may be clever and weird-funny in themselves, but they contribute little to Herbie's defined goal. In fact, with so much going on, readers may begin to feel as befuddled as poor Herbie.

Because the novel derives much of its humor from the situation, the characters suffer. It's not Herbie you laugh with or at or even get to know. It's what happens to him that amuses. And while the characters are vividly named as well as described ("Babbo Orgalescu, was extremely dark and hairy"), they are many, and they arrive and disappear forever with sometimes startling speed. Or they pop in and out, like puzzling Tyree Toledano (T.K.), a figment of Herbie's sensual imaginings, whose name is tenuously linked with other shapely characters who appear later in the story: "designer Mexican" Zippy, who sheds her sweatshirt for a surprised Herbie; and pretty Shali Sloan, who sheds everything.

Problematic, too, is the novel's idiom. Sometimes the language works extremely well, as in a funny scene with a high school counselor who parodies rap: " 'Hey! Herbivorous!' said Mr. Alexander Rex, his guidance guy that day '. . . I be tryin' to find you' RECORDS-Records-records, man,' he said. 'You' grades which whisper what you' *done,* you' test scores screamin' what you *can.*' " But speech patterns vary little from character to character. It's difficult to tell who's saying what at times. The cynical, slang-riddled descriptions of the narrator dominate; and, endeavoring to mimic funky talk, Thompson has larded them with asides—underlined, italicized, and, strangely, even put in parentheses: "Let's go she (simply) said." And he twists and stretches language to the limit, creating new words, upsetting clichés, and writing pure double-speak.

Certainly Thompson's way with words and his bizarre sense of humor are not to everyone's taste. But he is an innovative stylist: he has an ear fine-tuned to words and what they'll do; and he loves to turn reality on its head and challenge readers with his complicated visions. He spreads these talents very thinly here, though: the plot creaks under its zany load, and the experiments with language seem self-conscious and excessive; not even the novel's end is clear. Readers have to wade through a lot for their laughs. Those familiar with Thompson's audacity and inventiveness probably won't mind, but those who haven't read him in the past should not pick *Herb Seasoning* as the place to begin.

Stephanie Zvirin, " 'Herb Seasoning', by Julian F. Thompson," in Booklist, *Vol. 86, No. 18, May 15, 1990, p. 1792.*

"A lot of Herbie Hertzman's story sounds incredible to me, but yet I still believe it—Author's Disclaimer." And I agree: Thompson's latest is, well, incredible.

Thompson is in top form, his humor has never been better. And virtually every YA who has ever wondered what to do with themselves (in other words just about every YA) will appreciate Herb's journey—even if the trip itself is pretty unbelievable.

Stella Baker, in a review of "Herb Seasoning," in Voice of Youth Advocates, *Vol. 13, No. 2, June, 1990, p. 111.*

CUMULATIVE INDEX TO AUTHORS

This index lists all author entries in *Children's Literature Review* and includes cross-references to them in other Gale sources. References in the index are identified as follows:

Author Index

CUMULATIVE INDEX TO NATIONALITIES

Nationality Index

CUMULATIVE INDEX TO TITLES

Title Index

Title Index

Title Index

Title Index

Title Index

Title Index